INNOVATIONS

The Comprehensive Preschool Curriculum

Dedication

To Carla Newport Gwinn, the best and most intuitive preschool teacher I have ever known

and

To Katherine Ball Broussard, who shared both her love and her name with me—Kay

To my children, John and Kevin, who shared their delightful preschool years (and love) with me—Linda

Other Books by Kay Albrecht and Linda G. Miller

Innovations: The Comprehensive Infant Curriculum
Innovations: The Comprehensive Infant Curriculum: Teacher's Guide
Innovations: The Comprehensive Toddler Curriculum
Innovations: The Comprehensive Toddler Curriculum: Teacher's Guide
Innovations: Infant and Toddler Development
Innovations: Infant and Toddler Development: Trainer's Guide

Other Books by Kay Albrecht

Developmentally Appropriate Practice in School-Age Child Care Programs
The Right Fit: Recruiting, Selecting, and Orienting Staff

Other Books by Linda G. Miller

Making Toys for Infants and Toddlers: Using Ordinary Stuff for Extraordinary Play
Making Toys for Preschool Children: Using Ordinary Stuff for Extraordinary Play
Making Toys for School-Age Children: Using Ordinary Stuff for Extraordinary Play

INNOVATIONS

The Comprehensive Preschool CURRICULUM

Kay Albrecht / Linda G. Miller

Illustrations by Kathy Dobbs

Photographs by Masami Mizukami

gryphon house
Beltsville, Maryland

Printed in the United States of America.
Published by Gryphon House, Inc.
10726 Tucker Street, Beltsville, MD 20705
301.595.9500; 301.595.0051 (fax); 800.638.0928

Visit us on the web at www.gryphonhouse.com

Illustrations: Kathy Dobbs

Photographs: Masami Mizukami

Library of Congress Cataloging-in-Publication Data

Albrecht, Kay M.
The comprehensive preschool curriculum / Kay Albrecht/Linda G. Miller ; illustrations, Kathy Dobbs.
p. cm. -- (Innovations)
Includes index.
ISBN 0-87659-269-8
1. Education, Preschool--Curricula. 2. Curriculum planning. I. Miller, Linda G. II. Title.
LB1140.4.A43 2004
372.19--dc22

2003019499

Bulk purchase

Gryphon House books are available for special premiums and sales promotions as well as for fund-raising use. Special editions or book excerpts also can be created to specification. For details, contact the Director of Marketing at Gryphon House.

Disclaimer

Gryphon House, Inc. and the authors cannot be held responsible for damage, mishap, or injury incurred during the use of or because of activities in this book. Appropriate and reasonable caution and adult supervision of children are recommended at all times. Do not leave children unattended at any time. Observe safety and caution at all times.

Every effort has been made to locate copyright and permission information.

Acknowledgments

Innovations: The Comprehensive Preschool Curriculum is the third book in the ***Innovations*** series, which now covers birth through age five. Each book tells a story of the many people who contributed to its publication, and this one is no exception. We are especially grateful to the children, families, faculty at HeartsHome Early Learning Center and The Walden School, both of Houston, TX. Their photographs bring the pages of our book to life and provide wonderful visual images of high-quality care and early education at work in the real world.

The past year or so has been challenging for us. Sandwiched between children and parents, this life stage has provided many struggles. During all of them, the family at Gryphon House has been wonderful. In particular, Leah Curry-Rood provided unconditional support to us, which explains why Gryphon House authors are such a committed and productive lot. Our editor, Kathy Charner supported our ups and downs and waited patiently through each crisis until we were able to go back to work. We are also grateful for Kate Kuhn's careful editing. We hope our book is a resource to her obviously competent parenting.

As always, working with real teachers who work with real children in real classrooms is a cornerstone of our work. We had wonderful assistance from a team of educators, who collaborated with us to brainstorm, create, find, test, and refine the activities in the Possibilities Plans. Our heartfelt thanks go to Wendy Haardt, Brooke Harrington, Masami Mizukami, Tina Sabuco, and Shien Chun Wang for their invaluable contributions. We think you will want to know more about these talented teachers, so we are including a glimpse of some of their unique accomplishments.

Masami Mizukami

Masami Mizukami began his career in Japan, working with many different age groups before coming to the US to attend Houston Community College. An internship brought him to HeartsHome Early Learning Center where Masami so distinguished himself that he was offered a permanent position. He has now graduated two groups, providing continuous care and early education from infancy until graduation to kindergarten. Masami holds an associate degree in child development and is just a few hours short of completing his baccalaureate in human development at the University of Houston. He enjoys teaching through creative and experiential activities. Masami's interest in creative art shows up regularly in beautiful documentations of what children are learning over time. An avid photographer, he is responsible for most of the photos in this book.

Shien Chun Wang

Shien Chun Wang graduated from University of Texas at Austin with a Bachelor of Science in Child Development. She came to HeartsHome Early Learning Center seeking an assistant teacher position so she could start her career gradually. She didn't get that opportunity! She was instead offered a primary teacher position and has provided sensitive care and outstanding early education to two groups of children from toddlerhood to kindergarten. During this experience, she discovered that building relationships with children comes before teaching. She has recently accepted a new group of infants to grow up with, continuing her commitment to the co-construction of knowledge with children.

Brooke Harrington

Brooke Harrington holds a Preschool Child Development Associate degree and is working towards a bachelor's degree in her hometown of Normal, Illinois. She began her love affair with teaching in 1992 and has delighted in the magical nature of children's minds ever since. Brooke's dedication to individualized curriculum creates a classroom that encourages children to create their own knowledge about the world and their place in it as a creator, a problem solver, and a friend. Brooke creates and presents workshops on the subjects of creativity, music and movement, primary teaching or looping, documentation, emergent curriculum, and building community in the classroom. According to Brooke, "Children have a wisdom that, as adults, we have lost. They have the wisdom of freedom, imagination, and play; they have the wisdom of possibility. I learn from that wisdom every day."

Tina Sabuco

Tina Sabuco is Executive Director and creator of ARTS ALIVE! Inc., and holds a Master of Fine Arts degree in Creative Drama and Children's Theatre from The University of Texas at Austin and a Bachelor of Arts in Theatre from Northern Michigan University. She began dancing at age three in her hometown of Escanaba, Michigan and has never stopped! Since 1994, Tina has offered an integrated arts program for students of all ages and abilities in Houston, TX through ARTS ALIVE! Inc. Her innovative teaching methodologies combined with her extensive teaching experiences garner her frequent assignments training other teachers, as well as invitations to keynote early childhood education conferences. An adjunct faculty member at the University of Houston, Clear Lake, Tina looks forward to living out her personal motto—"You don't stop playing because you grow old. You grow old because you stop playing!"

Wendy Haardt

Wendy Haardt, director of ARTS ALIVE! Inc., specializes in preschool teaching in the Houston area. ARTS ALIVE! is an integrated arts program for children of all ages and abilities that builds self-esteem, confidence, and creativity through the expressive arts: creative movement, creative drama, dance, and music. A 13-year veteran, Wendy hails originally from Eustis, Nebraska, holds a BA in Psychology from the University of Houston, has a teaching certificate from the Houston Independent School District, and has completed graduate studies at the University of St. Thomas, Houston, TX. Her experience, creativity, colorful personality, and knowledge of Spanish make her a valued member of the ARTS ALIVE! Inc. family. Her enthusiastic love of children enables her to do what she loves, teach young children through play.

Tina Wendy Masami Brooke Shien

Table of Contents

Introduction

Welcome to the ***Innovations*** experience, a project that we began several years ago. From its inception, ***Innovations*** has been designed as a series. ***Innovations**: **The Comprehensive Preschool Curriculum*** is the third book in the series, following ***Innovations: The Comprehensive Infant Curriculum*** and ***Innovations: The Comprehensive Toddler Curriculum***. Together, they form a seamless, comprehensive, developmental approach to early childhood education for children from birth to five years of age.

Before we began our ***Innovations*** journey, we searched for a curriculum to meet the broad needs of teachers, parents, and the children who benefit from their efforts. Too often, we found books that were called "curriculum," but weren't. They provided activities or ideas and expected the teacher to determine the appropriate developmental skills. Or they approached skill acquisition as the result of didactic teaching. Some books equated "curriculum" with just the content that was included, as though facts are all that children need to grow and learn.

All of these approaches to "curriculum" are, in our view, too narrow. At the very least, curriculum for young children must include a focus on the relationships between the teacher and child and family, teacher observation, assessment, teacher training, and interactive responses; family participation, education, and appreciation as primary educators; integration of environment, toys, materials, health and safety, and room arrangement; knowledge of historical and emerging child growth and development theory and practice, the preschooler's experiences, interactions, reactions, cues, interests, and an understanding of the children's temperament.

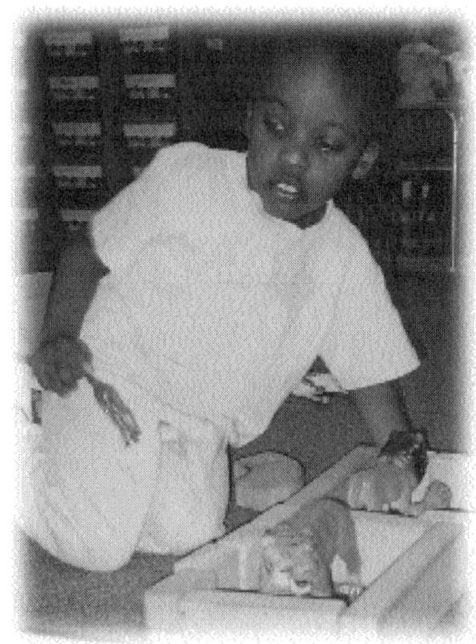

The focus of curriculum, we feel, must be squarely on the child and include all of the elements mentioned thus far. ***This curriculum advocates thinking about and planning for everything that can, by the nature of the setting (school vs. home), contribute to the child's development and the teacher's relationship with the child and the family.*** We think this is a paradigm shift, a way to move the discussion of curriculum out of the narrow range that leads to evaluating children's potential solely by high-stakes testing and outcomes toward a more comprehensive approach that embraces many different ways of knowing and learning. At the same time, we recognize the need for teachers to have something that is easy to use regardless of their educational background.

Innovations: The Comprehensive Preschool Curriculum meets the needs of teachers by providing everything to implement what we feel is "real" curriculum. The following diagram illustrates what we believe is the purpose of curriculum.

Curriculum is comprehensive—encompassing all aspects of growing and learning. This curriculum framework embraces the inter-relationship among teacher's planning, the child's interest and response, child development knowledge and best practices, the child's family context and culture, and the reactions and interactions of the adults and other children. Everything involved works together to build relationships with children.

We also embrace the open-ended nature of the teaching and learning process. Following children's interests is central to our view of curriculum with preschoolers. When activities or experiences are presented to young children, we never know what they are going to do with the experience! Preparing ourselves as teachers to consider alternatives allows us to recognize learning when it emerges in children's dialogue (an idea our colleagues at Reggio Emilia also embrace) and play. We also believe that the child's response is a cue to what to do next or where to go next. This dance between teacher and child—the gentle interplay that occurs over and over again during the day is what real teaching and learning are about.

It is our wish that ***Innovations: The Comprehensive Preschool Curriculum*** will insure that preschoolers are supported in learning, that teachers understand and embrace educating preschoolers in a comprehensive way, and that families and teachers work cooperatively to make sure it all comes together. We hope you enjoy and benefit from the ***Innovations*** journey as much as we have.

Kay Albrecht

Linda G Miller

CHAPTER I

Getting Started

Innovations: The Comprehensive Preschool Curriculum is designed for teachers of children three to five years of age. In this chapter you will prepare to use this book by exploring each component of the curriculum.

DEVELOPMENTAL TASKS

Chapters 2–7 each identify a major developmental challenge, called a developmental task, that children experience as they learn and grow. Most curriculum models focus on the sequence of emerging development. This curriculum, however, focuses on how development is encouraged, facilitated, and stimulated. It is interactional, viewing development as the complex interplay between the child and his world.

Developmental Tasks for the Preschool Years

- Adjusting to School
- Making Friends
- Exploring Roles
- Communicating with Parents, Teachers and Friends
- Problem Solving
- Expressing Feelings with Parents, Teachers, and Friends

The tasks are loosely sequential—that is, a teacher of preschoolers could start with Chapter 2, Adjusting to School, when the child enrolls in school or at the beginning of the school year, and continue to Chapter 3, Making Friends, then to Chapter 4, Exploring Roles, and so on. Or, teachers can begin by observing children to match emerging tasks with each child's current developmental needs and then begin using the curriculum in that task.

The developmental tasks of this curriculum are: Adjusting to School (Chapter 2); Making Friends (Chapter 3); Exploring Roles (Chapter 4); Communicating with Parents, Teachers, and Friends (Chapter 5); Problem Solving (Chapter 6); and Expressing Feelings with Parents, Teachers, and Friends (Chapter 7).

In addition, each of the above chapters contains the following essential elements:

- Innovations in Care and Early Education
- Innovations in Interactive Experiences
- Innovations in Teaching
- Innovations in Observation/Assessment
- Innovations in Family Partnerships
- Innovations in Environments
- Possibilities Plans Related to the Developmental Task

INNOVATIONS IN CARE AND EARLY EDUCATION

An understanding of child development theory, research, and best practices is the foundation of this curriculum. In each chapter, this section explains theories and early childhood education and child development principles, or content knowledge related to specific developmental tasks. Included in this section are topics such as primary teaching, literacy development, and theories about the social, emotional, intellectual, and physical development of preschoolers. Teachers can discover the *what* in the developmental tasks and the Possibilities Plans. This section provides the *why*.

INNOVATIONS IN INTERACTIVE EXPERIENCES

This curriculum advocates thinking about and planning for everything that can, by the nature of the setting (school vs. home), contribute to a child's learning and development and the teacher's relationship with the child and the family. It is grounded in developmental and interactional theoretical frameworks and views all children's experiences, not just formal experiences, as important. Children are always learning, and it is the teacher's job to support that learning in whatever form it may take.

The type and quality of interactive experiences children have with others is a component of curriculum. This section offers ideas and suggestions for creating positive interactive environments and ensuring that children's emotional needs are met.

Listed in Innovations in Interactive Experiences are the types of experiences that teachers must be aware of, observe for, plan, support, and provide. Many opportunities occur to capitalize on children's experiences as they happen during the school day. Because capitalizing on these experiences is so important, they should appear in curriculum plans as prompts for these crucial, often spontaneous experiences.

In addition, teaching roles vary in the preschool classroom. Teachers work individually with children, in small groups, in large groups, and supervise children working on their own or with their peers. Matching the teacher's role to children's needs is one of the most dynamic jobs of a preschool teacher. This section explores teaching roles that relate to each developmental task, helping teachers see how teaching roles can be used, modified, or enhanced to support children's growth during each developmental task.

INNOVATIONS IN TEACHING

This section discusses topics related to the developmental tasks that are important for teachers to know. Effective practices are often explored here. Topics in Innovations in Teaching further explain how good practices are implemented and how to modify these practices to fit different situations. This section also covers important topics such as classroom management, discipline and guidance, health and safety, and nutrition—all discussed in terms of the developmental task and application in the classroom.

Teacher Competencies

A list of behaviors teachers can use to reflect on their teaching skills is included in each Innovations in Teaching section. Use these skill lists to evaluate your own skill level or to have a mentor or supervisor assess your teaching competence, and make supportive professional development plans to improve your skills.

INNOVATIONS IN OBSERVATION/ASSESSMENT

Understanding each child's developmental age and stage, temperament, learning style, play interests, play themes, interactive style, and other characteristics forms the foundation of curriculum tailored to meet individual as well as group needs. ***Innovations: The Comprehensive Preschool Curriculum*** views three components of observation and assessment as necessary for curriculum planning. The first component is careful observation of children at work and play in the classroom recorded in the form of anecdotal notes. These observations form the basis of teachers' understanding of the individual nature of development and learning. Each developmental task contains several ideas and suggestions for what to observe and how to go about observing. The second is information gathered from developmental checklists or assessment instruments. Teachers need support in assuring that development is unfolding normally and that children's alternative developmental pathways are understood. Assessment supports the process of identifying uniqueness as well as skill strengths and areas for growth. The third component is documentation of children's learning both in the classroom environment and in individual portfolios. Documentation is a powerful form of communication among and between children and their families—sharing the process of learning, knowing, and understanding for all to see.

Several forms are included in the Appendix to support teachers in observation and assessment. An Observation Classroom Summary and a Concepts Learned Classroom Summary are included for each Possibilities Plan. These tools allow teachers to summarize their observations for all of the children in the group, pinpointing which skills, abilities, and concepts were observed as children participated in activity areas. Keep both of these summary forms on a clipboard in the classroom to remind you to observe and assess as children participate in planned activities and experiences. Another assessment tool, the Child Accomplishment Record, is also included in the Appendix. It is designed to help you share this important information with families.

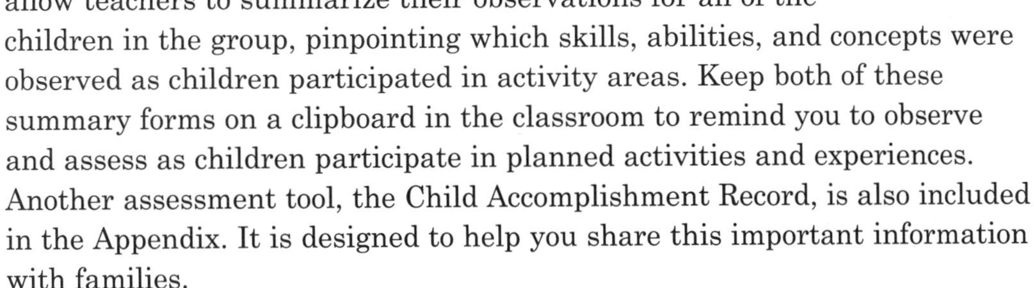

INNOVATIONS IN FAMILY PARTNERSHIPS

Creating a partnership with families is a crucial professional and curriculum planning skill. This section helps teachers seek an understanding of the unique cultural characteristics of families as they create respectful, reciprocal relationships and involve them in their children's development and learning. It offers many suggestions for creating and enhancing partnerships. Some suggestions involve families in their children's lives at school. Others support relationships with their children at home. Additionally, this section includes Parent Postcards, information that may be helpful to parents as they learn more about parenting, or that schools may want parents to have about child development, best practices, or curriculum. Postcards are designed to enhance the partnership between parents and teachers by creating a shared understanding of topics and issues. Postcards can be shared with parents as they show an interest in the topic of the postcard, at appropriate times during the enrollment cycle, or as developmental issues arise with individual children.

INNOVATIONS IN ENVIRONMENTS

The environment is a powerful contributor to children's learning. This section helps teachers create environments that support children's learning and growth and stimulate the wide range of play behaviors conducive to a beneficial early childhood experience. It covers appropriate environments, creativity, and safety. Individual interest areas are considered in detail to expand teachers' knowledge of enriching and modifying environments to support teaching goals.

Resources for Teachers

Additional suggested reading for teachers is included in this section. Connection with professional literature enhances teachers' understanding of child growth and development, theory, and best practices. Every effort was made to identify resources that lead to higher levels of understanding in these important areas. Add these resources to professional and school resource libraries and use them as references for curriculum ideas.

POSSIBILITIES PLANS RELATED TO THE DEVELOPMENTAL TASKS

Each of the six developmental tasks contains related curriculum plans, called Possibilities Plans. These plans give teachers a way to structure their activities and experiences with children. Each one begins with a brief discussion of appropriate content for the plan. Then, activities and experiences for use, modification, variation, or extension are detailed. Plans can be used in total, or activities and experiences can be selected and pulled out to use as appropriate with children in your group. The Possibilities Plans included in each chapter are designed to help teachers identify emergent curriculum ideas, expanding planning and implementation of curriculum while keeping it fresh and new with your own additions and extension ideas.

Webs

Webs show how this curriculum encourages emergent planning. Because ***Innovations: The Comprehensive Preschool Curriculum*** is interactional, teachers adjust their plans according to how children respond to the experiences. For example, the teacher's plan may focus on "my body," but children's interests may change the teacher's plan to focus on "eyes" or "things that I can do with my hands." Creating webs for children opens up the possibilities for interactions, experiences, and activities with children. In addition, webbing allows teachers to glean topics of interest from their observations of children and create Possibilities Plans that reflect those interests.

Activities and Experiences

Each plan is accompanied by numerous activities and experiences, called possibilities, so teachers can plan quality experiences for children in the classroom. Each activity or experience has some or all of the following sections:

Materials—This sections details all the materials and supplies you will need to complete the activity. This helps you determine if you have what you need and/or identify what you need to find, scrounge, or buy to make the activity successful. When possible, children's book suggestions that might connect or relate to the activity are also included.

Teacher Talk—This section offers examples and suggestions of appropriate language for teachers to use with young children during the activity or experience. Often, suggestions for commenting on children's work are included as well as examples of open-ended questions you might ask. Use these as a springboard for conversation related to the activity.

Instructions—Detailed instructions are included in this section. Because real teachers working with preschool children created the activities in this book, the instructions are clear, easy to follow, and lead to success in implementation.

Helpful Hints—These are hints about safety or ways to insure the success of the activity. Often, these tips help you avoid pitfalls and anticipate problems.

Observation/Assessment Suggestions—These suggestions focus your observations on what children might be learning as they complete the experience.

Extension Possibilities—Logical extension activities are listed in this section. If the experience can be extended, enhanced, or expanded, the suggestions for how to do so will be described in this section.

Because this curriculum is appropriate for children three to five years of age, activities are included to address that broad range. Knowledge of where children are developmentally will help you find activities that match. You can also modify activities by simplifying them or making them more complex to meet children's individual needs. Activities and experiences are included in the following activity areas:

- Dramatic Possibilities
- Art Possibilities
- Blocks/Construction Possibilities
- Science/Discovery Possibilities
- Sensory Possibilities
- Literacy/Writing Possibilities
- Math/Manipulatives Possibilities
- Rhymes/Fingerplays/Songs/Music Possibilities
- Group Time Possibilities
- Movement/Outdoor Possibilities
- Projects/Documentation Possibilities
- Field Trip Possibilities
- Snack Possibilities
- Family Participation Possibilities

During the preschool years, repetition of activities and experiences, such as playing with playdough, building with blocks, or doing a favorite art activity over and over again, creates important skill-building opportunities. As children repeat activities and experiences, they are perfecting techniques, exploring different outcomes, and connecting positive emotional meaning to what they are doing. Teachers will want to offer children many opportunities to repeat popular and enjoyable activities, both at the child's request and at the teacher's initiation through curriculum planning.

Dramatic Possibilities

Dolls, stuffed animals, costumes, and realistic props delight preschool children. Dramatic play activities contribute to children's understanding of the real world and support the development of self-concept, as well as the development of social interaction and problem-solving skills. Several options are included for each plan, allowing teachers to change Dramatic Possibilities to keep role-playing fresh and interesting to children.

Art Possibilities

Art activities for young children are opportunities for open-ended exploration, personal expression, and fun. Art allows children to exhibit creativity using many materials. While focusing on the process of creative art possibilities, children practice making choices that impact their experiences.

Blocks/Construction Possibilities

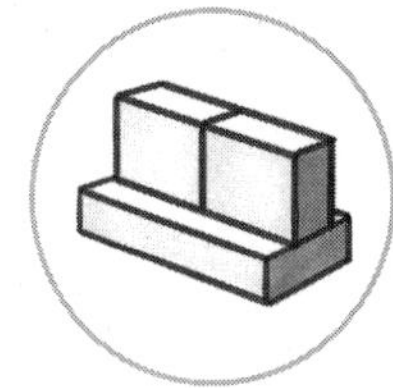

Putting things together, taking things apart, building with unit and other kinds of blocks, exploring numeracy skills such as figuring out how parts relate to the whole, discovering one-to-one correspondence, and creating and manipulating groups are skills facilitated by activities and experiences in Blocks/Construction Possibilities. Building and constructing, deconstructing, and building again are powerful opportunities for preschool children to experience control over their play environments. Enhancements and props are included here to ease into numeracy experiences in Blocks/Construction.

Science/Discovery Possibilities

Young children are naturally curious about the world in which they live. They enjoy exploring new things in the environment, and they want to find out how everything works. Opportunities for children to observe and manipulate materials are experiences that facilitate discovery of scientific concepts. Activities included in this area offer many opportunities for using scientific methods to explore children's natural curiosity.

Sensory Possibilities

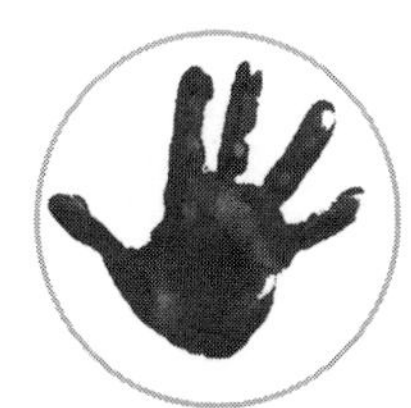

Sensory, sand, and water experiences are a mainstay of any preschool program. Water is soothing; water toys stimulate play; and the splashing and slapping of water and other sensory materials produce interesting reactions. Giving children opportunities to integrate the messages received though the senses with cognitive and language skills provides children experience with receiving, filtering, and processing sensory information. This section suggests ways to vary the type, quality, and source of sensory experiences.

Literacy/Writing Possibilities

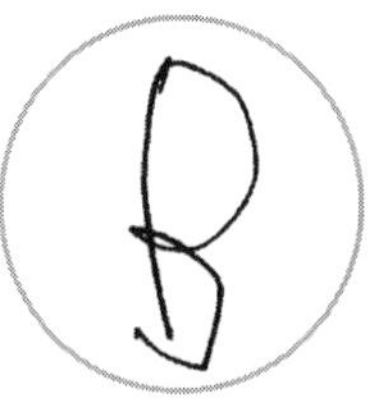

Supporting literacy development with a print-rich environment is the goal of this interest area. When children see how reading and writing work in everyday experiences, they begin to label objects, try out their own versions of writing, and practice communicating with each other. Providing many graphic experiences leads children toward functional use of symbols and the meaning they convey. Interesting, varied, and culturally diverse books are

included to bring the written word to life as adults read stories to children daily. Books are the source of interesting images and stimulation that form the foundation of literacy. Experiences with books increase children's ability to tell their own stories and expand their vocabularies as they explore the world of literature. Phonemic awareness and phonological skills grow as teachers introduce new vocabulary, connect sounds to letters, and provide children with experiences in rhyming words and the sounds of oral language. Children's books related to the developmental task are also included.

Math/Manipulatives Possibilities

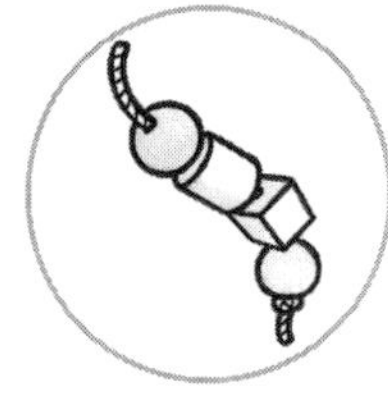

Grouping, sorting, matching, and ordering activities are numeracy skills that will prepare children for mathematics later in school. This area of the classroom introduces diverse materials that connect mathematical concepts to children's play.

Rhymes/Fingerplays/Songs/Music Possibilities

Music is a natural, enjoyable part of the environment for young children. A variety of musical experiences (singing as well as tapes or CDs) facilitates transitions, calms children for quiet time, and changes the pace of the day. Moving one's body to music and creating rhythms come naturally for young children and contribute to coordinating communication pathways in the brain. Rhyme and repetition in language expand children's vocabularies and teach the rules of grammar and syntax. Word play leads the way for these skills to emerge. When a rich language tradition is embedded in the school day, literacy skills flourish. This section expands teachers' repertoire of songs, rhymes, fingerplays, and music.

Group Time Possibilities

Preschool teachers often use group times to create and extend feelings of community among children—a sense of belonging to a group. Creating a community of learners who are curious, who want to know what is happening in the world around them, and who are interested in each other is celebrated during this time together. Teachers also use group time experiences to explore ideas, present didactic information, pose problems for the group to solve, and celebrate accomplishments of individual group members.

Movement/Outdoor Possibilities

Outdoor time is an important part of the day for young children, who need opportunities to run, jump, stretch, and use all of the large muscles of the body. The fresh air is a nice change from the classroom environment. In addition, activities that are moved from the inside to the outside take on new meaning. The sounds of the neighborhood, the way light changes because of clouds or shade, the feel of the breeze, running across the grass, and digging in the dirt all add to the richness of the outdoor experience.

Project/Documentation Possibilities

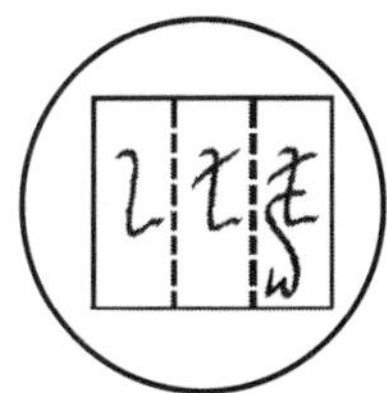

Projects are opportunities for children to engage in in-depth investigation as an individual, small group, or classroom activity. Projects are important because they provide opportunities for reflection on what children think, continuity of experience, as well as an opportunity to practice, perfect, and enjoy experiences again and again. Projects often focus on how children interpret what they are learning and what it means to them. Documentation communicates children's knowledge construction and provides children with the opportunity to revisit what they have learned. This section suggests project ideas and gives teachers suggestions about what might be included as documentation.

Field Trip Possibilities

When children participate in field trips, they are able to gather information first hand. Field trips are most beneficial when they are closely related to what is happening in the classroom and when teachers provide support for field trips before, during, and after the event. Suggestions for field trips are included in each Possibilities Plan for teachers to consider as out-of-school experiences for children.

Snack Possibilities

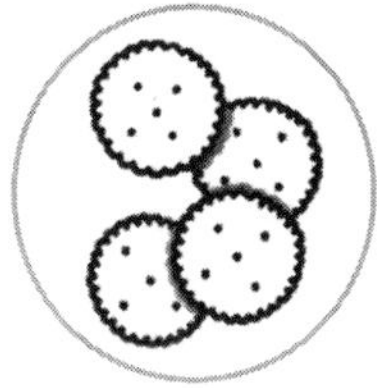

Each Possibilities Plan suggests snacks that are related to the topic. Snacks can be prepared by a group of children or included as self-service snack choices for individual children.

Family Participation Possibilities and Parent Postcards

Families are their child's first and most important teachers. For this reason, family participation in children's school experience is crucial. Suggestions for family involvement are either related to the Possibilities Plan or to the developmental task at hand. Parent Postcards are included in the Possibilities Plan sections as well as in the discussion of the developmental task. These postcards support the plan and are natural extensions of the activities and experiences that teachers are providing for children in the classroom.

Curriculum Resources

The Curriculum Resources section that accompanies each plan provides additional sources for support in planning. Suggested prop box materials, books, observation/assessment, concepts learned, and picture file/vocabulary for each Possibilities Plan are included.

Prop Boxes

In this section, prop boxes are listed with their contents. Prop boxes are a wonderful way to keep curriculum experiences fresh for children. Teachers can expand the collection of props for play and identify prop boxes that accompany the Possibilities Plans. Prop boxes help teachers keep materials organized and accessible as common play themes emerge. Suggestions of items for families to bring into the classroom that the children can use in the prop boxes are included here. Additionally, families can provide materials that are a part of the child's cultural context. As families learn about the topics explored in the classroom, they can support these activities and experiences at home.

Books

This section provides a full list of children's books related to each Possibilities Plan and to each developmental task.

Observation/Assessment

The observation and assessment section of curriculum resources includes strategies used to gather information to inform curriculum development and to make sure that each child's individual learning is on target. Sometimes this section refers to what the teachers could observe for or assess; sometimes it reminds teachers to be observant and continually assess when and where children are on a developing skill. Teachers get ideas about how to externalize what children are learning for all to see in this section.

Concepts Learned

What are preschoolers learning from their choices of activities? Teachers often see the range and depth of children's learning in the classroom. The Concepts Learned list is designed to help teachers share what children are learning with parents and families by identifying content, process, and pre-academic skills explored in each Possibilities Plan. Content knowledge includes discrete facts or concepts. Process knowledge is "how-to" knowledge learned through practice. Pre-academic skills are the precursors to more advanced skills that must be in place before subsequent academic skills such as reading, writing, spelling, and mathematics can be learned. These are skills that children are learning because of the planned environment, planned interactions, teaching, and planned experiences.

Concepts Learned lists are included in each Possibilities Plan. Post them in the classroom for parents to read, send the lists home, or use them during conferences. The result is making learning visible to parents and other stakeholders.

Picture File/Vocabulary

A Picture File/Vocabulary list is included for each plan. This list of suggested pictures provides a variety of different images related to the Possibilities Plan. Pictures also add information to the images that children have already experienced. In addition, the picture file is an inexpensive teaching tool that should be part of every preschool teacher's resources. Pictures support children's vocabulary development and remind teachers that focusing on expanding children's expressive language is excellent preparation for future academic success.

THE CURRICULUM PLANNING PROCESS

The period of three to five years of age is a dynamic time of life. Preschoolers are growing and changing quickly, and their interests often turn to the other children in the class. To make sure your curriculum planning is appropriate, follow the steps described below.

Curriculum planning always starts with observation and assessment. It is not possible to plan for children unless you know where they are developmentally and understand their interests and preferences. Observation and assessment are dynamic activities that take place continually and, when completed, lead teachers right back to the observation and assessment process again.

Observation should focus not only on emerging development, but also on emerging play themes and interests. As themes emerge (such as interest in restaurants or where we get clean water), they can be incorporated into the curriculum planning process. Teachers have the opportunity to expand content and skill knowledge by building on previous understanding and knowledge.

After teachers have a good picture of the preferences, interests, play themes, and ages and stages of the children in their group, many turn to curriculum resources to help them flesh out a complex and rich plan. ***Innovations: The Comprehensive Preschool Curriculum*** encourages teachers to plan not only activities and experiences, but also classroom environments; family participation activities; parent education activities; interaction possibilities;

the books that will be available and read to children; the fingerplays, rhymes, and transition activities that will be used; the songs that will be sung or music played; and so on. This comprehensive view of planning results in stimulating experiences for preschool children. Such planning often results in more ideas than you can use. Preparing more than you need isn't a problem. In fact, it gives you the ability to modify and individualize your plans by selecting among the activities and experiences you planned for just the right one to match a child's interest or age and stage. Or, it allows you to add complexity or simplify activities based on the child's response to what you planned.

Use the materials in this curriculum as a starting place. Then, pull additional activities and experiences from the wealth of resources that are available that contain many good curriculum ideas. Additional resources for teachers are included in each chapter.

While children are involved in the carefully planned environment and activities you have prepared, your role once again becomes that of observer. You gather valuable information about where to go next, what skills are being learned or practiced, and how learning can be shared or documented. From these new observations comes the knowledge of preferences, interests, play themes, and ages and stages that start the process again.

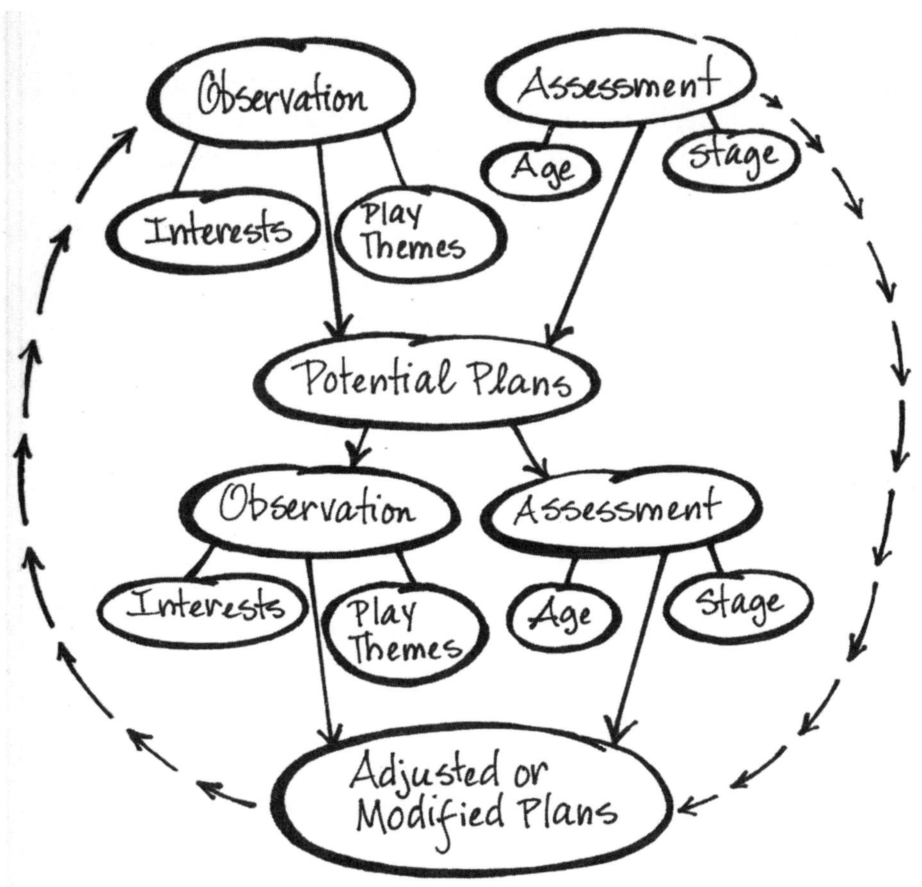

Observation—the Source of Emergent Curriculum Ideas

Where do emergent curriculum ideas come from? They come from observation. Developing a strategy for collecting play themes and ideas from observing children is the challenge. Begin by completing a series of brief observing children as they play. From these observations, identify play ideas and interests of particular children. Sometimes it takes only one observation to get ideas, other times it takes several observations for interests and play themes to emerge. For example, as a result of observing that children were playing with water, teachers may plan curriculum about experimenting with water. The resulting curriculum plan can capture the children's interest in water and explore it in a variety of ways. When curriculum ideas come from children's interests, they enthusiastically pursue the activities, materials, and experiences that teachers prepare for them, and teachers are able to modify their plans to fit individual interests.

But curriculum planning doesn't stop here. The teacher continues to observe, so she or he can adjust plans where needed and find ways to communicate to families what children are learning as a result of experiences. This completes the cycle and makes sure that parents see the teacher's plans and children's experiences as good early childhood education.

Viewed this way, curriculum planning is not an event—it is an ongoing process. Use the blank Possibilities Plan (see pages 615–617 in the Appendix) to reflect this process as it unfolds. Post these plans where parents and visitors can see and begin to understand the complex and thorough process that leads to exciting, integrated curriculum in your classroom.

Curriculum developed this way results in rich, meaningful experiences for children while accommodating the need to help parents and families see and understand the growth and development of skills. The first developmental task of preschool, adjusting to school, is where it all begins.

CHAPTER 2

Adjusting to School

INNOVATIONS IN CARE AND EARLY EDUCATION

Historically, three major strands of theories contribute to explanations about how children grow and develop. One strand views development as a result of the innate biological makeup of the child. Growth and development is then just a process of waiting and watching as the child follows her biological programming.

The second strand views development as a result of environmental influences on the child. The child comes into the world waiting for experiences to influence what will become of her.

The third strand views the process of development as influenced both by biological heredity (or nature) and environment (nurture), as well as by the dynamic interplay between the two. Interactional theories, as they are called, view development as much more complex than the nature or nurture strands.

Recently, interactional theories have identified additional components of influence. Educators now embrace the expanded role of culture in child development and early childhood education, recognizing that learning takes place within a child's cultural context. In addition, increased understanding of the role the child plays in her own development is showing educators how to structure learning in different ways for different children. Finally, theoretical work in the interactional point of view embraces the centrality of relationships in how children develop and learn.

Innovations: The Comprehensive Preschool Curriculum is grounded in theories that view human development as a dynamic, sequential, and cumulative process. But this view is not adequate to explain the individual nature of development and the uniqueness of each child. It must be supplemented with theories that view human development as occurring within the context of interactions—with significant others; with the social, cultural, and physical environment; and with the biological predispositions of individual genetics. Taken together, developmental and interactional theories are informative and useful for families, parents, and teachers.

The developmental view is a tradition within early childhood education, forming the foundation of how we think children grow and develop. Increased documentation of the impact of the early years on development, an improved understanding of the importance of nurturing relationships, and clearer information about the impact of relationships on children's development have informed and expanded our understanding.

An increase in our knowledge and understanding of how children learn also has occurred. The long-held views of children as active learners who construct their own knowledge and understanding of the world are rapidly being amended with insights from neuroscience about sensitive periods or timing effects of brain development. Teaching the right things at the right times has become an important educational issue.

In this chapter, the underlying principles of developmental and interactional theory are explained. The goal is to help teachers understand the contribution of these theoretical points of view, concepts, and ideas for understanding development during the preschool years.

Developmental Theory

Principles of Developmental Theory

Which of the following diagrams do you think best represents the way children develop?

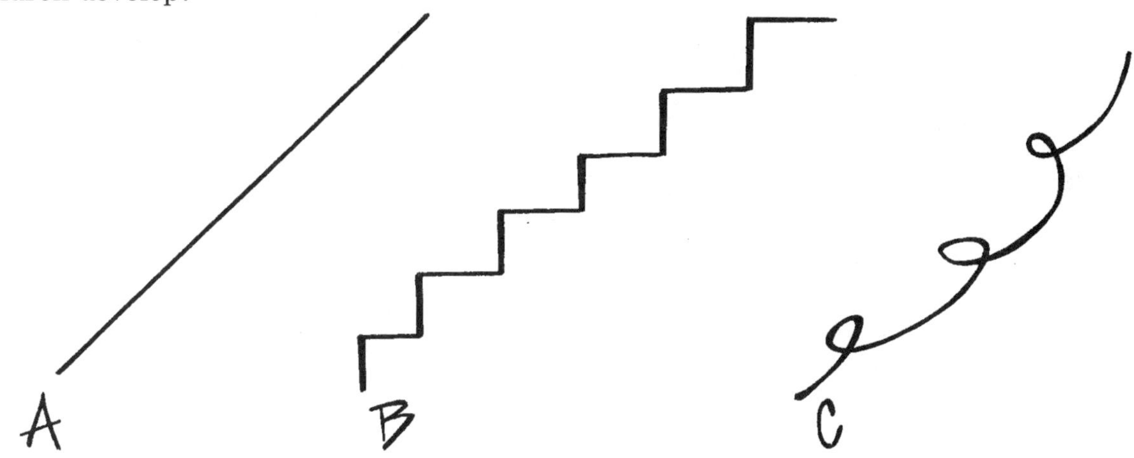

Based on what educators now know, the answer is C. Development is a continuous though uneven cycle of ever-increasing skills and abilities in which each period of growth is often preceded by a brief, sometimes turbulent regression. Guided by a set of underlying principles, developmental theory helps explain the amazing changes that take place during the early childhood years.

The first principle of developmental theory is that human development is integrated. All domains of development—physical, emotional, social, and intellectual (which includes language and cognition) are interrelated.

Development or growth in one area influences and is influenced by development and growth in another (Bredekamp & Copple, 1997).

The second principle is that growth follows a universal and relatively predictable sequence. Milestones of development are observable and are used to track children's progress along the growth continua. The relative predictability can be seen in each area of development—physical, social, emotional, and intellectual, including cognitive and language development. For example, in the area of literacy development, children proceed from scribbling to making basic shapes, to making symbol-like marks, to making letters, and then to making words. Almost every child follows this sequence of development.

The Five Principles of Developmental Theory

1. Human development is integrated; all developmental domains are interrelated.
2. Growth follows a universal and relatively predictable sequence.
3. Each child has an individual pattern and timing of growth.
4. Development proceeds from the simple to the complex and from the general to the specific.
5. The interplay of biological, environmental, cultural, social, and interactional experiences impacts development.

The third principle of development is that each child has an individual pattern and timing of growth. Although the sequence is relatively predictable, each child's individual progress through the sequence varies. For example, some children have the eye-hand coordination to cut with scissors around the age of three years while others may not be able to handle scissors well until closer to five years of age. This principle captures the sporadic and uneven nature of development. A child might work on physical development until she can hop on one foot and then move on to language development or cognitive skill acquisition. Or, a child might make no observable developmental progress at all for a few months and then all of a sudden make major strides in several domains. This component of development illustrates the uniqueness of each child (Perry, 2000).

This principle of developmental theory also explains why age is such a poor predictor of developmental stage. Each child's prenatal and birth experience, personality, temperament, preferred approach to learning, type of and variation in experiences, interests, strengths, needs, family structure and background, expectations of culture, motivation, energy level, health status, and so on, are individual and contribute to the child's unique pattern and timing of growth. This principle explains the many differences among and between children who are the same chronological age.

A fourth principle of developmental theory is that development proceeds from the simple to the complex and from the general to the specific. Simple skills must be acquired before more complex ones can build upon them.

Development also proceeds from behavioral knowledge to symbolic or representational knowledge. Children learn to do things long before they can describe them with language or represent them with pictures or in writing. For example, children can find the way to their bedrooms before they can read and follow maps or diagrams of the way to their bedrooms. This trend of increasing complexity in development is predictable and leads to greater organization and internalization of skills and abilities. Parents and teachers can see this principle at work as children become more independent, more self-controlled, and more able to coordinate their behaviors with the expectations of the people around them.

The fifth principle highlights the impact of biological, environmental, cultural, social, and interactional experiences on development. The interplay among these contexts and experiences influences not only the general direction of development, but also the short- and long-term outcomes for children. For example, children who have many experiences with books are more likely to be early readers.

These principles are the foundation of the developmental approach. Teachers need a thorough understanding of these concepts to serve as the foundation for their work with young children and their families.

Interactional Theories of Development

Principles of Interactional Theory and How Children Learn

Intimate, reciprocal, synchronous relationships form the foundation and core of healthy development. This first principle of interactional theory addresses the type of affective or emotional environment necessary for healthy development. Brazelton and Greenspan (2000) consider warm, nurturing interactions to be the first essential need of young children. Others point to the profound effect that these relationships have on how children grow up and what they learn (Berk, 1999; Shonkoff & Phillips, 2000).

The second principle is that interactions take place in and are influenced by a variety of different contexts, including social and cultural contexts. As individuals, we each live within our own culture. These social and cultural contexts determine how individuals communicate with each other (verbally and non-verbally) and what behavioral expectations are present. For example, some parents believe that schools are public places and that teachers should be respected and obeyed. Others view school as a part of the extended network of the family and approach relationships with teachers as extensions of family relationships subject to give and take. The expectations of each of these families will, to a large extent, control and shape the way children respond to their teachers.

The Five Principles of Interactional Theory

1. Intimate, reciprocal, synchronous relationships form the foundation and core of healthy development.
2. Interactions take place in and are influenced by a variety of contexts, including social and cultural contexts.
3. There is a dynamic relationship between biological heredity and experience.
4. Interactions between children and the social, cultural, and physical worlds direct children's learning.
5. Play is the interactive medium of development.

The third principle of interactional theory states that there is a dynamic relationship between biological heredity and experience. This interplay is continuous and influences development throughout the lifespan. Although genetics are fixed at conception, optimal experiences during the early childhood years serve as the key to unlock biological potential at sensitive periods during children's development. Further, experiences can serve as compensating factors, mediating early deprivation or mistreatment.

The fourth principle tells us that interactions between children and the social, cultural, and physical worlds direct children's learning, allowing them to construct their own knowledge and understanding. No matter how knowledgeable we are as teachers, we cannot *give* children knowledge and understanding. Instead, they *build* their own, using who they are, what experiences they have had, what relationships they have, what learning styles they use, and what interest levels they have at the moment. For example, even when children have been in the same school environment having very similar experiences, one child may develop a strong interest in trucks, another in playing outside, and another in reading books.

The fifth principle is that play is the interactive medium of development. Emotional, social, physical, and intellectual growth takes place within the context of play that occurs with objects and materials, in interactions with peers, and as facilitated by supportive adults. We observe children at play to determine their developmental stages.

Integrating Interactional and Developmental Theories

Developmental Tasks

Development is a lifelong task. It begins in infancy and continues throughout the lifespan. There are many different ideas about how humans develop into capable, productive, functional adults. ***Innovations: The Comprehensive Curriculum*** series proposes six life tasks that begin in infancy and continue as development emerges. Each life task is grounded in theory and the resulting practices that have emerged from developmental and interactional theory and research, and from our current understanding of how children learn.

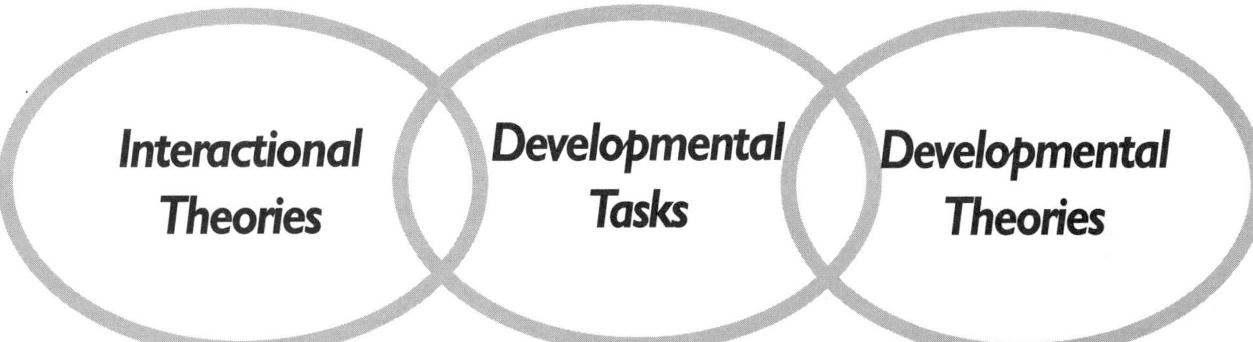

Developmental Tasks by Age

Birth–18 Months	18 Months–36 Months	3–5 Years
Separating from Parents →	Transitioning to School →	Adjusting to School
Connecting to School →	Making Friends →	
Relating to Self and Others →	Exploring Roles →	
← Communicating with Parents, Teachers, and Friends →		
Moving Around →	Problem-solving →	
← Expressing Feelings with Parents, Teachers, and Friends →		

In one case, the task for preschool children is different from the tasks for younger children, illustrating that different stages of development pose different maturation, learning, and interactional challenges. In others, the task continues to develop throughout the first five years of life, with each maturation, skill acquisition, and interactional experience building on and being influenced by the previous one.

These tasks and their supporting curricula are featured in ***Innovations: The Comprehensive Infant Curriculum*** and ***Innovations: The Comprehensive Toddler Curriculum*** (Albrecht & Miller, 2000). These resources can be used in conjunction with ***Innovations: The Comprehensive Preschool Curriculum*** to provide high-quality and appropriate school experiences for children from birth through age five.

Temperament

Regardless of the imprint of biology, environment, parents, and culture, every child is born with a personality—a temperament that guides and influences her approach to the world. Genetically determined, a child's temperament will manifest itself in a variety of character traits (Chess & Thomas, 1987). These stable differences in personality are a major consideration in predicting psychological health later in life.

Each of these traits varies along a continuum. Teachers can observe and identify where children are on each continuum. Psychologist Alicia Liebermann combined the characteristics of temperament into three groups and described them as flexible, fearful, or feisty (California State Department of Education, 1990).

The Flexible Child—The traits of flexible children include regular biological rhythms, adaptability to change and new situations, low intensity, low sensitivity, and positive mood. In school, flexible children are easily recognizable and can be overlooked because they do not often demand attention. It is important to the development of flexible children that adults devote attention to them although they do not demand it.

The Fearful Child—Fearful children avoid new situations and are slow to warm to new people and experiences. Their cautious ways mean that adults must go slowly with them, allowing them to observe a new activity or situation before approaching it. Teachers also may need to introduce fearful children to new stimuli and only gradually withdraw their support as caution gives way to interest and enjoyment.

Concern about perceiving this temperamental style as negative, rather than just a different style, has led some educators to call this temperamental style *cautious* rather than *fearful* or *slow to warm* (Klein, 2002). The intent of temperamental styles is not to label children's temperaments as positive or negative but to help understand the impact of temperament on development and learning.

The Feisty Child—Feisty children have irregular rhythms and are very active, intense, easily distracted, sensitive, and moody. Feisty children run rather than walk, push the limits, and respond impulsively with intense emotions. Well-planned transitions are important to feisty children who often will resist being rushed. Feisty children need opportunities for active play, as well as a chance to experience quiet play when the mood strikes.

Temperament is relatively stable, but not unchanging. Innate temperament is influenced by experiences, and these experiences can be compensating ones. For example, a cautious child can learn, with the help and support of caring adults, to approach new situations or to manage the fear of new experiences. Feisty children, in recovering from emotional outbursts, can learn to manage intense feelings and express them appropriately when supported by teachers. Flexible children can learn appropriate ways to ask for and receive needed attention even when the adults around them are busy. Sensitive parenting and teaching are mediating experiences that support children's temperamental characteristics.

Use the chart on the next page to explore children's temperaments. Then use the information to inform teaching.

Temperament Chart

Mark where each child's behaviors fall on the continuum. Use this information to help you plan.

1) activity level
2) regularity of biological rhythms (sleeping, eating, and elimination)
3) approach/withdrawal tendencies
4) mood, positive to negative
5) intensity of reaction
6) adaptability
7) sensitivity to light, touch, taste, sound, and sights
8) distractibility
9) persistence

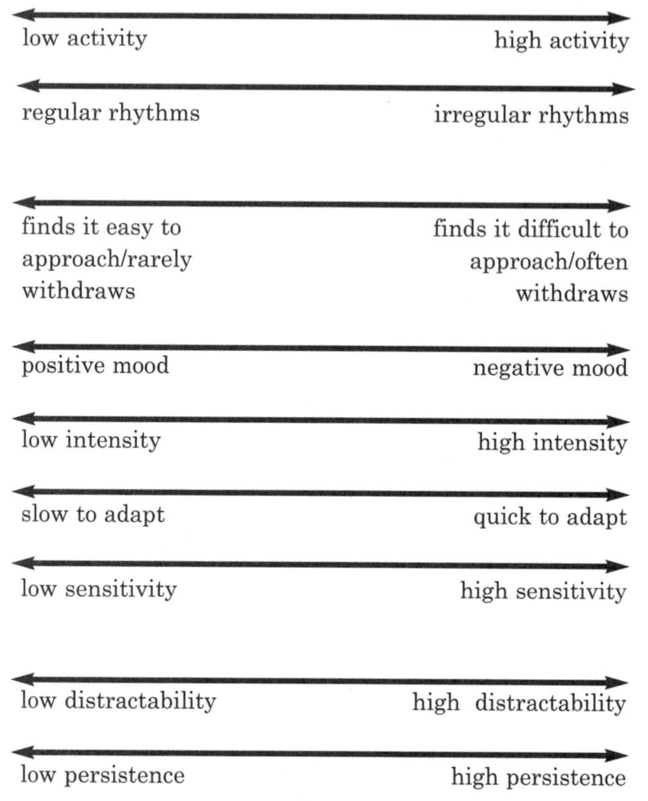

Adapted from California State Department of Education (1990). ***Flexible, fearful, or feisty: The different temperaments of infants and toddlers.*** Videotape. Sacramento, CA: Department of Education.

Components of Developmental Uniqueness

Although children's development follows a relatively predictable, identifiable sequence, there are components of uniqueness within that sequence. One of the components is the child's pace of development. Pace varies within and across domains of development. One example of this principle is seen as children learn to jump first with both feet and then to balance while jumping on just one foot. Children move sequentially through the steps of learning to jump on one foot. However, one child may learn to jump on two feet at three years of age while another might learn at four.

The methods children use to perfect jumping on one foot may also be different. One child might jump on one foot, falling when balance isn't maintained. Another might try jumping on one foot while holding hands with a friend or while holding onto a railing. Still another might watch others jump, learning from their successes and failures before trying the skill.

A second component of uniqueness is the child's integration of developmental domains. Development is integrated, with growth in one sphere closely tied to and influenced by development in other areas. For example, emotional development during preschool influences children's ability to access and use social skills with friends, while social interest in what others are doing emerges from stability in emotional relationships.

Yet, the way children's domains of development are integrated varies. Children may have a dominant domain that leads the developmental process (Perry, 2000). For example, a child may mature or learn skills in one domain before maturing or learning new skills in other domains. Alternatively, domains may dominate sequentially with a child learning new physical skills first, then emotional skills, then language skills, then cognitive skills, and then social skills. Or, domains may be so integrated that development proceeds in tandem in each area with teachers noticing maturation or skill acquisition in all areas of development at the same time. These subtle differences are important. Early indications of intelligences (Gardner, 1983) or learning styles (Scanlon, 1988), and risk factors (Shonkoff & Phillips, 2000) are often extrapolated from children's unique integration of developmental domains.

The Three Components of Developmental Uniqueness

1. The pattern and timing of development—the pace of development—is unique for each child.
2. Development is integrated, with growth in one sphere closely tied to and influenced by development in other areas.
3. Development is often sporadic and uneven.

A third component of uniqueness is the sporadic and uneven nature of development. Developmental growth in children seems to come in spurts. A child might make no developmental progress at all for a few weeks or months. Then, all of a sudden she may make major strides, acquiring new skills in several different areas seemingly all at once. Or, development may be steady and incremental.

An example of uniqueness within domains might be the child who works hard on physical development until the ability to skip is acquired, then moves on to language development or cognitive skill acquisition, acquiring new skills in separate domains sequentially. An example across domains of development can be seen in the child who works on the growth in each developmental domain until maturation or skill acquisition is gained (learning to hop on one foot, to use a full sentence to communicate needs), and then moves on to new skills in another domain.

Brain research has produced evidence that there are also biological components of uniqueness. When children's brains are developing, the process of synaptogenesis—the connecting of brain cells together in communicating neural pathways—is affected by experience. Some synaptogenesis is the result of experiences that the brain is biologically prepared to receive—genetically built-in pauses for external stimulation. Other synaptogenesis is dependent on experiences tied to happenings that most children experience as they grow and develop in the interactive world—that then triggers additional synaptic connections. Because each child's experiences (both experience-expectant and experience-dependent) are unique, they create a unique pattern of connections and neural pathways. As a result, no two brains form and strengthen exactly the same neural pathways (Shonkoff & Phillips, 2000; Shore, 1997).

Exploring Alternate Developmental Pathways

Variations in developmental growth are viewed as alternate developmental pathways—not deviant or delayed development, but development that proceeds uniquely. Children who never crawled or who pulled to a stand before they crawled, or children with physical impairments (such as blindness and deafness), who still develop basic abilities to communicate or navigate their environments, illustrate the concept of alternate developmental pathways. They got to the same or similar destination developmentally in a unique and different way. Because the components of uniqueness vary within the same child and across children, viewing these variations as alternate, yet normal, lessens the dependence on normative data as the only measuring stick of developmental progress.

Maslow's Hierarchy of Needs

Maslow (1954) conceptualized a hierarchy of needs that serves as a backdrop to how children develop and learn across the lifespan. The theory proposes that basic needs are arranged in a hierarchical order and that higher order needs cannot be addressed without satisfaction of previous levels.

The first level of needs is related to physiological survival and well-being. Food, water, clothing, shelter, hygiene, and health care are examples of some of the basic needs of this level. The second level of needs relates to physical safety and psychological security. This includes safety from physical dangers and psychological needs, such as the need for touch and responsive nurturing from significant adults.

Needs relating to love and belonging form the third level of the hierarchy. This is a reciprocal need. Emotional support from a limited number of consistent, responsive adults and interactions with other children are both required to meet this need.

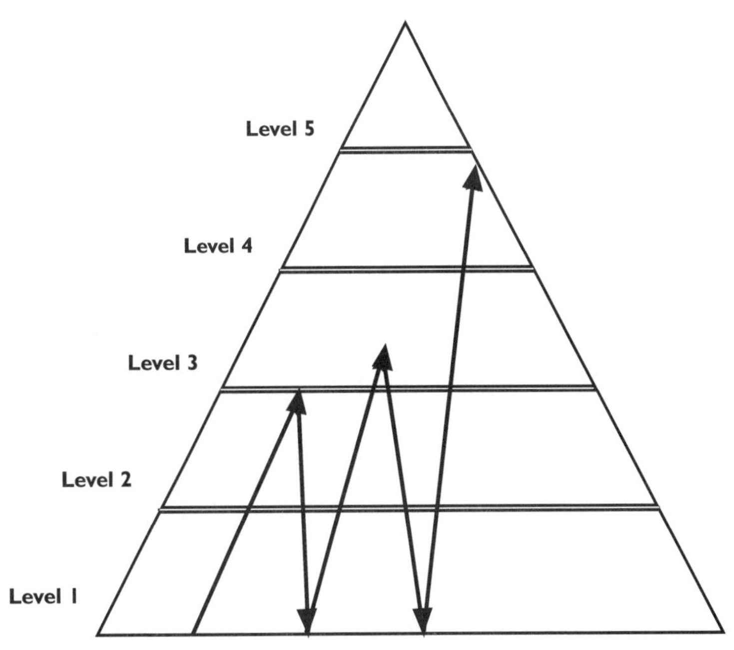

The need for self-esteem and self-worth is the fourth level of the needs hierarchy. When a feeling of love and belonging is established through emotional support, the child develops self-esteem and a feeling of self-worth. Finally, the need to know and understand is the fifth level of Maslow's Hierarchy of Needs. Human beings cannot get to this level until needs have been met at all of the other levels.

Maslow proposed that each need grows out of the satisfaction of the previous one and that the process of meeting needs can be regressive. In other words, if a child has progressed to the level of needing belonging and love, and suddenly is threatened physically by disease, her need level will revert from level three to level one until the need for physiological survival and well-being is once again satisfied.

INNOVATIONS IN INTERACTIVE EXPERIENCES

Children's experiences at school have so much to do with the way they will grow and develop. If they experience school as negative, frustrating, or insensitive, they will view the learning process as overwhelming and insurmountable. If, on the other hand, their relationships and experiences at school are supportive, nurturing, and positive, human development has an almost perfect plan for growing and learning. In fact, during the first five years, development unfolds naturally for most children. Many teachers view the activities and curriculum they plan as the most important part of their job. While these tasks are important, children are learning all the time—not just when teachers are providing direct instruction.

What is outside the realm of activities in the classroom (for example, a child who takes longer to transition from one activity to another, a child who naps for a longer or shorter time than expected, a child who is suddenly fascinated with another child's friendship) is all curriculum. Children are always learning. It is the teacher's job to support that learning in whatever forms it may take.

Interactive Experiences Checklist for Adjusting to School

Ask a mentor to observe you in your classroom to document the following interactive behaviors. Think about the following list of interactive experiences and make sure that the classroom reflects many of them.

- ☐ Prepare children for transitions. Talk with children about what is going to happen next. Use songs, fingerplays, and rhymes to support transitions.
- ☐ In full-day programs, leave written records for other teachers who are involved in children's care and early education. Written records prevent relying solely on verbal exchanges that may get lost in the midst of transitions.
- ☐ Watch the tone of your voice and your non-verbal cues during interactions. Congruence, between what you say and the way you say it, and between what you do and the way you do it, is communication.
- ☐ Support children during new experiences. When new things are happening in the school environment, children need support in taking in the new stimuli. Sometimes this support is anticipatory, such as warning children that the fire alarm is going to go off in a minute and make a loud noise, or reminding children that you are going to ask them to stop what they are doing and go outside.
- ☐ Know each child's temperament and learning style, so you can anticipate what each child will need. When physical support is no longer needed, visually support the child with eye contact and non-verbal cues such as smiling and nodding your head.

Create Positive Interactive Environments

In ***Innovations: The Comprehensive Preschool Curriculum***, guidance and discipline are approached from the point of view that adults create positive interactive environments between children and with their teachers. Specific techniques for managing, influencing, and teaching children appropriate behaviors are considered. This is one of the most important jobs teachers have. When children feel safe and secure, they are more likely to be self-responsible, exhibit self-control, and be empathetic with others.

Maslow's hierarchy gives teachers ideas about how children feel when they approach new interactive environments. Children must initially discover whether new environments will meet their needs, beginning at the bottom of the hierarchy. If children feel no threats to their psychological survival and security, they can move on to discovering ways to belong and feel good about themselves as they participate with others in the new environment.

Interactive environments that facilitate a feeling that emotional needs will be met have many of the following characteristics:

- Warm, caring adults who are responsive to children;
- Adults who have clear communication styles;
- A few clear, easily understandable limits;
- Many acceptable and interesting options for play and participation;
- Clear and reasonable expectations for interactions;
- Close supervision and monitoring to help children feel comfortable participating in play and to protect them from danger;
- Adults who have good reasons for rules and limits;
- Options for choosing what to do when problems arise;
- Adults who really listen to children's interests, concerns, and problems;
- A high level of acceptance of strong feelings and expressed emotions; and
- An expectation that hurting people and things is not acceptable.

Every one of these characteristics is under the teacher's control and can become part of the interactive environment.

Use a Variety of Teaching Roles

Teachers use a wide variety of roles in their work with young children. During the developmental task of Adjusting to School, two of the most important teacher roles are observer and facilitator.

The Teacher as Observer

Observation, rather than interaction or instruction, is the primary teaching strategy for getting to know all children and their families. Teachers observe to discover:

- The unique ways families communicate;
- The ways parents interact with their children;
- How children approach and respond to new situations;
- A child's sense of personal space—whether being close is acceptable or not;
- Children's interest in the physical world that is near them;
- Management strategies used by parents that might be used by teachers, as well;

- Children's temperamental traits; and
- Children's developmental uniqueness or alternate developmental pathways.

When observation is a focus, teachers need many ways to embed taking observation notes into their routine. Try placing observation tools near where you will use them. Or use Post-It™ notes to make notes that can be quickly sorted among children's portfolios. Then, organize observation records by having a readily accessible place to put the finished notes.

The Teacher as Facilitator

The role of facilitator emerges from the important task of planning and implementing gradual enrollment with children (see page 48). The task of adjusting is a challenging one for most children and families. When teachers see their role as facilitating this experience, rather than directing it, parents are free to use their skills and abilities to help their child adjust.

This means that teachers check in with the families often, asking if things are going well. They facilitate the expression of ideas, opinions, and points of view that differ from their own, and find ways to facilitate the connection among the child, teacher, parents, and school.

Facilitation can take many forms, and based on the teacher's observations during the process of gradual enrollment, can be modified to achieve a better fit along the way. Here are some areas for facilitation during the task of adjusting to school:

- Facilitate the transition from outside the classroom to inside the classroom.
- Help parents understand where things go.
- Facilitate the exchange of knowledge about the child from the family to the teacher, including information about typical schedules, security items, favorite comforting strategies, ideas for encouraging interactions, and so on.
- Facilitate the exchange of information about the cultural context of the child from the parent to the teacher.
- Facilitate the identification of concerns, fears, anxieties, expectations for learning and growing, hopes for the child's development, parental development needs, and so on.

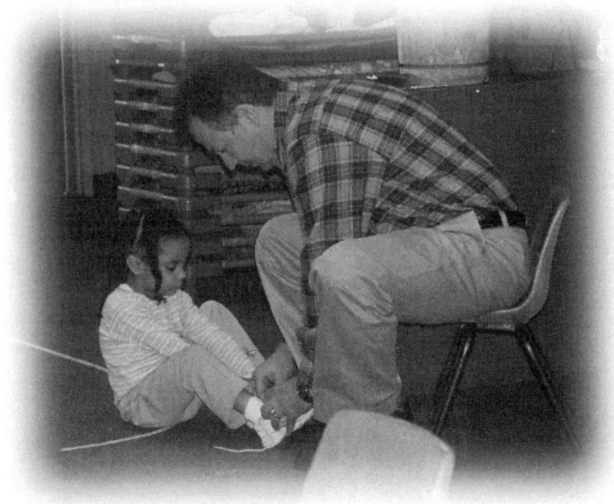

INNOVATIONS IN TEACHING

Knowledge leads to best practices. Understanding developmental theory, interactional theory, temperament, developmental uniqueness, and Maslow's Hierarchy of Needs guides teachers to conduct gradual enrollments and to actively facilitate adjustment to school.

Conduct Gradual Enrollment

One of the best ways to facilitate a child's adjustment to any new early childhood experience is to encourage important adults in the child's life to participate with the child and the teacher in a gradual enrollment process. Young children have little experience with change and need time to adjust to new settings. Parents need to understand how new environments work and how teachers will handle the dynamic tasks of early education. Gradual enrollment gives children, teachers, and families the necessary time.

Although there is no single way to do gradual enrollment, most often it looks like this.

1. The parent(s) or another familiar adult brings the child to the school.
2. The child's things are put away in an assigned location.
3. The parent sits with the child or moves about the room, allowing the child to watch the teachers, parents, and other children, or to play in the environment.
4. The child's teacher is near during this time but is not in a hurry to interact with the child. The teacher uses this time to observe the child and the parent in action as she or he continues to respond to other children and follow the day's routine.
5. As the parent and child settle in and the day progresses, the parent can talk with the teacher as she or he moves about the room. As this happens, the teacher's voice and communication style will become familiar to the child.
6. When the child needs help with toileting, a snack, lunch, or a nap, the parent proceeds with routine care. The teacher observes as the parent does this.
7. Gradually, as the day progresses or during subsequent visits, the parent and the teacher reverse roles, with the parent becoming the observer and the teacher interacting directly with the child.

In full-day, full-year programs, gradual enrollment can take place over a week or so with the parent and child staying one to two hours the first day and working up to staying for the full program day. Parents who can't should be encouraged to do gradual enrollment for at least two days. If this is not possible, the parents or a familiar family member should spend 20–30 minutes in the school before departing, return for lunch that day, and then spend another 20–30 minutes in the school at the end of the day.

For programs that have a traditional academic schedule and begin in the fall, gradual enrollment will look different. Some suggestions include starting the children in small groups, rather than starting everyone at once; staggering start times so that children arrive in two or three small groups rather than all at the same time; shortening the length of the day during the first few days or weeks to allow time for adjustment; or having one or two play days in advance of the beginning of school to acquaint children with the physical environment of the new school and to introduce the teachers to children and their families.

Although gradual enrollment is more than most schools ask or require of families, it is one of the most important components of the family/school connection. It helps both parties understand what to expect. When families cannot participate in the gradual enrollment process, they often have difficulty adjusting to school, complain more often, and make changes in the child's placement more frequently. Families who are unsuccessful in calibrating their expectations and who don't have the time to work cooperatively with the teacher and the school to make sure the child's adjustment is well-planned and implemented, will have more complaints and misunderstandings.

Don't skip gradual enrollment—it is the firm foundation upon which a mutual relationship between the families and the teacher is built. It also gives children the time they need to adjust to new places and new people.

Facilitate Adjustment

Facilitating adjustment is a shared job. Attachment to parents, family, and close relations is usually completed by the preschool years. Adjustment to school focuses on building secondary relationships with other adults and peers. Try some of the following suggestions for helping preschool children and their families adjust to school.

- Assign a primary teacher to every child—that first friend at school who

will work sensitively to match what individual children need to curriculum and interactions. (See page 132 for more about primary teaching.)
- Resist the tendency to look at children as more similar than different. Try to observe for and investigate differences to inform your teaching and curriculum planning.
- Differentiate the teacher's role from the parent's role. Both seem to do the same thing during different times of the day, but the roles are not the same. Teachers listen to parents, suggest solutions, raise issues, point out alternatives, and provide resources to families. These are appropriate roles for teachers. Directing child rearing or insisting on specific expectations (such as requiring the parent to teach the child to tie his shoes by the fourth birthday) are examples of inappropriate roles for teachers.

Think about the following questions to help choose appropriate boundaries.
- Who should be the first person to share the emergence of a new skill or change in growth?
- Who should suggest strategies for helping children learn specific table manners (such as not talking when your mouth is full of food)?
- Who should be responsible for providing a change of clothes or extra socks to use in case of toileting accidents or when messy activities result in wet clothes?
- Who should determine when a security item is banned from school?

There is no absolute right answer to each of these questions. Situations will vary, and teachers need to be aware of carefully differentiating between the family role and the teaching role. Success in creating these boundaries will help facilitate the child's adjustment by clarifying both the teacher's and the family's special and unique roles.

Why does facilitating adjustment to school matter? For some children, these types of experiences can be life altering. Positive, reciprocal, synchronous relationships with significant adults (including teachers) can compensate for early deprivation and stressful experiences caused by poverty, unskilled parenting, abuse, or neglect (Schweinhart & Weikart, 1997).

Teacher Competencies to Support Adjusting to School

Sometimes	Usually	Always	
☐	☐	☐	Looks up, acknowledges, and greets children and families as they arrive in the classroom.
☐	☐	☐	Accepts and respects each child as he or she is. Indicates this respect by giving children the kind of support they need as they transition from one activity to another.
☐	☐	☐	Allows children to follow their own interests; changes with the child as interests fluctuate.
☐	☐	☐	Uses routines of eating, resting, and toileting as opportunities to maximize reciprocal interactions.
☐	☐	☐	Monitors children's general comfort and health.
☐	☐	☐	Invests in quality time with children throughout the day during routines and activities.
☐	☐	☐	Structures group time that is short enough to maintain children's interest.
☐	☐	☐	Supports children's developing awareness by talking about families, using photographs, and celebrating accomplishments.
☐	☐	☐	Uses books, pictures, and stories to help children identify with events that occur in the world of the family and the school.
☐	☐	☐	Practices safety precautions in the classroom (for example, takes attendance, never leaves children alone, posts allergy list, checks toys and materials for safety).

Competencies for the Teaching Role of Observer

Sometimes	Usually	Always	
☐	☐	☐	Shows an awareness of each child's temperament and level of development.
☐	☐	☐	Is an alert observer of each child in the classroom.
☐	☐	☐	Develops and maintains a system for recording regular anecdotal notes.
☐	☐	☐	Uses observations to inform teaching.
☐	☐	☐	Uses observations to guide curriculum development.
☐	☐	☐	Structures time for observation into daily or weekly teaching routines.
☐	☐	☐	Uses webbing to identify the many different possibilities for activities and experiences and to create a picture of the direction in which children's learning might proceed.

Competencies for the Teaching Role of Facilitator

Sometimes	Usually	Always	
☐	☐	☐	Facilitates exchange of information from families to the teacher and back to families.
☐	☐	☐	Maintains a positive, pleasant attitude toward parents; thinks in terms of creating a partnership to support the child.
☐	☐	☐	Communicates regularly with families about the child's experience at school; uses a variety of techniques to keep communication flowing.
☐	☐	☐	Plans, implements, and evaluates regular family participation experiences, parent/teacher conferences, and parent education experiences.

INNOVATIONS IN OBSERVATION/ASSESSMENT

Assessment is the process of gathering and recording information for the purpose of making informed decisions about how children are adjusting to school, teaching approaches, individual needs, curriculum development, and intervention. ***Innovations: The Comprehensive Preschool Curriculum*** uses authentic assessment strategies. Authentic assessment is a collection of methods of assessment that occur in the context of the classroom. Observation to confirm developmental progress and documentation of children's learning experiences are the authentic assessment strategies recommended.

Documentation of children's development and learning is an integral part of authentic assessment. In this curriculum, documentation takes two forms. The first is documentation of children's classroom experiences. The second is the collection of teacher observations, materials, examples, work samples, and other appropriate material into a portfolio to document individual developmental and educational progress. Using authentic assessment strategies insures that teachers are able to meet children's individual needs and match their teaching strategies and curriculum to individual children.

Observation and Authentic Assessment Allow Teachers to See Children as Unique

Comparison of children begins to occur early in education programs. Families who visit the classroom upon arrival and departure get to know the children in the group and notice the developmental changes in children. Teachers, who have watched a number of children grow and develop, compare children across time. Parents, who are watching their own child grow up in a group, often compare their child's development with the development of other children in the group.

The Innovations approach focuses families' attention on the things children *can* do, instead of the things they cannot.

Authentic assessment creates common ground between families and teachers. As they watch skills emerge, it is logical to talk about new skills and how changes give further insight into the child's individuality. Discussion of developmental maturation also serves as a marvelous parent education tool. As parents see their child grow and develop, they come to understand the sporadic nature of development as well as ways to enhance further development with their children.

The ***Innovations*** approach focuses families' attention on the things children *can* do, instead of the things they cannot. This focus on successful activities and accomplishments enhances the child's self-esteem (Curry & Johnson, 1990).

Observation and Authentic Assessment Insure Developmentally and Culturally Appropriate Practice

Developmentally and culturally appropriate practice guides us to modify programs to fit children and respect culture rather than requiring children to fit programs which may not reflect their culture. The foundation of developmentally and culturally appropriate practice is:

- Knowledge of where each individual child is on the developmental continua,
- Understanding of the individuality of each child's development, and
- Knowledge and understanding of the multiple social and cultural contexts that influence development and learning (Bredekamp & Copple, 1997).

The ***Innovations*** approach to assessment guides teachers to gather this information in a truly noninvasive fashion—by careful observation of children involved in daily activities. Further, it helps to organize teacher behavior. There are times when the sheer demands of the classroom can seem overwhelming. Authentic assessment techniques continually orient teachers' behavior toward their selected goals and allow teachers to see progress as they merge routines (such as toileting, eating, and napping) with stimulation (such as directed activities, reading books, playing with stimulating materials, interacting with teachers and friends, playing inside and outside, and so on). What children can do becomes the focus of teachers' interactions with children. Because teachers are carefully observing emerging skills, they can give children repeated experiences with success. Success leads to enthusiasm toward new attempts and has a positive impact on the child's emerging sense of self.

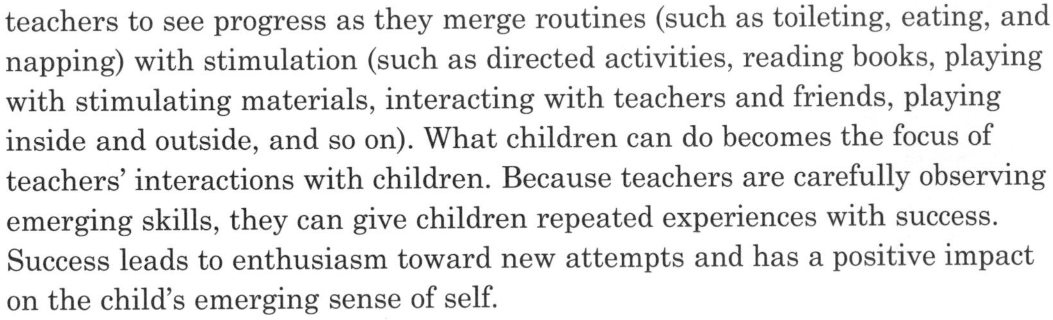

Children have to "live" in their school settings (Greenman, 1988). Because this is the case, curriculum must be balanced across the important dimensions of activity (quiet or active), location (indoor or outdoor), and initiator (child-initiated or adult-initiated) (Bredekamp, 1987; Bredekamp & Copple, 1997; National Academy of Early Childhood Programs, 1997). Knowledge of where each child is developmentally helps teachers keep a good balance among these important dimensions. Using authentic observation and assessment techniques helps teachers match curriculum to the developmental level of each child, preventing frustration yet insuring challenge.

Observation as the Foundation of Assessment

Observation begins the process of knowing about children, their play interests and themes, their individual interests, and the impact of socio-cultural contexts. It informs practice and serves as the foundation for matching the educational process to emerging development. Observing children at work and play in the early childhood classroom inspires good teaching and insures that educational objectives fit children.

Observation (and recording what is observed) is embedded throughout this curriculum. Using written anecdotal records of observations, teachers collect information for review, analysis, and reflection.

Resources for Assessment

In ***Innovations: The Comprehensive Infant Curriculum*** and ***Innovations: The Comprehensive Toddler Curriculum***, a structured assessment instrument is included. This is necessary because of the few resources available to organize observation and confirm developmental and educational progress for the infant and toddler age group. This is not the case for preschoolers—many observation and assessment resources for the preschool years are readily available. (See Appendix page 618 for a list of resources). In addition, ***Innovations*** includes three different assessment tools (see Appendix pages 558-609).

Many strategies to support authentic assessment are included in ***Innovations: The Comprehensive Preschool Curriculum***. In each developmental task, suggestions are made for focusing the teacher's observation and assessment on emerging skills and abilities that are important to children's continued growth and learning. Suggestions for building and expanding children's portfolios are also included. Further, each Possibilities Plan contains specific suggestions for observation and assessment as well as identifying content knowledge, process knowledge, and pre-academic skills to focus teachers' attention on skills and abilities that children are acquiring.

Observation/Assessment for the Task of Adjusting to School

Good teachers build an understanding of each child in their group through observation. Observation informs practice and serves as the foundation for matching the educational process to emerging development. This goodness of fit is crucial for maximizing potential. So powerful is the investment in observation that it is considered transformational to the teaching process (Curtis & Carter, 2000).

During the developmental task of Adjusting to School, observation is directed at understanding two areas:

1) each child's components of uniqueness or alternate developmental pathways, and
2) each child's temperamental characteristics.

Understanding each child's components of uniqueness may require continued observation, while studying the temperamental characteristics of each child may be uncovered more directly by completing a temperamental assessment.

Observe to Uncover Components of Uniqueness and Alternate Developmental Pathways for Each Child

The first goal of observation/assessment during the developmental task of adjusting is to uncover the components of uniqueness and alternate developmental pathways of each child (see page 40 for a discussion of the components of developmental uniqueness). Understanding each child's pace and timing of development in each domain (physical, social, emotional and intellectual, which includes language and cognition), and understanding the relationship among developmental domains are important areas of observation that illuminate learning styles and an understanding of each child's pattern of the fits and spurts that accompany growth.

Observe for Temperamental Differences

The second goal of observation during the developmental task of adjusting is to uncover each child's temperamental characteristics (see page 38 for a discussion of temperament). Temperament is innate. An understanding of temperament leads teachers to improve the goodness of fit between their interactions and the child's temperamental style.

Create Children's Portfolios

Children's portfolios are an important tool for accomplishing authentic assessment in the preschool classroom. Portfolios show a child's progress over time and can be created in many different ways. A wide variety of materials can be used as a part of the documentation process. Date and label everything that goes into the portfolio. Use expandable files, large folders, or even small boxes.

Consider including the following in children's portfolios:

- all types of children's artwork (drawings made with pencils, crayons, and markers; paintings made with fingerpaints, tempera, and watercolor; collages made with a wide variety of materials, such as stickers, construction paper, tissue paper, posterboard, and nature materials);
- photographs and drawings that show other class work (such as building with blocks, dress-up in dramatic play, math and manipulative experiences, sensory experiences with water, sand, and other materials, and emergent literacy experiences);
- assessment summaries;
- written summaries of family communication (parent conferences, selected communication logs, parent visit log, and incident/accident reports);
- anecdotal observations;
- audio and videotapes;
- books read lists;
- concepts learned lists; and
- copies of favorite fingerplays, poems, and songs.

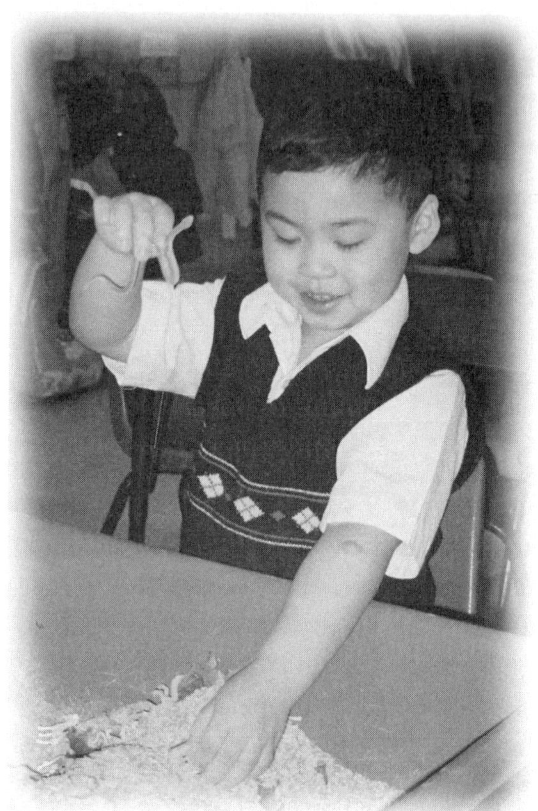

Add to Individual Portfolios to Highlight the Developmental Task of Adjusting to School

In each chapter you will find suggestions for what to add to individual portfolios related to the current developmental task. Consider adding the following to children's portfolios:

- The temperament chart (see page 40), along with your comments about how to modify your teaching classroom or curricula to accommodate the child's temperament
- The information you observe about components of developmental uniqueness and alternate developmental pathways

INNOVATIONS IN FAMILY PARTNERSHIPS

Create Home-School Partnerships

Parents often feel insecure in their role as their child's first and most important teachers. Some try to read everything possible on child rearing and development to overcome their feelings of uncertainty and inadequacy. Others ask many questions, seeking input from a wide variety of sources. Still others may try to defer parenting decisions to their child's teacher.

Teachers have the responsibility to become partners with parents. Respect for parents as their child's most important teachers allows teachers to work together with families to support young children as they grow and learn.

Family/teacher partnerships are not the same as parent involvement or parent education. Partnerships are characterized by mutual respect, sensitivity to the perspective of the other, two-way communication, common goals that are clear and agreed on, equal distribution of power, recognition and valuing the strengths of each partner, and shared decision-making (Stonehouse, 1995).

Establish Two-Way Communication

An important part of creating partnerships is to have accurate and frequent communication between families and teachers. This includes written and verbal communication systems.

Written communication systems support families in giving information to teachers and support teachers in sharing how things are going at school with families. Such systems can be as simple as a spiral-bound notebook in which families and teachers write sequential notes to each other as needed or as detailed as a daily or weekly communication log. An example of a Communication Log is on page 611 of the Appendix. Exchanging information creates a platform for the teacher to accurately anticipate and interpret children's needs. Likewise, families need to know information about what happens at school. Events in the child's day can be recorded and shared with families. Teachers can also record developmental notes and observations. Written communication helps families get a feel for the child's experiences at school.

Create many other opportunities for communicating with families. Conferences, phone calls, and notes are all additional examples. Help parents feel free to discuss any and all concerns. By doing so, concerns don't escalate into real miscommunication or problems.

Encourage Family Participation

Parents and family members who fill parenting roles are their child's first and most important teachers. For this reason, their participation in their child's educational experience is crucial. Family participation suggestions are listed here, as well as in each Possibilities Plan. Use them to provide opportunities for families to participate in their child's educational life.

Plan a Pre-enrollment Visit/Family Interview: Plan a pre-enrollment visit for the family and child to see the classroom. This is an excellent opportunity to identify what parents and their child may expect from you at school. You can also share information with parents about what to bring to school, the daily schedule, and curriculum plans.

Establish Rituals: Establish a separation and reunion routine that both the family and the teacher will use every day. Write it down, so everyone will know what the plan is. (See the Parent Postcard "Creating a Separation and Reunion Ritual" on page 59.)

My Friends at School Book: If time allows, send home a photo book of children in the classroom to new children. Write each child's name on a photo and laminate the pages of the book. Tie the pages together with yarn or string. This book will help children and their families identify the other children in the classroom.

Conduct Gradual Enrollment: Conduct a gradual enrollment where new families gradually increase the amount of time the child spends in school—first with the support of Mom, Dad, or another familiar adult, and then for increasing amounts of time without them. Adjust the gradual enrollment plan to fit each family.

Share Parent Postcards

Share Parent Postcards with parents as they indicate an interest, at appropriate times during the enrollment cycle, or as developmental issues arise. Copy the Postcards, cut them if necessary, address them to the parent(s), and then either attach them to the Communication Log, send home to the family, or hand them out personally.

Create a Separation and Reunion Ritual

The way the day begins and ends for your child is so important. It sets the tone for the day and supports the task of adjusting to school. What can you do to make these important times of the day work for you and your child?

Establish a predictable way to separate and reunite with your child. Having a predictable pattern helps children feel comfortable in the transition process and promotes a feeling of well-being and security for children.

Come into the room, talk a minute with your child's teacher, and assist your child in putting his or her things away. Next, help your child begin to settle in by offering a toy to play with or a book to read. Don't rush the separation process. It may take your child 10 minutes or more to get ready for you to leave. When it is time to leave, tell the teacher, kiss and hug your child, say goodbye and that you'll be back, and leave, waving all the while.

Do the same upon your return. Instead of rushing off to gather your child's belongings to go home, cherish the reuniting process. Get on your child's level, hug and kiss him or her, and then spend a few minutes getting reconnected. Don't be surprised if your child ignores you for a minute or two. Sit down and watch what your child is doing and follow his or her lead.

If your child attends a pre-kindergarten program in an elementary school, your separation and reunion routine might look very different from the one described above. A predictable routine will still provide security and help your child with the transition.

We Are Now Partners

Partnerships are special. Although no one is more important to your child than you, starting school means that someone else is sharing the job of providing early care and education for your child.

Clearly, family involvement in the school improves the quality of your child's experience. Part of being involved is regularly exchanging information with your child's teacher. Another part is coming into and looking around the classroom frequently to see the documentation your teacher has prepared to share with you concerning your child's experiences. Look for lesson plans, photographs, developmental banners, and work samples.

The following is a list of ways families can involve themselves in school. Look through it and find out which ways might fit your schedule, available time, and/or your particular talents and experiences. Check off the ones that you might like to try and put them in your monthly plan.

Parent Partnership Ideas for Adjusting to School

- ☐ Drop by to read a story to the children in your child's group.
- ☐ Save materials to convert into teacher-made toys.
- ☐ Schedule and attend conferences requested by your child's teacher. Conferences are an excellent time for you to get to know your child's teacher as you discuss your child's developmental progress.
- ☐ Read the parent handbook, newsletters, and other written information shared with you. When the school or teacher writes something for you, it is important for you to read it and know about it.
- ☐ Share family traditions with your child's classroom. Cultural celebrations and special family traditions make your family unique. Sharing these experiences with other children and your child's teachers adds a special quality to your child's experience and validates his or her uniqueness.
- ☐ Share your family with us. Bring pictures of your child's experiences to school. Come by for an extra visit when you have time. And, don't forget to share your unique expertise. Leisure activities, work-related activities, and your talents are potential resources to enrich our educational program.
- ☐ Attend special events planned by your child's teachers. Get-acquainted teas, toy swaps, book exchanges, potluck dinners, and happy hour visits are all planned to involve you and your family.

These are just a few of the ways you can be involved. Remember, we are now partners. Our shared goal is to provide the very best early childhood education we can for your child.

Resources for Families

Add this helpful book to your family library or post the title on your family bulletin board.

Brazelton, T. B. & J. Sparrow. (2002). ***Touchpoints 3 to 6: Emotional and behavioral development***. Reading, MA: Addison Wesley.

INNOVATIONS IN ENVIRONMENTS

Ease Adjustment with Supportive Environments

Often, the transition from home and family to school is a difficult one for children because the two environments are so different. Imagine going from a small, cozy, naturally lit home environment with familiar smells to a large, sanitized, classroom with bright lights and unfamiliar scents. No wonder the first week or more in a new school setting can be difficult! To create environments that support the developmental task of adjusting to school, consider the following environmental issues.

Create a Sense of Calm

A supportive environment begins by creating a sense of calm, even amid a high activity level of the children in the classroom. Use carpets, curtains, and other soft elements to absorb sounds and keep them from bouncing off hard surfaces. Include soft elements to make the environment more home-like and familiar.

Keep noise levels low by designing the classroom's activity areas to spread children throughout the available space. Provide a variety of quiet and active experiences for children, so everyone is not participating in noisy activities at the same time.

Create a Sense of Belonging

Feelings of security grow from having a place to put your things to keep them safe. A cubby with each child's photo and name on it and a set of hooks provide a place for coats, boots, extra clothing, security items from home, art projects, and notes between home and school. Keep family photographs in the cubby, covered with clear contact paper, so children can look at them when they feel the need to re-connect with family. Maslow's theory suggests that photos of important people, things from home, and places to safely store your personal things contribute to a child's and family's sense of belonging.

Establish a Predictable Environment

Preschool children need a predictable environment with both novel and familiar features. To provide predictability, arrange a wide variety of toys and materials on low shelves in clear containers labeled with pictures and words. Make sure enough toys and materials are available without cluttering up the display space. Novelty can be provided with mirrors, art projects, music, sensory experiences, sand and water play activities, and texture experiences.

While children are adjusting to school, make changes in the environment incrementally as needed instead of all at once. Make sure that most of the classroom environment looks familiar to children, creating a feeling that the classroom will be as expected when children return the next day.

Create Places to Be Alone and Regain Composure

Early childhood classrooms are stimulating places. Sometimes, they are too stimulating. Children need places in the classroom where they can get away from the hustle and bustle. Shelf units, area carpets, dividers, pillows, and throw rugs help create the places to play without interruption and provide a break from interaction and stimulation when needed. Preschoolers have intense emotions and are still working on regulating these powerful feelings. They need places where they can go to regain composure after getting upset. Make these spaces welcoming, soft, and comforting, separating them from other activity areas and equipping them with comfy chairs, pillows, and other soothing props.

Create Ways to Decrease and Increase Stimulation

Decreasing the amount of light, increasing it, or providing incandescent as well as florescent and full-spectrum lighting are examples of ways to change stimulation levels. Add quiet music, or remove all background noise and replace it with sounds of nature. Provide soothing activity choices such as sand, water, and sensory play, as well as creative activities using paint, clay, playdough, markers, watercolors, and other alternatives to more physical activities.

Create Places to Be with the Teacher

Plan classroom environments that allow for intimate communication and face-to-face contact between adults and children. Such intimacy helps create a feeling of security, supporting emerging relationships between children and their teachers. Make sure there are places where children can be near teachers by providing adult-sized furniture that encourages sitting side by side, on the teacher's lap, or next to her or him on the floor.

References

Albrecht, K. & L.G. Miller. (2000). ***Innovations: The comprehensive infant curriculum.*** Beltsville, MD: Gryphon House.

Albrecht, K. & L.G. Miller. (2000). ***Innovations: The comprehensive toddler curriculum.*** Beltsville, MD: Gryphon House.

Berk, L.E. (1999). ***Infants and children.*** Boston: Allyn and Bacon.

Brazelton, T.B., & S.I. Greenspan. (2000). ***The irreducible needs of children: What every child must have to grow, learn, and flourish.*** Cambridge, MA: Perseus Publishing.

Bredekamp, S. & C. Copple. (1997). ***Developmentally appropriate practice in early childhood programs, revised edition***. Washington, DC: National Association for the Education of Young Children (NAEYC).

Bredekamp, S. (1987). ***Developmentally appropriate practice in early childhood programs serving children from birth through age 8.*** Washington, DC: National Association for the Education of Young Children (NAEYC).

California State Department of Education. (1990). ***Flexible, fearful, or feisty: The different temperaments of infants and toddlers.*** Videotape. Sacramento, CA: Department of Education.

Chess, S. & A. Thomas. (1987). ***Know your child.*** New York: Basic Books.

Curry, N.E. & C.N. Johnson (1990). ***Beyond self-esteem: Developing a genuine sense of human value.*** Washington, DC: National Association for the Education of Young Children (NAEYC).

Curtis, D. & M. Carter. (2000). ***The art of awareness: How observation can transform your teaching.*** St. Paul, MN: Redleaf Press.

Gardner, H. (1983). ***Frames of mind:The theory of multiple intelligences.*** New York: Basic Books.

Greenman, J. (1988). ***Caring spaces, learning places***. Redmond, WA: Exchange Press.

Klein, S. (2002). Feisty, adaptable, and cautious: Recognizing and understanding children's temperament. ***Early Childhood News,*** 14(4): 34-42.

Maslow, A. (1954). ***Motivation and personality.*** New York: Harper & Row.

National Association for the Education of Young Children. (1998). ***Accreditation criteria & procedures of the National Association for the Education of Young Children***. Washington, DC: NAEYC.

Perry, B.D. (Nov./Dec. 2000). Emotional development: The developmental hot zone. ***Early Childhood Today***.

Scanlon, P. (1988). In search of excellent training: Tuning into right brain/left brain thinking. ***Child Care Information Exchange,*** 63, 7-11.

Schweinhart, L. & D.P. Weikart. (1997). ***Lasting differences: The High/Scope preschool curriculum comparison through age 23.*** Monographs of the High/Scope Educational Research Foundation, #12, Ypsilanti, MI: High/Scope Press.

Shonkoff, J.P. & D.A. Phillips (Eds.). (2000). ***From neurons to neighborhoods: The science of early childhood development.*** Washington, DC: National Academy Press.

Shore, R. (1997). ***Rethinking the brain: New insights into early development.*** New York: Families and Work Institute.

Stonehouse, A. (1995). ***How does it feel: Child care from the parents' perspective.*** Redmond, WA: Exchange Press.

Resources for Teachers

Ames, L. & F. Ilg. (1980). ***Your three year old***. New York: Delacorte Press.

Ames, L. & F. Ilg. (1980). ***Your four year old***. New York: Delacorte Press.

Ames, L. & F. Ilg. (1980) ***Your five year old***. New York: Delacorte Press.

Child Care Information Exchange. (2001). Beginnings workshop: Parent involvement. ***Child Care Information Exchange,*** 138, p. 43-62.

Derman-Sparks, L. (1989). ***Anti-bias curriculum: Tools for empowering young children.*** Washington, DC: National Association for the Education of Young Children.

Miller, K. (2001). ***Ages and stages***. Glen Burnie, MD: TelShare.

Mooney, C.G. (2000). ***Theories of childhood***. St. Paul, MN: Redleaf Press.

Neugebauer, B. (1992). ***Alike and different: Exploring our humanity with children.*** Washington, DC: National Association for the Education of Young Children.

Pelo, A. & F. Davidson. (2000). ***That's not fair.*** St. Paul, MN: Redleaf Press.

Smith, C.A. (1993). ***The peaceful classroom.*** Beltsville, MD: Gryphon House.

Rice, J.A. (1995). ***The kindness curriculum.*** St. Paul, MN: Redleaf Press.

Possibilities Plan— Saying Hello

Getting Ready to Plan

During the preschool years, much of children's learning is tied to the interactions they have with family and, increasingly, with friends. This Possibilities Plan explores four distinct but related interests in the lives of preschoolers—similarities and differences; emotions; families; and the experience of sending and receiving mail.

The purpose of Getting Ready to Plan is to support the planning process with a general overview of the content of this Possibilities Plan. Now is the time to think about what interests children and what you want them to learn about each of these topics. Topics are explored in general below.

Alike and Different: During the preschool years, children begin to understand similarities and differences. They enjoy learning about how they are similar to their friends and how they are different from their friends. They are beginning to explore relationships between their near environments of home and school with the larger world of their neighborhood and the community. All of these topics interest children who are three and four, while five-year-olds are beginning to recognize and think about differences among ideas, friends, and skills.

Emotions: Preschool children are just learning important emotional skills, although we are often surprised and pleased that they show empathy for others who are hurt or left out of social interactions. They are learning to understand their own emotions and to identify the emotions that other children are expressing. Emotion management skills such as waiting, delaying gratification, and impulse control are works in progress. Lessons in accurately recognizing and identifying emotions are usually learned in interactions with peers—often through conflict over toys, play partners, and what to play.

Families: Identification with family is usually strongly in place by the preschool years, and children are busy learning that the near environment of the neighborhood and the larger environment of the community have much to offer. At the same time, an increasing interest in family connections and traditions emerges as children recognize more details and information about their extended families.

Post Office: The process of getting and receiving mail is fascinating for preschoolers—what seems like magic in the early preschool years comes to be understood in the later preschool years. Explore how the post office gets and processes mail, simulate the process in your own classroom, and don't forget to consider new technologies such as email and facsimiles. The profession of postal worker or letter carrier is fun to explore as children begin to understand how the post office works.

Now that you have an idea about the general content of the Possibilities Plan, you are ready to proceed with developing your own plan. This section of Getting Ready to Plan identifies items you may want to buy, collect, or locate to implement your plan.

Toys and Materials*

Purchased

3-ring binders
butcher paper
chalk
chart paper
clear contact paper
collage materials
coloring supplies
construction paper
craft knife (teacher only)
cuddle toys
dishes
duct or masking tape
easel or art table
felt
glue
hot glue gun (teacher only)
markers (permanent and washable)
paints and brushes
pencils
pens
plastic food
plastic magnifying glasses
playdough
scissors
scrapbook
sheet protectors
silverware
stickers
tape
tape or CD player/music
toy cookware
unbreakable mirrors (locker size and full length)
unit blocks
watercolors
white butcher paper
wooden knob

Gathered

baskets
birthday candles
blankets
blue uniform shirts
books
books about the human body
brown paper bags
cardboard boxes (large and medium sizes)
clipboards
current photograph of each child
envelopes
fabric samples
fruit
greeting cards
hats
honey or syrup
intercoms and tape recorders
invitations
mail carrier bags
mailboxes
newspaper
old letters
old socks
old telephones
packages
paper cups
paper plates
papers
pencils
photographs of each child's family members
photographs of family pets
picture file for mail carriers
pictures of artists
pictures of dwellings
pillows
plastic knives and forks
plastic trays
pliers
postcards
rolling cart or table
ruler
safety glasses
self-portraits of artists
shoeboxes
short-handed screwdrivers
sit-on cushion
stamp pads
stamps
straws
strings
subscription cards from magazines
sunglasses
tablecloth
tubs
vanilla
vase with artficial flowers
yogurt

*Note: Please consider the ages and abilities of the children in your classroom. Use only safe, non-toxic materials.

Saying Hello

WEB

Saying Hello

PLANNING PAGES

Plan Possibilities

Group Time

ACTIVITIES AND EXPERIENCES FOR SAYING HELLO

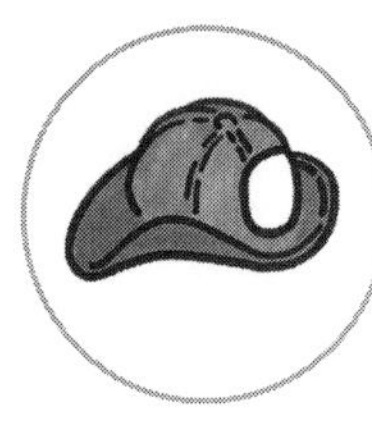

DRAMATIC POSSIBILITIES

Post Office

Materials
cardboard box • craft knife (teacher use only) • papers • pencils • old letters • postcards • stamps • stamp pads • envelopes • invitations • greeting cards • subscription cards from magazines • shoeboxes • tubs • baskets • books about the post office, such as *The Jolly Postman* by Janet and Allan Ahlberg • mail carrier bags • blue uniform shirts • hats • sunglasses • mailboxes • packages • clipboards

Teacher Talk
"What does your letter say?" "Tell me about the friend who's going to receive your letter."

Instructions
Create a mailbox out of a cardboard box. Use a craft knife (teacher only) to make a slot on one side of the box that is big enough to drop letters in. On the other side make a door that opens. Put different writing materials (postcards, greeting cards, invitations, envelopes, and old letters as well as stamps, stamp pads, stickers to use as postage stamps) in separate containers (shoeboxes, tubs, or baskets), so children have easy access to them. Also, add mail carrier uniforms, sunglasses, and clipboards, so children can role-play being mail carriers.

Start with a few props, perhaps the ones that are already familiar to children, such as stamps, postcards, or stamp pads and add to them as children learn more about the post office. Use boxes or baskets to give children the opportunity to categorize the materials by type (postcards, paper, envelopes, and so on) when it is time to clean up.

Observation/Assessment
Takes on various roles in dramatic play
Dresses and undresses in costumes

Houses with Different Rooms

Materials
Kitchen—cookware • plastic food
Bedroom—blankets • pillows • stuffed animals
Dining room—silverware • tablecloth • vase with artificial flowers
Office—cushions • books • papers • markers
books about houses, such as *No Mirrors in My Nana's House* by Ysaye M. Barnwell

Teacher Talk
"You are cooking in the kitchen." "What is your favorite room at your house?" "In which room do you play with your toys?"

Instructions
Provide props to divide the dramatic play area into individual rooms. Start with one room, such as the bedroom; then add others such as the living room, dining room, laundry room, play room, etc. You may need to redesign or enlarge the area dedicated to Dramatic Possibilities to accommodate the additional rooms. Include children in figuring out how to do this.

Observation/Assessment
Has particular play partners
Uses props to enhance dramatic play

Front Door Hello

Materials
craft knife (teacher use only) • two sides of a large box • duct tape • rolling cart or table • hot glue gun (teacher use only) • wooden knob

Teacher Talk
Knock, knock. "Who is it?" Talk about never opening the door to people we do not know.

Instructions
Use a craft knife (teacher use only) to cut one side and one-quarter of the adjacent side of a large box. Tape the smaller section to the side of a rolling cart or table. Use a hot glue gun (teacher use only) to attach the wooden knob. Children can play different front door situations with the teacher-made door.

Extension Possibilities: Add "Knock, Knock" jokes to the area. Write them on 3 x 5 index cards and read the cards to children using the door as a prop.

ART POSSIBILITIES

My Kind of House

Materials

pictures of many different dwellings including single-family houses, apartments, high-rise apartments, igloos, cabins, yurts, and so on • paper • markers, colored pencils, crayons, chalk, or paint and paintbrushes • easels • envelopes • books about houses, such as *The Little House* by Virginia Lee Burton

Teacher Talk

"Children and their families live in many different kinds of dwellings. Which house looks like your house?" "Which houses look different?"

Instructions

Children live in a variety of housing arrangements. This activity is designed to help children understand the living arrangements of many different families. Place the pictures from the picture file in Art Possibilities. Ask children to draw, sketch, or paint pictures of their houses. Offer a wide range of formats for creating their pictures—at the easel, on various sizes of paper, in three dimensions with boxes, with envelopes (the flap can be the roof), and a variety of media such as tempera paint, watercolors, crayons, markers, colored chalk, colored pencils, and so on.

Observation/Assessment

Draws, sketches, or paints using a variety of art media

I Can Draw Me!

Materials

close-up photos of each child's face or enlarged full-body photographs of each child • clear acetate film • easel • markers

Teacher Talk

"Trace your face on the clear acetate. Lift up the acetate. Does that look like your face?"

Instructions

Cover photos completely with clear acetate film. Place on easel with thin markers.

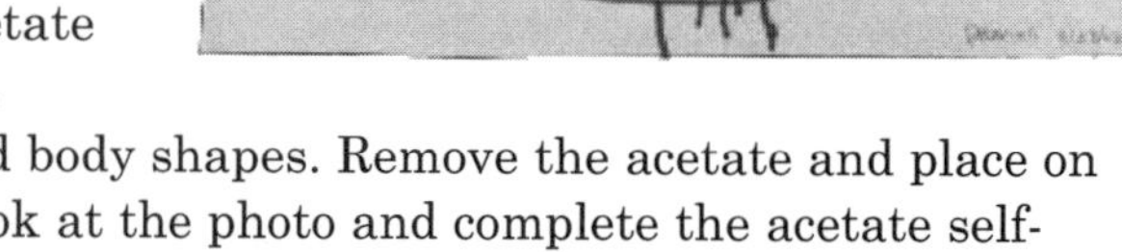

Children trace their facial features and body shapes. Remove the acetate and place on the art table. Encourage children to look at the photo and complete the acetate self-portrait. Laminate the photographs to extend their life.

Observation/Assessment

Draws self-portrait

Felt Faces

Materials
felt in a variety of different colors, particularly the range of skin and eye colors • scissors • glue • small, unbreakable locker mirrors with adhesive backing • fabric swatches • unbreakable full-length mirror • books, such as *From Head to Toe* by Eric Carle

Teacher Talk
"You selected the blue felt for your eyes."

Instructions
Collect or purchase different colors of felt, making sure that some of the felt is close to the skin and eye colors of the children in your classroom. Cut out face shapes (oval, round, oblong, and so on). Children cut felt to add features to the faces.

Helpful Hints: Encourage children to use the locker mirrors to look at their own faces as they make the felt faces.

Extension Possibilities: Send children to the full-length mirror to explore how to add arms, legs, and torso. Provide additional materials (felt, cloth, paper), so children can add the other features. Use a flannel board to display children's work.

Observation/Assessment
Accomplishes level of detail in felt people
Observes similarities and differences

Other Art Possibilities

- Make sock puppets with clean socks, craft glue, and collage materials.
- Make body tracings using butcher paper, markers, and other art materials.
- Make handprint and footprint murals.
- Create felt faces with face-shape pieces of felt and facial features cut out of felt.
- Make paper plate puppets that show different emotions. Match the paper plate faces with words written on index cards that describe the emotions.

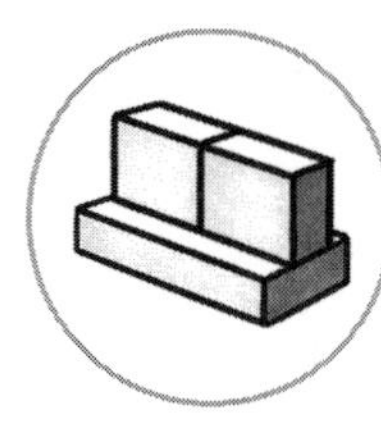

BLOCKS/CONSTRUCTION POSSIBILITIES

What's Inside?

Materials
telephones, intercoms, and tape recorders that are no longer working • pliers • short-handled screwdrivers • small unbreakable mirrors • unbreakable magnifying glasses • safety glasses

Teacher Talk
"The telephone has lots of different parts." "How are those parts different from these parts?"

Instructions
Obtain telephones, intercoms, and tape recorders, or ask parents to donate their old telephones, intercoms, tape recorders, or other inoperable electronic equipment for use in this activity. First, remove all power cords and any sharp or dangerous pieces. Then, demonstrate how to use the pliers, screwdrivers, and other tools to take apart the phones. Use the mirrors and magnifying glasses to examine the pieces.

Safety Note: Closely supervise the use of all tools and require children to wear safety glasses.

Observation/Assessment
Uses tools appropriately

Brown Bag Builders

Materials
brown paper bags in a variety of sizes • newspaper • duct or masking tape • books, such as *Block City* by Robert Louis Stevenson

Teacher Talk
"You are putting the big brown bag next to your block house." "What other buildings do you have in your neighborhood?"

Instructions
This is a two-part activity. Collect brown paper bags and newspaper from parents and the grocery store. Help the children crumple up the newspaper and stuff the bags. Fold the tops of the bags over, making the shape of the block as square as possible. Tape closed. Children can use the large blocks to build by stacking. They can place blocks end-to-end to form a maze or add three-dimensional buildings to the block structure. The ability to use the blocks for stacking will be more complicated because the bags are not rigid and firm like unit blocks. Children will discover how easily the blocks fall down!

Helpful Hints: Stuff the bags to different fullnesses to provide different sizes of paper blocks. Tape over the corners to extend the life of the homemade paper bag blocks and make them easier to stack. Monitor younger preschoolers for frustration, and help them develop strategies to use if they can't stack the blocks easily.

Observation/Assessment
Builds using various materials

You Blockhead!

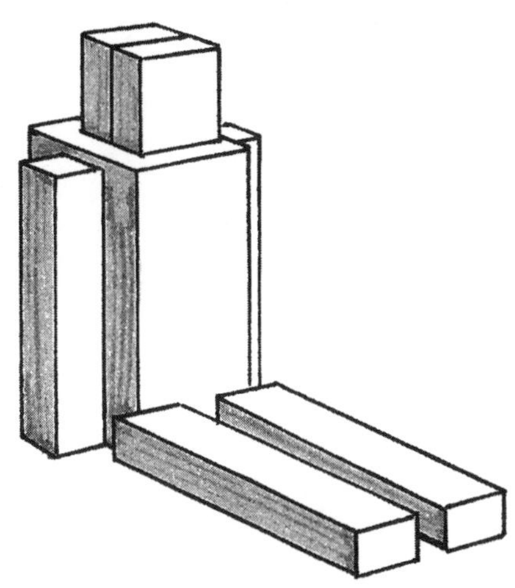

Materials
unit blocks • white butcher paper • markers • tape • clear contact paper

Teacher Talk
"You made your block person sit up." "What are the block people doing together?"

Instructions
Wrap the blocks with white butcher paper. Draw different features on the blocks. For example, use a square block for the head, a rectangle for the upper body, and another rectangle for the legs. Cover with clear contact paper to extend the lifetime of the block people.

Observation/Assessment
Builds using unit blocks

SCIENCE/DISCOVERY POSSIBILITIES

Close Up

Materials
plastic magnifying glasses • chart paper • pen or marker

Teacher Talk
"What do you see with the magnifying glass that you couldn't see without it?"

Instructions
Put the magnifying glasses out in Science/Discovery Possibilities area. Encourage children to look at themselves, their friends, and objects in the classroom. Record children's observations of similarities and differences as they discover them.

Observation/Assessment
Examines/observes using magnifying glass

Hello, Hello

Materials
paper cups • strings

Teacher Talk
"What do we use to communicate with people who live far away?" "How do you think people communicated with each other before the invention of telephones or email?"

Instructions
Punch a small hole on the bottom of the paper cups. Put the string through the hole and tie a knot at each end of the string. Pull the string tight to speak and listen.

Other Science/Discovery Possibilities

- Make handmade paper.
- Use unbreakable mirrors to look at and explore facial features.
- Use bendable straws to make simple telephones.

SENSORY POSSIBILITIES

Happy Birthday to Me!

Materials
playdough • candles • plastic knives • plastic trays

Teacher Talk
"Let's count how many candles you have on your cake." "You and Hannah have _____ candles."

Instructions
Set the trays on the table with the playdough, birthday candles, and plastic knives.

Helpful Hints: Family customs about birthday celebrations may vary. Find out about customary birthday celebrations before implementing this activity. Add props and materials to reflect what you learned so that different customs are equally validated. Be sensitive to families who may not celebrate birthdays (or holidays) because of religious reasons.

Observation/Assessment
Counts sequentially with birthday candles
Uses one-to-one correspondence with birthday candles to year of age

Body Parts Painting

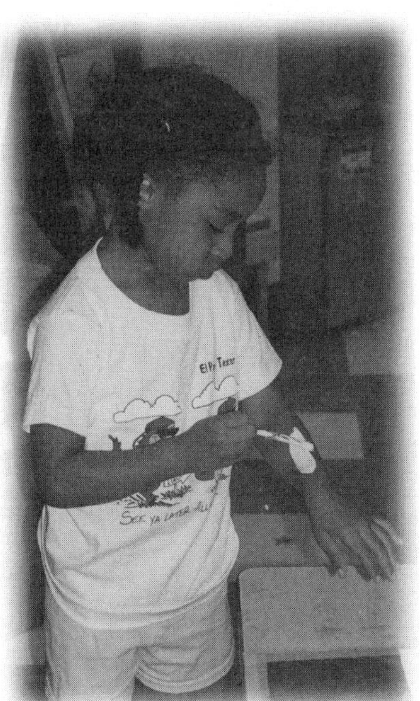

Materials
paints (non-toxic) • small paper plates • easel or art table • paper

Teacher Talk
"How does it feel to have paint on your elbow?" "Can you paint with your nose?"

Instructions
Squeeze small amounts of several different colors of tempera paint on the paper plates. Each child should have her own individual plate. Encourage children to use different body parts to paint on easel paper or at the art table. Children can experiment with elbows, wrists, fingers, and perhaps even noses or chins.

Helpful Hints: Be prepared for cleanup. Have wet washcloths/paper towels waiting near the sink for easy cleanup. Do not share paint plates.

Friendship Fruit and Fun

Materials
fruit • plastic knife • fork • yogurt • honey or syrup • vanilla

Teacher Talk
"What is your favorite fruit?" "Have you ever tasted ______?"

Instructions
Invite parents to help you create a friendship fruit salad by contributing their child's favorite fruit to the salad. When parents bring in the fruits, chart each one. Then, ask the children to check whether they like or don't like the fruit.

	John		Amalia		Kaylee		Kevin	
Fruit	Likes ☺	Doesn't Like ☹	Likes ☺	Doesn't Like ☹	Likes ☺	Doesn't Like ☹	Likes ☺	Doesn't Like ☹
banana		X		X		X	X	
kiwi		X	X		X		X	
red apple		X	X		X		X	
green apple	X		X		X			X

Wash the fruit. Help children peel and cut up the fruit they brought to school, adding it to a big bowl. Mix the yogurt with a little syrup or honey, adding a little bit of vanilla as flavoring. Serve the snack in a self-serve snack area. As children eat their friendship salad, comment on how interesting the salad is with so many different kinds of fruits. Compare what the salad might taste like with only one type of fruit.

Helpful Hints: Make sure that children are not allergic to any of the fruits or the honey.

Other Sensory Possibilities

- Make matching sound canisters using film canisters. To make this a self-checking activity, attach matching stickers to the bottoms of canisters with the same sounds.

LITERACY/WRITING POSSIBILITIES

Eyewitness News

Materials
newspapers • clipboard • paper • pen

Teacher Talk
"We have some questions." "Who can be a news reporter and find the answers?"

Instructions
Describe the job of a newspaper reporter. Show children the bylines of reporters in the newspaper. Identify questions children can ask their friends, such as, "Do you like apples?" or "Do you have a pet?" Write the questions on sentence strips and post them in the Literacy/Writing Possibilities area. Reporters ask children questions and use invented spelling or letter-like scribbles to write down their answers. Children can also dictate their answers to a teacher.

Observation/Assessment
Uses letter-like symbols or scribbles to represent print

These Are a Few of My Favorite Things

Materials
three-ring binders • plastic sheet protectors • paper • markers

Teacher Talk
"I learned that Timmy likes carrots." Comment on each child's illustrations. "What did you learn about your friend?"

Instructions
This teacher-supported activity will result in a unique book, complete with interesting information about each of the children in your classroom. Write sentences on the paper. Examples include, "My name is _______. I live with _______. My favorite food is_______." and others that are appropriate for the children in your class. Give children these book pages. As children visit the Literacy/Writing Possibilities Area, help them complete the sentences and draw an illustration. Ask children to share their pages at group time. Place the pages in sheet protectors and then in the three-ring binders.

Helpful Hints: Pick one or two children at a time, so you can help them write or copy the words. Make a place for these books that children have easy access to. Complete a set of pages yourself, so the children can get to know you better through the book.

Observation/Assessment
Identifies initial letter of own name
Identifies initial letter sound of own name
Indicates preferences and interests

Other Literacy/Writing Possibilities

- Make "I Can" books (showing photos or drawings of things each child can do).
- Make "Feelings" books (using photographs or magazine pictures that portray different emotions expressed in the classroom during actual interactions).
- Find a real pen pal to exchange correspondence.
- Create a "Family Identity" board. Glue each child's family photograph onto a sheet of paper. Add family information. Label all the family members in the photograph and display at children's eye level or put into a binder.
- Use index card to write, draw, or dictate letters, and then "mail" letters to each other.

MATH/MANIPULATIVES POSSIBILITIES

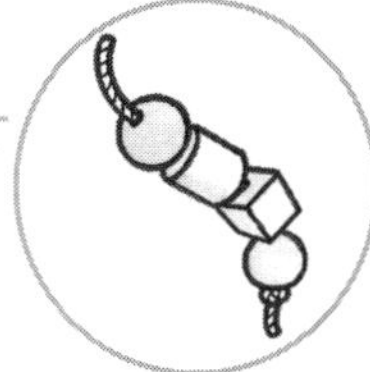

Family Composition Graphs

Materials
chart paper • markers • ruler • photos • stickers • books about families, such as *My Great Aunt Arizona* by Gloria Houston

Teacher Talk
"What is your family's composition?" "Let's put a sticker in each column that represents a member of your family." "Do you have a mommy? Daddy? Sister? Brother? Pet?"

Instructions
Create a graph for children to complete. They place a sticker in each column representing a member of their family. Summarize similarities and differences.

Helpful Hints: You need to be knowledgeable about family composition, so you can help children find their family components to mark. Prepare carefully for this activity, being ready to help children with different family compositions, particularly if a child is resistant or doesn't want to talk about this topic. Accept such preferences from children until you get to know them well and can discuss issues or concerns with them.

Observation/Assessment
Recognizes family members

Hair Color and So Much More!

Materials
paper • markers • ruler • photos • stickers • non-breakable locker mirrors • books about personal traits, such as *Purple Hair? I Don't Care* by Dianne Young

Teacher Talk
Talk about the features of children's faces (such as hair color, eye color, glasses, no glasses, etc., special abilities, and other features) "You have brown eyes like Eric."

	Craig	Amee	Sean	Connie
wink	Yes	No	No	No
Roll tongue	No	Yes	No	Yes
snap	Yes	Yes	Yes	Yes
Blow a bubble	No	No	No	No
Clap	Yes	Yes	Yes	No

Instructions
Use the paper to make several graphs of different features or characteristics (hair color, eye color, special abilities including winking, snapping fingers, or rolling tongues). Ask parents for photographs of children. Cover the charts with clear contact paper or laminate them, so they will be durable. Put them in a basket. Then, let the children use the stickers to mark on the graphs, using the photos as a reference or searching out answers from their friends. Introduce this activity at group time. Then place the photos, graph, and stickers in Literacy/Writing Possibilities Area.

Observation/Assessment
Sorts by one dimension (eye color) or two dimensions (eye color and hair color)
Uses graphing skills

How Many Fingers on the Floor?

Teacher Talk
"Let's count fingers." "Can you count the fingers with me? 1, 2, ...10" "Put your hands on the floor. We are going to count all the fingers in the room."

Instructions
First, count the fingers on each child's hand and then count everyone's fingers together. After perfecting counting one finger at a time, count by five fingers at a time, then ten. Also, do this activity with toes, legs, or eyes. Comment that every person's hands are different (size, handprints, fingerprints, coloration, and so on).

Observation/Assessment
Counts sequentially from 1-10, counts by 5's, 10's, and so on.

RHYMES/FINGERPLAYS/SONGS/ MUSIC POSSIBILITIES

Sylla-beats

Teacher Talk
"Ma-ry-Kath-er-ine has 5 syllables." "Ro-ber-to has 3 syllables."

Instructions
Ask children to count along with you as you clap the beats (or syllables) in their name, one clap for each syllable.

Observation/Assessment
Breaks words down into syllables

Make New Friends

Instructions
Sing these favorite songs often throughout the day and week.

"Make New Friends"
"The More We Get Together"
"Good Morning"

Observation/Assessment
Listens to stories, rhymes, fingerplays, and songs

Other Rhymes/Fingerplays/Songs/Music Possibilities

- Consider any of the following recorded selections:
  - "If You're Happy and You Know It"
  - "We Are Family" from *Pure Disco* by Sister Sledge
  - "Circle of Friends" from *Circle of Friends* by Parachute Express
  - "You've Got a Friend in Me" from Disney's *Toy Story* Soundtrack
  - "I Wanna Be a Friend of Yours" by Capitol Sings from *Kids Songs for Grownups*
  - "That's What Friends Are For" by Joanie Bartels from *Adventures with Family and Friends*
  - "Family Tree" by Tom Chapin from *Family Tree*
  - "Friends Forever" by Greg and Steve from *We All Live Together, Vol. 5*
  - "Friends Forever" from *Winnie the Pooh's Friends Forever*
  - "Alerta Sings Children's Songs" and "Songs for the Playground" by Suni Paz
  - "Positively Singable Songs" by Ronno
  - "World Playground" by Putumayo

GROUP TIME POSSIBILITIES

Counting Fingers: Cumulatively count each child's fingers. Extend this activity with toes, ears, and eyes. This activity exposes children to sequential counting and to the rhythm and sound of counting.

Birth Date Calendar: Mark each child's birth date on the calendar. As you regularly review the calendar, point out who is having a birthday during the week or month.

A Place for All Things: Take children on a "field trip" to Dramatic Possibilities. Point out where things go and the appropriate way to put props and materials away. Repeat this activity every time you change the theme and props in Dramatic Possibilities.

Slipper Day: Invite children to bring in their favorite slippers. Put them on before group time. Ask children to share something about their slippers with their friends.

Hello in Many Languages: Investigate the primary language spoken at home or by family members for children in your group. Read *Margaret and Margarita* by Lynn Reiser or a similar book that introduces different ways to say the same thing. Practice saying hello in the languages of the cultures represented by the children in your classroom. Then, add some new languages until you can say hello in many different languages.

Other Group Time Possibilities
- Share children's "These Are a Few of My Favorite Things" pages (see pages 78-79).
- Read any of the books listed for this Possibilities Plan (see pages 90-91).

MOVEMENT/OUTDOORS POSSIBILITIES

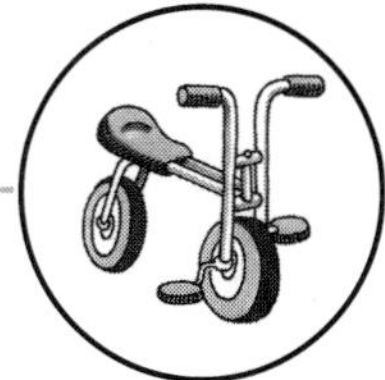

Mail Delivery

Materials
cardboard boxes • papers • envelopes • paint • shoulder bag • pictures from the picture file of mail trucks, mailboxes, mail carriers, shoeboxes, subscription cards from magazines

Teacher Talk
"How do mail carriers know which letter goes to which house?" "You can be a mail carrier."

Instructions
Make a mail truck out of a large cardboard box. Let children paint it. Make a mailbox or use the one prepared for Dramatic Possibilities (page 70). Encourage children to pick up letters and deliver them. Put the pictures from the picture file near the materials for the mail truck, box, and play props.

Helpful Hints: Laminating the letters will make them last longer. You can also write down numbers or words on letters and the same numbers and words on smaller boxes. Place boxes all over the playground for children to use as mailbox addresses. Use those numbers and letters for delivery purposes by matching the numbers on the mail to the numbers on the mailboxes.

Observation/Assessment
Identifies patterns in words and numbers (e.g., my name goes up in the middle, or that number is made up of circles)

Partner Choosing

Materials
CD or tape player

Teacher Talk
"Now find someone with eyes the same color as yours."

Instructions
Ask children to find a partner. Play the music, encouraging partners to dance. Stop the music and give children instructions about how to find another partner using similarities and differences, for example, same or different hair color, same or different shirt color, same or different shoe color, or same or different number of siblings.

Other Movement/Outdoor Possibilities

- Use a Plexiglas easel for tracing each child's body.
- Trace bodies on a wooden fence instead of a sidewalk, changing the dimension from horizontal to vertical.
- Partners take turns tracing each other on the sidewalk.
- Play "Guess Who!" by asking questions to identify a child that another child is thinking of. To help children learn how to ask questions, re-phrase comments or statements into a question.
- Play Follow the Leader—one child pretends to be a "mirror" and the rest copy her movements. If necessary, demonstrate for a while until the children get the idea.

PROJECTS AND DOCUMENTATION POSSIBILITIES

"These Are a Few of My Favorite Things" Book Grows!

Materials
paper • sheet protectors • markers or other art media

Teacher Talk
"Let's add the photograph of you in the block area to your favorite things book."

Instructions
Continue to add to "These Are a Few of My Favorite Things" Books (see page 79) from time to time. Add accomplishments, interests, favorite foods, favorite areas of the classroom, favorite activities, and so on.

Self-Portraits over Time

Materials

paper • markers • crayons • watercolors • tempera paint • mirror • self-portraits by artists from the picture file • books about self, such as *I Am Me* by Karla Kushen

Teacher Talk

"You added ears to your self-portrait." If children are reluctant to draw self-portraits, send them to the mirror to check out what they see.

Instructions

Tell children you would like them to draw a picture of themselves. Repeat the activity monthly, using different media and different techniques. This activity can be used for tracking the development of fine motor skills and artistic representation. As children's cognitive skills develop, they will begin to add details such as hair, fingers, nails, ears, and eye color. You will notice changes in the self-portrait as well as different skills in representing features of one's self as different media and techniques are tried.

Observation/Assessment

Adds details to self-portrait

Stamp Collection

Materials

stamps removed from mail received at the school and from mail received at home • scrapbook • glue

Instructions

Start a stamp collection with your children. Collect stamps; add them to the scrapbook along with a label of where the stamp came from and who brought it to school. Purchase a stamp collection kit on a visit to the post office.

Helpful Hint: This kind of project will hold children's interest for a long time, although interest may wax and wane. A new, interesting stamp or a pen pal from far away will rekindle the children's interest.

FIELD TRIP POSSIBILITIES

Corner Mailbox: Take a walk to the nearest mailbox and post a letter to a sick friend, a vacationing teacher, or a traveling family member.

Post Office: Visit the nearest branch of your local post office to buy stamps for a collection or to see the mail processing in action.

Neighborhood Ride: Take a walk, a bus, or a van ride through your neighborhood to view people saying "hello," mailing letters, or using delivery services such as UPS or Federal Express.

SNACK POSSIBILITIES

Friendship Fruit Salad: Make a fruit salad using directions for Friendship Fruit and Fun, page 77.

Friendship Faces: Use round crackers, cream cheese, olives, and pickles to make friendship faces.

Snacks from Home: Share a snack provided by families.

FAMILY PARTICIPATION POSSIBILITIES

"Family Identity" Pictures: Ask parents to gather the pictures to bring in for this activity (see page 79).

Our House Is a Very, Very, Very Fine House: Fill paper lunch bags with a few crayons. Send bags home with instructions for parents to decorate the bag with their child to look like their home, stuff the bag with newspaper, and seal the top. As the bags are brought back, place them in the block center for children to use in their block play.

Share a Family Heirloom, Cultural Tradition, Food, or Song: Invite family members to share a family heirloom, cultural tradition, food, or song with the children.

My Favorite Fruit: As an extension to the "Friendship Fruit and Fun" activity, ask parents to bring in their favorite fruit for the children to taste. Compare the children's favorite fruit to their parents' favorite fruit.

Add to Our Stamp Collection: Include parents in collecting stamps to add to the classroom collection.

Arrivals and Departures ARE Routines

Expect arrival and departure times to be transitions. Some transitions are handled better than others. In general, children resist being rushed or hurried. Parents have all been in the situation where they are running late. The harder they push, the slower and more resistant their child becomes! Knowing this is the case, plan arrival and departure routines to accept this inevitable reality.

Let your child's teacher know if your routine is going to change. Sometimes teachers can offset children's real discomfort about changes in schedule by preparing them for the change. Children know the sequence of which parent picks up first, then next, then next, and so on. If you let your teacher know, your teacher can help your child accommodate the increased time at school without going into the "waiting" mode too soon.

Develop back-up strategies before you need them and practice these routines, too. It's going to happen—a flat tire, a car accident, a last-minute work demand that can't be postponed. Plan now for these situations. And, don't forget to discuss the back-up plan with your child's teacher. Practice it once or twice before it is needed. Then everyone will know how to handle it if the plan is put into effect.

Predictable beginnings and endings to the day are important to you and to your child. Children need help from you to make transitions a pleasant part of their school experience.

Facilitating Adjustment—How Long Will It Take?

What can parents do to facilitate adjustment? First of all, be patient with the process. It typically takes a while for children to adjust to new experiences and settings. Begin the transition process with shorter days. Reduced hours will be easier for your child to handle.

Most children make the transition to school in about four to six weeks, but each child is different. Your child may take two weeks or ten weeks to fully adjust. This is normal and to be expected.

Good communication helps both you and your child succeed in adjusting. Stay in close touch with your child's teacher. Share the strategies you are using to help your child make the transition to school. Talk about your concerns, and ask your child's teacher to tell you how she or he is helping your child adjust and how you can be supportive of efforts at school. Taking time during the transition process to help your child will pay off for both of you.

Always Say Goodbye

Leaving your child may be as hard for you as it is for him or her. It might seem that leaving without saying goodbye could save you and your child from suffering through another separation. In fact, the opposite is true.

Young children are learning that the world in which they live is a predictable and responsive place to be, or that it isn't. They learn this important lesson from their parents and teachers. Those who provide sensitive, responsive, and predictable care teach children to trust them.

You can help your child learn that although you may leave him or her, you will never disappear without a hug and a promise to return. Through this repeated process, your child will learn that you mean what you say—that you will come back, just like you said you would.

Handling Pacifiers, Thumb or Finger Sucking, and Security Items

Pediatricians and child development experts view pacifier, thumb, or finger sucking as an extension of the strong rooting and sucking reflexes with which a child is born. They consider it a normal part of early development. Most children give up finger or thumb sucking on their own as they learn other self-soothing and self-comforting behaviors. By the time children are three, they usually have transitioned to alternate behaviors. If your child is still sucking a thumb, finger, or pacifier as a preschooler, you and your child's teacher can work together to address this concern.

As your baby matured, the sucking reflex disappeared and was replaced by your child's use of sucking as a comfort strategy. He or she may still use sucking for calming down after losing control or to relax enough to fall asleep. Both of these coping strategies are good ones, and we usually don't want to take away a coping strategy without helping children learn new ones. Many children transition from sucking a finger, thumb, or pacifier to using a security item of some kind. For some, the item is transitory and changing as long as it is something from home. For others, the intensity of the attachment requires parents to make sure the security object is always nearby.

Although attachment to a security item can become a problem, consider three issues when deciding about whether to be concerned about transitional objects: 1) the duration, 2) the intensity of the attachment, and 3) the distress caused by separation from the security item. For example, teenagers rarely carry around transitional objects from early childhood but may, quite normally, keep them in a safe place in their rooms. Children who are traumatized if they misplace their transitional objects as they near the end of the early childhood period (which actually lasts until age eight) may be indicating the need for help to solve an underlying problem.

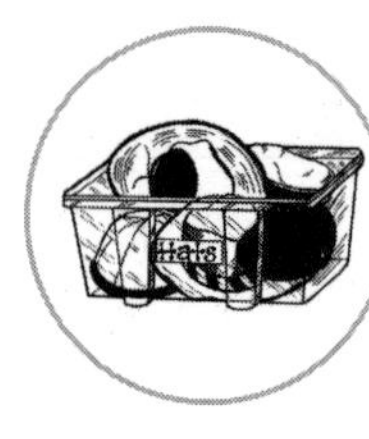

Curriculum Resources

Prop Boxes

Telephone Prop Box
toy telephones • real telephones with cords removed • telephone books • address books • pencils • paper

Mail Carrier/Postal Worker Prop Box
mail carrier bags • blue uniform shirts • hats • stamps • stamp pads • old letters • post cards • mail boxes • packages • papers • pencils • clip boards • envelopes • invitations • greeting cards

Books

Abuela by Arthur Dorros
All the Colors We Are: The Story of How We Get Our Skin Color by Katie Kissinger
All Kinds of Children by Norma Simon
All Kinds of Families by Norma Simon et al.
Beginnings: How Families Come to Be by Virginia Kroll
Benjamin Comes Back (Benjamin Regresa) by Amy Brandt
Best, Best Colors/Los mejores colores by Eric Hoffman
Block City by Robert Louis Stephenson
The Desert Is My Mother—El Desierto Es Mi Madre by Pat Mora
Eight Hands Round: A Patchwork Alphabet by Ann Whitford Paul
Fairy Houses by Tracy Kane
Friends Together: More Alike Than Different by Rochelle Bunnett
From Head to Toe by Eric Carle
Hawaii Is a Rainbow by Stephanie Feeney
Houses and Homes by Ann Morris
How to Lose All Your Friends by Nancy Carlson
I Am Me by Karla Kuskin
I Am Not a Crybaby! by Norma Simon
I Live With Daddy by Judith Vigna
I Was So Mad by Norma Simon
The Jolly Postman by Allen Ahlberg
Let's Go Home: The Wonderful Things About a House by Cynthia Rylant
The Little House by Virginia Lee Burton
Margaret and Margarita by Lynn Reiser
My Great-Aunt Arizona by Gloria Houston
Penelope's Amazing Imperfect People Eating Machine by 4th grade students at Village Elementary School in Coronado, CO
The Post Office Book: Mail and How it Moves by Gail Gibbons

Purple Hair? I Don't Care by Dianne Young
The Quilt by Ann Jonas
The Quilt Story by Tony Johnston
Today I Feel Silly and Other Moods That Make My Day by Jamie Lee Curtis
The Way I Feel by Janan Cain
To the Post Office with Mama by Sue Farrell
The Way Mothers Are by Miriam Schlein
We Adopted You, Benjamin Koo by Linda Shute
Wemberley Worried by Kevin Henkes
When Katie Was Our Teacher (Cuando Katie era Nuestra Maestra) by Amy Brant
When I Feel Angry by Cornelia Maude Spelman
Whoever You Are by Mem Fox
Will You Come Back for Me? by Ann Tompert
Will There Be a Lap for Me? by Dorothy Corey

Observation/Assessment

Takes on various roles in dramatic play, page 70
Dresses and undresses in costumes, page 70
Has particular play partners, page 71
Uses props to enhance dramatic play, page 71
Draws, sketches, or paints using a variety of art media, page 72
Draws self-portrait, page 72
Accomplishes level of detail in felt people, page 73
Observes similarities and differences, page 73
Uses tools appropriately, page 74
Builds using various materials, page 75
Builds using unit blocks, page 75
Examines/observes using magnifying glass, page 75
Counts sequentially with birthday candles, page 76
Uses one-to-one correspondence with birthday candles to year of age, page 76
Uses letter-like symbols or scribbles to represent print, page 78
Identifies initial letter of own name, page 79
Identifies initial letter sound of own name, page 79
Indicates preferences and interests, page 79
Recognizes family members, page 80
Sorts by one dimension (eye color) and two dimensions (eye color and hair color), page 80
Uses graphing skills, page 80
Counts sequentially from 1-10, counts by 5's, 10's, etc., page 81
Breaks words down into syllables, page 81

Listens to stories, rhymes, fingerplays, and songs, page 81
Identifies patterns in words and numbers, page 83
Adds details to self-portrait, page 85

Picture File/Vocabulary

bedroom
body parts (hands, arms, legs, feet, faces, eyes, noses, mouths, chins, etc.)
brother
Daddy
dining room
emotions (happy, sad, irritated, angry, enthusiastic, frustrated)
envelope
eye colors (brown, black, hazel, blue, green)
family
friends
half-brother
kitchen
letter carrier
living room
Mama
me
Mommy
Papa
post office
sister
step-sister
syllables

Concepts Learned in

Saying Hello

Content Knowledge

- ☐ All children are alike in some ways.
- ☐ All children are different in some ways.
- ☐ Fruits have different tastes.
- ☐ I know the members of my family.
- ☐ All families are not the same.
- ☐ I can determine the color of my friend's eyes, hair, skin color, and so on.
- ☐ Houses have different rooms.
- ☐ I can identify my emotions.
- ☐ I can count birthday candles.
- ☐ I can say hello in many different ways.

Process Knowledge

- ☐ I can cut with scissors.
- ☐ I can play post office.
- ☐ I can draw myself.
- ☐ I can make puppets.
- ☐ I can draw and paint to express my ideas.
- ☐ I can trace.
- ☐ I can make prints—handprints and footprints, and so on.
- ☐ I can find out what is inside a telephone, intercom, or answering machine.
- ☐ I can build with blocks.
- ☐ I can use a magnifying glass.
- ☐ I can taste different foods and tell others which ones I like.
- ☐ I can paint with different parts of my body.
- ☐ I can find things out from others by asking questions.
- ☐ I can communicate my thoughts in drawings and with letter-like writing.
- ☐ I know a lot about me.
- ☐ I can follow a leader.
- ☐ I can sing.
- ☐ I can dance.
- ☐ I can recognize my emotions.
- ☐ I can wait just a minute for my turn.

Pre-academic Skills

- ☐ I can count my fingers (one number to each finger).
- ☐ I can count the beats (syllables) in my name.
- ☐ I can identify the first letter of my name.
- ☐ I understand that words have meaning.
- ☐ I am interested in what words say.
- ☐ I can make a graph.
- ☐ I can listen to others.
- ☐ I can ask questions.
- ☐ I can answer questions.
- ☐ I can observe likenesses and differences.

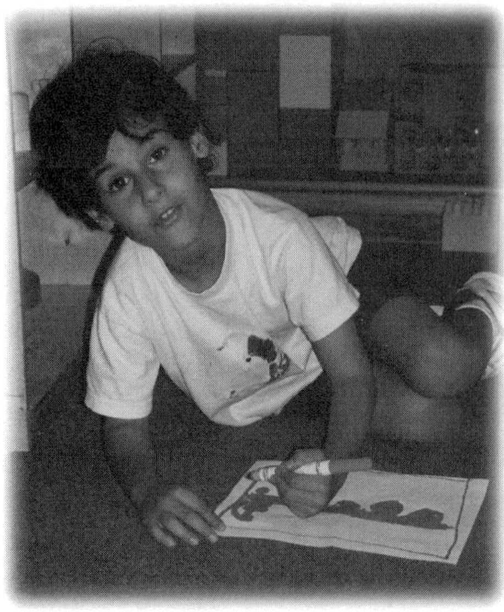

POSSIBILITIES PLAN— Castles

Getting Ready to Plan

Children are learning all the time—first from their own personal experiences and later from hearing about the experiences of others and from imaginative play. This section explores content that preschool children will find exciting related to Castles. The topics are people who lived in castles, parts of castles, special events at castles, people who worked in and around castles, and defending castles.

The purpose of Getting Ready to Plan is to support the planning process with a general overview of the content of this Possibilities Plan. Now is the time to think about what you want the children in your group to learn about each of these topics. Each of the topics is explored in general below.

People Who Lived in Castles: When exploring people who lived in castles, children see that a wide variety of people were associated with life in and around the castle. There were kings and queens and other nobles; merchants; farmers; peasants; builders and stonemasons, and so on. Children can explore the roles different people played—like different people live and work today.

Parts of Castles: Most preschool children have seen pictures of castles. Because castles are so different from our homes now, children will enjoy how castles are similar to our own houses and how they are different. Introduce new vocabulary words such as drawbridge, parapet, turret, and other words associated with castles.

Special Events at Castles: Children love celebrations, so learning about and acting out special events at castles will be especially fun. Organize a banquet (with the help of parents), plan for dancing, and explore how knights had special roles in the special events. Dress-up will be an important part of experiencing the celebrations.

People Who Worked in and around Castles: Just as adults have different roles in today's cities, individuals in castles had different tasks to perform. Children probably will be familiar with jobs such as cook, carpenter, soldier, stonemason, and laborer, but blacksmith and ruler may be new concepts. Show how adults had their own jobs, so the society around the castle worked.

Defending Castles: Children will be excited about the idea of defending a castle. This topic will bring up many opportunities to talk about how people get along as well as identifying reasons why they might not. Children may be familiar with some of the tools of defense and interested in understanding those with which they are not familiar. Plan ahead how you will address play that incorporates ideas from castle defense—including how you will help children play out these themes without hurting each other using miniature dramatic play manipulatives, setting reasonable limits, and enforcing them.

Now that you have an idea about the general content of the Possibilities Plan, you are ready to proceed with developing your own plan. This section of Getting Ready to Plan identifies items you may want to buy, collect, or locate to implement your plan.

Toys and Materials*

Purchased

Asian writing brushes
aluminum foil
baking soda
beach towel or non-skid rug
beads
beanbags
blocks
buckets
calligraphy pens
child-size rake
collage materials
colored tissue paper
construction paper
contact paper
craft knife (teacher only)
craft sticks
crayons
duct tape
food color
glitter
glue
hole punch
large pieces blue and green felt
Legos®
liquid water color
markers
masking tape
paints and brushes
paint cups with lids
playdough
poster board
PVC pipe and connections
red and blue spray paint
sand and water tub
sandbox
sandcastle molds
scissors
shovels
stickers
thin paintbrushes
toy figures
tracing paper
vinegar
writing (or calligraphy) brushes
yarn
yarn needles

Gathered

beads
boxes
branches
brown paper grocery bags
burlap or other loose-weave cloth
cardboard
castle toys
classical music
clear plastic containers
clothes
coins
costume jewelry
cups of different sizes and shapes
double sets of photographs relating to castles
eight tennis balls
examples of calligraphy
examples of materials with different alphabets/symbols (e.g., Chinese, Greek, Russian),
feather quills
flags
golf balls
golf tees
hair gel
horse toys
ink pens
labeled and decorated boxes
lamp
large marbles
large shallow container
large table
large tray
Mardi Gras masks
menus
milk jugs
natural items (seeds, nuts, pine cones, leaves, sticks)
old jewels
pebbles
pictures of castles
pictures of coats of arms, crests, emblems
pictures of horses
pictures of mazes
pictures of stained glass windows
ping-pong balls
ribbons
rocks
scarves
sheet or tablecloth
small toys
smooth pebbles
tablespoon and ¼ cup measuring cup ,
towel
toys of different weights
tray
two bowls
vests
water bottle
wood

*Note: Please consider the ages and abilities of the children in your care. Use only safe, non-toxic materials.

Castles

WEB

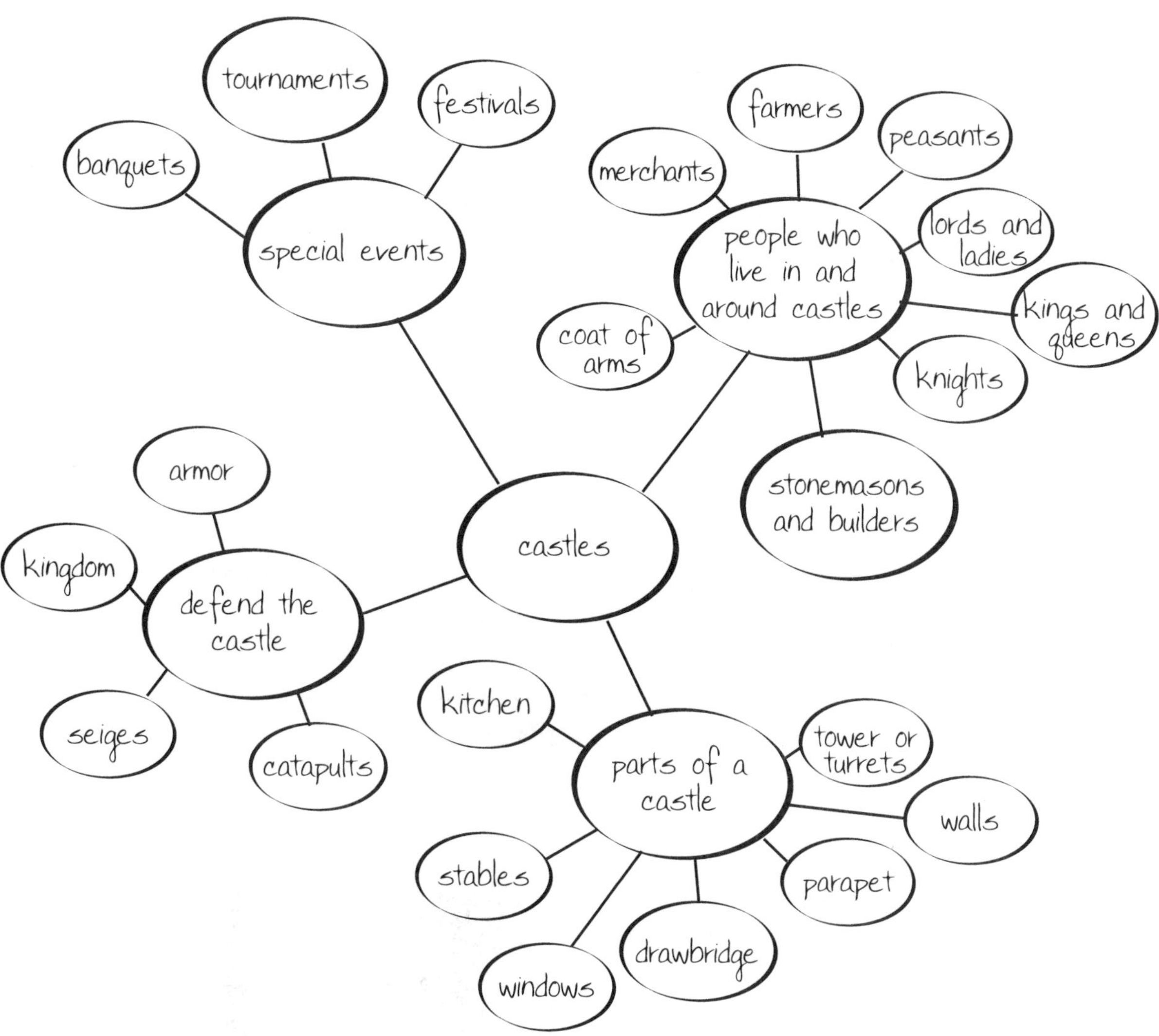
tournaments
festivals
banquets
special events
farmers
peasants
merchants
people who live in and around castles
lords and ladies
kings and queens
coat of arms
knights
stonemasons and builders
armor
castles
kingdom
defend the castle
seiges
catapults
kitchen
parts of a castle
tower or turrets
walls
stables
parapet
drawbridge
windows

Castles

PLANNING PAGES

Plan Possibilities

ACTIVITIES AND EXPERIENCES FOR CASTLES

DRAMATIC POSSIBILITIES

Classroom Castle

Materials
crowns (construction paper, foil) • tabards (old towels) • princess hats (cardboard and construction paper) • helmets (milk jugs) • costumes (skirts, cloaks) • armor (brown paper grocery bags) • lamp • big blocks (brown bags and newspaper) • flags • costume jewelry or beads • coins • rocks • books about knights and armor, such as *Knights in Shining Armor* by Gail Gibbons

Teacher Talk
"Tell me about the people who live in the castle." "Why do you think the lord of the castle needs such a big castle?" "Tell me about your costume." Talk about rules before children play in Dramatic Possibilities. Establish rules early because children may act aggressively when they are pretending to be knights.

Instructions
Make helmets out of milk jugs, crowns out of construction paper and foil, and armor out of brown paper grocery bags. Create big blocks out of brown bags with newspapers stuffed inside. Use beads, coins, and rocks as jewels. Make tabards out of old towels by cutting a slit (big enough for child's head). Have enough materials to let the children create and use their imaginations. Creating open-ended resources like these enriches children's play. Teacher-made materials can greatly enhance play. Don't worry about getting perfect costumes or materials. Use what is available from parents and at your school.

Helpful Hints: Ask families to donate old jewelry, toys related to castles that are no longer being used by their children, and old clothes that can be modified to fit into this plan. Different sizes of boxes are great building materials for the castle.

Observation/Assessment
Takes on various roles in dramatic play
Uses props to enhance dramatic play
Dresses and undresses in costumes

Medieval Banquet

Materials
materials from classroom castle • large table • sheet or tablecloth

Teacher Talk
"Our lords and ladies of the castle are all dressed for the banquet." "What will we be eating?"

Instructions
Cover table with tablecloth or sheet. Children dress and prepare for the banquet. Omit utensils since they were not used during this time.

Observation/Assessment
Dresses and undresses in costumes

Other Dramatic Possibilities

- Add a May Pole to the area. Make it out of a long mail tube with lots of ribbons attached.
- Add books about life in a castle.

ART POSSIBILITIES

Coats of Arms

Materials
brown paper bags • scissors • variety of different colored construction paper • glue • paints and brushes • markers • collage materials (natural items such as small pinecones, acorns, leaves, seeds, nuts, moss, buttons, cord, cotton balls, dried beans or peas, plastic or silk flowers, glass beads, mosaic pieces, lace, rickrack, and so on) • books and pictures of coats of arms, crests, emblems

Teacher Talk
"Most knights had their own family symbol. These were called coats of arms, emblems, or crests. Families used these crests to identify each other from far away. They put their coats of arms or crests on banners, their tunics, and their household items."

Instructions
Cut out a hole at the bottom of a brown bag. Cut off the sides of the bag. Create a coat of arms or crest on the bag. Place resource books about castles with pictures of coats of arms or crests on the Art Possibilities table to help children get a better idea of what coats of arms look like.

Observation/Assessment
Uses collage materials to decorate paper

Royal Bangles and Baubles

Materials
duct tape • colored tissue paper • construction paper shapes • small old toys • glitter • yarn • beads

Teacher Talk
"You made a bracelet." "I see you used the blue yarn to decorate your bracelet."

Instructions
Cut duct tape in pieces long enough to go around a child's wrist plus an overlap of one to two inches. Help children put a piece of duct tape around their wrists with the sticky side out. Children can decorate the duct tape with many different materials to create bracelets. It is easier to put duct tape together and make a bracelet before decorating it. Decorating the bracelet with only one hand will also be a fun challenge. Encourage children to make bracelets for both arms, using dominant and non-dominant hands for the activity and requiring that children cross the midline of their bodies to complete the activity (an important way to stimulate neural connections in the brain!).

Playdough Recipe (Cooking Required)
3 cups flour
1½ cups salt
3 tablespoons oil
2 tablespoons cream of tartar
3 cups water

Combine all ingredients into a saucepan. Cook over very low heat until mixture pulls away from the sides of the pan. Store in an airtight container.

Playdough Recipe (No Cooking Required)
6 cups flour
3 cups salt
2 cups water
½ cup oil
Food coloring

Mix together all the ingredients. Knead until smooth. Store in an airtight container.

Other Art Possibilities

- Draw dragons.
- Make crowns out of foil and cardboard.
- Make bracelets using thick postal rubber bands decorated with fine tipped markers.
- Use playdough to make knights or other castle-related figures.
- Make stained glass using jewel-toned paint, contact paper, and yarn.
- Make stained glass windows with tissue paper, construction paper, glue, and scissors.

BLOCKS/CONSTRUCTION POSSIBILITIES

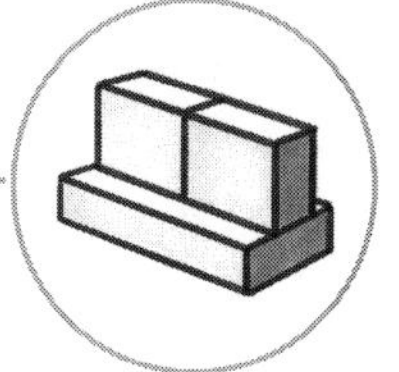

Castles around the World

Materials

blocks • pictures of castles from the picture file • books about castles in different countries, such as *A Samurai Castle* by Fiona MacDonald

Teacher Talk

"What is similar about the castles?" "What is different?" "What would you like your castle to look like?"

Instructions

Post the pictures of castles in the block area. Add block supports such as paper cones, drawbridges, crenellated blocks, and so on to support the castle-building activities.

Observation/Assessment

Builds using various materials

Amazing Playdough Maze

Materials

playdough • large tray • golf tees • golf balls • large marbles • ping-pong balls • pictures of mazes from picture file

Teacher Talk

"How can we make a ball stay in the maze?" "Which ball works best when it goes through the maze?"

Instructions

Make homemade playdough (see recipe on page 102) or use purchased playdough. Spread the playdough on the large tray or baking sheet. Place the golf tees in the playdough and create a maze for the ball. Be sure the playdough is thick and stiff enough to keep the golf tees stable.

Observation/Assessment

Spreads and pounds playdough

Other Blocks/Construction Possibilities

- Add horses and fencing to create stables.
- Add a balance scale for weighing and measuring blocks, and so on.
- Create block mazes.
- Add chess pieces as block accessories.
- Make castle scenes in the block center using blocks, boxes, and blue and green felt.

SCIENCE/DISCOVERY POSSIBILITIES

Magnificent Moats

Materials
Legos® • large shallow container • rocks • pebbles • wood • coins • craft sticks • water • books about moats, such as *I Wonder Why Castles Had Moats: And Other Questions About Long Ago* by Phillip Steele

Teacher Talk
"Why do you think a castle would have a moat?" "How can you make the Lego castle stand in shallow water?" "Why do you think it floats?"

Instructions
Creating a castle in shallow water is fun. The Legos float because they are made of lightweight plastic. The castle needs to be big enough and heavy enough to stay in shallow water. Explore different ways to keep the Lego castle standing in the shallow water with children.

How Does a Drawbridge Work?

Materials
medium cardboard box • craft knife (teacher only) • string • tape

Instructions
Cut the flaps off the top of a box. Then cut notches out of the top edge to give the appearance of a castle wall. Make the drawbridge by starting at the base of the box, cutting up about 8", across about 5", and then down about 8". Leave the drawbridge attached at the base. Punch holes about one inch to the outside of the cut corner of the box. Attach string to the corners of the flap using tape. Thread string through the holes. Children can pull on the string to close the drawbridge.

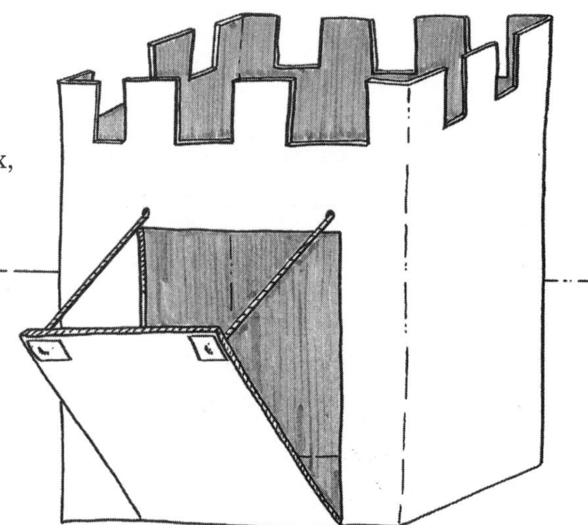

Other Science/Discovery Possibilities

- Explore catapults and how they work.
- Design and build catapults.

Gooey Castle

Materials
Legos® • non-toxic hair gel or starch • knight figures • dragon figures • other castle-related figures

Teacher Talk
"How does the gel make you feel?" "Would you like to live in a gooey castle or house?"

Instructions
This is an incredibly exciting sensory activity that uses a castle as the object for discovery. You can adapt this activity to fit any theme. Create a castle with Legos™ and then dump the hair gel on it. Build and rebuild the gooey castle, exploring the difficulties and challenges of building with the gel on the blocks. As an alternative to hair gel, make a gooey mixture out of starch mixed with water. Children can clean up the castle using vegetable scrubbers in the water table.

Ice Castles

Materials
sandcastle molds • food color/liquid watercolor • small toys • water

Teacher Talk
"How do you think people who lived in castles kept themselves warm when it was cold outside?" "What do you think people did to keep themselves cool when it was warm outside?"

Instructions
Color the water with variety of colors of food color or liquid watercolor. (Some types of food color/liquid water color will stain hands and clothes.) Pour the water into the sandcastle molds. Add small toys. Freeze in the freezer. Take the molds out and place them in the sensory table. Let children feel the ice castles and play with the toys inside the ice castles as they melt.

Wet and Dry Sandcastles

Materials
sand • water • different sizes and shapes of cups, toy figures (people, horses, and so on) • sand molds • beach towel or non-skid rug

Teacher Talk
"What makes a stronger castle—wet or dry sand?" "How could we find out?" "What do you think?" Talk about the castles that children build.

Instructions
Place dry sand and wet sand in different containers to explore making castles with molds, cups, etc. Put a beach towel or small non-skid rug underneath the sand activity to make cleanup easy.

Extension Possibilities
Take this activity outdoors for bigger wet and dry castles. Add pebbles, shells, and twigs as a variation.

Observation/Assessment
Uses wet sand to create shapes
Compares building with wet and dry sand

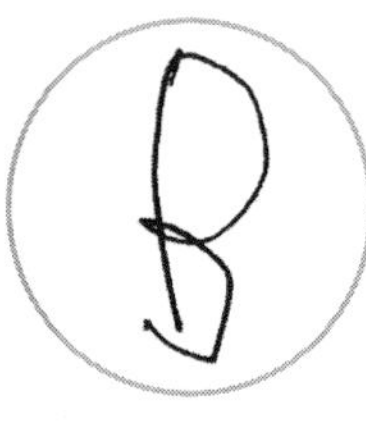

LITERACY/WRITING POSSIBILITIES

Writing in Style

Materials
examples of calligraphy (invitations, posters, and so on) • calligraphy pens and markers • tracing paper • menus • newspapers and magazines that use different alphabets, such as Chinese, Japanese, Greek, Arabic, Russian, and others

Teacher Talk
"Do these letters look different?" "How are they different?"

Instructions
Make supplies available to children in the writing center. Children can use the tracing paper to lay over the calligraphy examples and trace the examples or make their own calligraphy.

Observation/Assessment
Uses correct pencil grip
Traces letters

Ink a Dink, a Bottle of Ink

Materials
Paint cups with lids • liquid watercolors • paper • thin paintbrushes • regular ink pens preferably with see-through cylinders • feather quills • writing (or calligraphy) brushes

Teacher Talk
"Before we had pens with ink inside them, people had to dip their pens in the ink to write."

Instructions
Pour watercolors into paint cups. Make supplies available to children in the writing center. Let children dip the paintbrushes in the watercolors and use them to draw or to write words.

Observation/Assessment
Draws using paintbrushes and watercolors

Sewing Monograms

Materials
yarn, burlap or other loose weave cloth • masking tape • marker • yarn needles

Teacher Talk
"Up through the cloth, down through the cloth." "You are sewing!"

Instruction
Cut pieces of burlap or other loose-weave cloth into 12" by 12" pieces. Tape the edges, so they won't unravel as the children sew. Assist children in using the marker to write their initials on the cloth. Show children how to thread the needle, knot the yarn, and sew on the letters.

MATH/MANIPULATIVES POSSIBILITIES

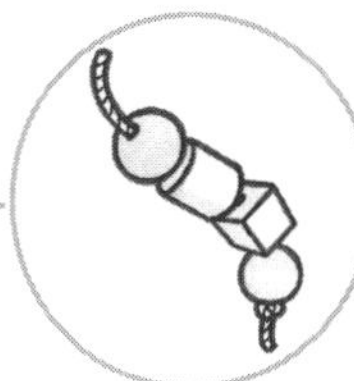

Horse Patterning

Materials
pictures of horses of different colors • paper to make patterning sheets • miniature horses • markers

Teacher Talk
"Look at the pattern and tell me about it." "Can you make your own pattern?"

Instructions
Make a patterning sheet with different patterns of horses (for example, black, brown, gray, dapple). Put the miniature horses in a basket. Place the basket on a tray with the pattern sheets. Ask children to make their own patterning sheet using the pictures of the horses to create a unique pattern. Start with simple patterns. When a child is making her own pattern, accept the child's idea of patterning.

Observation/Assessment
Creates a simple pattern

Turrets, Towers, and Tabards Lotto

Materials
two sets of photos or pictures of turrets, towers, walled villages • books about turrets and towers, such as *A Medieval Castle* by Fiona MacDonald

Instructions
Place the photos or pictures face down in rows. Children turn over one photo and try to find its match as they turn over another one. As more and more photos or pictures are turned over, children will increasingly be able to find the match for their photo or picture.

Observation/Assessment
Matches photos and pictures

Other Math/Manipulatives Possibilities

- Sort Legos®.
- Sort coins.
- Sort buttons by size, shape, or color.
- Make necklaces using yarn and beads.
- Use a balance scale, coins, and toys to explore weights.
- Use clear plastic boxes to sort pebbles, coins, and jewels.

RHYMES/FINGERPLAYS/SONGS/ MUSIC POSSIBILITIES

A Revel of a Good Time

Materials
classical music • Mardi Gras masks • crowns • scarves • vests

Teacher Talk
"Sir Nathan, may I have this dance?" "Lady Megan is turning in circles."

Instructions
Tell the children that the class will be having a special dance. Explain that these dances were called revels or balls in medieval times and that people liked to dress up in fancy costumes to attend. Make the costume options available for children to choose. After everyone has chosen what to wear, turn on the music. Encourage children to dance alone, in pairs, and in small groups. Have children try to imitate each other's movements. Try dancing in lines facing each other like people did in the castle halls.

Helpful Hints: Some children do not like to put on masks. Help them feel comfortable with their decision and encourage them to be a part of the activity by choosing another costume piece (crown, scarf, or vest).

Observation/Assessment
Moves to the musical beat
Freely explores space while dancing

Who's that Underneath that Crown?

Materials
crown

Instructions
Sing this song, adding your own tune. Identify different children as you sing.

Who's that Underneath that Crown?
Who's that underneath that crown?
Who's that underneath that crown?
I see Margaret underneath that crown!
Margaret is underneath that crown.

Other Rhymes/Fingerplays/Songs/Music Possibilities

- Sing "One Little, Two Little, Three Little Knights" to the tune of "Bumpin' Up and Down in My Little Red Wagon."
- Listen to and repeat Gregorian chants.
- Say the rhyme, "Humpty Dumpty."

- Explore any of the following recordings:
  - "William Tell Overture" by Telarc
  - "Queen's Goodnight" by Signum
  - "Courts, Kings, and Troubadours" by Medieval
  - "Renaissance Music" by Fine Tunes
  - "Music for a Medieval Banquet" by Classical Express

GROUP TIME POSSIBILITIES

Once upon a Time: Tell the children you would like them to write their own fairy tale to put in the Books/Library Possibilities area. Begin the story with "Once upon a time...." Move around the group until every child has added a sentence to the story, writing each child's sentence on a separate sheet of paper. Place the pages in the Literacy/Writing Possibilities area for children to illustrate their pages. **Helpful Hint**: Children may need you to read their page back to them as a reminder before they begin drawing. Punch holes in their pages (or use three hole paper), so the book can be put together when finished. Tie the pages together with yarn.

Find the Castle Features: Duplicate photographs or pictures of details of castles like drawbridges, moats, crenellated turrets, etc. Paste one set of photographs on a poster board or large chart paper. Hand out a second set of pictures, so each child has at least one photograph or picture. Ask children to match their photograph to one on the poster board. See if the children can identify common features of all of the castles.

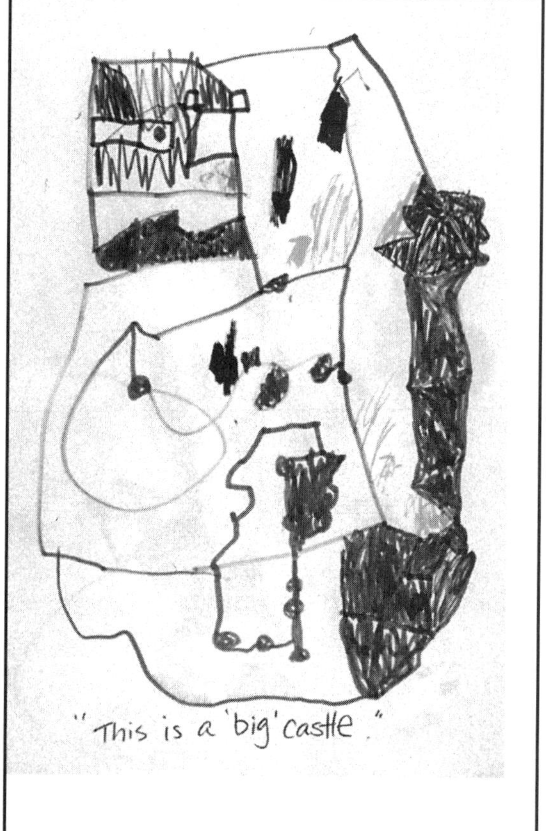
"This is a 'big' castle."

Other Group Time Possibilities
- Discuss sharing (fighting over land compared with fighting over toys).
- Compare castles around the world.
- Discuss gender role differences (then and now).
- Explore historical names of people and places.
- Read any of the books listed for this Possibilities Plan (see page 115).
- Look at pictures of castles and discuss what you see.

Bull's Eye!

Materials
cardboard from boxes (to make bull's eyes) • craft knife (adult use only) • white and red paint • yarn • beanbags

Teacher Talk
"Can you throw the beanbag hard/softly?" "You hit the red (or white) circle!" Talk about the archery tournaments nobles held during the medieval period.

Instructions
Cut two (or more) large circles out of cardboard using a craft knife (adult only). Paint a bull's eye or target pattern on a large piece of cardboard using one color at a time and allowing one color to dry before adding a second color. After paint has dried, use the knife to cut two holes in the top of the cardboard and thread the yarn through. Hang the bull's eyes outside and let children toss beanbags to try and hit them. Having two (or more) bull's eyes will cut down on frustration about waiting for a turn and still allow children to practice taking turns.

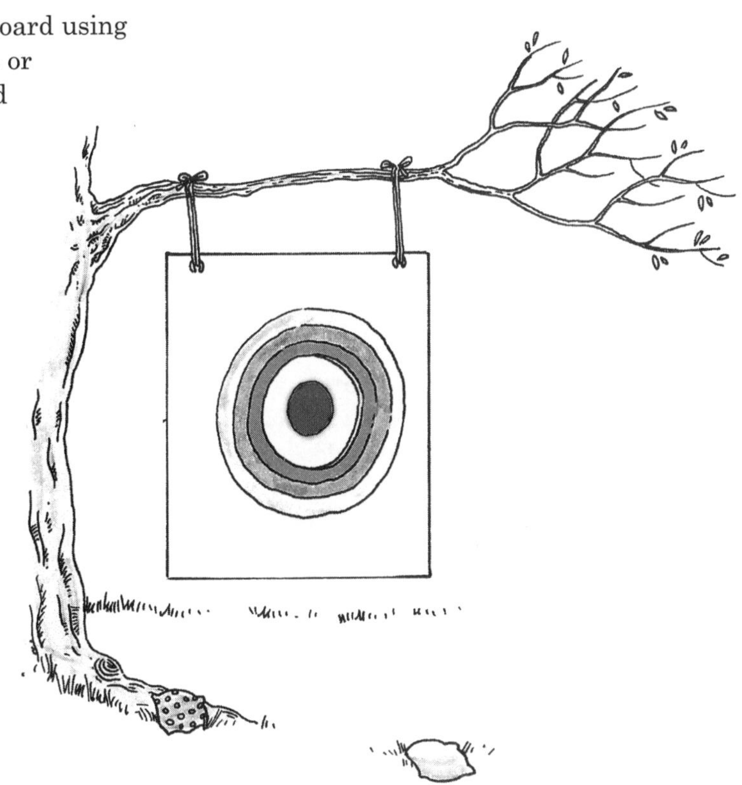

Helpful Hints: Set up this activity away from heavy traffic areas to keep beanbag accidents from occurring. Having bull's eyes in your classroom and on the playground is a good way to deal with aggresion that arises. Remind children to aim for the target (a more acceptable thing to shoot at) and not at people or other things.

Observation/Assessment
Throws beanbags at target

Other Movement/Outdoor Possibilities

- Play "Ring around the Rosie" and explain that this was a popular children's game in the time of castles.
- Put saddles on sawhorses or bales of hay or pine straw to ride, joust, and so on.
- Play Bocce ball.
- Use sand, buckets, sandcastle molds, rocks, leaves, and sticks to create sandcastles.

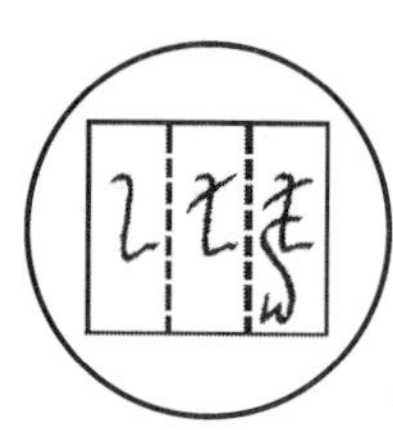

PROJECTS AND DOCUMENTATION POSSIBILITIES

What I Know about Castles

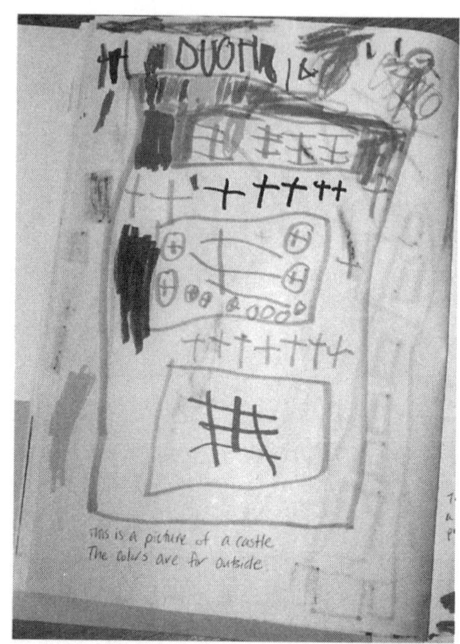

Materials
papers and writing/drawing materials • books about castles

Teacher Talk
"Tell me what you know about castles."

Instructions
Have each child dictate what she knows about castles before you start this Possibilities Plan. Once children have dictated what they know, ask them to draw what a castle looks like. Then, at the end of the Possibilities Plan on Castles, ask the children the same questions and have them draw another picture. When all are finished, put the papers together into a book with a page of what they knew when the project started next to the page of what they learned during the project. This gives teachers and children a chance to see what they learned about castles and document what children are learning in a format that can be shared with parents. It also can be used to revisit children's knowledge if children or teachers bring up the topic of castles again.

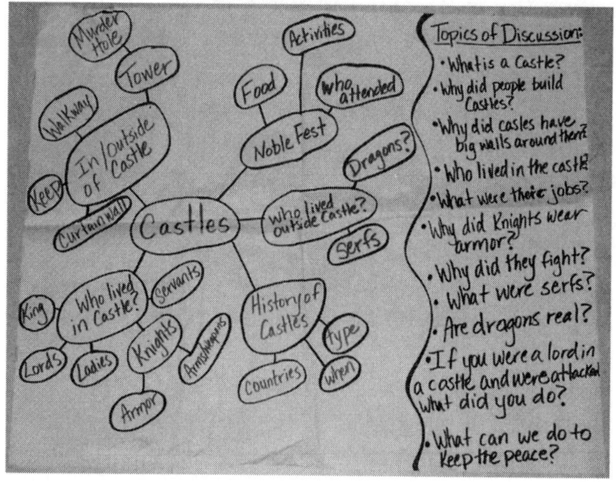

Renaissance Feast or Festival

Materials
same as Classroom Castle (see page 100)

Instructions
Plan a Renaissance feast with food and music, and encourage the children to dance. Ask the children to prepare for the feast by making things, such as crowns, masks, tabards, and so on. Explore the types of food the people usually ate at the Renaissance feast. Plan the food for the feast. Include parents by involving them in the food preparation. Invite parents to the feast. Write the invitations using feather pens and ink bottles.

FIELD TRIP POSSIBILITIES

City Hall: Visit a municipal building to compare modern-day city management to the management of cities during the castle period.

History Museum: Visit a history museum to see historical representations of times gone by.

Architecture Tour: Plan a walking or riding tour of your neighborhood to observe different architecture. Look for features of castles in local architecture.

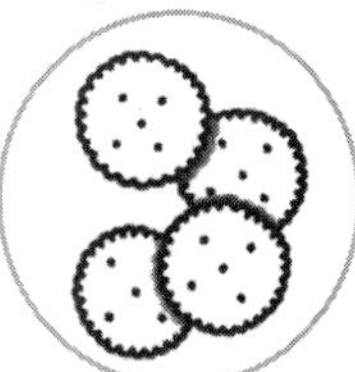

SNACK POSSIBILITIES

Jerky: Provide jerky for snack.

Turkey Legs: Provide barbequed turkey legs for snack or lunch.

Bread Plates: Toast large slices of bread to use as plates. Children can eat off the bread plates and then eat the toast.

FAMILY PARTICIPATION POSSIBILITIES

Have You Ever Seen a Castle?: Invite families to bring in photos of different kinds of buildings taken on vacation or while traveling for work.

Feast Fun: Ask families to prepare food for the Renaissance Feast or Festival (see page 112). Invite families to join the Renaissance Feast or Festival (see page 112).

Mood Music, Please!: Request recordings of period music (Gregorian chants, bugles or trumpet music, jousting music, and so on) from family music libraries.

Moving from Pretend Play to Dramatic Play with Miniature Play Sets

Ask any three-year-old in a Spiderman costume what his or her name is and usually the answer will be "Spiderman!" The interest in "being" the character lessens as children age and seek to act out their ideas, fantasies, and play themes by playing (rather than becoming) different characters. Older preschoolers enjoy playing a wide variety of roles, particularly the ones they see in their nearby communities, such as truck drivers, cashiers, and so on.

Preschoolers also develop an interest in creating and acting on miniature play sets. When pretend play moves to the miniature version, children create play settings that allow them to take figures through action sequences and to "act" on the play environments. Dinosaurs, insects, people, automobiles, airplanes, and action figures and props become very popular.

Pretend play with miniature figures serves some very important functions. Moving from being the character or acting "like" the character changes into playing with characters and action figures and acting "on" the play settings. This transition indicates an advance in children's thinking—they can now think about play themes and ideas, and then implement them.

Pretend play in miniature is also a wonderful way to handle intense feelings—like anger, sadness, and frustration. It may be acceptable to crash your car into your pretend friend's miniature house when she doesn't let you play the way you want. As the house is messed up by the crash, the intense feelings are expressed in an acceptable way, increasing the chances that the child will be able to process intense emotions in more acceptable ways as she grows up.

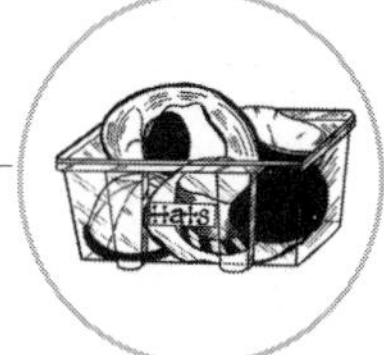

Prop Boxes

Medieval Prop Box
crowns • tabards • princess hats • helmets (from milk jugs) • costumes (skirts, cloaks) • armor made of cardboard covered with foil • big blocks • flags • costume jewelry • masks • coins or doubloons

Books

1,2,3 Draw Knights, Castles, and Dragons: A Step-by-Step Guide by Freddie Levin
Alexander and the Terrible, Horrible, No Good, Very Bad Day by Judith Viorst
Architecture and Construction: Building Pyramids, Log Cabins, Castles, Igloos, Bridges, and Skyscrapers (Scholastic)
Color of Light by Nomi Joval
DK LEGO Readers: Castle Under Attack by Nicola Baxter
DK Readers: Days of the Knights—A Tale of Castles and Battles by Christopher Maynard
The Good-bye Book by Judith Viorst
How Droofus the Dragon Lost His Head by Bill Peet
How to Behave Like a Princess by Ali Hokin and Dana Thompson
How to Draw Knights, Kings, Queens, and Dragons by Christopher Hart
How Would You Survive in the Middle Ages? by Fiona MacDonald
I Wonder Why Castles Had Moats: And Other Questions About Long Ago by Phillip Steele
King Bidgood's in the Bathtub by Audrey Wood and Don Wood
The Kissing Hand by Audrey Penn
Knights and Castles: 50 Hands-on Activities to Experience the Middle Ages by Avery Hart and Paul Mantell
Knights at Dawn by Mary Pope Osborne
Knights in Shining Armor by Gail Gibbons
Light by Donald Crews
Look Inside a Castle by Laura Driscoll
The Making of a Knight: How Sir James Earned His Armor by Patrick O'Brien
A Medieval Castle by Fiona MacDonald
A Medieval Feast by Aliki
Paper Bag Princess by Robert Munsch
A Samurai Castle by Fiona MacDonald
The Sand Castle by Shannon Yee
The Sun's Day by Mordicai Gerstein
The Truth About Castles by Gillian Clements
What Were Castles For? by Phil Roxbee Cox

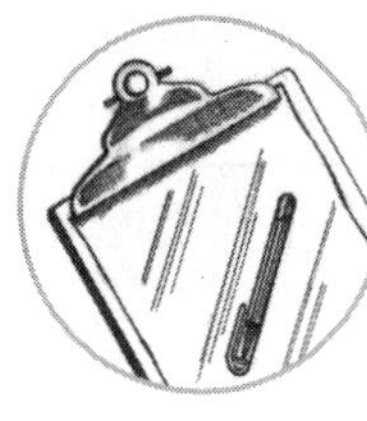

Observation/Assessment

Takes on various roles in dramatic play, page 101
Uses props to enhance dramatic play, page 101
Dresses and undresses in costumes, page 101
Uses collage materials to decorate paper, page 102
Builds using a variety of materials, page 103
Spreads and pounds playdough, page 103
Uses wet sand to create shapes, page 106
Compares building with wet and dry sand, page 106
Uses correct pencil grip, page 106
Traces letters, page 106
Draws using paintbrushes and watercolors, page 107
Creates a simple pattern, page 108
Matches photos and pictures, page 108
Moves to the musical beat, page 109
Freely explores space while dancing, page 109
Throws beanbags at target, page 111

Picture File/Vocabulary

armor
banquet
bishop
blacksmith
Bocce ball
castle
coat of arms
cook
costume
crossbow
crown
defend
duchess
duke
family crest
feast
festival
gown
helmet
hypothesis
jewelry
joust
king
knight
lady
longbow
lord
maze
medieval period
moat
parapet
peasants
princess
queen
renaissance
revel
stained glass
stonemason
tabard
target
towers
turrets

Concepts Learned in Castles

Content Knowledge

- ☐ Castles are a different kind of building than we have today.
- ☐ Knights wore armor for fighting.
- ☐ Castles from different countries look different.
- ☐ Coats of arms are symbols or crests that identify particular families.
- ☐ Castles have moats and drawbridges.
- ☐ Castles were built during the medieval period.
- ☐ People in castles worked in different ways.
- ☐ Kings, queens, and nobles ruled the castles.
- ☐ Knights rode horses.
- ☐ Castles were used for protection.
- ☐ Castles have walls and turrets.

Process Knowledge

- ☐ I can cut using scissors.
- ☐ I can play Bocce ball.
- ☐ I can throw a beanbag.
- ☐ I can build using different materials.
- ☐ I can make sandcastles.
- ☐ I can make stained glass windows.
- ☐ I can create mazes.
- ☐ I can dance.
- ☐ I can hit a target with a beanbag.
- ☐ I can roll balls.
- ☐ I can paint.
- ☐ I can clean up.
- ☐ I can put on and take off dress up clothes.

Pre-academic Skills

- ☐ I can make hypotheses.
- ☐ I can make a necklace out of beads and string.
- ☐ I can weigh things with a balance scale.
- ☐ I can sort by one dimension (color, weight, size, function, etc.).
- ☐ I can sort by two dimensions (color and size, function and weight, etc.).
- ☐ I can create a mathematical equation.
- ☐ I can create patterns.
- ☐ I can create a story with a beginning and an ending.
- ☐ I can create a story with a beginning, middle, and an ending.
- ☐ I can illustrate my words and thoughts.
- ☐ I can tell how things are different.
- ☐ I can match photographs and pictures.
- ☐ I can estimate.
- ☐ I can grip a pencil.

CHAPTER 3

Making Friends

INNOVATIONS IN CARE AND EARLY EDUCATION

Play

Play overlaps all areas of development—physical, social, emotional, and intellectual, which includes cognitive and language development. In fact, we often determine where a child is on one or more developmental continua by watching him play. The developmental process guides play behavior from the simple to the complex, from concentrating on the self to interacting with others, and from the concrete to the abstract, following the principles of developmental theory (see page 33).

The benefits of play for children are well documented (Oliver & Klugman, 2002.) Through play, children are able to explore their world, learn about themselves and others, build language and literary skills, and increase self-regulation. Because play is so integrated into the developmental context, it is helpful to look at the types of play behavior.

Piaget and Play

Piaget gave us a cognitive conceptualization of play as divided into three types of play behavior—practice play, symbolic play, and play-with-rules (Piaget, 1962). Practice play, the most common type of play during the first two years of life, is composed of repetitions of the same movements and actions, both with and without objects.

Symbolic play involves the beginning of the traditional "dramatic play," where children recreate in play what they see in the real world. Children play symbolically between ages two and seven. Play-with-rules is the last type of play behavior that emerges between ages seven and twelve, when children began to impose rules to govern play or to manipulate interactions.

Preschool children typically exhibit symbolic play—the ability to play out the roles and activities they see in the larger world of family, school, and community. An emerging sense of self as independent from their families entices children to explore being just like these important people, as well as to explore being very different from them. Increasing exposure to the larger community leads children to explore diverse roles seen in their neighborhoods and the community, such as firefighter, cashier, nurse, shoe salesperson, and so on.

Parten and Play

As children develop socially, they experience six increasingly complex types of peer play (Parten, 1932). The first type is unoccupied play where children watch others at play. Then, onlooker play emerges where children still watch others play, but seek to be near, and, perhaps even respond to the play of others. Solitary independent play comes next. Children play alone with objects without interacting with others, regardless of how near. Parallel activity emerges next, with children playing alongside each other with similar toys—beside each other rather than with each other. In associative play, interactions occur between children, although no specific roles are assigned or play goal identified. Cooperative play is the sixth form of play that finds children cooperating with others to create play situations. Group membership is defined, and group members play roles.

Preschool children may exhibit all of these types of play at various times during the school day. As the preschool years unfold, children spend more and more of their playtime in associative and cooperative play. Understanding play behavior gives teachers cues to where children are socially and emotionally. Information about such behaviors facilitates fine-tuning the interactive relationship between teachers and preschoolers.

Vygotsky and Play

Although all of these theorists believed that play links children to the larger society, Vygotsky's socio-cultural theory is based on the premise that children socially construct what they know in the context of their family and cultural experiences. In this theory, language is viewed as the primary strategy for communication and contact with the thoughts of others (Berk, 1994). In other words, Piaget believed children construct knowledge by interacting with objects and perfecting errors. Vygotsky stated that children construct knowledge through instructions from others and by talking about their ideas, mistakes, and actions.

Vygotsky is also known for the idea of the zone of proximal development (ZPD), which is "the range of tasks a child cannot yet handle alone but can accomplish with the help of adults and more skilled peers" (Berk, 1994, p.30). Vygotsky believed that play creates a ZPD in the child, preparing, through make-believe play, for the future development of abstract thought. Supportive teachers and more competent peers can raise the level of children's play. Called scaffolding, this support is essential to social-emotional, language, and cognitive development in the early years. When teachers engage in joint play with children, skills develop that can be used later in social play with peers.

Vygotsky also proposed that socio-dramatic play gives children practice in internalizing social norms and learning the skills to conform to the expectations of society. Children learn to self-regulate by separating thoughts from actions and by talking to themselves about the expectations they understand others have for them. Recent research confirms that socio-dramatic play supports the development of self-regulation, just as Vygotsky proposed (Elias & Berk, 2002).

Development of Peer Relations

The foundation for success in having friends and being friends is laid during the early childhood years. Successes in peer relationships matter. Successful friendships impact how children view themselves and their place in the social world, predict success with peer relationships in later life, and affect the type of children selected as friends during adolescence (Shonkoff & Phillips, 2000).

Children socially construct knowledge about peer relationships. Like social development in general, interaction and experience with peers influence friendships. Peers help each other learn lessons about social relationships that are different from the lessons learned within family relationships. They learn social skills such as joining in play, sustaining play, resolving disagreements and conflicts, and maintaining relationships. They learn to make social comparisons—to evaluate themselves compared with others. These self-evaluation skills contribute to children's emerging sense of self as competent and capable, affecting identity formation and self-esteem.

By three, children often choose who to play with by what they are playing with—the selection of toys and materials rather than who is playing with the toys and materials. By four, friendship becomes conditional—to play, you must agree to follow the play leader, or risk being rejected as a playmate. Cooperation is the hallmark of five-year-old play. Peers often select whom to play with first and then decide on what to play or how to play together with the outcomes being negotiated within the group.

To move through these steps, children need to pay attention to selected parts of environmental stimulation, to know how to take turns interactively, and to be mutually responsive to others, all lessons first learned in important relationships with significant adults in their lives.

Peer relationships are not always easy. As interest in peers increases, so do the mistakes children make in keeping interactions between themselves and others going. Miscues derail play often as children bump into each other, take each other's toys, lose track of play ideas, or hurt each other.

An important condition of peer relationships for children is familiarity. Children find it easier to play successfully with familiar playmates that have compatible temperamental styles (Howes, Phillips, & Whitebrook, 1992). Children who stay in the same peer groups throughout the preschool years remain friends and have better developed social skills (Howes, 1988). Continuity of care, also called looping and sustained instruction, creates the ideal setting for children to become better friends—by giving children time to become familiar with each other and to succeed in working out conflicts and problems with well-known peers.

Conflict plays a big role in children's construction of peer relations, particularly among friends. When children are friends, they are more likely to stay and try to work out conflicts than if the conflicts occur among acquaintances or unfamiliar playmates (Shonkoff & Phillips, 2000). When conflict occurs among friends, it can actually support emerging social competence as children try to work out ways to continue to play together. These interruptions create experiences with negotiation and problem solving, and encourage children to figure out what will maintain their play.

Emotional, social, and intellectual competence affects peer relations. Secure emotional relationships with parents, teachers, and other adults create the emotional foundation for friendships to grow. Social skills, such as the ability to gain entry into a play setting, join in play, and then sustain play by eliciting responses from others, help friendships grow. The ability to communicate clearly, both with gestures and with expressive language, and good observation abilities, are intellectual competencies that enhance peer relations. Opportunity affects friendships, also. When there are many opportunities to play successfully with friends, peer relationships grow.

Secure emotional relationships with parents, teachers, and other adults create the emotional foundation for friendships to grow.

The environments in which peer relationships operate make a difference. When responsive, supportive adults provide coaching and clear ideas about appropriate and inappropriate play behaviors, friendships and play mature. When adults view helping peers interact and play successfully as a key parenting or teaching role, children are more successful in making and keeping friends.

Bronfenbrenner's Ecological Model

Bronfenbrenner's ecological model of human development proposes that development occurs in the context of complex systems that influence, impact, and direct development. These systems are dynamic, as is the child's development occurring within them (Bronfenbrenner, 1979).

Four systems of influence are identified in Bronfenbrenner's theory—the microsystem, the mesosystem, the exosystem, and the macrosystem. The microsystem is composed of the child and the socio-cultural context of the family, including values, cultural practices, previous caregiving experiences, and reciprocal relationships between the child and her parents and teachers.

The mesosystem includes connections and relationships between the child and family and the neighborhood and other settings that foster development. The interface between and among cultural, religious, ethnic, family composition, extended family, racial, and socioeconomic backgrounds is part of the mesosystem.

The exosystem is composed of the broader community and includes values and practices of institutions such as schools, religious organizations, community agencies, and social groups. The macrosystem is composed of the broader society including economic resource allocation, business practices, employment, health and education priorities, government policies, demographic trends, and technological changes. The priority given to children by the community is usually evident at this level.

Howes proposed an extension of Bronfenbrenner's ecological systems theory. The primary difference in Howes' ideas "is the centrality of relationships in understanding development" (Howes, 2000, p. 88). This reconceptualization moves attachment relationships with extended family members, teachers, and peers much closer to the child into the microsystem. The emphasis is placed on the influence of a network of relationships, rather than simply the mother/child or parent/child relationship. This conceptualization is more consistent with children's real experiences.

The relationships between the family and care and early education are added to the social context (the mesosystem) of the child. The influences from relationships within the family and the relationship between the child and the quality of the care and early education arrangements are considered key variables in the child's social development, and as such, are socializing agents.

At the exosystem level, Howes places the influence of culture as it is "understood and enacted by the child's caregivers" (Howes, 2000, p.93). As teachers understand, interpret, and enact routines, children learn important lessons about how adults view the child's cultural background and characteristics. These lessons influence social development. Finally, society is placed at the macrosystem level, where social policy, racism, sexism, and beliefs about gender roles influence the social development of the child. A child's teachers operate within these societal expectations, influencing how the child's social development proceeds.

Erikson's Stages of Psychosocial Development

Erik Erikson proposed a stage theory of psychosocial development (Erikson, 1963). He viewed each stage as a struggle, a crisis to be negotiated before continuing to the next stage. The resolution of each crisis influences the way the crisis of the next stage unfolds.

Erikson's contribution to what we know about the development of young children hinges on the idea that development is cumulative, with each developmental step laying the foundation for the next and with each future step forward being influenced by previous ones.

The first stage of Erikson's theory is the struggle to develop a sense of trust in the interactive, physical, social, and cultural world. During the first year of life, babies discover that the world is a safe and responsive place to be or that it is not. During this stage, children learn whether caring and responsive adults will meet their needs, particularly when they are in distress. The direction of this struggle has much to say about developmental outcomes. Learning that their needs will be met results in a growing sense of connection and attachment—a condition crucial to continued emotional development.

Children are also learning to understand and use their own abilities to impact what happens to them. The result of these experiences is a sense of self-awareness and self-motivation—an "I can" and "I want to" attitude.

A feeling of trust, instead of mistrust, grows when there is a good match between children and the adults in their lives. If parents and teachers "read" non-verbal cues and respond appropriately, children become more intentional with their communication and seek to perfect it.

The second stage of Erikson's theory relates to feelings of autonomy versus shame and doubt. The struggle to hold on or to let go is evident in this stage. Feelings of autonomy (rather than shame and doubt) emerge from successful experiences with choosing when to hold on and when to let go, and from many successful experiences in letting go.

Growth in physical development contributes to feelings of autonomy as children try and succeed at new endeavors such as hopping, running, drawing, building with blocks and manipulatives, climbing, digging, and other motor skills. Language growth enables children to communicate their emotional needs successfully, resulting in less dependence by adults on gestural or non-verbal cues. Cognitive growth leads to the ability to wait a moment and to make simple predictions about what might happen and when.

Initiative versus guilt is the next stage—the one that predominates during the preschool years. As autonomy grows, preschool children seek to act on their newfound sense of independence, initiating actions and behaviors in many spheres of their world. They take the initiative to dress themselves, choose their own snacks, select playmates and friends, help with routine tasks at home and at school, and perfect emerging physical, social, and intellectual skills. Children are less oppositional to adult input than during the stage of autonomy versus shame and doubt, and more likely to want to please adults and succeed in accomplishing requested tasks.

During the stage of initiative versus guilt, children recover quickly from their mistakes and are usually willing to take risks to figure things out, particularly if the adults in their lives focus on their successes rather than their failures. This same behavior, though, explains why preschoolers often overextend themselves. Because they are not yet able to anticipate the outcome of activities accurately, they try dangerous or inappropriate activities. Children in this stage need clear, predictable ideas about expectations and limitations in order to feel competent and capable.

During this stage, there is a risk that children will begin to feel appreciated and successful, or guilt-ridden and unsuccessful, for what they do instead of who they are, particularly if more attention is given to their failures than to their successes. The prevalence of pushing down curriculum from elementary school to preschool and the increase in measuring outcomes through high-stakes testing are two examples of current educational practices that are guilt (stage 3) and shame and doubt (stage 2) producing experiences for children. From Erikson's perspective, neither of these experiences is likely to help children negotiate this stage with a positive outcome.

Erikson's theory offers hope for children whose early childhood experiences are less than optimal. Failure to resolve an early dilemma is not irreversible. Renegotiation of any stage is possible at later stages although Erikson cautioned that the renegotiation is not easy. For example, for children who do not develop a sense of trust, Erikson felt it was possible to help them renegotiate this struggle with consistent, responsive care. It takes a long period of sensitive, responsive care to reverse the mistrustful trend, longer than it would have taken to establish trust in the first place.

Erikson's Stages of Psychosocial Development

Age	Stage
0-1 year	Trust vs. Mistrust
2-3 years	Autonomy vs. Shame and Doubt
4-5 years	Initiative vs. Guilt
6-12 years	Industry vs. Inferiority
Adolescence	Identity vs. Role Confusion
Young Adulthood	Intimacy vs. Isolation
Middle Age	Generativity vs. Stagnation
Old Age	Ego Integration vs. Despair

Erikson's theory is a good fit with ideas about development and learning occurring within the context of relationships. The identity crises of each stage are obviously worked out in relationships with important people within the child's world. Children's experience in resolving these struggles is tied closely to repeated interactive and behavioral sequences of interactions that build to create feelings of one kind (trust, autonomy, and so on) or the other (mistrust, shame and doubt, and so on) (Howes, 2000).

INNOVATIONS IN INTERACTIVE EXPERIENCES

Children learn social skills through observation, and imitation or modeling. Although these strategies are also used to learn cognitive, language, and physical skills, it is in the social context that the results of these strategies are most apparent.

Imitation is copying or adopting the behavior of another person. Imitation begins early in children's lives as they mimic the facial expressions of their parents and teachers. Then, children imitate interactive patterns they see enacted by others in their interactions with the environment, adults, and friends.

To benefit from imitation, children must learn first to attend to what is going on around them. When children can attend, they are able to use their senses to gather data. Being able to focus on the sensory information that is being gathered is important as a means of social learning. Observing—watching, listening to conversations, and picking up on subtle differences in the emotional messages that are included in actions—serves as a means of social learning.

Many of the experiences that stimulate social development are part of all interactions. The following list of experiences/activities could be included in other tasks as well. This overlap is precisely what makes it challenging to explain the important teaching that is required to stimulate social and emotional learning. Long before children begin to show others their new skills, these experiences lay the foundation for future social and emotional success.

Interactive Experiences Checklist for Making Friends

Ask a mentor or peer to observe you in your classroom to document the following interactive behaviors. Think about the following list of positive interactive experiences and make sure that the classroom reflects many of them.

- ☐ Talk to children often, particularly during routines.
- ☐ Rotate toys and materials often enough to support new play themes.
- ☐ Create quiet places for children to play together.
- ☐ Establish a few consistent limits.
- ☐ Comment on what children are doing as they play.
- ☐ Imitate children's actions.
- ☐ Model play behaviors.
- ☐ Engage in joint pretend play.
- ☐ Point out interesting things in the physical and natural worlds.
- ☐ Help children recognize and accept intense feelings of joy, anger, jealousy, sadness, fear, and so on.
- ☐ Help children express their emotions by suggesting appropriate behaviors to substitute for inappropriate ones.
- ☐ Encourage children to control their impulses.
- ☐ Validate attempts to assert autonomy, independence, and initiative.
- ☐ Encourage early tries that fail as well as those that succeed.
- ☐ Support peer interactions by staying close by and scaffolding children's interactions.

What Is Guidance and Discipline?

Guidance refers to what teachers do before a problem is present. Discipline is what teachers do after a problem is present. Guidance techniques are preventive in nature; they guide children to maintain self-control without actual intervention. Although self-control begins to emerge during the early childhood years, children from three to five still depend on adults to help them maintain control, particularly in situations where there are other children present.

Teachers can use daily activity schedules, classroom arrangement, and the plans they make for children's activities to help guide and direct children's behavior.

Distraction

Distraction is a guidance technique that involves changing the child's focus from an activity that is unacceptable to one that is acceptable without directly confronting the inappropriate behavior. Use distraction when there is no danger to the child. Distraction also can be used to prevent the escalation of a minor problem into a major one.

Redirection

Redirection is a strategy requiring that teachers be particularly good observers of children. Redirection involves anticipating problems and intervening before they occur. The following are examples of redirection.

- Exchanging an inappropriate toy or activity (such as tossing sand at your friend) for an appropriate one (such as filling a bucket with sand);
- Quietly singing a song to redirect a child's focus from a separation event to what is going on in the classroom; and
- Giving children who have a hard time sitting still at group time something to hold in their hands or an alternate activity to do.

Redirection only works when alert teachers get to a situation before it erupts into a problem. Once children need more intervention, the opportunity to redirect is lost.

Ignoring as a Guidance Strategy

Ignoring inappropriate behavior is a guidance strategy that teachers often forget to use. The school day can be long, and some children exhibit behaviors that are irritating but not dangerous or really problematic. For example, children often rock back and forth when they are sitting in circle time or listening to a story. An observant teacher might ignore this behavior if it is not disrupting the group.

Use a Variety of Teaching Roles

Teachers use a wide variety of roles in their work with young children. During the developmental task of Making Friends, three of the most important teacher roles are initiator, investor, and partner. These roles have specific characteristics during this developmental task.

The Teacher as Initiator

Teachers easily take the lead in preschool classrooms—initiating actions that support the teaching role. For the task of Making Friends, initiation has a particular feel and timbre. Teachers take the lead with families to get information about the child, his schedule, the parents' hopes and dreams, parenting strategies, and so on. This information helps teachers see the school experience from the families' point of view and increases the likelihood that they are on the same page in their expectations.

Initiating connections with children during transitions comes next. Sometimes, initiations can be direct, such as inviting a child to join an activity. At other times, the initiations may need to be subtler, such as a non-verbal gesture (a smile), a toy (offering a toy you are playing with), or a planned activity (of high interest or novelty).

Making families feel welcome in the classroom can be initiated in many ways. More than any other role the teacher plays, this one can create a firm foundation for future collaboration and partnership. Families feel welcome when teachers accept their important role in the child's life and offer to support, validate, and strengthen it. Teachers may also need to initiate welcoming activities and experiences. Adult-size furniture, an invitation to sit on the floor with their child, a place to put things, and a nametag will help others recognize and acknowledge family participation.

Offering to listen is a wonderful gift, particularly for families who are experiencing transitions to school for the first time. When teachers initiate conversations with open-ended questions that tell parents they are prepared to listen, connections and partnerships flourish. Some good questions to ask might be "How are you feeling about the transition?" or "Should we make any changes in our plan for tomorrow?"

The Teacher as Investor

The role of teacher as an investor sounds so financial—so business-like. But this investor is looking for dividends beyond the monetary kind. Some families "warm up" to teachers faster than others. Teachers who invest in collecting information that might help them understand each child's uniqueness give parents an opportunity to fulfill their role as the experts on what their child needs from school.

Teachers may need to invest extra time in sharing information about the school, insuring communication between school and home, and sharing the new child's experiences during the school day with parents. Teaching behaviors for this role include investing in spending extra time, having more conversations, and interacting warmly with new children; and investing time in observing the child at school, the interactions between families and children, and the child at play. Because observation gives teachers insight into the child's individuality, unique skills and abilities, and family relationships, it leads teachers to know what to do or try next.

The Teacher as Partner

Assuming the role of partner with families and children begins early for teachers. Partner with the new child to bridge interactions between peers in the classroom. This may mean actively facilitating interactions so that initial ones go smoothly enough to give the child confidence to try other interactions independently. Partnering with families starts here as well. Teachers create partnerships with families when they sincerely listen, ask families for input into the educational lives of their children, and include families in decision-making about what should happen next in the child's education.

INNOVATIONS IN TEACHING

Theoretical knowledge leads to best practices. Understanding play, peer relations, Bronfenbrenner's ecological systems theory and Erikson's stages of psycho-social development guide teachers to invest in relationships by implementing primary teaching and continuity of care and early education and to teach social problem-solving skills.

Invest in Relationships

Good things happen to children in the context of abiding, mutual relationships. Ongoing, nurturing relationships characterized by consistency and intimacy are essential, and there are no short cuts (Brazelton & Greenspan, 2000). Investing in relationships with children and with the adults in their lives forms the foundation of accomplishing the goals and objectives of educational programs. For most children, the beginning of this relationship-building starts with the first teacher.

Teacher as the First Friend—Primary Teaching

Primary teaching typically involves assigning each child to a special person to get to know at school. The primary teacher then spends her or his time gathering information and knowledge about the child's family, culture, unique temperament style, cues, schedule, and personality, so the teacher can be responsive and appropriate in her or his relationships with the child and the family. The three components of primary teaching are outlined below.

The first component is the relationship between the family and the school. Because parents are the most significant people in a child's life, the relationship between the teacher and the family is paramount (Lally, 1995). Seeing each other as partners is an essential component of early education.

The second component of primary teaching is the responsive relationship between the child and teacher. This relationship is based on careful observation of each child's individuality and on a sense of personal and emotional involvement that is mutual (Leavitt, 1994). Many researchers, including Brazelton (1992), Greenspan (1999), and Howes (2000), have characterized the interactive relationship between teachers and young children as crucial. Children need to know that the human world in which they live is a caring one that is responsive to their bio-behavioral needs.

The Three Components of Primary Teaching

- Mutual relationships between families and teacher
- Mutual teacher-child relationships
- Balance among routines, interactions, stimulation, and play time alone or with friends

The concept of reciprocity and mutual trust includes much more than just stimulating interactions (Gerber & Johnson, 1997; Kovach & Da Ros, 1998; McMullen, 1999). Characteristics are:

- interacting with, rather than reacting to, children;
- working to read and interpret verbal and nonverbal cues accurately;
- anticipating needs and wants;
- responding quickly and affectionately;
- waiting for cues from the child that he is ready for some action to take place;
- including the child's individuality and temperament in decisions about cue interpretation;
- sensitivity to over- or under-stimulation from the environment, as well as the people (and other children) in it; and
- individualizing the schedule or pace of the day.

When the interactive climate has these characteristics, secure relationships emerge (Gerber & Johnson, 1998; Howes & Hamilton, 1992).

Each child is unique. Primary teachers take the time to learn each child's unique ways of being in order to foster positive communication. Teachers gather substantive information about the child from the families and from observations of the child with his parents at school. This information gives the teacher a start toward understanding each child's individuality so the teacher can match her or his interactive style to the young child's emotional and social needs.

The teacher-child relationship is based on mutual personal involvement between the child and the teacher that is reciprocal in nature. Reciprocity refers to the careful give-and-take of interactions between the child and the teacher and their mutual interdependence. Greenspan (1999) calls these interactions circles—the child says something to the adult; the adult responds, letting the child know that a dialogue has begun; the child adds more to the discussion; the adult smiles and expands the conversation with an open-ended question or further comment. The child is as active a participant as the adult, engaging in continued or modified interaction as a result of each other's responses.

The third component of primary teaching is the balance among routine, interaction, stimulation, and playtime alone or with friends. An unfortunate legacy of the early education movement is the mistaken idea that children need to have constant stimulation. In reality, children need balance in the interactive world. Preschoolers need sensitive responses to routines; warm, caring, intimate interactions with a primary teacher; stimulation from the environment; toys, adults, and children in the environment; and, most important, uninterrupted time alone or with peers to integrate the experience, usually through play.

Relationships between teachers and children are not formed overnight; they develop over time. The process of becoming familiar, learning each other's interactive styles, developing a joyful interest in each other's worlds, and learning to understand each other's communication style takes time (Fein, Gariboldi & Boni, 1993). Primary teaching leads children and their teachers to form such relationships by taking time with each step of the process and by not requiring the child or the teacher to be in a relationship "all at once."

Continuity of Care and Education and Friendship Groups

Continuity of early care and education, also called looping or sustained instruction, is an extension of primary teaching that works to keep all of the components of relationships intact. The teachers stay the same; the peers stay the same, and the context stays the same. Maintain as many of these components as possible during the preschool years.

Because it takes time to develop close, reciprocal relationships, teachers and children need long periods of time together. Continuity of early care and education involves keeping all components of the child's experience continuous—the teacher, the other children in the group, and the context of the child's experience. Frequent moves of children to new classrooms with new teachers disrupt the relationship-building process, forcing everyone (children, families, and teachers) to start over repeatedly.

Philosophically and experientially, primary teaching extends the length of time a teacher and a group of children stay together in the same place. Groups stay together for at least 9-12 months, and may stay together for up to three or more years. Extended time together allows children to form strong ties to their primary teacher and to form additional secondary relationships with other adults and children in the classroom. This much time allows families and teachers to get to know and understand each other's needs, expectations, and talents (Edwards, Gandini, & Forman, 1994).

Changes in context are also avoided. When children need changes in their environments, primary teachers make those changes in the familiar setting of the classroom, instead of requiring children to move to a new location.

Teaching Social Problem-solving Skills

Teaching social problem-solving skills is a process—one that parents and teachers start in infancy and continue until children become adept at reading social cues in different contexts. Identifiable steps in social problem solving can be taught to children during the preschool years that will support emerging social relationships and facilitate emerging friendships.

Calling for Help

The tendency to call for help emerges as children develop. Quick response to calls for help when children violate personal space, accidentally hurt each other physically, or get in each other's way as they work and play tells children that their communication is received. When teachers validate such cries for help, children learn that the world is responsive to their needs.

Children need to be reminded to call for help if the strategies they are using do not seem to be working. For example, when two children want the same toy, both may grab it and begin to scream for help. By responding and validating the call for help, teachers can help children begin to understand that although grabbing didn't work, some other strategies might.

Trading

The concept of sharing is still difficult for preschool children to understand. Trading something you have for something you want is a little easier. When two children both want a favored toy, the adult helps the child who is grabbing the toy find another one of equal interest to trade, saying, "Ask him to trade with you." Regular assistance with the concept of trading (which exchanges something for something rather than sharing, which exchanges something for nothing) facilitates social skills in young children.

Taking Turns

After children learn to trade, introduce the concept of taking turns. Taking turns requires children to delay gratification for a little while and participate as an onlooker or find something else to do until the other child is ready to take a turn. Again, sensitive adults need to help children learn this skill by explaining what is happening and providing the physical support and supervision to encourage children to take turns.

Walking Away

Walking away is a technique that helps children use language rather than actions to solve problems. Walking away can take two forms: I can tell you to walk away from me, or I can walk away from you if you won't leave me alone. Both techniques empower children to solve their own problems and to use language as the problem-solving tool. A sensitive teacher needs to be close and remind children to talk to their friends, and then, if necessary, she or he can provide the words and support the actions.

Plan-making

Finally, facilitated plan-making helps both children get a turn. Plan-making initially requires adult support. Tell the children that you have an idea about how to solve the problem. Both children will get a turn. One child will get the toy for five minutes, and then the teacher will help the child give the toy to the other child for five minutes. While the second child is waiting, the teacher helps him choose another activity—even if that activity is sitting and waiting for five minutes with the teacher's help! Plan-making keeps teachers from feeling like referees. One child has to delay gratification, but gets the teacher's help to do so. Plan-making keeps teachers from saying, "No." Having a plan is very different from not being able to do something.

Social Problem-Solving Skill Development—A Process over Time

Step One: Calling for Help

Step Two: Trading

Step Three: Taking Turns

Step Four: Using Words

Step Five: Walking Away

Step Six: Plan-making

When children learn to make their own plans, their social skills are growing. Although the plan may be uneven or unfair, support these spontaneous attempts at plan-making as long as the involved children accept the plan. Later, as skills increase, sensitive teachers can help children see the fairness or lack of it in their plans.

Dealing with Negative Social Behaviors

During the preschool years, children try and then abandon a number of negative social behaviors. These behaviors emerge and then are usually replaced with more sophisticated skills. Name-calling, taunting friends, whining, tattling, arguing, and lying are examples of these types of behavior. It is important to see these behaviors in the overall context of social development—as attempts to make and keep friends, and to understand the way the social world works—not as deviant or deficit behavior.

Name-calling is usually the first negative social behavior preschool children try. It emerges as children struggle with ways to be a friend and make friends. Teachers can handle name-calling directly by prompting children to tell name-callers to call them by their real names. "His name is John, and you can call him by his name." Then, help children use a similar response to name-calling ("Call me John."). Reflect with the name caller about how it might feel to be called a name.

Taunting and threatening friends is usually an exclusionary tactic—"You can't play with me" or "I'm not going to invite you to my birthday party." Teachers recognize the progress children make when they move from using physical aggression to using verbal aggression when things go wrong. Children who are taunting and threatening need support for the intense feelings that prompted the threat as well as opportunities to replace the threat or taunt with more authentic expressions of how they are feeling.

Sensitive teachers can rephrase threats and taunts, showing children how to identify their feelings and how to express them to their friends.

Sensitive teachers can rephrase threats and taunts, showing children how to identify their feelings and how to express them to their friends.For example, when one child threatens to exclude another, a teacher might point out "you are really interested in playing with Aaron without being interrupted. Tell José that you are busy with Aaron and don't want to be interrupted." Then help the excluded child find a way to share how he feels. In this example, the teacher might say to José, "It's hard to want to play and not get to. Ask Aaron if you can play later (or after lunch, or tomorrow)." These types of responses are much more effective than forcing children to play together or using punishment to stop threatening behavior.

Whining is a behavior that usually gets teachers' attention because it is so irritating! Children whine for the same reason they taunt or threaten. They tried to be included, and it didn't work. Children who whine need to work on two skills: asking for help from an adult for a play problem (one that the child can sometimes solve on his own but was unsuccessful this time), and using a normal speaking voice. Approach whining from the same point of view as you do taunting. Reflect the child's feelings ("You really wanted to play and didn't get to."), and then help the child pursue his goal another way ("Try again after snack" or "Ask if you can play with him tomorrow."). With the whiny voice, try something such as, "I will hear your important words when you can say them in your regular voice" to help children see that there is a different way to ask besides whining.

When children lie, it reflects their egocentrism. They are actually telling you what they "wanted" to happen rather than what "actually" happened. Experts recommend approaching lying without too much confrontation. Restate what really happened and help the children move on to solve the problem. For example, when children fight over toys, one will usually say the other initiated the conflict and the other will say, "No, I didn't!" Instead of picking who is telling the truth, say, "It seems that playing together in blocks isn't working for you right now." Then, focus on what needs to happen next. This means that your intervention is directed at solving the problem rather than identifying who is telling the truth. In this situation, you might suggest that the children divide the blocks in half and play in separate areas.

Negative social behaviors are opportunities to teach. When teacher intervention is required for these behaviors, focus your attention on helping children understand each other's feelings and finding a solution that works for them.

Teacher Competencies to Support Making Friends

Sometimes	Usually	Always	
☐	☐	☐	Shows she or he likes children and teaching with nonverbal and verbal cues.
☐	☐	☐	Bends over, stoops down, sits, and maintains eye contact while interacting with children.
☐	☐	☐	Uses a low, calm, soothing voice.
☐	☐	☐	Avoids interruption of child's activities; times requests wisely.
☐	☐	☐	Allows children some flexibility in following routines; does not insist on scheduling compliance that conflicts with individual schedules.
☐	☐	☐	Makes mealtime and other routine interactions a time for self-help skill practice and social interaction; makes mealtime a pleasant experience.

Competencies for the Teaching Role of Initiator

Sometimes	Usually	Always	
☐	☐	☐	Welcomes families in the classroom at any time during the school day.
☐	☐	☐	Comments to parents about strengths, accomplishments, and positive attributes of the child through conversation, notes, phone calls, and so on.
☐	☐	☐	Actively seeks meaningful exchanges with children.
☐	☐	☐	Plays social games with children.

Competencies for the Teaching Role of Investor

Sometimes	Usually	Always	
☐	☐	☐	Spends as much or more time listening to families as providing guidance.
☐	☐	☐	Asks questions to clarify parents' points of view or issues of concern before responding with program policies or procedures.
☐	☐	☐	Acknowledges and compliments parents on the unique contributions they make to their child's developmental progress.

Competencies for the Teaching Role of Partner

Sometimes	Usually	Always	
☐	☐	☐	Takes advantage of opportunities for social play during routines.
☐	☐	☐	Structures periods of social time with children; remains available to support, facilitate, or interact while children direct the activity.

INNOVATIONS IN OBSERVATION/ASSESSMENT

Observation and Assessment for the Task of Making Friends

During the developmental task of Making Friends, observation and assessment are directed at understanding the social world and skills of each child, signs of a growing relationship between teacher and child, stage accomplishments, and children's feelings.

This understanding starts with observing stages of development in relationship to the theories discussed in Innovations in Care and Early Education (page 32).

Teachers will want to observe for signs that the relationship between the teacher and child is growing. Mutual, synchronous relationships result in children using the teacher as a secure base—a place to go when confronted with problems, disappointments, or conflict. Observe to see if children are using you as a resource, an ally in getting support when things don't work out. Then, you will want to confirm that children also use you to celebrate accomplishments and validate successes. Observe for stage accomplishments, using Erikson's, Parten's, and Piaget's theories as a guide.

Finally, observe children at play to help you understand children's friendships and social skills. Observe to identify play partners, favorite play themes or interests, favorite roles, and other interactions. A clearer picture of children who are experiencing successful friendships and those who are experiencing difficulty is the result of this observation, leading teachers to plan appropriate and individualized curriculum for those who are having peer challenges.

Observation of children's knowledge construction is a powerful record of learning and growing. Consider the following ideas as you observe what children are learning, how they are constructing their own knowledge, and which skills they are building:

- Observe who plays with whom.
- Observe where play partners like to play the most.
- Observe where, with whom, and what kind of conflicts occur.
- Observe favorite roles or play themes.
- Observe for indicators of stage development based on various theories.

Use Documentation to Communicate about Learning

Exchanges between the educators in the Italian town of Reggio Emilia and educators in the United States have resulted in an intense interest in using documentation as a source of understanding the learning strategies children are using to construct knowledge. The goal of documentation is to communicate children's ideas, competence, and knowledge construction while engaging teachers in co-constructing their own knowledge about children, their interests, and their competencies. Teachers in Italy use many different strategies to provide a record of children's experiences in learning, often focusing on how knowledge is communicated through many languages. Documentation is more than a display, much more than an interesting bulletin board highlighting children's work (Sussna, 2000). It is a journey to understand how children are using their skills and abilities to make sense of the world around them.

There are many reasons to use documentation in work with young children. Documentation can be used to:

- gather information,
- communicate with the learners and others,
- guide further exploration of ideas,
- create flexible plans and experiences,
- make visible the process of children's learning, and
- create a sense of history and memory about children's experiences (Tarini, 1996).

What does documentation do for children? It allows them to revisit their work—thinking about what they were interested in then, what they are interested in now, and what they might be interested in later. It offers opportunities to discover errors in thinking, mistakes in judgment, as well as to discover new ways to think about what they know.

What does documentation do for teachers? It provides opportunities for reflection about the teaching/learning process and strategies used by teachers to understand children's interests and ideas. Documentation is also a professional development strategy—allowing teachers to grow in their own insight and understanding of children's thinking and development. It informs teaching by gathering a great deal of data for teachers to use in matching their curriculum to children's interests, emerging skills, and developmental challenges.

Documentation also plays an important role with parents. It creates a sense of belonging. It shows parents what children are thinking (how they are constructing their own knowledge) instead of just what they are learning from a content perspective. This broader perspective helps families understand that learning is not just about facts but also about skills, abilities, and understanding.

Progress from creating documentation that is cute to creating documentation that is truly reflective of the joint process of teaching and learning changes teaching. Documentation, as presented here, is much more closely aligned with the ideas of the Italian schools than with the usual idea of documentation as displays of children's work products. Although work samples are sometimes included, such samples are just part of the documentation process, not the entire display.

In ***Innovations: The Comprehensive Preschool Curriculum***, documentation is used as part of the observation, assessment, and planning process designed to inform classroom teaching. It is a mutual process that results in meaningful, visible, exciting records of what children are learning, how they are learning it, and how teachers are supporting the exploration of children's ideas.

Create Children's Portfolios

Children's portfolios are an important tool for accomplishing authentic assessment in the preschool classroom. Portfolios show a child's progress over time and can be made in many different ways. A wide variety of materials can be used as a part of the documentation process. Date and label everything that goes into the portfolio. Use expandable files, large folders, or even small boxes.

Consider using all types of children's creations, teacher records, observation forms, and so on:

- drawings made with pencils, crayons, and markers;
- paintings made with fingerpaints, tempera, and watercolor;
- collages made with a wide variety of materials, including stickers, construction paper, tissue paper, posterboard, and nature materials;
- photographs and drawings that show other class work, such as building with blocks, dress-up in dramatic play, math and manipulatives experiences, sensory experiences with water, sand, and other materials, and emergent literacy experiences;
- assessment summaries;
- parent communication summary (parent conferences, selected communication sheets, parent visit log, and incident/accident reports);
- anecdotal observations;
- audio and videotapes;
- books read lists;
- concepts learned lists; and
- copies of favorite fingerplays, poems, and songs.

Add to Individual Portfolios to Highlight the Developmental Task of Making Friends

Children's portfolios reflect evidence of growth, development, and learning. They are a rich resource to use in sharing with parents and others. In this section of chapters 3-7, ideas about possible additions to portfolios are suggested. Consider the following as potential entries into one or more children's portfolios:

- initial play partners, and how children's play networks expand or change over time;
- favorite activities over time
- resolution of conflicts—how children work things out, which strategies they use, and how their strategies change over time; and
- children's construction of knowledge about play themes—what they learn from playing roles over time (including content, process, and pre-academic skills).

Although each child's portfolio is a unique collection of information and examples, entries such as the ones listed above will enhance your understanding of each child.

INNOVATIONS IN FAMILY PARTNERSHIPS

Employ Family-centered Practices

An important part of one's self-concept comes from being a part of a family group within a culture. Cultures have different characteristics, and families within cultures vary as well. Race, ethnicity, religion, gender, primary language, family size, family composition, and cultural values are all components of culture. The way the school environment responds to children's cultural differences impacts self-concept.

Teachers have a marvelous opportunity to make sure that their classrooms are family-centered as well as culturally inclusive. They do this by using family-centered practices that acknowledge, respect, and support all families. Three specific principles are suggested as core ideas about family-centered practices (McBride, 1999). The first principle is to establish the family, not the child, as the focus. This validates the influential role of the family on children's development.

Three Principles of Family-centered Practices

1. Establish the family, not the child, as the focus.
2. Support and respect the family as decision-makers.
3. Provide flexible, responsive, and comprehensive services to families.

The second principle is to support and respect the family as decision-makers—both by acknowledging them and by including them in all decisions made about their child. Learning to make decisions about educational issues is sometimes challenging for parents. Supported and shared decision-making helps make sure the child's educational needs will be met at school and supports parents in participating in, learning from, and guiding those decisions.

The third principle is to provide flexible, responsive, and comprehensive services to strengthen family functioning. In most educational systems, teachers come and go. The family provides the context for the child's ongoing development and growth. Teachers' support for families to meet their children's needs builds confidence and competence at being able to do so.

Other characteristics of family-centered programs include providing parents with choices that address family needs and concerns, helping families make informed decisions by fully disclosing information, and providing support in ways that empower parents and enhance parental competence (Shonkoff & Phillips, 2000).

Family-centered practices have particular characteristics. Families are validated as the primary educators of their children. Teachers develop partnerships with families to enhance school experiences and validate home experiences. Partnerships require reciprocal communication—true two-way communication aimed at acknowledging the family and school's contributions to the relationship. Having a partnership also requires teachers to make sure families can be a part of the classroom by creating many ways for parents and other family members to participate and be involved.

Encourage Family Participation

Family participation suggestions are listed here, as well as in the Possibilities Plans. When you develop relationships with parents and other family members, you will be better able to support their child's development in the classroom.

Comfort from Home: Ask families to provide a photograph or security items that will remind children about home and family. A handkerchief, T-shirt, or a toy brought from home can connect a child with loved ones while at school.

Mid-day Reunion: Children, especially when they are beginning a new school, benefit from seeing their parents or family members during the day. Invite families to plan a mid-day reunion to reconnect with their child during the school day. Encourage them to sign a visit logbook to document their involvement in their child's school experience.

Share Your Biography: Ask families to provide a brief biography with a photograph, so you can talk about and make connections between children and their families during the school day.

Share Parent Postcards

Share Parent Postcards with parents as they indicate an interest, at appropriate times during the enrollment cycle, or as developmental issues arise. Copy the Postcards. Cut them out, if necessary, address them to parent(s), place them on the Communication Log, or hand them out personally.

Dear Parents

The Importance of Friendship

Making friends is a major task of childhood—and one that matters. The ability to make friends impacts how children see themselves and their place in the social world. It predicts success with relationships later in life and affects the type of friends selected during adolescence.

How do children make friends? Friendships are socially constructed from repeated interactions with others. They start out with an interest and proceed to give-and-take relationships. Children are better at playing with familiar playmates than with strangers. They are more successful at picking up where they left off if they are friends who play together often.

Preschoolers make many mistakes in early friendships. Miscues derail play as children bump into each other, take each other's toys, lose track of play ideas, and hurt each other. These conflicts are not necessarily negative. They create opportunities for learning to negotiate and problem solve.

Almost all friendships need some adult support—it is much easier to figure out how to play together successfully if someone helps you deal with conflicts. Clear ideas from parents about what won't be tolerated (such as hitting) and lots of coaching (such as asking, "What else might work?") are key parenting strategies. With this support, children learn quickly how to be friends and play together successfully!

Making Friends Matters!

As adults we understand that making friends is an important part of life, but how important is it for children to make friends? One of the greatest benefits of children being in school is that they have the opportunity to develop social skills with their classmates.

Initially, children are curious about one another. They watch from a distance and notice that other children in the class are like them and different from them. Younger preschoolers are more interested in objects than in other children. They are awkward in their interactions with others. Because they may still view themselves as the center of the universe, it is difficult for children to think of how another child will react to a situation or how a child will feel if a particular thing happens.

Parents and teachers are the key to children understanding how their actions will affect others. They facilitate social interactions, so children are successful. This happens when children learn to wait, take turns, and finally, share. Try the following suggestions to help your child make friends:

1. Tell your child when he or she is being kind. Be very specific in what you say. Let your child know specifically what he or she is doing that will help build a friendship, such as "You made Eliza happy when you gave her the toy you had."
2. Talk with your child about what it takes to be a friend. Children need to understand that friends are friends even when they are confused, unhappy, thrilled, or lonely. Share stories about friendships and read books that give examples of good friends.
3. Model friendship for your child. Speak and act respectfully to others. Courtesy is a great starting place for an eventual friendship.
4. Be patient. Making friends involves skills that may be difficult for children. Teach your child how to be a good friend through the positive, sensitive interactions that occur in your family.

Play a supportive role in helping your child make friends. Children who are able to establish stable friendships early in life are much more likely to be able to do the same as adults.

Resource for Families

Add this helpful book to your family library or post this recommendation on your family bulletin board.
Lickona, T. (1994). ***Raising good children***. New York: Bantam Doubleday Dell.

INNOVATIONS IN ENVIRONMENTS

Create Environments that Welcome Families

Classrooms are the purview of teachers. Families normally come in and out of them without really spending too much time. They may or may not feel comfortable being there. It should be a goal to make your classroom welcome families. A good place to start is to create places for adults to comfortably "be" in the classroom. This may mean having an area that has adult-sized furniture, leaving a clear pathway from the door to the child's cubby area, or even providing a place to put purses, keys, or personal items while parents are reconnecting with their children. Pair these kinds of accommodations with a stated and written "open door" policy. Clear explanations that families are not visitors, but a part of the classroom, will go a long way to make them feel welcome.

Post photos of parents, children, and families in the environment. Familiar faces and photos of children invite parents into the classroom. Make sure images of families posted in the classroom match the families enrolled in the classroom. Ask parents to share magazines and photographs from their collections to enhance the classroom.

Formalize your welcome by having a family sign-in book located near the adult-size furniture. Make a parent visit log in a loose-leaf notebook so that parents can record their visits to the classroom.

Create Places to Be with Friends

Friends are so important during the preschool years. Provide places where children can be with friends, selecting their own level of involvement. Some children initiate involvement. Others watch friends at play with toys and materials before joining in. Some children can play with more than one friend while others need the special experience of being the only playmate. Still others enter groups easily, finding new or novel ways to join in play. An environment that provides many activity areas and many choices of interesting things to do will enhance children's opportunities to be with and play with friends.

Creating varied and interesting learning centers or activity areas is the primary goal for creating places to be with friends. Blocks, manipulatives, and books are excellent examples of areas that encourage friends to be together as they play.

Environmental supports for playing with friends are important. Provide duplicates of popular toys, so children can play together with the same or similar toys and materials. Make sure there are enough toys. Sharing resources is not possible when resources are too scarce. When there are plenty of toys and materials to play with, children are less likely to have play derailed or interrupted because of conflicts over materials.

Consider duplicating popular or frequently selected activity areas. Two block/construction areas or two sensory areas will keep children from having to wait too long to get to play in a favorite area with their friends.

Make Toys and Materials Accessible

Young children are constantly exploring and learning from the environment. Carefully plan the classroom to take maximum advantage of the child's natural desire to explore and learn.

Children need to be able to go to the shelves or storage units and choose things that interest them. Toys and materials that are piled together or in toy boxes don't offer cues as to how to use and play with the toys. Display toys separately, with just a few on each shelf. When given a choice, children individualize for themselves, choosing toys that are just right for their current interests and stage of development.

Activity Areas

Art Possibilities

Art activities for young children are opportunities for open-ended exploration, personal expression, and fun. In this activity area, children use a variety of art materials such as paper, crayons, playdough, paste or glue, magazines for cutting, collage items, and watercolor and tempera paints in trays with brushes. An easel, complete with paint cups and a good paper supply, is always available in this area. Add a full-length mirror to the wall nearby so that children can watch what they are doing in the art center as well as check out physical images as they paint and draw one of their favorite representations—themselves!

For children who are at the beginning of their preschool years, stock art areas with a limited variety of supplies and media while children learn how to use the materials appropriately. As children reach the end of their preschool years, art areas can be completely stocked, so older preschoolers can use their own ideas and imagination to combine art media and techniques as they create.

Art is a messy activity. Position the art area near a sink with running water and on a floor that can be cleaned easily. If you don't have a sink nearby, position the art area on an easily cleaned surface and provide towels and spray bottles for cleanup.

During the preschool years, the art area may actually be a combination or cluster of areas. An easel, positioned in a well-lit location, a worktable or two for children to complete their creations, and shelf units to store materials are the usual components of art areas. Also have a large, closed storage unit near the art area to keep extra supplies and store recycled materials that will become art projects later.

A well-stocked art area will have the following supplies and equipment, perhaps not out at the same time, but accessible as needed to enhance children's creations:

- tempera paints, fingerpaints, and watercolor paints; crayons; and markers;
- one or two worktables of different sizes;
- vinyl or fabric smocks;
- double easel;
- chalkboards and chalk;
- non-spill paint cups in at least eight colors, easel paintbrushes, watercolor paintbrushes, paste brushes, and so on;
- child-sized safety scissors;
- clay tub and clay hammers, playdough, rolling pins, cookie cutters, and so on;
- plastic trays;
- collage materials, tissue paper, yarn and string, craft sticks; and
- a variety of paper, including newsprint, easel, watercolor, and recycled paper.

Sensory Possibilities

Sensory experiences heighten children's awareness of the world around them by stimulating the senses. Sensory awareness becomes more complex, coordinated, and organized during the preschool years as children have many experiences with touching, tasting, smelling, and listening.

Sensory experiences, such as sand and water experiences, are a mainstay of any preschool program. Water is soothing; water toys stimulate play; and the splashing and slapping of water produce interesting reactions. Preschoolers need a sensory table in the classroom that can be used with a variety of sensory materials.

Health and safety skills are learned in this area as children are reminded to wash their hands before they go to the sensory table and to help teachers clean and sanitize sensory tables, bins, and materials after use.

As children learn to coordinate small muscles of the hand and arm with small muscles of the eye, they perfect fine motor skills. Attention to detail, such as including what sensory materials smell like, how they feel, or the sounds materials make when manipulated, increases children's ability to receive and process information from the physical world, enhancing readiness for literacy, reading, and mathematical understanding.

Over-stimulation is an issue to consider when planning and placing the sensory activity area. The materials are stimulating enough that few additional cues from the environment are needed. In particular, keep the wall space and area around the sensory center uncluttered and undecorated. If possible, make music a part of your sensory center so that you can add interesting auditory cues to the sensory experience. A tape recorder or CD player will make this possible. An outlet for the CD player is also necessary although you will want to make sure that the plug and player are not too close to an area where water is in use.

The sensory center is where teachers can put a bottle of hand lotion—the perfect sensory experience for one. Children can use the lotion to calm their hands by rubbing and massaging them when they feel the need to get control over their bodies and calm down.

Store sensory materials in closed containers, near the area where they are to be used. Use small, non-skid area carpets to catch spills and keep a supply of towels on hand to keep the area dry. Appropriate clean-up equipment is important, including handheld brooms, dustpan, sponges, and paper towels. Make cleanup a shared job that children learn to do.

Educators have different views of what is appropriate to use as sensory materials. Some suggest that only non-food items should be used (West & Cox, 2001) while others suggest that some food items are an inexpensive source of sensory experiences. When making a determination about what materials to use as sensory materials, consider the families you serve, available resources, children's experiences, and community and cultural expectations and experience.

A well-stocked sensory center will have the following supplies and equipment, not out at the same time, but accessible as needed to enhance children's sensory experiences:

- A sensory table or a collection of tubs to hold sensory materials;
- A large collection of sensory materials stored in covered containers, such as birdseed, sawdust, shredded paper, cornstarch packing pellets, soap shavings, cornmeal, rock salt, sand, potting soil, large buttons, and other appropriate sensory materials;
- A large collection of interesting containers to use for pouring, sifting, mixing, and blending sensory materials, such as funnels, measuring cups, measuring spoons, recycled spray bottles, recycled yogurt or cottage cheese containers, recycled plastic bottles, and plastic tubing;
- A large collection of interesting items to use in sensory exploration of different media, such as cookie cutters, egg beaters, strainers, whisks, scoops, garlic presses, and other items;

- A large collection of enhancements to add to sensory media, including plastic cars, trucks, airplanes, tractors, trains, people, insects, letters, plants, animals, and dinosaurs;
- A tape or CD player (with the cord and outlet covered and protected);
- Vinyl smocks;
- Washable, non-skid area rugs to put down to prevent slipping hazards from spills; and
- Clean-up resources, such as hand-held brooms and dustpans, towels, sponges, and so on.

References

Berk, L. E. (2000). ***Development through the lifespan***. Boston: Allyn and Bacon.

Berk, L.E. (1994). Vygotsky's theory: The importance of make-believe play. ***Young Children***, 50 (1): 30-39.

Brazelton, T.B. (1992). ***Touchpoints: The essential reference***. Reading, MA: Addison-Wesley.

Brazelton, T.B., & S.I. Greenspan. (2000). ***The irreducible needs of children: What every child must have to grow, learn, and flourish***. Cambridge, MA: Perseus Publishing.

Bronfenbrenner, U. (1979). ***The ecology of human development: Experiments by nature and design***. Cambridge, MA: Harvard University Press.

Edwards, C., L. Gandini & G. Forman. (1994). ***The one hundred languages of children: The Reggio Emilia approach to early childhood education.*** Norwood, NJ: Ablex.

Elias, C & L. Berk. (2002). ***A study guide for child development***. Boston: Allyn and Bacon.

Erikson, E.H. (1963). ***Childhood and society***. New York: Norton.

Fein, G.G., A. Gariboldi & R. Boni. (1993). The adjustment of infants and toddlers to group care: The first six months. ***Early Childhood Research Quarterly***, 8, 1-14.

Gerber, M. & A. Johnson. (1997). ***Your self-confident baby***. New York: Wiley.

Greenspan, S.I. (1999). ***The six experiences that create intelligence and emotional growth in babies and young children***. Reading, MA: Perseus Books.

Howes, C. (2000). Social development, family, and attachment relationships of infants and toddlers. In D. Cryer & T. Harmes, (eds.) ***Infants and toddlers in out-of-home care*** (87-113). Baltimore: MD: Brookes Publishing.

Howes, C. (1988). Peer interaction of young children. ***Monographs of the Society for Research in Child Development***, 53 (1).

Howes, C. & C.E. Hamilton. (1992). Children's relationships with caregivers: Mothers and child care teachers. ***Child Development***, 64, 859-866.

Howes, C., D.A. Phillips, & M. Whitebrook. (1992). Thresholds of quality: Implications for the social development of children in center-based care. ***Child Development***, 63, 449-460.

Kovach, B.A. & P.A. Da Ros. (1998). Respectful, individual, and responsive caregiving for infants: The key to successful care in group settings. ***Young Children***, 53 (3): 61-64.

Lally, J.R. (1995). The impact of child care policies and practices on infant/toddler identity formation. ***Young Children***, 51 (1): 58-67.

Leavitt, R.L. (1994). ***Power and emotion in infant-toddler day care***. Albany, NY: State University of New York Press.

McBride, S.L. (1999). Family-centered practices. ***Young Children***, 54 (4): 62-68.

McMullen, M.B. (1999). Achieving best practices in infant and toddler care and education. ***Young Children***, 54 (4): 69-75.

Oliver, S. & E. Klugman. (2002). What we know about play. ***Child Care Information Exchange***, 147, 16-18.

Parten, M.B. (1932). Social participation among preschool children. ***Journal of Abnormal Psychology,*** 27, 243-269.

Piaget, J. (1962). ***Play, dreams, and imitation in childhood***. C. Gattegno & F.M. Hodgson (trans). New York: Norton.

Shonkoff, J.P. & D.A. Phillips (Eds.). (2000). ***From neurons to neighborhoods: The science of early childhood development***. Washington, DC: National Academy Press.

Sussna, A.G. (2000). Banning cute in the classroom. ***Dimensions***, Spring, 3-7.

Tarini, E. (1996). Reflections on a year in Reggio Emilia: Key concepts in rethinking and learning the Reggio way. In J. Hendrick (ed.) ***First steps toward teaching the Reggio way***. New York: Prentice Hall.

West, S. & A. Cox. 2001. ***Sand and water play***. Beltsville, MD: Gryphon House, Inc.

Resources for Teachers

Albrecht, K., M. Banks, G. Calhoun, L. Dziadul, C. Gwinn, B. Harrington, B. Kerr, M. Mizukami, A. Morris, C. Peterson, & R.R. Summers. (2000). The good, the bad, and the wonderful: Keeping children and teachers together. ***Child Care Information Exchange***, 136, 24-28.

Albrecht, K., L. Dziadul, C. Gwinn, & B. Harrington. (2001). The good, the bad, and the wonderful: Keeping children and teachers together (part 2). ***Child Care Information Exchange***, 137, 90-93.

Possibilities Plan—

Making Messes and Cleaning Them Up

Getting Ready to Plan

Messes are part of the everyday lives of preschoolers. Teachers and parents may even think that the majority of their day is involved in cleaning up the messes that children make. Some adults and children may feel that messes are always inappropriate. We don't. We think they are a natural part of the early childhood experience! In this Possibilities Plan, children will have an opportunity to explore the topics of making messes, cleaning up messes, and recycling trash.

The purpose of Getting Ready to Plan is to support the planning process with a general overview of the content of this Possibilities Plan. Now is the time to think about what you want the children in your group to learn about each of these topics. Topics are explored in general below.

Making Messes: Making messes can be fun! In this Possibilities Plan, children will be able to make messes in a variety of ways, including mud pies, dirt in the garden, and art products. Be aware of children's learning styles and preferences. One child may join the activity immediately, while another may watch before participating.

Cleaning Up Messes: Cleanup is a natural part of the routine at home and at school. Preschool children wash their own hands, but their experiences with washing other things, such as dishes, clothes, or the car, may have only been observed. Re-introduce clean-up routines into the class schedule. Labels on shelves and containers will allow children to do many tasks independently. In this Possibilities Plan, children will learn many ways to clean up for themselves.

Recycling Trash: Introduce the concepts of reusing and recycling materials with children. By reusing materials (instead of throwing them away) and recycling trash to be made into other materials, we can all help protect the environment. Sorting materials for recycling and finding out where trash goes can be fun activities.

Now that you have an idea about the general content of the Possibilities Plan, you are ready to proceed with developing your own plan. This section of Getting Ready to Plan identifies resources you may want to buy, collect, or locate to implement your plan.

Toys and Materials*

Purchased

assorted colors of paint
balloons
camera
construction paper
contact paper
craft paper (long pieces)
different types of pasta
display board
dramatic play sink or sensory tubs
duct tape
eggs
fingerpaint
flour
hot glue gun
markers
new fly swatters
non-toxic spray paint
paintbrushes
paint rollers
pen
plastic coins
scissors
scotch tape roll (one roll per child with one extra)
stickers
trays for paint
tricycles
utility knife (teacher only)
washable paint
white paint
zipper-closure bags

Gathered

aprons
basket
big and little bowls
big tub
bottle brushes
boxes, 2 medium
broom
bubble wrap
buckets
car wash sign
change purses
cheese slicers
clothes
collection of soap containers (shampoo, detergent, dishwashing soap, and so on) of all sizes and shapes
cups
different shapes/sizes and connectors of PVC
dish rack
dish rags
dish towels
empty laundry detergent containers
empty liquid soap bottles
forks
goggles
golf tees
hangers
hard hats
Ivory soap bars
knee-high pantyhose
large tube of hair gel
large tub or box for storage
laundry baskets
measuring cups
milk caps to make dials
mixing spoons
mop
newspaper
paper plates
pictures of handwashing steps
plastic bottles
plastic dishes
plastic hammers
plastic knives
plastic worms
plates
popcorn maker
popcorn kernels
purses
rolling pins
salt or fine sand
scrub brush
scrubbers
shallow trays
small laundry basket
smocks
spatulas
Styrofoam blocks and pellets
tapes
things that float (foam, acorn, boat, leaves, and so on.)
things that sink (steel, coins, seashells, and so on)
things to copy (word cards, headlines, logos)
toilet paper
trays
unclaimed artwork
utensils
variety of balls (big and small Nerf balls, tennis balls, textured balls, ping pong balls, and so on)
variety of clothes to wash
variety of matching socks and mittens
washcloths
whisks

*Note: Please consider the ages and abilities of the children in your classroom. Use only safe, non-toxic materials.

Making Messes and Cleaning Them Up

WEB

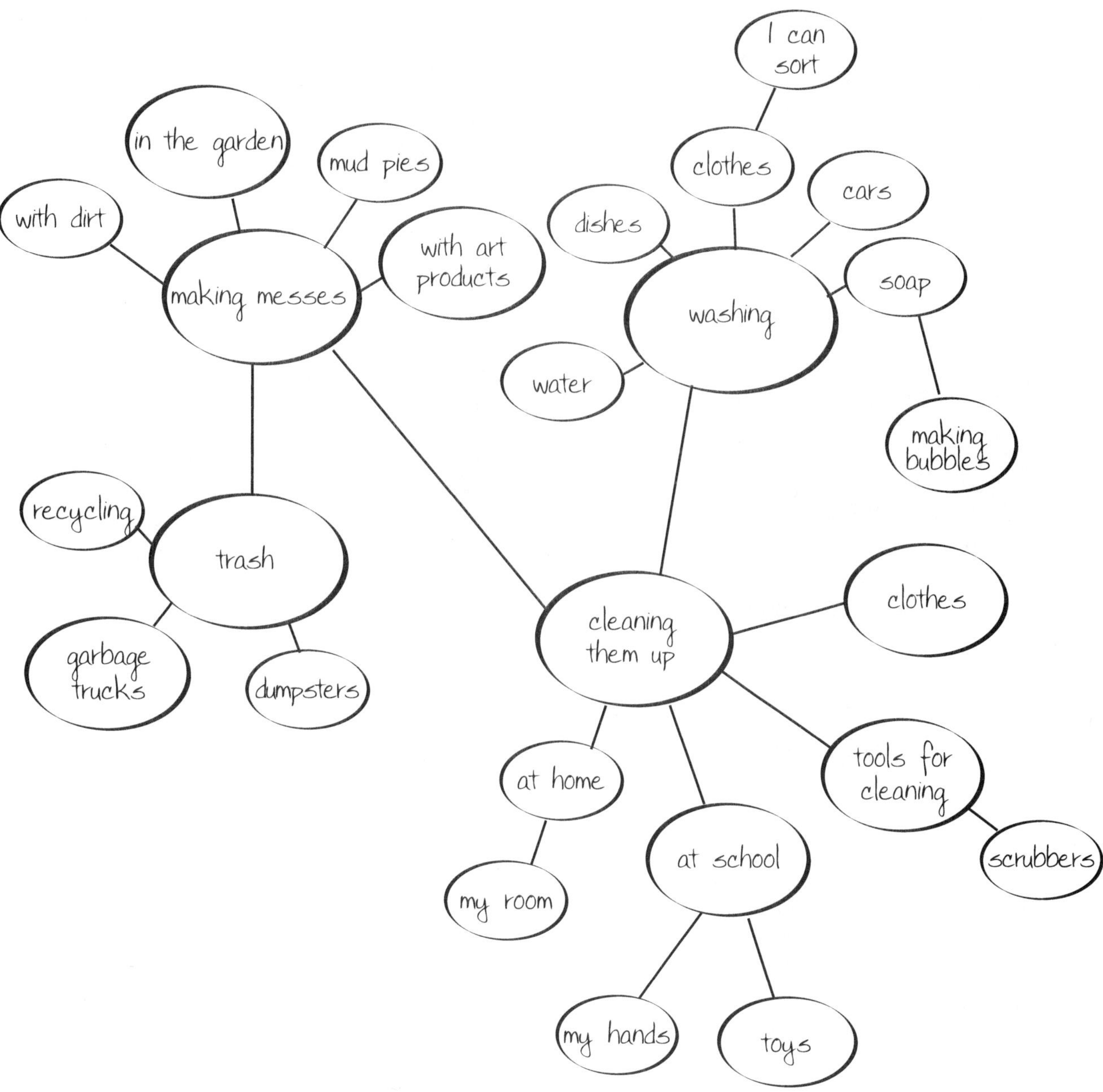

Making Messes and Cleaning Them Up

PLANNING PAGES

Plan Possibilities

ACTIVITIES AND EXPERIENCES FOR MAKING MESSES AND CLEANING THEM UP

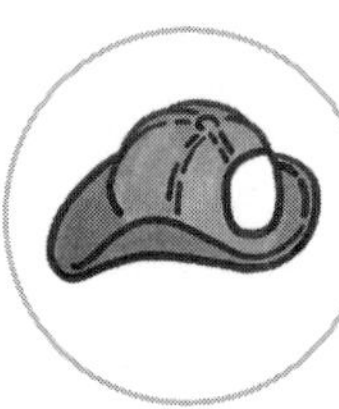

DRAMATIC POSSIBILITIES

Rub-a-Dub-Dub

Materials
dramatic play sink or sensory tubs • empty liquid soap bottles • dishcloths • dishtowels • scrubbers • bottle brushes • plastic dishes • utensils • plastic bottles • cups • dish rack • aprons • books about washing, such as *Ms. Sneed's Guide to Hygiene* by Dale Gotlieb

Teacher Talk
"Washing dishes is part of cooking." "First we cook, and then we clean up." Ask children how they might use the different scrubbers and clean-up tools.

Instructions
Place dishes to be washed in the sink and the cleaning supplies nearby. Children enjoy water and real soap in the sink, if appropriate for your setting. This activity is great for discussing how a family works together to make a house run smoothly. Collect empty dishwashing containers from parents and other teachers.

Observation/Assessment
Washes dishes
Dries dishes

This Is the Way We Wash Our Clothes

Materials
two medium-sized boxes • utility knife (teacher only) • hot glue gun • white paint • paintbrushes • milk caps to make dials • empty laundry detergent containers • laundry baskets • a variety of clothes to wash • hangers • plastic coins for the machines • change purses • books about washing clothes, such as *The Lowdown Laundry Line Blues* by Cynthia Millen

Teacher Talk
"How much money does the first load cost?" "Can you find all the pants? Shirts?"

Instructions
Cut a flap in the top of one box to make a door for the washing machine. Cut a flap in the front side of the other box to make a door for the dryer. Cut slots in the lids of the two small boxes to make coin boxes. Use a hot glue gun to glue the coin boxes to the top of the larger boxes next to the flaps. Hot glue the milk caps in place and label them to make the dials on the machines. Label the coin boxes with the cost of washing and drying a load.

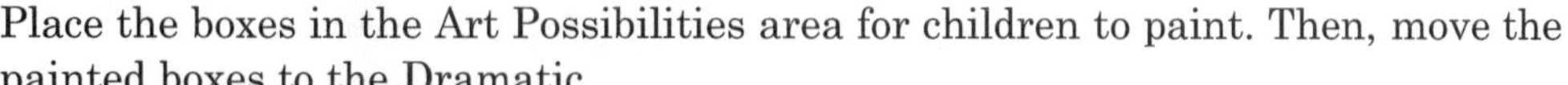

Place the boxes in the Art Possibilities area for children to paint. Then, move the painted boxes to the Dramatic Possibilities area. Let children sort laundry, load it into the baskets, and head off for a day at the laundromat. Introduce children to the value of coins as they use the plastic coins to pay for laundry loads in the washer or dryer. Sing, "This Is the Way We Wash Our Clothes" (see page 171) as children do the wash.

Observation/Assessment
Classifies laundry by type
Uses mathematical language (more, less, the same, bigger, smaller, smallest, most, least, and so on)
Recognizes that different coins have different values

Other Dramatic Possibilities

- Use spray bottles with water and cloths to clean up the classroom.
- Wash riding toys outside.
- Wash dolls in plastic tubs or sensory table.

ART POSSIBILITIES

Snap, Crackle, and Pop Painting

Materials
bubble wrap • tape • washable paint • paint rollers • paint • body-size pieces of craft paper

Teacher Talk
"Ask your friend, Simone, if she will help you paint with your back."

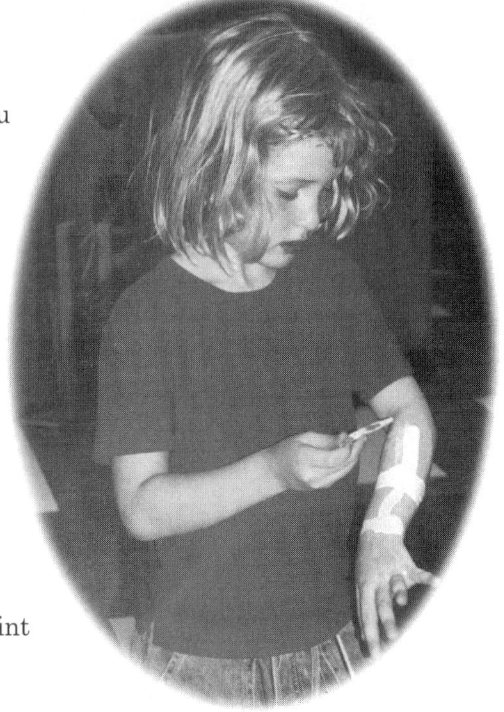

Instructions
Give children pieces of bubble wrap. Let them tape it on the parts of their body with which they wish to paint. Children can use the rollers to apply paint to the bubble wrap and make prints on the paper. This activity needs enough space for the children to move around without fear of getting paint in the wrong places. Consider setting it up outside.

Extension Possibilities: Isolate the body parts children can use to paint. "Can you paint just using your elbows and knees?"

Observation/Assessment
Uses problem-solving skills

Splatter Up!

Materials
variety of balls (big and small foam rubber balls, tennis balls, textured balls, ping-pong balls, and so on) • paint • trays for paint • tape • a large sheet of craft paper

Teacher Talk
"Which balls make the biggest splat?" Use sound effects as the children paint such as "splat," "boing," "swoosh," "splash," "bam," and so on.

Instructions
Pour the paint into the trays. Place the balls on the trays in the paint. Tape the paper onto a wall of the building outside. Let children roll the balls in the paint, stand back, and toss the balls at the paper.

Extension Possibilities: Instead of tossing the balls, anchor the paper on the ground and let children roll the balls down the paper. Compare the marks the balls made when children rolled the balls and when they tossed them.

Helpful Hints: Discuss the safety issues that could arise when throwing balls in high-traffic areas. Remind children to look out for friends who are passing by or watching the fun. Place a plastic shower curtain in front of the painting, so balls don't get too dirty as they fall and get reused.

Observation/Assessment
Throws a ball
Follows safety rules

Slap Painting

Materials
paper • tape • paint • paper plates for the paint • new flyswatters • knee-high pantyhose filled with sand and knotted at the top • spatulas

Teacher Talk
"What happens when you slap the paint onto the paper?"

Instructions
Tape a large piece of paper to the table or floor. Pour the paint onto the paper plates. Let the children dip their painting tools into the paint and then slap them on the paper.

Helpful Hints: Some pantyhose work better if you double them up before pouring in the sand. You can find a variety of common objects that create varied textures in paint. A few ideas are plastic combs, hand-held wooden massagers, potato mashers, cleaned corncobs, and, of course, fingers.

Observation/Assessment
Paints using different methods

BLOCKS/CONSTRUCTION POSSIBILITIES

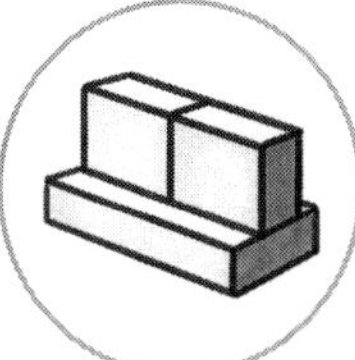

I Have a Hammer

Materials
goggles • hard hats • supply of golf tees • Styrofoam blocks • plastic hammers

Teacher Talk
Discuss safety precautions taken when using tools. Talk about what each safety article is used to protect and why. "Goggles protect our eyes from flying objects while we are hammering."

Instructions
Put on the goggles and hard hats. Use the hammers to hammer the golf tees into the Styrofoam blocks. This is a great way to introduce woodworking into your classroom. Make sure the goggles are adjustable and fit each child. Discard goggles when they get scratched. If children can't see through the goggles, they won't use them.

Observation/Assessment
Follows safety rules
Hits the golf tee with a hammer

Ticky, Tacky Tape

Materials
One roll of tape per child

Teacher Talk
"What will you do with your tape?"

Instructions
Introduce this activity at Group Time. Explain that children will each get a roll of tape to do with as they choose. Establish the limits you expect children to accept. Allow children to take their tape rolls with them to the Possibilities areas. After everyone is finished, recycle the tape together to create a giant tape ball. The children can use the ball inside and outside.

Observation/Assessment
Makes plans for using materials
Uses materials independently or with others
Works cooperatively to extend resources
Uses positional vocabulary, such as over, under, by, on top of, below, alongside, and between

Pipe Down, Pipe Up, Pipe All Around

Materials
various shapes and sizes of PVC piping • PVC pipe connectors • non-toxic spray paint (for teachers only) • a large tub or box for storage

Teacher Talk
"See what you can build with these pipes." "Where will you put the pipes in your structure?"

Instructions
Group pipe sections by size and shape. Away from the children and in a well-ventilated area, spray paint each group of PVC pipes a different color and allow to dry. Children then use the pipes to create structures.

Observation/Assessment
Groups objects by size
Builds using various materials

SCIENCE/DISCOVERY POSSIBILITIES

Humpty Dumpty's Great Fall

Materials
eggs • materials (newspaper, bubble wrap, Styrofoam or cornstarch packing pellets, and so on) to wrap the eggs • tape

Teacher Talk
Discuss different ways children can wrap the eggs to keep them from breaking when dropped. Repeat the rhyme, "Humpty Dumpty" as you test the various egg wrappings.

Instructions
Children use the materials provided to wrap the eggs. Cover the area to be used for testing with plastic sheeting, a shower curtain, or trash bags to help with cleanup.

Safety Note: Concerns about salmonella require that children wash their hands carefully after this activity. Discard broken eggs. Wash plastic sheeting or shower curtain with soap and hot water.

Sink and Float

Materials
big tub • water • things that float (foam pellets, acorns, boats, leaves, and so on) or sink (toys, coins, seashells, and so on) • basket

Teacher Talk
"The leaf is floating on the water." "Why do you think the coins are sinking?"

Instructions
Fill the tub with water and put the sink/float materials in a basket for children to experiment with by dropping them in the water to see what floats and what sinks.

Extension Possibilities: Add a literacy experience to this activity by creating a chart for children to complete as they try out the materials.

items	sink	float
rock	X	
feather		X
ball		X

Observation/Assessment
Sorts items by whether they sink or float

Other Science/Discovery Possibilities

- Use paper cups to catch the popcorn "blizzard" with a popcorn maker (no oil) and popcorn. Place the popcorn maker in the middle of a sheet and stand around the sheet. Tape the electric cord to the floor to prevent tripping.
- Mix various items in water (dirt, Styrofoam pellets, paper pieces, coins) to observe the results.

SENSORY POSSIBILITIES

Making Clean Mud

Materials
toilet paper (one roll per child) • Ivory soap bars (one bath-size bar per child) • cheese slicers

Teacher Talk
"Today we will slice up the soap, and tomorrow, we will tear up the toilet paper and add water to our clean mud." "Make sure to take your turn slicing soap."

Instructions
Collect the ingredients for this fun sensory experience. Consider asking each child (or family) to bring one roll of toilet paper and one bar of Ivory soap to school to show children that if everyone pitches in and brings a small amount of ingredients, they can be put together to make a large amount of clean mud.

Write out the directions on a rebus chart.

1. Shave soap into thin pieces or slivers with cheese slicers.
2. Mix equal parts soap—one bar, water—one cup, and toilet paper—one roll. (Adjust to make mixture the texture of cake batter.)
3. Mix well by squishing the mixture together with your hands and fingers.

Safety Note: Remind children to wash their hands before playing with the clean mud, so it will stay clean!

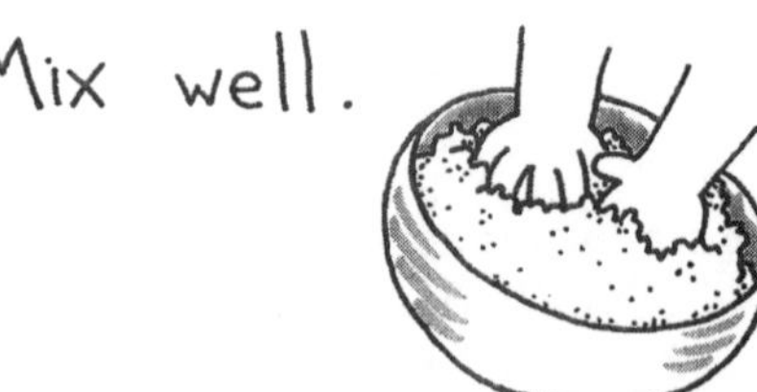

A Little of This, a Little of That

Materials
sensory tub • water • large quantities of flour • big and little bowls • measuring cups • mixing spoons • whisks • rolling pins

Teacher Talk
"How does it feel on your hands?" "It's fun to make a mess, and part of making messes is cleaning them up."

Instructions
Put flour in one tub and water in the other. Place tubs on a table with dishes and utensils. Let children mix and stir the water and flour. Children will enjoy making many different concoctions—some runny and some dough-like.

Helpful Hints: Talk about the responsibility of cleaning up a messy activity when children select this activity. Let the children know you will all be cleaning up together when you are finished and what their cleanup roles will be.

Observation/Assessment
Mixes, stirs, and measures materials

Wet, Wiggly Worms!

Materials
sensory tub or dishpan • two small bottles or one large tube of hair gel • plastic fishing bait worms • books about worms, such as *Wormy Worm* by Chris Raschka

Teacher Talk
"What do the worms in the gel feel like?"

Instructions
Place the worms in the sensory tub. Dump the hair gel on top and mix around until all the worms are covered. Children can squish their fingers around in the mixture for a gooey good time. Worms will stick to the side of the sensory tub with the help of the sticky hair gel.

Helpful Hints: This activity provides an appropriate outlet when children reach the stage where they are fascinated by "gross" things.

LITERACY/WRITING POSSIBILITIES

Squishy Bags

Materials
zipper-closure plastic bags • fingerpaint • duct tape

Teacher Talk
"You made a picture with your finger. What else could you use to draw?"

Instructions
Add fingerpaint to a zipper closure plastic bag (about one-third full). Then lay flat with the paint spread equally in the bag. Push out the air, seal the bag, and tape closed with duct tape. Use additional duct tape to secure the bag to a table in the Writing Possibilities area, creating a writing surface.

Observation/Assessment
Draws shapes
Writes letter-like marks
Writes letters

Salty Scribblers

Materials
salt or fine sand • shallow trays • a collection of things to copy, such as headlines • word cards and logos • dustpan • hand-held broom

Teacher Talk
"You are writing the letters of alphabet." "What sounds do the letters make?"

Instructions
Put the tray on the table and pour some salt or fine sand on the tray. Children use their fingers to draw or write. Shake the tray slowly to redistribute the salt or sand.

Observation/Assessment
Draws shapes
Makes letter-like marks
Writes letters

Other Literacy/Writing Possibilities

- Discuss the sequence of each step of handwashing. Photograph children demonstrating each step of handwashing. Label each step and post near the sink.
- Provide paper and writing materials in all areas of the room, so writing experiences can be spontaneous.

MATH/MANIPULATIVES POSSIBILITIES

The Sudsy Sort

Materials
magazines • scissors • glue • construction paper • a large variety of clean, rinsed soap containers (shampoo, bar soap, dish soap, dishwasher detergent, and laundry detergent) • markers • contact paper

Teacher Talk
"What do you wash with this kind of soap?"

Instructions
Collect pictures from magazines of different things that get washed (hair, clothing, cars, dishes, children, adults, and so on) Glue them on construction paper. Laminate or cover with clear contact paper to make more durable for children to use. Place the clean and dry containers of cleaning supplies in a large tub. Place the pictures on the table or floor. Children then match the boxes and bottles of soap to what they are used to wash (shampoo to hair, laundry detergent to clothes, and so on). Include a few containers that don't have a match. Observe to see how different children solve the problem.

Observation/Assessment
Groups similar containers
Sorts items according to how they are used

Laundry Patterns

Materials
variety of matching socks and mittens • a small laundry basket for storage

Teacher Talk
"Which one should come next?" Use positional vocabulary, such as first, last, next, after, under, in the middle, and so on.

Instructions
Put all the socks and mittens in the laundry basket. Encourage children to create patterns with the mittens and socks. Children can create simple 1, 2 patterns (mitten, sock, mitten, sock...) or more complicated 1, 1, 2 (mitten, mitten, sock), and 1, 2, 3 patterns (red sock, green sock, blue mitten, red sock, green sock, blue mitten). Encourage children to move on to the next level by setting up more complicated patterns (1, 2, 3, 2, 3 or 1, 3, 1, 2, 2, 1 etc.) to challenge patterning skills.

Extension Possibilities: Sing "Three Little Kittens Have Lost Their Mittens" as children make patterns. To add a literacy experience, ask children to copy the patterns they make onto paper, duplicating the pattern they made with socks with crayons or markers.

Observation/Assessment
Creates simple patterns
Uses positional vocabulary, such as first, last, next to, under, beside, and over

Other Math/Manipulatives Possibilities

- Count the number of toilet paper rolls and soap bars needed to make clean mud (see page 166).
- Make personal puzzles from unclaimed artwork. Cut each piece into 5 to 7 pieces. Number each piece (A-1, A-2, A-3, and so on for one puzzle and B-1, B-2, B-3, and so on for another). Store in zipper-closure plastic bags.

RHYMES/FINGERPLAYS/SONGS/MUSIC POSSIBILITIES

Clean-up Song

Instructions
Every classroom needs a clean-up song that serves as a notice to transition from independent, self-selected activities to other kinds of activities. Using the same song every time creates a classroom ritual that helps children accept the transition and serves as an auditory cue for children whose first language is not English. Sing the Clean-up Song.

This Is the Way We Wash Our Clothes

Instructions
Sing this song to the tune of "Here We Go 'Round the Mulberry Bush" as children wash clothes in the Dramatic Possibilities area.

This Is the Way We Wash Our Clothes
This is the way we wash our clothes, wash our clothes, wash our clothes,
This is the way we wash our clothes, so early in the morning.

Other Rhymes/Fingerplays/Songs/Music Possibilities

- Support the idea that we all make messes, and we are all responsible for cleaning them up. Use any of the following musical sections as clean-up songs:
  - "Heigh Ho" from *Snow White* by Disney
  - "Don't Worry, Be Happy" from *Simple Pleasures* by Bobby McFerrin
  - "Hakuna Matata" from *The Lion King Soundtrack* by Disney
- Sing "Whistle While You Work" from Disney's *Snow White* as children are working on activities.
- Sing " The Three Little Kittens" as children sort socks and mittens in the Math/Manipulatives area (see page 169).

GROUP TIME POSSIBILITIES

My Room: Ask a family member to take a photograph of their child's bedroom to bring back to school. Use the photographs as children talk about cleaning up their bedrooms. If photographs are not a possibility, ask a family member to sketch a floor plan of the room the child sleeps in and bring that to school.

Introduce Ticky, Tacky Tape: Introduce this activity (see page 164). Assure children that they will each get a roll of tape and that they can choose how to use it.

Tape Ball: The tape ball is made from the rolls of tape that children explored in Ticky, Tacky Tape (see page 164). Use this as a clean-up activity, with children collecting all of their pieces of tape from their exploration. Form the tape pieces into a ball. Then, ask the children to sit down in a circle. Start the activity by rolling the ball to a child and ask what he did with his roll of tape. Once the child shares his experience, he rolls the ball to someone who has not had a turn. The next person gets to share his experience with others and so on.

Pasta Tasting: Collect several different kinds of pasta (spaghetti, elbow macaroni, spinach pasta, bow ties, and so on), small plates, forks. Cook small amounts of the different pasta according to the package directions. Label each one and place the pasta in bowls. Once all the pastas are tasted, let the children have a chance to eat the pasta they like. Graph the results, letting children put stickers on the type of pasta that they liked. Review the results of the tasting with children.

Other Group Time Possibilities

- Read any of the books listed for this Possibilities Plan (see page 178).
- Discuss the importance of handwashing as a way to prevent spreading germs and dirt.

MOVEMENT/OUTDOORS POSSIBILITIES

Hey, Squirt!

Materials

rubber gloves • washable paint • string • wooden fence or butcher paper taped to a fence • smocks • needle (for teachers only) • clean-up supplies

Teacher Talk

"You squeezed the finger of the glove! What happened to the paint?" "Can you paint on the wall (or paper)?" "It is so much fun to make big messes! And, to clean them up!"

Instructions

Prepare rubber gloves by filling with enough paint to create some resistance when you tie the wrist of the glove. Use the needle to punch holes in the tips of the gloves (teacher only). Children squeeze the glove fingers, directing the paint at the fence or paper. Consider cleaning up as part of the activity.

Extension Possibilities: Turn this into a water play activity in warm weather, letting children use water to squirt the sidewalks, etc. and maybe even each other!

Observation/Assessment

Uses small muscles of hand to squeeze paint from gloves

Mop and Broom Painting

Materials
buckets • water • broom • mop • fence or sidewalk

Teacher Talk
"Use the mop to paint on the fence." "Which one do you like best—the mop or the broom?"

Instructions
Fill the buckets with water. Children can dip mops and brooms in the water and paint on fences or the sidewalk.

Extension Possibilities: Consider doing this activity with washable paint instead of water.

Observation/Assessment
Paints using different methods

Other Movement/Outdoors Possibilities

- Make mudpies.
- Use drum or lummi (rhythm) sticks to make the beat of popcorn popping.
- Put a car wash sign on the playground and scrub and clean the tricycles, wagons, and other riding toys.

PROJECTS AND DOCUMENTATION POSSIBILITIES

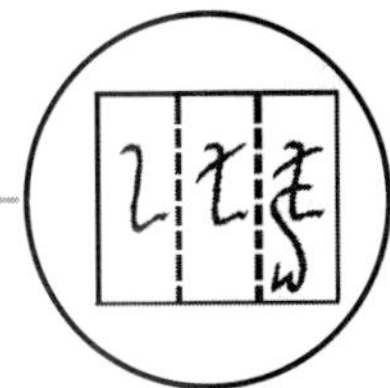

Where Does the Trash Go?

Materials
camera • markers • paper for recording dictation • display board • books about trash and recycling, such as *Trashy Town* by Andrea Griffing Zimmerman

Teacher Talk
"What will happen to the trash after we put it in the dumpster?"

Instructions
Introduce this project by talking about trash and letting the children hypothesize where it goes. Record their ideas. Then, follow the trash from the classroom to where it is discarded at your school. If a housekeeper or janitor collects the trash, ask him or her if the children can follow him or her on their trash collection run. Take pictures of important points in the process, such as trash bin or dumpster, who takes out the trash, when and how the dumpster is emptied, and the other steps in the process.

Then, explore with the children what might happen to the trash after it leaves the school. From this point, follow children's lead, exploring additional related ideas or questions generated by the children.

Helpful Hints: Add pictures to the classroom of dump trucks, trash collectors, landfills, and trashcans and bins.

FIELD TRIP POSSIBILITIES

City Dump: Follow the trash to the dump or recycling center to see how it is handled once it leaves school.

Recycling Site: Plan a field trip to a recycling site. Research what recycled materials will be made into.

Cleaning Company: Visit a cleaning company office or a site where the cleaning company cleans. Compare how the professional cleaners clean with how we clean our own homes.

Car Wash: Visit a car wash. This could be a great opportunity to get the school van washed!

SNACK POSSIBILITIES

Dirt Dessert: Give each child a small zipper closure plastic bag containing two chocolate cookies. Show children how to crush the cookies by mashing the bag. Scoop whipped topping or pudding into a cup and then pour the crushed cookies on top. Add a gummy worm for fun!

Guacamole: Peel and mash avocados to make guacamole. Add a bit of mayonnaise or sour cream and serve with tostadas.

Squeezed OJ: Show children how to pound, roll, and squeeze oranges to make juice. Recycle rinds into the compost bin.

FAMILY PARTICIPATION POSSIBILITIES

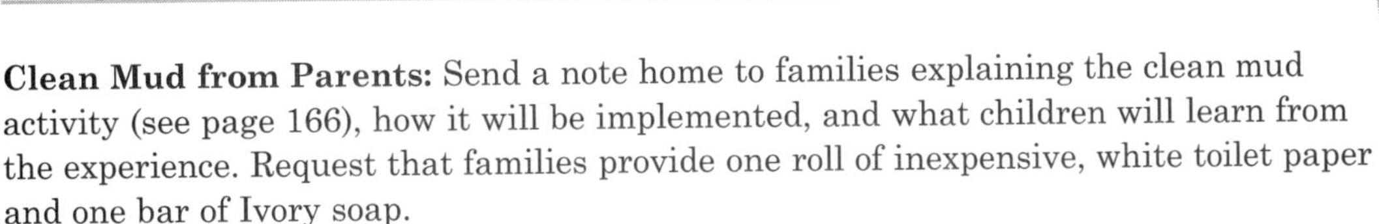

Clean Mud from Parents: Send a note home to families explaining the clean mud activity (see page 166), how it will be implemented, and what children will learn from the experience. Request that families provide one roll of inexpensive, white toilet paper and one bar of Ivory soap.

Pasta Cooking: Share your idea about pasta tasting with families. Invite them to attend and provide unique pasta for the children to taste.

Personal Puzzles: Share your idea about cutting excess artwork into puzzles with family members. Suggest that parents use the personal puzzles as children are waiting for meals.

I Can Make Messes, and I Can Clean Them Up!

An important life lesson is learning that most of life's fun activities have three phases. One phase is planning and preparing to do fun and interesting things. The second is implementing the plan, and the third phase is cleaning up after the fun is over. Including your preschooler in all three phases is a good idea.

Children benefit from understanding the process of planning fun and interesting activities. They need to see that interesting experiences do not just materialize out of thin air, but are planned in advance by someone. When you begin to make plans for a family outing, visits from extended family, or just an afternoon of playing outdoors, include your child in the planning phase.

Adults understand that cleanup is a part of every family activity. Preschoolers are just learning to understand this part. Yet, preschoolers love to do what adults do—modeling them and copying their activities. Take advantage of this interest to include your child in this important phase as well. Identify ways that your child can work alongside you during the cleanup process, doing a part of the cleanup that is within his or her developmental skill level. For example, after a picnic, give your child a small trash bag and ask him or her to pick up any stray trash that has not been discarded properly.

Sometimes adults think that cleaning up is just easier when they do it by themselves. Including children in the process can be a little more complex, but sharing this part of the fun with children while they are preschoolers is important. If this last phase of fun is included from the beginning, children will understand that cleanup comes with the territory.

Start now to include your child in all three phases of fun. Then, the next time your child asks to play in the rain, make playdough, or paint a picture, you can say, "Yes!" Planning, implementing, and cleaning up are all enjoyable and necessary parts of the process.

How to Talk to Children about Their Artwork

When children first learn to scribble, we are delighted that they can "draw." We encourage our child's efforts through praise and by sharing the pictures with other family members. As children develop their fine motor skills, they begin to make pictures with shapes and letter-like marks. So, all those art experiences are actually linked to being able to write.

As parents we are often tempted to say, "Oh, how beautiful!" Because children view art as a process, it may be more helpful for us to stress what children are doing. "I noticed that you used many different colors on your picture," will show a child that you have seen the details and that you really are interested in what he or she is doing.

Avoid single-answer questions, such as, "What is this?" You will learn much more about your child's experience by asking open-ended questions. You may also want to ask if there is a story or experience that goes with the picture. The following are additional suggestions for how you can talk with your child about his or her art:

- Show your interest in your child's artwork by asking him or her to tell you about it.
- Really listen as your child interprets what he or she has created.
- Avoid comparisons of your child's work to the work of others.
- Allow your child to evaluate how pleased he or she is with a drawing or art product.

Curriculum Resources

Prop Boxes

Rub-a-Dub-Dub Prop Box
dramatic play sink or plastic tub • empty liquid soap bottles • dishcloths • dishtowels • scrubbers • bottle brushes and plastic bottles • plastic dishes • utensils • cups • dish rack • aprons

This Is the Way We Wash Our Clothes Prop Box
washer and dryer (made from two medium-sized boxes) • empty laundry detergent containers • laundry baskets • variety of clothes to wash • clothes hangers • clothesline and clothespins

Books

Best Enemies Again by Kathleen Leverich
Blood and Gore, Like You've Never Seen by Vicki Cobb
The Cat Who Wore a Pot on Her Head by Jan Slepian
The Clean Up Surprise by Christine Loomis
Dirt and Grime, Like You've Never Seen by Vicki Cobb
Don't Need Friends by Carolyn Crimi
Earthworms: Ooey Gooey Animals by Lola Schaefer
The Fire Station by Robert Munsch
George and Martha by James Marshall
The Great Trash Bash by Loreen Leedy
I Like You by Sandol Stoddard
The Lowdown Laundry Line Blues by Cynthia Millen
Mary Ann's Mud Day by Janice May Udry
Miss Twiggly's Tree by Dorothea Warren Fox
Mouse Mess by Linnea Asplind Riley
Ms. Sneed's Guide to Hygiene by Dale Gotleib
Piggies by Audrey Wood
The Popcorn Book by Tomie dePaola
Puddles by Jonathan London
Sing a Song of Popcorn: Every Child's Book of Poems by Beatrice Shenk de Regniers
Ten Dirty Pigs, Ten Clean Pigs: An Upside-Down, Turn-Around Bathtime Counting Book by Carol Roth
Trash Trucks! by Daniel Kirk
Trashy Town by Andrea Zimmerman
Wash Your Hands! by Tony Ross
We Love the Dirt! by Tony Johnston
What's the Recipe for Friends? by Greg M. Williamson
Wormy Worm (Thingy Things) by Christopher Raschka

Observation/Assessment

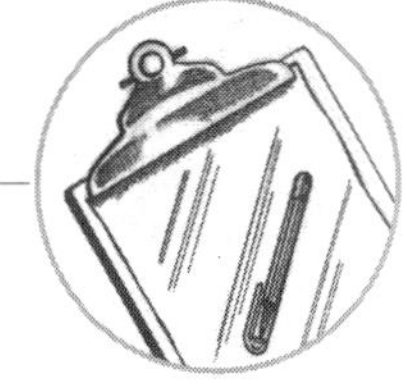

Washes dishes, page 160
Dries dishes, page 160
Classifies laundry by type, page 161
Uses mathematical language, such as more, less, same, bigger, smaller, most, least, and so on, page 161
Recognizes that different coins have different values, page 161
Uses problem-solving skills, page 162
Throws a ball, page 163
Follows safety rules, page 163 and 164
Paints using different methods, page 163 and 173
Hits golf tees with hammer, page 164
Makes plans for using materials, page 164
Uses materials independently or with others, page 164
Works cooperatively to extend resources, page 164
Uses positional vocabulary, such as over, under, by, on top of, below, and between, page 164 and 170
Groups objects by size, page 165
Builds using various materials, page 165
Sorts items by whether they sink or float, page 165
Mixes, stirs, and measures materials, page 167
Draws shapes, page 168
Writes letter-like marks, page 168
Writes letters, page 168
Groups similar containers, page 169
Sorts items according to how they are used, page 169
Creates simple patterns, page 170
Uses small muscles of hand to squeeze paint from gloves, page 172

Picture File/Vocabulary

aluminum
body parts
bottles
broom
bubbles
cheese slicer
clean mud
compost
dumpster
dustpan
first
fourth
glass
goggles
gooey
gravity
handwashing
landfill
last
laundry detergent
metal
middle
mop
muddy
mushy,
pipes
plastic
recycle
rubbery
scrubber
second
slimey
sort
sound effects ("splat," "boing," "swoosh," "splash," "bam")
sponge
squiggly
squishy
sticky
suds
third
tracks
wiggle

Concepts Learned in Making Messes and Cleaning Them Up

Content Knowledge

- ☐ Some messes are easy to clean up and others are hard.
- ☐ Coins have different values.
- ☐ Recycling saves resources.
- ☐ Cleaning up messes is the last step of making them.
- ☐ Some things float in water, and others sink.
- ☐ I need different tools to clean up different messes.
- ☐ Handwashing has many steps.
- ☐ Handwashing keeps me healthy.
- ☐ Singing while you clean up makes it more fun.

Process Knowledge

- ☐ I can make messes.
- ☐ I can clean up my messes.
- ☐ I can clean up my room.
- ☐ I can wash things (clothes, dishes, my hands, tricycles).
- ☐ I can sort (socks, mittens, laundry, coins).
- ☐ I can paint with many different objects (balls, flyswatters, potato mashers, spatulas, mops, brooms).
- ☐ I can hammer golf tees into Styrofoam.
- ☐ I have creative ideas.
- ☐ I can catch popcorn after it pops.
- ☐ I can complete puzzles.
- ☐ I can write letters.
- ☐ I can draw shapes.

Pre-academic Skills

- ☐ I can match soap bars to toilet paper rolls to see if we have the same number of each (one-to-one correspondence).
- ☐ I can make simple patterns.
- ☐ I can remember and repeat fingerplays and rhymes.
- ☐ I can figure things out (how to drop eggs without breaking them, what floats and what sinks, how to make clean mud, how to mix flour and water together, how to make plastic wiggly worms stick to the sides of the sensory tubs).
- ☐ I can trace figures, letters, and numbers with my fingers.
- ☐ I can make plans.

Possibilities Plan—

Creepy Crawlies (and Germs)

Getting Ready to Plan

During the preschool years, children are fascinated by bugs, insects, worms, butterflies, caterpillars, and all things with interesting textures, fragrances, colors, and shapes, both real and imaginary. This Possibilities Plan explores the topic of Creepy Crawlies (and Germs). It facilitates the exploration of the natural world as children learn about the scientific methods of observation, comparison, and prediction.

The purpose of Getting Ready to Plan is to support the planning process with a general overview of the content of this Possibilities Plan. Now is the time to think about what you want the children in your group to learn about each of these topics. Topics are explored in general below.

Insects: Preschool children will enjoy learning new vocabulary to help them talk about creatures that they are able to observe and discuss. Children will be interested to find out about entomologists, metamorphosis, the production of honey, and what an apiary is. Unlike spiders (who are creepy crawlies, but not insects at all), insects have six legs and three main body parts (head, thorax, and abdomen). Some are able to fly and some are not. Insects go through a life cycle stage called metamorphosis where they look like totally different creatures when they are young than they do when full grown. Extend the discussion begun in Saying Hello (see Chapter 2) of similarities and differences to that of insects and see how much young children already know!

Spiders: The most fascinating thing about spiders to preschool children is the fact that they are able to build intricate webs. Observing, drawing, and constructing webs will give children practice with noticing details and making patterns. Stress safety as children capture creepy crawlies to observe in the classroom. Release creatures after a short period of observation (a discussion of how long to keep caught bugs will be worth having early on in this plan). A field trip to a butterfly museum or natural history museum is a great way to begin the class discussion of creepy crawlies, or you may wish to use a field trip as a culminating activity.

Germs: Because children cannot see germs, they may have difficulty understanding the concept. Nevertheless, they benefit from discussions and experiences that expand their knowledge and understanding of germs and the role they play in health and wellness. Handwashing is supported in this Plan (as well as in Making Messes) because this health practice is such an important one.

Now that you have an idea about the general content of the Possibilities Plan, you are ready to proceed with developing your own Plan. This section of Getting Ready to Plan identifies resources you may want to buy, collect, or locate to implement your plan.

Toys and Materials*

Purchased

ant puppet
bee costume
black markers
bug catchers
bug houses
bulletin board
circle dots stickers
clipboard
construction paper
contact paper
craft eyes
craft glue
craft pipe cleaners
food for snacks (honey, graham crackers, celery, peanut butter, raisins, prunes, chop suey, lettuce, fruit, vegetables)
glue
grasshopper puppet
hole punch
index cards
markers
microscope
paper
pen set
pencils
plastic magnifying glasses
plastic petri dishes
plastic worms
playdough
pompoms
purchased pictures of steps in metamorphosis
safety goggles
sensory trays
silver rings
small and large plastic bugs
stickers
tempera paint
unit blocks
washable inkpads
water liquid color

Gathered

aluminum foil
ant mounds
beekeeper hat
bolts
branches
bug shapes
bugs
butterfly novelty items
clipboard
cookie cutters
cotton balls
dropper bottles
duct tape
forks
golf tees
heavy objects (rocks or pails with sand)
knives (plastic)
large zip-lock bags
leaf shapes
lightweight blanket
loose dirt and sand
net or plastic screen
pictures of ant tunnels and ant mounds
pictures of insects and leaves
pictures of scientists at work
pictures of spiders and webs
plastic caps
plastic containers in a variety of sizes
plastic eggs
plastic spoons
potato chip tins
rubber bands
silk and plastic flowers
small finishing nail
striped socks
trays
twigs
white shirts (for lab coats)
wood shavings and other nature items
worm tunnels

*Note: Please consider the ages and abilities of the children in your classroom. Use only safe, non-toxic materials.

Creepy Crawlies (and Germs)

WEB

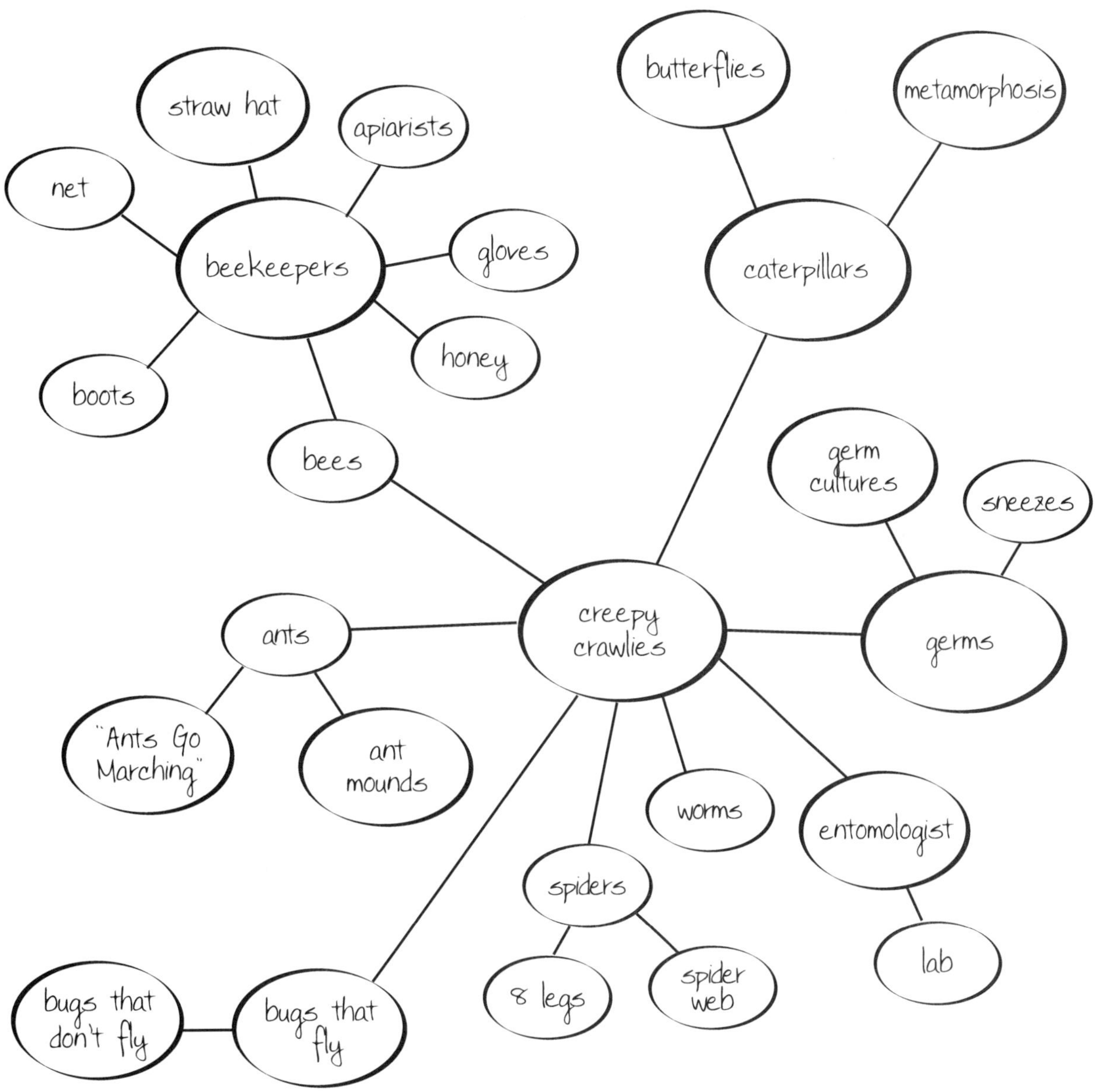

Creepy Crawlies (and Germs)

PLANNING PAGES

Plan Possibilities

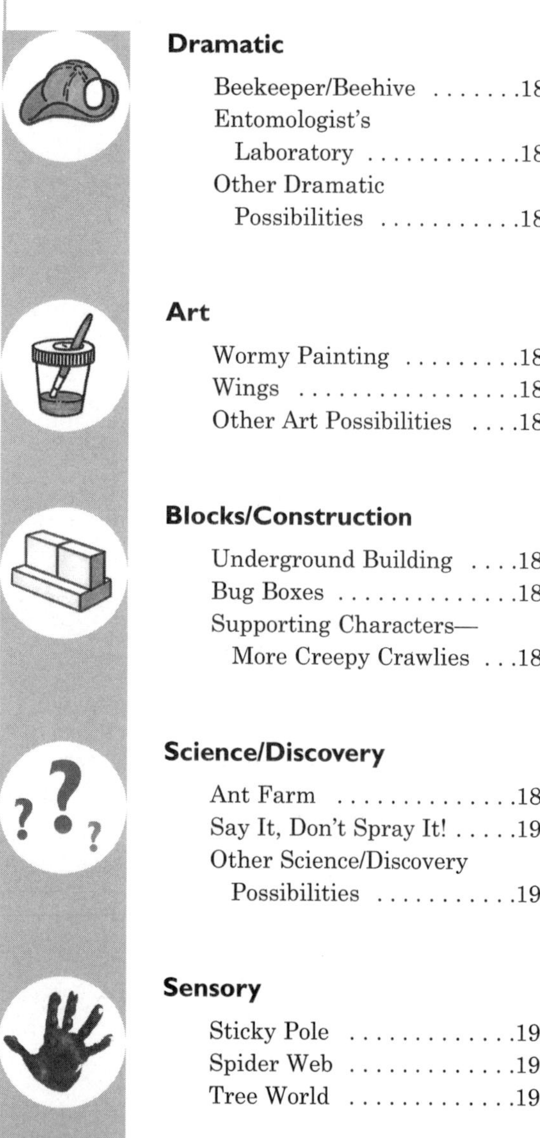

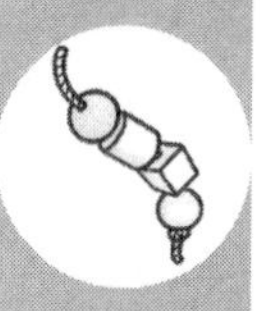

Movement/Outdoors

Projects/Documentation

Field Trip

Snack

Family Participation

Parent Postcards

Curriculum Resources

ACTIVITIES AND EXPERIENCES FOR CREEPY CRAWLIES

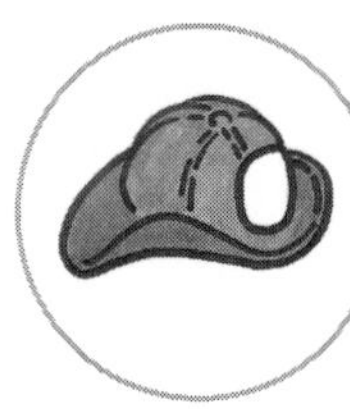

DRAMATIC POSSIBILITIES

Beekeeper/Beehive

Materials
straw hat • net • glue gun (teacher only) • plastic bees • flowers (real or plastic/silk) • yellow T-shirts • black marker or washable paint • tape or fabric • paper plates • stapler • pipe cleaners • hair band • gloves • boots • cardboard boxes • clipboards with paper and pen attached • bee puppets • books about bees, such as *Bees* by Gallimard Jeunesse

Teacher Talk
"Why do beekeepers wear hats with netting to cover their faces?" "What do bees need to make honey?" "How do bees help nature work?"

Instructions
Make a beekeeper's hat by cutting netting to go around the hat. Glue it onto the hat with the hot glue gun (teacher only). Create bee costumes by adding black stripes to the yellow T-shirts either with black washable paint, tape, or fabric. Make wings by stapling two paper plates together. Attach the wings to the T-shirt. Create antennae with hair bands and pipe cleaners. Add a beehive made out of a cardboard box, adding cardboard shelves to serve as the beehive honeycombs.

Create a garden area in the Dramatic Possibilities area using the flowers and bees. Plastic bees or bees made from black and yellow pipe cleaners will provide additional interest.

Observation/Assessment
Takes on various roles in dramatic play
Uses props to enhance dramatic play
Dresses and undresses in costumes

Entomologist's Laboratory

Materials
small and large plastic bugs • magnifying glasses • pen set • microscope • plastic containers in a variety of sizes • plastic petri dishes • safety goggles • white shirts (for lab coats) • clipboard • markers • pictures of insects, bugs • and scientists at work • silk and plastic flowers • bug catchers of various types • bug houses to hold captured bugs • aluminum foil • butterfly hairclips • bug novelty slippers or galoshes • ant puppet • grasshopper puppet • book about bugs and insects, such as *About Insects: A Guide for Children* by Cathryn P. Sill or *Bugs* by Nancy Winslow Parker

Teacher Talk
"What kind of scientist studies insects?" "A scientist who studies insects is called an entomologist."

Instructions
Modify the Dramatic Possibilities area by adding tables for the entomologist's equipment and materials. Add props to the area, along with pictures of insects, bugs, and scientists at work. A good place to look for bugs is underneath rocks and fallen logs.

Observation/Assessment
Observes insects using magnifying glass

Other Dramatic Possibilities

- Add plastic worms and fishing props.
- Add clean-up materials (empty, clean containers) that help fight germs.

ART POSSIBILITIES

Wormy Painting

Materials
tempera paint in small bowls • plastic fishing lures and fishing worms • books about worms, such as *Wonderful Worms* by Linda Glasser

Teacher Talk
"Paint a picture with the worms—a wiggly, wormy painting!" "Your picture has lots of green paint and lots of wiggly marks."

Instructions
Put paint in small bowls. Arrange a variety of fishing lures and worms around the bowls. Children can dip the worms and lures into the paint and use them to apply the paint to the paper.

Observation/Assessment
Paints using various media

Wings

Materials
paper plates • stapler • T-shirts • duct tape • markers • water • liquid color • paints • construction paper • pictures of bugs and insects • books about insects with wings, such as *Caterpillars, Bugs, and Butterflies* by Mel Boring

Teacher Talk
"How do insects fly?" "How many wings does a butterfly have?" "How many wings does a bee have?" "How many wings does a ladybug have?"

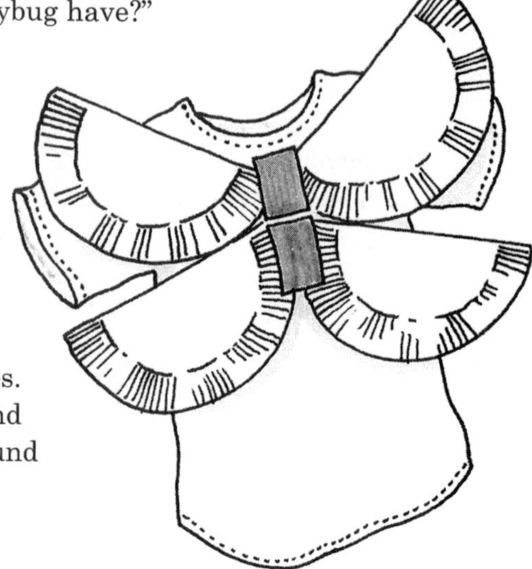

Instructions
Staple paper plates together to make wings (for example, one paper plate folded in half for a ladybug, two paper plates for a bee, four paper plates for butterfly. Tape them on the backs of old T-shirts with duct tape. Add to the Dramatic Possibilities area.

Helpful Hints: Pictures from the picture file are particularly helpful here. Add them to Art Possibilities. Some wings may need a different shape than the round paper plates. Experiment with oval platters or cut round paper plates to reflect the different shapes of wings.

Other Art Possibilities

- Make egg carton insects, animals, and germ molecules.
- Make a blot painting.
- Create a butterfly by placing blobs of paint on paper, folding it, and tapping the paper to spread the paint.
- Use homemade playdough and art supplies to make bugs.
- Use craft pipe cleaners, construction paper, and collage materials to create baby bugs to put inside plastic eggs.
- Use art materials to make insects with patterns and designs on their bodies. Look at books about insects for ideas.

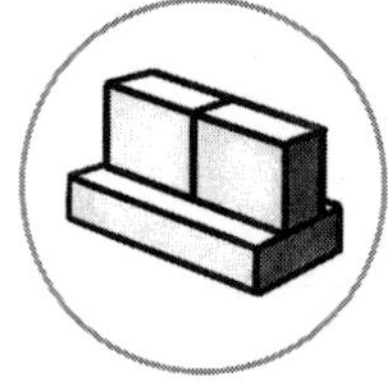

BLOCKS/CONSTRUCTION POSSIBILITIES

Underground Building

Materials
large, lightweight blanket • duct tape • four adult-size chairs • blocks • plastic ants • plastic worms • various toy insects that live underground • pictures of ant tunnels, worm tunnels, ant mounds, and so on

Teacher Talk
"What kinds of insects live in underground?" "What do you think it is like to move around without light?"

Instructions
Simulate the feeling of being underground by covering the Block Possibilities area with a lightweight blanket over the chairs. Use duct tape to attach the blanket to the floor. Add props for children to explore the feeling of being underground. Supervise closely when children are inside the structure.

Bug Boxes

Materials
shoebox • net or plastic screen • glue • rubber band • various live insects, spiders, and other creepy crawlies

Teacher Talk
"The net will allow us to observe the insects in the bug house." "Tomorrow we will let the insects go free."

Instructions
Cut large square sections out of the shoebox. Glue a net or plastic screen to the inside of the box with glue, so squares are completely covered. Use the rubber band to secure the top to the shoebox. Place bug houses in the Block Possibilities area as a prop or take outside to use on bug searches.

Observation/Assessment
Constructs bug box

Supporting Characters—More Creepy Crawlies

Materials
bug costumes • antennae made from craft pipe cleaners • books about insects, such as *One Hundred Hungry Ants* by Elinor J. Pinczes

Teacher Talk
"You used all the blocks to create a big beehive."

Instructions
Provide costumes and antennae made from craft pipe cleaners for children to wear as they build.

Observation/Assessment
Builds using blocks and other materials

SCIENCE/DISCOVERY POSSIBILITIES

Ant Farm

Materials
large, plastic, clear jar • hammer • small finishing nail • sand and loose dirt • shovel • gardening gloves • black construction paper • plastic magnifying glasses • tape • books about ants, such as *The Little Red Ant and the Great Big Crumb* by Shirley Climo

Teacher Talk

"Why do you think the ants are making tunnels?" "After the ants visit our classroom, we will let them go."

Instructions

Clean the large plastic jar. Punch tiny holes in the top using a hammer and a small finishing nail. Fill the jar about two-thirds full with sand and loose dirt. Locate an ant mound. While wearing gloves, use the shovel to put several scoops of a mound containing ants into the jar (teacher only). Screw the lid tightly on the jar. Tape the black construction paper on the sides of the jar. In a few days remove the paper, so children can observe the ants and tunnels using magnifying glasses. If you keep the ant farm for an extended period of time, give ants water by placing wet cotton balls on top of the dirt. Also, add small crumbs of bread to feed the ants. When the tunneling activity slows down, it is time to release the ants where you found them.

Observation/Assessment

Observes using magnifying glasses

Say It, Don't Spray It!

Materials

spray bottles • towels • tissues • washable paint • soap • water

Teacher Talk

"I got all wet! How can you stop the water from spraying all over me?"

Instructions

Introduce the concept of spreading germs by coughing or sneezing. Discuss how a squirt from the water spray bottle is just like a germ spray from a cough or sneeze. Demonstrate with the spray bottle. Then, cover the nozzle of the spray bottle with a tissue, demonstrating how the tissue stops the germs.

Many health practitioners recommend that children be taught to cover sneezes or coughs by turning their heads and using their shoulders, upper arms, or elbows. This avoids using the hands to cover the mouth and nose and helps to prevent the spread of germs. Demonstrate this technique and remind children to use it if they are not able to grab a tissue.

Finally, discuss handwashing following sneezing or coughing, particularly if the child covers his or her mouth with hands. To demonstrate this, put washable paint in the spray bottle instead of water. Spray children's hands to demonstrate how the germs go all over their hands when they sneeze or cough. Follow the demonstration by careful handwashing to get rid of all of the germs (paint).

Add spray bottles with a small amount of water in them to the Science/Discovery Possibilities, letting the children experiment with how far the germs spread without covering the nozzle.

Other Science/Discovery Possibilities

- Review the handwashing process and why it is important (see page 169).
- Observe hornets' nests or wasps' nests.

SENSORY POSSIBILITIES

Sticky Pole

Materials
contact paper • potato chip tins • small plastic bugs • branches or twigs • leaves

Teacher Talk
"Why are the bugs sticking to the pole?" "How do you think bugs stay on trees or walls?" "What makes walking on walls and trees possible for bugs?" This is a great question for the children to research (with adult help, as needed).

Instructions
Wrap the potato chip tins with contact paper, sticky side out. Put the remainder of the materials out in Sensory Possibilities. Children can stick plastic bugs and nature items to the sticky pole. Don't forget to add field experiences to this activity by observing for bugs on windows, trees, and other places.

Spider Web

Materials
homemade playdough • golf tees • yarn • sensory trays • plastic spiders and bugs • pictures of spiders, bugs, and spider webs • books about spiders and webs, such as *The Very Busy Spider* by Eric Carle

Teacher Talk
"How can you make spider webs out of these materials?" "Why do spiders make webs?"

Instructions
Place the playdough on a large tray and spread it out. Stick some golf tees in the playdough. Connect the golf tees with yarn and make a spider web.

Helpful Hints: Add pictures of spider webs to the Sensory Possibilities area, so children can look at them as they make their webs. Coach children on how to wrap the yarn around the golf tees twice before moving on to the next tee. This helps the yarn stay in place.

Playdough Recipe (No Cooking Required)
6 cups flour
3 cups salt
2 cups water
½ cup oil
Food coloring

Mix together all the ingredients. Knead until smooth. Store in an airtight container.

Tree World

Materials
wood shavings • twigs • leaves • logs • bark • roots • dirt • plastic insects

Teacher Talk
"Which insects eat leaves?" "What else do insects eat?"

Instructions
Add tree materials to the sensory table for children to manipulate and determine likenesses and differences.

LITERACY/WRITING POSSIBILITIES

Thumbprint Bugs

Materials
washable inkpads • black markers • thumbprint or bug books, such as Ed Emberley's *Great Thumbprint Drawing Book*

Teacher Talk
"You turned your thumbprints into insects. Which ones can fly?"

Instructions
Make thumbprints by pressing thumbs onto the inkpads and then onto paper. Add details with the black markers.

Helpful Hints: Activities like this often need a "starting point." Make a few thumbprints on paper and add features to give children ideas about where to begin.

Extension Possibilities: Children who are beginning to associate letters with their sounds can make thumbprints in the shape of the letters of their name or interesting creepy-crawly words.

Bug Matching

Materials
insect shapes (4 blue of one shape, 4 red of a different shape, 4 yellow of another shape, and so on, or a collection of bugs with many duplicates of each bug)

Teacher Talk
"That's right, Joshua. You have three yellow bees."

Instructions
Children can match similar bugs or bugs of the same color, use different colors to create patterns, and arrange insects in interesting ways as they play with them.

Observation/Assessment
Matches shapes and colors
Creates simple patterns using shapes and colors

Metamorphosis Book

Materials
purchased or teacher-prepared pictures of the steps in metamorphosis life cycle • construction paper • large zipper-closure plastic bags • hole punch • silver rings or yarn • small permanent markers

Teacher Talk
"This is called a pupa." "What is the difference between a caterpillar and a butterfly?"

Instructions
Mount pictures of metamorphosis steps onto construction paper. Cut to fit inside plastic bags. Talk with children about the steps in metamorphosis. Then write children's dictations of what is happening in each step under the pictures. Place pages in plastic bags. Attach bags together using silver rings or short lengths of yarn. Be sure to include a cover page with title, date, and children's names.

Observation/Assessment
Dictates ideas
Dictates sentences

MATH/MANIPULATIVES POSSIBILITIES

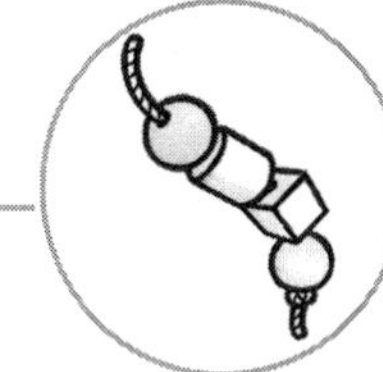

"The Ants Go Marching One by One" Game

Materials
plastic ants • pictures of ants • clear contact paper • pictures of foods that might attract ants • stick-on labels numbered 1-10

Teacher Talk
"How many ants go on the eight?" "What number is on ice cream?"

Instructions
Laminate pictures of foods that might attract ants such as sugar, ice cream, cookies, and so on. Tape pictures of food onto cardboard and cover with clear contact paper sticky side up. Tape the edges of contact paper to the cardboard. Stick one label with a number written on it on each sticky cardboard. Children stick the correct number of ants on the food pictures.

Extension Possibilities: Increase the numbers to 20 for five-year-olds. Continue to add higher numbers if children master 1-10 and 10-20.

Observation/Assessment
Uses one-to-one correspondence to 10 or 20

Bug Game

Materials
one sheet of large construction paper or poster board • construction paper • markers • thirty plastic insects • simple game pieces • dice

Teacher Talk
"Today, Jessica and Corrie won. Yesterday, Shawna and Derrick won."

Instructions
Make a simple addition board game by drawing an octagon on a piece of cardboard or poster board. Put circles at each "corner" of the octagon (see illustration). Create cards by writing instructions such as "Pick up 1 bug" or "Pick up 2 bugs" on pieces of construction paper. Place the insects and the cards face down in the middle of the game board. Children take turns rolling the die and moving their game piece the number of circles indicated on the die. When they finish moving their game piece, they pick a card and follow the instructions on it—taking one or two insects as instructed on the card. When all of the insects are gone, children count up their insects and the game is over.

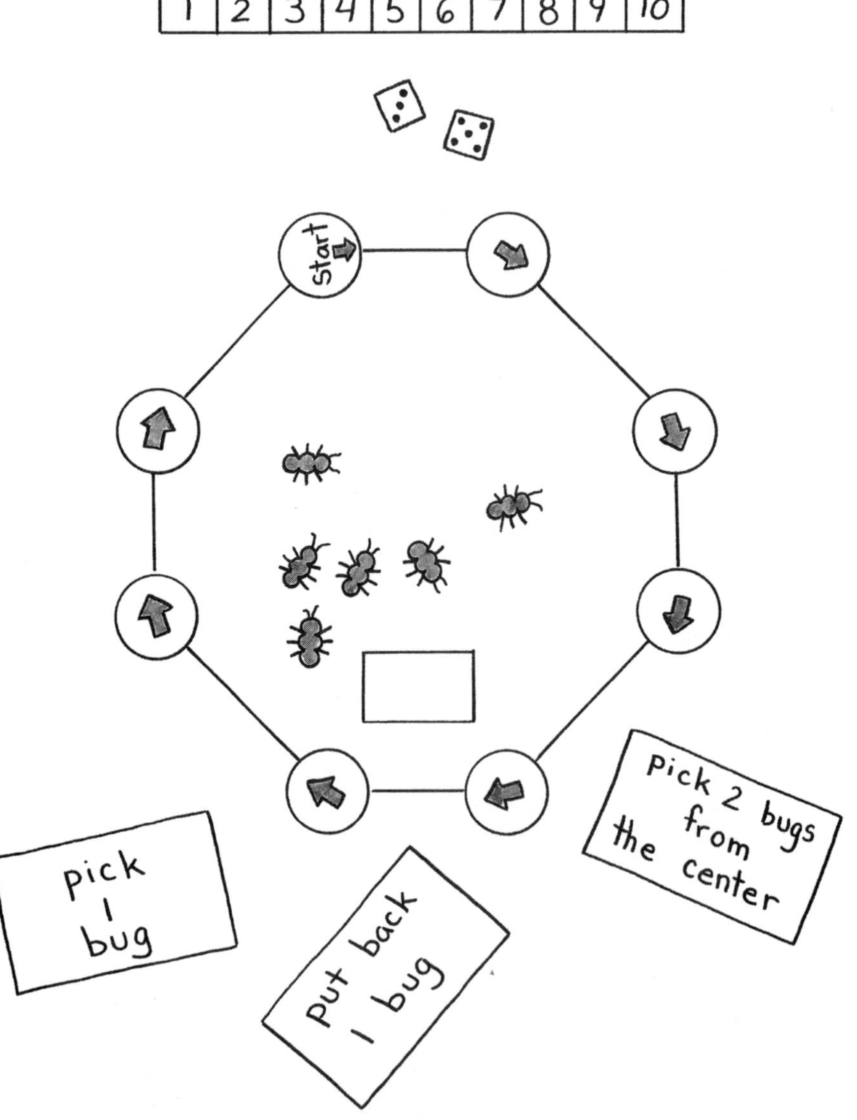

Introduce the rules of the game to children. Explain how to take turns rolling the die, moving the game piece the number of spaces on the board, drawing a card, and then collecting the number of insects on the card. When children complete the game, help them count their insects using bar graph counting strips (1-10).

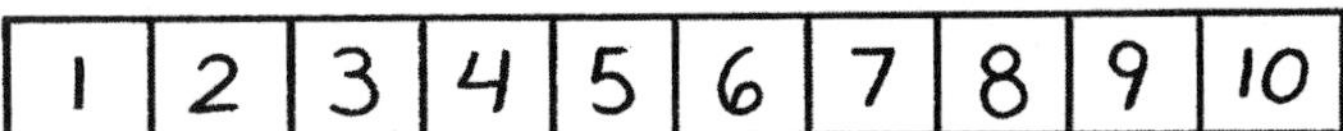

Helpful Hints: This game can be introduced at Group Time. Start with addition only—"Take 1 bug." Introduce complexity by increasing the numbers of bugs children take from the center of the game board. Start with numbers 1-5, then 1-10, and so on. Introduce the concept of subtraction—"Take away 1 bug"—as children master the idea of putting sets together and taking them apart. As with adding, when appropriate, increase the numbers of bugs the children must take away. To decrease the competition that regularly arises between preschoolers, play tournaments (best of 10), keeping track of who has the most insects over time to help children see that the occupant of the winner's seat changes. Chart the results and keep them with the game.

Observation/Assessment
Adds numbers 1-5 (then 1-10)

Some Bugs Fly, Some Don't

Materials
bugs • pictures of insects • 4" x 6" index cards • glue • markers

Teacher Talk
"I like bugs that don't bite!" "What kinds of bugs do you like?"

Instructions
Glue insect pictures on index cards. Add the insect name to the card. Ask children to sort the bugs into those they like and those they don't like. Then, add other dimensions, such as "insects that fly and those that don't," "insects that scare me and those that don't," or "insects I find around my house and those I don't."

Observation/Assessment
Sorts insects into categories

RHYMES/FINGERPLAYS/SONGS/MUSIC POSSIBILITIES

Musical Math—The Ants Go Marching

Materials
a recording of "The Ants Go Marching" such as "Ants" from *Ants* by Joe Scruggs (Shadow Play Records)

Teacher Talk
"Everyone has lined up with a partner—marching two by two."

Instructions
Begin by inviting the children to march to the music in a single-file line. When the verse ends, partner ants together in pairs to march "two by two." At the end of every verse, children change formation to reflect the new marching numbers. Practice this once or twice before trying it with the music or be prepared to pause the music as children figure out the math.

Helpful Hints: Give the children a chance to figure out the math before offering your help. Be patient—there is no hurry. Sometimes, the number of children in the group and the number of ants marching won't work out (there will be some ants left and not enough to make a new group). Encourage the children who are left over to participate as the audience until the next verse.

Caterpillar Metamorphosis

Teacher Talk
"We have learned about how caterpillars turn into butterflies. Now, we are going to be caterpillars and change into butterflies ourselves."

Instructions
Say and act out the fingerplay.

Caterpillar Poem

A caterpillar crawled to the top of a tree. *"I think I'll take a nap," said he.*	(two fingers crawling up on the other arm)
So under a leaf he began to creep.	(two fingers creeping down underneath the other hand)
To spin a cocoon;	(wrap one hand over the other hand)
Then he fell asleep.	(place both hands on the side of the face and close the eyes)
All winter he slept in his cocoon bed, *Till Spring came along one day and said,*	(wrap one hand over the other hand, again)
"Wake up, wake up, little sleepyhead. *Wake up, it's time to get out of bed."*	(move the fist out of the wrapped hand slowly)
So he opened his eyes that sunshiny day.	(pop the fingers out)
Lo! He was a butterfly, and he flew away!	(flapping the arms up and down)

Observation/Assessment
Recites and acts out fingerplays

Other Rhymes/Fingerplays/Songs/Music Possibilities

- Use any of the following recordings during this plan:
  - "I Love Bugs" from *Insects, Bugs, and Squiggly Things* by Jane Murphy
  - "The Parade" from *Ants* by Joe Scruggs
  - "The Worm" from *Songs about Animals and Other Things* by Kimbo
  - "The Inchworm" from *A Child's Celebration of Song, vol. 2* by Music for Little People
  - "Creepy Crawlin'" from *Mr. Al Sings and Moves* by Mr. Al
- Move like bumblebees as you listen to "The Bee Bop" from *Insects, Bugs, and Squiggly Things* by Jane Murphy, or "The Bumble Bee Boogie" from *Happiness Cake* by Linda Arnold, or "The Flight of the Bumble Bee" from *Cappuccino Classics* by RCA Victor.
- Say the fingerplay "Here Is a Beehive."
- Sing "The Itsy Bitsy Spider" by counting to the melody instead of singing the words. (Spiders have eight legs and the song is counted in eighths.) See if you end on the same number each time.

GROUP TIME POSSIBILITIES

"Say It, Don't Spray It!" Introduction: Explain this activity (see page 190).

The Bug Game Introduction: Explain the rules and demonstrate how the game is played. Then, place the game in Math/Manipulatives for children to play as they choose (see page 194).

I'm a Spider: Give children different instructions as they crawl like spiders. Crawl like a spider in different directions—forward, backward, and sideways. Take different pathways—straight, curving, zigzagging, and circling. Use different levels to crawl—high, medium, and low. And, finally, pretend you are a heavy spider, a light spider, a big spider, and a small spider. Make sure there is plenty of room to move.

Other Group Time Possibilities
- Read any of the books listed in this Possibilities Plan (see pages 203-204).
- Act out movements of worms and bugs while playing Follow the Leader.
- Use bug pictures from your picture file collection to start discussions.
- Ask children to describe their favorite bug.

MOVEMENT/OUTDOORS POSSIBILITIES

Spider Webs with Balls of Yarn

Materials
ball of yarn • heavy objects such as large rocks or pails with sand in them

Teacher Talk
"How do you make a spider web?" "Do you think we can make a spider web?"

Instructions
Sit in a large circle. Place a heavy object in front of each child. Place the end of the yarn under the heavy object. Throw the ball of yarn to a friend across the circle. When a child catches the yarn, he places it under the heavy object in front of him, and then throws it to another friend. Keep throwing the yarn until there is a thick web. Loosen some yarn before it is thrown. Remind children to toss the ball of yarn gently to their friends.

Flight of the Bumblebee

Materials
recording of "The Flight of the Bumblebee," "The Bee Bop," or "The Bumblebee Boogie" (see page 197 for recording information) • crackers • honey

Teacher Talk
"You are a fast-flying bee!" "Where can you get pollen?" "Are you a hungry bee?"

Instructions
Play the music as the children fly around pollinating flowers, gathering pollen to take back to the hive, chasing away predators, and coming home to the hive for a delicious dinner of honey.

Safety Note: Remind your "bees" to wash their hands before they eat their dinner. Confirm that none of the children in your group have allergies to honey before implementing this activity. Use filtered, processed honey.

Other Movement/Outdoor Possibilities

- Plant a garden.
- Go on a worm search.
- Play "bug" Simon Says.
- Use the fingerplay on page 196 outside and go through the metamorphosis on the grass.
- Go on an insect safari to discover how many insects are on the playground. Use a clipboard, paper, and a pencil to make a hash mark for each insect that you spot.

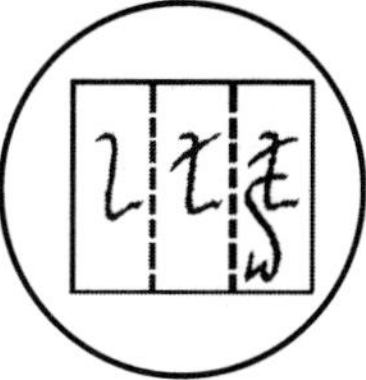

Field Science—Observing Ant Mounds

Materials

paper • markers • sand • glue • bowl • tray • spoon • sticks • grass • magnifying glasses • books about ants, such as *Are You an Ant?* by Judy Allen

Teacher Talk

"We are improving our observation skills. What details can we report?"

Instructions

Find an ant mound or mounds for children to observe. Discuss good field observation skills, including approaching ant mounds slowly, spending time quietly observing, and keeping a safe distance from the ant mound. Give each child a clipboard, paper, and markers, crayons, or colored pencils. Ask children to draw what they see and make field notes on the paper.

Next, hold a group discussion, making a list of what children learned as they observed the ant mounds. Encourage the children to use their field notes (drawings) to explain their observations. Make a list of what children observed and learned on chart paper.

Finally, explore with children how they could make an ant mound. Take a walk on the playground to collect materials that children suggest are needed to make the mound.

Children can try out their ideas, exploring techniques for creating ant mounds with the materials they collected. Encourage children to use their field notes (drawings) to help them consider ways to make the mounds. Record the ideas and processes that children explore, with anecdotal notes, photos, or videotape.

Observation/Assessment

Makes field notes (drawings)
Uses field notes to explain ideas or observations

Butterfly Metamorphosis

Materials

Dream Tree by Stephen Cosgrove • construction paper • craft glue • markers (any colors) • scissors • leaf shapes (made beforehand) • one pair of striped socks (optional) • cotton fiber filling or cotton balls • collage materials • pipe cleaners • papers • stapler • yarns • bulletin board

Teacher Talk

"You worked hard to create the models for our class. Who would like to tell me about the models?"

Instructions

Before you start the project, read *Dream Tree* by Stephen Cosgrove, to help the children know what they will be doing. Discuss the steps explained on the next page.

Step One (egg): Take a look at the size of the caterpillar eggs in comparison to a leaf before making caterpillar eggs. Let everyone make an egg with construction paper, markers, and scissors. Once finished, ask the children to glue their eggs on a paper leaf, made beforehand.

Step Two (larva): Work together to make a caterpillar for the second stage of the metamorphosis. Place a sock in front of the children. Take turns stuffing fiber filling or cotton balls in the sock. Once the sock is filled, fold the ends inward and use craft glue to seal or a stapler to staple the open end together. Decorate the larva with collage materials. Put the antenna on the larva by stapling or sewing. A larva is formed.

Step Three (chrysalis or pupa or cocoon): Use the rest of the fiber filling to form an oval-shaped pupa. Then, cut long strings of yarn about two feet long. Take turns spinning the string of yarn onto the pupa to hold the shape together. When finished, paint the pupa. Place the pupa on a tray. Put different colors of paints in small bowls. Mix a small amount of glue into the paint. When the children use their hands to paint the pupa, the mixed paint will help the strings stick to the pupa. Let the finished pupa dry completely.

Step Four (butterfly): Using the same methods as in Step Two, make another stuffed sock without the glued collage materials. Use the collage materials to decorate precut butterfly wings. When the glue on the wings is dry, staple the wings to the second stuffed sock.

As each step is finished, display the results to show children the stages of the butterfly metamorphosis.

Growing Germ Cultures

Materials
plastic petri dishes • different specimens • charts

Teacher Talk
Talk with children about growing germ cultures. "Look at the difference between the dishes." "What do you think will happen next?"

Instructions
Get a collection of plastic petri dishes. Number each dish. Ask children to identify things in the classroom that they would like to culture. Make a list. Discuss and demonstrate the correct way to collect samples to culture. Assign children to petri dishes, recording on the list the source of the sample they will collect. Then, send children out to collect their samples.

Chart the bacteria growth every other day on simulated petri dishes made out of paper circles. Have children shade in the circles where the bacteria grew with colored pencils. Label the chart with the number of days passed (+1 day, +2 days, and so on).
Ask children to report to you what they learned about germs from the petri dish cultures. Put their ideas together in a book.

Helpful Hint: Petri dishes can be found in science supply catalogs for teachers.

Observation/Assessment
Records observations

FIELD TRIP POSSIBILITIES

Community Gardens: Visit a community garden to see how vegetables are grown in your area.

Butterfly House or Museum: Visit a butterfly or horticultural museum to see how entomologists actually work.

Natural Science Museum: Visit a natural science museum to explore the wonders of nature.

Science Laboratory: Visit a laboratory to see science at work in the real world.

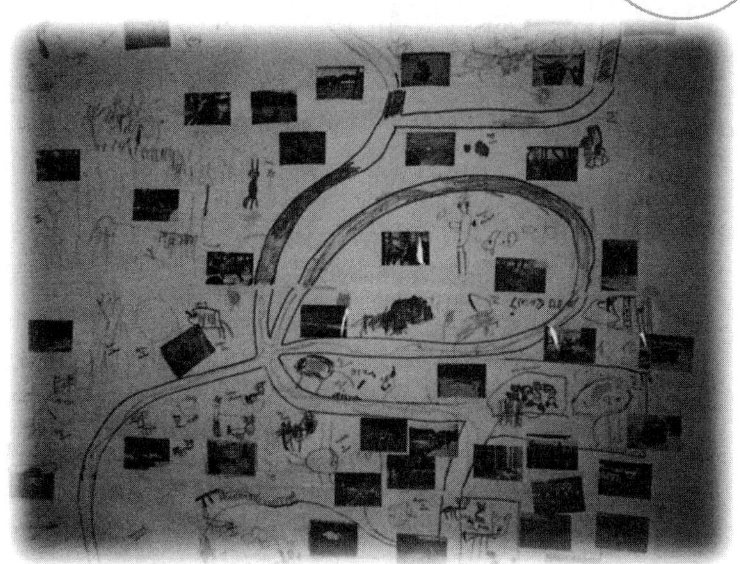

SNACK POSSIBILITIES

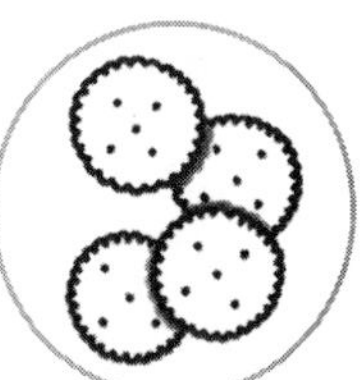

Honey and Graham Crackers with Milk: Use a special honey spoon to drip honey on graham crackers. Serve with milk. Check for allergies.

Ants on a Log: Stuff celery with peanut butter and dot with raisins to simulate ants on a log. Check for allergies.

Plum and Chop Suey Spiders: Stick chop suey noodles into a dried plum to create an edible spider.

Things Bugs Like to Eat: Consider a sampling snack of things bugs like to eat. Make the list with children and then serve these choices for snack. Some ideas might be lettuce or any green, leafy vegetable, apples, seeds, nuts, and so forth.

FAMILY PARTICIPATION POSSIBILITIES

Bug Boxes: Invite family members to participate in this activity, providing direct support for building the bug houses, contributing/loaning tools from home, or helping complete the bug boxes with their children at home.

"Here Is a Beehive" for Parents: Send the words of this fingerplay (see page xxx) home, so parents and family members can say it with their children.

Supporting Possibilities: Ask family members to bring items you need for this plan. Be clear about whether items are being loaned or donated.

Expectations with Friends

Preschool children are changing, becoming less egocentric. They enjoy being in groups and doing things with other children. They grow and develop so quickly that it may be difficult as parents to keep expectations about friendships realistic. The following are some general suggestions:

- Young preschoolers are beginning to understand and even demonstrate sharing. More often, however, they still need adult support and encouragement to take turns, share resources, and wait for a turn. Let your child know how his or her actions impact other children. This will help your child understand the impact of his or her behavior on friends and lead to being able to share.
- Preschool children enjoy learning about how they are similar to their friends and how they are different. They are beginning to explore relationships between the environments of home and school with the larger world of their neighborhood and the community. All of these topics interest younger preschoolers while older preschoolers are beginning to recognize and think about differences among ideas, friends, and skills.
- New situations may still be somewhat problematic for preschool children. Prepare your child for new experiences and meeting new friends by talking about what to expect and how your child might respond.
- Keep working on manners in the context of making friends. "Please," "Thank you," and "Excuse me" can go a long way in smoothing the rough edges of a new friendship.
- Emotion management skills such as waiting, delaying gratification, and impulse control are skills that are still "in process." Support your child as he or she begins to recognize and identify emotions more accurately. This is usually learned in interactions with peers—often through conflict. Expect conflicts, but recognize that this is a very powerful way to learn what works and what doesn't and how to relate to others.
- Preschool children are learning to understand their own emotions and to identify emotions that other children are expressing. Support your child's beginning skill of empathy for others who are hurt or left out of social interactions.

How your child makes and keeps friends as a preschooler can be indicative of future success in social skills and being a friend, so take the time to support beginning friendships. Try new situations, but let your child know that you are there if he or she needs support.

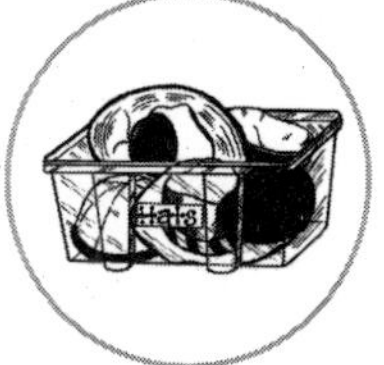

Prop Boxes

Beekeeper Prop Box
straw hat • net • gloves • boots • cardboard boxes • glue gun • plastic bees • flowers (real or plastic/silk) • yellow T-shirts • black marker • paper plates • pipe cleaner • hair band

Entomologist Prop Box
microscopes • magnifying glasses • bug boxes • small and large plastic bugs • pen set • plastic containers in a variety of sizes • petri dishes • safety goggles • white shirts (for lab coats) • clipboard • markers • pictures of insects • bugs, and scientists at work • silk and plastic flowers • bug catchers of various types • bug houses to keep captured bugs in • aluminum foil

Books

About Insects: A Guide for Children by Cathryn P. Sill
Are You an Ant? by Judy Allen
A Bad Case of Stripes by David Shannon
Bees by Gallimard Jeunesse
The Berenstain Bears and the Trouble with Friends by Jan and Stan Berenstain
Bugs! Bugs! Bugs! by Bob Barner
Bugs by Kees Moerbeek and Rodger Smith
Bugs by Nancy Winslow Parker
The Caterpillow Fight by Sam McBratney
Caterpillars, Bugs, and Butterflies by Mel Boring
Dirt and Grime, Like You've Never Seen by Vicki Cobb
Dream Tree by Stephen Cosgrove
The Eensy-Weensy Spider by Mary Ann Hoberman
The Foolish Tortoise by Richard Buckley
Friends at School by Rochelle Bunnett
Frog and Toad Are Friends by Arnold Lobel
Gotta Go! Gotta Go! by Sam Swope
The Greedy Python by Richard Buckley
The Grouchy Ladybug (La Mariquita Malhumorada) by Eric Carle
The Honey Makers by Gail Gibbons
How Do Flies Walk Upside Down?: Questions and Answers About Insects by Melvin and Gilda Berger
How to Lose All Your Friends by Nancy L. Carlson
Insects by Robin Bernard
Ladybug at Orchard Avenue by Kathleen Weidner Zoehfeld

Leo the Lightning Bug by Eric Drachman
Little Miss Spider by David Kirk
Little Miss Spider at Sunnypatch School by David Kirk
Little Miss Spider's Tea Party by David Kirk
The Little Red Ant and the Great Big Crumb by Shirley Climo
Monarch Butterfly of Aster Way by Elizabeth Ring
One Hundred Hungry Ants by Elinor J. Pinczes
A Pill Bug's Life by John Himmelman
Those Ooey-Gooey Winky Blinky but... Invisible Pinkeye Germs (Esos pringosos viscosos pestaneantes parpadeantes pero... invisibles germenes que causan conjunctivitis) by Judith Rice
Red-Eyed Tree Frog by Joy Cowley
A Remainder of One by Bonnie MacKain
The Roly Poly Spider by Jill Sardegna
Thinking About Ants by Barbara Brenner
Those Icky Sticky Smelly Cavity Causing but... Invisible Germs (Esos sucios pegajosos olorosos que causantes de caries pero... invisibles germenes) by Judith Rice
Those Itsy-Bitsy Teeny-Tiny Not-so-Nice Head Lice (Esos pequenines chiquitines para nada simpaticos piojos) by Judith Rice
Those Mean, Nasty, Downright Disgusting but... Invisible Germs (Esos deagradables detestables sucios completament asquerosos pero... invisibles germenes) by Judith Rice
The Very Busy Spider by Eric Carle
The Very Clumsy Click Beetle by Eric Carle
The Very Hungry Caterpillar (La Oruga Hambrienta, La Chenille Affammée) by Eric Carle
The Very Lonely Firefly by Eric Carle
The Very Quiet Cricket by Eric Carle
Waiting for Wings by Lois Ehlert
What's the Recipe for Friends by Greg M. Williamson
Wonderful Worms by Linda Glasser
Yikes-Lice! by Donna Caffey

Observation/Assessment

Observes using magnifying glasses, page 190
Matches shapes and colors, page 193
Creates simple patterns using shapes and colors, page 193
Dictates ideas, page 193
Dictates sentences, page 193
Uses one-to-one correspondence to 10 or 20, page 193
Adds numbers 1 to 5, then 1 to 10, page 195
Sorts insects into categories, page 195
Recites and acts out fingerplays, page 197
Makes field notes (drawings), page 199
Uses field notes to explain ideas or observations, page 199
Records observations, page 200

Picture File/Vocabulary

ant farm
ant mounds
ants
apiary
bee
beekeeper
beehive
bugs
boots
butterflies
camouflage
caterpillar
culture
entomologist
field study
firefly
germ
germ culture
gloves
hatch
honey
honeybees
laboratory
lady bugs
larvae
legs
lightning bugs
marching
matching
metamorphosis
molting
moths
museum
net
patterns
petri dish
predators
pupae
science
shapes
sneeze
spiders
tunnels
webs
wings
wiggly
worms

Concepts Learned in

Creepy Crawlies and Germs

Content Knowledge

- ☐ Beekeepers are called apiarists.
- ☐ Bees live in an apiary or beehive.
- ☐ Some bugs hide under logs, branches, rocks, etc..
- ☐ Some insects fly, and some don't.
- ☐ Bugs hatch from eggs.
- ☐ Baby bugs can look different from adult bugs.
- ☐ Caterpillars turn into moths and butterflies.
- ☐ Some insects have patterns on them.
- ☐ Insects use patterns and color to camouflage and protect themselves from predators
- ☐ Spiders spin webs.
- ☐ Webs catch insects so spiders can eat the body fluids.
- ☐ Insects can climb because their feet are made for gripping.
- ☐ Spiders crawl many different ways.
- ☐ Worms live underground.
- ☐ Worms make tunnels in the ground.
- ☐ Germs grow.
- ☐ Germs can make you sick.
- ☐ Covering a sneeze keeps you from spreading germs to others.
- ☐ Frequent handwashing keeps you from spreading your germs to others.

Process Knowledge

- ☐ I can create insects with playdough, collage materials, egg cartons, and pipe cleaners.
- ☐ I can express ideas, thoughts, or feelings through creative dramatics.
- ☐ I can move to music.
- ☐ I can collect objects to observe likenesses and differences.
- ☐ I can draw a two-dimensional image.
- ☐ I can create a three-dimensional image.

Pre-academic Knowledge

- ☐ I can count the beats of music.
- ☐ I can research my ideas to learn more.
- ☐ I can make predictions.
- ☐ I can recognize shapes in the natural environment.
- ☐ I can look at books to get information.
- ☐ I can read pictorial context clues in books.
- ☐ I am interested in print.

CHAPTER 4

Exploring Roles

INNOVATIONS IN CARE AND EARLY EDUCATION

The Importance of Cultural Context

Human development is deeply and dramatically affected by the multiple contexts in which growth and learning occur. These contexts include the interactive emotional context of the family and the social context of the community, as well as the expectations of the society in which the family lives (Bredekamp & Copple, 1997; Bronfenbrenner, 1979; Shonkoff & Phillips, 2000). Children's growth, development, and learning are all influenced by the culture of their families.

"Culture is defined as the customary beliefs and patterns of and for behavior, both explicit and implicit, that are passed on to future generations by the society in which they live and/or by social, religious, or ethic groups within it" (Bredekamp & Copple 1997, p.12). Within the context of culture, developmental and interactional theories merge with practice to facilitate each child's individual needs, competencies, abilities, and style of learning and growing.

Culture is the lens through which children, parents, and teachers see the world.

An increased understanding of culture as a mediating and influential contributor to maturation, development, and learning is one of the major modifications of the developmental viewpoint during the last decade. Educators have grown to understand that a child's culture influences many things. Prenatal care, attachment, child-rearing practices, food preferences, sleeping arrangements, peer relations, self-esteem, emotional regulation and expression, and physical, social, emotional, cognitive, and language development are all influenced by culture. These influences are a part of the child's experience and development and cannot be left out of the teacher's consideration.

Adults are a product of the cultural context they experienced during their childhood. These experiences influence how they view the world and interpret those views in the teaching role. Acknowledgment of this influence as well as the cultural context of the community in which they live allows teachers to consider multiple points of view in the teaching decision-making process (Bredekamp & Copple, 1997).

Culture influences the behavior of children, parents, and teachers. Relational styles are embedded in the cultural contexts of the child and adult and may differ dramatically from the community's dominant culture and from the culture of the school or classroom. Culture is the lens through which children, parents, and teachers see the world. Points of view vary depending on the experiences of children and adults within their families and their cultures. These points of view come to school with both children and adults and mediate and modify the experiences they have at school and in the community.

The Development of Positive Self-concept

By age three, an increasing awareness of self leads children to view their actions, interactions, and behavior as observers. This ability to watch one's own interaction and evaluate one's own "performance" is a crucial social skill that is uniquely human. It means that children can learn to anticipate the social responses and interactions of others before they occur, and choose to modify their behavior to match the situation.

This process is neither simple nor objective. Children's views of self are influenced by how they think others view them. If adults, the community, the school, and other children view them as competent, capable, or confident and communicate this view, then children are likely to see themselves as competent, capable, and confident. If adults, the community, the school, and other children view them as incompetent, incapable, or lacking in confidence, then children may see themselves similarly. So, how we see (and therefore, interact and communicate with) children directly influences their developing self-concepts.

The creation of self-concept begins at birth and continues throughout life. It is an emerging process to which children contribute actively, influencing their own development. The self-concept is constantly shaped and reshaped as we interact with the important people in our lives and experience the interactive environment.

Curry and Johnson (1990) view self-concept as the way individuals value themselves and others. Rejecting the view that self-concept is fixed or unresponsive to change, these authors conclude that acceptance, power and control, moral virtue, and competence are the lifelong issues that impact emerging self-concept. Each of these important issues requires consideration by teachers. Wardle (1995) expands on the issues that influence self-concept, describing themes that are present throughout life. Each theme is summarized in the following chart.

General Themes that Impact Self-image	
Love and Acceptance	Feeling unique, special; feeling cared for and loved; feeling like a worthwhile individual
Power and Control	Feeling in control of one's destiny; having control over some parts of one's experience
Moral Value	Feeling a sense of belonging; feeling fairly treated; feeling like a worthy person
Competence	Feeling like it is worth trying; feeling capable of accomplishing tasks and skills

Notice the emphasis on "feeling." The way we "feel" about things is often different from the way things look or the way we respond. Creating feelings of acceptance, control, value, and competence is related to but different from planning activities that encourage acceptance, control, and so on. One is external to the child (plans, activities, questions, props); the other is internal (how I evaluate and feel about those activities, plans, questions, props as I experience them). It is this internal arena that is so important to the child's emerging sense of self.

Why Is Exploring Roles Such an Important Task?

What, then, does exploring roles have to do with emerging self-concept? As children play, they take on different roles they see being used in the broader social setting. Preschool children observe roles such as mommy, daddy, friend, teacher, firefighter, police officer, sister, brother, puppy, fast runner, tricycle pedaler, helper, and many others. Then, through play, children get images of themselves as they attempt to play these roles. Children evaluate these play experiences and use their evaluations to alter their views of themselves. If the role player feels positive about the response of others to the role-playing experiences and feels successful in figuring out what to do and how to do it, the likely result is an enhancement of self-concept.

But children don't have only positive play experiences. They often have disagreements over whether others can play, what they can play with, and the possible roles they can play. How children handle negative experiences is just as important as how they handle positive ones, and also influences self-concept. If they are able to find another way to play (i.e., joining in the play as an onlooker, finding another place to play, calling to the teacher to help figure out how to play, and so on), the experience can still enhance self-concept. They will evaluate themselves as successful in finding a way to play. If, on the other hand, children feel rejected and evaluate that rejection as a valid part of their view of themselves, the experience can influence their self-concepts negatively.

Teachers have an important role to play in supporting children's views of themselves and the evaluation of those views. First, they are responsible for setting up the environment to facilitate taking on interesting and varied roles successfully (see the Dramatic Possibilities sections of the Possibilities Plans for numerous good ideas). Second, teachers are responsible for creating interactive relationships with children that give them many messages about love, acceptance, control, value, and competence—the themes that influence self-concept throughout life. Third, teachers are responsible for being observant enough to help children with limited views of self or negative evaluations of self. And, lastly, teachers are responsible for making sure that their interactions support children who are bumping up against their own or others' negative views of self.

Teachers are responsible for creating interactive relationships with children that give them many messages about love, acceptance, control, value, and competence.

Throughout the ***Innovations*** series are repeated references to the importance of the interactive environment—the way adults and children interact with each other and the messages those interactions give children. It is during the early childhood years that teachers begin to see the results of creating this warm, interactive environment and relationships as children approach exploring roles with confidence, competence, and capability.

INNOVATIONS IN INTERACTIVE EXPERIENCES

When it comes to self-concept development, children's experiences and their evaluation of themselves as participants are crucial. Teachers are always influencing a child's self-concept. Children are always influencing their own self-concepts. Positive experiences can lead to a feeling of competence and confidence. Negative experiences can lead to an integration of new ideas about how to succeed and motivation to do it differently next time. Or, negative experiences can stifle and damage the emerging view of self. Life's minutiae build to create experiences. Teachers must be attuned to these everyday, yet important, experiences. They are the foundation upon which skills and abilities grow. When teachers plan interactive experiences such as the ones that follow, children's self-concepts will have opportunities to flourish.

Interactive Experiences Checklist for Exploring Roles

Ask a mentor to observe you in your classroom to document the following interactive behaviors. Think about the following list of interactive experiences and make sure that the classroom reflects many of them.

- ☐ Support children's feelings of belonging. Make it clear that all children belong in your classroom.
- ☐ Provide understandable and consistent limits.
- ☐ Use encouragement (instead of praise) to describe completed tasks and recognize effort.
- ☐ Validate children's uniqueness, focusing on your positive feelings about their unique qualities.
- ☐ Give children opportunities to have your undivided, personal attention regularly.
- ☐ Provide lots of opportunity for choice.
- ☐ Provide opportunities for exploration, investigation, and development of new alternatives.
- ☐ Let children know that you believe they can succeed.
- ☐ Encourage children to make and keep their own rules.
- ☐ Make sure interactions are characterized by mutual respect.
- ☐ Help children handle failure by being close and recognizing effort.
- ☐ Help children persist.
- ☐ Help children cooperate and work together to accomplish things.
- ☐ Be an ally to help identify potential solutions to solving problems.
- ☐ Accept children's solutions to their own problems.
- ☐ Prevent frustration that comes from unrealistic expectations.

Provide Close Supervision and Monitoring

As teachers create interactive environments for children, the issue of safety becomes an important consideration. When a child feels physically safe and emotionally secure, she is better able to be self-responsible, exhibit self-control, and be empathetic with others. Beginning with the appreciation of all children as important members of the classroom, teachers work to establish a community of learners who feel a connection with each other. Classroom teachers cannot ensure the total absence of conflicts—nor should they try. How children work through conflicts and interact with each other is an essential part of social growth and development. Protect children by closely supervising their interactions. Set the expectation that all children can participate (though maybe not all at the same time), and protect children from being bullied or intimidated by others as they play.

Use Encouragement

Cautions about the rampant use of praise, stickers, and other examples of external motivation are included throughout early childhood literature, particularly the literature about self-concept development. External motivation prevents children from placing their own evaluations on their experiences. This, in turn, can interfere with their emerging sense of self. For example, preschool children may draw on a portion of a piece of paper and then request another. When teachers praise children's work ("Good job!") and then ask the child to draw more on the same sheet to prevent paper waste, children can be confused. If the first (limited) drawing was good, why is more drawing on the page needed?

Some early childhood educators propose that teachers reconsider their use of praise to foster self-concept and to motivate children. Instead, they suggest that teachers use encouragement (Hitz & Driscoll, 1988; Grey, 1995). Encouragement acknowledges the effort or attributes of the work without evaluation or judgment. Encouragement has the advantage of being sincere and authentic, putting teachers in the role of honestly responding to children's experiences and efforts. The following guidelines support the use of encouragement instead of praise.

Guidelines for Using Ecouragement

Be specific.	"Your painting has many bright colors in it." "Your construction is built with lots of different shapes of blocks." "You pulled your friend in the wagon all over the playground." "You chose one of my favorite books to read."
Encourage individually and privately.	"You were able to find all the different pieces to the puzzle, Caitlin." "All of the Duplos™ are in your construction!"
Focus on effort, improvement, and progress rather than products or outcomes.	"You made it closer to the gate on the scooter." "You finished gluing all the feathers on your duck." "You built with 20 of the Duplo™ blocks. Last time you built with 14."
Be sincere and authentic.	"You worked hard on that." "You kept working until you finished everything."
Help children see their successes.	"Your tower is three feet tall." "You set the table for us to have lunch." "You put on the costume all by yourself."
Help children appreciate their own achievements.	"You are able to jump all the way out the door!" "You helped clean up the snack table." "You helped her feel better."
Avoid comparisons and competition.	"You are ready to go on our field trip." "You finished cleaning up all the pieces of paper."

Use a Variety of Teaching Roles

Teachers use a wide variety of roles in their work with young children. During the developmental task of Exploring Roles, three of the most important teacher roles are play partner, model, and director. These roles have specific characteristics during this developmental task.

The Teacher as Play Partner

Vygotsky's socio-cultural theory validates the importance of adults as play partners for children (Berk & Winsler, 1995, see page 121). The teacher is in a unique position to partner with children as they play.

Teachers are the most interesting element in any classroom. No matter where the teacher is physically in the classroom, it is usually a popular place to be. Children often choose teachers as play partners. Teachers are able to enhance play by providing props and ideas, extending play, and scaffolding play ideas that would be too difficult for the child without support. Make playing with children a regular part of your teaching.

The Teacher as Model

Children learn from watching, modeling, and imitating others. From this initial play, more complex play often emerges. Teachers show children how to use complex social skills such as entering a playgroup or getting a desired toy and support attempts to try out the new skills. With the teacher's help, practicing these new skills might be possible.

As you model for children, it is important to do what you want children to do. If you want children to sit on the floor or in chairs instead of on tables or furniture, then sit on chairs and the floor yourself. If you want children to keep their belongings in their cubbies, always put your belongings in your cubby. Modeling appropriate behavior is an important teaching role. Children are intensely interested in the behaviors of adults. As children observe how teachers play and interact, they see behaviors they can try themselves.

The Teacher as Director

Teachers direct a large amount of a young child's life, telling children what to do, where to go, and when things will happen. The type of direction meant here is that of play director. Teachers create stages for play—providing props, play cues, and materials that children can incorporate into their play. Sometimes these props are tied to play themes that children enjoy revisiting often in play, such as mommy, daddy, or baby. Sometimes they are tied to emerging interests in things (for example, trucks or animals). Other times they are tied to new experiences, such as going to get a haircut or watching a play at the children's theatre. Teachers also direct children to fill roles that are challenging yet rewarding.

As teachers help children explore roles, they create an environment that supports children's explorations. Adding materials, especially props, to the classroom creates interest and variety for children's early role-playing experiences. Change materials regularly to refresh the classroom setting.

Teachers in the director role must be cautious to support but not to dominate the child's play. Scaffolding play, by adding to children's ideas, asking interesting and thought-provoking questions, and playing roles assigned by children are appropriate. Telling children what to play or how to play isn't.

INNOVATIONS IN TEACHING

Theoretical knowledge leads to best practices. Understanding the socio-cultural context and self-concept guides teachers to implement multicultural practices, facilitate self-concept development, teach children to use pro-social behaviors, create and support role exploration, and expand role exploration with field trips that include families.

Implement Multicultural Practices

Children (and adults) learn within their own cultures. Examine your own cultural background and how it impacts your view of early childhood education and your teaching role. Look carefully at all of the components of your classroom for subtle and unintended messages of discrimination, separation, isolation, or biased images, ideas, toys, books, materials, and so on. Be certain every child in your classroom can see herself in the images in the classroom. Also, be sure that children from other cultures are represented.

Read more about the impact of culture on early childhood programs, such as *The Anti-Bias Curriculum: Tools for Empowering Young Children* by Louise Derman-Sparks and *Alike and Different: Exploring Our Humanity with Children* by Bonnie Neugebauer. Ask yourself, What makes my particular classroom unique? How do I welcome all families into my classroom? When families join your school community, find out about their unique cultural background and experiences. Consider collecting this information on all families, finding out if they can teach a skill, share a hobby, food, a cultural artifact, experience, oral history, or celebration with the children in the class or school. Sharing information about cultural backgrounds early in the new relationships supports families as they join in and try to find positive ways to contribute to their child's school experience.

Facilitate Positive Self-Concept

Make sure that your interactions support children who are bumping up against their own or others' negative views of self. Because young children are still learning to modify their behavior to fit the situation and to understand the impact of their behavior on others, they need help when things don't work out. When they don't get to play, when they're not first, when someone else chooses the bike they wanted to ride— opportunities for teachers to influence self-concept are created. In the process of social problem solving, teachers help children convert an experience that could be evaluated as negative into one that recognizes a new skill is being tried out or learned. (To learn more about social problem solving, see page 135). For example, teachers provide support for children as they narrate situations in the classroom. Instead of viewing not getting to play, not being first, or not getting a favorite bike as negative, the teacher can show a child that these situations are opportunities to learn new things and try different experiences.

Teach Children to Use Prosocial Behaviors

Prosocial behaviors are those that precede and lead to successful social interactions. When teachers are supporting social skill development, they are often modeling, teaching, validating, and supporting prosocial behaviors that will predict success in future social situations. Teachers serve as important role models. Their actions must coincide with the expectations they have for children. For example, if teachers expect children to touch each other softly or to respect each other's personal space, then they must model these social behaviors for children by touching children softly and requesting permission to look into a child's cubby.

Teachers actively create the social climate of the classroom. They start by anticipating needs, so children can get their needs met with certainty. They continue by getting to know individual cues and by validating that verbal and non-verbal cues were received and understood. Additionally, the teacher helps children solve social problems by learning new skills, including waiting a moment, trading, taking turns, and making plans.

The teacher's most important role in prosocial behavior is supporting interactions between children—helping them to interact successfully. Being close to where children are in the classroom helps facilitate social interaction. With the teacher nearby, children are able to try new experiences, knowing help and support are close at hand.

Create Opportunities to Explore Roles

Dramatic play is the area that is most conducive to supporting the exploration of roles, but children also play roles on the playground, through movement and music, and with their artistic creations. Dramatic play themes usually start close to home with the roles children see their significant others filling. Then, themes move on to the roles that interest children, frequently based on their experiences. Going grocery shopping, to the shoe store, to the doctor or hospital, and to Mommy or Daddy's work setting provides children with rich opportunities to explore roles. These interests are usually followed by preferences for types of materials, types of play, or types of roles. Truck driver, hairstylist, and dance teacher all become interesting as children are exposed or introduced to these people in the course of experience.

Creating and using prop boxes gives teachers the play props children need and the ability to change the dramatic play areas to create a wide variety of roles for children to explore. When boxes are prepared and available, they can be pulled out to enhance, support, and scaffold children's play as needed.

Support Children's Role Exploration

It is not the aim of the preschool teacher to treat every child the same.

Relationships form the core of curriculum during the preschool years. Teachers enhance children's self-concept by maintaining close connections to them and supporting them as they begin to evaluate themselves and their actions.

Central to this connection is an understanding of children's uniqueness and individuality. It is not the aim of the preschool teacher to treat every child the same. Some children need the teacher very close to try new roles whereas others can pick up a prop and explore a role without much more than a smile from the teacher. Figuring out these differences is part of the observation/assessment job of the teacher.

Teachers may want to look at their curriculum plans for chances to provide children with messages about love, acceptance, control, value, and competence, the themes that influence self-concept throughout life. Exposing and validating these messages is important curriculum and an important teaching skill.

Expand Role Exploration with Field Trips

Field trips broaden children's view of the world, incorporating experiences that are new and exciting. Field trips develop children's observation skills; reinforce children's prior knowledge about the neighborhood or community; help children practice planning, prediction, and sequencing skills; and create a sense of shared community. Additionally, field trips invite firsthand experiences and creative expression/representation of experiences in different media.

Suggestions for Field Trips

- Bakery
- Bookstore
- Bank
- Construction site
- Deli
- Department store
- Dentist's office
- Doctor's office
- Farm
- Farmer's market
- Florist
- Fire station
- Garden center
- Grocery store
- Gym or fitness center
- Hairdresser
- Hardware store
- Ice-cream parlor
- Library
- Neighborhood elementary school
- Pet shop
- Pizzeria
- Police station
- Post office
- Radio station
- Restaurant
- Television station
- Shoe repair shop
- Tailor
- Veterinarian's office

Include Families in Field Trips

Family involvement is an important aspect of any early childhood program. Planning for this involvement is part of curriculum planning. Teachers can invite parents to participate in their child's education by participating in field trips in any number of ways. Volunteers may choose specific helping roles, such as arranging activities with the destination; communicating with other parents; planning transportation, meals, and snacks; accompanying the class on the field trip; taking photographs/videos; and sending thank-you notes.

Plan an orientation session to let families know the expectations you have for children and for them concerning field trips. Communicate the time commitment that is required, so parents can make adequate arrangements. Provide clear limits for children by putting the limits in writing and reviewing them at orientation. Participating in field trips can be a wonderful learning experience for families.

Field Trip Planning

Why do some teachers regularly schedule field trips while others may have only one (or even none) in the period of a year? Field trips can be added work for the teacher and added worry and liability for the school. Early childhood professionals are committed to providing young children with real, hands-on learning experiences that allow them to question, explore, and discover. Field trips are an excellent way to accomplish this.

The most meaningful field trips are often ones that result from a question or concern that surfaces in the classroom. Children may wonder where the trash goes, how they get clean water to drink in the classroom, what makes a car go, where the rain water goes, and so on. These all make for perfect field trips based on inquiry.

After determining possible destinations, call to see if the field trip is a possibility. If so, obtain dates and collaborate with the staff at the destination to see what kinds of services are available. (Some field trips may be more basic, for example, a walking field trip to observe site preparation for a new building. However, these basic field trips still require planning.) At any step in the planning process, you may want to involve families.

After gathering this information, put the event on the calendar. Then call the field trip destination back to confirm. Besides the specific details concerning the field trip, you will need to plan pre-trip activities, en route activities, and follow-up activities. The value of a field trip experience rests on how well you are able to integrate it into the educational experience of the classroom. Field trip safety considerations are crucial. Review all regulatory requirements, so all the details will be arranged.

Teacher Competencies to Support the Developmental Task of Exploring Roles

Sometimes	Usually	Always	
☐	☐	☐	Does not treat every child the same—bases interactions and teaching on understanding of each child's developmental age and stage, as well as the child's uniqueness.
☐	☐	☐	Supports children's feelings of belonging—all children belong in the classroom.
☐	☐	☐	Uses encouragement (instead of praise) to describe completed tasks.
☐	☐	☐	Validates children's uniqueness, focusing on positive feelings about their unique qualities.
☐	☐	☐	Provides opportunities for exploration, investigation, and development of new alternatives.
☐	☐	☐	Helps children handle failure by being close and recognizing effort.
☐	☐	☐	Is an ally to help identify potential solutions to solving problems.
☐	☐	☐	Recognizes and supports developmental tasks in the classroom
☐	☐	☐	Plans field trips that support learning in the classroom.

Competencies for the Teaching Role of Partner

Sometimes	Usually	Always	
☐	☐	☐	Shows support for parents as primary educators by developing a partnership of respect, information exchange, and collaboration.
☐	☐	☐	Finds many different ways for family members to be involved in the school experience of the child.
☐	☐	☐	Recognizes and acknowledges the unique contributions that parents make to their child's developmental progress.

Competencies for the Teaching Role of Model

Sometimes	Usually	Always	
☐	☐	☐	Recognizes, accepts, and celebrates cultural similarities and differences.
☐	☐	☐	Assures that interactions in the classroom are characterized by mutual respect.
☐	☐	☐	Serves as a partner to introduce new play themes.

Competencies for the Teaching Role of Director

Sometimes	Usually	Always	
☐	☐	☐	Creates stages for play by equipping activity areas with appropriate props and play supports.
☐	☐	☐	Provides props, play cues, and materials that children can incorporate into their play.
☐	☐	☐	Directs children to fill roles that are challenging and rewarding.

INNOVATIONS IN OBSERVATION/ASSESSMENT

Observation/Assessment for the Task of Exploring Roles

During the developmental task of Exploring Roles, observation and assessment are directed at understanding children's role explorations in the following areas:

- the child's view of herself, and
- the child's prosocial skills.

Observation emerges once again as a crucial teaching skill. In this case, teachers are observing to see when they might need to help children with experiences that challenge the child's view of self. When a child has a limited view of the roles she can play, or negatively evaluates a role-playing experience, observant teachers step in. Their goal is to help the child understand what is happening and learn from the experience.

For example, entering a playgroup is often difficult for young children. Some children stand back and watch until others notice them and invite them in. Other children jump in the middle and try to take over. One child might find a similar toy and begin to play beside the other players. Another child might complain, "They won't let me play." Each of these responses offers teachers an opportunity to help children learn.

The observant teacher might help the "watchers" to use appropriate language to ask if they can play and support them if the answer is no. The teacher might help the "jumpers" see how others feel about their intrusion into their play and explore other ways to join in. The teacher might help the parallel player offer the additional toy to the players as a way to join in. The teacher might stay close to the complaining child to help her see that a different approach might be worth a try. All of these examples show how dynamic the role of the teacher is in supporting children's exploration of roles and emerging self-concepts.

Additionally, teachers can observe children for progress in the development of prosocial behaviors. Are children able to touch each other softly? Do they respect each other's personal space? When teachers first identify appropriate behaviors, model appropriate responses, and then observe children's behaviors to see where children are in their development, they are better able to support children's progress in role exploration.

Add to Individual Portfolios to Highlight the Developmental Task of Exploring Roles

Consider the following as potential entries to one or more children's portfolios:

- List of child's favorite play roles
- Photos of children playing various roles
- Memory book from a field trip
- Photographs from cultural sharing experiences by families
- Play-partner chart (see below for example) and how play partners changed over time

Play Partner Chart

Dramatic Possibilities

10/15/04
10:15-11:05am

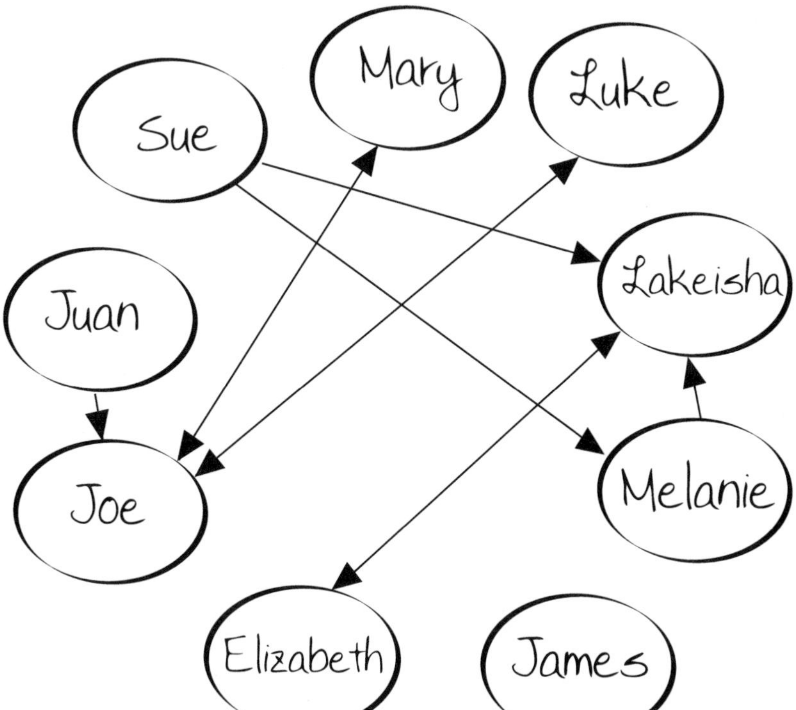

Mary
Luke
Sue
Lakeisha
Juan
Joe
Melanie
Elizabeth
James

Lakeisha and Elizabeth set up housekeeping with dishes and dolls. Melanie joined them. Sue asked Lakeisha if she could play.

Juan, Joe, Mary, and Luke joined together to play the puppies in the house.

James asked if he could be a puppy. Everyone said no.

INNOVATIONS IN FAMILY PARTNERSHIPS

Encourage Family Participation

Parents are their child's first and most important teachers. For this reason, their participation in their child's educational experience is crucial. Suggestions for participation by family members are listed here, as well as in the Possibilities Plans. By developing relationships with parents and other family members, you will be better able to support their children's development in the classroom.

Anecdotal Note Calendar: Families love to hear news about what their child experiences and accomplishes. For this activity, use calendars with plenty of space for writing. Calendars may be bought, created with computer programs, or drawn. The anecdotal comments on the calendar make a wonderful gift for birthdays or when children move away or graduate. Decorate calendars using photographs you have taken of children.

Family Members' Clothing: Create connections with family members during the day by using their discarded clothing in dramatic play. Ask parents for clothing that their child will associate with them. Let family members know how the clothing will be used. Label each piece of clothing with the parent's name. Talk about the child's family members as the child dresses in the clothing.

Invitation for Families to Participate: Invite family members to come to school to share their work roles.

Share Parent Postcards

Share Parent Postcards with parents or other family members as they indicate an interest; at appropriate times during the enrollment cycle; or as developmental issues arise. Copy Postcards, and cut if necessary. Address them and place them on the Communication Log, or hand them out personally.

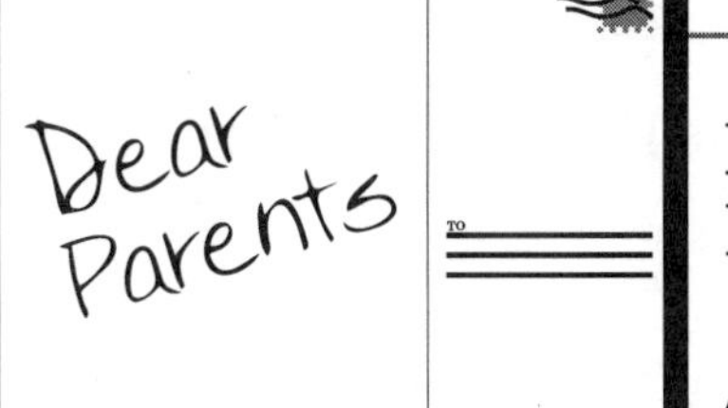

How Parents Support Exploring Roles

A child's positive view of self emerges as a result of interactions with other children and adults. When a child has a limited view of the roles he or she can play or negatively evaluates a role-playing experience, as an observant parent, you can step in. Your goal is to help your child understand what is happening and learn from the experience.

For example, entering a playgroup (at home, at a family gathering, in the park, at school) is often difficult for preschoolers. Some preschoolers stand back and watch until others notice them and invite them in. Others jump in the middle and try to take over. Another might find a similar toy and begin to play beside the other players. Another might begin to cry and wail, "They won't let me play." Each of these responses is an opportunity to help your child learn.

You might help the "watcher" to use words to ask if he or she can play. "Ask her if you can play." Of course, you also need to be there to support your child if the answer is "no" by reminding your child that he or she can try again later. If your child "jumps" into play, you might help him or her see how others might feel about the intrusion into their play, as well as explore other ways to join in. "Those faces tell me your friends didn't like that. What would happen if you…?" You might help the parallel player offer a toy to others as a way to join in. You might stay close to the crying child to help him or her see that crying isn't working, but words might be worth a try. "Tears don't seem to be getting you anywhere. What else can you try? Try these words…" All of these examples show how dynamic your role can be in supporting your child's exploration of roles and his or her emerging self-concept.

Facilitating a Positive Self-concept for Your Child

Because your preschooler is still learning to modify his or her behavior to fit the situation and to understand the impact of that behavior on the feelings of others, he or she will need help when things don't work out. When your child doesn't get to play, when he or she is not first, when someone else chooses the tricycle he or she wanted to ride—each of these examples creates opportunities for you to help your child learn new social skills.

As your child learns to interact in new ways, you are his or her support. A look, a pat, a word of encouragement—all let your preschooler know that you are there and that you know he or she can be successful. Your acceptance and love contribute to your child's emerging sense of self and clearly communicate that your child's place close to you is secure.

Participating in Field Trips with Your Child

Accompanying your child on a field trip is a wonderful way for you to support your child's school experience. If you are unable to schedule the time to actually go on the field trip, show your support in other ways. You may volunteer your time on the phone committee, make sandwiches, or write thank-you notes. All parents can support their child's excitement by talking about the trip, asking good open-ended questions, and showing that school events are important.

Resource for Families

Add this helpful book to your family library or post the title on your family bulletin board.

Glenn, H. & J. Nelsen. (1998). ***Raising self-reliant children in a self-indulgent world.*** Rocklin, CA: Prima Publishing.

INNOVATIONS IN ENVIRONMENTS

Create Multicultural, Bias-free Classrooms

Teachers must understand the contributions of their own culture and ethnicity to their personal teaching style, parent relations, and biases. We are all products of culture. Make the classroom a place where both your culture, as well as the cultures of the families of children in your classroom, are shared and appreciated.

One way to create multicultural and bias-free classrooms is to include diverse images of children in your classroom. Photographs of the children and their families are important ways for children to connect with their families during the day. Additionally, include images that reflect the children in your classroom from posters, books, and magazines. Avoid pictures that are cartoon-like or that show children as having the same features with different skin tones.

Add Diverse Cultural and Anti-bias Props to Activity Areas

Use the information you gather from families about their unique cultural heritages to enhance and enrich activity areas with specific multicultural and anti-bias props and materials.

In Dramatic Possibilities, include items such as:

- Clothing worn by both genders and all ages;
- Props used by people of differing abilities and all ages, such as crutches, eye glasses (unbreakable), braces, and so on;

- Cooking and eating props that reflect a variety of cultures; and
- A balance of dolls of both genders and all ages (particularly those from the cultures represented in the school, including dolls with differing abilities).

Don't forget to add photographs of children playing in Dramatic Possibilities with various props and interactive experiences that show diversity.

In Art Possibilities, include items such as:

- Shades of paint (tempera, watercolors, fingerpaint) and other media (chalk, colored pencils, markers) that represent the diversity of skin colors;
- Unbreakable mirrors for children to view themselves as they record their own images in their artwork;
- Artwork completed by both genders depicting people of many cultures; and
- Dolls, puppets, and props of people of various ages.

In the Literacy/Writing Possibilities, include items such as:

- Printed materials (photographs, posters, books, newspapers, etc) that reflect the racial and cultural groups of children and adults in the program as well as others in the community;
- Printed materials with a balance of genders, ages, and racial, ethnic, and cultural differences and similarities;
- Books and magazines with varied family groupings including single-parent families of both genders, two-parent families, extended families, bi-racial families, and family members of all ages and differing abilities;
- Printed materials that reflect different occupations;
- Printed materials that reflect varied family celebrations and lifestyles; and
- Printed materials that reflect different languages, including Braille, sign, and the written and spoken languages of the children, families, and staff of the school.

In Music/Movement Possibilities, include items such as:

- Songs/recordings that reflect various types of cultural music, including children's music;
- Music played by both males and females;
- Dances that reflect cultural connections of children in the classroom and the community;
- Games that reflect various cultures; and
- Music that reflects the home languages of children in the class and the community.

The best source of many of these materials, and a good way to help families understand the importance of multicultural, anti-bias experiences and materials, is to include the entire community of the school and the neighborhood in the collection and addition of resources. When families share cultural experiences at school and offer their own cultural artifacts for sharing or use, the understanding of similarities and differences is broadened and enhanced.

Provide a Variety of Play Cues and Play Props

The play cues and props that are part of the environment invite children to play. When classrooms are full of play cues and props that lead to appropriate, exploratory play, children are able to look at an activity, area, or planned experience, and figure out what to do and where to get started.

Creating an environment that stimulates play is one of the teacher's most important roles, as the stage manager, costume designer, orchestra conductor, and set designer. When all of these elements of the environment are planned, children can find many varied and interesting places to play, both alone and with their friends.

Both over-stimulation and under-stimulation are issues in school settings. Over-stimulation can occur from too much noise, light, color, activity, or too many instructions. Under-stimulation can occur from too few interactive experiences, physical isolation, or too few toys and materials in the environment.

Play cues or invitations come from many sources. The first and best source of play cues is you. A teacher who plays a role in Dramatic Possibilities sends out exciting and enticing invitations. Called triangulation, this strategy for inviting play and interactions is an excellent way to initiate interactions and to interest children in new materials or props.

The second source of play cues or stimulation is color. Graphics, photographs, and pictures from the Picture File lists (included for each Possibilities Plan), and colorful toys all interest preschoolers. But, color also can be overwhelming. Children benefit from color in the toys they play with and colors worn by the children and adults in the environment. They need soothing, neutral colors to serve as the backdrop. Avoid adding color in bold swatches to the walls and floors of the classroom. This will help insure that the stimulation comes from child-directed and -initiated activity and not from the background (Cherry, 1976).

The third source of play cues is the way toys are displayed. Make toys available where children are in the classroom, on low shelves, in clear plastic containers, in baskets, on trays, and in tubs. Separate toys on shelves, so children can consider each type of toy. Label shelves and containers with a picture of the toy or object and with the name printed in lowercase letters.

Preschoolers are developing their ability to explore roles as they play. Toys that are real items from the child's world (purses, wallets, pots, pans, clothes, shoes, hats) are important supports for beginning role-play efforts. Provide duplicate items, so more than one child can play.

Dramatic Possibilities is a natural area to support emerging literacy skills. Add plenty of food containers with labels, paper to write grocery lists, and pencils, markers, or crayons. When children are pursuing various play themes, support their play by adding the natural reading and writing supplies that a person in that role might need. When the props are tied to the role, such as blueprints and construction plans for architects and contractors, or prescription pads and charts for physicians, play becomes practice in using literacy skills. Props like these allow children to represent their ideas by drawing or writing them down. As they use functional language for the role, children expand vocabulary to include the words that support the roles they are playing.

When children lose interest in the props and play cues in an area, they will let you know. They won't go there to play. This indicates that it is time to change materials to add interest, change the roles that are being explored, or supplement the area with additional props and play cues.

Dramatic Possibilities

In Dramatic Possibilities, children develop communication skills, learn to be both leaders and followers, practice cooperation skills, and play out the roles that interest them. This area encourages play that truly emerges from children's lives, homes, and cultural context. It is one of the most spontaneous and natural of play settings in the preschool classroom, where children are free to play, feel, and act on their ideas and interests.

Children need dramatic play spaces and props that allow them to continue to express the complete range of emotions they feel—not just the positive ones. They need to practice acting out anger, fear, hostility, and eagerness, as well as empathy, altruism, curiosity, and so on, in acceptable ways that do not cause conflict. They practice the roles they see adults using in the real world. They also begin to separate what is real from what isn't and understand when and how to switch from fantasy to reality.

Teachers who foster Dramatic Possibilities plan exciting, interesting, and changing dramatic play centers. They play along with children as they act out these experiences, facilitating and enhancing the experience. And, they spend lots of time observing children as they play, watching for emerging interests, new abilities being practiced or tried out, and ideas about what play themes they can expand or support.

In addition to the supplies and materials listed on page 236, a well-stocked Dramatic Possibilities area will have the following supplies and equipment. You will not put all items out at the same time, but keep them accessible to enhance children's dramatic play.

- Kitchen utensils, pots, pans, food sets, dishes, spoons for cooking, utensils for the table, cleaning supplies such as brooms, mops, dust pans, and spray bottles, measuring cups, bowls, spatulas, cookie sheets, and so on;
- Photographs of children playing with various props and creating dramatic roles—particularly the photos of your children in Dramatic Possibilities;
- Child-sized dramatic play furniture that is similar to the furniture in the rooms of children's houses, including kitchen equipment such as stoves, refrigerators, sinks, cupboards, kitchen tables and chairs, etc., bedroom furniture such as baby beds, strollers, and storage for clothes), telephones, computers, radios, or CD players;

- Storage units for displaying dramatic play props;
- Puppets (of both genders, of various ages, cultures, and abilities) displayed on stands; and
- Props to support emerging literacy such as books, tablets, note pads, pens, pencils, and markers, and play props to match roles such as order forms for flowers in the florist shop or dental x-rays in the dentist's office.

Curriculum Resources

The Resources section that accompanies each Possibilities Plan provides additional sources for help in planning. Because the classroom environment is an important part of curriculum, suggested prop box materials and picture file/vocabulary lists are provided for each Possibilities Plan. These resources enrich Dramatic Possibilities and expand children's ideas about where to start and what to play.

Prop Boxes: Creating and using prop boxes gives children the play props they need in Dramatic Possibilities and other activity areas. It also gives teachers the ability to change the dramatic play area to create a wide variety of roles for children to explore.

A real advantage to prop boxes is that teachers are able to build their curriculum resources over time. Start with a few popular play themes, and create prop boxes to support these. Themes such as grocery store, construction, firefighters, restaurant, and travel are a good place to start. Every Possibilities Plan in the ***Innovations*** series provides a list of items for prop boxes that support the different plans.

Use a uniform method for compiling and storing materials. Copy paper boxes work well as do sturdy plastic bins. Label the containers on the ends and top. Then place a list of the contents on the lid, so you can return materials to the correct box when it is time to store them. As you plan your curriculum, include plans for adding to your growing wealth of prop boxes. This will increase your different curriculum options to enrich children's play.

Picture File/Vocabulary List: Each plan has a Picture File/Vocabulary List. Preschoolers are building cognitive images of the things they are experiencing. Using pictures helps give children a variety of different images. It also adds information to the images that they have already experienced. In addition, it is an inexpensive teaching tool that should be part of every teacher's resources.

Collect pictures from a variety of sources, including magazines, calendars, and so on. Look for pictures that show one image clearly. Laminate them or cover with clear contact paper to make them more durable, and store them in file folders or boxes by category. You might start with categories that match the Possibilities Plans topics, such as Saying Hello, Castles, and Making Messes. Then, as categories become filled with pictures, separate them into smaller categories. For example, in Castles, divide pictures into outside castles, inside castles, people in castles, and so on. Eventually, your picture file collection will become filled with images to assist you in presenting diverse and interesting mental images to enhance, challenge, and inform children's play.

Your picture file collection will become filled with images to assist you in presenting diverse and interesting mental images to enhance, challenge, and inform children's play.

Don't forget photographs. Photos of the children in your group now, children in your last group, and other children you know are wonderful additions to picture files. Never throw away a good photo; add it to your picture file.

There are many uses for the pictures in your file. The first is to provide interesting additions to the environment. Post laminated pictures at eye level for children to see. Put collections of pictures in the Possibilities areas (for example, pictures of food in the Dramatic Possibilities during Where Does It Come From? and Where Does It Go?).

Second, help children create connections between pictures and vocabulary by labeling the pictures. Start with one label (such as Daddy), and then expand your labeling (Kaylee's daddy, Miguel's daddy). When you relate a picture to a child's experience in this way, connections between the image, the vocabulary, and the child's experience are made. These connections form the foundation for additional information. The next time you talk about daddies, you can move on to what daddies do or where daddies work. Over time, children will look at a picture of a daddy and connect it to ideas and images of their daddy, then to where their daddy works and what their daddy does, all on their own. Next, extend vocabulary further by adding other ways to label Daddy, such as Papa and Padre, which will expand the image and connections even further while validating home languages.

Third, use pictures to celebrate diversity. Images that are familiar—such as pictures of other people who look like me as well as others that don't look like me—celebrate the diversity of the human experience. Work hard to make your picture files reflect images of the children in your group as well as those that aren't. Both are important and enriching.

Fourth, use pictures to teach. When you want to extend a child's knowledge with mental images, use pictures. For example, when a child is interested in dogs, pull out all of the pictures of dogs. Add pictures from your file to the library shelf, so children can "read" pictures as well as books.

References

Berk, L.E. & A. Winsler. (1995). ***Scaffolding children's learning***. Washington, DC: National Association for the Education of Young Children (NAEYC).

Bredekamp, C. & C. Copple. (1997). ***Developmentally appropriate practice in early childhood programs, Revised edition***. Washington, DC: National Association for the Education of Young Children (NAEYC).

Bronfenbrenner, U. (1979). ***The ecology of human development: Experiments by nature and design***. Cambridge, MA: Harvard University Press.

Cherry, C. (1976). ***Creative play for the developing child: Early childhood education through play***. Belmont, CA: Fearon.

Curry, N.E. & C.N. Johnson. (1990). ***Beyond self-esteem: Developing a genuine sense of human value.*** Washington, DC: National Association for the Education of Young Children (NAEYC).

Grey, K. (1995). Not in praise of praise. ***Child Care Information Exchange***, 104, 56-59.

Hitz, R. & A. Driscoll. (1988). Praise or encouragement? New insights and implications for early childhood teachers. ***Young Children***, 43(5): 6-13.

National Association for the Education of Young Children (NAEYC). (1996). Responding to linguistic and cultural diversity: Recommendations for effective early childhood education. ***Young Children***, 51 (2): 4-12.

Shonkoff, J.P. & D.A. Phillips (Eds.). (2000). ***From neurons to neighborhoods: The science of early childhood development***. Washington, DC: National Academy Press.

Wardle, F. (1995). How young children build images of themselves. ***Child Care Information Exchange***, 104, 44-47.

Resources for Teachers

Barbour, A. & B. Desjean-Perrotta. (2002). ***Prop box play: 50 themes to inspire dramatic play***. Beltsville, MD: Gryphon House.

Boutte, G.S. (1999). ***Multicultural education: Raising consciousness***. Atlanta: Wadsworth.

Child Care Information Exchange. (2001). Beginnings Workshop: Field trip stories and perspectives. ***Child Care Information Exchange***, 139, 39-58.

Derman-Sparks, L. (1989). ***Anti-bias Curriculum: Tools for empowering young children***. Washington, DC: National Association for the Education of Young Children.

Kohl, M.F. (1999). ***Making make-believe***. Beltsville, MD: Gryphon House.

Neugebauer, B. (1992). ***Alike and different: Exploring our humanity with children***. Washington, DC: National Association for the Education of Young Children (NAEYC).

Possibilities Plan—
Maps

Getting Ready to Plan

As preschoolers become more and more proficient at doing things on their own, they begin to understand concepts associated with playing roles and travel. In this Possibilities Plan, children will explore many different types of maps and also have opportunities to go on field trips connected with various roles.

The purpose of Getting Ready to Plan is to support the planning process with a general overview of the content of this Possibilities Plan. Now is the time to think about what you want the children in your group to learn about each of these topics explored in general below:

Maps: The concept of maps can be a difficult one for preschool children, so start simple. First, talk about things children are familiar with, such as what their house or apartment looks like and what school looks like. Then talk about how to get from one place to the other and show this on a map. Because maps are representational, provide as many concrete experiences as possible to get the concept across. Begin with neighborhood maps before expanding to state or national maps.

Travel: Most children are familiar with travel in one form or another. Children travel from home to school, but people can also travel far away to different destinations. Support children's play by providing information about traveling to places of interest.

Field Trips: When a child goes on a field trip, she is able to experience something new firsthand. Preschoolers are especially interested in field trips because they are developing a sense of independence and competence. Plan field trips that are a natural extension of classroom inquiry, or use children's curiosity as opportunities for learning.

Exploring Roles: As children play, they take on roles they see being used in the broader social setting. From initial roles involving family members, children progress to more varied and imaginative roles. They get images of themselves as they attempt to play these roles. Children evaluate their play experiences and alter their views of themselves as they play. Exploring roles can be an important part of self-concept. With the support of teachers who help interpret children's experiences, they can learn to view themselves as competent, capable, and successful. Plan for children to explore many roles that support viewing their play experiences as successful.

Now that you have an idea about the general content of the Possibilities Plan, you are ready to proceed with developing your own Plan. This section of Getting Ready to Plan identifies resources you may want to buy, collect, or locate to implement your plan.

Toys and Materials*

Purchased

- 10' to 12' piece of lumber
- airplanes
- black paper
- blocks
- butcher paper on roll
- cars
- charts
- coins of different types
- colored pencils
- construction paper
- glue
- glue sticks
- hole punch
- index cards
- Liquid Watercolor paints
- magnetic alphabet letters
- magnifying glasses
- markers
- pens
- people figures
- permanent markers
- pin
- scissors
- sentence strips
- small unit blocks
- stickers
- tape
- toy buildings
- toy sea creatures
- train set
- trucks
- variety of art and collage materials
- white cloth
- white drawing paper

Gathered

- backpacks
- bandanas
- bar magnet
- basket
- bike
- binoculars
- bowls for categorizing
- broomstick
- cameras
- camp kit (metal dishes, and so on)
- cardboard boxes
- chairs
- clear contact paper or laminating film
- clothes
- coins of different types
- compass
- containers
- cotton swabs
- crayons
- duct tape
- eye patches
- fishing pole
- flags
- flashlights
- gemstone pebbles
- hats
- hiking boots
- jewels
- large needle
- large paper world map
- large tub
- maps of campgrounds
- maps of the state divided into counties or other divisions
- marbles
- muffin tins
- nature items
- necklaces
- neighborhood map or neighborhood rug
- oars
- paints
- paper clips
- pictures of each child's and teacher's house/apartment
- pictures of pirates and ships
- picture of your school
- pole
- postcards
- sand
- scented potpourri
- small cork
- shallow pan
- sleeping bags
- state maps with counties
- stones
- straw hats
- suitcases
- sunglasses
- swimsuits
- telescope
- tent
- tickets, different kinds
- traffic sign pictures
- treasure box
- vacation posters and brochures
- water can
- yarn

*Note: Please consider the ages and abilities of the children in your classroom. Use only safe, non-toxic materials.

Maps

WEB

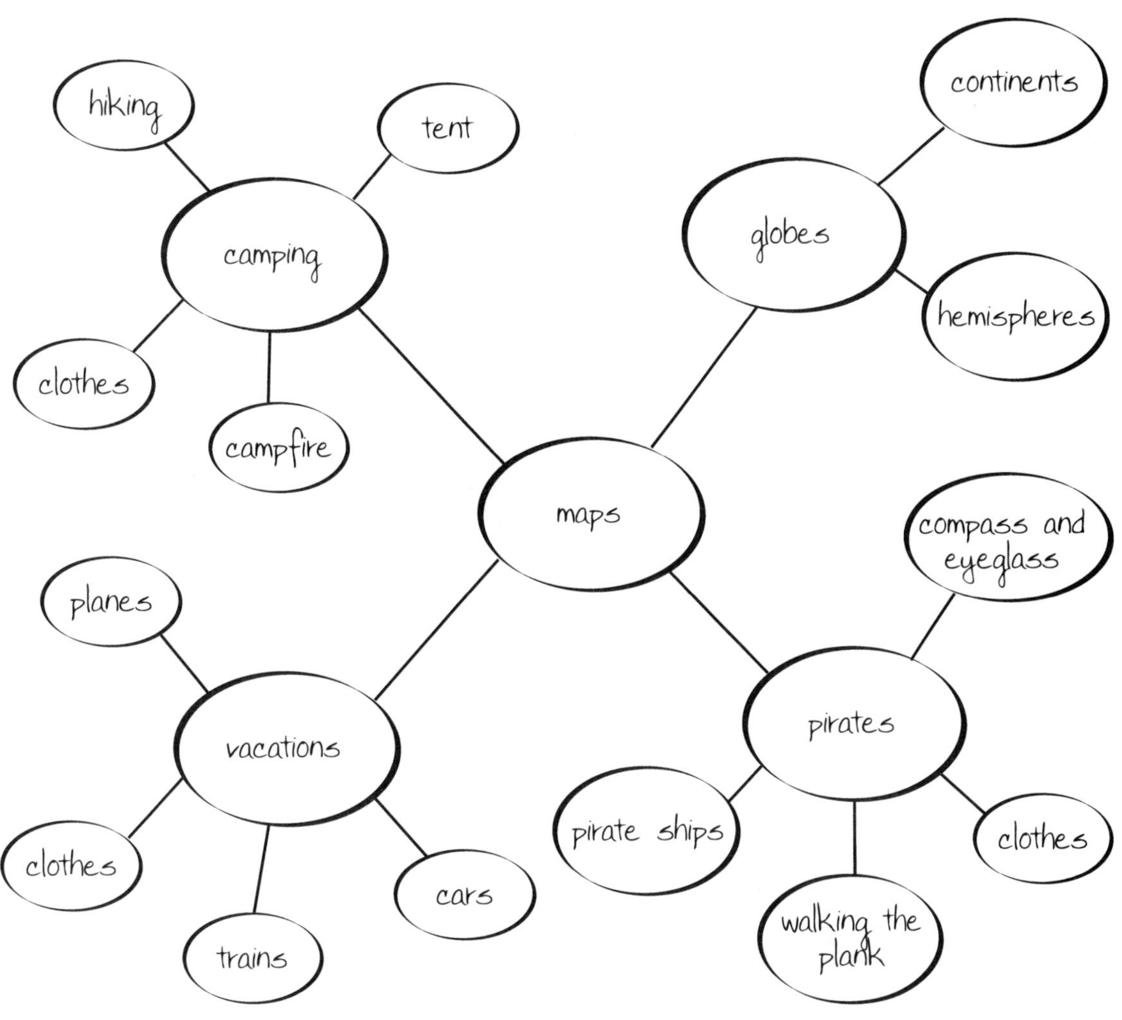
hiking
tent
continents
camping
globes
hemispheres
clothes
campfire
maps
compass and eyeglass
planes
vacations
pirates
pirate ships
clothes
clothes
cars
walking the plank
trains

Maps

PLANNING PAGES

Plan Possibilities

Dramatic

Art

Blocks/Construction

Science/Discovery

Sensory

Literacy/Writing

Math/Manipulatives

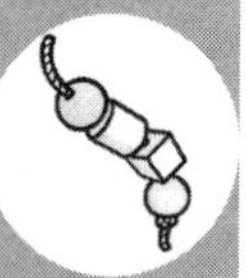

Rhymes/Fingerplays/Songs/Music

Group Time

ACTIVITIES AND EXPERIENCES FOR MAPS

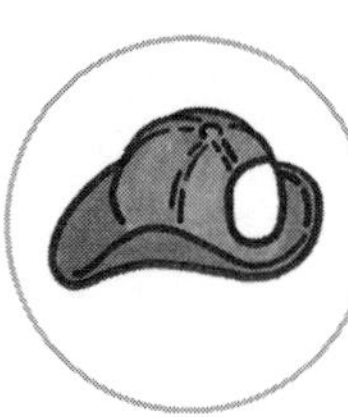

DRAMATIC POSSIBILITIES

Shiver Me Timbers!

Materials
large and small cardboard boxes • paint or crayons • duct tape • a broomstick to use as a mast for the boat • yarn or tape • flags, jewels • treasure box • oars • compass • telescope • bandanas • eye patches • books about pirates, such as *Pirate Pete* by Kim Kennedy

Teacher Talk
Talk about what pirates like to do. "Where do you think the treasure is buried?"

Instructions
Make a ship with cardboard boxes. Use a large box in the center and medium-sized boxes on either end. Use duct tape to tape all the boxes together. Take it outside so children can paint it, or use crayons to decorate it indoors. Use duct tape to tape the broomstick mast on the ship. Hang the flags on the mast with lengths of yarn or secure with duct tape. Place jewels, necklaces, and small silver or gold objects in a small box to make a treasure chest. Provide compass and telescope (made from cardboard tubes) as play props.

Campsite

Materials
camping supplies • such as tent • sleeping bags • compasses • binoculars • water cans • flashlights • straw hats • backpacks • camping food kit (metal dishes, and so on) • hiking boots • maps of campgrounds • topological maps with hiking trails • books about camping, such as *Arthur Goes to Camp* by Marc Brown

Teacher Talk
Ask children questions about their camping experiences. "Why is having a compass on a camping trip important?" Talk about personal identification in case of injury. "What is your last name?"

Instructions
Ask families and staff for sleeping bags and camping supplies. If items come from families of children who are in the classroom, discuss with the children that the personal items from homes are on loan to the classroom and can be used by all of the children, not just their owners. Label each item with the owner's name written on a piece of masking tape.

Helpful Hints: As you convert the Dramatic Possibilities area to a campsite, invite a family member or community resource person (for example, Eagle Scout, camping supply store manager, or family member who camps frequently) to come to group time to talk with children about camping and hiking.

Observation/Assessment
Takes responsibility for others' possessions
Shares resources for play

Other Dramatic Possibilities

- Explore ways to travel on vacation or for work (car, train, airplane, ship, and so on)
- Correlate this area with travel experiences of children. For example, if a child is going to Grandma's house, add the things children will need to take to Grandma's house to the area.
- Correlate this area with travel experiences of families, particularly if parents are traveling for work. Match Dramatic Possibilities to the destination of a traveling parent, adding the types of props that might be needed by the parent who is traveling.
- Add supplies and materials to Dramatic Possibilities that are used to prepare for taking a trip or vacation.

ART POSSIBILITIES

Arrrgh! Pirates We Be!

Materials
pieces of white fabric • watercolor paints • paint holders • markers • permanent markers • cotton swabs • pictures from a picture file of pirates and ships

Teacher Talk
"Use the watercolors on your pirate bandana." "What color are you planning to use next?" Talk about their bandanas and pictures that children may have seen of pirates.

Instructions
Cut the fabric in 20" x 20" pieces. Pour the different colors of paint in paint holders. Use the materials to make a pirate bandana. Cotton swabs, such as Q-tips, make good applicators for the paint. Demonstrate how bandanas can be used around the neck or over the head.

Observation/Assessment
Paints using various materials

Coin Rubbings

Materials
coins of different types • white drawing paper • crayons • colored pencils • construction paper • and scissors

Teacher Talk
"You made the image of the coin by rubbing it with the yellow pencil." "What details do you see in the coin rubbing?"

Instructions
Collect a variety of types and sizes of coins. Demonstrate how to make a rubbing by placing a coin under the drawing paper and holding the crayon parallel to the paper. Rub the side of the crayon over the coin repeatedly until the complete image appears. Cut out the center portion of a piece of construction paper leaving a one- to two-inch border. Glue the construction paper border over the white drawing paper to mount the rubbing. Help children write their names on their rubbings. When children get proficient at making rubbings with crayons, move on to colored pencils, charcoal pencils, or chalk. Novelty coins such as those thrown at Mardi Gras parades work especially well for making the rubbings. You may also want to use coins from other countries. Save the scraps of construction paper for future art projects.

Other Art Possibilities

- Include books about pirates in the area for children to use as a source of art ideas.
- Add striped cloth, sequins, and bird feathers to other art materials.
- Add sand mixed with powdered tempera paint to do sand art.
- Make travel collages using travel brochures, and art and collage materials.

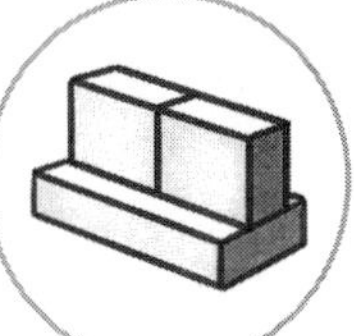

Construction Zone

Materials
Large map showing your neighborhood or a neighborhood rug, such as those available from school supply stores and catalogs • small unit blocks • buildings • people figures • traffic signs

Teacher Talk
"You have built three buildings on this street."
"Where can the cars go?"

Instructions
Provide a map or a rug with a neighborhood scene on it to build on. Give children small blocks, buildings, and figures. Create a sign saying "Construction Zone Created by _________." List all the names of children who helped in the construction.

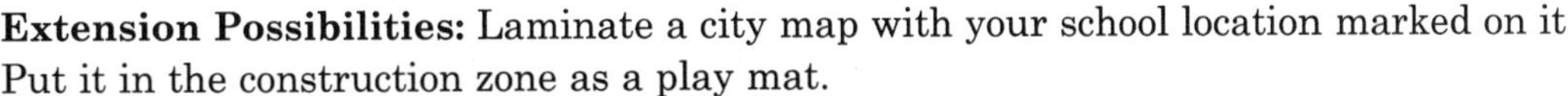

Extension Possibilities: Laminate a city map with your school location marked on it. Put it in the construction zone as a play mat.

Observation/Assessment
Builds using blocks and other materials

Down by the Station

Materials
blocks • wooden train set • people figures • trees • books about trains, such as *Freight Train* by Donald Crews

Teacher Talk
"Many people depend on trains for transportation to and from work and also for traveling to other cities." "How does a passenger know when a train is coming down the track?"

Instructions
Provide all the materials for children to build a train station. Sing "Down by the Station" as they build.

Observation/Assessment
Experiences dramatic play in miniature

Other Blocks/Construction Possibilities

- Build an airport, ticket counter, and even an airplane in the block area.
- Add strips of paper for roads and various vehicles for making a highway system.

SCIENCE/DISCOVERY POSSIBILITIES

Constellation Navigation

Materials
scissors • black paper • pin (teacher only) • tape • large flashlight

Teacher Talk
"How can you tell if you are going in the right direction in the middle of an ocean or desert?" "What do you see in the sky during the day and during the night?"

Instructions
Cut out a large circle and use the pin (teacher only) to make lots of pinholes in the black paper. Place it over the large flashlight and tape it in place. Turn on the flashlight to make stars on the ceiling. The "stars" will show up better in a darkened room. You can make the constellations look real by using a reference book to help you know where to make pinholes.

Making a Compass

Materials
shallow pan of water • small cork • large metal needle, bar magnet • paper • marker

Teacher Talk
"We are going to make a simple compass. First, we will have to magnetize the needle."

Instructions
Pour about one inch of water into the pan. Float the cork in the water. Stroke the needle on the magnet going in the same direction over and over again until the needle is magnetized. Lay the needle flat on the cork. It will point north. Tape a sign that reads north in the direction that the needle points. Tape a sign that reads south opposite the north sign. Then place the east and west signs in the appropriate directions.

Helpful Hint: Practice this activity before demonstrating it.

Sniffing Sort

Materials
a few different types of scented potpourri • large tub • magnifying glasses • bowls

Teacher Talk
"I see you are using the magnifying glass to look at the different things in the tubs." "What things do you see in the tub?"

Instructions
Pour different scents of potpourri into the tub. Have the magnifying glass and the bowls for categorizing nearby for children to explore.

Observation/Assessment
Uses the five senses for exploration

SENSORY POSSIBILITIES

Digging for Treasure

Materials
sand • gemstone pebbles • necklaces • paper clips • marbles • containers

Teacher Talk
"Look at the colors of the gemstones you have found." "Can you separate them by color?"

Instructions
Layer the sand and the different materials in the sensory table. Provide containers for sorting objects. When the child is finished digging, make sure she buries the objects back in the sand, so the next person can dig up the treasures again.

Terra Firma

Materials
aquarium rocks • dirt or potting soil • water • shaved ice • ice cubes • sand • sensory table or tubs • globe or map of the world

Teacher Talk
"When we go outside, what do we find under our feet?" "What would people who live in Antarctica have under their feet?" Explore with children what people might find under their feet in different parts of the globe.

Instruction
Fill sensory tubs with different media that represent the surfaces of the Earth. Children explore the various materials in the tubs.

Other Sensory Possibilities

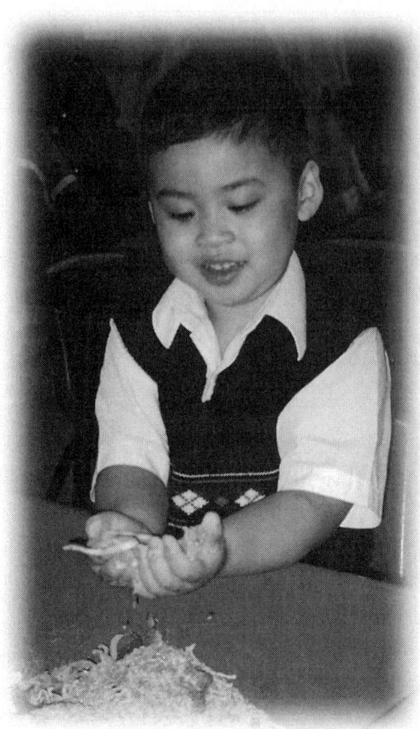

- Carve a map in playdough.
- Create trees for the area by placing twigs in playdough.
- Play music as children manipulate sensory materials.
- Add sand buildings, vehicles, and street signs to the sensory table.
- Use nature items and art materials to make nature prints.
- Tint bubble solution with food coloring or Liquid Watercolors, blow lots of bubbles, and make bubble prints.

LITERACY/WRITING POSSIBILITIES

Where Is My House?

Materials
maps of your local area • stickers • markers • drawing paper • books about maps, such as *Me on the Map*, by Joan Sweeney

Teacher Talk
"How can we find the way to a place where we have never been?" "Can you find your house on the map?"

Instructions
Ask children, "How can we find a way to your house?" Discuss the route and then look at the map. Find each child's house on the map, and mark it with a sticker or marker. Show children the way from school to each child's house. Ask each child to draw and illustrate a map to her house from school.

Helpful Hints: You may ask children to draw their maps at home with families. Suggest they look at the map while they are driving to and from school.

Observation/Assessment
Makes simple diagrams and maps
Knows home address

On the Way Home

Materials
paper • markers

Teacher Talk
"What do you see when you are on the way to school from your house? Do you see a grocery store?"

Instructions
Write "On the way to school, I see ____, _____, and ____ on blank paper. Offer a page for each child to complete by dictating and illustrating the answer. Record additional dictation of the artists' descriptions of their drawings.

Observation/Assessment
Explores maps and globes
Shows curiosity about where places are on maps and globes

Other Literacy/Writing Possibilities

- Match cards with traffic sign pictures to cards with traffic sign words.
- Create a group trip story.
- Use a fishing pole to "catch" magnetic letters in a tub. Add non-magnetic letters for additional interest.

MATH/MANIPULATIVES POSSIBILITIES

Are We There Yet?

Materials
maps with same scale of miles • strips of paper • fine-tip markers

Teacher Talk
"How far is it on the map to the next town?"

Instructions
Provide several maps using the same scale of miles. Help children make their own scales using strips of paper and fine-tip markers. Show children how to hold the strips on the map to measure distances. Get maps from state travel agencies, welcome centers, or rental car agencies.

Observation/Assessment
Estimates distance

County Counting

Materials
simple map of your state divided into counties, parishes, or other divisions • clear contact paper or laminating film

Teacher Talk
"The state is divided into counties. Before we start, let's guess how many counties there are. Now, let's count and see how many there are." "What is the county next to your county?"

Instructions
Provide maps of your state. Laminate or cover with clear contact paper. Introduce this activity during Group Time Possibilities. Show children how to put a mark on each county as they count. Repeat this activity to observe for increasing rote counting skills.

Observation/Assessment
Counts using one-to-one correspondence

Nature Counting

Materials
paper • scissors • muffin tins • markers • stones • bowl or basket to hold stones

Teacher Talk
"You are finding the number of stones needed for each tin." "Put the stones back in the basket (or bowl) when you finish."

Instructions
Cut round pieces of paper to fit into the bottom of the muffin tins. Write a number on one side of the paper and draw the same number of circles on the other side. Place the paper in the tins with the number face up. Children can place the corresponding number of stones in the tins. (Small river stones work best.) The children can flip over the paper to check their answers.

RHYMES/FINGERPLAYS/SONGS/MUSIC POSSIBILITIES

Going on a Vacation

Materials
suitcases • maps • other items mentioned in the song

Teacher Talk
"Remember the 'Going on a Bear Hunt' game we used to play? Today we will do the same activity in a little different way. Today we will be 'Going on a Vacation.'"

Instructions
Recite "Going on a Vacation" using "pack my bags," "put the suitcases in the car," "get out the maps," "plan the route," "get everyone in the car," "drive the car," "stop to buy gas," and other appropriate actions as the verses. Be creative and have fun! The activity is even more fun when you provide the materials mentioned in the story, such as suitcases, maps, and other items as props.

Observation/Assessment
Repeats familiar stories

"This Is the Way" Transitions

Teacher Talk
"All the toys are put away. Now we can fly to the playground. This is the way we fly a plane."

Instructions
Use "This Is the Way We ..." as a transition activity. Children can pretend to fly a plane, drive a car, ride a bus, walk to work, and so on."

Helpful Hints: Songs are a way for children to go from one activity to another during the day. Using songs gives children something to do as they transition. They are wonderful literacy activities, as well.

Other Rhymes/Fingerplays/Songs/Music Possibilities

- Sing "The Ship Went Over the Ocean" to the tune of "The Bear Went Over the Mountain."
- Sing "One Little, Two Little, Three Little Pirates" to the tune "Bumping Up and Down in My Little Red Wagon."
- Use the following recordings during this Plan:
  - "Twinkle, Twinkle" from *One Light, One Sun* by Raffi
  - *Bedtime Stories for Pirates* by Kevin Hendrickson and Lorin Hoskins
- Sing "The Wheels on the Train" to the tune of "The Wheels on the Bus" with appropriate phrases that the children make up themselves.

GROUP TIME POSSIBILITIES

Here a Map, There a Map, Everywhere a Map, Map: Compare the variety of maps (world map, U.S. map, state map, city map, and so on) and discuss the different purposes of maps. If possible, have enough maps for each child to hold a map during this discussion. Assist the children in finding your state.

We've Got the Whole World in Our Hands: Use a large globe, and position it so all children can see where you are pointing. First, talk about the fact that the world is round. Show the difference in land and water on the globe. Point to the different countries as you name them.

Group Time Charts: Charts are a great way to introduce new topics. Write a question dealing with the topic, such as "How can we use maps?" at the top of the page. Then write each child's name on the left side of the paper. As each child answers the question, write the response next to his or her name. Post the chart, so families will see what children have been discussing. A week or so later, repeat the activity and compare answers. Observe the difference in children's responses at the beginning and at the end of the Possibilities Plan. Spell out letters in each child's name.

How can we use maps?

Tanya	To go home
Le	To find where to drive our car
Allison	To color
Tinsley	For folding
Gene	To go on a business trip

Introduce County Counting: Introduce the maps and ideas about counties (see page 248) at group time.

Other Group Time Possibilities

- Read any of the books listed in this Possibilities Plan (see page 256).
- Create a map of the classroom with children.
- Create a map of the playground with children.

X Marks the Spot

Materials
box • jewels • coins • paper • marker

Teacher Talk
"Can you find the treasure chest without a map?" "To find a treasure what do you need to do?"

Instructions
Decorate the box like a treasure chest. Bury the treasure chest in the sandbox. Draw a map to the treasure. Let children figure out where the treasure chest is by following the map.

Helpful Hints: For young children make the map very simple. For older children you may try using a compass to figure out the direction by reading the direction of east, west, south, and north.

Fun with a Compass

Materials
compass • index cards • markers • four lengths of yarn or streamers

Teacher Talk
"Do you know how to use a compass?" "How can we find the direction for south?" "What direction is the object if it is between south and east?"

Instructions
Place the compass in the middle of the playground. Set the compass to north. Look around the playground to see what can you find in each direction. Write down the object's name and direction on the index card and tape it on the object. For example, write "see-saw—west," "big tree—southeast."

Observation/Assessment
Labels directions by name—north, south, east, and west

Walking the Plank

Materials
10–12-foot piece of lumber • chart paper • markers

Teacher Talk
"How far do you think you can walk on the board?" "One, two, three, four, five steps. Let's write down the number of steps by your name on the chart." Talk about using your arms to help balance.

Instructions
Talk with children about how pirates would sometimes make people "walk the plank" as punishment for particular actions or deeds. Place the piece of wood on a padded surface inside or outside. Count the number of steps as each person "walks the plank." Record each child's number of steps on the chart. Ask children if they would like to balance on the board before they attempt to "walk the plank." Offer your assistance, if needed.

Observation/Assessment
Balances on a beam

PROJECTS/DOCUMENTATION POSSIBILITIES

On the Road Again

Materials
butcher paper on a roll • colored markers • pictures (real or child-drawn) of each child's and teacher's dwelling • a picture of your school • glue sticks • books about maps, such as *Mapping Penny's World* by Loreen Leedy

Teacher Talk
"Is your house close to the school or far away?" "What other buildings are by your house?"

Instructions
Cut a sheet of butcher paper large enough to make a map including your school and the neighborhood. Glue all of the pictures on the map. Let the children draw roads and the landmarks on the route they take to school.

Extension Possibilities: Let children make maps of the school, their classroom, and the playground. Refer to "Where Is My House?" (see page 246).

Observation/Assessment
Knows home address
Understands the concept of direction
Knows name of city or location of residence

The Melting Pot

Materials
large world map • thin bright-colored yarn • tape • pens • sentence strips

Teacher Talk
"We all live in ______. Look at all the different places our families are from."

Instructions
Gather information about what countries the families of the children in your class came from or where their ancestors came from. Make a nametag for each child on the sentence strips. Post the world map on the wall. Help each child locate the countries where they or their ancestors lived. Tape each child's name around the sides of the map, and tape a piece of yarn from the child's nametag to the country.

Extension Possibilities: Use a map to mark where the children were born. Have children send postcards when they go on vacation and use the postcards instead of nametags to mark your map.

Helpful Hints: Take this opportunity to talk about same and different in regards to cultural origin.

FIELD TRIP POSSIBILITIES

Museum Visit: Plan a museum visit. Use a city map to determine the route you will take. Discuss where you are on the map as you travel. Point out map milestones as you travel to the museum.

Map Destination: Visit a river, creek, or lake visible on a map. Talk about where it is and how you will get there.

Courthouse Visit: Go to the county courthouse to get copies of county maps to use in the classroom.

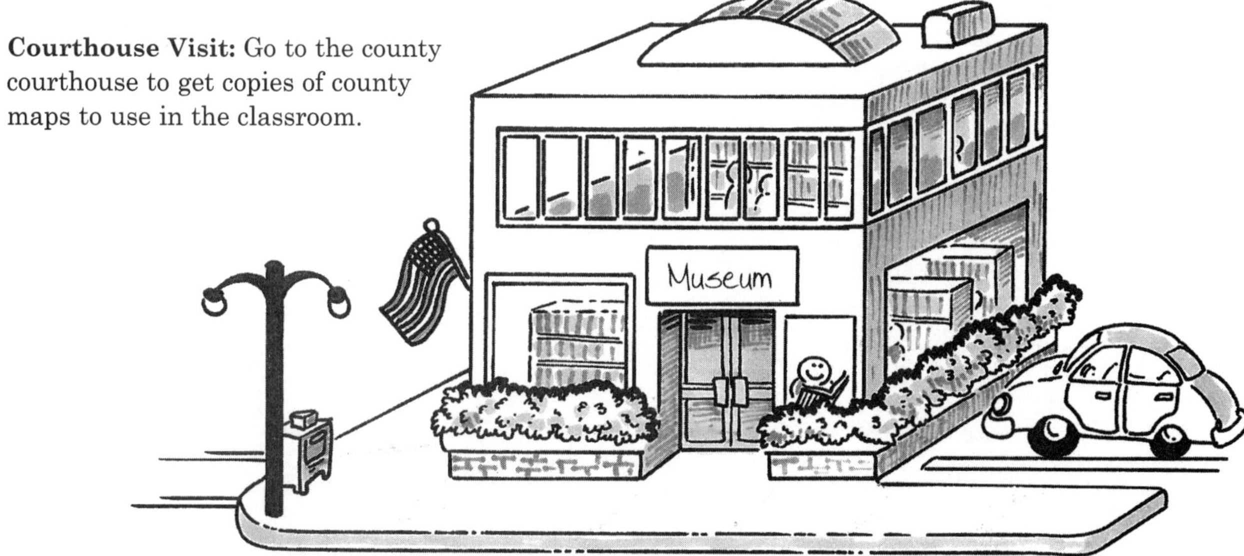

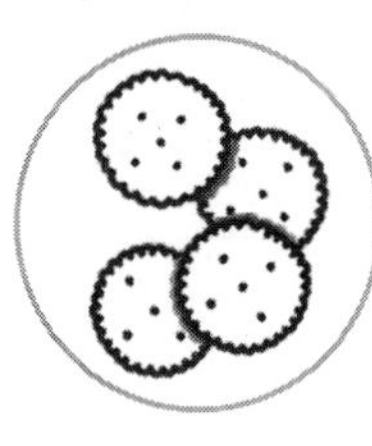

SNACK POSSIBILITIES

Field Trip Snack: Pack simple snacks (cheese and crackers, apple slices, grapes, cookies) to carry along on one of the field trips.

Pirate Sandwiches: Create stripes (such as on pirate shirts) on bread by squeezing jelly from individual jelly packets (available at fast food restaurants) or from jelly in plastic squeeze bottles.

Tropical Drinks: Juice oranges, grapefruit, limes, and tangerines to make tropical drinks.

FAMILY PARTICIPATION POSSIBILITIES

Making Maps: Send home construction paper and pencils for parents and children to work together to make a floor plan of their house.

The Melting Pot: Have parents come in and talk to the children about their families' cultures and traditions.

Map Library: Have parents bring in old road maps, building floor plans, hotel or convention center maps, and other map-related materials. Laminate and place them in the library for children to examine.

On the Road: Ask traveling parents and family members to save travel paraphernalia to add to this area. Maps from rental cars, airline magazines, ticket jackets, ticket stubs, postcards, tickets, and travel posters are all good additions to dramatic play and involve parents in the Possibilities Plan.

Being Away from Your Child

When a parent or family member leaves home for work-related travel or family business, things are disrupted. Schedules, caregiving patterns, and routines change. What can families do to help children adjust to parental absence?

Preschoolers are able to deal with absences reasonably well after they have had some experience with separations. They have already learned that Mommy or Daddy will actually come back. Preschoolers still benefit from being included in the discussion, planning, and preparation for the trip. Try some of these ideas to help your preschooler cope with your absence:

- Mark the trip on a calendar that everyone can see. This helps preschoolers see that the duration of the trip is limited and helps them prepare for you to be away.
- Include your child in the planning process. Let him or her help you get your luggage and pack, find a photograph for you to take along, pack his or her own bag just like yours, and so on.
- If you anticipate that your child will have trouble while you are gone, make some plans to ease this difficulty. Cover a photo of yourself with contact paper and put it under your child's pillow for him or her to pull out whenever he or she misses you.
- Get a map and mark your destination so that your child can classify trips by distance from home and duration. Compare the upcoming trip to past ones.
- Maintain your child's normal schedule as much as possible. Predictability is an important part of routine.
- Call home and talk to your child if you can. Arrange in advance to call at a certain point during the trip and make sure your call comes in on schedule. If calling is not an option or can't be done reliably, don't promise to do so.
- Don't forget to bring home a souvenir. It doesn't have to be a big-ticket item. Share your experience—postcards that show what the things looked like, photographs of the area you visited, and a taste of a different food that you sampled are great choices. T-shirts are good if they reinforce the geography of the trip. If you bring home toys, be prepared to do so for every trip after this one. It will be expected.

As children get older, parental travel gets easier for both you and your child. Careful planning can keep your trip from being disruptive or challenging for you and for your child.

Curriculum Resources

Prop Boxes

Pirate Ship Prop Box
striped shirts • eye patches • maps • compasses • pictures of oceans and beaches • pirate ships • a treasure chest • jewels • flags • a compass • a spyglass or telescope

Vacation Prop Box
maps • postcards • travel posters • airline tickets • sunglasses • hats • bags • pictures from vacation • collapsible bags

Camping Prop Box
sheet (for tent) • sleeping bags • camping cook kits • hiking boots • binoculars • compass • maps • nature collections • flashlights • backpacks

Books

A Pirate's Life for Me!: A Day Aboard a Pirate Ship by Julie Thompson, et al
Amelia Bedelia Goes Camping by Peggy Parish
Arthur Goes to Camp by Marc Brown
As the Crow Flies: A First Book of Maps by Gail Hartman
Berenstain Bears Go to Camp by Jan and Stan Berenstain
Blast Off to Earth: A Look at Geography by Loreen Leedy
Curious George Goes Camping by H.A. Rey
Do Pirates Take Baths? by Kathy Tucker
Edward and the Pirates by David McPhail
Everything I Know About Pirates: A Collection of Made-Up Facts, Educated Guesses, and Silly Pictures About Bad Guys of the High Seas by Tom Lichtenheld
Freight Train by Donald Crews
It's Okay to Be Different by Todd Parr
Leon the Chameleon by Melanie Watt
Madlenka by Peter Sis
Mapping Penny's World by Loreen Leedy
Me and the Measure of Things by Joan Sweeney
Me on the Map by Joan Sweeney
My Map Book by Sara Fanelli
Pirate Pete by Kim Kennedy
Pirates by Dina Anastasio
Pirates Past Noon by Mary Pope Osborne
Pirates: A Nonfiction Companion to Pirates Past Noon by Will Osborne and Mary Pope Osborne
Round Trip by Ann Jonas
Sally Goes to the Mountains by Stephen Huneck
School Bus by Donald Crews

Simple Signs by Cindy Wheeler
Somewhere in the World Right Now by Stacy Schuett
The Secret Birthday Message by Eric Carle
The Whole World in Your Hands: Looking at Maps by Melvin Berger, et al
Tough Boris by Mem Fox
Truck by Donald Crews
Where Do I Live? by Neil Chesanow

Observation/Assessment

Takes responsibility for others' possessions, page 241
Shares resources for play, page 241
Paints using various materials, page 242
Builds using blocks and other materials, page 243
Experiences dramatic play in miniature, page 243
Uses the five senses for exploration, page 245
Makes simple diagrams and maps, page 246
Knows home address, page 246 and 252
Explores maps, globes, page 247
Shows curiosity about where places are on maps, page 247
Estimates distance, page 247
Counts using one-to-one correspondence, page 248
Repeats familiar stories, page 249
Labels directions by name—north, south, east, and west, page 251
Balances on a beam, page 252
Understands the concept of directions, page 252
Knows name of city or location of residence, page 252

Picture File /Vocabulary

address
airport
beach
boat
compass
destination
directions
east
highway
itinerary
Jolly Roger
legend (for a map)
map
mast
neighborhood
north
pirate
road
route
ship
south
street
tickets
train station
treasure
vacation locations, such as mountains, Grandma's house
west

Concepts Learned in Maps

Content Knowledge

- ☐ Maps are drawn to scale.
- ☐ A scale represents distance.
- ☐ Maps help us find things.
- ☐ Maps give directions.
- ☐ North, south, east, and west are directions.
- ☐ Pirates sailed on the seas in ships.
- ☐ Wind makes sailing ships move.
- ☐ A compass shows direction.
- ☐ Long ago, people navigated by using the stars.
- ☐ Luggage carries clothes and personal belongings on a trip or on vacation.
- ☐ People camp in tents.
- ☐ People travel to different locations.
- ☐ I can find my house on a map.
- ☐ I can find my state and city on a map or globe.
- ☐ I know what country my ancestors lived in.

Process Knowledge

- ☐ I can balance on a "plank."
- ☐ I can use a map.
- ☐ I can search for hidden treasure.
- ☐ I can play the role of pirate.
- ☐ I can pack a suitcase.
- ☐ I can make rubbings.
- ☐ I can build a replica of my neighborhood.
- ☐ I can build an airport.
- ☐ I can build a train station.
- ☐ I can build a working compass.
- ☐ I can dig for treasure.
- ☐ I can use a compass to find North.

Pre-academic Skills

- ☐ I can read signs (stop, yield, no right turn, etc.).
- ☐ I can count.
- ☐ I can read a map.
- ☐ I can categorize.
- ☐ I can investigate and test my ideas.
- ☐ I can predict.
- ☐ I can identify letters in my name.
- ☐ I know my last name.
- ☐ I know my address.

Possibilities Plan—

Spin Me a Tall Tale

Getting Ready to Plan

Learning about stories is an important part of literacy development. In this Possibilities Plan children will explore many different types of stories, and have opportunities to tell, retell, and act them out.

The purpose of Getting Ready to Plan is to support the planning process with a general overview of the content of this Possibilities Plan. Now is the time to think about what interests children and what you want them to learn about each of the topics explored below.

Exploring Roles: As children play, they take on roles they see being used in broader social settings. From initial roles involving family members, children progress to more varied and imaginative roles. They get images of themselves as they attempt to play these roles. Children evaluate their play experiences and alter their views of themselves as they play. So exploring roles can be an important part of self-concept. Plan for children to explore many roles that support viewing their play experiences as successful.

Story Telling: As children have more experiences with stories, they learn that stories have a beginning, middle, and end. They discover that they can learn from stories and that stories can be about many different topics. Children enjoy retelling stories, and may tell a different version than the one that was read to them. Repetition is an important way for children to learn, so retelling stories is a good use of your time. Include the many different ways to tell stories, including telling stories with music, dance, and creative dramatics. Encourage children to tell their own stories and write them down.

Characters: Children sometimes think of characters in stories as old friends. Acting out stories is a great way to reinforce story sequencing skills and have fun dressing up! Children can also act out stories using puppets. This provides opportunities for role-play and expressing emotions. Asking children questions about why characters do the things they do increases their understanding of the motivations of characters and gives children practice in anticipating what might happen next.

Now that you have an idea about the general content of the Possibilities Plan, you are ready to proceed with developing your own plan. This section of Getting Ready to Plan identifies resources you may want to buy, collect, or locate to implement your plan.

Toys and Materials*

Purchased

12" x 18" paper
8 ½" x 11" white paper
black cloth
CD or tape player
classical music (that tells a story)
clear contact paper
colored pompoms
construction paper
craft knife (teacher only)
craft sticks
crayons
electric skillet or griddle
fabric glue
geometric pegboard (or make one)
glue
hot glue gun (teacher only) and glue
large sheets of white paper
Liquid Watercolor paints
magnifying glasses
music collections
paint
paintbrushes
paper plates
pencils
permanent and washable markers
pig masks
pipe cleaners
purple washable paint
scissors
sensory tub
sheet protectors
tape
tracing paper
tuning fork
variety of puppets
whoosh tube or other toys that make sounds
wiggle eyes
wolf masks

Gathered

architecture magazines
assorted materials that make different sounds
black and clear film canisters
books about houses
cardboard brick blocks
clean socks (one per child)
coffee filters
cookie cutters
examples of invitations
eyedroppers
fabric ribbons and scarves
fabric scraps
felt
flannel board with characters
flashlight
large cardboard box (refrigerator or dryer)
long piece of string
magazines
materials and ingredients for making pancakes
nature items (pinecones, small branches, seashells, rocks, sheets of bark, moss, and leaves)
newspapers and magazines in different languages
opaque shower curtain
photographs of children and photographs of family members
plastic or paper cups
PVC pipe 4' long and 1 ½" around
rebus pancake recipe
ribbon
rubber bands
sequins
shoeboxes, large
shower curtain rings
small cups
straw
string
Styrofoam blocks of different sizes
tempera or finger paints
three-ring binder
toothpicks
towels, large
twine
various dress-up clothes for costumes
wipe-off markers
wood

*Note: Please consider the ages and abilities of the children in your classroom. Use only safe, non-toxic materials.

Spin Me a Tall Tale

WEB

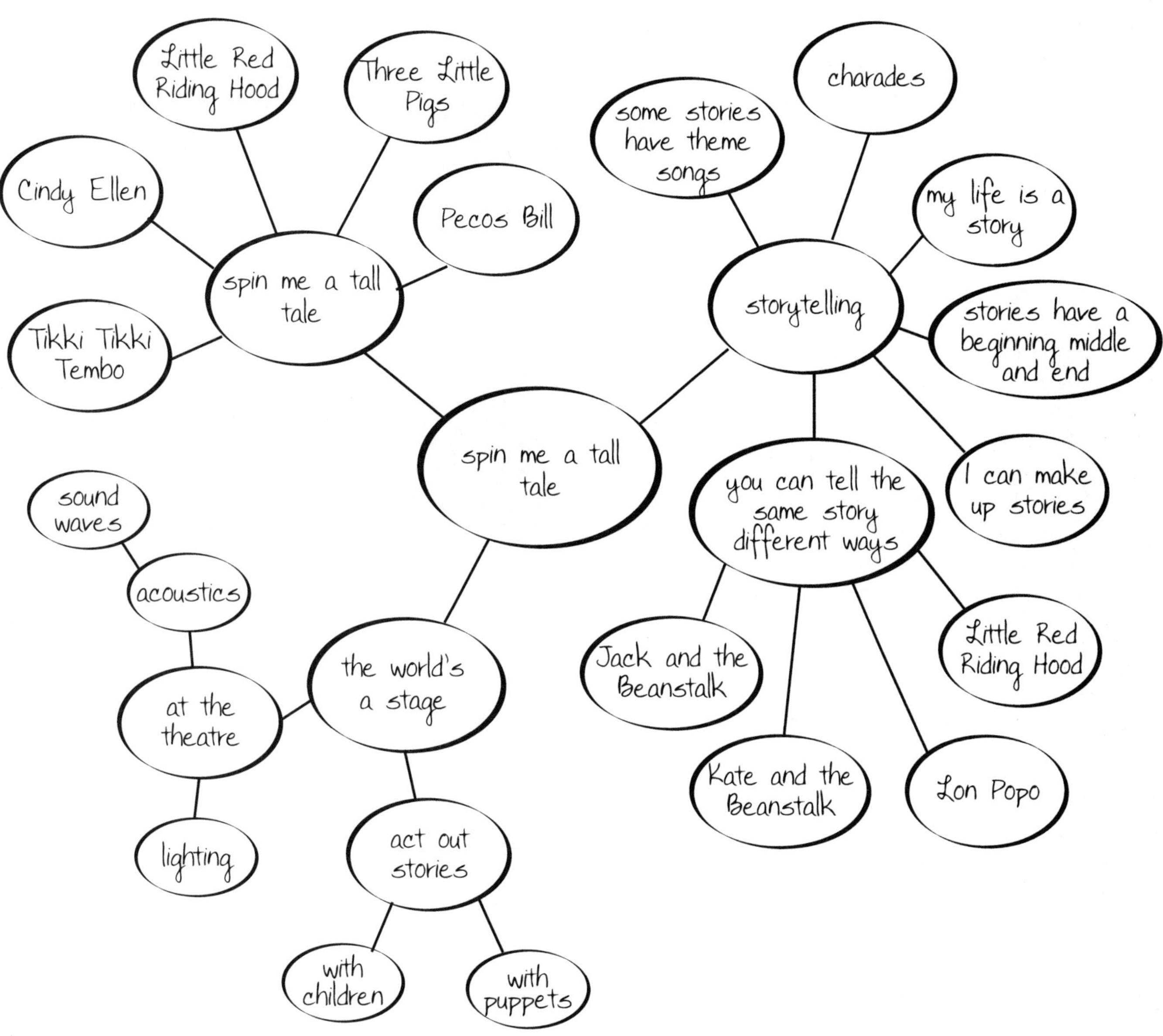

Spin Me a Tall Tale

PLANNING PAGES

Plan Possibilities

Dramatic

Art

Blocks/Construction

Science/Discovery

Sensory

Literacy/Writing

Math/Manipulatives

Rhymes/Fingerplays/Songs/Music

Group Time

ACTIVITIES AND EXPERIENCES FOR SPIN ME A TALL TALE

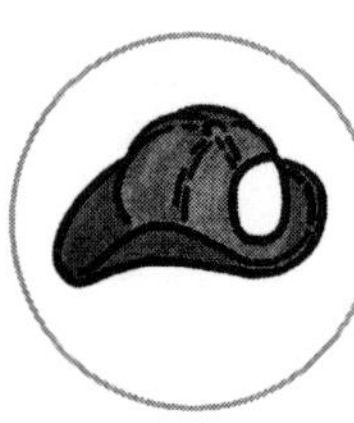

DRAMATIC POSSIBILITIES

The World's a Wonderful Stage

Materials
opaque shower curtain • shower curtain rings • PVC pipe 4' long and 1½" wide • twine • various dramatic play props (hats, scarves, ties, masks, shoes)

Teacher Talk
"What is the role of the actors?" "What about the role of the audience?"

Instructions
Put the shower curtain rings on the PVC pipe and attach the shower curtain. Tie a piece of twine on each end of the PVC pipe. The twine needs to be long enough to hang the curtain. Attach the curtain to the ceiling in the Dramatic Possibilities area using ceiling clips or expansion bolts, depending on your ceiling type. Add the costume materials. Encourage children to act out familiar stories or make up performances of their own. Observe the stories the children act out.

Observation/Assessment
Tells stories with a beginning, middle, and end

Puppet Theatre

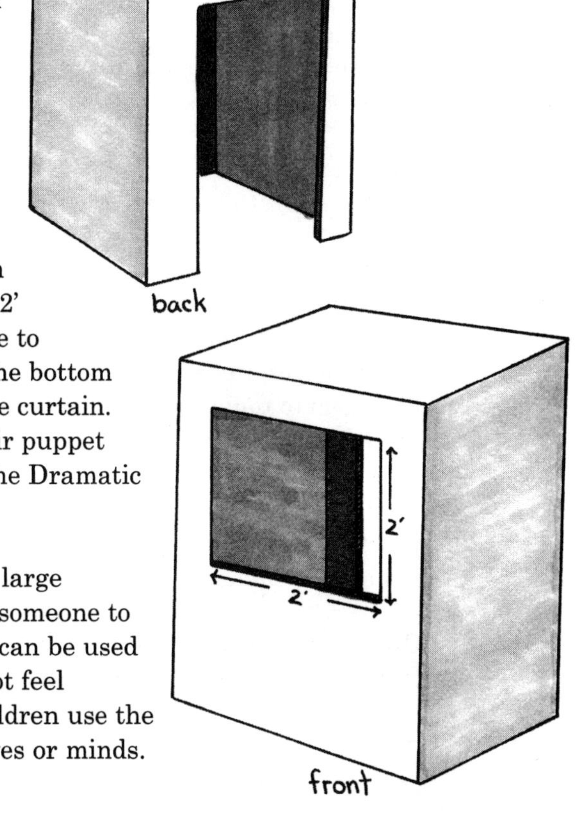

Materials
variety of puppets • large cardboard box (refrigerator or washer/dryer) • craft knife (teacher only) • a 2'1" x 2'1" piece of black material • tape • paint, paintbrushes • or a purchased puppet theatre

Teacher Talk
"You have a pig puppet, Bethanie. Tell me a story!"

Instructions
Cut an opening into the back of the box large enough for children to enter the box "stage." Next, cut a 2' x 2' square on the side opposite the opening. Use the tape to attach the material at the top of the square. Leave the bottom loose, so children can stick the puppets in front of the curtain. Children can use paints and brushes to decorate their puppet theatre. When the paint dries, place the theater in the Dramatic Possibilities area with a collection of puppets.

Helpful Hints: Many appliance stores will set aside large boxes, if requested. Collaborate with parents to find someone to pick up the box and deliver it to the school. Puppets can be used to help children express emotions or ideas they do not feel comfortable expressing themselves. Observe how children use the puppets to communicate what is going on in their lives or minds.

Observation/Assessment
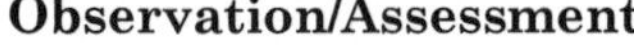
Expresses emotions using puppets

Other Dramatic Possibilities

- Add books from the books list (see page 284) to the area to give children play ideas.
- Add props to support the different stories.

ART POSSIBILITIES

Once Upon a Quilt

Materials
construction paper cut into squares • markers • crayons • ribbon • sequins • felt • fabric scraps • scissors • tape • *Tar Beach* by Faith Ringold

Teacher Talk
"Tell me the story of your quilt square." "You used sequins on your square to make it sparkle."

Instructions
Make supplies available in the Art Possibilities area. Talk with the children about using images and pictures to tell a story without words. Tell the children you would like them to tell a story without words and introduce the new supplies available in the Art Possibilities area. Read *Tar Beach* by Faith Ringold. Let children decorate their squares using the supplies. As the squares are finished, tape them together to form your group's story quilt. Place the quilt in the center of your Group Time circle when you are reading a story. The teacher may want to go back and draw "stitches" in around the squares to give the quilt a hand-sewn look.

Observation/Assessment
Participates in art activities

Sock It to Me!

Materials
clean socks (at least one for every child) • felt • fabric scraps • wiggle eyes • yarn • ribbon • fabric glue • scissors

Teacher Talk
"Deborah, your puppet has brown hair just like you do." Talk about the differences in appearance of children in your classroom (short hair vs. long hair, tall vs. short).

Instructions
Make supplies available in the Art Possibilities area for children to create puppets. Observe children's conversation as they work. Are they accepting of puppets that look different (one eye, purple hair)? Using fabric glue makes the puppets more durable for children's play.

Observation/Assessment
Makes sock puppets

Story Collage

Materials
magazines • scissors • glue • construction paper • markers • pens

Teacher Talk
"You are right! That looks like the bear in 'The Three Bears.'"

Instructions
Children cut out pictures that remind them of stories. Use the pictures and other materials to create a story collage.

Observation/Assessment
Creates collages using various art media

Other Art Possibilities

- Paint to classical music that tells a story, such as such as Prokofiev's "Peter and the Wolf" or Tchaikovsky's "Nutcracker Suite."

BLOCKS/CONSTRUCTION POSSIBILITIES

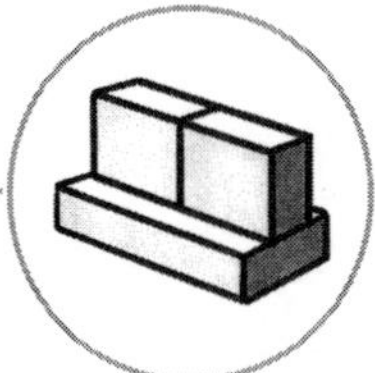

Constructing with Mother Nature

Materials
items from nature, such as pinecones, small branches, seashells, rocks, sheets of bark, moss, and leaves

Teacher Talk
"Animals use many different materials to build their homes." "I would like to walk barefoot in a house made out of moss."

Instructions
Children love to collect items from outside. Go on a nature walk and let them do the gathering. The activity will be more meaningful to children if they take part in the preparation. Set materials out in the Block Possibilities area. Suggest that children use the materials as enhancements to their building.

Observation/Assessment
Adds details to block constructions

Styrofoam Block Houses

Materials

permanent markers (for teachers only) • different sizes of Styrofoam blocks • picture file pictures of houses • architecture magazines • books about houses, such as *Mr. Pine's Purple House* by Leonard Kessel, *Fairy Houses* by Tracy Lane, *The Village of Round and Square Houses* by Ann Grifalconi, *Building a House* by Byron Barton, or *Houses and Homes Around the World* by Ann Morris

Teacher Talk

"The house you made is very colorful." "Who lives in that house?"

Instructions

Use the permanent markers to decorate Styrofoam blocks to resemble the houses in books, magazines, and pictures. (Washable markers do not adhere to the Styrofoam and will rub off on hands and clothes.) Add these to the Block Possibilities area to encourage children to tell stories about their houses.

Safety Note: Use permanent markers in a well-ventilated area.

Observation/Assessment

Constructs with blocks

Rubber Band Geometric Peg Board

Materials

rubber bands • geometric pegboard (purchased or constructed) • crayons or wipe-off markers • journal*

Teacher Talk

"Look, Kevin. You used all the different colors of rubber bands to make your design."

Instructions

If you don't have a geometric pegboard, make one with a square piece of wood and some nails. Hammer nails into the wood about half way, leaving enough of the nails sticking out for children to wrap the rubber bands around the nails. Place the nails evenly, so children can use the board to make shapes, patterns, and designs. Then, draw or sketch a copy of their work in the journal.

* To make a reusable journal, cut 8 ½" x 11" white paper in half. On the top of some pages, write, "I discovered..." or "I made...." Leave some pages blank. Laminate all the pages. Punch two holes in the pages and hold the journal together with rings.

Helpful Hints: Remind children to sign their work. Store the sketchbook with the geometric board and put it out whenever you put out the board. Encourage children to revisit their work.

Observation/Assessment

Uses geometric boards to make designs
Records sketches of designs

SCIENCE/DISCOVERY POSSIBILITIES

Shake, Shake, Shake Your Bottles

Materials

film canisters (black opaque and clear) • assorted materials that make different sounds • hot glue gun (teacher only)

Teacher Talk

"You matched the bottles that make the same sound."

Instructions

Use film canisters to make sound cylinders. Fill the canisters with materials that make different sounds, filling one clear and one black or opaque canister with each material. Glue the lids with the hot glue gun to secure (teacher only). Match the clear canisters with the black or opaque ones, just by listening.

Observation/Assessment

Differentiates among sounds by listening

Riding Sound Waves

Materials

plastic or paper cups • string • toothpicks • whoosh tube • tuning fork

Teacher Talk

"Hello, Maurice. How are you today? It sounds like you are in the same room with me."

Instructions

Make a homemade phone with plastic or paper cups, string, and toothpicks. Punch a hole in the bottom of the cups. Thread the string through the holes in the bottom of the cups. Break the toothpick into two. Tie a piece of the toothpick on the end of the string, pulling it inside the cup. Repeat on the other end of the string. When children use the phone, make sure the string is pulled tight for the sound waves to travel. The cups can be used for talking and listening. Toys that make noise, such as whoosh tubes and tuning forks, are other ways to show how sound waves work.

Shadows with Flashlights

Materials
large shoebox • scissors • a piece of white butcher paper • glue • cutouts of people or animals • pipe cleaners • craft sticks • pencils • construction paper • blocks • tape • flashlight

Teacher Talk
"You are telling a story with the shadow puppets. What is going to happen next?"

Instructions
Cut the bottom out of the shoebox, leaving ½" along the edges. Cut out one side of the horizontal panel from the shoebox. Now, cut a piece of white butcher paper as big as the shoebox. Glue or tape the paper on the opened bottom to make a paper screen.

Make puppets. Use cutouts of people or animals from the picture file or hand draw simple silhouettes. Tape one end of the puppet to pipe cleaners and wrap the other end of the pipe cleaners to the craft sticks. Maneuver the puppets behind the paper screen.

Stack one or two blocks together and wrap the blocks with a piece of tape. Now, tape the flashlight on top of the stacked blocks with the switch facing up for easy access.

Set the paper screen towards you with the cut panel facing up. Place the flashlight on the back of the paper screen. Drop the paper puppets down into the cut panel and move the craft sticks around behind the screen to tell a story.

Observation/Assessment
Tells stories using puppets

Purple Paint Palette

Materials
table • washable purple paint • paper plates

Teacher Talk
"How does the paint feel between your fingers?" "What other shapes could we make?"

Instructions
Pour washable paint onto paper plates. Set the plates on the art table in the Art Possibilities area. Children dip their hands into the paint and paint directly on the table focusing on how the paint feels as they manipulate it.

Extension Possibilities: After children paint on the top of the table, lay large pieces of craft paper on top of the paint to create one or more prints. Display the prints in the classroom.

Observation/Assessment
Paints using various materials

Hot and Cold Paints

Materials
tempera or fingerpaints of various colors • large pieces of white paper • stories with a "cold" focus, such as *Polar Bear, Polar Bear, What Do You Hear?* by Bill Martin Jr. and Eric Carle (illustrator) or a "hot" focus, such as *Curious George and the Hot Air Balloon* by H.A. Rey

Teacher Talk
"Tell me about your cold painting." "Does it remind you of something?" Talk about temperature and read stories related to hot and cold as children paint.

Instructions
Place paint in the refrigerator to get cold, or on a sunny window ledge or in a hot water bath to get hot.

Other Sensory Possibilities

- Add figures, trees, and buildings to sand in sensory table.
- Provide different colors of playdough for children to manipulate.
- Create rainbows with coffee filters and Liquid Watercolors.

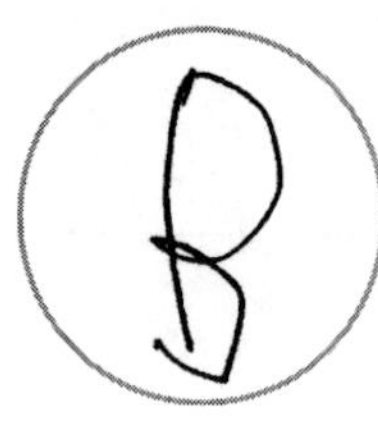

LITERACY/WRITING POSSIBILITIES

Come One, Come All!

Materials
papers • scissors • basket • examples of invitations • writing materials

Teacher Talk
"Are you going to invite your friends to watch your play?" "Don't forget to tell them when and where your production will take place."

Instructions
Cut pieces of 8 ½" x 11" paper in half. Put sheets in a basket along with some examples of invitations. The children can look at the examples to get ideas about what an invitation looks like. The cards also provide words such as "time," "place," and "date" that children can copy for their invitations.

Booklets

Materials
paper • scissors

Teacher Talk
"Would you tell me about your story?" "You made a picture book."

Instructions
Fold a letter-size piece of paper vertically in half. Open the paper. Then fold in half horizontally. Fold another fold of the half. Now, unfold the fold back to halves. Use the scissors to cut on the folded vertical line. Stop cutting when the scissors reach the intersection of the horizontal and vertical folded lines. Open the paper up to the original shape. There should be a slit in the middle of the paper vertically. Fold the paper vertically again. Hold your paper horizontally and place hands on each end. Push both hands toward the center. The slit in the middle of the paper should help to make a cross. You should have four paper leaves. Fold all paper leaves together to form a book.

Place the booklets in Literacy/Writing Possibilities area for children to illustrate or write books.

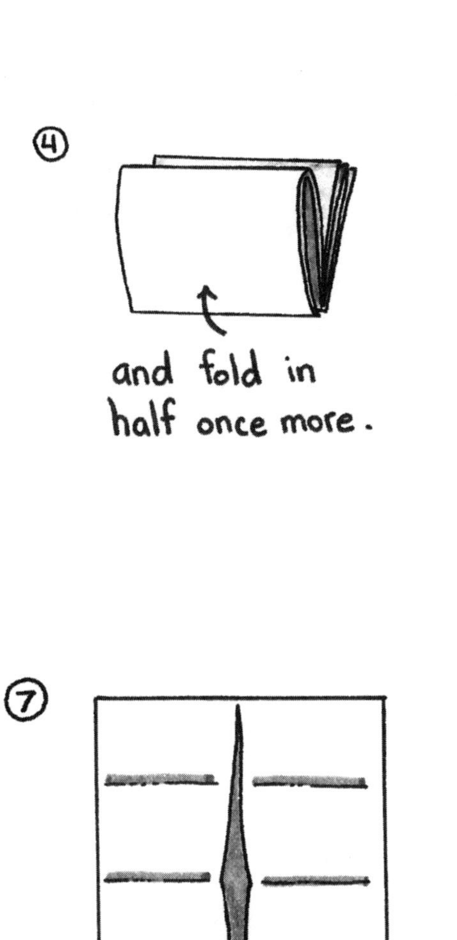
4
and fold in
half once more.

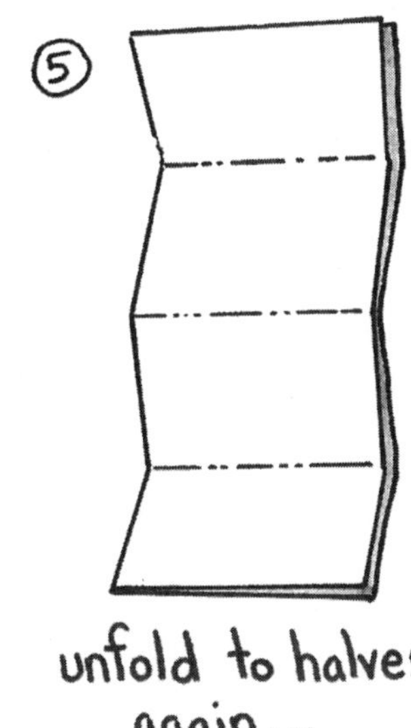
5
unfold to halves
again...

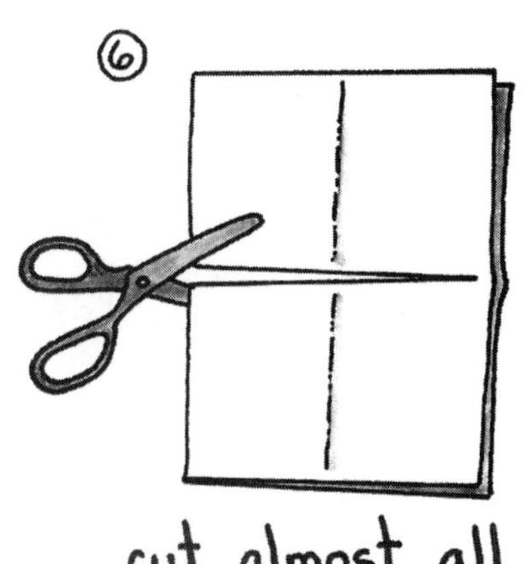
6
cut almost all
the way to the end.

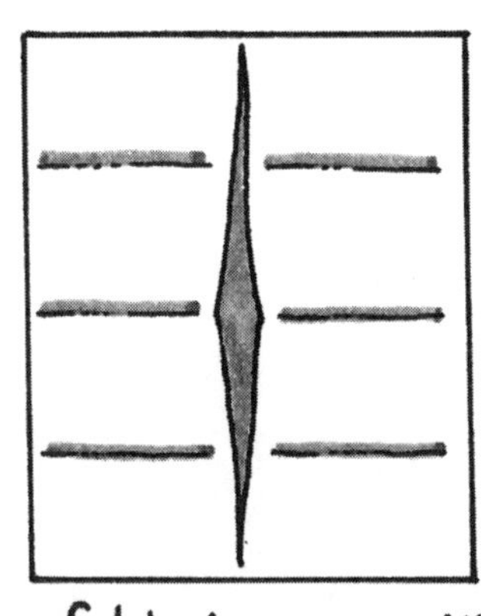
7
unfolded paper will
look like this...

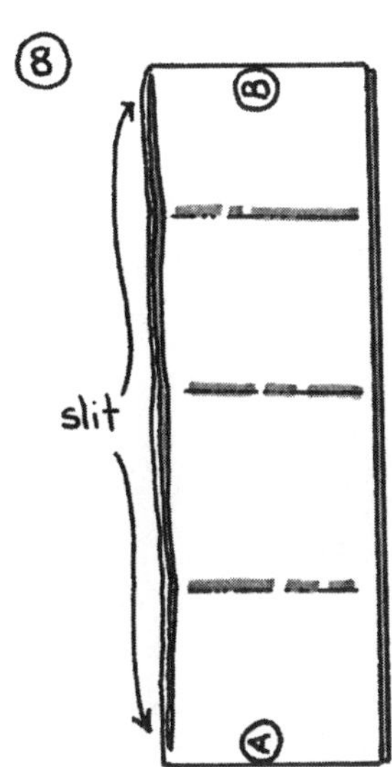
8
B
slit
A

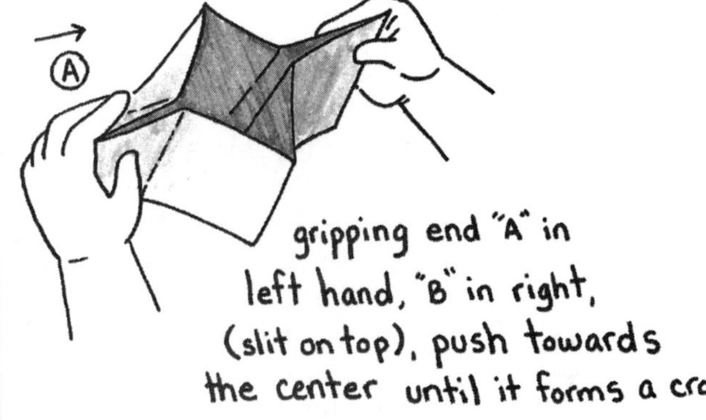
9
A
B
gripping end "A" in
left hand, "B" in right,
(slit on top), push towards
the center until it forms a cross.

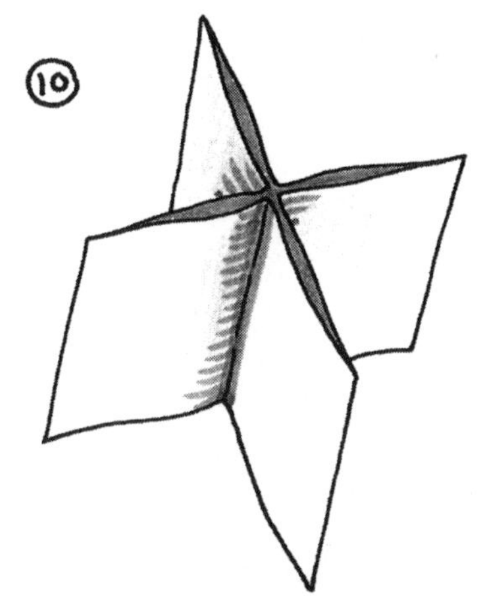
10

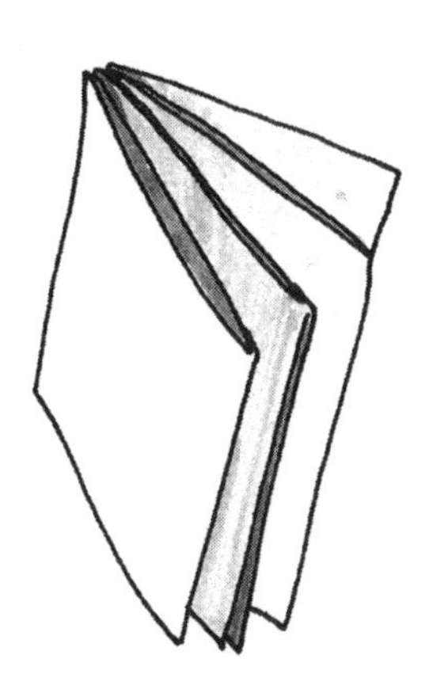
11

12
MY
BOOK

Extra! Extra! Read All About It!

Materials
newspapers and magazines in different languages • magnifying glasses • tracing paper • writing materials

Teacher Talk
"You are looking at a Chinese newspaper. See if you can trace the characters using tracing paper."

Instructions
Collect the materials. Use the magnifying glasses to look at the words closely and the tracing papers to trace words or characters.

Observation/Assessment
Traces letters

Other Literacy/Writing Possibilities

- Keep copies of children's dictations. Read the story back to individual children and underline all the characters in the story. Ask children to count characters.
- Create accordion books following the instructions below.

One Little, Two Little, Three Little Piggies

Materials
paper • markers • clear contact paper • colored pompoms

Teacher Talk
"If 'The Three Little Pigs' has four characters and 'Rapunzel' has five characters, which story has more?"

Instructions
As you read stories during this Plan, create a graph illustrating the number of characters in each book. Let children use the colored pompoms to represent the characters from the fairytales, and graph them on the chart. Cover the graph with clear contact paper.

Number of characters in the story			
	1	2	3
Little Red Riding Hood			
Three Little Pigs			
Stone Soup			

Helpful Hints: Put pictures of book covers (from a book or school supply catalog) on the graph to help children identify the stories on the graph.

Observation/Assessment
Uses one-to-one correspondence
Uses basic graphing skills

Numbers in Stories

Materials
books read during this Possibilities Plan (see page 284) • big books • flannel board and flannel board story characters

Teacher Talk
"How many pigs do you see in the picture? That's right. One, two, three."

Instructions
As you read books throughout this Possibilities Plan, notice and comment on the numbers of things in the stories. This is especially easy to accomplish when reading big books with vivid illustrations or using flannel board stories.

Observation/Assessment
Counts objects in book illustrations

Size Comparisons in Stories

Materials
books read during this Possibilities Plan (see page 284) • big books • flannel board and flannel board story characters

Teacher Talk
"Yes, the watermelon was enormous. What else is enormous?"

Instructions
As you read books throughout this Possibilities Plan, notice and talk about the sizes of objects in the stories. Encourage children to use words that describe size, such as small, medium, large, huge, tiny, giant, teeny, and so on.

Observation/Assessment
Labels objects according to size

RHYMES/FINGERPLAYS/SONGS/MUSIC POSSIBILITIES

Ribbons and Scarves

Materials
collection of fabric ribbons and scarves • CD or tape player • several musical selections

Teacher Talk
"You are using the ribbon to move with the music." "Try the scarf, now."

Instructions
Place the ribbons and scarves together with the tape or CD player. Let the children explore with scarves and ribbons as they play the musical selections. Try this activity outside on a windy day.

Music Tells a Story

Materials
storytelling music such as "The Nutcracker," "Twinkle, Twinkle Little Star," and "Sleeping Beauty" • CD or tape player • books about the musical selections

Teacher Talk
"Do you remember which story this music is from?"

Instructions
Place the books and musical selections near the CD or tape player. Children listen to the music and look at the books.

Other Rhymes/Fingerplays/Songs/Music Possibilities

- Use any of these recordings during this Plan:
  - "Nursery Rhymes" from *Abracadabra* by Joe Scruggs
  - "Itsy Bitsy Spider" from *Late Last Night* by Joe Scruggs
  - "Itsy Bitsy Spider" from *For Our Children* by Disney
  - "Nursery Rhyme Melody" from *Children's Favorites 3* by Disney
  - "London Bridge" from *Elephant Show Record* by Sharon, Lois, and Bram
  - "Earth Dance" from *Earth Quest* by Richard Searle
  - "Twinkle, Twinkle" from *One Light, One Sun* by Raffi
  - "Rock 'Round the Mulberry Bush" from *We All Live Together Volume 3* by Greg and Steve
  - "Waltzing with Bears" from *Minneapolis Concert* by Bok, Muir, and Trickett
- Sing "Whistle While You Work" from Disney's Snow White, "The Three Little Pigs Blues" from *Greg & Steve's Playing Favorites*, or similar theme music.

GROUP TIME POSSIBILITIES

Once Upon a Quilt: Read *Tar Beach* by Faith Ringold to introduce children to the Once Upon a Quilt art activity on page 266.

Riding Sound Waves Introduction: Introduce the concept of sound waves by showing children a slinky toy. The slinky illustrates how sound travels. The sound moves up and down in a wave.

Pass It On!: With children sitting in a circle, start the game by whispering a short phrase to the child sitting next to you, making sure the other children don't hear what you say. Then, the child passes the phrase that she heard to the next person, until the message goes all the way around the circle. The last person repeats the phrase out loud. The person who started the game repeats the initial phrase to see how similar or different it is to the one heard by the last person in the circle. Remind the first person to remember his or her phrase. You will find children often forget.

Sign Language: Talk about the different ways people communicate—with music, with words, with hands, and so on. Read *The Handmade Alphabet* by Laura Rankin. Explore ways communicate with signs.

Acting Out Dictated Stories: Offer children opportunities to act out the stories dictated to you in Literacy/Writing Possibilities (see page 272). Read the dictated story out loud to children first, making sure to mention the title of the story and the writer who dictated the story. Ask the author to identify children to play each character. Re-read the dictated story one sentence at a time slowly, giving the actor time to act out what is said. Start the applause when the story is finished. Talk about why everyone is not in the story. "Hannah gets to pick who she wants in her play." "Not everyone will get to act this time." "We also need an audience to watch the story being acted out."

Other Group Time Possibilities

- Read any of the books listed on page 284.
- Let shadow puppet theatre producers put on a shadow play (see page 265).
- Play related theme music before you read books.

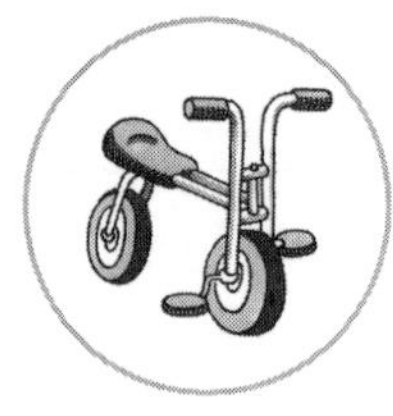

MOVEMENT/OUTDOORS POSSIBILITIES

Story Adventures

Teacher Talk
"What do you think is going to happen next?" "Tell me how I should go on with the story."

Instructions
When you are outside on the playground, tell children a story using the children as characters. Create stories based on old favorites, such as "Three Little Pigs" and "Hansel and Gretel." Tell the story as children act it out. Spontaneous literacy experiences like these are great to add to children's time outdoors. The children are more likely to follow the story if you participate while you tell the story.

Observation/Assessment
Acts out stories

Mother Goose on the Loose

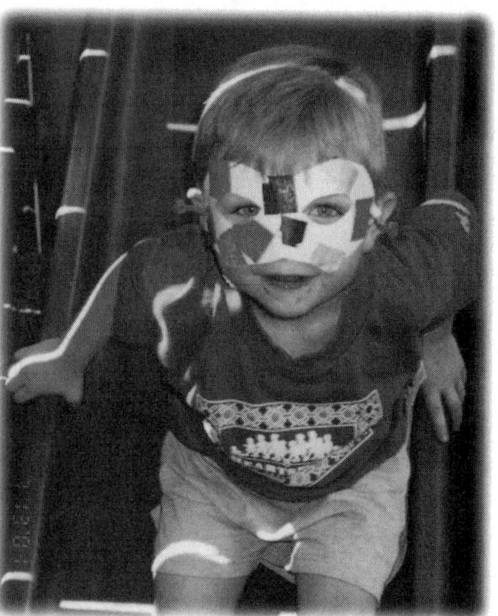

Materials
"The Three Little Pig Blues" from *Greg and Steve Playing Favorites* • wolf and pig puppets • "Rocking Around the Mulberry Bush" by Greg and Steve, *We All Live Together Volume 3* • "London Bridge" from Sharon, Lois and Bram, *Elephant Show Record* • tambourines • "Nursery Rhymes" from Joe Scruggs' *Late Last Night*. • puppets • other similar nursery rhyme selections

Teacher Talk
"You used all the different props to act out the story."

Instructions
Play nursery rhymes from any of the recordings mentioned, using the suggested props to support children's dancing and creative dramatics. Enjoy this activity outdoors.

Observation/Assessment
Acts out stories using props

Three Little Pigs Outside

Materials
straw • wood • brick cardboard blocks • clothes • wolf mask • pig masks

Teacher Talk
"Acting out stories can be fun, especially when we are outside."

Instructions
Dramatic play outdoors can be even more fun than indoors. Provide props so that children can act out and narrate favorite stories. Make sure masks do not obscure vision or lines of sight.

Observation/Assessment
Acts out familiar stories

PROJECTS/DOCUMENTATION POSSIBILITIES

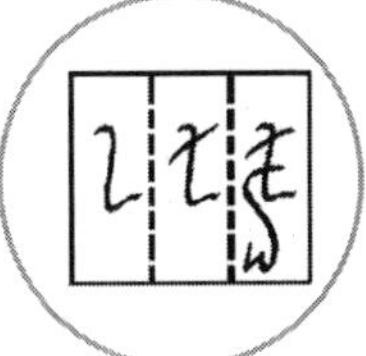

Making Pancakes

Materials
Pancakes for Breakfast by Tomie De Paola • instructions for making pancakes in rebus chart form (see page 280) • materials and ingredients for pancakes • pancake mix boxes • mixing materials • clean-up materials • electric skillet or griddle (teacher only)

Teacher Talk
"Even though this book does not have a lot of words, it tells a story." "This time you are going to read to me."

Instructions
Because *Pancakes for Breakfast* is a picture book, most preschoolers are able to read the pictures and understand the story. Let the children read the book to you together as you turn the pages. Assist them if needed. When you finish the book, ask children to list the ingredients in pancakes, writing their list on chart paper.

Plan a visit to the supermarket to purchase the ingredients for pancakes identified by the children as they read the book. If a field trip is not possible, include families in providing the ingredients, or order them from your school's kitchen.

Use the rebus instructions of the steps of making pancakes (see page 280). Include each child in preparing the pancakes. Once the mixing is complete, cook the pancakes on the griddle or skillet (teacher only). Talk about safety rules when cooking in the classroom, helping children understand that the skillet or griddle is hot and poses a burn risk. If cooking in the classroom is not allowed in your school, check to see if children can stand at the door of the kitchen or watch through an observation window as pancakes are being cooked.

Observation/Assessment
Follows directions

Making Pancakes

Spin Me a Tall Tale Wall

Materials
tall tales books from the list on page 284 • construction paper • contact paper • markers • scissors • glue

Teacher Talk
"Which tale is your favorite?" "Why do you like this tall tale best?"

Instructions
As children get to know the tall tales and stories in this Possibilities Plan, ask each child to pick one or two favorites. Make a chart of each child's favorite tales and stories. As children make their selections, give them paper to illustrate their favorite tales. Because this is a project, children may work on their illustrations more than once, perhaps several times, perfecting and adding to the illustration. When children tell you that their illustrations are complete, post them on the wall, creating a "Spin Me a Tall Tale Wall."

Children's Biographies

Materials
photographs of children (preferably one for each year of life) • construction paper • page protectors • hole punch • three-ring binder

Teacher Talk
"This is a picture of Karl as a baby. Does he look like Karl?" "Everyone was little once."

Instructions
Collect photographs (or copies) of children from their families. Help children attach the photographs to paper, if necessary, and put the photographs in the page protectors. Put the pages into a three-ring binder. Ask children to tell you something about each photograph, compiling their comments into an autobiography.

Extension Possibilities: See if children can identify each other as babies. See if children can identify their parents or family members from the family photos brought in by parents and family members. Play guessing games such as "Whose Grandfather Is This?"

FIELD TRIP POSSIBILITIES

Children's Theater: Plan a field trip for children to experience live theater. Bring an activity for children to enjoy as they wait for the play to begin.

Bookstore or Library: A field trip to a bookstore or library can show children many different versions of similar stories.

Library Story Time: Many local libraries have visiting storytellers to tell stories or read to children. Check local schedules and arrange for your class to participate.

SNACK POSSIBILITIES

Pancakes and a Story: A number of books have stories about pancakes in them. Serve pancakes for snack and read one of the children's favorite pancake stories while they eat. Some favorites are *If You Give a Pig a Pancake* by Laura Joffe Numeroff, *Pancakes for Breakfast* by Tomie dePaola, and *Pancakes, Pancakes* by Eric Carle.

Cheese and Crackers and a Mouse Story: Serve cheese and crackers and read a mouse story for snack.

Food in a Basket: Any snack can be fun if you put it in a basket and take it outside to eat! Read any version of "Little Red Riding Hood" (complete with different character voices) for added fun. Don't forget handwashing before snacking.

FAMILY PARTICIPATION POSSIBILITIES

Story Time with Parents or Family Members: Invite parents and family members to come to the class and read their favorite tale to children. They can provide their own books or select one from the classroom and read as they drop off their children, during their lunch break, or at the end of the school day during pick-up time.

Parent Baby Books/Photographs: Ask parents to bring their family photo albums from their childhoods or photographs of themselves when they were their child's age to share. Make a plan to keep photo albums and photographs safe (restrict the times when children can look at them, supervise directly, and so on) and to return them to families.

Songs and Fingerplays from Parents' Childhoods: Ask parents to come and share favorite songs and fingerplays from their childhood. Write them down to repeat or sing at a later time.

What Do Children Learn in Dramatic Play?

We all know that children love to pretend—to be something they aren't while they play. Why do children enjoy dramatic play so much and what do they learn from it? Children use play as the context for learning—learning in all domains of development.

There is much for children to learn about social relationships during dramatic play. It is hard to play with another child without getting his or her attention and agreeing on what to play. The problem-solving and negotiation process that unfolds as children decide what to play and who will play which role is a proving ground for social learning. Children learn to be the leader and direct play, as well as learn how to follow another child's play ideas. They also learn to find many ways to play with others.

Children use dramatic play to express emotions. It is often possible to act out feelings that are not easy to identify, to express fears and concerns in helpful ways, and to be able to play out life issues and challenges many different times, experimenting with different outcomes and strategies. Dramatic play also engenders a whole range of emotions, happy feelings, sad feelings, feelings of frustration, anger, and irritability as well as empathy, sympathy, and altruism. During the preschool years, children all have these feelings and more. They are just not yet able to identify this wide range of different feelings. In dramatic play, they practice connecting feelings with actions and clarifying the differences between emotions.

Dramatic play benefits intellectual development, as well. While playing, children often have to solve problems. This process is worked out through dialogue during play— not only stimulating problem-solving skills but also stimulating language and vocabulary.

Children gain experience with creating different outcomes, using imagination and fantasy to explore creative ideas and adventures. Many of these adventures are actually the children's attempt to make sense of their experiential world. Play is the perfect medium for allowing children to use and explore these fantasies without the limitation of the physical world. Fantasies really do come true as children play—they can be the pirate, the princess, the mom, or the dad.

Dramatic play allows children to practice and learn a wide range of skills. Physical, intellectual, social, and emotional development is supported as children participate in dramatic play. Encouraging this natural and educational experience in your child's life virtually guarantees growth in many different areas.

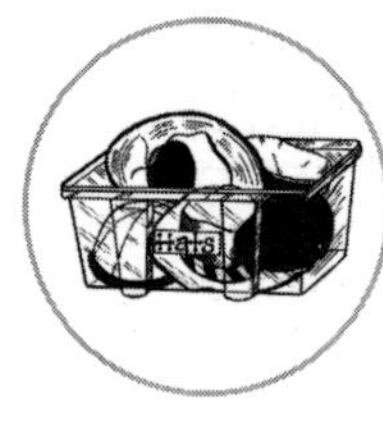

Curriculum Resources

Prop Boxes

The World's a Wonderful Stage Prop Box
shower curtain • shower curtain rings • twine • PVC pipe 4' long 1 ½" wide • various dress-up clothes for costumes (hats, scarves, ties, masks, shoes)

Puppet Theatre Prop Box
large cardboard appliance box (refrigerator or washer/dryer) • craft knife • 2'1" x 2'1" piece of black material • tape • paint • paintbrushes • variety of puppets or a purchased puppet theatre

Books

Abiyoyo: Based on a South African Lullaby and Folk Story by Pete Seeger
Abiyoyo Returns by Pete Seeger
Angkat: The Cambodian Cinderella by Jewell Reinhart Coburn
Cindy Ellen: A Wild West Cinderella by Susan Lowell
Curious George and the Hot Air Balloon by H.A. Rey
Davy Crockett Saves the World by Rosalyn Schanzer
Eric Carle's Treasury of Classic Stories for Children by Aesop, Hans Christian Andersen, and the Brothers Grimm by Eric Carle
The Girl Who Loved Wild Horses/La Nina Que Amaba Los Caballos Salvajes by Paul Goble, Spanish version
The Golden Sandal: A Middle Eastern Cinderella Story by Rebecca Hickox
The Handmade Alphabet by Laura Rankin
Harold and the Purple Crayon by Crockett Johnson
Heckedy Peg by Audrey Wood
If You Give a Moose a Muffin by Laura Joffe Numeroff
If You Give a Pig a Pancake by Laura Joffe Numeroff
Johnny Appleseed: A Tall Tale by Steven Kellogg
Kate and the Beanstalk by Mary Pope Osborne
Lon Po Po: A Red-Riding Hood Story from China by Ed Young
Mufaro's Beautiful Daughters: An African Tale by John Steptoe
Pancakes for Breakfast by Tomie dePaola
Pancakes, Pancakes by Eric Carle
Pecos Bill: A Tall Tale by Steven Kellogg
Polar Bear, Polar Bear, What Do You Hear? by Bill Martin Jr. and Eric Carle (illustrator)
The Rough-Face Girl by Rafe Martin
Sally Ann Thunder Ann Whirlwind Crockett: A Tall Tale by Steven Kellogg
Seven Chinese Brothers by Margaret Mahy et al.
Tar Beach by Faith Ringgold
The Three Pigs by David Wiesner

Three Tales of My Father's Dragon by Ruth Stiles Gannett
Tikki Tikki Tembo by Arlene Mosel
Where the Wild Things Are by Maurice Sendak
Yeh-Shen: A Cinderella Story from China by Ai-Ling Louie

Observation/Assessment

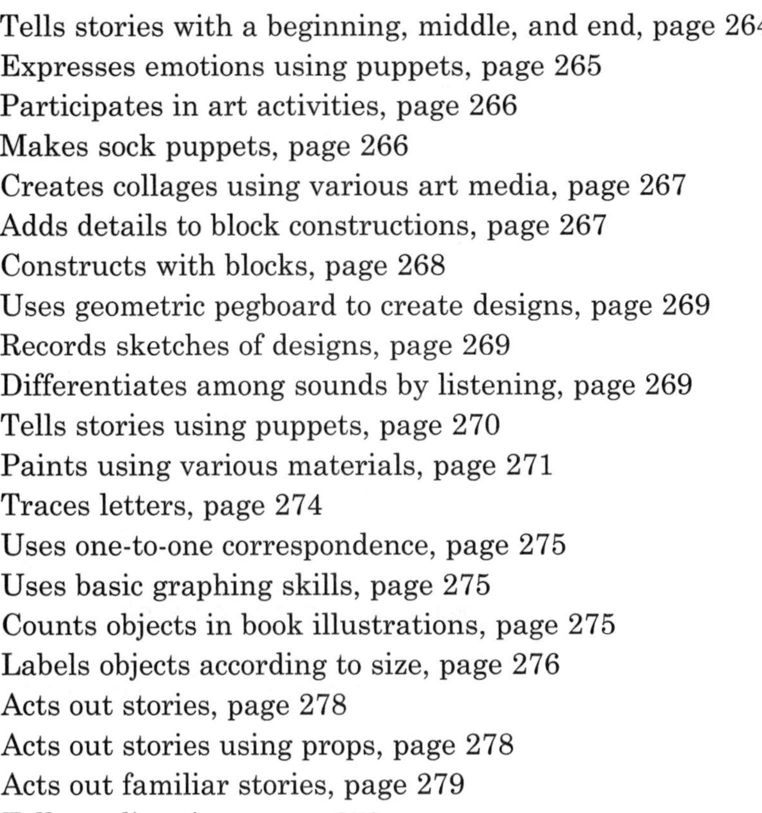

Tells stories with a beginning, middle, and end, page 264
Expresses emotions using puppets, page 265
Participates in art activities, page 266
Makes sock puppets, page 266
Creates collages using various art media, page 267
Adds details to block constructions, page 267
Constructs with blocks, page 268
Uses geometric pegboard to create designs, page 269
Records sketches of designs, page 269
Differentiates among sounds by listening, page 269
Tells stories using puppets, page 270
Paints using various materials, page 271
Traces letters, page 274
Uses one-to-one correspondence, page 275
Uses basic graphing skills, page 275
Counts objects in book illustrations, page 275
Labels objects according to size, page 276
Acts out stories, page 278
Acts out stories using props, page 278
Acts out familiar stories, page 279
Follows directions, page 279

Picture File/Vocabulary

applause
audience
author
bang
beginning
boom
characters
cold
conclusion
ear
end
exaggeration
hot
illustrator
introduction
main idea
middle
mime
mouth
music
numbers
prediction
puppet theater
quilt
recipe
ring
sequence
size
sound wave
throat
warm
whoosh

Concepts Learned in

Spin Me a Tall Tale

Content Knowledge

- ☐ Stories have characters.
- ☐ Quilts are made up of many squares.
- ☐ There are many ways to tell a story.
- ☐ Music can tell stories.
- ☐ Hand signs can tell stories.
- ☐ Pictures can tell stories.
- ☐ Words can tell stories.
- ☐ Invitations ask people to attend special events.
- ☐ You can tell the same story many different ways.

Process Knowledge

- ☐ I can perform.
- ☐ I can make puppets.
- ☐ I can produce a puppet show.
- ☐ I can paint to music.
- ☐ I can make books in several different forms.
- ☐ I understand how sound moves through the air in waves.
- ☐ I can follow a recipe.
- ☐ I can act out stories.

Pre-academic Skills

- ☐ I can differentiate between sounds just by listening (auditory discrimination of sounds).
- ☐ I can figure out pictures that tell a story (reading context clues to discern meaning).
- ☐ I can identify how many characters there are in a story.
- ☐ I can dictate a story with a beginning, middle, and ending.
- ☐ I can predict what will happen next in a story.
- ☐ I can sequence a story.

CHAPTER 5

Communicating with Parents, Teachers, and Friends

INNOVATIONS IN CARE AND EARLY EDUCATION

Language Development

During the early childhood years, children go from being non-verbal to communicating effectively. Various language development theories propose different ideas about how children learn language. Noam Chomsky (1957) proposed that children are born with a genetic system that primes them to learn language. This view is used to explain why children all over the world follow roughly the same language acquisition process.

Other theorists propose that language learning occurs as a result of the child's response to environmental stimuli. Called operant conditioning, this learning is a direct result of the child's actions and the responses received. When the experiences are pleasant, the likelihood of the child repeating the action increases. So, when Mom and Dad are delighted when their child learns the names of dinosaurs, their reactions of excitement and enthusiasm increase the child's desire to repeat and learn names of other dinosaurs. If no one responds or if a hearing loss prevents the child from getting auditory feedback, the continued learning may not happen. It further suggests that children model the actions of adults who talk and interact with them. Such interaction reinforces children's language efforts, promoting language acquisition.

Still other theorists view language as a much more complex process, one that depends on innate predispositions as well as responsive, interactive adults and environments. As children experience language, innate abilities are stimulated (nature viewpoint) and supported by observation, participation, and exploration (nurture viewpoint). These experiences combine to support children's construction of knowledge about language and understanding of form, content, similarities, and differences of language. This theoretical point of view is called interactional.

From this perspective, relationships create the context for language acquisition. Reciprocal language, starting with gestures and facial expressions, creates shared meaning between children and the adults in their attachment networks, intensifying and facilitating the mutuality of relationships (Stern, 1985). Language has a primary influence on relationship development—facilitating both non-verbal and verbal communication between children and the important adults in their lives.

Language competence is fostered when children and adults give joint attention to reciprocal conversations about the experiences going on in their lives. From these conversations, children learn to pay attention to others, take turns, acquire new vocabulary, and talk with peers and significant adults (Katz & Snow, 2000).

During the early childhood years, children typically go from babbling to using grammatically correct sentences. Language development follows the developmental principle of proceeding from the simple to the complex and the general to the specific.

Language development follows the developmental principle of proceeding from the simple to the complex and the general to the specific.

For speech and language acquisition, the sequence follows these developmental principles:

1. Motorically simple to motorically complex; for example, (m) as in mama to (kw) as in queen
2. Acoustically simple to acoustically complex; for example, (p) as in pie to (thr) as in throw
3. Visible (simple) to less visible (complex); for example, (b) as in boy to (r) as in red

The sequence of initial sound articulation is also predictable. During the first five years, a child will typically master the following sounds:

(b), (d), (f), (g), (h), (j), (k), (m), (n), (p), (s), (t), (v), (w), (y), (z)

Other initial sounds are acquired after the fifth year (Smith et al., 1990).

Children's language behaviors also follow a fairly predictable developmental pattern. The language behaviors chart on the following page lists skills that can be expected to emerge within a few months following chronological ages.

Preschool Language Behaviors

Age	Language Behaviors
3-4 Years	• Uses sentences of 4-6 words routinely • Talks about activities at school • Uses speech that is usually understood by people outside the family • Asks who, what, when, where, why, and how questions • Pays attention to stories • Says most initial sounds correctly; makes a few mistakes with l, s, r, v, z in some words • Uses speech that contains hesitancies and repetitions (disfluencies or nonfluencies) caused by the thinking process getting ahead of the speaking process • Recognizes print and symbols in the environment • Displays reading and writing attempts—says, "look at my story" • Loves rhyming words and word games, often using them to get a reaction or to be silly or funny
4-5 Years	• Uses sentences that give lots of details • Retells stories; tells stories that stick to the topic • Communicates easily with other adults and children • Begins to isolate the initial sound in words • Uses the same grammar and syntax as the rest of the family members • Reports on past and present experiences • Knows some alphabet letters, particularly those in his own name
5-6 Years	• Has a vocabulary that continues to grow • Corrects most grammar and syntax errors • Uses complex sentences • Creates and tells original stories • Identifies all of the alphabet letters; may still confuse some letters • Connects letters to the sounds that they make

As these skills emerge, children's language becomes more readily understandable. About 60%–65% of a three-year-old's language is understandable to strangers and 75%–90% for a four-year-old. By age five, adults should be able to understand almost all of children's expressive language.

Children's language development before age three is explored in ***Innovations: Infant and Toddler Development***. If children are exhibiting speech and language delays, it may be helpful to refer to the developmental milestones (found in ***Innovations: Infant and Toddler Development***) that precede those in the preschool years.

Almost all children follow the relatively predictable path of language acquisition, regardless of culture. This is not to say that the cultural context doesn't influence language—it does. But the influence of culture seems independent of the developmental process of acquiring language (Shonkoff & Phillips, 2000).

The influences of culture are usually seen in children's language learning styles (Berk, 1999). Some children view language learning as a mechanism to label and identify objects while others view language learning as a way to get their needs met and express their feelings. These style differences originate in the interactive style of the adults and others in the cultural context of the child.

Expressive, Receptive, and Pragmatic Language

During the early childhood years, children have three kinds of language skills. One set is expressive language skills, meaning the production of language, those things children can say, the size of the spoken vocabulary, and the grammar and syntax of language. The second set of skills is related to receptive language, which refers to children's comprehension of language, the words they can understand, regardless of whether they use them in expression. Pragmatic language refers to the third type of skills where children use language appropriately in social settings—knowing what to say, how to say it, when to say it, and how to use language to be with others socially. As they approach three, children have usually acquired receptive language skills and developed the expressive language skills to use language functionally.

It is during the preschool years that children work on the pragmatics of language, perfecting how to use language to get their social and interactive needs met. They are learning to use language for different purposes, such as greeting, promising, instructing, or asking. Following the rules of language, such as when to talk and when to listen or how to read non-verbal cues, is also being practiced and learned. By far the hardest pragmatic skill is learning how to adapt or change language to fit the situation and the other people in it. Modifying the way you ask to be the leader to get others to agree, asking to play in a way that gets a "yes" answer rather than a "no" answer, or responding to one playmate's request to play differently than another's request are examples of pragmatic language skills.

Literacy Learning and Development—Teaching Children to Read and Write

Reading and writing are interdependent processes—the ability to read and write develops in tandem with oral language. During the early childhood years, children construct their own knowledge of the written word. Some children learn by hearing stories read to them; others learn by talking about literature, exploring the clues in pictures, learning the sounds letters make; still others learn by remembering or memorizing the patterns of letters that make up words. For most children, though, repeated and varied experiences coupled with extensive exploration of books and print materials help them begin to make sense of the written word. Adults facilitate most of children's early exposure to literacy. From reading aloud to children to connecting oral language to the printed word, the teacher's role in supporting emerging literacy is a dynamic one.

Most children use many different strategies to understand print before they learn to read or write. Although controversy exists about the best ways to teach children to read and write successfully, consensus has emerged that no one teaching method or approach is likely to be effective for all children. It takes a cadre of good methods, strategies, and approaches that include many appropriate literacy experiences to ensure that all children gain the necessary skills they need to read and write and use these skills successfully in the learning process.

Like so many skills and abilities, literacy skills evolve along a developmental continuum in which simple skills are acquired before more complex ones. The first phase is awareness and exploration. During this phase, children enjoy listening to and discussing storybooks, begin to understand that print carries a message, engage in reading and writing attempts, identify labels and signs in the environment, participate in rhyming games, identify letters, make sound/letter matches, and use approximations of letters and letters to represent writing (NAEYC/IRA, 1998). The preschool years are the prime time for these experiences.

Reading Aloud, Developing Vocabulary, and Phonemic Awareness

A strong correlation exists between reading aloud to children and building the understanding and skills needed to read successfully in elementary school. Children whose parents and teachers read aloud to them at least 30 minutes a day read more easily than children who aren't read to by the significant adults in their lives. When children are read to, they learn many concepts about how print works and how to access the written word.

Vocabulary size is predictive of reading success. When children have many opportunities to listen to books, to talk about the stories and pictures in the books they read, and to ask and answer questions about the print and the story, the size of their vocabularies increases. Children with larger vocabularies are well prepared to access the world of print (Hart and Risley, 1999).

Phonemic awareness is also considered an oral language skill that leads to success in reading. It is the ability to hear, identify, and manipulate the separate sounds in spoken language. It is the capacity to understand the way that language is constructed—the structure of sounds, words, phrases, and sentences.

A strong correlation exists between reading aloud to children and building the understanding and skills needed to read successfully in elementary school.

Rich and varied oral language experiences at home and at school, plenty of interactions with print in books and other forms, and specific attention to the sound structure in spoken words create the best literacy environment for young children.

Intellectual Development

The intellectual development of children is stimulated by virtually everything teachers do with children. In fact, during the early childhood years, intellectual and language development is motivated naturally as children explore and interact with the people and things in their environment.

Piaget's Cognitive-development Theory

According to Jean Piaget, children learn cognitive skills by making mistakes, by actively experimenting with the real world, and by trying to understand how things work (Piaget, 1977). Piaget viewed active experimentation, experiences with concrete objects and the environment as the best way to stimulate intellectual development.

Piaget's theory of cognitive development is a stage theory. It proposes four periods of development. The first two of Piaget's stages occur during early childhood. During the first stage, the sensori-motor stage, children use information gathered through their senses and motor movement to construct an understanding of the world. Beginning with reflexes, then with purposeful motor movement, and finally, through manipulation of objects, children discover and explore the environment.

Two complementary cognitive processes are responsible for construction of knowledge during the early childhood years, according to Piaget. The first, called assimilation, is the process of interpreting new information or learning into existing ideas or thought. The second process, called accommodation, is the creation of new ideas or the adaptation of old ones when new information is received from exploration and manipulation of objects.

The second stage of Piaget's theory is the pre-operational stage. During the pre-operational stage, Piaget believed that children's cognitive skills are very different from adult skills. Children's cognitive development is dominated by the formation of cognitive images that are based on direct, interactive experiences.

Many mistakes in thinking occur in this period. Children's thought is characterized by egocentrism—the inability to understand or envision situations from perspectives other than one's own. Thinking errors that children make during the pre-operational period include reasoning errors and misunderstandings of causal relationships. Children in this stage reason from one particular to the next, which is called transductive reasoning. This thinking error is related to applying one experience to other, unrelated experiences. Children also focus on one aspect of a situation or problem rather than considering all of the possibilities. This thinking error is called centration. An example might be refusing to eat anything that is green, even when the color of the food has little to do with its taste or texture.

Children in this stage also attribute lifelike and human qualities to inanimate objects. This thinking error is often seen when children ascribe names and human qualities to security items or toys. The inability to reverse or undo actions is another thinking error, called irreversibility. Children in this stage are often unable to think of an alternative behavior they might use when adults ask them to stop the behavior they are using. Children also have many magical thoughts during this stage. The child's inability to separate fantasy from reality results in the child believing that what he thinks is connected to what he can do.

The inability to conserve size, shape, mass, and volume is another thinking error. Many classic examples come to mind of the conservation thinking errors. Children often think other children got "more" than they got (of juice, cookies, or clay) when the perceptual presentation of the materials is different (big cup, little cup, for example).

These errors explain so well what every adult understands about children this age—that they are much more interested in figuring things out for themselves than they are in having adults tell them how things work (Mooney, 2000).

The chart on the following page summarizes the characteristics of Piaget's stages of cognitive development.

Piaget's Stages of Cognitive Development

Stage 1	**Sensori-motor Stage**	Birth–2 years	• Adaptation (through assimilation and accommodation) to environment does not include the use of symbols or oral language • Child develops schema (cognitive pictures)
Stage 2	**Pre-operational Stage**	2–7 years	• Characterized by the beginning of symbolic thought and the use of mental images and words • Child has flaws in thinking: egocentrism, centration, irreversibility, transductive, or illogical reasoning • Child has flawed beliefs of causal relationships: animism, artificialism, participation
Stage 2A	**Pre-conceptual Stage**	2–5 years	• Develops ability to classify objects: child will group similar objects together but will not appear to have an overall plan to complete task • Develops the ability to serialize objects: child will serialize sporadically without plan or goal • Cannot conserve quantity, substance, or volume
Stage 2B	**Intuitive Stage**	4–7 years	• Classification of objects can be done by classes and sub-classes • Serialization develops to constructing an ordinal arrangement with some difficulty
Stage 3	**Concrete Operations Stage**	6–11 years	• Characterized by performing concrete mental operations with symbols (numbers, letters) and by organizing objects by their distinct qualities

Recent consideration of Piaget's ideas reveals limitations in his observations about cognitive development, particularly in light of the advances in brain theory and research, and in our understanding of the role of emotion and social relationships on cognitive development (Cryer & Harms, 2000; Mooney, 2000). Nevertheless, Piaget's basic ideas are still useful in understanding how children construct their own knowledge.

Vygotsky's Socio-cultural Theory

Vygotsky (1978) shared many of Piaget's ideas, but felt that the child's social and cognitive worlds are much closer than Piaget did. This theory placed increased emphasis on the importance of the family and the cultural context where the child lives and experiences learning. Vygotsky viewed social interactions between children and supportive adults or more competent peers as a significant part of the learning process.

Language, particularly language used in play, is the primary mechanism for advancing children's construction of knowledge, according to Vygotsky. As children participate in play, their conversations, discussions, conflicts, and negotiations extend and enhance cognitive skills and abilities.

Vygotsky's theory validates the importance of the teacher as a keen observer of children. The goal of observation is to allow teachers to understand each child's zone of proximal development (ZPD). The ZPD is the range of tasks children cannot handle on their own but can manage with the help of a supportive teacher or more competent peers. To be able to challenge children cognitively, Teachers have to be aware of children's socio-cultural contexts and their zones of proximal development.

Encouraging conversations, interactions, and play experiences in small groups is the optimal way for children to learn. Within small groups, scaffolding of children's learning by peers is most likely to occur. Vygotsky also considers the teacher's role in supporting learning as a challenging one. Knowing when to intervene with which teaching strategy is a crucial teaching skill. When to ask a questions, which question to ask, what idea to offer, which suggestion to make, and when to let children proceed on their own are delicate considerations that can disrupt the flow of children's learning or scaffold it to an even higher level.

Gardner's Theory of Multiple Intelligences

Gardner's theory of multiple intelligences proposes that children have several kinds of intelligence that operate at the same time in complementary ways (Gardner, 1983). Theorists and researchers who think children have multiple intelligences believe that there are many ways for children to learn and for teachers to teach.

Gardner's Theory of Multiple Intelligences

Intelligence	Description
Linguistic	Sensitivity to the meaning and order of words
Logico-mathematical	Ability to handle chains of reasoning and recognize patterns and order
Musical	Sensitivity to pitch, melody, rhythm, and tone
Bodily-kinesthetic	Ability to use the body skillfully and handle objects adroitly
Spatial	Ability to perceive the world accurately and to recreate or transform aspects of that world
Naturalist	Ability to recognize and classify the numerous species of an environment
Interpersonal	Ability to understand people and relationships
Intrapersonal (also called emotional intelligence by Goleman)	Access to one's emotional life as a means to understand oneself and others

This theory proposes that all of the multiple intelligences are present at birth. Early indicators of different intelligences can be seen in children. For example, some children are watchers—they like to observe as others try new things. Some are doers—they have to be in the middle of any experience embracing it all. Still others listen carefully to what goes on around them before they begin to interact. These differences emerge from the individual's unique collection of intelligences and are part of what makes each of us different from one another.

One type of intelligence—intrapersonal intelligence—is thought to be an important type to support during the early years. Also called emotional intelligence, it includes self-awareness, managing emotions, emotional self-control, recognizing emotions in others, and handling relationships (Goleman, 1998). Every interaction between children and their parents or teachers carries emotional messages that can influence emotional intelligence. If messages are positive and responsive, children learn that the world is a supportive and caring place. If children receive curt, insensitive responses, or worse, abusive or cruel responses, these emotional encounters negatively mold children's views of relationships. Both experiences affect functioning in all realms of life, for better or worse.

Another tenet of Gardner's theory is that interactions are cumulative—each interaction matters. The actions and reactions of adults, the teaching plans, and school schedules tell children if and how much we care for them.

Gardner's theory of multiple intelligences validates that every child is unique and that our programs must be modified to fit each child, rather than requiring children to fit into our programs. Further, the theory of multiple intelligences helps us support parents in viewing their child's unique skills rather than comparing their child to other children.

INNOVATIONS IN INTERACTIVE EXPERIENCES

Theories of language acquisition and intellectual development suggest that appropriate stimulation of language and cognition results in many advantages for children later in life. For language, appropriate stimulation means giving children many repeated experiences with language. It also means having good language models that add complexity and extend children's language, stimulate vocabulary development, associate letters with the sounds they make, and connect language to the broader functional world of literacy.

Stimulation of cognitive development happens naturally as children explore the world around them. Interests serve as springboards for providing more information about the things that intrigue them, adding vocabulary and expanded language related to their interests, and increasing interactions with their peers.

Interactive Experiences Checklist for Communicating with Parents, Teachers, and Friends

Ask a mentor to observe you in your classroom to document the following interactive behaviors. Think about the following list of interactive experiences and make sure that the classroom reflects many of them.

- ☐ Make and keep eye contact with children as they play. Preschool children still need reminders that you are available to help if needed.
- ☐ Narrate routines as you implement them. This gives children ideas about what is going to happen, serves as a reminder that the next steps are familiar and predictable, and associates vocabulary with routines.
- ☐ Converse with children, labeling objects, pointing out actions, and describing actions and reactions.
- ☐ Ask open-ended questions that require a real response. Avoid questions that have only one right answer or only one-word answers. Try, "What is your idea?" as a starting response for questions asked by children.
- ☐ Wait for responses to questions. Resist the tendency to answer your own questions. Give children time to put together their responses. Then, accept their responses, posing another open-ended question rather than correcting the answer.
- ☐ Sing and dance with preschoolers, and use fingerplays as routine, stimulation, and transition activities.
- ☐ Stimulate vocabulary development by expanding sentences used by children. Simply restate their sentences with additional words that expand the sentence's complexity.
- ☐ Interpret nonverbal cues and give them word descriptions.
- ☐ Respond to children's actions, particularly when they are too excited, frustrated, or angry to find the words themselves.
- ☐ Ask children with limited language skills or whose home language is not English to show you, take you to, or point to objects of interest, particularly if you don't understand what they need or want. Success in communicating, even non-verbally, supports an interest in learning more language.
- ☐ Play "what if" games.
- ☐ Support emerging concentration skills by avoiding interruptions of children when they are playing.
- ☐ Time interruptions to avoid distracting children from interesting tasks, particularly if they are favorite ones.

Create Positive Interactive Environments

Creating a positive interactive environment for communication starts with good listening skills. Attentive teachers listen to children carefully, using their listening skills to further their understanding of what children are thinking and feeling.

Positive interactive environments for language development embed language in interactions, routines, transitions, and activities. This communication between children is very much a part of learning. Talking about what you are doing with your peers as you do it is just as important as what you are doing. At the same time, positive interactive environments help children understand when talking is not appropriate or when it should wait. Part of pragmatic language skill development is learning when to talk, when to listen, and when to keep quiet.

Value each child's attempts to communicate. Help children learn skills such as not interrupting, taking turns, and saying what you want to say succinctly. "I will hear your important words when Angi is finished" is a good example of a teaching technique to help children who have a hard time waiting their turn.

Resist the temptation to tell children all they need to know. For preschool children, getting the answer from you is unlikely to result in learning. Interactive environments that focus on what children think rather than what the answer is encourage cognitive exploration and problem solving.

Give children time to think before they answer—value the pause. Offering children time to think about their ideas, form a response in their minds, and then communicate their ideas is not an instantaneous activity. When teachers value the exploration of what children think as much as they value the answers children form, cognitive development is encouraged and stimulated.

When teachers value the exploration of what children think as much as they value the answers children form, cognitive development is encouraged and stimulated.

Protect opportunities to share points of view and differences. As preschool children explore their thoughts, egocentrism makes them want everyone to see things the same way they do. Yet, different thought processes, various intelligences, and different temperaments and learning styles lead to different thinking outcomes. Embrace this creativity and diversity while helping children see that people can have different points of view and ideas and still work cooperatively together as they learn. "He has a different point of view (or idea) than you do" helps children understand that situations can be approached from more than one perspective.

Use a Variety of Teaching Roles

Teachers use a wide variety of roles in their work with young children. During the task of Communicating with Parents, Teachers, and Friends, teachers encourage frequent, clear communication between children and plan experiences that support reciprocal communication and receptive, expressive, and pragmatic language skill acquisition. They work on expanding vocabulary and teach thinking skills, challenging children to construct their own understanding of how the things that interest them work.

During the developmental task of Communicating with Parents, Teachers, and Friends, two of the most important teacher roles are instructor and documenter. These roles have specific characteristics during this developmental task.

The Teacher as Instructor

One of the traditional roles of a teacher is instructor. Vygotsky's socio-cultural theory supports the idea of the teacher as an instructor with specific characteristics. He believed that children learn best when they are assisted in learning. Vygotsky's instructor role includes explaining, demonstrating, prompting, interpreting, analyzing, probing, illustrating with examples, clarifying, summarizing, questioning, and supporting peer collaboration and cooperation. These teaching tasks are used when the child is near his zone of proximal development (ZPD), so that learning can scaffold to the next level (see page 297 for more information).

This view of instruction as embedded in intimate knowledge of individuals, not applied to everyone at the same time, differentiates the instructor's role during the preschool years from the traditional elementary classroom instructor.

Knowing when instruction will support children's learning is based on observation and knowledge of each child's ZPD. This view of instruction as embedded in intimate knowledge of individuals, not applied to everyone at the same time in the same way, differentiates the instructor's role during the preschool years from the traditional elementary classroom instructor.

The Teacher as Documenter

In this role, teachers observe, record, reflect on, and synthesize children's learning processes into documentation. The goal of documentation is to communicate—communicate children's ideas, competence, and knowledge construction while engaging teachers in co-constructing their own knowledge about children, their interests, and their competencies.

Documentation is a cycle of inquiry that proceeds in fits and starts (Gandini & Goldhaber, 2001). It begins with framing questions to focus thinking on the types of appropriate experiences for children. Then, teachers collect evidence of children's experiences. The techniques of collection can be quite varied, including written notes, photographs, samples of children's work, videotapes, or audio recordings.

Organizing, analyzing, and interpreting the results of the observation process is the next step. This synthesis step often leads right back to reconsidering the questions that were framed in the beginning of the process. Then, teachers use the results of the organizing process to guide what to do next with children. It is at this stage that documentation becomes "public," resulting in an opportunity to share children's ideas and thinking with others, as it was observed and recorded during the process of documentation.

This brief introduction to the documentation process is only a beginning. Teachers who are interested in expanding their teaching roles to include documentation will need to explore these ideas further. Check the resource list (pages 327-328) for helpful references.

INNOVATIONS IN TEACHING

Talk to Children Often Using Language Stimulation Techniques

The field of speech and language development offers indirect language stimulation techniques that teachers will find useful. These techniques, called description, parallel talk, self-talk, expansion, and expansion plus, direct the adult's language behaviors and encourage the continuation of language acquisition for children.

Description

Description is a technique in which the teacher narrates or describes what is going on in the child's world by putting word labels on things. For example, if a child looks toward the door as a parent enters the room, the adult might say, "That's Jenny's mother. She must be here to pick up Jenny." Description is also helpful in communicating mutual respect. When a teacher tells a child what will happen to him before it happens and waits for the child to indicate that he is ready for the action or activity, the teacher is showing mutual respect for the child (Gerber, 1979). A teacher might say, "In five minutes, it will be time to wash hands so we can eat lunch," as a description of what and when it will happen.

Parallel Talk

Parallel talk is a short phrase that focuses on the child's action. Parallel talk usually begins with "you." For example, "You're playing with the cars and the trucks," is parallel talk. Focusing on the action helps the child put word labels on behavior and more importantly, connects the word labels into a sentence describing the action. Use this technique as you observe children at play, showing that you are interested and involved as you watch.

Self-Talk

Self-talk focuses on adult behavior, labeling and describing what the adult is doing. Adults who use self-talk usually start their sentences with "I." For example, a teacher might say to a child who is getting tired, "I think it is time for Maureen to take a nap." Self-talk is particularly helpful in preparing children for transitions. When you announce and remind children about transitions with self-talk, you help children prepare for the transition, an important guidance technique. To use self-talk this way, say things such as, "In 10 more minutes, I will get the mats out to get ready for naptime."

When you announce and remind children about transitions with self-talk, you help children prepare for the transition, an important guidance technique.

Expansion and Expansion Plus

Expansion and expansion plus are techniques to use with children as their vocabularies begin to grow. These techniques take what the child says and expand on it (expansion) or add to what the child says (expansion plus). For example, when a child says, "cracker," the teacher might say, "You want another graham cracker," or "Jason would like another saltine cracker, please," to expand what the child says into a complete sentence. If the child says, "Outside," the teacher might say, "You'd like to go outside." For expansion plus, the teacher adds a little more to the sentence a child uses. An example might expand, "Time to go bye-bye," said by the child, to "It's time to get your things and go home now." Expansion and expansion plus restate what the child says in complete and sometimes expanded sentence form. Vocabulary development correlates strongly with later literacy development. Adults can support vocabulary development significantly with this technique.

Notice that these techniques require nothing of the child. The child is not asked to repeat the longer sentence, to repeat the label of an object identified by description, or to respond further to the teacher. These techniques are teaching techniques that add information to the child's language skills and foster language development.

Build Vocabulary

Most preschoolers' expressive vocabulary has increased to over 2,000 words and will continue to grow to as many as 10,000 by the end of the early childhood period. Teachers and parents help children develop vocabulary when they use the following techniques:

- Provide word labels for things in the environment, increasing the sophistication of the labels as children age. For example, when you are on a walk, start by pointing out birds, clouds, trees, and other features of the environment. Then, add descriptive characteristics as you label the birds. "That's a blue bird; that one is called a mockingbird; that one's a crow."
- Use pictures to enhance and expand vocabulary. Continuing with the bird example, post pictures from your picture file of different species of birds along with their written names so that you can point out and use new vocabulary words. Exposing children to words, whether they use them expressively or not, is a great literacy activity. 
- Play word games with children. Children love to be entertaining with language—playing nonsense games with words. Encourage and expand on this interest by enjoying word games, too. Change the initial letter of a child's name (Baitlin instead of Caitlin). Or, use sequential initial sounds, such as Aitlin, Baitlin, Caitlin, and so on, to explore initial sounds. Chant, repeat rhymes and fingerplays, and sing songs, all with the idea of expanding vocabulary.
- Add vocabulary words to your curriculum plan to focus your attention on new words and to remind parents that you have identified new words for vocabulary development.

Support Linguistic and Cultural Diversity

English is not the primary language of a growing population of children who are in school settings (Tabors, 1998). This creates the need for increased understanding of linguistic and cultural diversity. Teachers also need strategies for supporting emerging oral language and literacy skills while accepting and validating each child's home language.

Young children are capable of learning more than one language at a time. Children learn language by having caring, responsive adults use language with them long before they begin to use language themselves. When children are exposed to second languages during the first five years, each language develops as a primary language, without slowing overall language development (Shonkoff & Phillips, 2000).

There are components of language that are not specific to the language spoken. Non-verbal communication develops in young children as they are developing verbal communication. Facial expressions, crying, whimpering, wiggling, running away or toward something or someone, all communicate without words.

Children whose primary language is not English need support bridging the two language worlds. They need validation of their home language and time to begin the process of acquiring receptive and expressive language skills in the second language at the same time. Try some of the following suggestions to support families and children for whom English is not the primary language.

- Collaborate with families to support the home language. Ask parents to help you learn a few words, of the child's home language, particularly needs-meeting words, such as "more," "Mother," "Daddy," "bathroom," and the words used to express hunger, sleepiness, and fear. Specifically, learn to say "hello" and "goodbye" and how to communicate changes in routine in the child's home language.
- Use both English and the child's home language when you say these familiar words. Use the home language first, and then repeat the word in English. This helps children begin to understand that the two languages they are hearing are different but communicate the same thing.

- Ask parents to help you translate fingerplays and rhymes into the home language, and to provide fingerplays and rhymes in the home language for you to use in the classroom. Encourage parents to record lullabies, songs, and other oral language traditions of the home language for you to use at school.
- Expand your children's book collection to include books in the home language of children in your group.
- Maintain eye contact and physical proximity during transitions, so you can provide non-verbal cues as well as verbal ones to children whose home language is not English.

- Create predictable routines—particularly those cued by oral language. For example, if you sing a clean-up song when it is time to clean up and go outside, non-English speaking children can pick up on other cues besides the words, in this case, the action and the tune. Think about transitions and try to support them with cues other than just oral language.

Support Emerging Literacy

What teachers do in their classrooms with children is so important for supporting emerging literacy. Try some of the following strategies in your classroom:

- Label your classroom with pictures and words. Children learn to read pictures easily, and connecting the picture to the word emphasizes the pattern of the word as well as its letter components. Label the important things, starting with 10-12 word/picture labels and building up to 20 or so over time, adding and changing the ones you have posted as children come to understand the word labels.
- Label storage containers with pictures and words to indicate what goes inside them. Label cubbies with pictures and names. Make copies of children's photographs and use them for labels, charts, and so on.
- Develop patterning skills by coding shelves indicating where thing go, particularly in the Blocks/Construction Possibilities area. Returning unit blocks to the shelves by following a picture pattern of the blocks is an excellent literacy experience as well as an appropriate mathematical, visual-motor, and figure/background discrimination experience.
- Make and use signs in your classroom. When you leave your classroom to go to the playground, put a simple sign on the door that says so. When a child finds something special on the playground or on a nature walk, post a sign that tells everyone about the discovery.
- Add real reading materials to your classroom—cookbooks, newspapers, magazines, appropriate junk mail advertisements, and so on. These are functional reading materials, not ones just for children.
- Read to all children. Read to individual children, to children in small groups of three or four, and to the whole group. Frequent book reading should be a mainstay of the preschool classroom.
- When you consider adding or changing an area of the classroom, also consider what kinds of reading and writing materials will go along with the change.
- Write down children's ideas, words, and stories. When ideas, words, and stories are written down, they take on a special meaning for children (Cooper, 1993; Paley, 1981). Children can dictate the words they want you to add to their work. Offer to do so often. Make your offer open-ended, "Would you like to tell me some words to write down?"

Frequent book reading should be a mainstay of the preschool classroom.

- Connect functional writing to children's behavior. For example, when a child does (or doesn't) like something at snack or lunch, you might ask the child if he would like to write a note to let Mom or Dad know about the preference. If he says yes, provide a piece of clean paper and a marker or crayon for him to do so. Then, make sure you tell the parent about the importance of the written note by including additional information for the parents or interpreting the child's early writing attempts so that family members understand them.
- Explore initial and final sounds—particularly initial sounds of names, words, and toys, objects, and materials. This exploration should not include drills as these are still inappropriate. But songs, chants, poems, fingerplays, and action rhymes are excellent ways to explore initial sounds. For example, when you call a child by name, say, "Rodney, it's your turn to paint with the red paint. Red, Rodney, those words start with the same sound." Or, use fingerplays, rhymes, and songs to reinforce the connection between sounds.

- Use description to connect initial and final sounds to word labels. This exploration is teachers' work in the beginning. Teachers point out the obvious connections between sounds and letters as they use them in daily experiences.

Ask Good Questions

Asking good questions is an important teaching skill—one that does not necessarily come naturally to all teachers. Good questions are open-ended or divergent in nature and encourage children to experiment with their thoughts and ideas. Open-ended questions promote higher order thinking skills and require children to use problem-solving skills. They also promote expressive language skills, requiring that children form responses in words that express what they are thinking.

Good open-ended questions focus on higher order thinking skills, such as comparing, inferring, and problem solving. When children use these thinking skills, they are involved in intellectual activities that enhance their knowledge and skills.

The following tips can guide you to ask the right kinds of questions to keep children thinking:

- Start your questions with how, what, or why. "What's your idea?" "How could we find out?" or "Why do you think _______?" are examples of good beginnings.
- Ask questions that do not have one-word or specific answers. When we ask children, "What color do you get when you mix red and blue?" the only right answer is purple. A better question might be, "What happens when different colors get mixed together?" This question lets children pick any color combination or create a new idea.
- Focus questions on new knowledge, not on what has been already learned. For example, when children know the names of dinosaurs, focus on finding and naming new species rather than on just naming and reporting the ones the children already know.
- Ask children to tell you more about their ideas. Expanding on an original thought is a valuable skill. When children offer their ideas, ask them to tell you more about them.
- Listen to children's answers carefully. Often their answers will lead you to identify the best question to ask next.
- Accept new ideas and unusual answers. Sometimes divergent questions will cause children to think about ideas that are not very well formed or thoroughly thought through. When this is the case, they need more time to think about their ideas.
- Encourage risk-taking when children offer ideas that are just beginning to form. When children share new ideas, recognize their work.
- Resist the urge to ask convergent questions—questions that have one right answer, that probe only previous knowledge, or require habitual responses such as "yes" or "no." This type of question may teach children to limit exploration of ideas because they don't find the desired answer.

Use Multi-age Grouping

If Vygotsky is right, children need frequent opportunities to learn from more competent peers as well as to scaffold learning in younger children. Multi-age grouping is the way to insure that children have role models to watch, peers who need help, and peers who can help. Widening the age range of children in classroom groups is the first step in providing multi-age experiences.

In today's society, children have fewer opportunities to relate to children of different ages because of smaller family size, extended time in out-of-home care and early education settings, and isolation from extended family members. Children glean both social and intellectual benefits from being in mixed age groups (Katz, 1998; Katz, Evangelou, & Hartman, 1990). Older children benefit from being the experts and being able to model for younger children. Younger children benefit from having older children for interactions. All children benefit from decreased pressure to be like other children the same age. Teachers also benefit from not having all the children going through similar developmental issues at the same time.

Teachers can create opportunities for younger children to have interactions and experiences with older children. These can be formal, such as visits to each other's classrooms, or informal, such as being on the playground at the same time.

Teacher Competencies to Support Communicating with Parents, Teachers, and Friends

Sometimes	Usually	Always	
☐	☐	☐	States directions in positive terms.
☐	☐	☐	Communicates effectively with children and adults.
☐	☐	☐	Speaks in simple, understandable terms.
☐	☐	☐	Understands how to use voice as a teaching tool.
☐	☐	☐	Uses positive nonverbal techniques to communicate desired behavior.
☐	☐	☐	Uses existing materials and equipment effectively.
☐	☐	☐	Devises new materials to stimulate and challenge children.
☐	☐	☐	Rotates and adapts materials to insure children's interest.
☐	☐	☐	Encourages language by expanding sentences used by children.
☐	☐	☐	Narrates routines throughout the day.
☐	☐	☐	Makes and keeps eye contact with children.
☐	☐	☐	Talks with children, labeling objects, pointing out actions, and describing actions and reactions.
☐	☐	☐	Waits for responses to questions.
☐	☐	☐	Asks open-ended questions that require more than a one-word response.
☐	☐	☐	Sanitizes toys and materials.

Competencies to Support the Teaching Role of Instructor

Sometimes	Usually	Always	
☐	☐	☐	Creates opportunities for peer collaboration in activities and experiences.
☐	☐	☐	Associates letters with the sounds they make.
☐	☐	☐	Demonstrates skills to children, teaching them "how to" by showing them.
☐	☐	☐	Summarizes what is happening in the classroom for children. Helps children notice what is happening beyond their immediate play environment.
☐	☐	☐	Participates in professional development experiences.
☐	☐	☐	Keeps records of professional development experiences.
☐	☐	☐	Sets short-term and long-term goals for professional development.
☐	☐	☐	Continues professional development.
☐	☐	☐	Keeps a record of training coursework and conferences attended.
☐	☐	☐	Participates in professional organizations.

Competencies to Support the Teaching Role of Documenter

Sometimes	Usually	Always	
☐	☐	☐	Collects work samples that show evidence of children's learning and discovery.
☐	☐	☐	Organizes collected documentation materials.
☐	☐	☐	Interprets children's learning to parents and family members in many ways.
☐	☐	☐	Uses documentation to guide future curriculum development.
☐	☐	☐	Documents children's progress through the use of individual portfolios.

INNOVATIONS IN OBSERVATION/ASSESSMENT

Observation/Assessment for Communicating with Parents, Teachers, and Friends

During the developmental task of Communicating with Parents, Teachers, and Friends, observation and assessment are directed at literacy and cognitive skills of each child. This understanding starts with observing the stages of development in relationship to the theories discussed in Innovations in Care and Early Childhood Education.

Teachers will want to observe for signs that language development is proceeding. Start by checking off the sounds that children have mastered expressively. Then, use the Preschool Language Behaviors chart (see page 290) to confirm the language behaviors children are demonstrating. Finally, confirm children's articulation by checking to make sure that each child's oral language is understandable within normal ranges.

With this in mind, focus observations on children's pragmatic language, looking for examples of children using language to get their social needs met and to adapt their behavior to fit different situations.

For literacy learning and development, focus observations on children's interest in being read to, vocabulary use, and phonemic awareness—the growing understanding of how language is constructed. Observe for connections between oral language and print, particularly interest in the printed word.

For cognitive development, focus your observations on identifying or confirming the stage of development using Piaget's and Vygotsky's theories. Observations of children's assimilation and accommodation experiences and the thinking errors will also inform your work.

Observation can reveal some very interesting information about each child's zone of proximal development (ZPD). As you learn more about individual children, observation will lead you to scaffold children, either directly with teaching support or by pairing them with a more competent peer.

Finally, observe for signs of the different intelligences in Gardner's theory of multiple intelligences. Because early indicators of particular combinations of intelligences are present during the preschool years, you will want to uncover and offer curriculum support to children's various intelligences.

Add to Individual Portfolios to Highlight the Developmental Task of Communicating with Parents, Teachers, and Friends

Many products of children's work can be added to portfolios during the developmental task of Communicating with Parents, Teachers, and Friends. Collect samples of children's literacy and thinking skills.

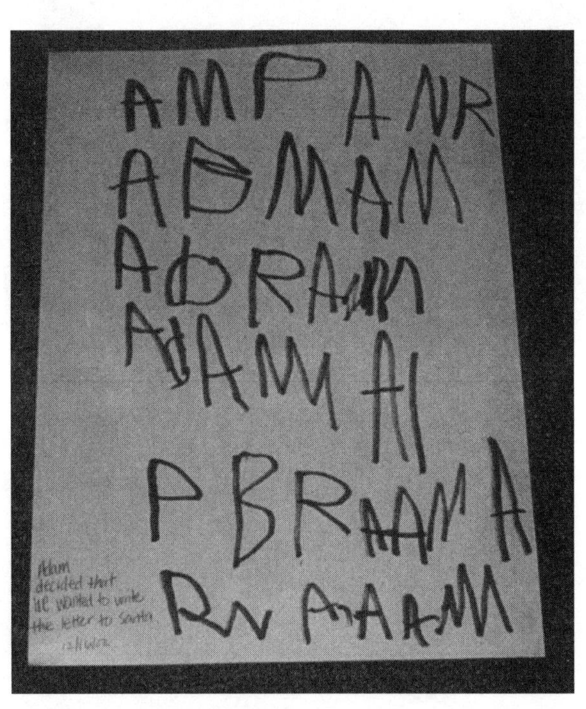

Additions to Portfolios that Highlight Literacy Learning

A valuable addition to each child's portfolio is a list of books the child has read. Teachers read many books to children during the preschool years, and this list can include all of them. Use the list to reflect a child's favorite books over time, recording favorite books at several times during the preschool years, or perhaps construct a list of the books that the child knows well enough to tell or "read" to others.

Books I've Read

	Book Title	Date
1.		
2.		
3.		
4.		
5.		
6.		
7.		
8.		
9.		
10.		
11.		
12.		
13.		
14.		
15.		
16.		
17.		
18.		
19.		
20.		
21.		
22.		
23.		
24.		

My Favorite Books

	Book Title	Date
1.		
2.		
3.		
4.		
5.		
6.		
7.		
8.		
9.		
10.		
11.		
12.		
13.		
14.		
15.		
16.		
17.		
18.		
19.		
20.		
21.		
22.		
23.		
24.		

Books I Can Read to My Friends

	Book Title	Date
1.		
2.		
3.		
4.		
5.		
6.		
7.		
8.		
9.		
10.		
11.		
12.		
13.		
14.		
15.		
16.		
17.		
18.		
19.		
20.		
21.		
22.		
23.		
24.		

Collect the vocabulary words that children have learned. When children use new vocabulary words in their conversations with others, add them to the vocabulary list of words the child knows and uses. As this list grows, teachers will be able to document the size and complexity of the child's vocabulary as well as find many other ways to use the lists to expand literacy experiences.

Collect samples of children's writing as it emerges through the stages of scribbling, adding shapes to the picture, making letter-like and word-like marks, and representational or invented writing. In particular, look for work samples that show transitions between theses stages. Include examples where children begin to add recognizable letters (such as the first letter of their name), examples that indicate children recognize the difference between drawing and writing, and examples of using both drawing and writing to clarify and enrich the expression.

Collect examples of children's dictation taken over time by teachers. Children will go from telling you to write down their disconnected ideas to telling stories with a beginning and an end, and then with a beginning, middle, and end. As their vocabularies grow, the length of their stories will increase, and the stories will become more complex. Teachers can also help children find letters and words in their stories by underlining letters and words that are repeated or used frequently.

Across the preschool years, add the alphabet letters and numbers that children have learned to write. Writing samples with this information will guide teachers to identify which letters and numbers have been learned.

Additions to the Portfolio that Highlight Cognitive Learning

Several tools in ***Innovations: The Comprehensive Preschool Curriculum*** help document children's growth in cognitive and intellectual development. The first is the Concepts Learned Lists. Each Possibilities Plan has a list of the content, process, and pre-academic skills that children might be learning and integrating into their experiences. Use these lists to confirm skill acquisition, as well as to document growth in each type of skill.

Another tool is the Observation/Assessment suggestions in activities in each Possibilities Plan. This curriculum uses observation to inform assessment. Write anecdotal notes that include naturalistic observation about whether children use and how they apply specific skills and abilities in play and interactions with others. These notes, in turn, become sources of documentation that can be added to the child's portfolio. Suggestions for observation are included in individual activities (see page 335, for an example).

INNOVATIONS IN FAMILY PARTNERSHIPS

Encourage Family Participation

Picture Nametags: Make picture nametags for parents to use during their time at school, especially during family meetings. Take a photograph of each child and mount it on a cardboard rectangle. Write the child's name and the parent's name under the picture. Cover with clear contact paper or laminate it. Punch a hole above the photo and string on a length of yarn or raffia.

Parents' Voices: Children love to hear their parents' voices during the day. Provide a cassette tape and recorder. Ask parents to record favorite stories to place in the Literacy/Writing Possibilities listening area.

Supporting Possibilities: Decorate a medium-size cardboard box to send home for storing discarded items that you can use in activities for children at school. You may want to attach or include a list of everyday items that you can use, such as cardboard tubes, clean plastic bottles, magazines, boxes, subscription cards from magazines, appropriate junk mail, and so on.

Visiting Readers: Invite family members to sign up to read in the classroom. They may bring a favorite book or choose one from the school library when they arrive. Or, ask parents to bring one of their child's favorite books to school, so you can read it to children during the day. This will make a connection between home and school for the child. Keep a list of the books parents read to their child at school and add it to the child's portfolio or send it to the family member as a thank-you recognition.

Share Parent Postcards

Share Parent Postcards with parents or other family members as they indicate an interest, at appropriate times during the enrollment cycle, or as developmental issues arise. Copy Postcards. Cut if necessary. Address to parent(s) and attach to the Communication Log or hand out personally.

Dear Parents

TO

How Children Learn

In our society a tendency exists to push early formal education down into younger years. However, preschoolers are not yet ready to be elementary students. Children are best prepared for future success by fully experiencing and growing through this stage without being hurried or pressured to perform or learn about how they will be in the next stage.

Preschool children learn through their senses (touching, tasting, listening, seeing, doing, manipulating). This is a period of rapid growth characterized by excitement, frustration, confusion, and wonderful feelings of accomplishment for both preschoolers and their parents. Every parent knows that this is a "let me do it," not a "make me do it" time. Children often resist adult efforts to guide, support, and help, even though they may not be able to accomplish the tasks they are trying. It is through exploration, trial and error, and practice that children perfect emerging skills.

The experiences children have with books and rhymes prepare the way for learning to read. The experiences they have with sorting, patterning, and grouping prepare the way for learning to add, subtract, and understand mathematics. And, the experiences children have with their parents, teachers, and friends prepare them to establish and maintain relationships that will nurture future developmental growth.

Good Books for Preschool Children

Reading to young children is a great way to get them interested in books. In fact, early experiences with books help ensure that children will have successful literacy experiences later.

What kinds of books do young children need? Picture and story books are best. Books with realistic (not cartoon) illustrations are recommended. Expect children to want to read the same books over and over again. Children learn from repetition (and adults get to practice patience with the repetition)!

What do children learn from being read to? Children learn that print goes from left to right and from top to bottom, and that books are read right side up. They perfect page-turning skills and discover that the books go from the front to back. They connect the meaning of the story to the illustrations and then to the printed word.

When you read to your child, start with the title and the author. Then talk about what the book is about. Read each page, pointing out things of interest in the story and the illustrations. Read the book with expression. Enjoy this wonderful, close time with your child as you support his or her interest in books and emerging pre-reading and reading skills.

The Amazing Brain

New imaging techniques are providing neurobiologists with fascinating new information about how the brain develops. This research confirms that the early years are learning years and that parents and teachers need to make them count.

Brain development is the result of a complex "dance" between the genetic makeup of a child, which is predetermined, and the child's experience, which is open to many possibilities. Scientists have always thought of this development as a lifelong one. They now know that what happens to a child in the first 10 years of life has a profound impact on the way the dance proceeds.

Before a child is born, neurons or brain cells are developed. It is after birth that connections (called synapses) are developed between the neurons. From birth to about a year, millions of connections between neurons are developed—almost like making roads between towns and communities. During this stage of brain development, it is a use-it-or-lose-it time. Neurons that aren't stimulated simply don't get connected to other neurons.

After these initial connections are formed, the brain begins the process of improving the connections, or highways, between neurons and connecting smaller roads to larger ones. As this process progresses, communication and coordination among areas of the brain begin. For the next 10 or so years, well-stimulated neural pathways get bigger, stronger, and more coordinated, while under-stimulated ones are abandoned.

What makes brains strong and capable? Experience is the chief architect of the brain. Stimuli from people, places, and things provide the nutrients for healthy brain development. What a wonderful thing to know—the way you provide early experiences to children develops their brains!

Windows of Learning: Brain Development and the Young Child

While the brain has a remarkable capacity to change, the timing of experiences and stimulations that influence the change can be crucial. It is during these "prime times" that the synapses (connections) and the coordination between different sections of the brain grow. After these periods, the brain's capacity to change does not disappear, but it does diminish.

Prime times for learning occur throughout the early years of a child's life. Brain scientists now think that windows of learning occur for emotional, visual, and motor development during the first two years. A window of learning is open between birth and age three for music and for thinking skills between birth and age four. During these windows, connections in the brain are developing at their most rapid pace, and brain activity is at its greatest.

Stimulating the emotional development of the brain comes easy for most parents. Warm, responsive, intimate relationships with primary caregivers create "construction sites" in the developing brain that buzz with activity and create synaptic connections at an amazing rate. Snuggling, holding, and loving your preschooler all help develop his or her brain.

Try some of these ideas for stimulating your preschooler's developing brain visually, motorically, and musically:

- Learn the fingerplays and songs that your child's teacher is using at school and teach your child your favorites. Shared, repeated musical and rhythmic experiences are great brain "food."
- Offer things to each of your child's hands—not only the right or the left one. This motor movement enhances connections between areas of the brain and increases coordination. It also stimulates brain connections for both sides of the brain.
- March, hop, crawl, slink, creep, strut, or wiggle to get from here to there. It will be more fun and will send all kinds of stimulating messages to the developing brain.
- Read stories to your child, visually tracking the words and pointing out the pictures.
- Give your child choices. Emotional health for children emerges from positive experiences with control and autonomy.

What Is Developmentally Appropriate Care and Early Education for Preschoolers?—The Role of Curriculum Activities and Experiences

The content of curriculum for preschoolers is not the same as content for older children. Children learn in a variety of ways during the early childhood years. They learn by interacting with and acting on their environment—touching, tasting, smelling, feeling, manipulating, and seeing the world around them. This interaction with people and things forms the core of curriculum for young children.

Although good early childhood settings may look similar to one another, part of curriculum is preparing the environment to have pleasing, stimulating, and interesting objects in it. What is available, what gets added or taken away, what is new, and what is familiar are all important parts of curriculum for preschoolers. Adults plan experiences that will be fun to do alone, with a caring adult, or with a friend or two.

This curriculum is less didactic, or teacher-directed, than it is in the elementary classroom. Teachers of preschoolers do direct instruction with children all the time, but not usually with a large group. Direct instruction is at the child's initiation or request and with only a few other interested children. The direct instruction done by teachers includes reading books; playing with children; helping children play with each other and with interesting toys; counting with children; singing; repeating fingerplays and rhymes; helping children try new motor skills or perfect emerging ones; going outside with children; preparing, serving, and eating snacks and lunch; observing children; suggesting play ideas; and supporting building with and manipulating objects.

Resource for Families

Add this helpful book to your library or post it on your family bulletin board.
Levine, M. (2002). ***A mind at a time***. New York: Simon & Schuster.

INNOVATIONS IN ENVIRONMENTS

Create a Classroom that Values Multiple Intelligences

Classrooms that value multiple intelligences recognize that how long children take to complete an activity is one of the variations in intelligences. Teachers make every attempt to embrace these variations rather than trying to eliminate them.

Teachers who understand multiple intelligences recognize that different children like different types of stimulation. For example, a child with highly complementary spatial and body kinesthetic intelligences might love exploring tight spaces, such as the inside of boxes and behind furniture. One who has complementary spatial and logico-mathematical intelligences might prefer to manipulate items in an open space. These examples illustrate the individual nature and variety of multiple intelligences.

Perhaps the best way to support multiple intelligences is to make sure your classroom environment provides opportunities for all types of learning. Make sure you have places for children to find interesting and stimulating things to do with their different combinations of intelligences. Are there musical choices in your classroom to stimulate the musical intelligence? Do you bring natural things inside to stimulate naturalist intelligence? Where do you support intrapersonal intelligence in your classroom? Where do children have opportunities to transform their environment using their spatial intelligence?

Classrooms that value various intelligences integrate experiences, allowing children to use preferred intelligences while stimulating other styles. Isolated experiences in music, movement, outdoor exploration, and so on, don't meet the intent of supporting multiple intelligences unless they incorporate experiences across and within children's preferred learning styles. For example, music experiences for children, whether done in the classroom or by a specially trained music teacher, need to include a wide range of topics and techniques. Children can sing, dance to music, draw to music, learn about musical instruments, play real instruments, read stories about musicians, go to a concert, and so on, supporting all types of intelligence, not just the ability to sing or play a musical instrument.

Create Literacy-rich Environments

A literacy-rich environment includes so much more than just books. It means creating an environment that connects children to the functional or useful aspects of oral language and the written word. Literacy-rich environments have some common characteristics.

The first is the inclusion of books of all kinds in the classroom, both in the Literacy/Writing Possibilities area, as well as throughout the classroom. Objects around the room have labels on them (printed in large, lowercase letters). Sentences are also visible (printed in large letters using both uppercase and lowercase where appropriate, as well as appropriate punctuation). Other elements of environmental print include signs, posters, charts, big books, and art experiences where teachers have written descriptions of what actually happened in the classroom or the words that children asked to have added to their work.

A literacy-rich environment has many places for preschool children to write at a variety of angles (on low tables with chairs, on taller tables while standing, on easels, on fences outside, on the floor on big paper, and on a surface with little paper) with a variety of writing materials, including markers, crayons, paintbrushes, chalk, and pencils. These materials are readily available.

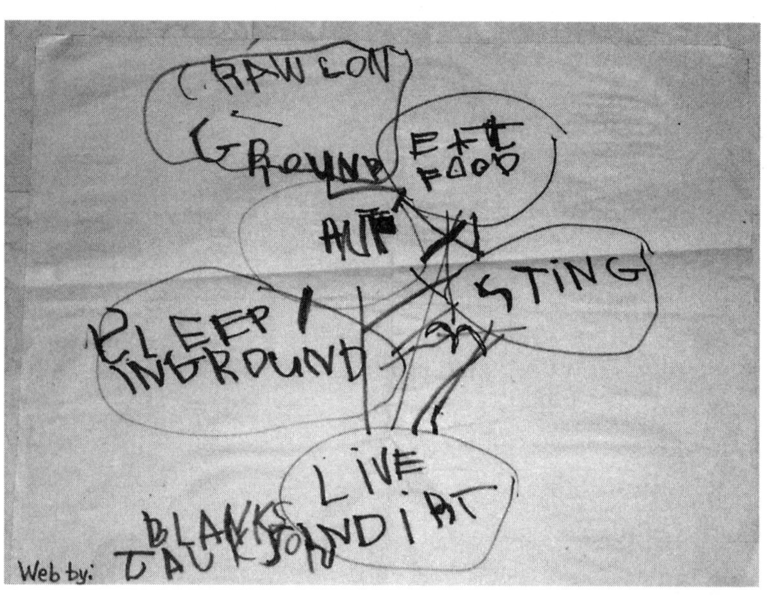

Many open-ended materials are in literacy-rich environments. These materials help young children learn gross and fine motor control and eliminate the pressure of getting something "right" the first time. Magic slates, clay, playdough, sand trays, flour pans, and fingerpaint enable preschool children to practice in a "forgiving," open-ended environment.

Because young children are not yet good conservationists, literacy-rich environments provide as many "free" or recycled materials as possible. Magazines and catalogs show pictures with print and are useful as concept books. Junk mail shows how letters are sent and provides practice with opening, unfolding, holding, writing, and turning. Recycled paper from copy machines and offices and used computer paper are free sources of paper to use for writing and drawing throughout the classroom.

Literacy-rich environments include teachers who exhibit teaching behaviors that support the development of young children's literacy. The most critical one is reading to children each day. Teachers also discuss how letters, words, and sentences are formed; create group drawing experiences; read to small groups of interested children; show individual attention to children's language efforts; narrate and describe things to children; and engage in sustained and extended conversations about things that interest children throughout the day.

From this rich environment, children learn that language has meaning when it is written down as well as when it is spoken. These experiences form a strong foundation for formal reading, writing, and spelling instruction to take place during the kindergarten and elementary years.

Activity Areas

Literacy/Writing Possibilities

In Literacy/Writing Possibilities, children have opportunities to practice and experiment with functional reading and writing activities. The physical arrangement of this area includes two separate components. The first is a library area where many children's books and written resources are displayed in attractive and inviting ways. A bookrack that displays books with the covers facing out is typically the foundation of the children's library and can be supplemented with bookshelves to catalog and store books that are not in use. Consider having several different kinds of seating available for children near the books. A rocking chair gives a child the chance to look at books all by himself and creates a way to be with books without interruption from others. Cushions, pillows, and beanbags give children the opportunity to relax and look at books and printed material together as well as by themselves.

The second component of Literacy/Writing Possibilities area is a sturdy table that seats 3-6 children, depending on your group's size. A well-stocked shelf unit needs to be close to the table. Fill it with a good collection of pencils, a pencil sharpener, other writing materials such as crayons, markers, colored pencils, chalk, watercolors, and so on. Paper is essential to this area. Paper can be stored in stacking bins and should be of various sizes, textures, and weight. Don't forget to add a roll of craft paper so that children can use it when large amounts of paper are needed for their writing projects. This area is also a resource area where children come to find the implements they need to express themselves through drawing or writing in other activity areas.

A well-stocked Literacy/Writing Possibilities area will have the following supplies and equipment, perhaps not out at the same time, but accessible as needed to enhance children's early literacy skills:

- Crayons, markers, chalk, regular and colored pencils;
- A pencil sharpener;
- Stacking bins to hold paper in an accessible format;
- Index cards, note paper, white paper, colored paper, paper of different weights, textures, formats, and sizes;
- Greeting cards, subscription cards from magazines, envelopes, notebooks, and paper folded and stapled or stitched into books ready for creating;
- Clipboards with pencils attached with string to use as a writing surface;
- Alphabet letters in various formats including one copy of the alphabet written sequentially, alphabet magnets, alphabet letters made of sandpaper to trace, felt board letters to attach to a felt board, alphabet lacing beads, alphabet stamps, alphabet puzzles, alphabet beanbags, alphabet floor puzzles, foam letters;
- A felt board, a white board with an eraser, and/or a chalk board;

- Laminated name cards with each child's name written in upper- and lowercase letters on sentence strips;
- A collection of shapes, both magnetic and felt;
- Numbers written sequentially, number magnets, numbers made of sandpaper to trace, felt board numbers, foam numbers; and
- Magnetic or felt story kits with the characters of the story and the book included.

Group Time Possibilities

As you plan for group time, think about ways to communicate what to do in the group by defining this area with a carpet, carpet squares, or another environmental support. Many preschool teachers conduct group time as a large group activity with all of the children at the same time. A better strategy is to conduct group times in smaller groups. Try repeating group times so that you can keep the size of the group small enough to prevent waiting for a turn, not getting a turn, or not having time to get to hear everyone's ideas. Another approach is to divide children into smaller groups and conduct simultaneous group times. If you have more than one teacher in the classroom, accommodating group time this way is as easy as dividing children into two groups.

Many teachers view group time as the way to start or end the day, or to culminate certain activities. The ***Innovations*** curriculum encourages you to also consider group time as an opportunity to teach, model, demonstrate, and support children's learning throughout the day. Viewed this way, children can join in group-time activities when they are interested and continue their work and play in other Possibilities areas if they are not. This approach also allows teachers to individualize their group-time experiences, focusing on the interests or needs of a subset of children within the classroom instead of all of the children. When they choose not to participate, remind them that there is a place for them when they are ready.

Group time is often used to set up or introduce topics or activities that will be going on in the classroom. New materials added to activity areas and activities that need introduction or explanation are often shared during group time. Discussions about classroom happenings, particularly problem solving about experiences and conflicts, can also take place at group time. And, don't forget to use group times to celebrate observations, insights, experiences, and happenings that go on in the classroom.

Good group times are often fairly short, lasting no more that 10 or 15 minutes. You will know when group times are getting too long because children will begin to fidget, lose interest, and interrupt. When this happens, children are usually ready for a change of pace and to move on.

Curriculum Resources

Rhymes, Songs, Fingerplays, and Music: Rhymes, songs, fingerplays, and music are additional literacy opportunities. The rhyme and repetition in language are important for literacy development. In fact, some reading specialists believe that the ability to use rhyme and alliteration is correlated with reading success. Include many opportunities during the day to involve children in this kind of interaction.

Create a collection of rhymes, songs, fingerplays, and music using index cards. Write the words on the cards or attach copies of the music to the cards. Laminate and store them in a readily accessible location in your classroom.

A good way to use rhymes, songs, fingerplays, and music is to include them in your transitions during the day. When the same rhyme, song, fingerplay, or music is used regularly, it becomes a guidance strategy that helps children anticipate what comes next.

References

Berk, L.E. (1999). ***Infants and children***. Boston: Allyn and Bacon.

Chomsky, N. (1957). ***Syntactic structures***. The Hague: Mouton.

Cooper, P. (1993). ***When stories come to school: Telling, writing, and performing stories in the early childhood classroom***. New York: Teachers and Writers.

Cryer, D. & T. Harms. (2000). ***Infants and toddlers in out-of-home care***. Baltimore, MD: Brookes Publishing.

Gandini, L. & J. Goldhaber. (2001). Two reflections about documentation. In L. Gandini & C.P. Edwards (Eds.), ***Bambini: The Italian approach to infant/toddler care***. 121-145. New York: Teacher's College Press.

Gardner, H. (1983). ***Frames of mind: The theory of multiple intelligences***. New York: Basic Books.

Gerber, M. (1979). ***Resources for infant educarers: A manual for parents and professionals.*** Los Angeles: Resources for Infant Educarers.

Goleman, D. (1998). ***Working with emotional intelligence.*** New York: Bantam Doubleday Dell.

Hart, B. & T. Risley. (1999). ***The social world of children: Learning to talk***. Baltimore, MD: Brookes Publishing.

Katz, J.R. & C.E. Snow. (2000). Language development in early childhood. In D. Cryer & T. Harms (Eds.), ***Infants and toddlers in out-of-home care*** (49-87). Baltimore, MD: Brookes Publishing.

Katz, L.G. (1998).The benefits of the mix. ***Child Care Information Exchange***, 124, 46-49.

Katz, L.G., D. Evangelou, & J.A. Hartman. (1990). ***The case for mixed-age grouping in early education***. Washington, DC: National Association for the Education of Young Children (NAEYC).

Mooney, C.G. (2000). ***Theories of childhood: An introduction to Dewey, Montessori, Erickson, Piaget, and Vygotsky.*** St. Paul, MN: Redleaf Press.

National Association for the Education of Young Children/International Reading Association (NAEYC/IRA). (1998). Learning to read and write: Developmentally appropriate practices for young children. ***Young Children,*** 52 (4): 30-46.

Okagaki, L. & K.E. Diamond. (2000). Responding to cultural and linguistic differences in the beliefs and practices of families with young children. ***Young Children,*** 55 (1): 74-80.

Paley, V.G. (1981). ***Wally's stories.*** Cambridge; MA: Harvard University Press.

Piaget, J. (1977). ***The origins of intelligence in children.*** New York: International Universities Press.

Shonkoff, J.P. & D.A. Phillips (Eds.). (2000). ***From neurons to neighborhoods: The science of early childhood development.*** Washington, DC: National Academy Press.

Smith, A.B., L. Hand, J.J. Frelinger, J. E. Bernthal, & A. Bird. (1990). The Iowa articulation norms project and its Nebraska replication. ***Journal of Speech and Hearing Disorders,*** 66, 779-798.

Stern, D. (1985). ***The interpersonal world of the infant: A view from psychoanalysis and developmental psychology.*** New York: Basic Books.

Tabors, P.O. (1998). What early childhood educators need to know: Developing programs for linguistically and culturally diverse children and families. ***Young Children***, 53(6): 20-26.

Vygotsky, L. (1978). ***Mind in society: The development of higher psychological processes***. Cambridge, MA: Harvard University Press.

Resources for Teachers

Athouse, R., M.H. Johnson, & S.T. Mitchell. (2002). ***The colors of learning: Integrating visual arts into the early childhood classroom***. New York: Teacher's College Press.

Child Care Information Exchange. 2001. Beginnings workshop: Projects and themes. ***Child Care Information Exchange***, 141.

Child Care Information Exchange. 2002. Beginnings workshop: Projects and themes, part 2. ***Child Care Information Exchange,*** 141.

Carter, Margie. (2000). Literacy development: Back to the real basics. ***Child Care Information Exchange***, 14-17.

Cadwell, L. (2002). ***Bringing learning to life: The Reggio approach to early childhood education***. New York: Teacher's College Press.

Cadwell, L. (1997). ***Bringing Reggio Emilia home: An innovative approach to early childhood education.*** New York: Teacher's College Press.

Dever, M.T. & D.C. Burts. (2002). Using family literacy bags to enhance family involvement. ***Dimensions of Early Childhood***, 30(1): 16-20.

Edwards, C., L. Gandini, & G. Foreman. (1998). ***The one hundred languages of children: The Reggio Emilia approach to early childhood education—Advanced Reflections***. Norwood, NJ: Ablex.

Hart, B. & T. Risley. (1999). ***The social world of children: Learning to talk***. Baltimore, MD: Brookes Publishing.

Helm, J.H., S. Beneke, & K. Steinheimer. (1997). ***Windows on learning: Documenting young children's work***. New York: Teacher's College Press.

Owocki, G. (2001). ***Make way for literacy***. Washington, DC: National Association for the Education of Young Children.

Raines, S.C. & R.J. Canady. (1989). ***Story stretchers***. Beltsville, MD: Gryphon House.

Raines, S.C. & R.J. Canady. (1991). ***More story stretchers***. Beltsville, MD: Gryphon House.

Redleaf, R. (1993). ***Busy fingers, growing minds***. St. Paul, MN: Redleaf Press.

Rockwell, R., D. Hoge, & B. Searcy. (1999). ***Linking language and literacy: Simple language and literacy throughout the curriculum***. Beltsville, MD: Gryphon House.

Schiller, P. (2001). ***Creating readers***. Beltsville, MD: Gryphon House.

Possibilities Plan—
What Will I Be?

Getting Ready to Plan

During the preschool years, dramatic play becomes more and more important. Children are intensely interested in what their parents and other adults do in their jobs. The What Will I Be? Possibilities Plan provides many opportunities to explore what adults do in the world of work.

The purpose of Getting Ready to Plan is to support the planning process with a general overview of the content of this Possibilities Plan. Now is the time to think about what interests the children and what you want them to learn about each of these topics, which are explored in general below.

Community Workers: Because preschool children are curious about what happens in their school and community, the topic of community workers is interesting to them. Talk about situations that are familiar to children (such as firefighters coming to help in an emergency), and then talk about situations that may be less familiar (such as surgeons who help people through operations). Provide different costumes and props, so children can play different roles, making sure to offer a wide variety of occupations and options. Stress the importance of working together as a community.

Consider the work that is done by parents and family members as you construct this Plan. Adding this point of view and content, which relates to the child's home context, validates the connections between home and school, and opens the door for rich exchanges of resources, information, and support.

Construction Workers: Because children like seeing how things change, the idea of working in the area of construction is popular. Talk about the different roles involved in building (architect, electrician, engineer, plumber, truck driver, brick mason). Provide many hands-on activities where children can build and see the changes in their creations and buildings over time.

Farmers: Animals and plants are two topics that preschool children can easily connect with farming. Pets in the classroom and field trips to see farm animals are two ways to show children how interesting and complex animals can be. Allow children to experience gardening, use gardening tools, dig, and plant. Record observations as plants grow. Consider bringing this topic into the school setting by designing, planting, and harvesting your own garden.

Teachers: Teachers are interesting for preschool children because you are such an important part of their lives. Don't be surprised if you see yourself acted out as children role play! This interest creates a wonderful opportunity to include many materials used in the areas of math and literacy.

Now that you have an idea about the general content of the Possibilities Plan, you are ready to proceed with developing your own Plan. This section of Getting Ready to Plan identifies resources you may want to buy, collect, or locate to implement your plan.

Toys and Materials*

Purchased

battery
books about careers
brushes
chart paper
child-size gardening tools
coloring materials
community worker figures
construction paper
craft paper
dolls
flexible wire
glue
hole punches
index cards
laminator or clear contact paper
magnets, variety
markers
paper
pen
people figures
plastic trees, bushes, cars, and houses
playdough
safety glasses
scissors
toy airplanes, animals, gardening tools, medical items, telephone, tools, trains and tracks, vehicles of all types, wagons
unbreakable mirrors
unit blocks
washable tempera paint
water table or tub
weather charts
white board and markers or chalkboard and chalk
yarn

Gathered

art paper
bags
blocks
blue plastic sheet
boards
books, various types
bottles, clear plastic
boxes, various sizes
brown paper bags
buckets
cardboard
child-size trowel
clothes/costumes
cloth measuring tape
computer
container, small
dictionary
gloves
gravel or dried peas
hammer
hats
heavy whipping cream
index cards
items teachers use
light bulb, small
magazines
marbles
marshmallows
mirrors
nails, nuts, bolts
nature items
paper towel tubes
pictures and books showing careers
pictures of buildings
pictures of butcher, baker, and candle maker
pictures of workers and equipment
plastic knives
pretzel sticks
PVC pipes and connectors
ribbon
rocks of different shapes and sizes
rulers
sand
sentence strips
shoes of different types and sizes
shovels
soil
sprouting vegetables (carrots, potatoes)
sticks
table, small
toothpicks
utensils, variety of
variety of large nuts and bolts
vegetables
watering pail
wire
yard sticks
zoo pictures and brochures

*Note: Please consider the ages and abilities of the children in your classroom. Use only safe, non-toxic materials.

What Will I Be?

WEB

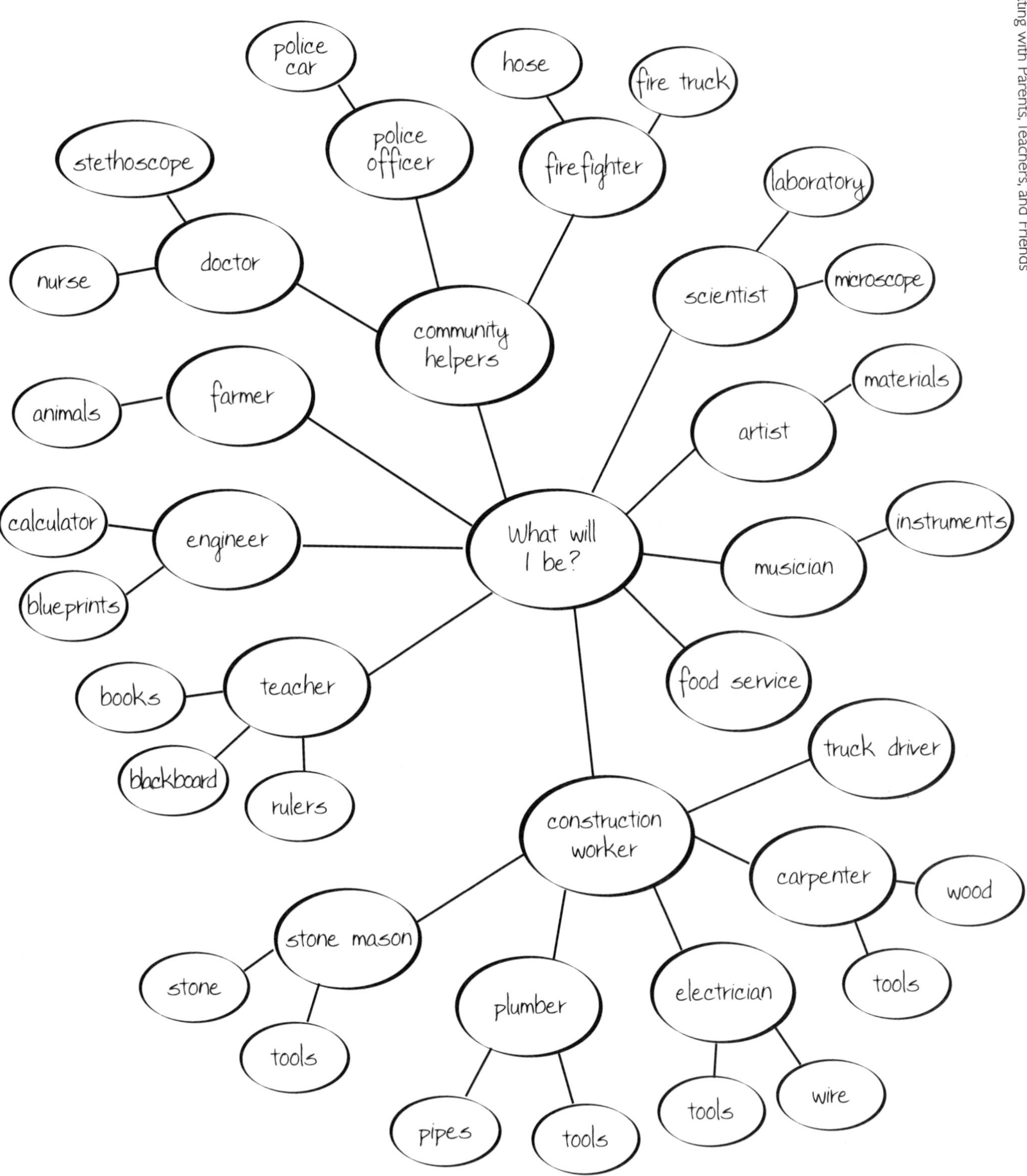

What Will I Be?

PLANNING PAGES

Plan Possibilities

Dear Parents

ACTIVITIES AND EXPERIENCES FOR WHAT WILL I BE?

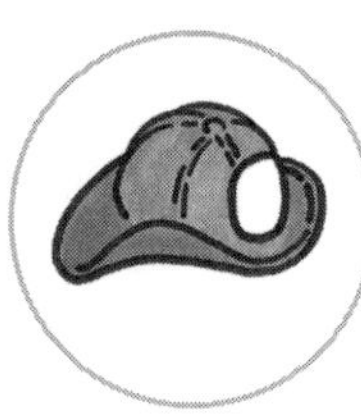

DRAMATIC POSSIBILITIES

What Will I Be?

Materials
variety of clothes/costumes (doctor, pilot, musician, baseball player, firefighter, suits, dresses, and so on) • bags • hats • tools • medical items • computer • telephone • paintbrushes • dolls • pictures of different occupations

Teacher Talk
"What will you be when you grow up?" "Why is that a great job for you?"

Instructions
Put different kinds of clothes and props in the dramatic possibilities area, so children can play any role they wish. Attach pictures of different occupations to the wall in the area. Ask parents to donate their children's old costumes, as well as other dress-up materials.

Extension Possibilities: Brainstorm different roles with children to determine what costumes and props are appropriate now and as play emerges. Make a list of the results of the brainstorming, add photos of the occupations, and post in the Dramatic Play Possibilities area.

Observation/Assessment
Uses props to enhance dramatic play

Classroom

Materials
dolls • books • small table • white board or chalkboard (small) • markers or chalk • other items teachers use in the classroom

Teacher Talk
"What does a teacher do?" "Who wants to be the teacher? Who wants to be the students?"

Instructions
Support children as they play the role of teacher and do what a teacher does. Children can use dolls or other children as students.

Observation/Assessment
Takes on various roles in dramatic play

Dramatic Play with Prop Boxes

Materials
prop boxes created for this Possibilities Plan (Community Helper, Construction, Food Service, Farmer, Shoe Store, Musician, and so on)

Teacher Talk
"We have children interested in so many different careers in this classroom!" "Who wants to be the farmer next?"

Instructions
Use the prop boxes created for this Possibilities Plan to keep a number of choices present in the area. With a good collection of different prop boxes, teachers can change the props in the area every few days. As children have extended periods of time in Dramatic Possibilities, their play will become more complex. Provide additional materials as play changes.

Observation/Assessment
Uses props to enhance dramatic play

ART POSSIBILITIES

"What I Want to Be" Puppet

Materials
brown paper bags • art paper • scissors • glue • markers • paint

Teacher Talk
"We are making puppets that show what children want to be." "What do you want to be?"

Instructions
Children draw faces of a person they want to be. Next, they cut out the faces and glue them to the bottom part of a paper bag. Children can draw or paint clothes, cut them out, and glue them onto the bags, or they can draw directly on the bags. Keep a long list of career possibilities at the art table. Read the list if children ask. Repeat this activity using cloth to create clothes for the puppets.

Observation/Assessment
Draws using markers

Careers and Food

Materials

chart paper • markers • magazines • pictures of people involved in a variety of career choices

Teacher Talk

"What might an ice skater eat for a snack?" "Which foods go well with dancing?"

Instructions

Explore foods and snacks that might "fit" with various careers, such as graham cracker teddy bears with zookeepers, carrots for gardeners, jerky for ranch hands, and hotdogs for baseball players. Challenge children to think creatively about various careers and their connections to foods. Place career pictures on the art table. Use the magazines to find foods that might go with the careers pictured.

Other Art Possibilities

- Make tool paintings using toy tools from a variety of jobs.
- Roll vehicles through paint and then roll them on paper to create transportation paintings. Repeat over a number of days using different colors of paint and different vehicles.

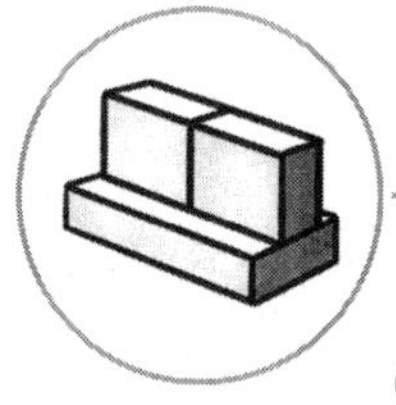

BLOCKS/CONSTRUCTION POSSIBILITIES

City Project

Materials

pictures of buildings (fire station, police station, restaurant, warehouse, bank, apartment building, houses, manufactured housing) • blocks • boxes • glue • community worker figures • cardboard • books, such as *Old MacDonald Had an Apartment House* by Judith Barrett

Teacher Talk

"Where do people work in the city?" "Who works in this kind of building?"

Instructions

Collect pictures of a variety of buildings. Mount these on cardboard and glue them onto the sides of the boxes. Children use blocks and boxes to build a city. Include books that show concepts related to the city. Make streets by drawing them on a large piece of cardboard, making them from construction paper, or using a play mat. Make a sign saying "Construction Zone," "Construction in Progress," or "Construction provided by (children's names). Place the sign in the area, so children can leave the city overnight and extend work the next day.

Observation/Assessment
Builds a variety of structures with blocks and block supports

Zookeeper

Materials
nature items including grass and rocks • toy animals • blue plastic sheet • blocks • construction vehicles • zoo pictures and brochures

Teacher Talk
"What do zookeepers do at the zoo?" "How is a zoo built?" Talk about people who are involved in building a zoo, including an engineer, designer, and construction workers.

Instructions
Collect nature items and small animal toys for children to create their own zoo. After they look at pictures and brochures about zoos, compare natural habitats with habitats in the zoo.

Train Station/Airport

Materials
trains • train track • blocks • people figures • planes • trucks • wagons

Teacher Talk
"Many people travel throughout the world. What are some of the different types of transportation they use?" "How do we get the goods we need?"

Instructions
Children can build transportation systems including train stations and airports, and highway systems. Be conscious of children's experiences. Start with the children's familiar frame of reference. If your city has an airport but no train station, begin with the airport.

Observation/Assessment
Builds a variety of structures using blocks

Growing Vegetables

Materials
clear plastic bottles • toothpicks • sprouting vegetables (carrots, potatoes) • soil • water • yarn • books, such as *Busy Farm Trucks* by R.W. Allery

Teacher Talk
"Do you know anyone who grows vegetables?" "What do they grow?"

Instructions
Clean the clear plastic bottles. If the opening is too small for the vegetable to fit, cut the top out of the bottle. Use toothpicks to position the vegetable where about ¼ to ⅓ of it will be above the top of the bottle. You may use water or soil in the bottle. Water will make the root growth more visible. Sit the bottle on the windowsill, or use a hole punch to make holes at the top rim of the bottle. String yarn through the holes. Hang the bottle in the window. Observe the vegetable each day to determine any changes. If using soil, try to position the vegetable by the side of the bottle, so some of the root growth will be visible. Discuss the children's observations.

Extension Possibilities: Use two potatoes or two carrots and position them in the same way in the clear plastic bottles. Place the bottles in two different places (one dark and one light, one damp and one dry, or one hot and one cold). Observe to determine how the different growing conditions will change how the vegetables grow. Record the children's observations.

Observation/Assessment
Observes plant growth
Names parts of a plant including the stem, leaves, and roots

Electricity

Materials
flexible wire • small light bulb • battery

Teacher Talk
"Electricity makes it possible for us to have lights."

Instructions
Purchase or make an electricity tester. Touch the probe or an uncovered end of the wire to one post of the battery. Then touch the other probe or uncovered end of the wire to the other post of the battery. The light will then go on. Testers are inexpensive, so you may want to buy one. It is easier to make one when you have an example to follow.

Other Science/Discovery Possibilities

- Plant a garden outside.
- Plant an herb garden in a windowsill to use in cooking or snack preparation.
- Sprout various seeds in seed pots or zipper closure plastic bags.
- Make a worm habitat (see page 429).
- Make a weather chart using cards with different weather conditions drawn on them.

SENSORY POSSIBILITIES

Nuts and Bolts

Materials
variety of large bolts and nuts • magnets

Teacher Talk
"What are nuts and bolts?" "Can you find the right size of nut and bolt so that they will fit together?"

Instructions
Provide a variety of nuts and bolts that match. Children can match the nuts to the bolts and connect them. Test the nuts and bolts to see if they are attracted to the magnets. Provide nuts and bolts that do not match as well as those that do. Introduce materials that are attracted to the magnets and that are not.

Observation/Assessment
Matches nuts and bolts

Landscaping

Materials
water table or tub • plastic trees, bushes, cars, and houses • plastic buckets or trays containing soil, sand, different shapes and sizes of rocks • shovels

Teacher Talk
Talk with children about what landscapers do. Stress how they plan the landscape.

Instructions
Children use the materials to create a model landscape. Include children in determining the materials to use in the landscape. Real sticks and branches gathered on the playground can work well. Also, provide individual plastic trays, so children can make their own individual landscapes.

Observation/Assessment
Creates landscape using various materials

Other Sensory Possibilities

- Knead bread (using a recipe or biscuit dough) as a baker would.
- Plant seeds in trays like a gardener preparing young plants for the garden.
- Wash dishes like a dishwasher or windows like a window washer (or a great helper at home).
- Create figures using clay or playdough as a sculptor would.
- Measure flour, water, and other materials using a measuring cup as a cook would.
- Connect short lengths of PVC pipes and then pour water through them as a plumber would.

LITERACY/WRITING POSSIBILITIES

What Do I Need?

Materials
pictures of workers who wear uniforms (police, fast food worker, firefighter, mail carrier, cook, pilot, soldier, doctor) • pictures of items and equipment related to the workers • names of the workers' occupations • markers • index cards

Teacher Talk
"What does this person need to do his or her job?" "Can you help find things this person needs?"

Instructions
Collect pictures of different workers who wear uniforms or who have specific tools of the trade. Collect the actual items that are related to the workers, such as helmets, boots, fire jacket, hose, fire engine, mask, and air tank for a firefighter. Ask children to sort items according to what worker uses them. After using the real object, use a picture of it in the sort.

Helpful Hint: You can find pictures in books, on the Internet, or in magazines. Cover the pictures with clear contact paper or laminate them. Also, make and cover index cards with clear contact paper.

Observation/Assessment
Matches pictures of occupations with objects or tools used

"What Will I Be?" Words

Materials
pictures of people in the uniforms of different careers • pictures of tools or equipment used by different professions • index cards • markers

Teacher Talk
"The person who works in this job wears a white coat." "You asked a good question."

Instructions
Glue or draw a picture of a job on one side of the index card and write the name of the job on the other side. Include a variety of professions that are both familiar and unfamiliar to children. To play, one child holds all the cards, selects one, and then hides it (behind his back, under his seat, or any other place that is out of sight). The rest of the players each ask one question about the profession on the hidden card. The cardholder answers the players with "yes" or "no." The child who guesses the profession gets that card. If no one guesses, the card is discarded, and the next child holds the cards and selects a card. The child with the most cards at the end of the game wins.

Helpful Hint: Play the game with children at least one time to help them understand how it works.

Observation/Assessment
Plays simple games

Other Literacy/Writing Possibilities

- Read any of the books listed for this Possibilities Plan (page 350-351).
- Take dictation from children about careers when they are dressed in costumes. Take photographs to go with dictations.
- Interview each child asking what he wants to be when he grows up. Print the child's response. Children use the words as patterns.

MATH/MANIPULATIVES POSSIBILITIES

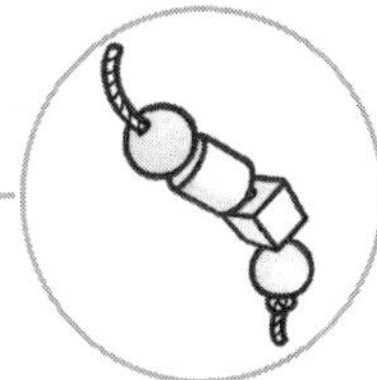

Job Survey

Materials
chart paper • marker

Teacher Talk
"What does your mother (father, aunt, uncle, grandfather, and so on) do at her (his) job?"

Instructions
Interview children to get their descriptions of their family's occupations. Use the information to make a graph.

	cook	lawyer	salesperson	mechanic	teacher
Jessica's Mom					
Jessica's Dad					
Antoine's Mom					
Julian's Dad					
Wiebke's grandmother					

Helpful Hint: Accept children's answers. If a child lives with another relative or caregiver, you will need to ask the question accordingly. Be aware of each child's individual situation before you implement this activity so you can pose the question appropriately.

Extension Possibilities: Make another chart showing what children want to be when they grow up.

Tape Measure and Boards

Materials
cloth measuring tapes • rulers • yard sticks • short boards of different lengths and widths • paper • pencils

Teacher Talk
"Look at the number that lines up with the end of the board." "That's right, Chen. The board is 11 inches long."

Instructions
Provide practice measuring using linear measurements. Demonstrate how to line up the tape, ruler, or yardstick and look at the number across from the end of the board. After children have mastered this skill, show them how to determine which board is longer using the tape measure. This is a good task for children to work on cooperatively in small groups of three. Two children can hold the tape measure (one at each end) while the third copies the numbers off the tape measure.

Extension Possibilities: Measure other items in the classroom or outdoor environment.

Observation/Assessment
Measures using a tape measure, ruler, or yardstick
Copies numbers
Compares length

Job Patterns

Materials
blank sentence strips (or strips of paper about four inches wide and three feet long) • small materials people use in their jobs (10 pencils, 10 spoons, 10 erasers, 10 pens, 10 index cards, 10 napkin rings)

Teacher Talk
"Can you create the same pattern?" "What comes next in the pattern strip?"

Instructions
Divide the sentence strips into sections about four inches wide. Draw lines to divide the sections. Create a pattern strip using the materials. For example, a pattern might be: napkin ring, napkin ring, eraser, pen, spoon. Children then use materials to create a like pattern on the sentence strip lined up below the pattern strip. After children catch on to how the activity works, invite them to create their own pattern strips with the collection of materials.

Observation/Assessment
Creates a matching pattern of materials

Other Math/Manipulatives Possibilities

- Use cloth tape measure to measure the height of all the children.
- Use playing cards to label the number of objects in storage boxes.
- Use food boxes (or blocks) for children to arrange in the order of smallest to largest or vice versa.
- Use small vehicles to sort by color.
- Write a number on a piece of paper and the corresponding number of dots on the back of the paper. Place these pieces of paper in muffin tin cups. Children count out the correct number of counters for each muffin tin.

RHYMES/FINGERPLAYS/SONGS/MUSIC POSSIBILITIES

Rub-a-Dub-Dub

Materials
pictures of a butcher, a baker, and a man with a candle • dictionary

Teacher Talk
Talk with children about what a butcher does, what a baker does, and what a candlestick-maker does. "Some jobs that people had long ago are still jobs today."

Instructions
Teach children the rhyme and use it as a transition activity. Different children can hold up pictures during the rhyme. Look up "knaves" in the dictionary to help children understand this unusual word and what it means. Post a copy of the rhyme, so families can repeat it with their children.

Observation/Assessment
Listens to and repeats rhymes

Old MacDonald

Teacher Talk
"What are some of the jobs a farmer might do?"

Instructions
Sing the song. Choose which animal comes next.

Additional verses:
Pig—oink, oink
Cat—meow, meow
Dog—bow-wow
Horse—neigh, neigh

Extension Possibilities: Sing "Old MacDonald" outside. Expand the animal choices to include a greater variety, for example, an ostrich, an emu, an aardvark, an anteater, a lizard, etc. Discuss the possibilities of having such animals on a farm. Sing "Ms. MacDonald" in the song, saying "on the farm SHE had a ________; then " The MacDonalds', THEY had _______", varying the use of pronouns in the song.

Observation/Assessment
Matches animal sounds to animal names
Sings songs

Other Rhymes/Fingerplays/Songs/Music Possibilities

- Consider any of the following recorded selections:
  - "When I Grow Up" from *25 Fun Adventure Songs* by Twin Sisters Production
  - "Blanket for a Sail" from *For Our Children* by Disney
  - "Yellow Submarine" from *Rockin' Down the Road* by Greg and Steve
  - "Dragnet," "Mission Impossible," "Get Smart," and Charlie's Angels" from *TV Hits* and *TV Hits Volume 2*
  - "Dumptruck Song" from *Children's Favorites, Volume 2* by Disney
  - "Color Medley" from *Mr. Al Sings Colors and Shapes* by Mr. Al

GROUP TIME POSSIBILITIES

Group Time

Family Careers: Have parents or other family members visit to talk about their careers. Explain how long they should talk and ways to keep children interested. Suggest that family members bring a uniform and/or tools of their trade to share with the children.

Introduction of Prop Boxes: This plan features a number of different prop boxes. Before placing materials in dramatic play, introduce them during group time. This is a great time to expand vocabulary by introducing new words.

Other Group Time Possibilities

- Read any of the books from the Book List (page 350-351).
- Wear different uniforms/costumes and have children guess who you are.
- Make a chart of what the children want to be when they grow up.

MOVEMENT/OUTDOORS POSSIBILITIES

Gardening Tools

Materials

child-size trowel • rake • shovel • buckets • gloves • hat • watering pail

Teacher Talk

"Let's pull all the weeds out of the dirt before we start to plant."

Instructions

Provide tools and a place to dig on the playground. If the season is right, provide plants or seeds for planting. Read directions to children and show how planting varies according to the plant or seed.

If the season isn't right for planting outdoors, use small plastic tubs for planting the seeds and plants. These can be taken inside when the temperature is extreme and returned to the playground when children are outside.

Extension Possibilities: This activity can be easily turned into a project by planning a garden, planting it, tending plants, harvesting vegetables, and cooking with vegetables.

Observation/Assessment
Uses tools for gardening
Digs holes in dirt using tools

Shoe Scramble

Materials
pairs of shoes of different types and sizes

Teacher Talk
"You've matched the tap shoes." "Look at the work boots Susan has!"

Instructions
Collect many different pairs of shoes (enough for each child to have a pair with several left over). Clean them and check them for safety. Pile the shoes on the grass on the playground. Children line up and race, one at a time, to the pile of shoes. Each child finds a match and puts the shoes on his feet. The child then races back to the original line.

Helpful Hint: Thrift stores sell inexpensive shoes if families don't donate enough pairs. Wash tennis shoes in the washing machine and use a spray disinfectant to disinfect leather shoes.

Extension Possibilities: Add hats to the pile or gloves to make the process more challenging and interesting.

Observation/Assessment
Matches pairs of shoes

Other Movement/Outdoors Possibilities

- Bring career prop boxes outside for dramatic play.
- Provide lengths of garden hose and fire hats for playing firefighter, large blocks for playing contractor or engineer, PVC pipe for playing plumber, art supplies for playing artist, silk and plastic flowers and vases for playing florist, and so on. Make sure to include diverse occupations.
- Pound large nails halfway into a thick board. Children pound the nails the rest of way into the board. **Safety note:** Supervise closely and require children to wear safety glasses while they work.

PROJECTS/DOCUMENTATION POSSIBILITIES

Self-portraits with What Will I Be?

Materials
paper • crayons • markers • unbreakable mirrors • pictures and books showing different careers

Teacher Talk
"You have brown eyes. Let's find the brown marker."

Instructions
Provide art materials, so children can create self-portraits. Children will need mirrors to see their own features. The books and pictures will help children determine how they might look in their chosen careers.

Observation/Assessment
Draws self-portrait using crayons or markers

FIELD TRIP POSSIBILITIES

Farmer's Market: Visit a local farmer's market to purchase produce for snacks.

Hospital or Ambulance Company: Visit a hospital or ambulance company to see how they work.

Dentist or Doctor: Plan a field trip to a dentist or doctor in the neighborhood. As a follow-up, write a thank-you note.

Costume Shop: If your community has a costume shop with appropriate costumes, plan a trip for children to explore the different costumes. A community or university theater may have a wide variety of costumes to explore.

Visiting Mom or Dad: Visit the worksite of parents or family members of children in the classroom.

SNACK POSSIBILITIES

Garden Vegetables: Purchase vegetables at a local farmer's market. Children can clean and prepare the vegetables for snack.

Cream to Butter: Pour a half-pint of heavy whipping cream into a one-pint plastic jar. Children take turns shaking the jar until butter starts to form. Serve the butter on crackers. Extend this activity by adding different flavors to the butter. Make honey butter, dill butter, lemon butter, and so on.

Career Snacks: Serve snacks that might be popular in various careers such as popcorn for a movie producer, hot dogs for a baseball player, jerky for butcher, ice cream for a dairy farmer, etc. Let children help you come up with possible snacks for various careers, and then plan to serve them, as well.

FAMILY PARTICIPATION POSSIBILITIES

Family Career Chart: Ask parents or other family members what career they wanted when they were children and what career they actually chose. Chart the information to show that children often want to have one career when they are young and then choose a different career when they grow up.

Family Career Information: Ask parents or other family members to provide printed materials (brochures, magazines, signs) related to their careers. Use these items to make books or provide as props in Dramatic Possibilities.

"What I Want to Be" Dress-up Presentation: After exploring what children want to be when they grow up, help them create, make, or find costumes. Invite family members to a presentation where children share their costumes and tell what they want to be. Take lots of pictures for documentation.

Getting Your Preschooler Ready to Read

We have some good news! Teaching your child to read is a relatively simple process. Surprised? Puzzled? Most parents are. Reading seems to require such a complex set of skills. How can we be a part of making it happen without expert assistance from educators?

Only one behavior predicts success in reading: being read to by parents. Research has found that children who are read to daily are the best readers during the elementary years.

Here are some tips for reading to your preschooler, so he or she is bound to succeed.

- In the beginning, don't read. Point! Reading pictures is an important pre-reading skill that your child will perfect first.
- Move your finger across the page to help your child learn left-to-right progression—a key pre-reading skill.
- Point out familiar things first, and then gradually add unfamiliar pictures and words as you read the book again.
- Start with books that can be used for different purposes. For example, if a book tells a story about animals, use the book to explore the different sounds animals make as well as to tell the story.

How much time is enough? Read to your child at least 30 minutes a day. If you can't find 30 minutes, grab 5 minutes here and 10 minutes there to add up to 30 minutes a day.

Curriculum Resources

Prop Boxes

Community Helper Prop Box
clipboard • paper • pencil, • hats • uniforms • city maps • pictures of community helpers doing their jobs • gloves • shoes

Construction Prop Box
toy tools • construction magazines • tool catalogs • newspaper ads and announcements about construction bids, gloves • hard hats • clipboard • paper • pencil • tape measure • level

Food Service Prop Box
uniforms from fast food restaurants • hats • bags and boxes with logos • magazines and newspaper ads • trays • napkins • pizza boxes

Farmer Prop Box
plastic animals • pictures of animals and farms • overalls • plaid shirts • hats and caps • buckets • farm equipment catalogs • pictures of farm equipment • toy gardening tools

Shoe Store Prop Box
shoeboxes • variety of shoes • shoe sizer • cash register • receipts • magazine and newspaper ads • mirror

Musician Prop Box
real and toy musical instruments • song books • sheet music • pictures of musicians playing • catalogs of musical instruments

Books

Bakers (Community Helpers) by Tami Deedrick
Best Times Ever by Richard Scarry
Busy Farm Trucks by R.W. Alley
Career Day by Anne F. Rockwell
Charlie Parker Played Be Bop by Chris Raschka
Community Helpers from A to Z by Bobbie Kalman
DK Readers: Jobs People Do: A Day in a Life of a Dancer by Linda Hayward
DK Readers: Jobs People Do: A Day in a Life of a Firefighter by Linda Hayward
DK Readers: Jobs People Do: A Day in a Life of a Musician by Linda Hayward
DK Readers: Jobs People Do: A Day in a Life of a Police Officer by Linda Hayward
Do You Want to Be My Friend? by Eric Carle
Fire Engine Shapes by Bruce McMillan
I Am an Artist by Pat Lowery Collins
I Want to Be a Cowboy (Firefly Books)
I Want to Be a Vet by Daniel Leibman
Jobs People Do by Christopher Maynard
Just Us Women by Jeanette Caines
New Blue Shoes by Eve Rice
Night Shift Daddy by Eileen Spinelli
Old MacDonald Had an Apartment House by Judi Barrett
Plumbers (Community Helpers) by Tracy Boraas
Shoes by Elizabeth Winthrop

The Very Hungry Caterpillar by Eric Carle
What Do Authors Do? by Eileen Christelow
What Can You Do with a Shoe? by Beatrice Shenk De Regniers
Who Drives This? by Charles Reasoner
Who Uses This? by Margaret Miller
Zin! Zin! Zin!: A Violin by Lloyd Moss

Observation/Assessment

Uses props to enhance dramatic play, page 334 and 335
Takes on various roles in dramatic play, page 335
Draws using markers, page 335
Builds a variety of structures using blocks and block supports, page 337
Observes plant growth, page 338
Names plant parts including the stem, leaves, and roots, page 338
Matches nuts and bolts, page 339
Creates landscape using various materials, page 340
Matches pictures with objects or tools, page 340
Plays simple games, page 341
Measures using a tape measure, ruler, or yardstick, page 341
Copies numbers, page 342
Compares length, page 342
Creates a matching pattern of materials, page 343
Listens to and repeats rhymes, page 344
Matches animal sounds to animal names, page 344
Sings songs, page 344
Uses tools for gardening, page 346
Digs holes in dirt using tools, page 346
Matches pairs of shoes, page 346
Draws self-portrait using crayons or markers, page 347

Picture File/Vocabulary

airplane
ambulance
baker
boots
briefcase
bull
calculator
career
carpenter
chef hat
chicken
construction site
construction worker
cow
dentist
doctor
drum
electrician
electricity
emergency
engineer
farmer
fire truck
firefighter
guitar
hammer
hat
helmet
horse
hose
hospital
librarian
musical instruments
musician
nails
nurse
photographer and other career names
pig
pilot
pipe
plumber
portrait
profession
rooster
safety glasses
shoes
stethoscope
suitcase
teacher
tools
train
trumpet
uniform
veterinarian
wagon
weatherrench

Concepts Learned in What Will I Be?

Content Knowledge

- ☐ Adults have different jobs.
- ☐ Firefighters, police officers, and medical workers are community helpers.
- ☐ Farmers grow crops and animals.
- ☐ Construction workers build.
- ☐ Carpenters build using tools and wood.
- ☐ Plumbers install pipes for water.
- ☐ Teachers help children and adults learn.
- ☐ Plants need light and water to live.

Process Knowledge

- ☐ I can play different roles.
- ☐ I can explore anything I want to be.
- ☐ I can explore career options.
- ☐ I can play with different partners.
- ☐ I can dress/undress in different costumes.
- ☐ I can build with blocks and boxes.
- ☐ I can glue, paint, cut, and draw.
- ☐ I can build a train station/airport.
- ☐ I can match nuts and bolts.
- ☐ I can use a tape measure.
- ☐ I can use tools for gardening.
- ☐ I can hammer nails.
- ☐ I can draw my self-portrait.

Pre-academic Skills

- ☐ I can count to 10.
- ☐ I can observe and discuss my observations.
- ☐ I can identify careers by uniforms and equipment used.
- ☐ I can use printed words as a pattern for writing.
- ☐ I can dictate.
- ☐ I can copy numbers.

Possibilities Plan—Space

Getting Ready to Plan

During the preschool years, children enjoy learning about strange and unusual things. Space is a topic of strong interest because children are familiar with some of the mysterious aspects of space, and they want to know more information. Before beginning this plan, teachers may need to learn more about planets and the solar system so they can co-construct knowledge with children.

The purpose of Getting Ready to Plan is to support the planning process with a general overview of the content of this Possibilities Plan. Now is the time to think about what interests the children and what you want them to learn about each of these topics. Topics are explored in general below.

Space Travel: The idea of traveling in space is an exciting one. Establish the difference between what people have imagined or made up and what has actually happened. You can accomplish this through looking at models of actual spaceships and rockets and exploring the space shuttle.

Sun: Children are familiar with the concept of the sun; they can explore solar energy and learn about the sun in relation to planets. Because you will be using a telescope and binoculars, talk about safety with children. They should never look directly at the sun.

Planets: Take this opportunity to show how planets differ from each other and from the Earth. Posters or a solar system model will help children understand how planets are positioned.

Earth: Talk about the Earth as a planet. How is it alike and different from other planets? What is its relationship to the sun? Use a globe to talk about characteristics of Earth (oceans, rivers, lakes, deserts, air, mountains, and so on). Explore the different habitats of Earth, such as the rain forest, the savannah, the tundra, and the plains.

Now that you have an idea about the general content of the Possibilities Plan, you are ready to proceed with developing your own Plan to implement with the children. This section of Getting Ready to Plan identifies items you may want to buy, collect, or locate to implement your plan.

Toys and Materials*

Purchased

aluminum foil
art paper
astronaut figures
balls of different sizes
binoculars
blocks
books about space travel
butcher paper
carbon paper
cloth
construction paper
countdown audio tape
craft paper
craft sticks
duct tape
flashlight with large lens
globe
glue
magnifier
map of constellations
maps of moon and planets
markers
microscope
models of rockets and spaceships
moon walk
paint brushes
paint, yellow, blue, red, black
paper
papier-mâché
pastels
pattern blocks
pencils
people figures
pictures of moon craters
playdough of different colors
poster of the solar system
posterboard, large black
scissors
silver gel pen
silver glitter
small permanent markers
space music
stapler
star-shaped and other types of stickers
string
tape
telescope
tempera paints, powdered, red
toy cars, planes, and trucks
toy space helmets, boots, and suits
toy space shuttle
zipper-closure plastic bags

Gathered

air tank
animal cage
backpacks
balloons
basket
blank mailing labels and name tags
boxes (small, medium, large, very large)
cardboard tubes
chalk
circle patterns (lids, glasses, jars)
coat hangers
cookie cutters
crayons
digital watches
felt of various colors
foil
food coloring
headsets
hole punch
ice trays
large rubber bands
men's shirts
muffin tin
notebook
old computer
old keyboard
paper cups
paper dishes
pictures of outer space
pictures of planets and stars
planet shapes
plastic bags
plastic cups and glasses
plastic utensils
rocks, variety of
rope
snow boots
sand
scientific materials
sharp pencil
shaving cream
silver items
silver paint
sleeping bags
small rocks
stainless steel items
stapler
straps
stuffed animals
Styrofoam balls of different sizes
thread or dental floss
toothpaste tubes, used
toothpicks
variety of rocks
water jugs

*Note: Please consider the ages and abilities of the children in your classroom. Use only safe, non-toxic materials.

Space

WEB

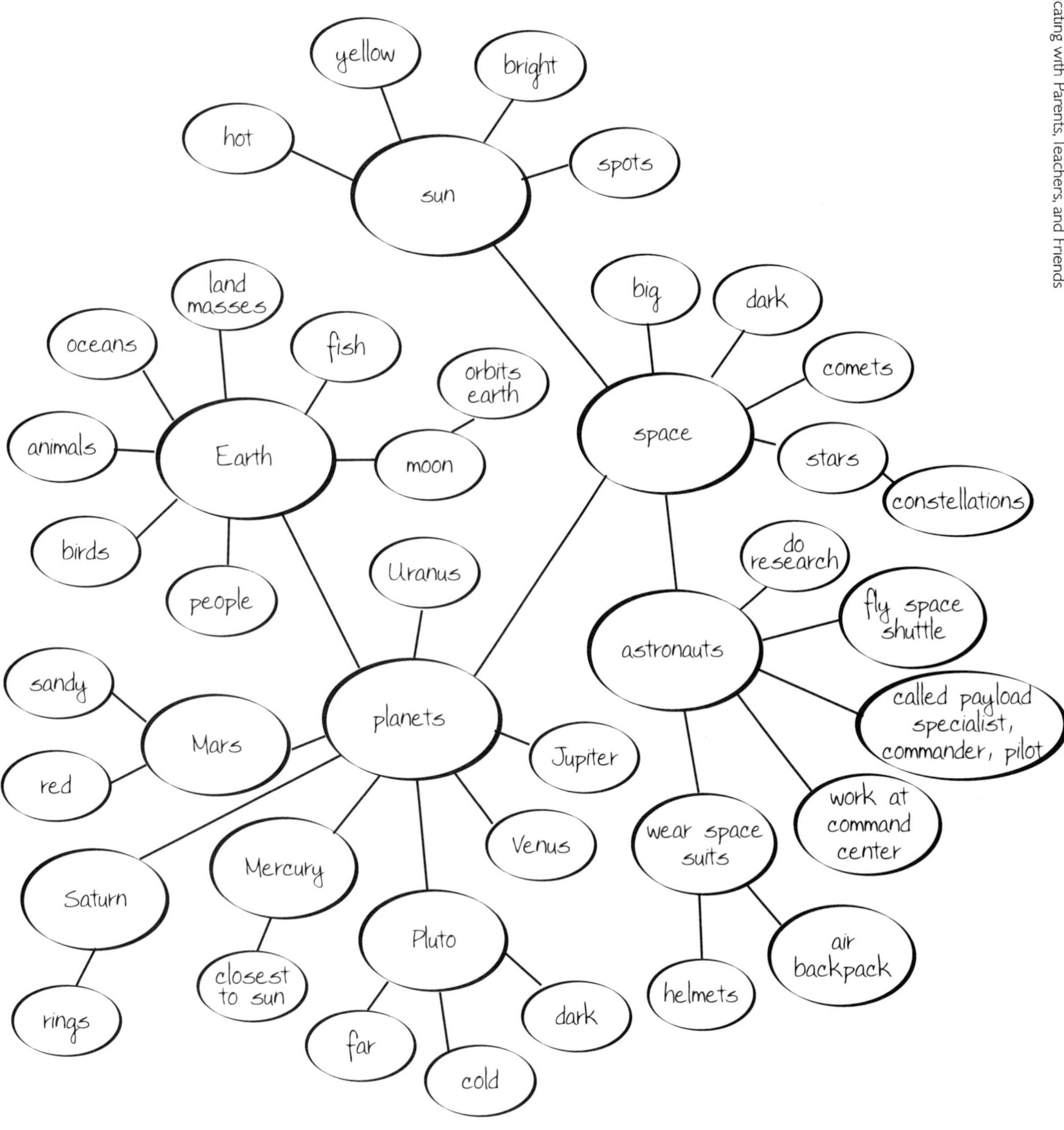

sun
yellow
bright
hot
spots
space
big
dark
comets
stars
constellations
Earth
land masses
oceans
fish
orbits earth
animals
moon
birds
people
astronauts
do research
fly space shuttle
called payload specialist, commander, pilot
work at command center
wear space suits
helmets
air backpack
planets
Uranus
Mars
sandy
red
Jupiter
Venus
Saturn
rings
Mercury
closest to sun
Pluto
far
cold
dark

Space

PLANNING PAGES

Plan Possibilities

Dramatic

Art

Blocks/Construction

Science/Discovery

Sensory

Literacy/Writing

Math/Manipulatives

Rhymes/ Fingerplays/ Songs/ Music

Group Time Possibilities

Movement/Outdoors

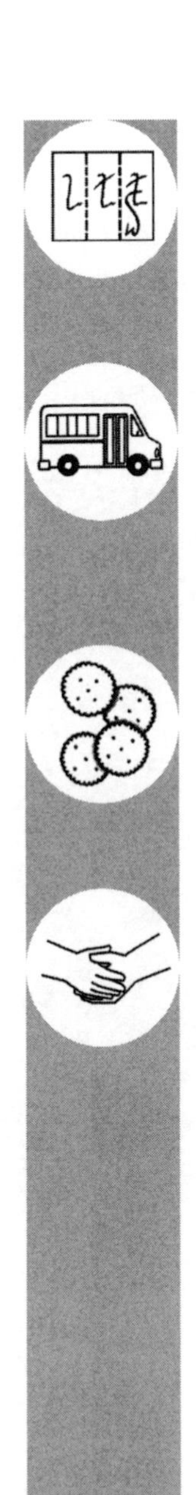

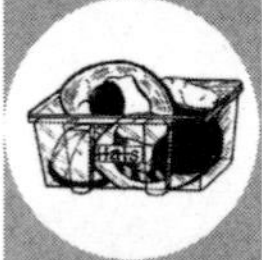

ACTIVITIES AND EXPERIENCES FOR SPACE

DRAMATIC POSSIBILITIES

Space Control Center

Materials

old keyboard • big box • construction paper • small box • aluminum foil • clear contact paper • rope • cloth • water jugs • snow boots • pictures of outer space • countdown audio tape • space helmets • space boots • space suits • head sets (discarded) • space pictures from picture file • books, such as *Astronauts Today* by Rosanna Hansen or *Floating in Space* by Franklyn Mansfield Branley

Teacher Talk

"Who helps astronauts when they are working in space?" "What do astronauts do?"

Instructions

Create the space control center by using old keyboards and monitors made with boxes. To make the monitor, put construction paper on one side to make a screen. On the screen you may write or draw pictures of a spaceship and planets. For astronauts you will need an air tank (carried as a backpack) and a helmet. For the air tank, find the right sized box to fit on a child's back. Cover the box with aluminum foil. Then cover it again with clear contact paper. Attach ropes or strips of cloth to make straps for the backpack. For the helmet, cut the top part off the water jug and use the remaining portion. For the spaceship, decorate a large box and use extra cardboard boxes to make wings. For the space control center, use an old computer or any discarded electronics.

Explore NASA's website for more ideas: http://kids.msfc.nasa.gov/.

Observation/Assessment
Uses props to enhance dramatic play

Space Station

Materials
air tank • helmet • magnifier • microscope • variety of rocks • scientific materials • toy animals with a cage • notebook • pen • sleeping bags • used toothpaste tubes • zipper closure plastic bags • old keyboards • men's shirts • head sets • telescopes made from cardboard tubes • books, such as *Life of an Astronaut* by Niki Walker or *I Want to Be an Astronaut* by Craig Ryan.

Teacher Talk
"What do astronauts do in the space station?" "How do they sleep in space?"

Instructions
Create the inside of a space station. Make a room for science experiments using the materials listed. Make a sleeping place by using the sleeping bags. Use empty toothpaste tubes and small zipper closure plastic bags to make pretend food containers.

Observation/Assessment
Takes on various roles in dramatic play

Silvery Shiny Things

Materials
materials covered with foil • aluminum • stainless steel items • digital watches

Teacher Talk
"You have discovered items from the space station."

Instructions
Use shiny items to represent items from the space station. Any item can be made shiny by covering it with aluminum foil. Hide the items in the Dramatic Possibilities area so children can find them and use them as they play.

Observation/Assessment
Finds hidden items

ART POSSIBILITIES

UFO?

Materials
stapler • paper plates • string • aluminum foil • glue • permanent markers • stickers • collage materials

Teacher Talk
"Do you think there are space aliens?" "If there are space aliens, how would they travel to Earth?"

Instructions
Staple two paper plates together to make a UFO. Punch a hole in the top and attach a string. Cover the plate with aluminum foil. Use permanent markers, stickers, or collage materials to decorate it. Hang the UFOs from the ceiling in Dramatic Possibilities.

Blast Off!

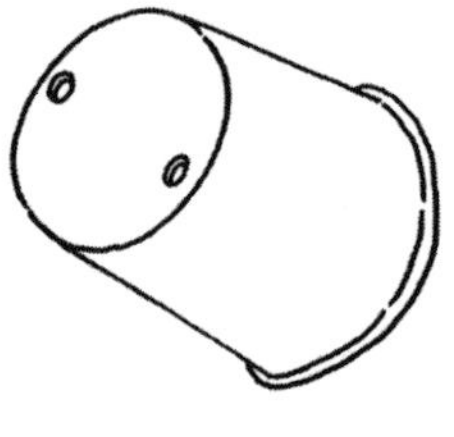

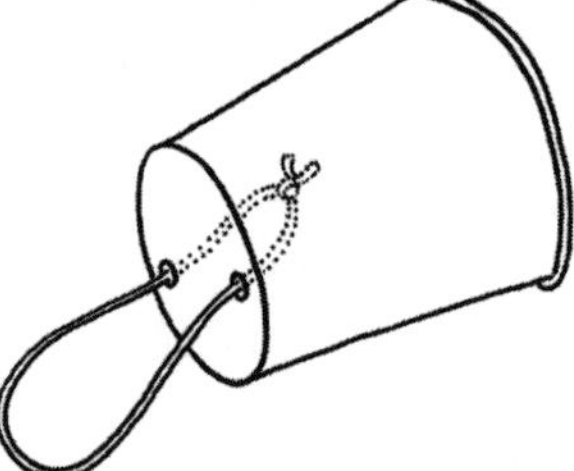

Materials
paper cups • sharp pencil (teacher only) • hole punch • tempera paint • paint cups and brushes • permanent markers • large rubber bands

Teacher Talk
"How do rockets fly?"

Instructions
On half of the cups make two holes in the bottom using the sharp pencil or hole punch (teachers only). Provide paint and brushes or permanent markers for children to decorate the cups. The rocket works best if the holes are punched on opposite sides close to the rim. Cut a rubber band and string it into one hole and out of the other. Then tie the rubber band back together again using a double knot. If the rubber bands are too short, tie two or more rubber bands together to make a longer rubber band. Place a cup inside the one with the rubber band. Pull the rubber band down, and then let it go. See how high the cup will fly into the air.

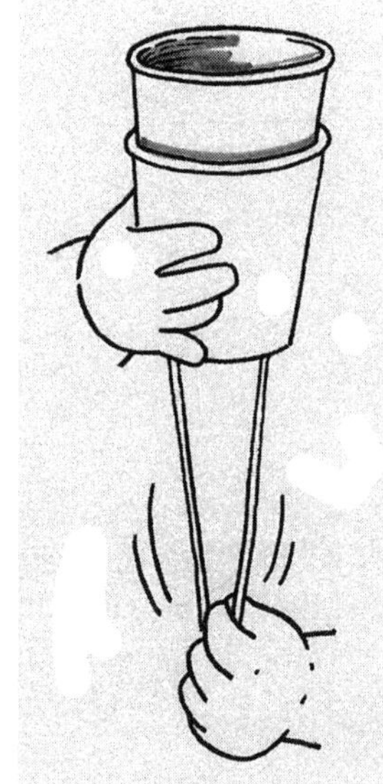

Observation/Assessment
Uses fine motor skills for art expression

Other Art Possibilities

- Make five-pointed stars and cover with foil to add to the ceiling of the space station.
- Make bubble wrap prints as moon craters. Talk about how the moon rotates around the earth.
- Make telescopes out of cardboard tubes.
- Paint with two circles—one with cold, blue paint (chilled in a refrigerator) and one with warm, yellow paint (warmed in hot water) on black paper. The blue circle represents cold planets such as Pluto and the yellow circle represents the sun.

BLOCKS/CONSTRUCTION POSSIBILITIES

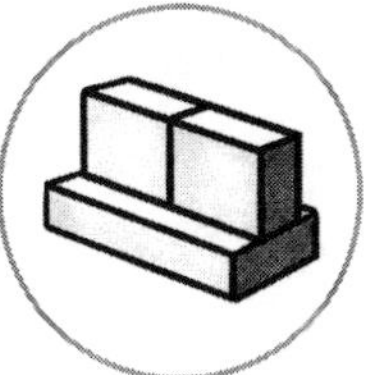

Space Station on the Moon

Materials
blocks • toy space shuttle • astronaut figures • books, such as *Man on the Moon* by Anastasia Suen

Teacher Talk
"What kind of buildings do we need in order to make a space station on the moon?"

Instructions
Use blocks and other materials to create a space station. Supplement this activity with related reading materials.

Observation/Assessment
Builds using blocks

People in Space Suits

Materials
figures in space suits or people figures • duct tape

Teacher Talk
"You placed all the astronauts in the space station." "Now where are the rockets?"

Instructions
Make astronauts by wrapping figures with duct tape to create space suits.
Add figures in space suits to the area as children play.

Silver Car, Rocket

Materials
Non-toxic silver spray paint (teacher only) • cars • trucks • rockets • books, such as *The Magic School Bus Lost in the Solar System* by Joanna Cole

Teacher Talk
"Where are all the space cars going?" "You have them all lined up."

Instructions
Add silver vehicles and paper cup rockets (see page 360) to the area to use as space vehicles. Spray paint (teacher only) old toy vehicles and rockets. Spray paint cars, trucks, and rockets in a well-ventilated area away from the children.

SCIENCE/DISCOVERY POSSIBILITIES

3, 2, 1 Blast Off!

Materials
models or toys of rockets and spaceships • books about rockets and spaceships (see page 374) • globes • books, such as *Do Stars Have Points?* by Melvin Berger

Teacher Talk
"You are counting down the numbers." "I guess it's time for blast off."

Instructions
Place the models, books, and globe in the Science/Discovery Possibilities area for children to explore. Talk about how rockets and spaceships go into outer space. Include books, such as *Do Stars Have Points?* by Melvin Berger. Children may be able to add space toys from home to this area. Discuss with children any rules pertinent to your setting about bringing toys from home and sharing with friends.

Extension Possibilities: Take dictation from children about their ideas of what happens after the rocket or spaceship blasts off.

Observation/Assessment
Counts backward from 5, from 10

Star Map

Materials
black construction paper • flashlight with large lens • pencil • tape • map showing different constellations

Teacher Talk
"You are pointing at the star formation that looks like a lion."

Instructions
Provide materials listed. Cut out black construction paper in circles the same shape and size of the flashlight lens. Children punch holes using the pencil to create the patterns on the star map. Place the black construction paper circles on a piece of Styrofoam to make punching the holes easier. Tape the construction paper over the lens. Shine the flashlight on the wall to see the star patterns.

Other Science/Discovery Possibilities

- Make a relief map of the moon using golf balls and plaster of Paris poured in a box top.
- Using a moon map, make a relief map of the moon using sand and golf balls.
- Look at a map of the moon or planets using a telescope, binoculars, or a magnifying glass.
- Create craters on paper. Cut a piece of paper to fit a box. Place it in the box. Put carbon paper (carbon side down) on top of the paper, add golf balls, and shake up and down.

SENSORY POSSIBILITIES

Sand from Mars

Materials
sand • red paint • toy astronauts • space shuttle • paintbrushes

Teacher Talk
"You are painting with paint that is the color of Mars." "Tell me about painting with red sand."

Instructions
Mix sand with red paint to make red sand. Let children paint with the sand. Allow children to experiment by adding other materials to paint (saw dust, soil, glitter, dots of paper from hole punch).

Observation/Assessment
Paints using paint and brushes

Ice Planet

Materials

food colors • balloons • toy astronauts • space shuttle

Teacher Talk

"Some planets are very cold, even colder than ice."

Instructions

Mix water with food colors. Fill the balloons with colored water. Keep the balloons small so they freeze faster. Put them in the freezer. Fill the sensory table with ice cubes or water. When frozen, remove the ice shapes from the balloons and discard. Place the colored ice balls in the sensory table as ice planets.

Other Sensory Possibilities

- Use playdough and cookie cutters to make planets and stars. Display on cardboard with the child's name written on it.
- Make colorful clouds in the sensory table with colored shaving cream and a variety of balls.

LITERACY/WRITING POSSIBILITIES

Captain Nametags

Materials

blank name tags • markers • star stickers • books, such as *Dogs in Space* by Nancy Coffelt

Instructions

Write the word titles for astronauts, such as captain, commander, lieutenant, first officer, science officer, payload specialist, and so on, at the top of each label. Each child can use the markers to write his own name underneath the title. Children can use the star stickers to decorate their tags. Wear the tags in the Dramatic Possibilities Area. Children might want to make a tag each day, because the stickers will not re-stick on clothes. Call children by their space titles when they are wearing the tags.

Observation/Assessment

Writes own name

Captain
Juan

Solar System Felt Board

Materials
piece of felt for each planet and the sun • scissors • small-tipped permanent markers • basket or box • solar system poster

Teacher Talk
"The planets orbit around the sun." "Which planet is closest to the Earth?" "P is for p-p-p-Pluto."

Instructions
Cut out the nine planets and the sun from the felt (make sure that each felt planet resembles the color of the real planet). Use the permanent markers to write the names of the planets and the word "sun" on the pieces. Place the planets and sun in a box or basket next to the felt board for children to create the solar system on the felt board. To add complexity, put the planet names on separate felt pieces so that children have to match the names to the planets as they sequence them.

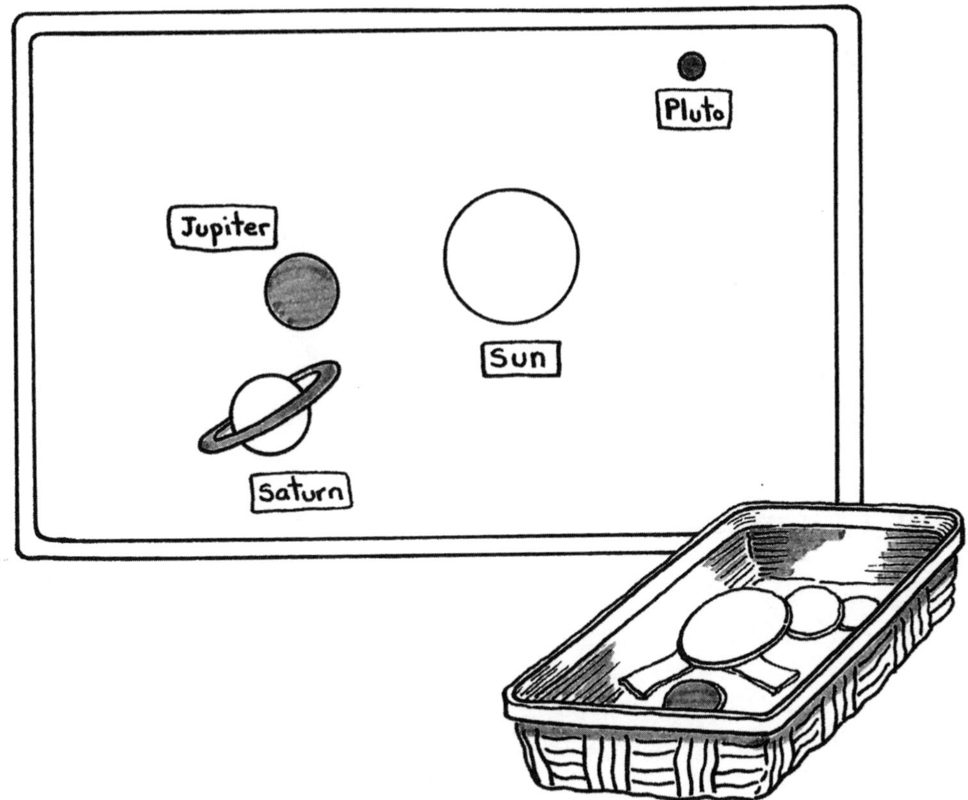

Observation/Assessment
Sequences the planets according to position
Matches names of planets to their images

Writing in Space

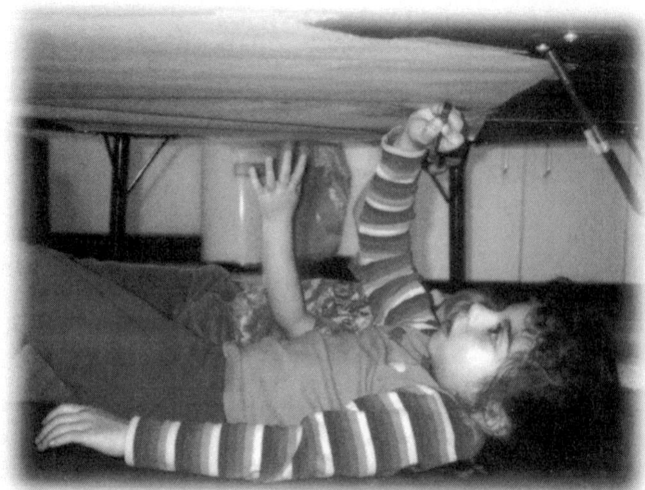

Materials
table • butcher paper • variety of crayons • markers • chalk • other writing materials

Teacher Talk
"Writing upside down is different!"

Instruction
Simulate writing in space by taping paper to the undersides of a table. The children can write while lying on their backs with the paper overhead.

Other Literacy/Writing Possibilities

- Read the books listed in the Book List (page 374).
- Create a space story as a group.
- Use a sand tray in the area for beginning letter formation.
- Make journals for children to write their own space stories.
- On black paper, use a silver marker to write children's dictation about what they would do in space. Children illustrate their answers with metallic pens and glitter markers.

MATH/MANIPULATIVES POSSIBILITIES

Matching Planets

Materials
planet shapes • construction paper • scissors

Teacher Talk
"How many red planets can you find?" "That's right. Mars is called the red planet."

Instructions
Use the different-sized circles to cut out planets from different colors of construction paper. Children can match the same shapes and colors and then count them.

Extension Possibilities: Increase the number of planet shapes to 20, then to 30.

Observation/Assessment
Matches colors
Matches shapes

Moon Rock Counting

Materials
circle of construction paper • muffin tin • markers • small rocks • scissors

Teacher Talk
"You have five moon rocks on the number five."

Instructions
Cut circles from construction paper to place in the bottoms of each cup of the muffin tin. Write a number on each circle. Children count out the number of rocks to match the number in each cup of the muffin tin.

Extension Possibilities: Continue increasing numbers as children develop their counting skills. Count by 2's, using the muffin tin cups as groups.

Observation/Assessment
Counts to 5, then 10 or more using one-to-one correspondence
Counts by 2s

Other Math/Manipulatives Possibilities

- Use tinker toys for building planets.
- Add space puzzles to the area.
- Create space puzzles by gluing a space picture on cardboard and cutting it into pieces.
- Create matching, counting, and sorting games with space stickers.
- Create spaceships with Styrofoam balls and toothpicks.
- Put star stickers all over a black poster board. Children use pattern blocks to create space and spaceships.

RHYMES/FINGERPLAYS/SONGS/MUSIC POSSIBILITIES

Space Music

Materials
space music (see page 368 for suggestions)

Instructions
Start the music. Encourage children to move to the music.

Observation/Assessment
Moves body to the rhythm of a song

Where Is Space Man?

Instructions
Teach children the following song to the tune of "Where Is Thumbkin?" Use the song to call children to group time in the morning.

Where Is Space Man?
Where is space man?
Where is space man?
Here I am.
Here I am.
How are you today, sir?
Very well, I thank you.
Blast off! Blast off!

Other Rhymes/Fingerplays/Songs/Music Possibilities

- Consider any of the following recorded selections:
  - "Somewhere Over the Rainbow" from *Wizard of Oz Soundtrack*
  - "You Are My Sunshine"—any version using first stanza only
  - "Star Trek Theme" from *TV's Greatest Hits*
  - "Lost in Space" from *TV's Greatest Hits*
  - *Journey into Space* by Kimbo
  - "What Will I Take to the Moon" from *Happy to Be Here* by Parachute Express
  - "Star Trek Movie Theme" from *Star Trek Movie Soundtrack*
  - "Moon Rock Rock" from *Journey into Space*
  - "Star Wars Theme" from *Star Wars Movie Soundtrack*
- Sing "Twinkle, Twinkle Little Star" with hand motions.

GROUP TIME POSSIBILITIES

Eating Like an Astronaut: Talk about how astronauts eat in a weightless environment. Provide Jell-O in zipper-closure plastic bags. Teachers can cut off a corner of the bag so children can squeeze the snack into their mouths like astronauts in space. Try this with pudding, applesauce, peanut butter mixed with jelly, and other appropriate foods. **Safety Note:** Check for food allergies and carefully dispose of corner pieces.

Space Ice Cream: Provide dried ice cream on a paper plate. Talk about how this ice cream is different from ice cream we usually see because it is dehydrated. Divide the ice cream, so everyone can have a taste. Taste other dehydrated snacks, such as raisins (grapes), prunes (plums), dried apples, peaches, pears, or other dried fruit.

Space Book: Read any of the books about space listed in this Possibilities Plan (see page 374).

Star Sit-upons: Make seats for group time by folding a short stack of newspapers and wrapping it with duct tape. Decorate them with star stickers.

Star Map: Introduce a constellation map. Connect the stars to form the constellations.

Solar System: Introduce the concepts related to the solar system. Talk about each planet at a separate group time.

MOVEMENT/OUTDOORS POSSIBILITIES

I'm Too Heavy

Materials
sand • plastic bags • backpack

Teacher Talk
"What do you think would happen if you tried to walk on a planet with more or less gravity than on Earth?"

Instructions
Put sand into a plastic bag and place in the backpack. Let children put on the backpack and walk around the playground feeling that it is harder to walk with added weight.

Helpful Hint: Go to the NASA website to find out the gravitational pull of different planets.

Ice Art

Materials
powdered tempera paint • craft sticks • white construction paper • craft or freezer paper • ice trays

Teacher Talk
"This is a messy activity, so outside is a great place for us right now."

Instructions
Fill a plastic ice tray about one-half to two-thirds full of water. Add powdered tempera to the different sections. Place one craft stick in each cube. Freeze the cubes until solid. Remove ice cubes and use for painting. Place newspaper under the art paper to absorb the extra water from the melting cubes. To create a banner or a group art piece, use a length of art paper or the unwaxed side of freezer paper taped to a table or a fence.

Extension Possibilities: The product of this activity works well as a background or backdrop for other art creations.

Observation/Assessment
Paints using various media

Other Movement/Outdoors Possibilities

- Use space prop boxes outside.
- Create a spaceship outside using a large appliance box.
- Turn the playground into a space station. Put on astronaut gear before entering space (air packs, helmets, and so on).

PROJECTS/DOCUMENTATION POSSIBILITIES

Solar System

Materials
balloons of different sizes • thread • papier-mâché • newspaper • scissors • paint • brushes

Teacher Talk
"You are using the red paint on the planet Mars."

Instructions
Blow the balloons to different sizes to represent the different planets. The sizes of the planets should vary between the size of a tennis ball (Pluto) to the size of a basketball (Jupiter). After you tie a knot in each balloon, tie a piece of thread on it. Cut the newspaper into strips. Soak the strips in the papier-mâché solution. Lay the newspaper strips on the balloons, making circles around the balloons. Continue until there are at least two layers, allowing time for each layer to dry. Talk with children about the different sizes and colors of planets. After completely dry, planets can be painted. Recreate the solar system by hanging the planets from the ceiling by the thread.

Observation/Assessment
Paints using brushes
Creates with papier-mâché

Space Mural

Materials
large sheet of paper (art or butcher) • paint • brushes • construction paper • scissors • glue

Teacher Talk
"Do you remember which planets are cold and which planets are hot?" "How are the planets arranged?"

Instructions
Paint a large sheet of paper with black paint using hands, feet, or brushes. Next, cut circles for the sun and the planets. Paint the sun with warm yellow paint; paint Mars with red paint mixed with sand. For planets covered with dense clouds, use cotton to represent the clouds. For cold planets, use cold paint. After painting each planet, glue it on the space mural. Add the sun. Add moons, where appropriate. Children can decorate the space mural with additional creations of spaceships, stars, rockets, shooting stars, etc. Hang the mural on the wall or suspend the mural by its corners from the ceiling. Write down all the things that the children say about the space mural.

Observation/Assessment
Participates in group projects

Planet Mobile

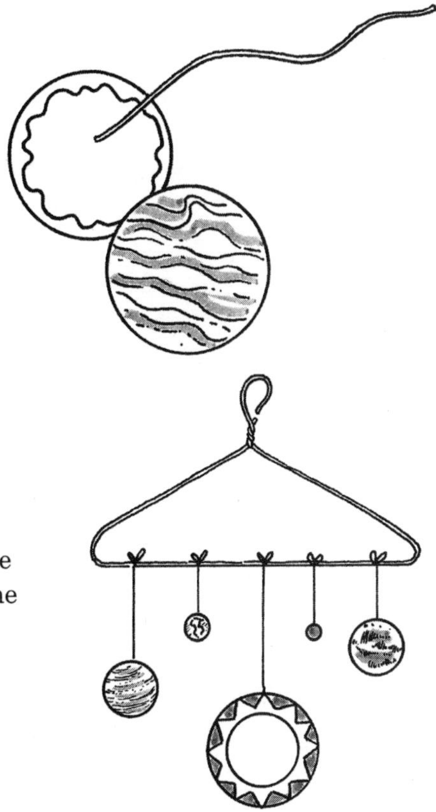

Materials
circle patterns (lids, glasses, jars) • construction paper • markers • glue • dental floss or thread • coat hangers

Teacher Talk
"You have made five planets to hang on your mobile."

Instructions
Make planets by tracing circle shapes on paper, making two circles of each size. Decorate the planets and then cut them out using scissors. Show children how to put glue on one undecorated side of a planet, sandwich the floss or string in the middle, and then place the other undecorated side of a planet on top of the floss or string. Hang the planets from the bottom of a wire coat hanger. Decorate the classroom with the mobiles.

Observation/Assessment
Makes circles on paper using patterns

FIELD TRIP POSSIBILITIES

Planetarium: Plan a trip to a local planetarium. This is an excellent way to introduce space concepts. You may also want to use the field trip as a culminating activity.

Museum of Natural Science: A trip to a natural science museum can help children recognize the relationship between the environment and how animals live. Talk with children about how Earth has a perfect environment for many types of plants and animals.

Weather Station: Many of the concepts children explore in space are also a part of weather (temperature, humidity, clouds, sunlight, and so on). Talk about how different areas have different climates.

SNACK POSSIBILITIES

Squishy Space Snack: Assist each child in placing one-third of a banana and a large spoonful of peanut butter in a small zipper closure plastic bag. Children can "squish" the contents until smooth. Cut a corner out of the bag, so children can squeeze the space snack into their mouths. For children with peanut allergies, substitute apple butter.

Cheese and Crackers: Talk with children about how some people joke that the moon is made from cheese. Children can make their own snack of cheese and crackers.

Other Space Snacks: Try pudding, applesauce, peanut butter and jelly, all eaten astronaut style.

FAMILY PARTICIPATION POSSIBILITIES

Star Gazing: Suggest that families look at the night sky as an at-home activity.

Come with Me!: Invite families to assist with field trips. Use the guidelines on page 219 to determine ways that families might help in the process.

Supporting Possibilities: Ask families to bring in items that you will need during the space plan. Also, ask if any family members are involved in careers related to the space program. Invite them in to share with the children.

Appropriate Expectations for Academic Skills

Many child development specialists believe that the foundation for learning is built during the early childhood years. This may be a scary thought because many people remember academic experiences starting at age five or six. You may think that you have no idea how to teach your children, but you do!

Everything parents do with their children is teaching. You have been teaching your child from the very beginning. You started by teaching your child that you love him or her. Then, you taught your child to depend on you. You helped your child learn to scoot, crawl, walk, and so forth. Now you are probably thinking of teaching more academic skills.

Each time you interact with your child you are teaching him or her. Each positive, playful experience a child has builds potential for academic readiness and success. The following is a list of activities are guaranteed to lay the foundation for success in academic skills after age six.

- Read to your child every day. Early positive experiences with books will help make your child a good reader.
- Share your work with your child. Children learn from real, hands-on experiences. Sorting laundry, cooking, counting out utensils for a meal, reading a grocery list—all can be learning experiences and important opportunities for you to spend time with your child.
- Talk about what you are doing and why. Conversations are chances for children to increase vocabulary and learn new things.
- Avoid telling your child too much. The early years are years of doing and experimenting—not being taught by telling.
- Don't be tempted to have your child memorize numbers out of context. It is far more important for him or her to be able to use math (knowing that three means one, two, three of a particular thing, knowing that a full cup is more than a half cup).
- Don't be tempted to have your child memorize letters of the alphabet out of context. Real experiences with words and books are far more important.

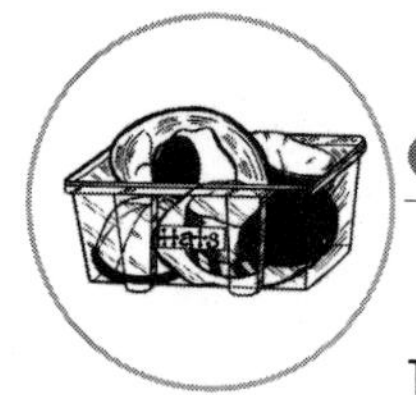

Curriculum Resources

Prop Boxes

Space Prop Box
space boots (silver painted) • notebook • pen • keyboard • helmets from milk jugs, books about planets • books about space travel • models of rockets and spaceships • astronaut figures • space suits • head sets • countdown audio tape

Astronomy Prop Box
telescope • binoculars • graph paper • pen/pencil • clipboard • pictures of constellations • books about space • star maps

Books

Astronaut: Living in Space by Kate Hayden
Astronauts Today by Rosanna Hansen
Children of the Sun by Arthur L'Hommedieu
Do Stars Have Points?: Questions and Answers about Stars and Planets by Melvin Berger
Dogs in Space by Nancy Coffelt
Draw Me a Star by Eric Carle
Earth, Sky, and Beyond: A Journey Through Space by Jean-Pierre Verdet
Floating in Space by Franklyn Mansfield Branley
Full Moon by Michael Light
Handshake in Space: The Apollo-Soyuz Mission by Sheri Tan
I Want to Be an Astronaut by Byron Barton
Ice Is… Whee! by Carol Greene
Kingdom of the Sun by Jacqueline Mitton
Life of an Astronaut by Niki Walker
The Magic School Bus Lost in the Solar System by Joanna Cole
The Man on the Moon by Anastasia Suen
The Moon Book by Gail Gibbons
My Brother Is from Outer Space by Vivian Ostrow
One Giant Leap: The Story of Neil Armstrong by Don Brown
Papa, Please Get the Moon for Me by Eric Carle
The Planets by Gail Gibbons
Postcards from Pluto: A Tour of the Solar System by Loreen Leedy
The Rain Puddle by Adelaide Hall
Rain Rain Rivers by Uri Shulevitz
Roaring Rockets by Tony Mitton
Stargazers by Gail Gibbons
The Storm Book by Charlotte Zolotow
Sky All Around by Anna Grosnickle Hines
Sun Up, Sun Down by Gail Gibbons

Observation/Assessment

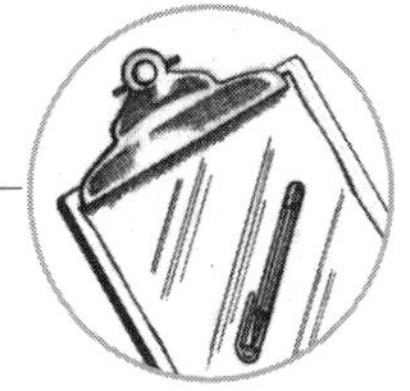

Uses props to enhance dramatic play, page 359
Takes on various roles in dramatic play, page 359
Finds items hidden from sight, page 359
Uses fine motor skills for art expression, page 361
Builds using blocks, page 361
Counts backwards from 5, from 10, page 362
Paints using paint and brushes, page 363
Writes own name, page 364
Sequences planets according to position, page 365
Matches names of planets to their images, page 365
Matches colors, page 366
Matches shapes, page 366
Counts to 5, then 10, using one-to-one correspondence, page 367
Counts by 2s, page 367
Moves body to the rhythm of a song, page 367
Paints using various media, page 370
Paints using brushes, page 371
Creates using papier-mâché, page 371
Participates in group projects, page 371
Makes circles on paper using patterns, page 371

Picture File/Vocabulary

air
air tank or backpack
astronaut
binoculars
clouds
cold
command center
computer
constellation
dark
Earth
gravity
hot
Jupiter
magnifying glasses
Mars
Mercury
moon
moon rocks
Neptune
orbit
papier-mache
planets
Pluto
position
rocket
rotate
Saturn
shuttle
space
space helmet
spaceship
stars
Sun
telescope
texture
Uranus
Venus
yellow

Concepts Learned in Space

Content Knowledge

- ☐ A control center controls the space ship.
- ☐ Different planets are different colors and sizes.
- ☐ Planets rotate around the sun.
- ☐ The moon rotates around the earth.
- ☐ The sun is very hot.
- ☐ Planets can be hot if they are close to the sun or cold if they are far away from the sun.
- ☐ Gravity is different on different planets.
- ☐ Astronauts travel in space.
- ☐ Astronauts wear space suits in space.

Process Knowledge

- ☐ I can find hidden objects.
- ☐ I can paint with hot or cold paint.
- ☐ I can build with blocks.
- ☐ I can stack cups and glasses.
- ☐ I can use a telescope/binoculars to see things.
- ☐ I can punch holes in a pattern.
- ☐ I can paint using colored ice.
- ☐ I can shape playdough with cookie cutters.
- ☐ I can build using Styrofoam balls and toothpicks.
- ☐ I can sing and move to music.
- ☐ I can carry a backpack.
- ☐ I can create with papier-mâché.

Pre-academic Skills

- ☐ I can identify planets.
- ☐ I can sequence planets by position.
- ☐ I can count backwards from 10.
- ☐ I can use letters to represent words.
- ☐ I can connect a sound to a letter.
- ☐ I can write letters.
- ☐ I can write my name.
- ☐ I can recognize familiar words.
- ☐ I can match colors and shapes.
- ☐ I can count (forward or backward) using one-to-one correspondence to 5 (to 10).

CHAPTER 6

Problem Solving

INNOVATIONS IN CARE AND EARLY EDUCATION

Brain Development

Every day we learn more and more about the brain, how it works, and what influences it. McCall and Plemons (2001) suggest that two principles should be considered fundamental with regard to the brain. The first is that the brain influences everything. Changes in the brain affect behavior, and changes in behavior affect the brain. The second is that there are negative consequences for the brain when there is inadequate stimulation or poor environments.

What influences how the brain develops? Old arguments of nature versus nurture have changed from a discussion of which is more important to considering the impact of each on brain development. Advances in neuroscience highlight the dynamic interplay between nature and nurture. An intricate "dance" occurs between what a child is born with and what happens to that potential. As the dance continues, genetic predispositions often cannot be separated from what is influenced by experience (Shonkoff & Phillips, 2000).

How Does the Brain Grow?

An understanding of how the brain grows reveals a sequence of overlapping stages, some of which occur in the prenatal stage. The first stage is neural proliferation—the creation of billions of nerve cells called neurons. The neurological hardware and wiring of the brain are produced during this stage. Brain cells (neurons) begin the process of brain development by connecting to other brain cells. Neurons are designed precisely with this goal in mind. Each cell has an axon and many hair-like extensions called dendrites.

The second phase, called neural migration, is completed during gestation. This process sends out nerve connections throughout the brain and joins them together. The third stage is synaptogenesis—the process of connecting neurons together to form neural networks. Synapses are created when an axon of one brain cell connects with a dendrite of another neuron. This process is repeated millions of times as the young child's brain is developing. During the early childhood years, the brain creates far more connections than it will ultimately need to process information. The over-development of synapses insures that children are primed and ready for continuing brain development.

The potential for positive as well as negative influences on synaptogenesis exists. For example, adequate nourishment provided to children when they are hungry is an environmental necessity for continued brain development. Yet, if nourishment is withheld or unavailable, or provided by an uncaring and unresponsive adult, the brain's vulnerability is exposed, and brain development may be compromised (Shonkoff & Phillips, 2000).

Neural pathways are strengthened by repeated experiences and by good teaching (Shore, 1997). The goal of this stage of brain development, called selective elimination or degeneration, is to strengthen and reinforce connections between and among neurons to the point that they will always be maintained. This goal is accomplished through repeated interactions that use the communication links between neurons.

During this period of brain development, neural pathways are pruned and eliminated if they are unused, underused, or if the brain is stressed by environmental factors. Pruning continues throughout the lifespan, with the brain continually creating synapses as a result of stimulation and abandoning those that are not being used.

The last stage of brain development, myelination, is the process of coating the nerve cells with a fatty substance that insulates nerve endings and increases the speed and efficiency of connections. This, in turn, increases the ease of communication between neural networks and facilitates coordination among them.

What Affects Brain Growth?

Environmental Conditions Affect Brain Growth—The development of the brain is influenced by many environmental conditions. Nourishment, type and quality of routine care, warm, nurturing interactions, stimulating and interesting surroundings, and stimulation experiences from objects and people in the environment are examples of potentially positive environmental conditions. Maternal depression; trauma; abuse; social deprivation; drug, alcohol, or nicotine use; and institutionalization are examples of potentially negative environmental conditions.

These affects can be immediate (as in drug use during pregnancy) or influence the general direction of brain growth positively or negatively (as in mother-child interactions that are warm and reciprocal). The direction of these effects is pervasive and cumulative, affecting children throughout their lives, not just during early childhood years (Bredekamp & Copple, 1997).

Normal Maturation Affects Brain Growth—Nature equips young children with a mechanism for developing the brain. Developmental maturation is a powerful stimulus that continues the process of connecting neurons, strengthening synapses, and coordinating neural pathways.

Some of these experiences are anticipated by the developing brain. That is, genetics prepare the brain to receive certain kinds of stimulation that, when received, allow for further organization and development. An "expectant" experience happens to the brain during the development of visual acuity.

As children are exposed to variations in natural light and the patterns of early visual experiences after birth, the brain uses these inputs to further normal visual development. Unless something interferes with this experience (like cataracts or strabismus), the brain detects and registers the expected experience and uses it to continue to develop the brain's wiring for visual acuity (Shonkoff & Phillips, 2000).

Continued brain development is also "dependent" on experiences. Normal development offers many of these "dependent" experiences. For example, children gain coordination of fine and gross motor skills by repeating the patterns of those skills over and over again, strengthening the communication and coordination between neural networks. Children who do not have experiences playing on the floor, exploring the environment, climbing stairs, and so on may not receive enough stimulating experiences to increase synaptic coordination and communication.

Understanding that normative development supports brain development is wonderful news for early childhood educators. Teachers have always known that authentic assessment is not designed to compare children to each other but instead to monitor emerging skills and abilities. Teachers do so to modify educational experiences to match the child's emerging skills.

The crucial importance of monitoring maturation as a teaching activity is validated by brain research. Because normally emerging skills and abilities support experience-dependent synaptogenesis, keeping a keen eye on emerging development is a teaching technique for facilitating continued brain growth. Alert teachers can identify potential interruptions in normal development early enough to intervene with remediation, preventing interruption or compromise of brain development.

Warm, Reciprocal Relationships Affect Brain Growth—Intimate, enduring, reciprocal interactions between children and adults in their attachment networks are crucial to brain growth. These relationships protect children from the impact of less-than-optimal life experiences, allow children to learn and benefit from life situations that are stress producing, and provide a firm foundation for the natural exploration and experience that continue the wiring of the brain during childhood.

Relationships that are most beneficial to the brain are warm, responsive, caring, and available. There is a good fit between the interactive style of the adults and the gestural and verbal communication of the child, so communication between them can be sent and received efficiently and effectively. Finally, an enduring nature to the relationships that children have with adults is required. Intermittent relationships with other adults and with peers are important for social development, but consistent, enduring relationships create the environment for continued brain and emotional development.

Consistent, enduring relationships create the environment for continued brain and emotional development.

Sensitive Periods Affect Brain Growth—Sensitive periods (also called critical periods and timing effects) are periods when specific structures of the brain are most susceptible to experience. These experiences alter future brain structures and functions. The impact of sensitive periods or timing effects can be positive if they result from normal, beneficial experiences, or negative if they result from abnormal, harmful, or withheld experiences.

Currently, there is some controversy about sensitive periods. Some neuroscientists say too much emphasis on sensitive periods negates the brain's plasticity and ability to compensate and change, a situation that continues throughout the lifespan (Bailey, 2002; Bailey, Bruer, Symons, & Lichtman, 2001; Shonkoff & Phillips, 2000). Nevertheless, there is enough evidence to support that there are sensitive periods for certain kinds of brain development to occur.

Most neuroscientists now view sensitive periods as rather long periods for brain development instead of narrow windows. They believe that the windows are open for longer periods of time and close gradually instead of abruptly. Opportunities to rewire or further strengthen neural pathways extend throughout the lifespan, although creating and strengthening pathways may not be as easy after these sensitive periods are over.

Physical Development

Physical development during the early childhood years is an uneven process. Within the body, physical asynchrony is visible in the size of child's head in proportion to the rest of the body. Because brain growth is rapid during the early childhood years, the head grows faster than the rest of the body initially; then it slows down. Other body systems, like the skeletal system, grow rapidly in infancy, slow down during early and middle childhood, only to return to rapid growth during adolescence.

Cephalocaudal/Proximodistal Trend

During the early childhood years, children's bodies change dramatically. Seemingly helpless newborns grow into physically competent preschoolers. As with all development, physical development follows predictable patterns even though individual progress may be highly variable.

For physical development in general, and motor development specifically, the sequence of development is from the head to the foot and from the center to the periphery of the body. This is called the cephalocaudal/proximodistal trend. Children develop their bodies from the top down and from the center out. For example, most normally developing children can swipe at and hold objects by the age of 5 or 6 months, pick up objects between the thumb and forefinger by about 11 or 12 months, scribble with a crayon before 18 months, complete puzzles around age 3, and write some of the letters of their name by age 4, illustrating the proximodistal trend. Similarly, normally developing children usually sit without support by about 7 or 9 months, walk by 12 to 16 months, ride a tricycle around their third birthday, and learn to kick a ball around 4 years, illustrating the cephalocaudal trend.

Both of these trends are affected by the components of uniqueness and the opportunities available for experience and practice of developing skills. Children continue to have an individual pace in acquiring skills, and experience and practice can support or hinder motor development. For example, children who do not have opportunities to go up and down stairs as they develop their motor skills may seem to lag behind those who do, although they catch up quickly when given opportunities to practice.

Gross and Fine Motor Development

The milestones of physical development are usually broken down into two major components—gross motor and fine motor. Gross motor development refers to the large muscles of the legs, arms, and torso, whereas fine motor refers to the smaller muscles of the body including the muscles in the hands, feet, and eyes. Physical development milestones for both gross and fine motor development from age 3–6 are charted below.

Physical Development Milestones

Age	Fine Motor Skills	Gross Motor Skills
3 Years	Puts on clothing Zips and unzips; buttons and unbuttons Builds a tower of blocks Uses eating utensils (fork, spoon) effectively Jumps, landing on two feet Grasps a pencil or crayon Scribbles; draws shapes	Jumps Pushes riding toy with feet Throws balls; catches with upper body and arms Walks upstairs, usually leading with one foot
4 Years	Uses scissors to cut paper Copies vertical and horizontal lines Draws person Copies some letters and numbers	Balances on one foot Pedals and steers tricycle Walks downstairs, alternating feet Gallops
5 Years	Draws person with up to six or more parts—eyes, ears, feet, arms, legs, eyebrows, etc. Copies numbers and simple words Pours from pitcher into glass	Skips using alternating feet Runs fast, changes directions easily Rides bicycle with training wheels Walks backwards
6 Years	Writes numbers and letters, and words, often reversing or confusing b/d and other similar combinations of letters Traces objects Ties own shoes	Is physically very active; moves almost constantly Runs, jumps, climbs, and throws with success Demonstrates increased physical coordination; clumsiness begins to decline

Health

Health Policies

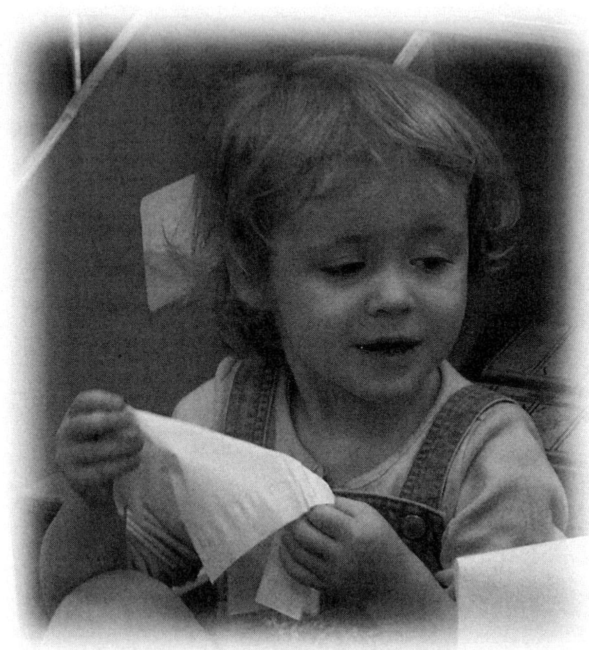

When to send children home and when to let them stay at school is one of the most important decisions a teacher must make. Every school needs a carefully crafted set of health policies. Clear policies are used as the foundation for determining whether or not a child can stay in school when she becomes ill or exhibits symptoms indicating the onset of illness. Policies should be developed in conjunction with a consulting physician and reviewed regularly to make sure that the latest information is included. Policies should also be shared with families in written form during the enrollment process and discussed with families in detail by the child's teacher during gradual enrollment.

The Pennsylvania chapter of the American Academy of Pediatrics has published excellent guidelines for parents and caregivers to follow to protect both well and ill children (Aronson, 2002). Though not substituting for advice from a physician, the guidelines provide an appropriate starting place. However, children's individuality and the teacher's attitude toward demanding children are variables that cannot be reduced to rules and regulations. Helping teachers understand how to make decisions about sending children home works better than trying to make health policies cover each and every potential situation.

Illness and the Young Child

Every teacher has heard the accusation, "He got sick at school." Teachers are in the position of helping families understand the infectious disease process and what steps are taken to prevent the spread of contagious diseases at school. Teachers also find that they are often the ones identifying the onset of illness.

The hardest part of understanding the spread of contagious disease is that children who do not look sick can be spreading infection by leaving their secretions in the environment. Typically, children are contagious before they show signs of illness. This makes careful observation and effective sanitation procedures in the classroom even more important.

Teachers need to be excellent observers of children's behavior to support parents in early intervention if an illness is suspected. In general, children should see a physician if they have a temperature over 101° under the arm or have other symptoms of illness, such as irritability, crying that cannot be comforted, frequent loose stools, coughing, wheezing, repeated vomiting, and so on.

Loose stools are also a normal part of children's experience. New foods, too much of a favorite food, and changes in diet can cause changes in the consistency and frequency of bowel movements. Diarrhea, though, is emptying of the bowel caused by spasms in the intestinal tract that are more frequent than normal for the child. For children in school settings, diarrhea is usually defined as stool that cannot be held until the child is on the toilet. Because of the risk of contamination, children with uncontained stool are usually excluded from school.

Infectious diseases are diseases caused by specific microorganisms such as viruses, bacteria, fungi, or parasites. Contagious diseases are infectious diseases that are spread from one person to another (Aronson, 2002; Kendrick, et al., 1995). The challenge for teachers is to prevent the spread of contagious diseases by careful sanitation procedures and appropriate health practices.

Environmental Sanitation

Environmental sanitation involves two steps. The first is removing the warm, moist conditions under which microorganisms thrive. The second is destroying or removing microorganisms that arrive at school through the respiratory tract (via secretions from the mouth, nose, lungs, or eyes); through the intestinal tract (via stool); through direct contact or touching; and through contact with blood. Keep classrooms well-ventilated with fresh air, and give opportunities to go outside often. As children open doors to move inside and outside, fresh air is introduced into closed, centrally air-conditioned classrooms, airing out the collected airborne contaminants.

Sanitize surfaces that children touch, including the floors, walls, and furniture as well as the toys and materials that children put in their mouths or touch with their hands. In addition, keep toileting and eating areas as far away from each other as possible. Sanitize eating areas need before and after each use and clean bathrooms at least once a day and as needed throughout the day. Bleach solution is usually the sanitizing agent of choice because it is inexpensive and easy to mix. Use ¼ cup of bleach to 1 gallon of water mixed fresh daily as a sanitizing solution.

Nutrition

What Do Children Really Need to Eat?

The following is a recommended 24-hour food guide for preschool children. Use it along with the information gathered from families as a resource to help confirm the nutritional needs of the children in your classroom.

Food Pyramid Guide for Young Children

Food	Number of Servings	Serving Size
Milk, Yogurt, and Cheese	2 servings	¾ cup of milk or yogurt, 2 oz. of cheese
Water	Offer 4–6 servings	4–6 oz. between meals, particularly in warm weather or after vigorous exercise
Cereals and Breads	6 servings of whole wheat or enriched bread, crackers, pasta, macaroni, rice, unsweetened cooked or ready-to-eat cereals, or graham or saltine crackers	½–1 slice of bread per serving, ½ cup of rice or cooked cereal per serving, 1 oz. ready-to-eat cereal per serving, 2–3 crackers per serving
Fruits	2 servings of 100% fruit juice, fresh fruit, canned fruit, or dried fruit	¾ cup of juice per serving, 1 piece or ½ cup of fresh fruit per serving, ¼ cup of dried fruit per serving
Vegetables	3 servings of raw or cooked vegetables or green leafy vegetables	½ cup raw or cooked vegetables per serving, 1 cup of green leafy vegetables per serving
Meats and Protein	2 servings of lean meat, fish, poultry, eggs, dried beans, peanut butter, or tofu	2–3 oz. meat, poultry, or fish per serving, or ½ cup cooked dry beans, or 1 egg, or 2 tbsp. of peanut butter substituted for 1 ounce of meat (2–3 ounces needed to make one serving)
Fats, Oils, and Sugar	Use margarine, butter, lard, mayonnaise, bacon, sausage, candy, cookies, soft drinks, and fruit punch in very limited amounts.	

Adapted from the USDA Food Pyramid Guide for Young Children, US Department of Agriculture, Center for Nutrition Policy and Promotion<www.usda.gov/cnpp>

Science, Mathematics, and Technology

Science, mathematics, and technology are not new to preschool classrooms. Although not usually thought of as the primary focus of care and early education, science and mathematics fit well into the preschool curriculum. Play, the child's venue of learning, is the context for exploration of science and mathematics learning.

Most child development specialists confirm that science and mathematics as well as exposure to technology, are important curricula topics for children to explore. The foundation of future scientific and mathematical knowledge and technological literacy is formed during the preschool years. These content topics are not seen as discrete or separate from the process experiences of the preschool classroom. Cooking activities, exploring the natural world, and understanding how our bodies work all illustrate the integration. When children are cooking, they need measuring and counting skills. When they understand what happens when a cake batter changes from batter into a cake, they are using scientific thinking.

Both science and mathematics require children to think about their ideas and theories. This ability to think about a person's own thoughts is called metacognition and is a major change in thinking that occurs during the preschool years. As children think about their thoughts, they revise, reconsider, and update mathematical and scientific concepts, and begin to apply what they have learned to their work and play. As they play, they test their ideas, constructing and re-constructing their understanding in the process.

It is extremely important to children's construction of knowledge in science and mathematics to avoid focusing on just the right answer, particularly if an adult provides that answer. Children's skills and abilities don't grow and expand when adults provide all the answers to questions or answer their own questions. The metacognitive process, thinking about your thoughts and whether they hold up to exploration, is at the heart of helping children learn about science and mathematics.

Science and Discovery

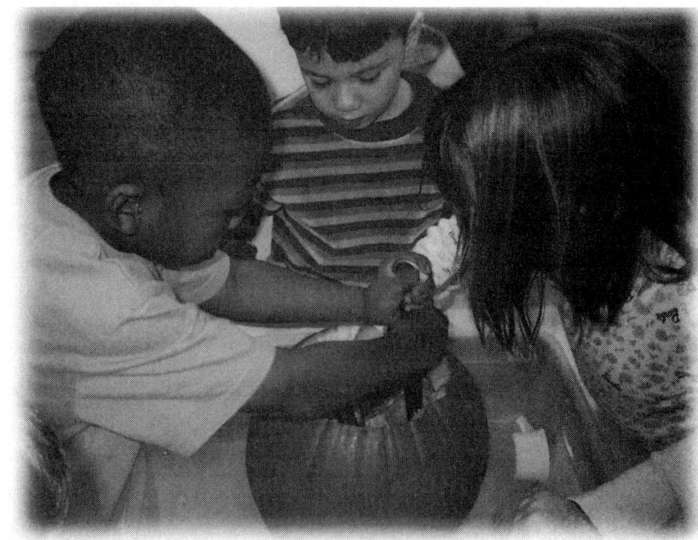

Science is a way of thinking and trying to understand the world (Charlesworth & Lind, 2002; Lind, 1999). Anyone who works with young children knows that the scientific exploration process begins early. Like other learning processes, science and mathematics learning starts with awareness and continues as children explore their ideas and discoveries. Then, children analyze and compare what they are exploring with their previous experience and observations. Finally, they begin to apply what they have learned to new situations.

Active, hands-on experiences provide preschool children with the most meaningful learning. Doing "scientific things" means asking and answering questions, doing investigations, and applying problem-solving techniques. When children have many and varied opportunities to apply what they have learned or figured out, expand what they know through exploration, and develop new knowledge and skills, they create a foundation for further scientific study in the elementary years.

Like other areas of development, there are identifiable steps to scientific exploration. Data collection is usually where exploration starts. The process of collecting and organizing data emerges as children explore the physical and natural worlds. Then children enter a phase of discovery through problem solving. Throughout the preschool years, problem solving and thinking about the experiences explored predominate children's scientific experiences.

Mathematics and Numeracy

Children actually have a great deal of knowledge about numeracy by the time they reach the preschool years (Copley, 2000). They have figured out, through experience, many mathematical concepts. More, enough, and too much are readily understood. Many preschool children are counting and already fascinated with numerical problem solving. The ability to see and understand patterns in their everyday experiences is growing every day. Although each child figures these things out in her own unique way during the first three years of life, by age three, mathematical thinking and reasoning is a regular part of children's experience.

Numeracy has developmental phases like so many other areas of growth. Children first learn about the relationships between quantities, such as five being more than two. Then they begin to attach verbal labels to different amounts and sizes, such as "lots," "big," "small," "little," and "more." At the same time, they also begin to count, first by just repeating the words they hear others use—usually without understanding the individual meanings of what they count. This "onetwothreefourfive!" counting lays the foundation for discovering one-to-one correspondence—the mathematical idea that every object counts separately and that there is only one object for each number.

Between the ages of three and four, the understanding of one-to-one correspondence supports increased accuracy in counting. Children are often able to count objects by pointing to the object and sequencing out the right word label. Counting becomes object-centered—one object for each number—and children experiment with counting higher and higher, even though they often lose track and have to start over.

Sometime during the preschool years, children figure out the idea that the last number in the counting sequence tells you how many objects you have or the quantity of the set. This important idea lets children count further to determine the number. They no longer need to go back to the beginning and start with one.

Experience with numbers is an important component of mathematics learning. When children are exposed to numbers and related mathematical concepts as their intuitive skills grow, they develop and maintain an interest in understanding and using number ideas in their daily experiences.

Technology

Computers are reaching into the early childhood classroom, offering promise and opportunity along with challenge. The promise is an added source of developmentally appropriate strategies for individualizing learning experiences; the opportunity is to introduce children to technology in ways that ensure their successful use of technology in future educational

pursuits. The challenge is to carve out appropriate usage along with appropriate limitations to prevent technology from infringing on other appropriate childhood and educational experiences or exaggerating educational inequalities.

Research gives some guidance about how to use computers in the classroom most effectively. Computers can foster social interaction between children, particularly when the computer is centrally located and available to children to work together and to get support from each other and from teachers. Language and thinking skills are encouraged as children try to figure out software applications. What children are learning is also important. Software that merely requires drill and practice is less useful to children's learning than open-ended software that encourages exploration and discovery. And, most importantly, computer use needs to be integrated with other developmentally appropriate experiences, not isolated as the place to practice mathematics or to learn colors.

INNOVATIONS IN INTERACTIVE EXPERIENCES

The physical domain of development responds so well to experience and practice. Practice is what "wires" the connections in the brain to bring muscles under voluntary control. Children need to repeat motor movements again and again. Movement sends messages to the developing brain and strengthens the connections between neurons. Muscle movement becomes more coordinated as these pathways become stronger.

Provide numerous opportunities for children to practice motor skills every day. You might also want to use the following list to make notes on the Communication Log (see page 612) or in Anecdotal Records (see page 610) to document the types of motor experiences children have had during the day.

Interactive Experiences Checklist for the Task of Problem Solving

Ask a mentor or a peer to observe you in your classroom to document the following interactive behaviors. Think about the following list of interactive experiences and make sure that the classroom reflects many of them.

- ☐ Encourage flexibility.
- ☐ Exercise the long muscles of the legs and arms.
- ☐ Offer practice reaching and stretching.
- ☐ Provide toys to pull and push and ride.
- ☐ Add surprises to favorite experiences.
- ☐ Provide challenges for small muscles in the hands.
- ☐ Raise children's heart rates as they run, jump, and move around.
- ☐ Encourage investigation and experimentation with mathematical concepts.
- ☐ Ask good questions to focus children's attention on what they know instead of what they don't know.

Encouraging and experimenting with science, mathematics, and technology are also an important part of interactive experiences. Because children need encouragement to pursue scientific, mathematical, and technological interests and activities, planning for interactive experiences to occur regularly and frequently is an important teaching task.

As you plan curriculum for the children in your group, be alert for opportunities to encourage and stimulate these content areas. Add good questions to your curriculum plans, embed them in your dialogues and conversations with children, and make sure to plan for the spontaneous yet natural opportunities to enhance scientific thinking, mathematical concepts, and appropriate experiences with technology. Consider the following as strategies for keeping these content areas in the forefront of your interactive experiences with children.

- Tie numeracy ideas to many different interactions, not just during mathematics instruction.
- Count often. Count how many children are present, figure out how many children are absent.
- Create chances to see how math functions. Ask for a second helping at lunch or snack, count the number of minutes until time to get up from rest time, and so on.

- Provide many manipulative collections to embed practice in manipulative play.

All of these experiences excite children about numeracy and mathematics. When teachers embed many of these experiences in their curriculum for young children, they are teaching children about mathematics.

Create Positive Interactive Environments

The way teachers guide and direct children contributes to their emerging skills in social problem solving. The following teaching techniques create the kind of interactive environment that fosters self-control and internalization of the expectations of the classroom.

- State directions in positive terms. Tell children what you want them to do rather than saying "No!" or "Don't!"

Negative Statement	Positive Statement
Stop running!	Walk! March! Crawl!
Don't throw sand!	Leave the sand in the sandbox.
Don't touch.	Put your hands in your pockets.
Don't whine.	Use a regular voice.
Don't touch the markers.	Put that in my hand.

- Show empathy and encourage children's empathic reactions toward each other. Validate what children want even when you don't intend to give it to them. Children feel motivated to cooperate if they feel that you understood how they are feeling. "I know you don't want to stop playing; you're having such a good time." "I know you're upset. We'll go inside soon." Statements such as these tell children that you understand their emotions, even if you are not going to respond to the request that accompanies the feelings.
- Modify the environment. Where children live and play is a minefield for an independence-seeking child. Tables and chairs look very much like climbing structures. Doors are there to be opened. Rather than deal with constant limit-setting, change the environment. Put safety latches on doors that need them. Create a place to climb that is safe. Any effort put into this area will make classroom life calmer.

Use Positive Discipline Strategies

Positive discipline is any disciplinary practice that treats children with respect and dignity. The goal of discipline is to lead children increasingly toward self-discipline or self-control (Swift, 1995). Discipline involves

Discipline focuses on what the child needs to continue to learn self-control rather than what adults need or want the child to do.

teaching children, not just on changing their behavior. It focuses on what the child needs to continue to learn self-control rather than what adults need or want the child to do. A wide variety of positive discipline strategies have been proposed that help children internalize the expectation of their parents, teachers, and the community. Two strategies, using natural and logical cosequences and setting appropriate limits, are discussed on the following pages.

Use Natural and Logical Consequences

Applying natural and logical consequences is a great tool for teachers to use to help children gain self-control. A natural or logical consequence is a consequence that develops from the situation. Consequences help children accept responsibility for their behavior and lead them to choose appropriate behaviors to avoid the consequences of inappropriate ones. The following example illustrates the concept of logical consequences:

Two children are playing together in the Blocks/Construction Possibilities Area. They have constructed a large block building, adding almost every block support to the building including cars, animals, and other props. The building takes a long time to build, and the children are proud of their work. When it is time to put the blocks and block supports away, the children don't want to do so. They arrive at an agreement with their teacher to leave the building up until the next day and proceed to make a sign that tells other children not to disturb the block building. In addition, the teacher takes a photograph of the building for the children to have later.

When the time comes to put the blocks and block supports away on the next day, the children decide they are still not interested in putting the building away. This time, the teacher explains to the children that the building has all of the blocks and block supports in use and other children are interested in having a turn with them. The children still refuse to pick up the blocks. The teacher then suggests to the children that the blocks will be off limits to them until next week if they are not willing to pick up the blocks.

The next day, the children head to the block/construction area and start to take some blocks off the shelf. The teacher stops them, reminds them that they weren't willing to pick up the construction project from the previous day, and tells them that they can have another chance to play in this area next week. The logical consequence of not picking up construction materials when it came time to do so was not getting to play with the construction materials for a while.

When children have many experiences with the consequences of their actions and their effect on what happens next, they come to understand and embrace the rules and restrictions that adults put on childhood activities and behaviors. The goal of applying consequences is not just to keep children safe, but also to help them understand and then integrate the expectations of their home, school, and community into their behavior.

Set Appropriate Limits

Adults have two reasons to set rules and limits. The first reason is to protect children and keep them safe—reason enough for a good set of limits. The second reason is to help children grow toward self-control. Rules should have the following elements (Bredekamp & Copple, 1997; Marion, 1999):

- First, rules and limits must be humane. Humane rules do not humiliate, embarrass, belittle, or degrade the child. Here is an example of an inhumane rule: "Children who cry don't get to play." This kind of rule has no place in care and early education settings.
- Second, limits should not be arbitrary. Each rule should have several good reasons for existing. The following is an example of an arbitrary rule: "I won't help you solve your problem unless you stop crying."
- Third, rules should be overt, out in the open. Children, particularly young children, cannot guess what the rules are. They need to be told, reminded, and reminded again. If there is a rule that children use a cup to get a drink from the water fountain (to avoid contaminating the water spout), then children need to know about the rule as well as where the cups are stored.
- Fourth, limits should be clearly stated and enforceable. Rules should refer to the expected behavior and be clear enough for children to know immediately when they have broken the

rule. An example of a clearly stated rule with a reference to behavior: "Leave the sand in the sandbox, or I will have to ask you to play somewhere else."

- Fifth, rules should be accompanied by reasons. Research has shown that children who are given the reasons behind the rules are more likely to listen and follow the rules later without adult reminders. It is important to be brief and to the point. "Leave the sand in the sandbox. When you throw it, someone's eyes could be badly hurt."
- Sixth, remember to update rules. This is particularly important during the preschool years when children are maturing and developing so quickly. As children perfect new skills, for example, climbing competently high up on the climbing structure, update the rules. The teacher might say, "Climb only to the third rung of the ladder" to a new climber. Then, drop the rule when he becomes an experienced climber.
- Finally, rules and limits should be firmly enforced (Brazelton & Greenspan, 2000). As children grow, they will test limits that adults set for them. If parents, teachers, and others use repressive controls, such as coercion, testing will continue. If adults do not set limits and do not enforce rules, children will never find the psychological safe place to learn about limits. Firm, consistent responses to broken rules will result in children who learn to understand and follow the rules set for them by their parents and teachers.

When out-of-bounds behavior occurs, the easiest way to enforce the limits is to ask the child to move the child to another setting. This technique uses logical consequences to help children remember the rules. If the child is throwing sand, take her by the hand and ask her to find another place to play until she can remember the sandbox rules.

Use a Variety of Teaching Roles

Teachers use a wide variety of roles in their work with young children. During the developmental task of Problem Solving, two of the most important teacher roles are supporter and guide/limit setter. These roles have specific characteristics during this developmental task.

The Teacher as Supporter

The teacher's role in supporting the developmental task of Problem Solving is a broad and complex one. She or he must support exploration of the environment, encourage social interaction between children, and support emerging self-regulatory skills. To be effective, this support must be overt, consistent, and regular.

The teacher is also a supporter of safe risk-taking behavior. Supporting this kind of behavior is important to give children the feeling that they can try novel experiences and succeed in their chosen activities. Helping children identify risk-taking behavior is another supportive role. Differentiating between activities that are safe and likely to result in interesting outcomes and those that are dangerous and likely to result in harm to oneself or to others is a learning process for children that needs the teacher's support.

The Teacher as Guide and Limit Setter

Guidance is a positive discipline strategy designed to improve self-regulation and self-control. Teachers serve as guides when they suggest play ideas for children to enable them to play successfully together, identify alternatives to strategies that aren't working, and clearly support problem solving as the strategy for resolving conflicts and disagreements. They also use guidance techniques such as redirection and ignoring to influence children's behaviors without direct intervention.

Guidance is a positive discipline strategy designed to improve self-regulation and self-control.

The role of limit setter involves setting limits on behavior by making rules and enforcing them. These two roles—guiding and limiting—go hand in hand. As a guide, teachers help children understand what is expected in different classroom and school situations. As a limit setter, teachers help children understand when their behavior is not consistent with expectations for behavior, alerting children to incongruence between expectations and children's behavior. Both roles support children's acquisition of self-control.

In the guidance and discipline role, teachers assess when to apply rules and limits and to whom. Because each child is an individual, in this role teachers are constantly modifying their techniques for individual children and individual situations, intervening frequently for one child with many reminders about appropriate behavior, redirecting another when needed, enforcing limits on safe behavior with still other children, and applying consequences for children who are not able to comply with expectations. This dynamic role creates challenges and opportunities to turn almost any interaction into one that helps children acquire more sophisticated self-regulation skills.

INNOVATIONS IN TEACHING

Support Brain Development

Knowledge of brain development guides teachers to monitor normative development to make sure experience-dependent and experience-expectant opportunities are maximized. Teachers can also use their careful monitoring of normative development to determine if there are any developmental problems that need intervention.

Embracing repetitive experiences as brain stimulation comes naturally for most teachers. Creating opportunities for repeated experiences that reinforce and strengthen neural pathways is a preschool curriculum staple.

Creating opportunities for repeated experiences that reinforce and strengthen neural pathways is a preschool curriculum staple.

Knowledge of brain development suggests that teachers keep in mind the cumulative nature of development. This releases teachers from the pressure to accomplish everything at once and from forcing activities, experiences, or interactions on children before they are ready for them. There is time to individualize responses to children and to plan many more activities and experiences that will contribute to children's brain development as well as their developmental growth.

Monitor environmental factors that can affect brain development. Some potentially negative environmental factors are under the direct control of the teacher, such as the amount and type of nourishment provided to the child, the warmth of the interactive relationship with the child at school, and the amount and type of stimulation available in the school environment. Other environmental factors, such as poverty; trauma; abuse; social deprivation; drug, alcohol, or nicotine abuse; and maternal depression may require referral to resources outside the school to help families support the child's well-being.

Investing in relationships has such wide impact that it is mentioned as a primary strategy for furthering total development. When information about brain development is added to this understanding, the importance of relationships broadens still further.

Support Physical Development with Regular and Frequent Opportunities to Go Outdoors

Trips outdoors provide a change of pace, freedom from being so close to other children, and a constant source of interesting stimuli. Plan a minimum of at least two trips to the outdoors daily, three or four are even more likely to please children.

Outdoors is where children can perfect gross and fine motor skills. On playgrounds, climbing structures for children need to be sturdy to be safe. Don't forget equipment and materials that children can arrange in a variety of ways—providing experiences with controlling the environment. Children like to rearrange boxes, blocks, and toys. They also like tents to create places to climb into, under, or around.

Balancing is another skill to explore. Balance beams low to the ground will limit spills to tumbles instead of falls. Investigations of how to balance on a beam compared to balancing on a climber are examples of the way children create their own skill practice when the outdoor environment is conducive.

Push toys and tricycles are also popular. With paths through the playground, these important gross motor toys also contribute to dramatic play when paired with play props and supports brought outdoors.

Digging in the sand or soil is another great outdoor activity for children. Not only are the materials stimulating and enjoyable, but also the ability to rearrange sand and soil makes children feel powerful and able to influence the environment. Water added to dry sand and soil or placed in a water table will add interest as children explore the natural world.

When children are given ample opportunities to play outdoors, they can practice and experience many developing skills. The ability to impact and influence the environment communicates powerful messages of success about the things they can do. It is for this reason that many children love the outdoors—it is a "can do" place.

The fast-paced activity of the outdoors can also be over stimulating and overwhelming. Don't forget to have quiet places for children to cool off or calm down and water available to quench their thirst. A blanket in the shade serves nicely and also can provide a place for children to spend some time with the teacher, refueling and recharging before heading back out to explore the world again.

Support Scientific, Mathematical, and Technological Exploration

Children use three major strategies to explore science. The first is naturalistic exploration where spontaneously initiated daily activities expose children to opportunities to construct knowledge and understanding about the natural world. The role of the teacher is to observe what and how children are exploring and acknowledge the activity and experience.

A second strategy for science exploration is informal exploration where teachers see opportunities to offer cues, encouragement, or ideas about what might happen next.

Structured exploration is the third strategy. Teachers can put the glue and liquid starch out in sensory tubs to introduce children to the idea that combining two different materials in the right proportions creates a third substance, in this case, silly putty. The teacher structures the exploration and discovery process, providing suggestions and guidance along the way as the mixing of ingredients works or doesn't.

Teachers can be a roadblock to instilling scientific curiosity and mathematical literacy. Lack of content understanding and different interests make some adults feel that they are poorly prepared to teach science and mathematics. This obstacle can be overcome by an understanding that co-construction of knowledge is part of the process of planning and implementing good science and mathematics curriculum. Teachers can learn right along with children as they discover new information. It is not necessary for them to have all the answers.

Scientific, mathematical, and technological exploration also highlights the integrated nature of early childhood experiences. When children explore what adults do in their careers, scientific and mathematical careers can be among those represented. When children wonder about the weather, the bugs they find under rocks, or any of the other myriad questions that children ponder, they are showing us the way to integrate science and mathematics into their lives, their learning, and their play.

When children wonder about the weather, the bugs they find under rocks, or any of the other myriad questions that children ponder, they are showing us the way to integrate science and mathematics into their lives, their learning, and their play.

One important strategy for building science and numeracy skills is with gathered and found materials. Collect nature items to give children numerous ways to count, explore, and observe natural things. These materials can be used to practice one-to-one correspondence, patterning, and counting. Even common household items, such as paper towel tubes, jar lids, and junk mail, are useful as children determine the differences in materials, textures, shapes, and sizes.

Support Health and Wellness through Daily Health Conversations

Health is an important part of every daily conversation with parents. This conversation has two goals. The first is to make sure the parent or family member who is dropping off the child at school shares information about the time spent at home. The second is to make sure the child is healthy enough to stay at school.

When the school day starts, teachers need the following information about time spent at home:

- What time the child went to sleep and how long she slept,
- What time the child ate last,
- Changes in the child's behavior and disposition, and
- Any special instructions for the child's day.

Collecting this information is important because children's health and behavior at home are often indicators of their health and behavior at school.

Use a quick health check that can be completed before family members leave for the day. The check includes a quick look at the child's general physical condition for indicators of health problems. Place a hand on the child's abdomen to determine if she is running a temperature, and look at her face, eyes, the skin on the abdomen, and the inside of her arms to screen for signs of infectious or contagious disease such as rashes, bumps, or blisters.

Talk with the family member in detail about the child's behavior and disposition. Irritability, sleep interruptions, and changes in general demeanor and mood can be cues to a child's general health. Ask the parent if the child is on any medication.

Health checks won't prevent children from getting sick during the school day, but they will help spot ill children who are exhibiting symptoms and assure parents that you are diligent about preventing the spread of disease.

Determine When to Send Children Home

When teachers consider sending children home, a number of criteria need to be taken into consideration. Some of those are:

- **Symptom severity**. Severity of symptoms refers to the number and type of symptoms as well as the intensity of the symptoms. In general, the more symptoms a child has, or the more intense the symptoms, the more comfortable the teacher can be with a "go home" decision.
- **Time of the day**. Symptoms that begin at the end of the school day pose a different picture than symptoms that begin early in the school day. Some symptoms unrelated to disease onset are cyclical, such as having a fever after a temper tantrum or waking from a nap with an elevated temperature. Children who begin to get sick late in the day can probably stay at school until their families pick them up. When this occurs, teachers need to make sure to tell the family members whether or not the child can return to school the next day if symptoms persist.
- **Speed of onset of symptoms**. Symptoms that emerge rapidly need to be recorded on the child's Communication Log (see Appendix page 612) and watched for 15 to 30 minutes to determine if they go away or get worse. Don't forget to record what happens after the time lapse as well, particularly if you decide not to send the child home.
- **Daily pattern of behavior**. All symptoms need to be compared with the child's pattern of behavior. Two weeks of Communication Logs should be kept handy. Then, teachers can look back to bring behavior changes or symptoms into focus in the broader perspective. If symptoms have a pattern (such as loose stools every afternoon after eating spinach at lunch), you can be fairly sure they are not the result of onset of illness.
- **Consistency with health and sick child policies**. Schools have these policies for a reason. It is to protect teachers and other children from the spread of contagious disease when something can be done to impact that spread.
- **Sanitation procedures needed.** Because many of the types of diseases that are contagious are contact borne, the amount and frequency of environmental cleaning that is necessary is a consideration. Carefully follow sanitation procedures, such as hand washing, toy washing, and disinfecting areas affected by toileting accidents. When these duties prevent normal teaching activities, the child should go home.
- **Review of health policies**. The first thing a teacher should do if a child exhibits symptoms is read the school's health policies to determine any

guidance for the situation. If the policy is clear and the child is exhibiting the symptoms listed, send the child home. If the policy is not clear-cut, teachers may want to check their preliminary decision with others before acting. Getting a second opinion helps teachers gain confidence in their ability to make good decisions about whether a child should be sent home.

- **The family's unique situation**. Some families have several options for the care of sick children; others do not. Think in terms of helping the family when at all possible. Sending children home must be viewed in light of what the family can handle, particularly if the school can meet the child's needs.

Children who are too ill to be cared for at school need to be at home. But those decisions are usually easy to make. It is more difficult to determine whether mildly ill children or those who are only exhibiting one or two symptoms should stay at school. Letting the child's teacher and family make that decision in conjunction with the school's health policy seems appropriate.

Parents or family members should be informed about changes in children's health status as changes occur. Notification enables them to begin to plan ahead if they decide the child should be at home. It allows time to call a physician for advice or an appointment, and it makes the stay-at-school/send-home decision a shared one—made by the people who know the child best. It allows the child's teacher to consider the needs of the whole group of children. If the teacher feels she or he cannot meet the child's needs, she or he is free to say so to the parents and get their assistance in developing other strategies for getting the child's needs met.

When a contagious disease is documented, families of other children should be notified. Notification serves two purposes. One is to give families advance warning of possible contagious diseases with which their children have come in contact. Letting parents and family members know in advance what to look for can limit the number of children who come to school when they are contagious because parents notice symptoms more readily when they are alerted to them. Second, working families often need advance warning of impending absence from their jobs. Use the Communication Log (see Appendix page 612) to make a note for family members to read upon reuniting with their child.

Establish a Few Clear Limits and Enforce Them

Brazelton and Greenspan (2000) consider limit setting and the structure that results from clear limits as one of the irreducible needs of children—what they absolutely must have to grow, learn, and flourish. Children want to please the important people in their lives. Thus, adults, in the context of the meaningful relationships, can put in place a few clear rules to support children's compliance with expectations.

Young children need just a few rules, combined with plenty of nurturing and supportive guidance. The rules have to be clear and enforceable, and enforced consistently by the adults in the child's world.

When rules are applied intermittently, or when expectations of adults vary, children lose touch with a "psychologically safe" place to be. Only when the rules and expectations of adults are clearly defined and consistently applied can children feel safe and secure enough to continue the important exploratory work of childhood.

Only when the rules and expectations of adults are clearly defined and consistently applied can children feel safe and secure enough to continue the important exploratory work of childhood.

Respond Consistently to Individual Limit-testing

Children test the limits that adults have for them. When they do, they find out if the rules apply to each and every situation. Some children can test limits only once and then are able to remember or internalize and follow the rule. Most, however, need repeated reminders and frequent run-ins with limits to make progress in self-regulation of behavior.

Individual children need consistent responses to their own limit-testing experiences. When children are treated individually, teachers and families in their lives can adjust their responses to limit-testing to fit the child and the situation.

Teacher Competencies to Support Children's Problem Solving

Sometimes	Usually	Always	
☐	☐	☐	Is aware of the activities of the entire group even when dealing with a part of it.
☐	☐	☐	Guides children to develop increasingly effective ways of making social contacts and solving social problems.
☐	☐	☐	Sees that children are dressed appropriately for existing temperatures throughout the day.
☐	☐	☐	Models the behavior being encouraged and taught to children.
☐	☐	☐	Assures that all children have frequent opportunities for success.
☐	☐	☐	Provides regular and varied outdoor experience.
☐	☐	☐	Provides ample opportunity for and encouragement of large muscle activity.
☐	☐	☐	Asks good questions that stimulate metacognition or "thinking about one's thoughts."

Competencies for the Teaching Role of Supporter

Sometimes	Usually	Always	
☐	☐	☐	Supports children's explorations and discoveries.
☐	☐	☐	Supports children's exploration by helping them identify the things they need to figure things out.
☐	☐	☐	Helps children locate the resources they need to further the discovery process.
☐	☐	☐	Helps children find ways to take risks without endangering themselves or others.

Competencies for the Teaching Role of Guide and Limit Setter

Sometimes	Usually	Always	
☐	☐	☐	Establishes and carries out reasonable limits for children and activities.
☐	☐	☐	Uses non-punitive ways of dealing with behavior; can exert authority without requiring submission or undermining the child's sense of self.
☐	☐	☐	Redirects, distracts, or channels inappropriate behavior into acceptable outlets.
☐	☐	☐	Anticipates confrontations between children and intervenes before aggressive behavior arises.
☐	☐	☐	Anticipates problems and plans to prevent their re-occurrence.
☐	☐	☐	Does not avoid problem situations, can generate alternative ideas, and implement and evaluate solutions selected.
☐	☐	☐	Reinforces appropriate behavior by encouraging children's appropriate behavior.
☐	☐	☐	Uses praise and encouragement effectively; differentiates between the behavior and the child when using praise.
☐	☐	☐	Knows and uses a variety of guidance techniques, such as redirection, distraction, and ignoring.
☐	☐	☐	Uses room arrangement and schedules to support appropriate behavior. Uses each approach appropriately.
☐	☐	☐	Helps parents develop realistic expectations for children's behavior in ways that help avoid disciplinary problems.

INNOVATIONS IN OBSERVATION/ASSESSMENT

Observation/Assessment for the Task of Problem Solving

During the developmental task of Problem Solving, observation and assessment are directed at understanding the physical development and the development of numeracy, mathematics, scientific, and technological skills. This understanding starts with observing each child in gross and fine motor development, child health and nutrition, numeracy, and scientific inquiry.

Pediatricians normally monitor children's growth patterns, keeping track of their height, weight, head circumference, and normative position on the growth curve. Teachers and children should also monitor growth patterns. Chart children's growth in height and weight, confirming continued growth and development, as well as teaching children about measurement and comparison.

Assessment of science and numeracy and mathematical skills is also important. Similar to other areas of development, observation and listening are important skills for teachers to use as they try to understand children's intuitive numeracy knowledge and to support scientific investigation of new skills and knowledge. Teachers look for multiple sources of evidence that show children's construction of knowledge.

Teachers are also responsible for assessing their own teaching effectiveness with each child in relationship to physical development and numeracy, mathematical, scientific, and technological skills. Because each child has her own way of constructing knowledge, teachers need a variety of teaching strategies to make sure all children continue to consider mathematics, science, and technology fun and informative. This is particularly true for girls, who lose confidence in their intuitive abilities early in their school careers (Copley, 2000). Early dispositions such as task persistence, risk taking, and self-regulation all contribute to creating a lifelong interest in mathematics, science, and technology. These dispositions develop during the preschool years and can be supported and encouraged by teachers and curricula.

Add to Individual Portfolios to Highlight the Developmental Task of Problem Solving

Consider the following as rich sources of additions to individual portfolios:

- height and weight growth charts;
- emerging mathematics skills and abilities, such as rote counting, counting with one-to-one correspondence, extending patterns, and so on;
- anecdotal records with evidence of informal mathematics operations occurring naturally in play;
- examples of appropriate mathematical language used in appropriate contexts spontaneously by children;
- work samples including charts, graphs, drawings, or illustrations with shapes, numbers, or mathematical concepts;
- photographs of constructions with blocks and drawings of block buildings done by children to preserve their constructions;
- children's collections of interesting things, along with their organizational strategies for maintaining the collections;
- both deductive and inductive scientific explorations; and
- observations of the natural world, recorded by teachers or by children.

INNOVATIONS IN FAMILY PARTNERSHIPS

Encourage Family Participation

I Can Do It!: Find ways to celebrate children's developmental progress through developmental banners, notes, signs, and pictures. Invite parents to share information concerning their child's developmental progress at home. Try instituting a Family Sharing Board where family members can share information not only about the children in your classroom, but also about other children or family members.

We Are Family: Invite parents and other family members to be a part of school events. This can be accomplished through special events at the center, such as appreciation days for parents and staff, as well as through introductions of staff members to parents or family members.

Share Parent Postcards

Share Parent Postcards with parents as they indicate an interest, at appropriate times during the enrollment cycle, or as developmental issues arise. Copy Postcards. Cut if necessary. Address to parent(s) and place with the Communication Log or hand out personally.

Setting Appropriate Limits

Families have two reasons to set rules and limits. The first reason is to protect children and keep them safe. The second reason is to help children grow toward self-control. Where do you start to establish reasonable limits and rules? Start by following these guidelines.

- Make rules humane. Humane rules do not humiliate, embarrass, belittle, or degrade the child.
- Limits should not be arbitrary. Rules should convey to children that you make rules thoughtfully.
- Rules should be out in the open, not secret. Children cannot guess what the rules are. They need to be told, reminded, and reminded again.
- Limits should be clearly stated and enforceable. Rules should refer to the expected behavior and be clear. Avoid "don't" rules. Try to state your rules from a positive perspective (walk in the house, sit on the couch).
- Rules should be accompanied by reasons. Research has shown that children who are given the reasons for rules are more likely to listen and to follow the rules without parental reminders. But, be brief and to the point. No lectures needed!
- Remember to update your rules. Limits should reflect new skills. For example, young children need strict climbing rules such as, "Hold on tightly with both hands when you climb." As children become proficient in climbing, the rule can simply be, "Climb safely."
- Most important, rules and limits should be firmly enforced. As children grow, they will test limits. If families do not set limits and do not enforce rules, children will heed no adult guidance.

Young children get a sense of security and support from rules. Setting limits along with enforcing them is a loving and responsive thing to do.

Discovering Math and Science at Home

Parents have a unique opportunity to provide hands-on, appropriate math and science experiences for their children. What better way to learn about numbers than sorting, folding, and counting socks or gathering the right number of utensils to set the table? Measurement becomes real when using a measuring cup to get the correct amount of milk to add to a mixing bowl to create a favorite family recipe. When you create opportunities for your child to help you with household tasks, your enthusiasm for mathematical and scientific concepts will support your child's enthusiasm.

Science is also a topic that fits naturally in the context of the home. Using detergent in the washing machine, observing the difference in batter before it is baked and after it is finished, and observing herbs growing in the windowsill are all examples of science experiences. Support a spirit of inquiry with your child as you interact and learn about the world in which you live.

Resources for Families

Add these helpful books to your library or post this list on your family bulletin board.

Bailey, B. (2002). ***10 principles of positive discipline***. Oviedo, FL: Loving Guidance.

Coleman, R. (2001). ***Around the family table.*** Beltsville, MD: Robins Lane Press.

Mitchell, G. (1998). ***A very practical guide to discipline with young children***. Glen Burnie, MD: Telshare.

Nelson, J. (1998). ***Positive discipline for preschoolers***. Roseville, CA: Prima Publishing.

INNOVATIONS IN ENVIRONMENTS

What Does Brain-based Care and Early Education Look Like in the Classroom?

Brain-based early education looks like developmentally appropriate early education. It supports teachers in spending time with children to develop close connections. Children's brains work best in the context of healthy relationships. Warm, consistent, responsive interactions make brain growth and development proceed as planned. So, the time teachers spend connecting with children, increasing their understanding of non-verbal cues, observing play, and caring for and cuddling them is early education for growing brains.

Use warm, responsive touch to stimulate, strengthen, and reinforce neural connections. Rough, insensitive touch, however infrequent, puts children at risk for shutting down the emotional connections that are forming between adults and children. This is particularly important when children take more risks exploring the environment by climbing, reaching, and exploring every nook and cranny. When adults view risk-taking as a dangerous activity that should be stopped, the tone of their voices, as well as gestures and physical restraint may convey messages that interrupt rather than encourage exploration of new experiences.

Children are highly motivated to explore and discover. Children see and explore minute details that interest them and are able to use a large variety of physical points of view to do so. Teachers in brain-based classrooms understand this interest and create environments that can be explored from different points of view. Further, teachers view exploration as important and desirable—not an activity to be curtailed or stopped. This doesn't mean that there are no rules for safety or reasonable behavior. It means that the rules and the way teachers implement the rules are consistent with an understanding of exploration as a positive stimulation activity, not a negative one.

Talking to and with children about their discoveries is crucial to the future development of science, mathematics, and technology skills. Expanding vocabularies help children succeed in their interactions with peers, widening the social world in the process. The ability to initiate and interact with little direct support from adults launches children into the world of exploration, discovery, and language competency.

Stimulation that matches the child's interest and ability without overwhelming or over-stimulating is another part of brain-based early education. This goodness of fit refers to the match between the child's individuality and the actions, interactions, and facilitation of adults. Individualizing these interactions—making sure there is a match between the child's interest and the teacher's goals and plans—is crucial to brain development. Without this match, there is a risk of interrupting or negating the brain development underway.

This match between the ability and interest is particularly important to girls. Discrepancies between science and mathematics abilities among boys and girls surface early in children's lives. If there isn't a match between their abilities (particularly their cognitive abilities), children's interests get turned off as they figure out that teachers don't think they can do the work.

Basing children's experience on child-directed and initiated experiences, confirming prior knowledge—what children already know—before moving on to teach, and offering input that matches children's level of ability are all ways that brain-based classrooms stimulate and encourage ongoing learning.

Activity Areas

In each developmental task, a thorough consideration is given to two or three activity areas in the preschool classroom. The section is designed to support well-stocked and arranged learning areas or centers. Ideas about setup, room arrangement, and equipment and supplies are included for each activity area.

Blocks/Construction Possibilities

Putting things together, taking things apart, building with unit blocks and other kinds of blocks, figuring out how parts relate to the whole, discovering one-to-one correspondence, and creating and manipulating groups of objects are all facilitated by activities and experiences in Blocks/Construction Possibilities. The teacher plays an important role supporting the exploration of materials and bridging old skills to new skills. Building and constructing, destroying constructions, and building them again are powerful opportunities for preschool children to experience control over their lives.

A well-stocked Blocks/Construction Possibilities Area will have the following supplies and equipment, perhaps not out at the same time, but accessible as needed to enhance children's construction and building experiences:

- A complete set of natural, hardwood unit blocks and adequate labeled storage units to display the blocks;
- A variety of additional block types, such as cardboard blocks, plastic jumbo building blocks, waffle or grid blocks, and construction bricks;
- A complete set of large, hollow blocks for constructions;
- Specialty blocks, such as castle blocks, architectural blocks, foam blocks, plank blocks, tree blocks, interlocking wood logs, Legos®, Flexi blocks, magnetic blocks, thistle blocks, pyramid builders, brick blocks;

- A collection of manipulatives to support block play such as wild, forest, farm, and jungle animals; dinosaurs;
- A collection of vinyl figures of families, professional and occupational figures, figures with diverse abilities, figures with different functions;
- A collection of props, such as cars, trucks, airplanes, construction vehicles, emergency vehicles;
- Road signs and symbols;
- Construction sets with usable tools;
- Construction manipulatives, such as nuts and bolts, workbenches, pounding benches, gear-building sets, pipe construction sets, nuts and bolt boards, lock and latches boards;
- Puppets related to block play themes, such as animals, dinosaurs, careers;
- A large dollhouse;
- Train tracks and trains, including tunnels and bridges;
- Play sets for miniature play such as farm sets, school sets, garage play sets, building/construction play sets, marble maze play sets; and
- Woodworking materials and equipment stored in a locked cabinet along with a good supply of soft wood, safety glasses, nails, screws, bolts, and other fasteners.

Math/Manipulatives Possibilities

As preschoolers increase their fine motor skills, they are increasingly interested in the manipulation of different types of hands-on materials, such as puzzles, Duplos®, linking rings, lotto games, and cards. Grouping, sorting, matching, and ordering activities are beginning math skills that will prepare children for more formal math skills that develop later. During the preschool years, task persistence and the ability to cooperate both increase. As children improve their abilities to stay on task, they also develop the ability to cooperate with each other as they play, sometimes working together to accomplish a play goal or to complete an interesting task.

The teacher plays an important role in introducing new materials, helping children learn to use the materials safely, and expanding learning by connecting mathematical concepts to play. When mathematical concepts are discussed as children play, they develop a common mathematical language that can be used as they explore mathematical ideas.

A well-stocked Math/Manipulatives Possibilities Area will have the following supplies and equipment, perhaps not out at the same time, but accessible as needed to enhance numeracy skills:

- A variety of manipulative sets, such as nuts and bolts, slotted parts that fit or push together like prism blocks, linking sets, and interlocking building sets;
- Mosaic boards, geometric boards, magnetic boards, peg boards with a selection of pegs of various sizes;
- Wooden lacing materials including beads, rings, straws, tubes, and buttons, with laces;
- Number tiles, parquetry blocks, cubes, and shapes, shape sorters, dominoes, cylinder blocks;
- Wooden, cardboard, vinyl, and foam puzzles of various kinds (pegged, knobbed, jig saw) and levels of complexity (8-100 pieces), addressing a variety of topics including numbers, letters, shapes, types of animals, types of food, seasons, occupations, and so on;
- Puzzle stands to store wooden puzzles; bins to store manipulative sets;
- Giant floor puzzles;
- Sequencing and sorting materials, sound cylinders, and texture cylinders;
- Lotto cards and games, concentration games, card games, checkers;
- Calculators, cash registers, and play money;
- Clocks, both digital and analog;
- Balance scales;
- A computer station, equipped with at least two chairs side by side in front of the monitor and a chair for the teacher next to the monitor; and
- A variety of developmentally appropriate software.

Science/Discovery Possibilities

Young children are curious about the world in which they live. They want to find out what is in it and how everything works. They enjoy exploring new things in the environment. Include quality sensory experiences and opportunities for children to observe and manipulate materials. Provide a class pet (fish, gerbil, mouse, rabbit) that is approved by the regulatory agencies in your area.

A well-stocked Science/Discovery Possibilities Area will have the following supplies and equipment, perhaps not out at the same time, but accessible as needed to enhance children's scientific exploration and discovery:

- A collection of magnifying glasses of various sizes and various strengths; binoculars, prisms;
- Collections of natural items, such as shells, leaves, acorns, and rocks, stored in clear plastic containers;
- Growing plants, a terrarium filled with plants, sprouted vegetables, such as sweet potatoes, carrots, and potatoes;
- Plastic insects, bugs, animals, and dinosaurs;
- Simple microscopes;
- Bug catchers;
- Ant farms and worm farms;
- A variety of magnets, including horseshoe, bar, magnetic wands, magnetic marbles, and magnetic chips;
- Sound cylinders, texture boards, scent cylinders; and
- Plants and other living things, such as plant-filled hanging baskets, potted plants, fish tanks with fish, and so on.

Snack Possibilities

A self-service snack center is a wonderful addition to every preschool classroom. When snack is self-serve, rather than served in a large group, children learn to listen to their own bodies to determine whether they are hungry, and eat what they want (or what is designated as a serving size) rather than eating as much as everyone else eats. They also apply many skills, such as reading rebus charts depicting serving size, counting out a serving, pouring juice or milk into a cup, and cleaning up after one's self.

Snack is a social time. Friends can talk and share their experiences as they eat and drink their snacks. Finding a friend to have snack with you or having snack all by yourself as you decide where to go to play next are both possible.

The following materials and supplies are necessary to make a self-service snack center work:

- Child-size cups, forks, spoons, and napkins, paper or washable;
- Serving bowls, plates, platters, and baskets;
- Utensils such as serving spoons, forks, tongs, and spatulas;
- A wipe-off board, hung near the snack area for teachers (and children) to draw pictures of serving sizes and portions; and
- Tables and chairs appropriate for children and teachers.

References

Aronson, S. (2002). ***Healthy young children: A manual for programs.*** Washington, DC: National Association for the Education of Young Children (NAEYC).

Bailey, C.B., J.T. Bruer, F.J. Symons, & J.W. Lichtman. (2001). ***Critical thinking about critical periods.*** Baltimore, MD: Brookes Publishing.

Bailey, D.B. (2002). Are critical periods critical for early childhood education? ***Early Childhood Research Quarterly,*** 17(3), 270-280.

Brazelton, T.B., & S.I. Greenspan. (2000). ***The irreducible needs of children: What every child must have to grow, learn, and flourish.*** Cambridge, MA: Perseus Publishing.

Bredekamp, C. & C. Copple (1997). ***Developmentally appropriate practice in early childhood programs.*** Revised edition. Washington, DC: National Association for the Education of Young Children (NAEYC).

Charlesworth, R. & K. Lind. (2002). ***Math and science for young children***. Albany, NY: Delmar Publishing.

Copley, J.V. (2000). ***The young child and mathematics.*** Washington, DC: National Association for the Education of Young Children (NAEYC).

Kendrick, A.S., R. Kaufman, & K.P. Messinger. (1995). ***Healthy young children: A manual for programs.*** Washington, DC: National Association for the Education of Young Children (NAEYC).

Lind, K. (1999). ***Exploring science in early childhood: A developmental approach.*** Albany, NY: Delmar Publishers.

Marion, M. (1999). ***Guidance of young children.*** Upper Saddle River, NJ: Merrill.

McCall, R.B. & B.W. Plemons. (2001). The concept of critical periods and their implications for early childhood services. In D.B. Bailey, J.T. Bruer, F.J. Symons, & J.W. Lichtman (Eds.), ***Critical thinking about critical periods.*** (267-287). Baltimore, MD: Brookes Publishing.

Shonkoff, J.P. & D.A. Phillips (Eds.). (2000). ***From neurons to neighborhoods: The science of early childhood development.*** Washington, DC: National Academy Press.

Shore, R. (1997). ***Rethinking the brain: New insights into early development.*** New York: Families and Work Institute.

Swift, M. (1995). ***Discipline for life.*** Grapevine, TX: Stairway Education Programs.

Resources for Teachers

Appleton, J., N. McCrae, & C. Patterson. (2001). ***Do carrots make you see better?*** Beltsville, MD: Gryphon House.

Child Care Information Exchange. (2002). Beginnings workshop: Child nutrition. ***Child Care Information Exchange***, 145, 37-49.

Child Care Information Exchange. (2000). Beginnings workshop: Fitness and Health. ***Child Care Information Exchange***, 131, 41-56.

Charner, K. (1998). ***The giant encyclopedia of science activities for children from 3-6.*** Beltsville, MD: Gryphon House.

Copley, J.V. (2000). ***The young child and mathematics***. Washington, DC: National Association for the Education of Young Children.

Falk, J.H., R.L. Pruitt II, K.S. Rosenberg, & T.A. Katz. (1998). ***Bubble monster and other science fun***. Chicago, IL: Chicago Review Press.

Flicker, E.S. & J.A. Hoffman. (2002). Developmental discipline in the early childhood classroom. ***Young Children*** 57 (5): 82-89.

Foote, R.J. (1998). ***Cup cooking***. Lake Alfred, FL: Early Educators Press.

Gardner, H. (1983). ***Frames of mind: The theory of multiple intelligences***. New York: Basic Books.

Gartrell, D. (2004). ***A guidance approach for the encouraging classroom***. Albany, NY: Delmar Learning.

Guha, S. (2002). Integrating mathematics for young children through play. ***Young Children,*** 57 (3): 90-92.

Hurwitz, S. (1999). The adventure outside your classroom door. ***Child Care Information Exchange***, 127, 55-57.

Kamii, C. & L.B. Housman. (2000). ***Young children reinvent arithmetic: Implications of Piaget's Theory.*** New York: Teachers College Press.

Kohl, MA. & C. Gainer. (1996). ***MathArts: Exploring math through art with 3-6 year olds***. Beltsville, MD: Gryphon House.

MacDonald, S. (1998). ***Everyday discoveries: Amazingly easy science and math activities using stuff you already have***. Beltsville, MD: Gryphon House.

MacDonald, S. (2001). ***Block play: The complete guide to learning and playing with blocks***. Beltsville, MD: Gryphon House.

Moomaw, S. & B. Hieronymous. (2001). ***More than letters: Literacy activities for preschool, kindergarten, and first grade***. St. Paul, MN: Redleaf Press.

NAEYC & NCTM. (2002). Math experiences that count! ***Young Children***, 57 (4): 60-62.

NAEYC. 1996. NAEYC Position Statement: Technology and young children: Ages three through eight. ***Young Children***, 51 (6): 11-16.

O'Brien-Palmer, M. (1998). ***Sense-abilities: Fun ways to explore the senses***. Chicago, IL: Chicago Review Press.

Schiller, P. & P. Phipps. (2002). ***The complete daily curriculum for early childhood: Over 1200 easy activities to support multiple intelligences and learning styles***. Beltsville, MD: Gryphon House.

Seefeldt, C. (2001). ***Playing to learn: Activities and experiences that build learning connections***. Beltsville, MD: Gryphon House.

Sherwood, E., R. Williams, & R. Rockwell. (1990). ***More mudpies to magnets***. Beltsville, MD: Gryphon House.

Smith, C.J., C.M. Hendricks, B.S. Bennett. (1997). ***Growing, growing strong: A whole health curriculum.*** St. Paul, MN: Redleaf Press.

Swift, M. (1999). ***Discipline for life: Getting it right with children***.Grapevine, TX: Stairway Education Programs.

Possibilities Plan—

Where Does It Come From and Where Does It Go?

Getting Ready to Plan

The purpose of Getting Ready to Plan is to support the planning process with a general overview of the content of this Possibilities Plan. Now is the time to think about what interests the children and what you want them to learn about each of these topics.

Grocery Shopping: Going to the grocery store is a common experience for most preschool children. The connection between how food is grown and processed and how it looks at the grocery store may be a new concept for them. Seeing freshly harvested, unprocessed food at a farmers' market and preparing and serving food helps make the connection. Buying foods is an opportunity for applying emerging numeracy skills as children figure out how much things cost, why one kind of food is more expensive than another, how many items come in a package, or which container has more. Grocery shopping is also rich in literacy and writing opportunities.

Cooking Foods: This is a good topic for dramatic play and gives children an opportunity to interact and take on family roles. Explore not only how families cook foods, but also how restaurants prepare foods for customers. This topic lends itself to exploring and validating children's cultural backgrounds related to food traditions within their families, and supporting scientific and numeracy skills with cooking activities.

Food Pyramid: Information from the U.S. Department of Agriculture will provides great ideas for how to use the food pyramid with preschool children. Attach a food pyramid chart to the wall and refer to it during snack and lunch. There are ideas in the Possibilities Plan for children to categorize food according to where it belongs on the food pyramid.

Recycling: The idea of recycling foods may be a new one for children. Talk about leftovers served in a different way as a form of recycling. Setting up a recycling program to allow children to develop sorting skills and will help children understand that they can do their part for the environment.

Now that you have an idea about the general content of the Possibilities Plan, you are ready to proceed with developing your own plan. This section of Getting Ready to Plan identifies resources you may want to buy, collect, or locate to implement your plan.

Toys and Materials*

Purchased

assorted art paper
black construction paper
blocks
bricks
butcher paper on a roll
circles cut to fit inside salad spinner
collage materials
display board
duct tape
food coloring
food pyramid poster
glue, glue sticks
index cards
labels
markers
marshmallows
mortar and pestle
packing tape
page protectors
paint holders
paints, liquid
ping-pong balls
plastic foods
playdough
play money
plastic or real muffins
scissors
stickers
straws
tape
three-ring binders
toothpicks
toy cash register
toys
wire coat hangers

Gathered

5 to 10 one-gallon milk jugs
5-gallon water bottle
2-liter plastic bottles
aprons
blender (teacher only)
bowls
baskets
bins for recycling
camera, 35 mm or digital
carrots
carts
cellophane packing tape
chef hats
chocolate graham crackers
chocolate pudding mix
circles cut to fit inside salad spinner
clothes
coffee filters
coins or poker chips
containers to store materials
cookbooks
cookware
cornstarch
cups
cutting board
different types and shapes of boxes (shoe boxes, gift boxes, toy boxes)
display board
dried fruit
droppers
earthworms
felt
food boxes
food coloring
food labels
food magazines
forks
gummy worms
handheld strainers
hay
knife
labels
large brown sacks
magazines
mashed potatoes, instant
measuring cups
milk
milk cartons
newspaper
old socks
paper bags
peanut butter
pebbles or beads
pictures of foods
pictures of pizza wedges with different toppings
pictures of the ingredients in pizza toppings
pitchers
pizza boards or cardboard cut into 8- or 10-inch circles
pizza boxes
pizza cutters
plastic bottles of various sizes
plastic containers with lids
plastic cups, small
plastic hammers, small
plates
potatoes
purses
rice cakes
rolling pin
rocks, small
salad spinner
scoops
screen
shopping basket
silverware
slices and/or circle cut-outs of pizza dough and cut-outs of different toppings
soil
spoons
toothpicks
trash cans
trays, small
wallets
water
world map
zipper-closure baggies

*Note: Please consider the ages and abilities of the children in your classroom. Use only safe, non-toxic materials.

Where Does It Come From and Where Does It Go?

WEB

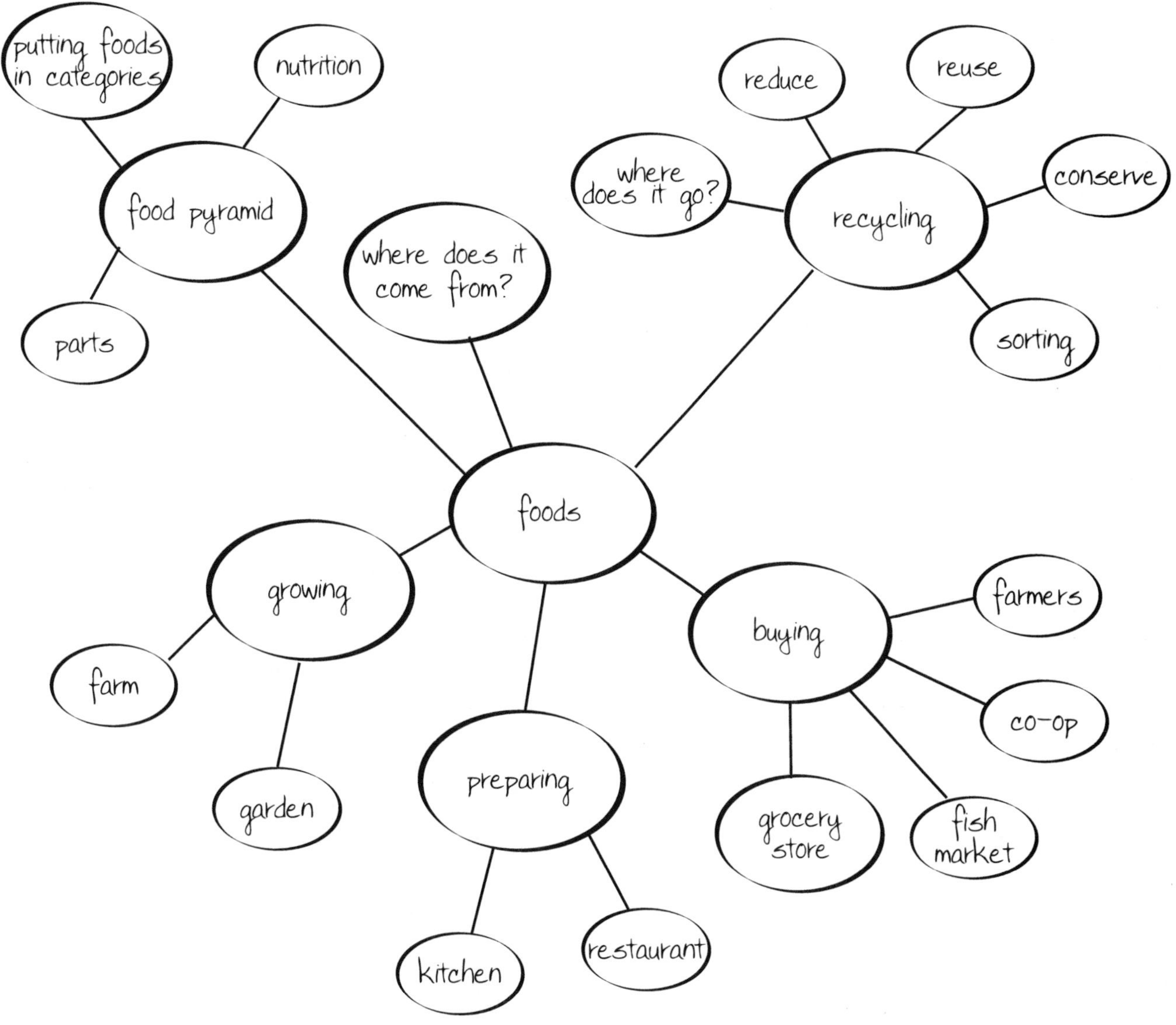

Where Does It Come From and Where Does It Go?

PLANNING PAGES

Plan Possibilities

Activities and Experiences for Where Does It Come From and Where Does It Go?

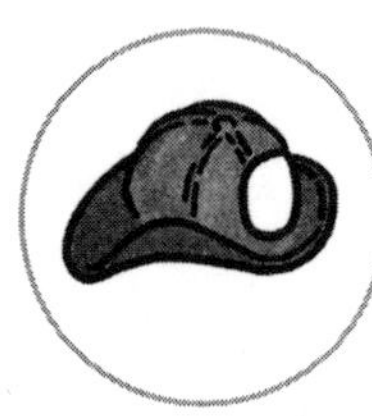

DRAMATIC POSSIBILITIES

Pizza Kitchen

Materials
paper slices and/or circle cutouts of pizza dough • paper cutouts of different toppings • pizza boxes • pizza cutters • rolling pins • aprons • chef hats • plates • silverware • bowls • books, such as *A Gardener's Alphabet* by Mary Azarian

Teacher Talk
"You are using the rolling pin to roll out your pizza dough." "Tell me your favorite toppings."

Instructions
Use brown felt to cut out the shapes (slices/circle) of pizza dough and the necessary colors for each topping (mushrooms, pepperoni, cheese, bell pepper, etc). Clean, unused pizza boxes are available at many pizza or box shops. Place all the toppings in different labeled containers in the Dramatic Possibilities area. Include books, such as *A Gardener's Alphabet* by Mary Azarian.

Observation/Assessment
Uses props to enhance dramatic play
Manipulates small objects

Kitchen

Materials
cookware • silverware • plates • bowls • cups • plastic or real foods • food pyramid poster • books, such as *Eat Your Peas* by Kes Gray

Teacher Talk
"What food group does your egg belong to?" Use the terms (vegetable group, fruit group, milk group, meat group, fats and sweets group, and grains and cereal group) in conversation as children are playing.

Instructions
Provide various examples of different food groups. Label baskets with the names of the different food groups. Ask children to put the foods in the appropriate food group baskets.

Helpful Hint: The United States Department of Agriculture has adapted the language of the food pyramid for preschool children in a publication called "Tips for Using the Food Guide Pyramid" for children from 2–6 years old. The booklet includes suggestions for using the pyramid with preschoolers, including both activities and recipes. The booklet is available from the Consumer Information Center or it can be downloaded from the website (www.usda.gov/cnpp).

Observation/Assessment
Takes on various roles in dramatic play
Has particular play partners

Grocery Store

Materials
different food boxes • baskets • carts • plastic foods • purses • toy cash register • play money • wallets • paper bags • books, such as *Good Enough to Eat: A Kid's Guide to Food and Nutrition* by Lizzy Rockwell

Teacher Talk
"You bought cereal, hotdogs, and mustard from the grocery store." "What are planning to cook today?"

Instructions
Collect a variety of empty food boxes. Stuff empty food boxes with newspaper and tape them with packaging tape to make the boxes last longer.

Extension Possibilities: Ask each child to bring a can of food to school. Encourage families to send food items that represent their favorite foods, insuring a diverse collection. Include the cans in Dramatic Possibilities. When you are finished talking about food, open a discussion with children about whether everyone has enough food to eat. After your discussion, explore with children a way to donate the cans to a local food pantry to be distributed to those in need.

ART POSSIBILITIES

Discarded and Recycled Material Collages

Materials
large paper bags • a large collection of collage materials • glue • baskets or plastic containers with lids • labels • books, such as *The Great Trash Bash* by Loreen Leedy

Teacher Talk
Talk about discarded and collected materials. "I can use this rubber band to make a number eight." "What can you make with the paper towel tube?"

Instructions
Send home a paper bag. Invite children to use the bag to bring discarded and collected materials back to school. When everyone has brought the bags back, look at each bag, considering how materials can be used. Categorize and store the materials for use in

Art Possibilities. When using recycled materials, be certain that they are safe and clean before making them available to children.

Extension Possibilities: Measure the weight or volume of the materials used and/or chart their use.

Observation/Assessment
Sorts recycled materials according to how they can be used in art

Salad Spinner Art

Materials
circles cut to fit inside the salad spinner • salad spinner • liquid paints • spoons

Teacher Talk
"You are turning the salad spinner." "What color will you add next?"

Instructions
Put a paper circle in the salad spinner. Drop different colors of paint on the paper with a spoon. Then, turn the handle of the salad spinner, spinning the paint into patterns. After use, clean the salad spinner using soapy water or take it to the sensory table for soaking and scrubbing.

Extension Possibilities: Do salad spinner art over a number of days or even weeks. See how the children's techniques change over time. Put the child's name and date on each piece of art.

Observation/Assessment
Paints using salad spinner

Potatoes, Carrots, and Toothpicks Sculptures

Materials
apples • carrots • toothpicks • paper plates • books, such as *The Ugly Vegetables* by Grace Lin

Teacher Talk
"You used many toothpicks." "You have more apples in your sculpture than carrots."

Instructions
Wash the apples and carrots. Cut some carrots into one-inch pieces. Core and slice some of the apples. Leave the rest whole. Give children a suggestion of what to do by sticking some toothpicks into some of the carrot and apple pieces. Give each child an

art tray covered with a paper plate (labeled with the child's name) to work on. Cleanup will be much easier if you cover the table completely with a large piece of art paper or use a plastic tablecloth. Children can use whole apples or whole carrots in their sculptures as well. Children can eat sculptures for snack.

Extension Possibilities: Substitute cut-up vegetables (such as cauliflower, broccoli, carrots and cherry tomatos) to create an "edible" centerpiece for a family event. Or, convert the sculpture into vegetable soup for a snack.

Observation/Assessment
Builds sculptures using toothpicks, apples, and carrots

BLOCKS/CONSTRUCTION POSSIBILITIES

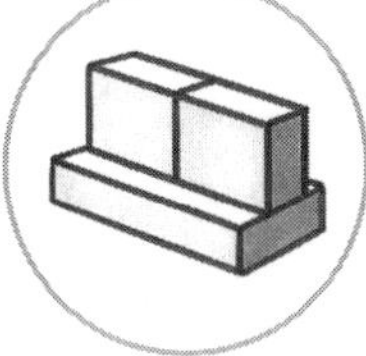

Box Blocks

Materials
different types and shapes of boxes (shoeboxes, gift boxes, toy boxes) • newspapers • packing tape • books, such as *Trash Trucks!* by Daniel Kurk

Teacher Talk
"You are using both wooden blocks and box blocks in your creation."

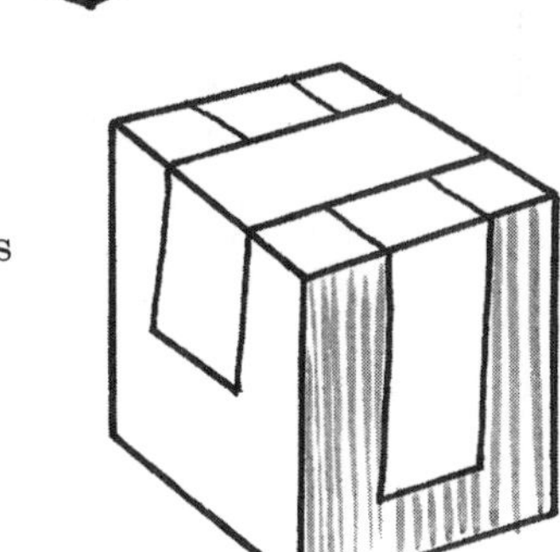

Instructions
Collect a variety of boxes, small and large. Create box blocks by stuffing the boxes with newspaper and taping them shut. Place box blocks on the shelves with the wooden blocks. Additions like this enhance construction activities for children. You can add interest to unit blocks easily by adding a collection of box blocks. Use small boxes as stands for cardboard figures.

Observation/Assessment
Builds using unit blocks and a variety of box blocks

Stock the Shelves with Food Boxes

Materials
grocery store food boxes • newspaper • packing tape

Teacher Talk
"You are using food boxes instead of blocks to build." "Some things can be used in more than one way."

Instructions
Collect a variety of cereal, oatmeal, cracker, and cookie boxes. Stuff them with newspapers and tape the top and bottom of the boxes shut. Use wide packing tape or clear contact paper to make the food boxes last longer. Add these unique blocks to the Block/Construction Possibilities area. Make extras, so boxes can be added to dramatic play. Include books in the area, such as *In the Night Kitchen* by Maurice Sendak.

Observation/Assessment
Builds using food boxes of various sizes and shapes

Other Blocks/Construction Possibilities

- Use small and large marshmallows and straws to make sculptures.
- Use empty, clean milk and juice cartons to make blocks.
- Use plastic bottles of various sizes and weighted in different ways (sand, water, Styrofoam pellets, peanut shells, marbles, stones, dirt, leaves) for building.

SCIENCE/DISCOVERY POSSIBILITIES

Clean Water

Materials
2-liter water bottle • coffee filter • small rocks • pebbles • hay

Teacher Talk
"How does the water in the rivers, streams, and lakes get clean and clear enough to drink?" Explore children's ideas about where clean water comes from.

Instructions
Cut off the bottom part of a plastic 2-liter bottle. Turn the bottle upside down with the open end at the top and the cap at the bottom. Wash rocks and pebbles before placing them in the bottle to make sure the layers will not contribute additional dirt to the water. Place two or three coffee filters at the bottom and then add hay, sand, pebbles, and small rocks. Pour dirty water into the bottle. Remove the cap to see how the filter works. Ask children to tell you in their own words how filtration works and why. Write down their descriptions.

Extension Possibilities: Try using various types of dirty water to determine differences in how well the filter works. Use water that contains soil, dye, oil, or juices. Children may observe, smell, and touch the water, but they should not taste or drink it.

Observation/Assessment
Observes and discusses how water is purified

Making Recycled Paper

Materials
paper of different types • blender (teacher only) • water • screen (at least 3" x 5" and up to as large as a window screen) • large bowl • hand-held strainers • felt • bricks or wood blocks • books, such as *Trashy Town* by Andrea Zimmerman

Teacher Talk
"Why is it important to recycle paper?" "How does our paper look different from paper we may buy?"

Instructions
Tear paper into small pieces. The teacher places paper into the blender until it is about half full and then fills it with water. Blend until the texture is fairly consistent (teacher only). Pour the mixture into a large bowl. Children scoop the mixture into strainers, strain the mixture, and then pour the strained mixture onto the screen. Smooth out the mixture on the screen and cover with a piece of felt. Place objects like wood blocks or bricks on the mixture to press the water out. Place the screen where air can circulate around it. Allow paper to dry completely before removing the bricks or blocks.

Extension Possibilities: Use various types of paper for different colors and textures. Try making paper thinner or thicker.

Observation/Assessment
Scoops, strains, and pours to make paper

Worm Farm

Materials
5-gallon plastic water bottle • black construction paper • tape • soil • earthworms • books, such as *Earthworms (Ooey, Gooey Animals)* by Lola M. Schaefer

Teacher Talk
"What do earthworms eat?" " Why do we cover the outside of the bottle with black paper?"

Instructions
Cut off the top part of a 5-gallon plastic water bottle. Cover the outsides of the bottle with black construction paper. Add soil and press down firmly. Leave at least five inches clear at the top of the water bottle. Place the earthworms in the bottle. Give the worms some time to settle in the container. Then, begin feeding the worms scraps of vegetables and fruits and coffee grounds. Mist lightly with water. Keep the worm farm in a cool place. Leave the worm farm undisturbed for several days before checking for tunnels. Plan time for a discussion of worm tunnels. Children can remove the construction paper to make their observations and then tape the construction paper back again. Provide tape in the area, so children can independently re-tape the paper.

Extension Possibilities: Count the worms before you add them to the worm farm. Count them periodically and chart the results.

Observation/Assessment
Observes and discusses worm farm

Other Science/Discovery Possibilities

- Start a recycling program at your school.
- Put on latex gloves to pick up trash on the playground. Categorize the trash and discuss how it got on the playground.
- Eat an "Edible Worms in the Garden" snack of chocolate pudding (mud), chocolate graham cracker crumbs (dirt), and gummy worms (worms). Make a rebus of the recipe, so children can make their own snacks.

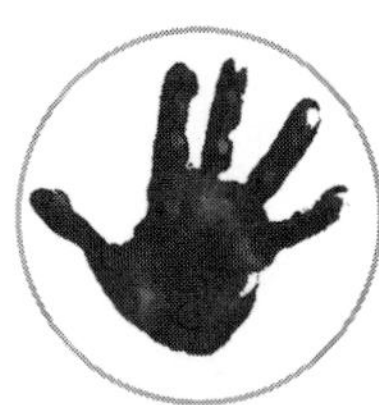

SENSORY POSSIBILITIES

Playdough Worms

Materials
playdough of different colors • books, such as *Wormy Worms* by Chris Raschka

Teacher Talk
"The more you roll the playdough, the longer the worm becomes."

Instructions
Show children how to roll playdough into ropes. Use different colors of playdough to make the worms. Include books, such as *Wormy Worms* by Chris Raschka.

Observation/Assessment
Rolls playdough to form worms

Peanut Butter

Materials
roasted peanuts in shells • mortar and pestle

Teacher Talk
"We are making peanut butter." "Everyone will get a chance to mash the peanuts."

Directions
Check for food allergies before beginning the activity. Teach children the song "Peanut, Peanut Butter." Children first shell peanuts and rub off the skins. As you sing the song, children can take turns mashing the peanuts. When the peanuts become paste, mix them with jelly. Spread on crackers for snack.

Helpful Hint: Recycle the peanut shells into collage material. Place in a sealed container and add to the collage materials in Art Possibilities.

Other Sensory Possibilities

- Use cornstarch, water, and food coloring to make goop.
- Make instant mashed potatoes. Serve as part of snack.
- Use peanut shells in the sensory table with plastic figures.

LITERACY/WRITING POSSIBILITIES

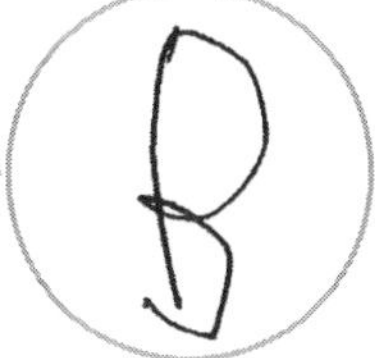

I'm a Great Chef

Materials
cookbooks • index cards • food magazines • scissors • shopping basket • books, such as *A Chef (How We Work)* by Douglas Florian

Teacher Talk
"I'm hungry." "Tell me about the recipe you are using." "How many potatoes do you need?"

Instructions
Ask children to tell you their favorite food. Then, ask them to tell you how it is cooked. Write down their directions. Encourage children to illustrate their recipes or to add pictures from food magazines to the recipe. Laminate them and place them in Dramatic Possibilities. Use 5x8 index cards or full-page sized card stock, so children will have the space they need to illustrate their recipes.

Extension Possibilities: Write children's recipes on chart paper and post them for families to enjoy. Add children's recipes to their portfolios.

Observation/Assessment
Dictates ideas to teacher

My Food Book

Materials
pictures of foods • three-ring binders • paper • markers • page protectors

Teacher Talk
"Do you know to which food group this food belongs?"

Instructions
Collect many pictures of food, including popular logos of snack food and pre-packaged food. Children select pictures of food picture they like, gluing one food on each piece of paper. Divide the three-ring binder into six sections, one for each of the food groups on the food pyramid. Help children label their food selection. Place in sheet protectors and add to the appropriate sections of the book.

Helpful Hint: If the children bring their lunches or snacks to school, lunch boxes will be a rich source of labels and logos. Other good sources of food pictures are food magazines and mail flyers from grocery stores and supermarkets.

Observation/Assessment
Identifies food according to its place on the food pyramid
Associates written words with their pictures
Identifies logos

Other Literacy/Writing Possibilities

- Use school menus to practice labeling food according to food pyramid.
- Write thank-you notes for field trips.
- Use colored cornstarch in a sealed and taped zipper closure plastic bag, so children can practice letter formation.
- Locate on a map or globe where children's toys and clothes are made.
- Cut out pictures from newspapers, magazines, and advertisements. Cut out large print words that accompany them. Glue the pictures and words on index cards. Help children "read" the cards.

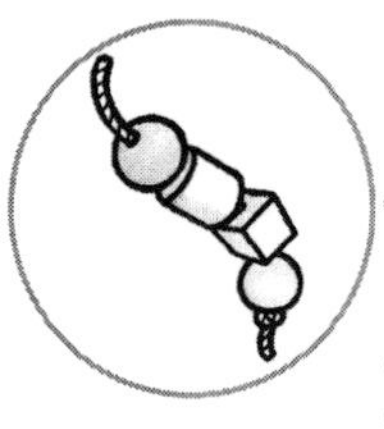

MATH/MANIPULATIVES POSSIBILITIES

Pizza Bingo

Materials
pictures of pizza wedges with different toppings • pizza boards or cardboard cut into 8- or 10-inch circles • pictures of the ingredients in pizza toppings (cheese, pepperoni, bacon, mushrooms, onions, sausage, olives, green peppers, anchovies, and peppers) • coins or poker chips for markers

Teacher Talk
"Call 'Pizza Bingo' when you have covered all of your pizza toppings with coins or chips."

Instructions
Glue the pizza pictures on the cardboard rounds. Glue ingredient pictures onto pizza wedges. Use the wedges as call out cards. Turn the pizza ingredient wedges face down on a table. Children take turns

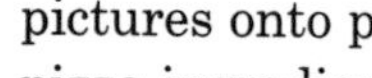

drawing a wedge and calling out what is on it. Each time children have a matching pizza wedge on their pizza, they mark it with a coin or poker chip. When they get all of their pizza wedges marked, they call out "Pizza Bingo."

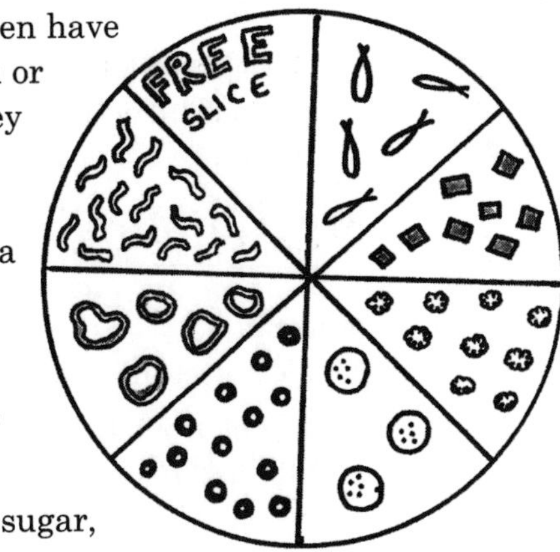

Helpful Hint: A computer with the Clip Art program will help a great deal. You can choose pictures and print any number you need.

Extension Possibilities: Instead of using the usual pictures of pizza ingredients, use food items from each section of the food pyramid (fruits, vegetables, meats, breads and grains, fats and sugar, etc.) and pyramid-shaped bingo cards.

Recycling Sort

Materials
items to sort • four baskets or trash cans • labels—paper, plastics, aluminum, non-recyclable

Teacher Talk
"How can we sort this piece of cardboard?"

Instructions
Collect different washed items that could be grouped into three different recycling groups—paper, plastic, and aluminum. Have three baskets or cans with labels and drawings of the three groups. Help children locate the recycle symbol on plastic to determine if it is recyclable. Invite parents to participate in this activity. Each family can bring in two or three things from each recycling group. If you want to, add another basket or can that can be used for non-recyclable products.

Observation/Assessment
Sorts materials into recycling categories

Other Math/Manipulatives Possibilities

- Make a food pyramid game with cards that have a food name and the pyramid category on them. Play the game as you would play "Go Fish." Each player tries to get all the cards in one pyramid category.
- Sort kitchen materials—forks, spoons, cups, napkins, and so on—by a variety of attributes.
- Use utensils for making patterns (spoon, fork, knife, knife, fork, spoon…).

RHYMES/FINGERPLAYS/SONGS/MUSIC POSSIBILITIES

Muffin Man Song

Materials
basket • pretend or real muffins

Teacher Talk
"Many people eat muffins for breakfast." "What is your favorite breakfast food?"

Instructions
Teach children "The Muffin Man." As you sing the song one child can be the muffin man and give out muffins from the basket.

Other Rhymes/Fingerplays/Songs/Music Possibilities

- Consider any of the following recorded selections:
  - "Home Grown Tomatoes" from *Country Roads—Very Best of John Denver*
  - "This Land Is Your Land" from *This Land Is Your Land—A Collection of Woody Guthrie*
  - "Everything Grows" from *Everything Grows* by Raffi
  - "The Worm" from *Songs About Animals and Other Things* by Kimbo

GROUP TIME POSSIBILITIES

Collecting Recycled Materials for Collages: Brainstorm a list of discarded and collected materials that would be interesting to have as sources for collage material. Send children home with a copy of the list and a large brown paper bag to fill with any of the items that might be available to add to your collage collection.

Unpack Recycled Materials Bags: Unpack one bag at a time to see what children brought and how it might be used.

Introduce Edible Worms in the Garden: Demonstrate how to make this snack (page 430), demonstrating the steps. Children can then prepare the snack independently at the snack table.

Under Our Sink: Take a "field trip" to the sink to examine the plumbing underneath the sink. Return to Group Time and look at PVC pipes, plumbing tools, and pictures of pipelines that run underground. Ask children to think about where the pipes go. Write down their ideas about where pipes and plumbing go.

Trash, Trash, Where Do You Go?: Collect clean paper, plastic, and aluminum objects that are recyclable and a few that are not. Put the objects in a box. Make a chart with five columns—one for the name of the item, then one each for paper, plastic, aluminum, and unknown. Give each child a pair of disposable gloves to put on. Ask them to draw an object out of the box and select which recycling group it might belong to. Place in the appropriate recycle bin.

Trash, Trash, Where Do You Go?

Item	Paper	Plastic	Aluminum	Unknown

Other Group Time Possibilities

- Read any of the books from the Books List in Resources (pages 442-443).
- Cut out articles about recycling from the newspaper to read to the children.
- Chart items from recycled materials bags by category.

MOVEMENT/OUTDOORS POSSIBILITIES

Milk Jug Basket

Materials

old socks • pebbles or beads • 5 to 10 one gallon milk jugs

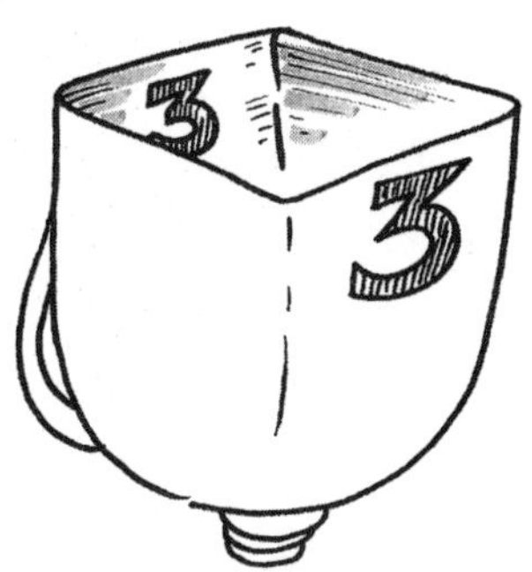

Teacher Talk

"Out of 10 beanbags, how many beanbags can you put into the milk jug?"

Instructions

Put pebbles or beads inside the socks. Tie a knot in the top of each sock to make beanbags. Cut off the bottoms of the milk jugs. Hold each bottle upside down and write a number on each milk jug. Partially bury the jugs in the sand with the bottom side up. Let children toss the beanbags into the milk jugs.

Helpful Hint: Start with 1-5, add 5 more, then five more, and so on as children learn one-to-one correspondence and counting skills. You can also attach milk jugs to walls, fences, or trees. Take off the caps, so water can go through the milk jugs when it rains.

Paddle Ball Rackets from Recycled Materials

Materials
wire coat hangers • washed old pantyhose • duct tape • ping-pong balls

Instructions
Bend a wire coat hanger, so the opening has a round shape. Bend the hanger portion double. Tightly stretch pantyhose leg (2 layers) over the round shape and secure with tape at the hanger portion. Use plastic coated wire hangers for best results. Bend and wrap the hanger portion with tape to form a handle for the racket. Use the racket and ping-pong balls to play paddle ball.

Extension Possibilities: Coat hangers can be used in much the same way and made into butterfly or bug nets. Instead of tightly stretching the pantyhose over the round portion of the hanger, cut off a leg of the pantyhose and attach the top portion of the leg to the round portion of the hanger using duct tape.

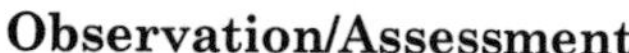

Observation/Assessment
Plays using racket and ball

Other Movement/Outdoor Possibilities

- Play Drop the Handkerchief using a food box.
- Fill a mesh fruit bag with recycled string, thread, yarn, and pieces of cloth. Hang outside, so birds can use the materials for nest building.
- Plant a vegetable garden, grape or wistera arbor, or fruit tree.
- Find toy food and food boxes on the playground that have been previously hidden by the teacher.

PROJECTS/DOCUMENTATION POSSIBILITIES

Food Pyramid

Materials
butcher paper on a roll • tape • a marker • pictures of foods from different food groups • glue sticks

Teacher Talk
"Katherine added her picture of black beans to the protein section. Protein gives us energy and helps us grow."

Instructions
Cut a large triangle out of the paper. You may need to cut out three separate pieces and tape them together to make the pyramid large enough. Use a marker to separate the paper into the six sections of the food pyramid. Attach the pyramid to a wall low enough for children to reach each section. Ask children to find pictures in magazines or food advertisements from the different food groups. As the children bring in pictures, they can glue them onto the correct sections of the pyramid. The lunch table is a good place to introduce this activity and talk about the food groups.

Extension Possibilities: Talk about where most of us get our food. Take a field trip to the grocery store. Most grocery stores have the food separated by food groups (produce, meat, bread, candy, etc.). Go on a scavenger hunt to see where the foods on your pyramid are located in the grocery store.

Observation/Assessment
Categorizes food according to where it belongs on the food pyramid

Start a Recycling Program

Materials
Gobble! Gobble! Munch! by Babs Bell Hajdusiewicz • bins for recycling • markers • paper • and tape

Teacher Talk
"Some trash rots and breaks down to go back into the Earth. This trash is called 'biodegradable.'" "Some of our trash does not break down. This kind of trash may not be good for our Earth."

Instructions
Read *Gobble! Gobble! Munch!* by Babs Bell Hajdusiewicz. Talk to the children about trash that is not biodegradable and what happens when we throw it away. Introduce the idea that some trash that does not break down can be remade into something new and that this is called recycling. Suggest that your class begin separating the trash that can be thrown away and the trash that can be recycled. Let the children make and decorate labels for the recycling bins to designate which items go in which bins. Tape the labels on the bins. Find out if there is a recycling pick-up service in your area. If not, ask families to volunteer to take turns dropping off your recyclables at a local recycling location and report their experiences back to the children.

Extension Possibilities: Take a field trip to drop off one of your loads of recyclables. This gives children the opportunity to see where recycled materials go and how they are recycled.

Where Does the Trash Go?

Materials
Trashy Town by Andrea Zimmerman • instant, 35 mm, or digital camera • markers • display board

Teacher Talk
"What will happen to the trash after we put it in the dumpster?" Discuss what happens to trash.

Instructions
First, talk about trash or read the book *Trashy Town* by Andrea Zimmerman. Then talk about conservation (reduce, reuse, recycle). Take children on a walking field trip to visit the dumpster where trash is collected for disposal. Take pictures of important points, such as the garbage can, the person who takes out the garbage, the dumpster, and so on. Next, talk about what will happen to trash after it is placed in the dumpster. After developing the pictures, create a display board with what you learned about trash for children to read and review. Add pictures of dump trucks, garbage collectors, landfills, and other related objects from your picture file.

FIELD TRIP POSSIBILITIES

Recycling Site: Plan a field trip to a recycling site. Ask where materials go when they leave the center. What are they recycled into?

Dumpster: Visit the dumpster when it is time for it to be emptied. Find out from the dumpster driver what happens to trash after it leaves school.

Grocery Store: A field trip to the grocery store can be a wonderful learning experience. Make a grocery list of labels or pictures of the items you want to locate. Identify different food types, match cans and boxes, count items, learn about different fruits and vegetables, count money, compare prices, and see how different foods must be stored to protect them from spoilage.

SNACK POSSIBILITIES

Triangle Crackers and Toppings: Talk about the food pyramid as children prepare snack using a variety of different toppings (olives, cheese, ham, butter, jam) on triangle (pyramid) crackers.

Fruit Salad: Create a fruit salad with children by providing fruits and vegetable peelers. Soft fruits like bananas or strawberries can be sliced using plastic knives.

Other Snack Possibilities

- Use any of the other snacks mentioned in other Possibilities Plans.
  - Apples, Carrots, and Toothpick Sculptures
  - Marshmallow Construction
  - Edible Worms in the Garden
  - Funny Face Feast
  - Instant Mashed Potatoes
  - Peanut, Peanut Butter

FAMILY PARTICIPATION POSSIBILITIES

Food Pyramid for Families: Ask families to cut out pictures of food from magazines and product labels from advertisements and junk mail flyers to use in this project.

Taste Test: Invite families to bring in their favorite bread from home for everyone to taste. Chart the bread varieties and who liked which one. This is an excellent way to include cultural variations in a participation activity. Try this same activity with other foods.

Collected and Recycled Materials for Collages: Ask families to bring in materials from home to add to the collage collection. Attach the list made by the children in group time to a brown lunch sack, so children can load things into the sack and return to school with it.

Picky Eaters

Almost all families are concerned about how much preschoolers eat (or don't eat) and whether their nutritional needs are being met. Children are capable of adjusting their own food intake, and nutritionists recommend letting children decide what and how much to eat without being overruled too much by adults.

Try some of the following strategies with your child to help him or her develop healthy, lifelong eating habits.

- Offer new foods many times. Your child will probably need to see food and try it several times before it is familiar enough to eat.
- Be a good role model. Try new foods and comment on them.
- Make meals a shared family time. Turn off the television and enjoy eating and talking together.
- Don't pressure your child. Accept your child's choices.
- Eat at regularly scheduled times. Three meals and two scheduled snacks are recommended. Don't offer additional snacks.
- Give children choices of nutritious foods; avoid fats and sugars.
- If your child regularly avoids one type of food, introduce it in an interesting or different way. For example, if he or she isn't drinking milk, substitute other foods high in calcium, such as yogurt or dried beans.
- Do not use food as a reward. This can contribute to problems with weight and self-esteem.
- Keep calm. If you are frantic about eating behavior, your child will feel like he or she has to continue the behavior that is problematic. If you avoid making a fuss and allow your child to control his or her nutritional intake, your child will learn to listen to the cues from his or her body about when and how much to eat—avoiding over- and under-eating.

Using the Food Pyramid with Your Child

Preschool children understand much more than we think they do. When talking about foods and nutrition, try using the food pyramid with your child. Children like the idea of eating in a healthy way, and the food pyramid is a visual way to support good nutrition in your family.

Get a food pyramid chart for your family and post it on a wall or the refrigerator. You can get information from many different sources including the U.S. Department of Agriculture. Get "Tips for Using the Food Guide Pyramid for Young Children 2 to 6 Years Old" (1999) by calling 202-512-1800 and asking for stock number 001-0004665-9, or download it from the USDA website, www.usda.gov. Include your child in meal planning by saying, "How many servings of fruits and vegetables have we had today? How many more do we need?" Soon your child will recognize where different foods fall within the food pyramid and will realize why you are offering apple slices instead of brownies.

Enjoying Mealtime Together

Mealtime is an important family time. Having meals together gives families a chance to reconnect after being away from each other during the day. Children can learn about what their parents did during the day and share important events in their lives.

Turn off the television, so the time is reserved only for communicating with each other. Talking with adults helps preschool children to increase vocabulary and understand events in the world. If your child is reluctant to share information about his or her day, find out about events in the classroom through talking with your child's teacher or reading the Communication Log. That way you can ask more specific questions, such as, "What did you learn when the chef visited your class today?"

According to research, children who eat evening meals with their family are more likely to do well in school. So enjoy a family meal together.

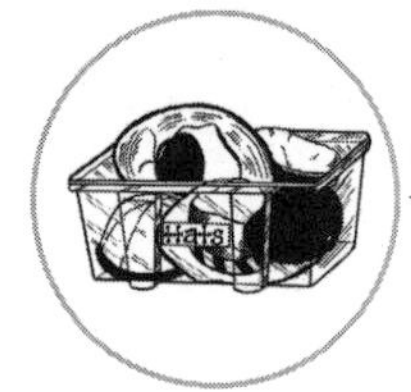

Curriculum Resources

Prop Boxes

Pizza Kitchen Prop Box
pizza boxes • pizza cutters, rolling pins • slices and/or circle cutouts of pizza dough • cutouts of different toppings • aprons • chef hats • plates • silverware • bowls • wooden spoons • logo items

Kitchen Prop Box
plastic bowls • utensils • spatula • large spoons • tablecloth • vase and flowers • cookbooks • napkins • food boxes • menus • aprons • cutting board • toy foods • plastic dishes

Grocery Store Prop Box
cash register • coupons • food boxes • toy foods • grocery store basket • magazines • artificial flowers • name tags • cash register receipts • grocery bags of different sizes

Garbage Collection Prop Box
trash containers • liners or bags • clean food boxes • plastic foods • plastic bottles and containers • aluminum cans • labels for recycling containers (paper, plastic, aluminum, glass) • schedule for trash pick-up

Books

A Is for Salad by Mike Lester
A Chef (How We Work) by Douglas Florian
City Green by Dyanne DiSalvo-Ryan
Cows in the Kitchen by June Crebbin
Each Living Thing by Joanne Ryder
Each Orange Had 8 Slices: A Counting Book by Paul Giganti
Earthworms (Ooey, Gooey Animals) by Lola M. Schaefer
Eat Your Peas by Kes Gray
Eating Fractions by Bruce McMillan
Eating the Alphabet by Lois Ehlert
A Gardener's Alphabet by Mary Azarian
Gobble! Gobble! Munch! by Babs Bell Hajdusiewicz
Good Enough to Eat: A Kid's Guide to Food and Nutrition by Lizzy Rockwell
The Great Trash Bash by Loreen Leedy
Growing Vegetable Soup by Lois Ehlert
I Will Never Not Ever Eat a Tomato by Lauren Child
If You Give a Moose a Muffin by Laura Joffe Numeroff
If You Give a Mouse a Cookie by Laura Joffe Numeroff
In the Kitchen by Susan Canizares and Betsey Chessen
In the Night Kitchen by Maurice Sendak
Jake Baked the Cake by B.G. Hennessy

On Market Street by Anita Lobel
This Is the Pumpkin by Abby Levine
Trash Trucks! by Daniel Kirk
Trashy Town by Andrea Zimmerman
The Ugly Vegetables by Grace Lin
The Wee Little Woman by Byron Barton
Who's Sick Today? by Lynne Cherry
Wonderful Worms by Linda Glaser
Wormy Worms by Christopher Rascka

Observation/Assessment

Uses props to enhance dramatic play, page 424
Manipulates small objects, page 424
Takes on various roles in dramatic play, page 425
Has particular play partners, page 425
Sorts recycled materials according to how they can be used in art, page 426
Paints using salad spinner, page 426
Builds sculptures using toothpicks, apples, and carrots, page 427
Builds using unit blocks and a variety of box blocks, page 427
Builds using food boxes of various sizes and shapes, page 428
Observes and discussed how water is purified, page 428
Makes recycled paper, page 429
Observes and discusses worm farm, page 430
Rolls playdough to form worms, page 430
Dictates ideas to teacher, page 431
Identifies food according to its place on the food pyramid, page 432
Associates written words with their pictures, page 432
Identifies logos, page 432
Sorts materials into recycling categories, page 433
Plays using racket and ball, page 436
Categorizes food according to where it belongs on the food pyramid, page 437

Picture File/Vocabulary

apron	dumpster	meal	same
carbohydrates	fats	meat	small
conserve	food groups	pizza	snack
curved	food pyramid	plain	straight
dairy	fruits	portions	utensils
decorated	grains	protein	vegetables
different	logos	recycle	worms

Concepts Learned in Where Does It Come From and Where Does It Go?

Content Knowledge

- ☐ I can make recycled paper.
- ☐ Worms recycle fruits and vegetables into compost.
- ☐ I can make mashed potatoes.
- ☐ I know many different types of pizza toppings.
- ☐ I can sort recycled materials into paper, plastics, and aluminum.
- ☐ I know many songs and fingerplays about food.
- ☐ I know about the food pyramid.
- ☐ I can identify four different food groups on the food pyramid.
- ☐ I can eat five fruits or vegetables a day.

Process Knowledge

- ☐ I can play roles in Dramatic Possibilities.
- ☐ I can create with recycled materials.
- ☐ I can create sculptures.
- ☐ I can construct things.
- ☐ I can stock the shelves in the grocery store.
- ☐ I can build with lots of different kinds of blocks.
- ☐ I can make my own snacks.
- ☐ I can throw beanbags into milk jugs.
- ☐ I can play paddle ball.

Pre-academic Skills

- ☐ I can write alphabet letters.
- ☐ I can sort kitchen utensils like forks, knives, spoons, etc..
- ☐ I can recycle words and pictures from printed materials.
- ☐ I can read the logos of my favorite snack foods.
- ☐ I know the sounds that vowels can make.
- ☐ I can count to 5, or 10, or 15, or 20.

Possibilities Plan—

Building Up and Tearing Down

Getting Ready to Plan

During the preschool years, children enjoy exploring actions and reactions, and they enjoy having some control over their environment. This Possibilities Plan will allow children to practice skills in construction, as well as explore topics related to Building Up and Tearing Down.

The purpose of Getting Ready to Plan is to support the planning process with a general overview of the content of this Possibilities Plan. Now is the time to think about what interests the children and what you want them to learn about each of these topics.

Building Up: Construction is a popular topic for preschool children. Ideal construction activities are hands-on in nature and allow children to learn spatial concepts (what is in front of/in back of/beside) and comparisons (longer/shorter, heavier/lighter). Easily seen as an activity for the Blocks/Construction area, children can also build up in many areas of the classroom including Art, Sensory, Library/Writing, and so on.

Recycling: The concept of recycling is explored in a different way in this Possibilities Plan. What can be made from discarded materials? How can we create with discarded materials? It also connects recycling to helping sustain our environment.

Tearing Down: Children love to experiment with deconstruction—and often explore this concept thoroughly in the Blocks/Construction area by deconstructing their own projects. As their interest in dramatic play in miniature grows, children are more able to do with objects and toys what they used to do with their whole bodies (for example, having one block person hit another block person instead of hitting a friend who doesn't follow your directions).

Focusing on how things are deconstructed gives children experiences with reversing the building-up process. Explore topics, such as the steps of deconstructing a block construction, safety rules for deconstruction activities, getting agreement among the players about when to initiate the deconstruction and who will play what role, appropriate safety equipment, such as goggles, hard hats, or work gloves, taking thing apart in steps, and so on.

Now that you have an idea about the general content of the Possibilities Plan, you are ready to proceed with developing your own plan. This section of Getting Ready to Plan identifies resources you may want to buy, collect, or locate to implement your plan.

Toys and Materials*

Purchased

2-3" diameter Styrofoam ball
architectural blocks
books about construction, engineering, demolition, and birds' nests
box cutter (teacher only)
calculator
chalk, colored
compass
computer
construction paper
construction vehicles
craft sticks of various sizes
dominoes
eraser
foam blocks
gel pens
graphing paper
hollow blocks
hole punch
iodized salt
Jenga blocks
jumbo waffle blocks
large, wheeled vehicles
Legos®
liquid glue
manipulatives
markers
musical tapes and CDs
notebooks
novelty paper with patterns (bricks, stones, siding, etc.)
packing tape
paint
paintbrushes
paper
paper cone cups
paper plates
pencils
pens
people figures
Ping Pong balls
plastic magnifying glasses
playdough
poster paints
printer
project board (chart, blackboard or whiteboard)
protractor
rubber cement (teacher only)
safety glasses and gloves
scissors
silver rings
stapler
tape/CD player
toy sandwiches, tools, trees
triangle rulers
unit blocks
washable paint
water table
whiteboard with markers or blackboard with chalk
zipper-closure bags

Gathered

24" x 4" piece of wood
alphabet cards
aprons
art trays
baby food jars with lids
baking soda
balls of different sizes
blueprints
bowls
boxes of various sizes
broken appliances
calendar
cardboard
carpenter's folding ruler
clipboards
cloth measuring tape
cloth of different textures
drawing table
floor plans
construction and engineering magazines
file folders
floor plans from newspapers and magazines
food coloring
hard hats
index cards
large nails, nuts, and bolts
leaves
letterhead
lunch boxes
magnifying glasses
mail
net bag
newspaper
old business cards
old computer and printer
old Daytimer
old palmtop organizer
old bank statements
phone book
phones
pictures of construction sites and buildings
plastic thermos
rocks
rolodex
pliers
sanding block
sandpaper
scoops, small
smocks
straws
tool boxes
tub
twigs and branches
twine
various shapes of wood
vehicles
vinegar
yarn

*Note: Please consider the ages and abilities of the children in your classroom. Use only safe, non-toxic materials.

Building Up and Tearing Down

WEB

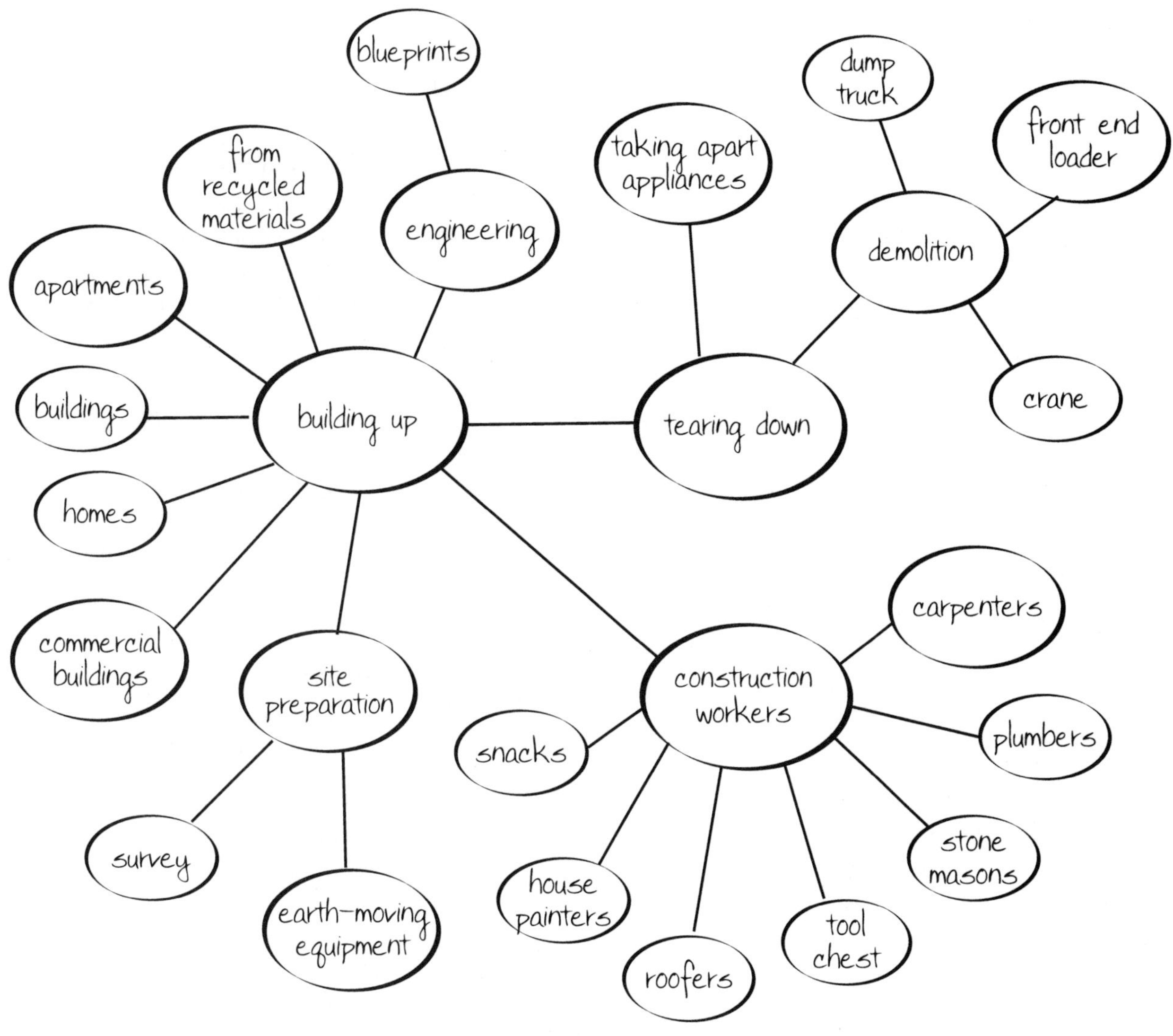

Building Up and Tearing Down

PLANNING PAGES

Plan Possibilities

Activities and Experiences for Building Up and Tearing Down

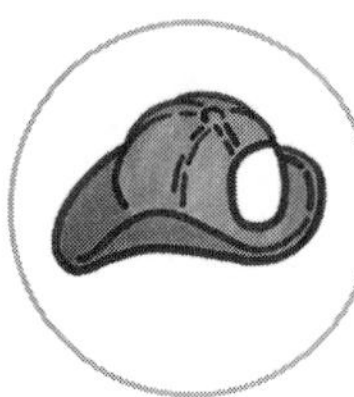

DRAMATIC POSSIBILITIES

Construction Site

Materials
tools • blueprints • tool boxes • aprons • lunch boxes • plastic thermos • hard hats • electrical tools • paint brush • rollers • pencil • paper • floor foam blocks • wooden hollow blocks • books, such as *This Is the House that Jack Built* by Pam Adams

Teacher Talk
"You are hammering this piece of foam block into place." "The corners are a bit tricky."

Instructions
Place materials in the area according to type (all electrical tools together). Attach one or more blueprints to the wall for children to explore. Floor plans may work even better for a crowded space. If you have plenty of room, you may want to include a drawing table for the plans. Make the rest available for children to use as part of their imaginative play. Continue to shape the area as play develops.

Observation/Assessment
Takes on various roles in dramatic play

Office for Construction/Demolition Company

Materials
file folders • alphabet cards • index cards • computer • calculator • phones • paper • printer • notebooks • clipboards • pencils • pens • stapler • mail • construction catalogs • phone book • project board (chart, blackboard, or whiteboard) • eraser • calendar • books, such as *Houses and Homes* by Ann Morris

Teacher Talk
"When is your deadline for the big project?" "Do you think we can do that?"

Instructions
Set up the area as a construction or demolition company office. Help children set up file folders for different projects. Select a project manager for each one. Write the names of the projects on index cards, so children can use them as patterns to label the file folders.

Observation/Assessment
Uses props to enhance dramatic play

Other Dramatic Possibilities

- Create a city planner's office with city maps and office materials. Help children find their houses.
- Create a highway department office with county maps, state map, and highway signs. Help children find their city on the maps.
- Create an engineering office with computer, blueprints, telephone, clipboards, and other related materials.

ART POSSIBILITIES

Paint Pendulum

Materials
hole punch • cone paper cups • twine • newspaper • two chairs • 24" x 4" rectangular block or piece of plywood • paint • water • paper

Teacher Talk
"Does the paint make a pattern?" "What happens when you swing the pendulum back and forth? Side to side?" "What color paint do you choose next?"

Instructions
Punch holes in the sides of the paper cup near the top. Also punch a smaller hole in the cone of the cup. Thread the twine through the two holes near the top of the cup and tie it securely creating a loop that goes about 4 inches up from the top of the cup. Cover a space on the floor with newspaper and place chairs on top about 12 inches apart. Balance the block on the seat of the two chairs and attach the cup so it hangs down, but does not touch the floor. Thin the paint with water, just enough to help it flow through the hole smoothly, but slowly. Lay art paper on the newspaper. Help children pour paint into the cup and swing the pendulum to make designs on the paper. Introduce this activity at group time, so children will be clear about how to do it.

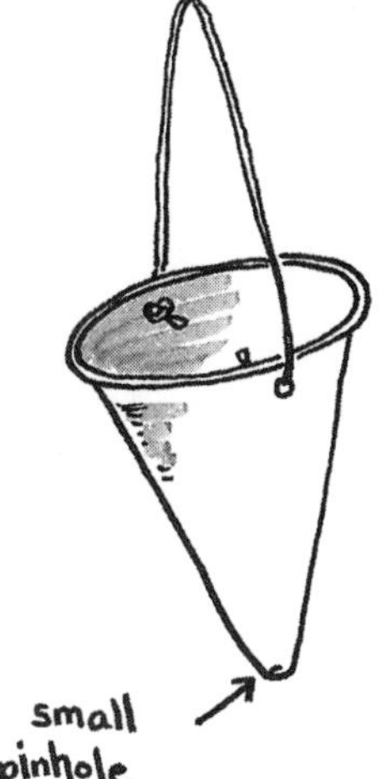

Extension Possibilities: Tie washable markers to the string to create a marker pendulum or tie paintbrushes to the string to create a different paint pendulum. The tip of the marker or brush will need to barely touch the paper.

Observation/Assessment
Follows simple directions

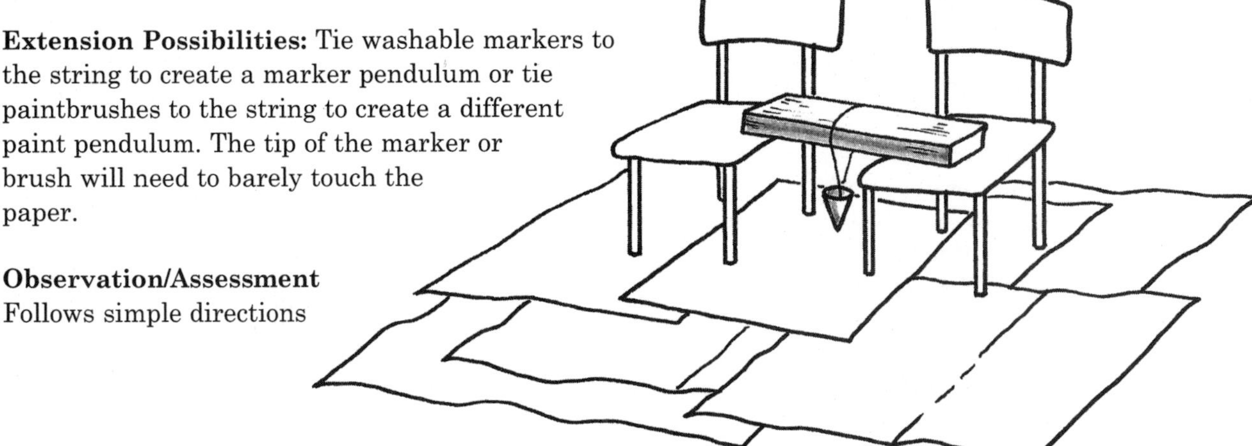

Accordion Art

Materials
construction paper cut into strips • glue • 8" x 11" pieces of cardboard

Teacher Talk
"How did you get that piece of paper to stand up?"

Instructions
Fold the strips of paper accordion style and them let them unfold naturally. Make supplies available for the activity. Children use the accordion strips to glue onto their piece of cardboard. As children begin to have three-dimensional understanding in art, they will discover that the accordion strips can be glued in ways that make them stand up, e.g., as arches, on one edge of the accordion, by connecting accordion strips, etc. It may take several experiences with new concepts like this for children to figure out how things work. Give children time to experiment on their own to discover the idea that art creations can be three, as well as two dimensional. Add other materials that will create depth in the artwork (foam shapes, craft sticks and stems, pieces of cloth).

Observation/Assessment
Creates three-dimensional art

Other Art Possibilities

- Gadget paint using large nails, bolts, screws, and nuts.
- Create box cars from shoeboxes.
- Grate colored chalk over salt to create colored salt. Layer in baby food jars.

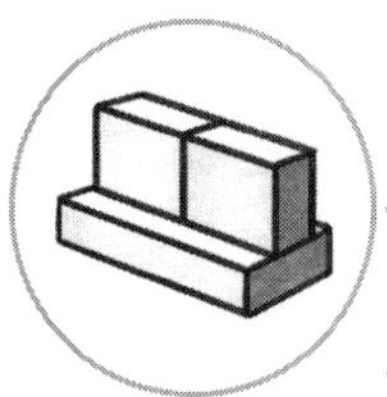

BLOCKS/CONSTRUCTION POSSIBILITIES

Mini-pendulum

Materials
three long unit blocks • a Styrofoam ball 2" or 3" in diameter • yarn • dominoes

Teacher Talk
"You have built a creation with dominoes." "Do you plan to knock your creation down with the pendulum?"

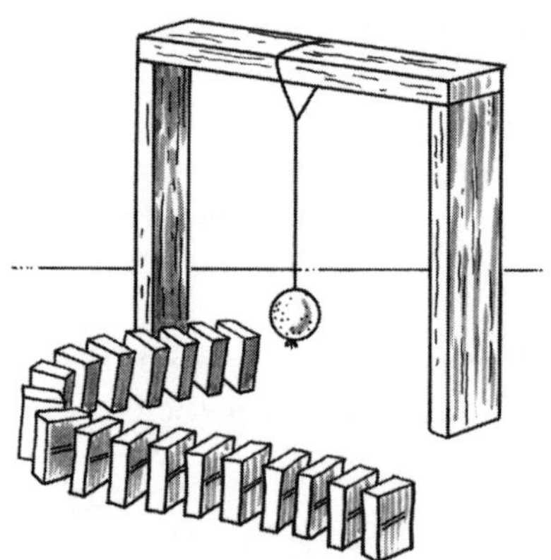

Instructions
Create an arch with three long unit blocks. Make a hole through the middle of the Styrofoam ball. Insert and tie the yarn. Then tie the other end of the yarn to the unit block that will bridge the tops of the other

two blocks. The ball should be low enough to knock down the dominoes. When the pendulum bridge and dominoes are knocked down, children can rebuild them on their own.

Observation/Assessment
Rebuilds block constructions after knocking them down

Brick Building

Materials
novelty paper with different appearances (bricks, blocks, stones, siding) • unit blocks • architectural blocks • tape • books, such as *Block City* by Robert Lewis Stevenson

Teacher Talk
"What building materials will you use for the porch?"

Instructions
Provide paper with different exterior appearances (available from school supply stores) or make your own by cutting it from magazines or drawing the different materials. Cover blocks with the paper by wrapping them like a present. Cover the blocks completely with clear packing tape to increase durability. Put the materials blocks and architectural blocks (windows, arches, doors, columns) in the block area. Provide housing magazines to give children construction ideas.

Extension Possibilities: Provide a large piece of poster board for each child to build houses on. Label the constructions. Have a Parade of Homes when the houses are complete. Invite families to view the houses.

Other Blocks/Construction Possibilities

- Add construction vehicles and make signs to add to blocks.
- Show children how to draw shapes and then build on them.
- Provide vehicles and people figures for building a construction site.
- Make an outdoor pendulum for children to explore.

SCIENCE/DISCOVERY POSSIBILITIES

What's Inside?

Materials

broken small appliances such as radios, telephone answering machines, keyboards, adding machine • magnifying glasses • safety glasses • screwdrivers • pliers • art trays

Teacher Talk

"What did you find inside the telephone?" Talk with children about exploring the insides of appliances safely.

Instructions

Provide a variety of broken appliances. You may want to assist children in getting inside the casings of the appliances. Discuss what children find inside. Sort the pieces of the appliances into categories on trays or paper plates.

Helpful Hint: Remove all plugs and sharp objects before letting children explore the appliances. Discuss safety issues, including use of tools, especially screw drivers. Require children to wear safety glasses while they are using the tools. Supervise closely. When appliances are completely disassembled, children can recycle the parts to build their own creations.

Observation/Assessment

Uses tools to take apart appliances

Volcanic Explosion

Materials

tub • playdough • rocks • toy trees • bowl • small scoop • baking soda • vinegar • food coloring

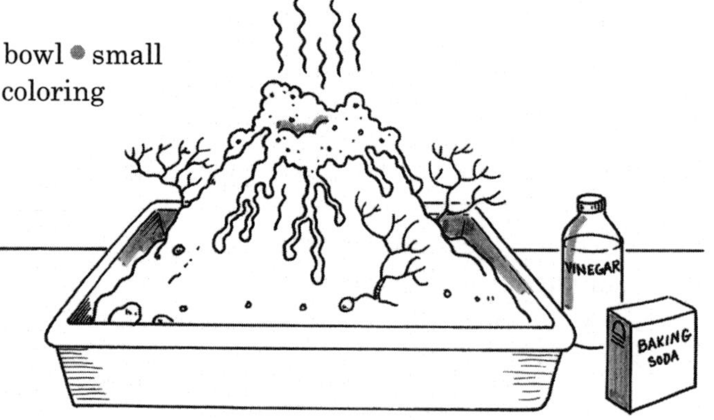

Teacher Talk

"You are putting some rocks and trees on the mountain." "You have noticed that the more baking soda you add, the greater the eruption it makes."

Instructions

Provide the large tub, playdough, rocks, and tree branches, so children can build a mountain in the tub. Dig a hole in the top of the playdough mountain. Add a bowl with a scoop of baking soda in it. Add vinegar to make a volcanic explosion.

Helpful Hint: Make or purchase the playdough. Tint with brown tempera paint or mix all the colors together to make brown. Add food coloring to the vinegar to make the eruption colorful.

Observation/Assessment
Forms shapes using playdough
Observes and discusses chemical reactions

Other Science/Discovery Possibilities

- Make structures using plaster of Paris.
- Create bricks using clay or mud.
- Make a maze with blocks or dominoes. Use straws to blow ping-pong balls through the maze.

SENSORY POSSIBILITIES

Sanding Wood

Materials
coarse to fine sandpaper • sanding block • various shapes of wood • work gloves • safety goggles

Teacher Talk
"What would you like to sand next?" Talk about the difference in fine and coarse sandpaper.

Instructions
Show children how to attach sandpaper to the sanding block and then use the sanding block to sand wood. Add wood glue and various sizes and shapes of wood, so children can build, sand, and paint their creations.

Observation/Assessment
Uses sandpaper to sand wood
Wears safety glasses when working with wood

Water World

Materials
water table or tub • water • Legos®

Teacher Talk
"How can you connect the two structures to each other?"

Instructions
Add enough water to be able to tell that the Legos are floating. Add various types of Legos to the water, so children can build with the Legos in the water.

Extension Possibilities: Add various other floating objects (such as packing pellets). You may also like to add color to the water or soap to make bubbles.

Observation/Assessment
Builds using Legos®

Build with Textures

Materials
pieces of cloth (fake fur, burlap, velveteen, rayon, felt, corduroy, etc.) • sandpaper • scissors • rubber cement (teacher only) • wooden or cardboard blocks

Teacher Talk
"Can you build something using these blocks?" Talk with children about the various textures.

Instructions
Cut pieces of textured material to fit each side of the block. Apply a coat of rubber cement to the block sides, then another coat to the back of each texture piece. Wait 10 to 20 seconds, or until about dry. Then carefully place the texture pieces on the blocks. Make about 15 to 20 medium or large texture blocks, or 25 to 30 small ones. To restore the blocks later to their original state, tug on the edges of the texture pieces; then pull the fabric off. Use your fingers to rub off any remaining rubber cement.

LITERACY/WRITING POSSIBILITIES

Reading Floor Plans and Blueprints

Materials
floor plans from the home sections of newspapers or home magazines • blueprints • paper • blue pens and pencils

Teacher Talk
"You are looking at the floor plan of a house. Let's see where the bathrooms are." "Can you draw a floor plan of your house?"

Instructions
Place different floor plans and blueprints on the writing table for children to look at and explore. Provide paper and pencils if children want to draw their own plans. Introduce floor plans and blueprints during Group Time.

Extension Possibilities: Provide pictures of the house with the plans. Talk about how it is the same house seen in two different ways. Provide gel pens and black or blue construction paper, so children can draw their own floor plans, blueprints, and houses.

Observation/Assessment
Explores house plans and blueprints
Draws house plans

Construction Bag Books

Materials
pictures of construction sites, vehicles, and buildings • construction paper • zipper-closure plastic bags • yarn or silver rings

Teacher Talk
"Our class books have many different kinds of buildings."

Instructions
Mount pictures on construction paper and cut to fit zipper-closure bags. Punch holes on the side and join pages together using silver rings or yarn. Use the books to discuss how buildings are built. Always include a title page on homemade books. Besides the name of the book, include the date and names of the children who contributed to it.

Observation/Assessment
Turns pages in a book

Other Literacy/Writing Possibilities

- Add construction magazines, real estate flyers and newspaper ads with homes for sale, and catalogs for construction machinery.
- Add a site safety poster to the Literacy/Writing area.
- Add any of the books listed in the Book List on page 465-466.

MATH/MANIPULATIVES POSSIBILITIES

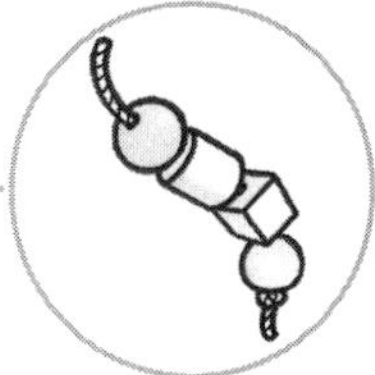

I Can Knock It Down

Materials
variety of blocks and manipulatives such as Wedge-its™, Ringamajigs™, Kapla Building System™, Tree Blocks™, and Lincoln Logs™ • tub of different-size balls

Teacher Talk
"Which blocks knock down the buildings the easiest? Hardest? Why?"

Instructions
Let children use the different blocks to build structures. If they choose, they can then roll balls at their structures to demolish them. Encourage children to come up with a system to communicate when a structure is ready for demolition. This will reduce hurt feelings and the frustration of someone knocking down a building that was not scheduled for demolition.

Extension Possibilities: Test the durability of constructions made of different kinds of blocks. Children build the structures and predict whether the buildings will be partially or completely knocked down. Knock the buildings down, and then chart the results. Complete the activity by discussing the accuracy of the predictions.

Observation/Assessment
Builds using a variety of blocks
Predicts outcomes related to block building

Construction Counting and Measuring

Materials
large nails • large nuts and bolts • cloth measuring tape • clipboard • pencil • wood scraps • folding wooden carpenter's ruler

Teacher Talk
"That board is over three feet long. Let's measure its exact length."

Instructions
Use materials typically found on a construction site to provide children with an opportunity for real, hands-on experiences with counting and measuring. Show children how to use measuring tools. The folding carpenter's ruler must be folded carefully or it will break.

Observation/Assessment
Measures using construction tools
Counts using one-to-one correspondence

Other Math/Manipulatives Possibilities

- Add wooden construction puzzles.
- Add a variety of manipulatives like Ringamajigs™ or Towerifics™ for sorting and building on a smaller scale.
- Talk about the tools that are used for building and describe how they are used.

RHYMES/FINGERPLAYS/SONGS/MUSIC POSSIBILITIES

Block Music

Materials
several sizes and types of blocks (wooden, cardboard, plastic) • tape or CD player • music with variety of beats • large paper • markers • chart paper

Teacher Talk
"That song has a really fast beat!"

Instructions
Gather the different blocks, tape or CD player, and music into one area of the room. Write a list of children's favorite songs on the chart paper and post at children's eye level, and turn on a favorite tape or CD. Sit on the floor and tap two blocks together in time to the music. Ask each child to get two blocks and join you. As the music plays, encourage children to tap out a beat with you. Use the list of favorites to provide a variety of beats. When children are familiar with the activity, invite them to try different ways to make the beat (hitting two different blocks together, patting a block on your hand, tapping blocks on the floor, etc.).

Extension Possibilities: Create beats with natural objects children find outside. They can also hop, walk, and run to the beats you make.

Observation/Assessment
Keeps time to the beat of music

The Dump Truck Song

Teacher Talk
"This song sounds like 'The Wheels on the Bus.'"

Instructions
Teach children "The Dump Truck Song" to the tune of "The Wheels on the Bus."

The Dump Truck Song

The front-end loader fills up the truck,
Fills up the truck, fills up the truck.
The front-end loader fills up the truck,
At the construction site.

The dump truck dumps out the dirt,
Dumps out the dirt, dumps out the dirt.
The dump truck dumps out the dirt,
At the construction site.

The driver of the dump truck waves hello,
Waves hello, waves hello.
The driver of the dump truck waves hello,
At the construction site.

Helpful Hint: List favorite songs and their words on chart paper and hang on the wall. Point to the song when you introduce it and to the words as you sing it.

Other Rhymes/Fingerplays/Songs/Music Possibilities

- Consider any of the following recorded selections:
  - "Circle of Friends" from *Circle of Friends* by Parachute Express
  - "Dumptruck Song" from *Children's Favorites Volume 2* by Disney
  - "That's What Friends Are For" from *Adventures with Family and Friends* by Joanie Bartels
  - "London Bridge" from *Elephant Show Record* by Sharon, Lois, and Bram
  - "The Three Little Pigs" from *Minneapolis Concert* by Bok, Muir, and Trickett
- Sing "Johnny Works with One Hammer."

GROUP TIME POSSIBILITIES

Thingamajig: Collect materials for each child in your group (bubble blower, scarf, bowl, spoon, fork, boa, straw, rubber band, paper clips, blocks, etc.). Give one object to each child. Ask children to look at the objects and think of another way they could use them. Demonstrate with your object. Give each child a chance to share her idea about another way to use the object. Accept children's answers without evaluating them. This is a creative, open-ended activity. Use children's responses to each other's ideas to facilitate a discussion about how the group's reaction made children feel.

Things that Build Other Things: Ask children to look around the room and find things that help us make other things. After children gather objects and return to the group, they can each tell the name of the object and how it helps her create.

Construction Site Safety: Glue pictures of constructions workers, construction sites, heavy machines (truck, bulldozer, cement trucks), hard hats, gloves, boots, and goggles onto a very large piece of art paper. Talk with children about how construction sites are not safe places for children. Talk about why construction workers wear safety gear. Share a construction site safety chart and interpret the symbols.

Other Group Time Possibilities

- Read any of the books from the Book List (see page 465-466).
- Discuss things that children tear or cut up to make other things in the classroom.
- Make a list of safety rules that will apply to classroom construction projects. Post the list near the Blocks/Construction area.

Big Boxes for Building

Materials
big boxes of different sizes

Teacher Talk
"You are trying to figure out how to stack these boxes to make your building. Maybe you can ask a friend to help you."

Instructions
Collect different appliance and supplies boxes. Tape up some of the boxes closed with packing tape and leave the rest of the boxes open. Put them all on the playground and watch children cooperate to create constructions.

Helpful Hint: Collect boxes from furniture stores, grocery stores, or from family members.

Extension Possibilities: After children have built their creations, provide paints and brushes to add details.

Observation/Assessment
Builds using big boxes

Other Movement/Outdoor Possibilities

- Add large vehicles to the sandbox for making a construction site.
- Add construction logos to riding toys; add traffic signs.
- Use large paintbrushes, paint trays, and water to paint a wall or fence.
- Build a community using waffle blocks outside.

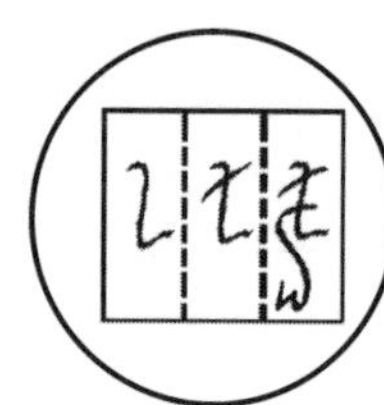

PROJECTS/DOCUMENTATION POSSIBILITIES

Box City

Materials
small boxes • tabletop size piece of thick cardboard • construction paper • scissors • glue • twigs and branches • toy vehicles

Teacher Talk
"We are creating a community." "Where should the fire station go?"

Instructions
Provide materials for children to create a city using small boxes. Start with a planning stage where children have ideas about what should be in the community. Then discuss where different buildings might be located. Children can create a building on their own and then add it to the box city or build buildings together. Label the different buildings (hospital, courthouse, school) and add the names of children's who contributed to the construction. The cardboard makes it possible to work on the box city and then move it to a protected area when the table is being used for something else.

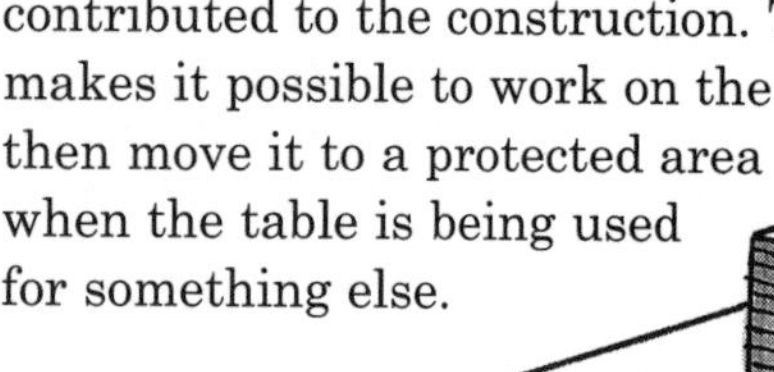

Extension Possibilities:
When the box city is complete, invite parents and family members to come see it. Take photographs to document the project.

Observation/Assessment
Cooperates with classmates to reach a goal

Outdoor Box City

Materials
large boxes • packing tape • coarse sandpaper • box cutter (teacher only) • paint • brushes • scissors • markers • duct tape • books, such as *Harry the Dirty Dog* by Gene Zion

Teacher Talk
"We'll have lots of fun playing in the big boxes." "What color will you paint the store?"

Instructions
Collect large boxes. Remove staples and cover any rough edges with duct tape or sand them smooth with coarse sandpaper. Use the box cutter to add lots of doors and windows (teacher only) so you can maintain visual supervision of children. Children can paint and draw on the boxes.

Extension Possibilities: Arrange buildings around the bike path to increase play possibilities with riding toys.

Observation/Assessment
Paints and draws on large surfaces

FIELD TRIP POSSIBILITIES

Construction Site: Observe a construction site from a safe observation point.

Construction or Demolition Company Office: Plan a field trip to a construction company or demolition company. Ask the owner or a project manager to talk with children about the process of building up or tearing down.

Engineering Firm: Plan a field trip to an engineering firm. Request that someone show children how plans can be made manually or on a computer.

SNACK POSSIBILITIES

Snack in a Bag: Provide children's snacks in individual brown bags, so they can eat at the construction site.

Construction Sandwiches: Provide materials, so children can build their own sandwiches. Provide a board or balance beam, so children can eat their sandwiches on the job (after handwashing, of course).

Graham Cracker Structures: Provide graham cracker sections, jelly, and peanut butter, so children can make structures for snack. Start with a cracker and spread it with a combination of jelly and peanut butter; add another cracker and spread it, too. Continue building until the snack is several stories high. Eat the "buildings"!

FAMILY PARTICIPATION POSSIBILITIES

Building Visitors: Ask a parent or family member in the building trades to visit the school to talk with children about building up or tearing down. If possible, ask the person to bring something he or she uses on the job.

Dream Junk House: Ask children to work with their own family to build a house. The house can be made out of anything (drawing, craft sticks, cereal boxes, plaster, etc.). Provide plenty of time to complete the house. Invite families to come to school to share their buildings.

Creating Meaningful Play with Recycled Materials

Families want to give children what is best for them. While many parents are tempted to think that the latest new toy on the market is the best choice, children often respond just as well or better to found or discarded items used in a new way. In addition, using recycled materials communicates to children that they can make creative choices about how to use materials.

Recycled materials make great art supplies. Save magazines for your child to cut pictures out of, computer paper that has a blank back side, packing pellets, tissue paper used in gift wrap, old bows and ribbons, and even discarded costume jewelry and buttons. These materials are perfect for creating cards for relatives, pictures to hang on the wall or refrigerator, or even a centerpiece for the table.

Boxes work well for art projects. Your child can decorate a small box by using markers, gluing on colored paper, or attaching pieces of cloth from discarded clothing. This box can be a place for your child's keepsakes. Larger boxes make great playhouses. Remove all staples, reinforce with tape, and eliminate all rough edges by sanding with coarse sandpaper. Don't forget to add doors and windows. Playhouses can be used inside (especially welcome on rainy days) or outside for play and creativity. Encourage your child to personalize the playhouse by adding your family name, flowers, and other decorations.

Plastic bottles can be used in a variety of ways. They make great pins for bowling using an inflated ball. Large bottles can be cut in two and used as planters, terrariums, or sand toys. Fill smaller bottles with glitter and a small object like a bead, and then fill to the top with cooking oil. Tape and glue the top securely on the bottle. Your child can manipulate the bottle to track the object. Make rhythm instruments by adding sand, beans, or bells to plastic bottles. Always tape and glue the top on securely.

The key to using found and discarded items is being open to the limitless possibilities and the imagination of your child. Think of the difference between a child having a toy car that is always a car and having a box that can be a house, a car, a truck, a train, a step, and so on. It is the open-ended nature of these items that makes them better than many bought toys, and a great way for your child to learn.

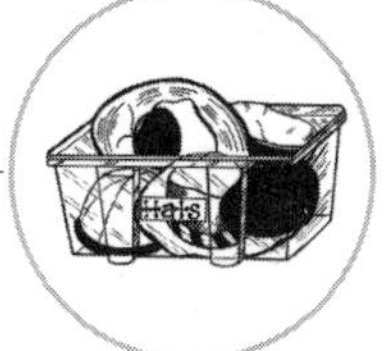

Prop Boxes

Construction Site Prop Box
toy tools • tool boxes • carpenter aprons • lunch boxes with toy sandwiches • plastic thermos • hard hats • toy electrical tools • paintbrush • rollers • pencils • paper • floor foam blocks • wooden hollow blocks • blueprints • books about construction

Construction/Demolition Company Office Prop Box
computer • calculator • phones • paper • printer • notebooks • clipboards • pencils • envelopes • letterhead • pens • stapler • mail • construction catalogs • telephone books • project board (chart, blackboard, or whiteboard) • eraser • calendar • file folders • books and magazines about construction and demolition

Engineering Firm Prop Box
computer • printer • drawing table • floor plans • blueprints • telephone • telephone book • old Daytimer • old palmtop organizer • project board • rolodex • stapler • file folders • clipboards • engineering magazines • business cards • statements • letterhead • pens • pencils • paper • stapler • paper clips • books and magazines about engineering • suits • ties • dress shoes • golf shirts • briefcase • purses

Books

26 Letters and 99 Cents by Tana Hoban
Alphabet Under Construction by Denise Fleming
B Is for Bulldozer: A Construction ABC by June Sobel
Big Red Barn by Margaret Wise Brown
Block City by Robert Louis Stevenson
Bridges by Susan Canizares
Building a House by Byron Barton
Cathedral: The Story of Its Construction by David Macaulay
City: A Story of Roman Planning and Construction by David Macaulay
Construction Trucks by Betsy Imershein
Diggers and Dump Trucks by Angela Royston
DK Readers: Jobs People Do: A Day of the Life of a Builder by Linda Hayward
DK Readers: Big Machines by Karen Wallace
Earthquakes by Seymour Simon
Fairy Houses by Tracy Kane
The Fire Station by Robert Munsch
First Aid by Susan Canizares
Get to Work, Trucks by Don Carter
Goldilocks and the Three Bears by James Marshall
Harry the Dirty Dog by Gene Zion
Here are My Hands by Bill Martin, Jr.
Houses and Homes by Ann Morris
I Have a Cold by Grace MacCarone
In My House by Susan Hood

The Little House by Virginia Burton
Make Way for Ducklings by Robert McCloskey
The Napping House by Audrey Wood
Pyramid by David Macaulay
The Shape of Things by Dayle Ann Dodds
Storms by Seymour Simon
Ten Black Dots by Donald Crews
This Is the House that Jack Built by Pam Adams
The Three Pigs by David Wiesner
Tornadoes by Seymour Simon
Underground by David Macaulay
Volcanoes by Seymour Simon
The Wheels on the Bus by Maryann Kovalski
Where the Wild Things Are by Maurice Sendak
Whistle for Willie by Ezra Jack Keats

Observation/Assessment

Takes on various roles in dramatic play, page 450
Uses props to enhance dramatic play, page 450
Follows simple directions, page 451
Creates three-dimensional art, page 452
Rebuilds block constructions after knocking them down, page 453
Uses tools to take apart appliances, page 454
Forms shapes using playdough, page 455
Observes and discusses chemical reaction, page 455
Uses sandpaper to sand wood, page 455
Wears safety glasses when working with wood, page 455
Builds using Legos™, page 456
Explores house plans and blueprints, page 457
Draws house plans, page 457
Turns pages in a book, page 457
Builds using a variety of blocks, page 458
Predicts outcomes related to block building, page 458
Measures using construction tools, page 458
Counts using one-to-one correspondence, page 458
Keeps time to the beat of music, page 459
Builds using big boxes, page 461
Cooperates with classmates to reach a goal, page 462
Paints and draws on large surfaces, page 463

Picture File/Vocabulary

beam
blueprints
chemical reaction
crane
demolition
dump truck
fine
floor plans
front end loader
salvage
scale
sky scraper
tools
wood
wrecking ball

Concepts Learned in

Building Up and Tearing Down

Content Knowledge

- ☐ Blueprints and house plans are drawn to scale.
- ☐ Blueprints are plans to help people build.
- ☐ I can find my house on a map.
- ☐ I can find my city on a county and state map.
- ☐ People build using different tools and materials.
- ☐ Demolition is when something is torn down.
- ☐ Recycling is when something is used again.
- ☐ Construction vehicles can be very big.
- ☐ Safety is important at a construction site.

Process Knowledge

- ☐ I can sort and recycle.
- ☐ I can build using blocks and boxes.
- ☐ I can create three-dimensional structures.
- ☐ I can build a replica of a community.
- ☐ I can cooperate with classmates to reach a goal.
- ☐ I can keep time to music.
- ☐ I can build using Legos®.
- ☐ I wear safety glasses when I work.
- ☐ I can use simple tools.
- ☐ I can create using various art media.

Pre-academic Skills

- ☐ I know my colors.
- ☐ I can count using one-to-one correspondence.
- ☐ I can read a house plan.
- ☐ I can predict what will happen.
- ☐ I can plan before I begin an activity.
- ☐ I can solve problems.
- ☐ I can measure using rulers and measuring tape.
- ☐ I can form letters.

CHAPTER 7

Expressing Feelings with Parents, Teachers, and Friends

INNOVATIONS IN CARE AND EARLY EDUCATION

Emotional Development

Throughout the ***Innovations*** series, the value of enduring, close, reciprocal, and synchronous relationships is viewed as crucial to all early development, not just emotional development, but also physical, social, and intellectual development. How do these kinds of relationships develop? What can teachers do to develop and maintain relationships that support children's continued development?

Relationships and Emotional Development

Interactional experience is responsible for shaping how relationships are co-constructed by children and adults. If the nature of the relationship has certain positive characteristics, it is likely to lead to positive emotional relationships. If the nature of the relationship has certain negative characteristics, the relationship may lead to a disruption in the relationship-forming process.

There is agreement in the field of care and early education about the characteristics of the relationships that foster optimal growth and development (Howes, 2000; Shonkoff & Phillips, 2000). The characteristics include:

- Contingent, dependable responses from reliable adults,
- Warm, nurturing, affectionate, loving interactions,
- Sensitivity to cues by caregivers, including gestural, non-verbal, and verbal cues,
- Reciprocal, mutual interest in each other,
- Synchronous, perceptive, and insightful interactive styles with a goodness of fit between the child's style and temperament and the caregivers' styles, preferences, and temperaments,
- Protective, caring support,
- Dependable, stable, abiding, recursive availability, and
- Predictable, consistent, believable responses from caregivers.

Characteristics of relationships that may not foster optimal growth and development include:

- The presence of maternal depression,
- Abusive or neglectful parenting behaviors,

- Institutionalization of the child,
- Disrupted patterns of interactions,
- Lack of emotional availability,
- Coercive parenting techniques,
- Asynchrony in interactive styles, and
- Socioeconomic, relational, and societal stresses, such as poverty, malnutrition, lack of medical care, limited family support, marital discord, and so forth.

Parents and Others

The security of attachment between parents or primary caregivers and children influences emotional development more than the relationships children have with other adults and peers in their attachment networks. However, children can develop close relationships with more than one adult. Having a few caring adults who are emotionally dedicated to the child may, in fact, prepare children to deal with the complex world of relationships and people in the broader social context (Howes, 2000). So, while emotional development benefits from secure attachment relationships with parents, having several selective attachments to extended family members and teachers can be beneficial as well.

Five Characteristics of Interpersonal Relationships that Foster Children's Emotional Well-being and Psychological Resilience

1. Collaborative communication
2. Reflective dialogue
3. Repairing disruptions in communication
4. Coherent narratives
5. Emotional communication

Siegel (1999) proposes five characteristics of interpersonal relationships that foster emotional well-being and psychological resilience in young children. The first characteristic is collaboration. The ability to develop and maintain collaborative communication and perfect non-verbal communications forms the foundation of reciprocal relationships. Reading non-verbal communication, interpreting the difference between needing nourishment and needing social contact, and anticipating what children might need so they don't have to wait, are all examples of collaborative communication for adults. An example of collaborative communication is when children read the verbal and non-verbal cues that Mom, Dad, or teacher is going to get them a cup of juice right after he or she finishes folding the laundry and they then find something to do while they wait for their juice. The result is an interpersonal closeness where each individual feels the other can understand his or her emotional point of view.

The second characteristic of interpersonal relationships is reflective dialogue. When parents and teachers understand the "states of mind" or internal experiences of the child, they are able to put into words the emotions, thoughts, intentions, and memories of the child. When children learn that these emotional states can be communicated and understood, they are able to share conversations with their caregivers and teachers, non-verbally at first, and then verbally. Communication then begins to go both ways, with the child learning to understand the emotions and intentions of important adults. When both members of the relationship are involved in reflective dialogues, supporting emotional experiences becomes the focus of the relationship.

Examples of reflective dialogues for adults include telling the child that you know he is hungry and that you are getting lunch out as quickly as you can, and naming and describing emotions that are being expressed to help the child get in touch with the way he is feeling. For children, reflective dialogues are often expressed emotions—crying, screaming, withdrawing, or being aggressive. Learning to communicate specific emotional states and having important adults understand how the child feels is a reflective dialogue that helps children understand they have communicated and been understood.

The third characteristic is repair. Disruptions in communication are just as common as collaborative communication in the early stages of emotional development. The ability of the adult to repair these disruptions reconnects the child to significant adults. Reconnections help children understand that life is filled with misunderstandings and disconnections, and that these can be fixed. To be able to repair disconnections, adults must be comfortable with children's intense emotional states. They must regain control over their own emotions quickly enough to reconnect before damage or negative effects are caused. Reconnecting every few minutes with a child whose crying won't stop, to remind him or her that you are still there; accepting the ambivalence of a child who has just recovered from an upsetting situation and wants to reconnect, but is still too angry; and accepting that clinging may relieve anxiety in new situations are examples of repair at work.

The fourth characteristic is coherent narratives. "Adults can teach children about the world of self and others by joining with them in the co-construction of stories about life events" (Siegel, 1999, p. 51). Talking about the past, the present, and the future creates shared stories that help children make sense of their experiences. When teachers, family members, and children tell their own emotional stories to each other, shared meaning is created for feelings.

Adults who tell stories about "when I was a baby" or "when I was your age" are creating narratives. Narratives are also created when adults express their inadequacies and fears ("I don't know what to try next!" or "I wish I could help you calm down and go to sleep."). When children share their own narratives, they add an insight and understanding that they are not alone in the way that they feel.

The fifth characteristic is emotional communication. Adults in close relationships with children amplify and share life experiences with the child—creating moments of heightened awareness that lead to a positive view of self and others. By emphasizing some experiences, and not others, adults help children live in an emotional environment without being overwhelmed by all that is happening in it. Staying connected to the child emotionally when negative or uncomfortable emotions are present and when soothing intense or negative emotional states are examples. This means being emotionally available to the child even when one's own intense emotions make him or her want to move away from the child.

Emotional Expression and Regulation

Emotional development in the preschool years focuses on two primary areas—emotion expression and emotions regulation (Berk, 2001). By the third year of life, children experience and express a wide range of emotions even if they are able to identify and label only some of them. The challenge of the preschool years is to learn to regulate intense emotions to be able to function in family, school, and community settings.

Greenspan (1997) describes this stage of emotional development as creating an internal world. An expanding sense of self helps children move from "being" the way they feel—acting on the emotions physically—to symbolically representing the way they feel. The ability to symbolically represent emotions allows children to use the emotional idea of anger to replace the physical manifestation of anger. In other words, the image of physically being angry is represented by an emotional thought of being angry.

This stage is characterized by images, ideas, and symbols. It is the beginning of the creation of an inner picture of the interactive world. This transition from the behavior as "being" to symbols and ideas as "being" is one of the significant accomplishments of the preschool years. It is made as children gain experience in creating symbolic images in their minds that are then used to explain to others what they need, want, and think.

Next, children begin to think emotionally. Emotional thinking is forming connections between one's own thoughts and ideas and the thoughts and ideas of others. Children now connect the reasons for the behavior to the emotional meaning that explains it. For example, when a child says, "No!" to a doll while playing in Dramatic Possibilities, he can tell you that he said it because the doll did something the child did not like or did not want the doll to do. This ability to understand that what you do now relates to what will happen to you in the future leads to emotional regulation based on the consequences of what might happen.

In addition to a stage theory of emotional development, Greenspan offers another important idea. He proposes that all intelligence is emotional, that is, each intellectual skill or ability is first organized by the emotional interaction that accompanies it. The emotional interaction or reaction creates the ability to apply that cognitive skill or ability to the interactive world. Intellect and emotion are integrated, not separated. Greenspan views emotions as the "architects, conductors, and organizers of the mind" (Greenspan, 1999, p. 9). Without the emotional connection, individual skills within domains cannot be accessed and applied.

Moral Development

Moral development is also a developmental process. Children's morality starts out being externally controlled by adults, then gradually moves toward self-control by a set of inner standards that apply to behavior and interaction. During the preschool years, children are developing an understanding of the standards and rules of the social world as they learn to understand the feelings of others (Buzzelli, 1992).

Children construct and reconstruct their knowledge of morality through interactions. They think about social rules (do this but not that), learn the conventions of social behavior (be quiet here but not there), and attempt to comply with the standards they adopt in their social interactions (friends don't hurt friends). Children learn these standards as their actions and behavior are approved and disapproved by important adults and peers and from emerging feelings of mastery of skills, particularly cognitive and language skills.

As children's social skills grow, so do their abilities to understand the feelings and emotions of other children and adults around them. Insight into how others feel comes from many experiences with seeing and processing the impact of one's behavior on others. From the security of a trusting and loving relationship, children share experiences about keeping and breaking rules and standards of the social world while adults teach the impact of their actions on others. This process creates a conflict for children as they get a clear picture of what is seen as appropriate and what is not. The emotions that are experienced as a result of compliance or transgression result in progress toward internalization of the expressed standards for behavior.

Children also come to understand the social world by adopting the social rules of their family, school, and cultural groups. These rules relate not to "right" or "wrong" behavior but to appropriate and inappropriate behavior in specific social settings, such as not interrupting someone who is speaking or waiting until everyone is at the table to start eating dinner. Over time, children come to understand, for example, that they can have only one serving of snack at the self-service snack center until after everyone has had an opportunity to have snack. Then children who want more can have seconds.

Coming to understand what is culturally and socially acceptable is a developmental process. The ability to access and use the understanding is influenced by the ability to regulate the emotions that accompany situations where appropriate behavior must be used. During the preschool years, children make great strides in understanding the standards and rules of the social world. This understanding is part of the moral developmental process.

Self-regulation and the Internalization of Self-control

Self-regulation begins with the process of communicating needs and wants to others, then proceeds to developing the capacity to regulate emotions, attention, and behavior. The early childhood years are characterized by increasing capacities for self-regulation. Teachers see the progress in self-regulation as children become more able to function independently in the classroom without direct adult support.

Shonkoff and Phillips (2000) consider self-regulation "a cornerstone of early childhood development that cuts across all domains of behavior" (p.3). Early in infancy, self-regulation focuses on sleeping, eating, crying, and communicating needs and wants to significant others. During the preschool years, children begin to connect their own emotions to the emotional responses of others and to predict how others might feel. These highly interrelated dimensions of self-regulation influence each other and children's success in achieving the competencies needed to manage independently. Competent regulatory functioning predicts later social competence. It is also related to success in school and self-control during adolescence (Brunson, 2000).

Greenspan (1997) cites increasing evidence from neuroscience for the connection between emotions and cognition. Once viewed as separate and different, cognition and emotions are now considered as interdependent. As children gain control over their emotions, they are increasingly able to focus their attention and behavior. The reverse of this is also true. If children can't manage their emotions well enough to focus their attention and behavior, they are less likely to be able to benefit from external stimulation of cognitive capacities or teaching from others.

Vygotsky emphasized the role of language in the development of self-regulation. As children learn to communicate thoughts, needs, and intentions through language, they increase their ability to self-regulate. Language serves as a shared experience to give meaning to children's self-regulatory efforts. As children listen to what others say about their behavior, they modify and adjust their behaviors, incorporating what others say into their self-regulation (Mooney, 2000).

Information-processing theories propose that children learn to engage in more organized, efficient, and effective cognitive processes as they develop "executive functions" that control action. Executive function is a term used to describe a collection of interdependent cognitive and attention skills that are necessary for purposeful, goal-directed activity (Shonkoff & Phillips, 2000). These include the ability to self-regulate, sequence behavior, control impulses, delay gratification, and plan and organize behavior.

The skills that lay the foundation for executive function usually begin to emerge around age three. Three important skills that lead to executive function have been identified. The first is orienting to relevant and important features of the environment while screening out the irrelevant ones. This means choosing the right features of the environment to attend to and ignoring unimportant features. Then, the child needs to be able to anticipate accurately what might happen next.

The second skill is being able to plan and implement goal-directed behavior. In order to plan and implement, children must be able to think about how they might make their desires happen. As they visualize the intent of their ideas, symbolic representations impact what they choose to do and how they choose to do it.

The third executive function skill is self-control. Self-control is the ability to comply with external expectations, often involving delaying gratification or controlling impulses. Preschool children often struggle to exercise self-control. For this reason, we will explore this component of self-regulation further.

The Internalization of Self-control

The third skill related to executive function is of particular interest to preschool teachers. Gaining self-control means that children are making progress in self-regulation and are beginning to understand and adopt the expectations of others for their behavior. Often considered a guidance and discipline issue, gaining self-control is actually a developmental task just like learning to skip or jump.

A continuum helps explain the process of how self-control moves from external control, to adult-assisted self-control, to independent self-control. At each point on the continuum, self-control is supported or influenced by

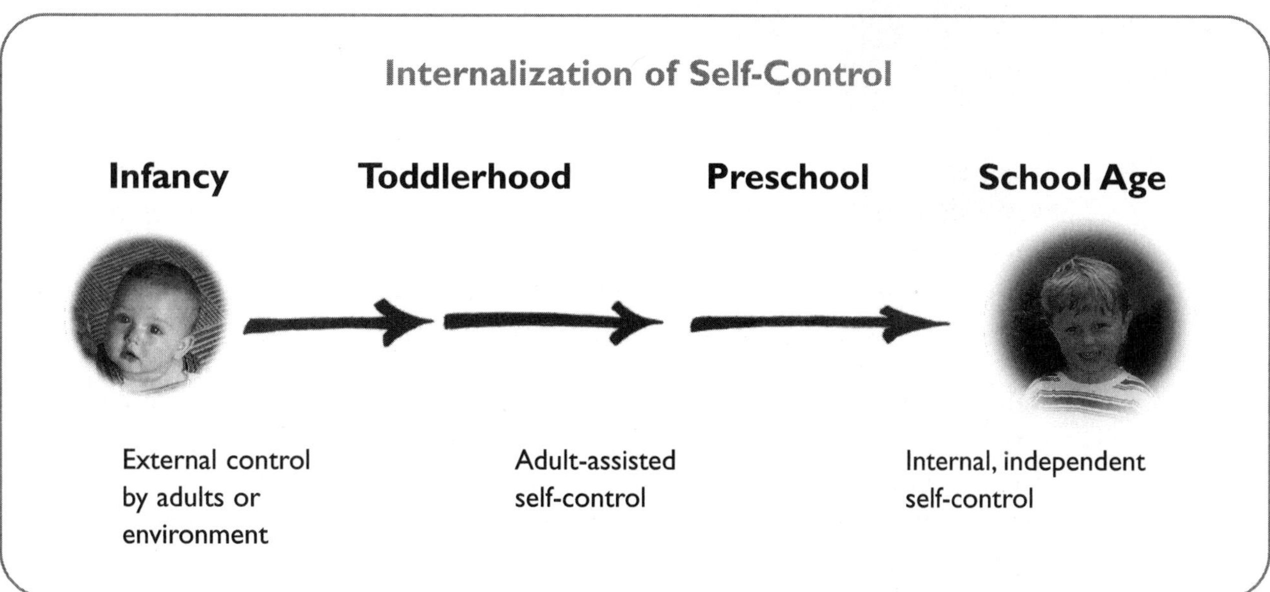

important adults in the child's family and school and the context of their relationships with the child. Self-control begins outside the child and then moves inside the child through the process of internalization.

Precursor Skills Support the Internalization of Self-control

Some skills are too advanced for children to learn directly. When children need additional growth and development to acquire skills, educators often identify the tendencies that develop in advance of these skills. These precursor skills indicate that the child is approaching or learning the sub-skills or tendencies that come before the actual skill. For example, sharing is often thought by adults to be a positive social skill. But, before children can demonstrate the relatively sophisticated skill of sharing, they must be able to demonstrate skills that will lead to sharing, such as taking turns or dividing resources. Taking turns and dividing resources come before, and lead to, the ability to share.

In order to gain self-control, children need to learn four key precursor skills:

- To control emotional and physical impulses
- To tolerate frustration
- To delay gratification
- To make and implement plans

Controlling emotional and physical impulses is difficult for young children. As with so many other developmental tasks, this one is learned within the context of important relationships with adults. Positive adult relationships scaffold children's emotional and physical responses, guiding how they respond by encouraging them to hold in their minds a symbolic representation of what they want to happen.

Tolerating frustration is also difficult for children. Children feel frustration when there is a discrepancy between what they want and what they get. Many parts of growing up are frustrating. Sometimes the frustration comes from not having the necessary skills needed (such as wanting to make the bicycle go but not understanding how to do so), and sometimes frustration comes from wanting something you know you can't have (such as a cookie before dinner). Either way, tolerating these experiences is necessary to the emerging self-control process.

Delaying gratification means postponing participation in a pleasurable activity or experience or delaying getting what you want. Egocentrism in young children makes them want almost everything now, as soon as it occurs to them. By learning to delay gratification, children learn that they can experience and recover from not getting what they want and that life goes on in the process.

A final precursor skill to self-control is the ability to make and implement a plan to get what the child wants or to solve a problem. The ability to make a plan shows a giant leap in understanding of the social and physical world. Plan making involves thinking of ways to make things happen and then implementing the plan. As children learn that there are ways to get what you want if you can control impulses long enough to make a plan, tolerate the frustration of waiting for the plan to work, and delay gratification while the plan is implemented, their emotional and social worlds become less conflicted and more satisfying.

As children develop these four behaviors, the number of meltdowns, tantrums, and conflicts diminishes. But this success is not guaranteed. It takes time and support from adults to practice and perfect these skills. Typically, children are able voluntarily to use these skills in multiple situations as they approach the end of the third year (Vaughan, Kopp, & Krakow, 1984).

Aggression

Aggression between and among children in school gets frequent media coverage. To be able to help children learn to manage aggression, it is important to understand what aggression is and how children learn to manage it.

Kinds of Aggression

Aggression is defined as any behavior that injures or diminishes a person or thing or damages or destroys property. All aggression is not the same. There are three different types (Marion, 1999). Accidental aggression occurs during the process of sensory exploration, play, or interactions. It is not intended to hurt others. Children often bump into each other, knock over play materials, crawl over hands, and accidentally run into each other as they play. When these acts are not intentional, they are called accidental aggression.

Instrumental aggression is aggression aimed at getting something you want, such as a toy or a particular experience. Typically, instrumental aggression has no deliberate intent to hurt the other person. For example, when one child pushes another out of a favorite caregiver's lap, he is not really intending to hurt the other child; he is intending to take his place in the caregiver's lap.

Hostile aggression is aggression that is intended to harm another person. There are usually two types: overt aggression and relational aggression. Overt aggression is physical aggression that is intentional. The child who wants a toy, bites or hits the child who has it so he will drop it, and then runs away to play with the toy, is exhibiting overt aggression. It is this type of aggression that seems to bother teachers the most. Overt aggression seems deliberate, focused, and intentional. Although research shows that overt aggression peaks between two and three years of age and declines during the preschool years (Shonkoff & Phillips, 2000), preschool teachers are still very concerned about it. Overt aggression declines as children acquire the ability to use language to solve problems, the ability to think about and symbolize what might happen, and the ability to delay gratification.

Relational aggression is designed to modify relationships between peers or between children and adults. Relational aggression occurs as children gain an understanding of other children's motivations and discover that they are often in conflict with their own motivation (Berk, 1999). Children use relational aggression when they call their friends mean names or attempt to exclude them from play. Relational aggression is common in the early preschool years. For example, when one child tells other children they can't come to his birthday party, he is using relational aggression to change the play relationships between himself and his playmates.

How Aggression Develops

Theories of how aggression develops focus on the influences of the family, peers, society, and the media. These ideas come from ecological systems theory (Bronfenbrenner, 1979, see pages 124-125), which looks at children in the context of the systems that impact their growth and development.

The family is one of the most important systems that influence children's growth and development, and therefore, their behavior. Aggression develops within families when children are exposed to violent and aggressive behaviors and see solutions to problems addressed in aggressive ways. Then, children model the behaviors they see in the context of the family to solve their own interactive problems.

Families learn many of their behaviors for coping from the context of the culture, community, and the society in which they live. When a culture or community accepts violent behaviors as normal, aggressive behaviors are likely to increase. As families accept the norms of the culture and community, they pass on what they have learned to their children. So, cultural behavior that allows or encourages aggressive solutions to problems will teach children to solve problems aggressively.

Peers also influence aggression. When peers have similar experiences with aggressive behaviors, they use the aggressive behaviors that they have observed to work out problems in the context of their friendships. As peers use aggressive behaviors to solve problems, children's responses are reinforced and become patterns for responding.

Children also learn aggressive behaviors from observing them in broadcast, print, and video media (Levin, 1998). Young children are not good at distinguishing fantasy from reality or at making logical causal connections. They focus on one aspect of a situation at a time. As a result, the many acts of violence and aggression in cartoons, commercials, and video and television programming can have a profound influence on them. Children learn from these sources that fighting is an acceptable way to solve problems, that conflict is normal, that violence is fun and exciting, and that the world is a dangerous place, so fighting is necessary. None of these lessons matches most children's real situations.

Some Aggression Is Normal

For most children, some aggression is normal—a byproduct of growing, becoming in control of and responsible for one's behavior, and of being in a group of peers at school. Children construct their knowledge about how to respond to aggression as well as what to do when aggression doesn't work for them by watching others. Both are part of learning to interact with peers and siblings.

Continuum of Aggression—As children grow, they usually go through a continuum of aggressive behaviors in the process of constructing their knowledge of how aggression works or doesn't work (see graphic on next page). At one end of the continuum is indiscriminant aggression—aggressive responses that are directed at everyone and everything in the child's environment, both people and things. Then, children usually direct their aggressive behaviors at others—adults and peers with whom they share the interactive world. The next point on the continuum is aggression that is limited to things—the toys and the environment. Finally, children learn to control their aggressive behavior and substitute words and language as the means of expressing aggression.

At each point on this continuum, children can learn or be taught other strategies to cope with and solve their problems. Learning non-aggressive strategies and being taught problem-solving strategies to address problems can lead children to replace aggression with more appropriate and more acceptable behaviors and strategies.

Continuum of Aggression

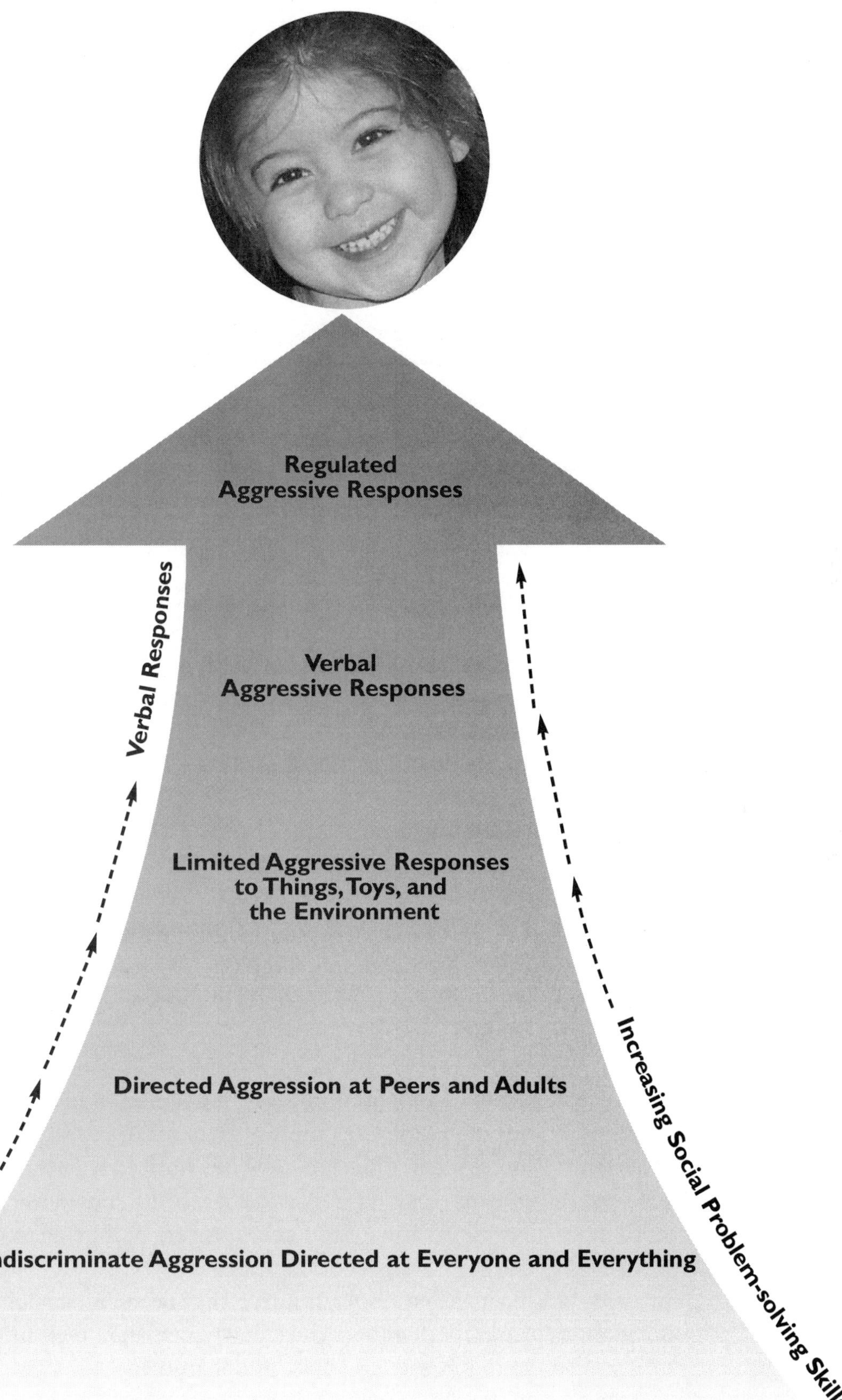

Child Abuse Prevention

The safety and well being of the children in care and early education programs are of foremost concern. Teachers are required by federal law and the Code of Ethical Conduct and Statement of Commitment (1999) to report any suspected child abuse, regardless of who is suspect or where the abuse may have occurred. The teacher, school principal, or program director does not determine whether actual abuse has occurred. It is the responsibility of the appropriate regulatory agency, usually the department of human services, to investigate the allegation and make a judgment.

Documentation of Suspected Abuse

The best way to assure thorough and accurate documentation of suspected child abuse is to have a system for anecdotally recording data on each child in the classroom on a regular basis. The Communication Log (see Appendix page 612) or Anecdotal Record (see Appendix page 610) can serve this purpose. Record any and all information related to the child as you notice it.

For example, if a child arrives in your classroom with a scratch or bump on his cheek, a quick note of the date, time, and description of the scratch is recorded under the teacher comments section or on an anecdotal record. Facts, not opinions, are recorded. Note the following example.

Jason arrived at the center at 7:55 a.m. When he took off his hat, a silver dollar-size bump and bruise were noticed above his right eye. His mother reported that he had walked into the corner of the dining room table over the weekend.

This account is accurate, factual, and non-accusatory. It indicates when and where the injury was noticed and establishes the explanation given for the injury. It does not indicate that Jason is abused or neglected. It is just a record of the incident.

If Jason had severe or repeated injuries or seemed to behave in a considerably different way after the injury, a report to the appropriate agency may be necessary. Or, if the teacher noticed a pattern in the injuries over time that Jason received, reporting might be considered. The better the records, the more likely the child's best interest will be served.

The same is true for even minor injuries that occur at school. Record the information for family members to review when they pick up the child. Parents deserve to know even about minor injuries.

INNOVATIONS IN INTERACTIVE EXPERIENCES

Create Positive Interactive Environments

When internal regulation of emotion or behavior is low, as it is during the preschool years, external regulation of structural components of the environment needs to be highly ritualized and predictable (Albrecht & Forrester, 2001). Structural components of the environment include the predictability of the environment (e.g., where things are), the familiarity and predictability of schedule (e.g., normal sequence of the day), and the appropriateness of individual schedules (e.g., being able to sleep shorter or longer periods of time at nap).

Repetition increases structure and supports emotional development. The more often an activity is repeated in a predictable format, the more likely children will take comfort from the structure of it. Try creating structures for separations, reunions, what happens before and after naptime, and when the primary teacher leaves the classroom.

Ritualize routines and transitions. If hectic times, such as transitions outdoors, transitions indoors, snack time, or lunch time are ritualized, children take cues from the ritual to give them indications of what comes next and how to act or behave as the routine or transition occurs.

Give children choices among appropriate alternatives. When children are trying to do things on their own, giving them choices among appropriate alternatives works for everyone. For example, "Do you want saltine crackers or graham crackers for snack today?" gives children a choice between two acceptable ones. Children benefit from practicing making decisions like these as they perfect decision-making skills.

Say "Yes" more than "No." This simple strategy for supporting children's emotional development tells them that they will get to do what they want. For example, if a child wants to go outside during snack time, say, "You can go outside, AND we will finish our snack first." Notice the AND. When adults use "but" with children, children often take it as saying "no." Using "and" instead of "but" says that children will get their wish and tells them when it will happen.

These characteristics are under the teacher's control and can be used to create a positive interactive environment.

Interactive Experiences Checklist for Expressing Feelings with Parents, Teachers, and Friends

Ask a mentor or a peer to observe you in your classroom to document the following interactive behaviors. Think about the following list of interactive experiences and make sure that the classroom reflects many of them.

- ☐ Label expressions of emotions, for example, "What a happy smile!" or "You didn't want him to take that toy."
- ☐ Act authentically. Figuring out emotions requires good models. Children deserve to see authentic emotional models in their classrooms.
- ☐ Support practice play that deals with emotional issues.
- ☐ Prepare children before strangers enter the classroom. Stay close to keep them from getting overwhelmed.
- ☐ Keep a predictable schedule during the school day. Times may vary, but the sequence stays the same.
- ☐ Be available when children are playing together. Facilitate appropriate behavior.
- ☐ Model appropriate interactions.
- ☐ Provide multi-sensory experiences for children.
- ☐ Spend floor time with children.
- ☐ Support emerging creativity by letting children choose their activities among a selected range of appropriate ones.
- ☐ Validate novel ways of doing things. When children make things happen in a new or different way, recognize and celebrate their excitement.

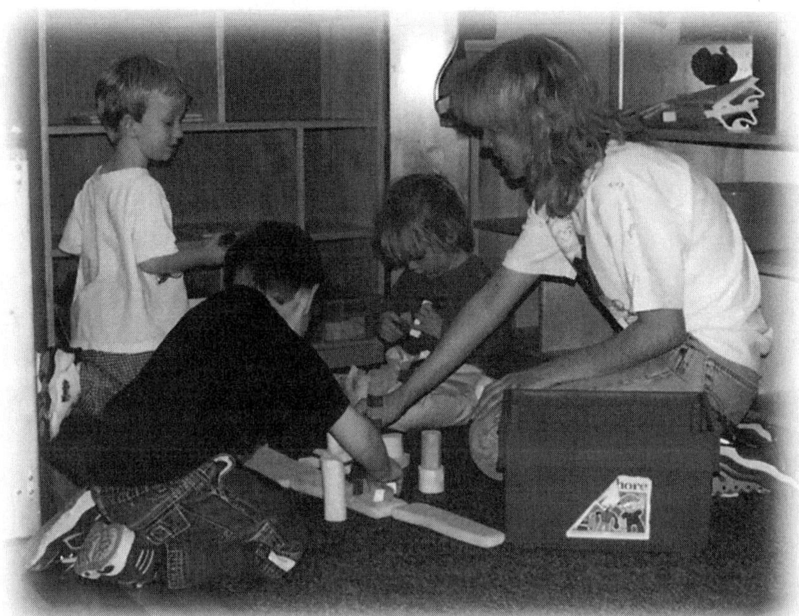

Use a Variety of Teaching Roles

Teachers use a wide variety of roles in their work with young children. During the developmental task of Expressing Feelings with Parents, Teachers, and Friends, two of the most important teacher roles are problem solver and emotions validator. These roles have specific characteristics during this developmental task.

The Teacher as Problem Solver

In this role, teachers approach problems in interactions as opportunities to teach children social problem-solving strategies and offer them practice in trying them out. Interactions that don't work or end in aggression are viewed not as major crises, but as platforms for helping children see the consequences of their behaviors for others, opportunities to help children assess whether behaviors should be used again, and openings to consider more appropriate alternatives.

Being a good model of appropriate social problem solving for children to see is an important teaching role. Children imitate and model the behaviors they see others use. As teachers interact with parents and other adults in appropriate and positive ways, children get ideas they may be able to use in their interactions with others.

As teachers interact with parents and other adults in appropriate and positive ways, children get ideas they may be able to use in their interactions with others.

Teachers also provide important scaffolding of children's efforts to solve problems. When teachers help children solve problems that are too complex by being near, offering suggestions about what might work, and supporting attempts even if they don't work, children are often able to use those experiences to solve problems that are beyond their ability to solve on their own.

The Teacher as an Emotions Validator

When teachers identify, acknowledge, and validate feelings for children, emotional development is encouraged and supported. This important teaching role is ongoing. Soon, children are able to label their own feelings and share with their peers how interactions make them feel. Monitor impressions of the emotional climate of the classroom to avoid under-recognizing feelings.

Support children when intense emotions are present. One of the most difficult times for children in school is when their emotions overtake and overwhelm them. Teachers serve as a cushion when this occurs, providing support to weather the emotional storm and connections that help children move on when the emotion subsides.

INNOVATIONS IN TEACHING

This section discusses topics related to the developmental tasks of Expressing Feelings that are important for teachers to know. Recognizing feelings, facilitating emotional thinking, managing normal aggression, practicing floor time, supporting moral development and internalization of self-control, controlling media exposure, and identifying developmental challenges are explored here.

Provide Experiences to Facilitate Emotional Development

Recognize, Identify, Acknowledge, and Validate Feelings

Recognizing, identifying, labeling, and validating feelings in young children are important teaching strategies for supporting emotional development in young children. For teachers and parents, this means being able to put word labels on feelings.

When children feel that their emotional expression is understood, an interpersonal closeness develops that supports development in all domains, not just the emotional domain. This concept, called "feeling felt" (Siegel, 1999), allows children to join with adults in experiencing primary emotions such as happiness, sadness, anger, frustration, and irritation. Children then come to understand, through signals communicated verbally and non-verbally, that someone understands exactly how they feel. Knowing that their emotions are perceived and understood by another person is one of the ways that adults help children accomplish the important task of understanding and controlling emotions.

Emotions are feelings—and as such do not need amending or fixing. It would be a mistake to try to eliminate or remove emotions from the child's experience, or to assume the responsibility for taking away intense and powerful feelings in young children. When emotions are recognized, identified, labeled, and validated, children are more able to handle these intense feelings.

When emotions are attached to behaviors or physical action, teachers are called on to do something. Intervention often takes the form of keeping children from hurting themselves or others, giving children time to recover from the intensity of emotional expression in order to talk about and work on a solution or resolution, and comforting children until they recover emotionally. Then, teachers help children create symbolic images of the other things that they could have done instead of acting on their emotions by talking about what happened and offering other problem-solving strategies that might work.

The following are examples of words and phrases that teachers can use as they recognize, label, and validate feelings with children.

Helpful Words and Phrases that Recognize, Identify, Label, and Validate Children's Feelings and Their Messages to Children

Helpful Words and Phrases	Skills or Abilities Being Learned or Practiced	Message to the Child
I think you are feeling ...(sad, happy, mad, angry, irritated, frustrated, bothered, pressured, excited, etc.).	Identifies and labels feelings Models the ability to talk about feelings Shows children how to think about feelings	Validates feelings and helps children "feel felt" by others Supports the development of emotional self-regulation
I bet that feels yucky.	Identifies and labels feelings	Modulates emotions by recognizing them
You are a boy (or girl) who can tell me how you are feeling.	Models the ability to talk about feelings	Validates feelings and helps children "feel felt" by others Supports differentiation of self from others
Shucks!	Shows children that they can control themselves even when they feel intense emotions	Shows non-judgmental concern about feelings Helps children "feel felt" by others
I am not sure how you are feeling.	Supports children's ability to label their emotions	Modulates emotions by helping identify and label them
It makes you mad (sad, frustrated, lonely, upset, happy, etc.) when ...	Connects one's feelings to the actions of others	Acknowledges the behaviors that cause feelings Clarifies emotional responses Supports reflection about past and future behaviors
This is hard for you.	Labels intense feelings	Acknowledges the feelings related to behaviors

Facilitate Emotional Thinking

Emotional thinking requires that children learn to translate the way they feel and what they need and want into symbolic ideas and images. Learning to make this transition is facilitated when teachers help children reflect. Reflection stops the momentum toward action by asking children to represent symbolically what they need or want. For example, when a child tells you he wants a snack, rather than saying "yes" or "no," ask him what he wants for snack or why he is ready for snack now. Both of these good questions give the child experience with creating symbolic representations of his emotions, desires, wishes, and impulses. Teachers who help children reflect before they provide answers, lead children toward more complex symbolic abilities, helping them contemplate and communicate rather than just act.

Teachers who help children reflect before they provide answers, lead children toward more complex symbolic abilities, helping them contemplate and communicate rather than just act.

Manage Normal Aggression

Aggression is a normal part of young children's experiences. Aggression results from powerful emotions that are not yet under the child's direct control. Children hit, pinch, bite, slap, and grab when their emotions cause them to act before they can think about doing something else.

Children learn to manage aggression when supportive adults connect consequences with aggression. Using aggression to stop aggression only teaches children that they must submit to adults who are bigger and more powerful. It does not help children gain control over aggressive behavior or replace it with more appropriate skills. Replacing aggressive behavior with more sophisticated skills is a process—just like learning to express feelings appropriately is a lifelong task.

The following are examples of ways supportive teachers can meet aggression with consequences from the earliest stage.

- Set clear limits for your classroom about aggression. If children know you will not tolerate aggressive behavior as a way to get what you want, they will feel safe enough to work on developing other strategies.
- Teach social problem solving. Help children learn to call for help, trade, take turns, walk away, use words, and make plans.
- Give children the words to use when they are having trouble communicating with each other. You might say, "Did you want him to take your toy?" If the child says "no," then help him say "no" to the child who took the toy. "Then tell him with words, 'I don't want you to take my toy. Please give it back to me.'"

- Recognize cooperative behaviors. When children are successful in working things out without losing control, recognize their success. When children

fail to work things out, remind them that they did it once before and that you expect them to try to work it out next time.
- Apply appropriate consequences to situations where children use aggression.

With help, children will find out that they don't get what they want when they use aggression, and that there are consequences for acting aggressively. Early experiences with the consequences of aggression help children learn over time that aggressive behavior doesn't accomplish much. After they learn this lesson, children can begin the process of becoming assertive enough to prevent being victimized and becoming authoritative enough to be seen as a problem solver. Both of these important lessons will never be learned unless both teachers and families help children learn to manage normal aggression and convert it into constructive assertion and problem solving.

Practice Floor Time

Floor time is a teaching practice that supports children's emotional development (Greenspan, 1999). Floor time looks something like this. The teacher prepares an area of the classroom with an attractive display of toys and materials. One or two children who are ready to play are invited to join the teacher in an area that is set up for floor time. The teacher starts the practice of floor time by watching, listening, and being with the children as they begin to play. She or he lets the child or children direct the time together. If a child smiles at the teacher, the teacher smiles back. If the children include the teacher in the play, she or he responds by joining in the play. Following the child's lead is the important part of floor time. When a child picks up toys, the teacher expands and extends the play to enhance the child's experience.

These interactions support interest in the social world and validate that the teacher is a part of it. They also fill children with feelings of competence. Once initiated by a supportive adult, the child will be able to reconnect with the feeling of support without the adult's actual support at a later time.

Teachers may find it hard to identify time when they can practice floor time with just a few children. Try some of the following ideas:
- Pick a time of day that naturally lends itself to calm play. Some ideas might be the beginning of the day as children are arriving one by one, or after naptime as the first few children wake up, during the time spent in self-selected activities in the classroom, or the end of the day as children are leaving and the group size is decreasing.

- Try to spend floor time with one or two children each day during the week. Keep track of who has had floor time each week—indicating it on your curriculum plan, so you know who has and hasn't had special time with the teacher.
- When children are having developmental difficulties or are experiencing stress from other sources (such as a family member who is traveling or recovering from an illness), give them extra floor time. Stress increases children's need to feel connected. The child who is demanding the most attention may be able to cope better on his own if he gets what he needs—a feeling of being filled up with attention and connected through play to his teacher.
- Enlist the help of others. Invite parents, students who are studying early childhood education, and grandparents to spend some time playing with children in your group so that you are freed up to practice floor time.

Support Moral Development

Support for moral development is embedded in the classroom community created by teachers. As children are learning about standards of acceptable and unacceptable behavior and differentiating between appropriate and inappropriate behavior for different social situations, they need to be able to figure out the expectations for both behavior and social participation. The interactive climate of the classroom creates the source of this understanding. Classrooms that have simple, understandable rules about what children can and cannot do that are agreed upon by the children are the place to start.

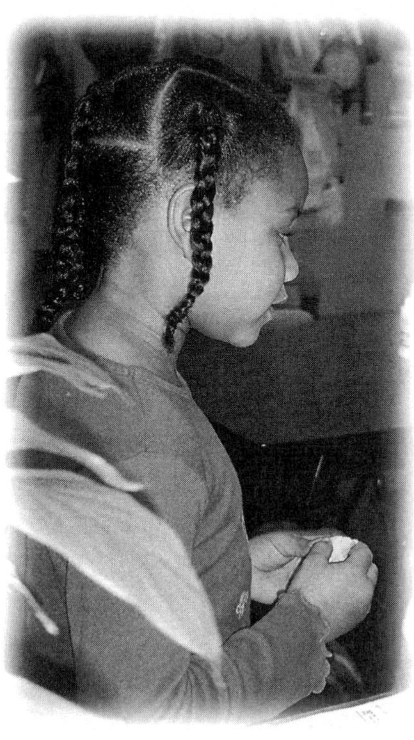

The other way children learn about the rules and social conventions is by experiences with non-compliance or disobedience. When children are supported in understanding what they did wrong, why it is important not to do it again, and see the impact of what they did on others, they learn about the standards and behaviors that could be used instead.

So, if children aren't adopting and learning the rules, it may be because the rules are unclear or in conflict with the rules they understand from other settings. It may also be that they don't understand the consequences, don't see the importance of complying with the rules, or haven't developed the empathy necessary to understand the impact of their behavior on others. All of these situations create opportunities for teachers to support emerging skills through their teaching. Try some of the following to support children's emerging moral development:

- Be very clear with children about the few things that are absolutely unacceptable in your classroom. Hurting others and damaging and destroying toys and materials are two examples of fundamental rules for unacceptable behavior.
- Help children figure out what causes events that lead to conflict or problems.
- Validate mastery when you see it in action. When a child chooses the appropriate behavior in a given situation, comment on the choice.
- Provide labels for children's behavior related to breaking the rules—particularly pride, shame, and guilt. "You are proud of yourself for using your words," or "Your feelings are hurt because I had to ask you to stop," are examples.
- Think about ways to talk about standards for behavior outside of disciplinary situations. Remember that most moral development lessons occur during other interactions besides disciplining.
- Apply consequences. Having a good collection of ideas of what to do in different situations prepares you to come up with good consequences.
- Identify both the effect of inappropriate behavior on the child as well as on others in the situation. For example, talk about whether other children will want to play with them if they destroy property as well as the consequences of destroying property.
- Remember that a child's cultural and social experiences outside of the classroom impact emerging moral development. Explore these with families so that you are aware of any of incongruence or sources of conflict.

Support Self-regulation and Internalizations of Self-control

There are many techniques that help children control impulses and gain self-control. The following are strategies to use to support children's emerging self-control.

- Use physical proximity and touch. Staying close is the best tool to use to provide children with external support for regulating themselves. When adults are close, they can support children with non-verbal cues (nods and smiles), verbal cues (suggestions of what might work), or physical support (holding the child back a minute while he thinks about what might work or what he might try).
- Give children choices. When children are given choices between acceptable alternatives, they feel independent and successful in solving their own problems. Examples include juice or milk, tennis shoes or sandals, and socks or no socks.
- Cue children to their lapses in self-control. Reminders from adults about the likely outcome of the chosen path may help them re-center and regain control. Examples include "I think you are getting upset" and "Take a deep breath and try again."

- Give children opportunities to comply on their own or with your help. Sometimes, children need adult support to accomplish their goals. At other times, they need reminders that they can do it, with support from an adult or they can do it on their own. Sometimes, just the reminder helps make it happen. For example, "Do you want to do it on your own or with my help?"

Use techniques to help children learn to tolerate frustration.

- Empower children to set their own limits in interactions with their friends. For example, when a child takes a toy away, empower the child who lost the toy to ask for the toy back. If the child lacks the expressive language or the self-confidence to ask for himself, help him do it by suggesting what to try.
- Support waiting by helping children think of alternative activities to do while they wait for a turn or a chance to play. For example, "Let's read a book while we wait."

Use techniques to help children learn to delay gratification.

- Use non-verbal signs to indicate that children are capable of waiting. A hand (held up like a stop sign), touch (such as a hand on the shoulder), and reminders ("one more minute until your turn") are examples.
- Provide hand-over-hand help for waiting. Hold the child's hands as you remind the child that he can wait. Touch communicates to children that you think that they can do it.
- Ask children for ideas about what would help them wait. They may have some good ideas that are worth trying.

Control Media Exposure and Develop Critical Media-viewing Skills

Concerns about the appropriate use of media in early childhood education have lead teachers to consider carefully the use of passive media viewing with young children. An interest in appropriate media has led to the production of some excellent media productions, mostly in the form of videotapes and CDs. Teachers who want to use media in their curricula can follow the guidelines below to ensure that the experiences are educationally appropriate.

- Limit viewing. Use of media should be an infrequent event. Look for good examples of children's media to use. Never use media as a way to fill up time.
- Always give children options and encourage them to consider them.

- Preview all media before showing it to children. As you preview the material, consider questions you might ask, what part of the media event you might draw closer attention to, and how to help children use the information.
- Develop a list of critical viewing questions to ask children before, during, and after the media event.
- Follow up media events with many additional developmentally appropriate experiences that contain the same content and information.

Identify Developmental Challenges

Teachers have many opportunities to observe children as they grow and learn. When a teacher notices that a child is outside of the typical age range for accomplishing a task or skill, she or he should remember that differences in development are normal. Continue careful observations and data collection. If the trend continues and the child is still not demonstrating widely held expectations for behaviors and skills within his chronological age range, talk to the child's family. Suggest that the family discuss the observations first with their pediatrician and then (if needed) with a developmental specialist, such as a developmental psychologist, or a specific specialist, such as a speech, physical, or occupational therapist.

Children who are six months or more behind their chronological age need to be evaluated further to determine if the delay observed is related to maturational factors, developmental uniqueness, or alternative developmental pathways. Early identification of developmental delays is an important role for teachers. They are not diagnosticians, but teachers can be excellent observers, setting the stage for early intervention that can completely remediate problems.

Brazelton and Greenspan (2000) suggest that a full evaluation is in order for any of the following developmental signs:

- By two months of age, if there are no signs of looking or listening;
- By four to five months, if there are no signs of relating to caregivers with joyful smiles, and sounds;
- By eight to nine months, if there are no signs of back and forth communication (e.g., reaching for a rattle in Dad's hand or initiating and reciprocating different emotional expressions and sounds);
- By 12 months, if there are no signs of multiple circles of communication in a row (e.g., back and forth exchange of emotional gestures sounds and even a word or two);
- By 16 months, if there are no signs of complex problem-solving interactions (e.g., taking caregiver by the hand to help get toy or food);
- By 24 months, if there are no signs of beginning pretend play (hugging a doll) or understanding or using words to get needs met (e.g., "give juice");

- By 36-48 months, if there are no signs of the logical use of ideas with caregivers and peers (e.g., answering where, when, why, and what questions as part of conversation lasting at least a few minutes);
- At any time, if there are signs of serious family or emotional difficulties in Mom or Dad or other family members (Brazelton & Greenspan, 2000).

When teachers experience concern about children's normative development, exploring whether the important milestones suggested by these authors emerged as expected might be a place to start a conversation with parents, family members, and caregivers.

Teacher Competencies to Support Expressing Feelings with Parents, Teachers, and Friends

Sometimes	Usually	Always	
☐	☐	☐	Assures that children have frequent opportunities for success.
☐	☐	☐	Delights in each child's success; expresses kindness and support when children are struggling with developmental challenges.
☐	☐	☐	Invites children to play with each other; participates in play as a partner.
☐	☐	☐	Allows children to direct and manage their own play.
☐	☐	☐	Uses vocabulary, materials, activities, and experiences that are suitable.
☐	☐	☐	Exhibits flexibility in carrying out activity and experience plans.
☐	☐	☐	Shows imagination and spontaneity in building on children's interest for developing curriculum.
☐	☐	☐	Plans, implements, and evaluates parent-teacher conferences, intake interviews, and gradual enrollment.
☐	☐	☐	Serves as a social role model by building a relationship with each child and family and by maintaining positive relationships with other teachers.
☐	☐	☐	Watches and observes children at play and throughout the school day.
☐	☐	☐	Uses observation to inform curriculum planning and provide insight into interactions with children.
☐	☐	☐	Has, uses, and adds to a file of rhymes, fingerplays, songs, and music.

Competencies for the Teaching Role of Problem Solver

Sometimes	Usually	Always	
☐	☐	☐	Uses modeling to help children interact successfully.
☐	☐	☐	Provides children with a break from social interaction or over stimulation as needed.
☐	☐	☐	Suggests problem-solving strategies that might work.

Competencies for the Teaching Role of Emotions Validator

Sometimes	Usually	Always	
☐	☐	☐	Models the recognition and expression of feelings by naming her or his feelings.
☐	☐	☐	Identifies, labels, and validates emotions expressed by children.
☐	☐	☐	Plans, implements, and evaluates parent participation activities.
☐	☐	☐	Understands that social roles and expectations for children in their family setting may be different than at school.
☐	☐	☐	Helps children make the transition between these two different sets of expectations and understand how to behave appropriately in each.

INNOVATIONS IN OBSERVATION/ASSESSMENT

Observation/Assessment for Expressing Feelings with Parents, Teachers, and Friends

Observation for the task of Expressing Feelings with Parents, Teachers, and Friends focuses on gaining an understanding of each child's emotional development. Observe to identify the quality of the relationships children have with parents and significant others. In particular, watch interactions between family members and children for the characteristics of relationships that support children's emotional growth, such as collaboration, dialogue, repair, narratives, and emotional communication. Look for evidence that children are creating an inner world of thought about feelings and doing emotional thinking.

Observing children for increasing skills in managing aggression and sharing your observations about their growth in developing these skills with families are important teacher activities for this task. Also important is observing for progress related to teaching interventions, which is evidence that children are learning the standards and rules for social behavior in your classroom. Success in learning these standards and rules is a true accomplishment for preschool children.

Add to Individual Portfolios to Highlight the Developmental Task of Expressing Feelings with Parents, Teachers, and Friends

Consider adding any of the following to children's portfolios:

- Lists of the feelings children can identify, label, and manage.
- Examples of anecdotal notes that indicate the creation of symbolic representation of emotions.
- Descriptions of play situations where children indicate an understanding of standards and rules.
- Anecdotal records showing children's progress on the internalization of self-control.
- Photos of positive interactive friendships at work.

INNOVATIONS IN FAMILY PARTNERSHIPS

Encourage Family Participation

Supporting Possibilities: Help families support their children's learning through gathering materials that will be needed in the Possibilities Plans of Fantasy Figures and More! and Saying Goodbye. Lists are provided at the beginning of each section on pages 527 and 552.

Developmental Banners: Communicate with families with developmental banners. As children acquire skills (e.g., waits for a turn), abilities (e.g., stays on task for 10 minutes), or dispositions (e.g., shows interest in figuring out how to play with Jude), communicate the child's progress by creating a development banner. For example, on a sheet of paper, invite the child to make handprints and footprints. Then add accomplishments in emotional development in pen or marker. Don't forget the child's name and the date. Or, take a picture of the child exhibiting the new skill and post the picture along with an anecdotal note recounting when you saw the skill used. Add these banners, photographs, and notes to the child's emerging portfolio.

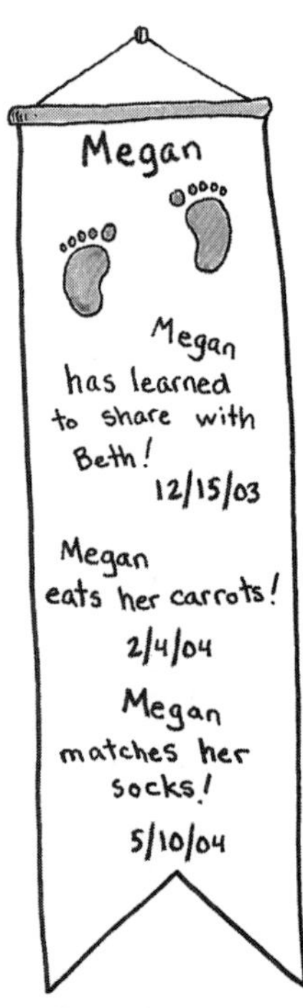

Note: Developmental banners are individual in nature. A wall full of the same banner for each child is not appropriate. Make each accomplishment noted on the banner specific to the child's emerging skills. Pick different domains of development to highlight for different children or focus on one or two children at a time, identifying new skills as they emerge.

Family Day: Invite families to visit at any time during Family Day. Provide decorated nametags and have children's art "in process" as families visit.

Share Parent Postcards

Share Parent Postcards with parents as they indicate an interest, at appropriate times during the enrollment cycle, or as developmental issues arise. Copy Postcards. Cut if necessary. Address to parent(s), and place on Communication Log or hand out personally.

Managing Normal Aggression in Young Children

Every parent dreads the day when the teacher reports that his or her child is responsible for hurting another child. But that day will probably come. Aggression is a normal part of young children's experiences. Children hit, pinch, bite, slap, and grab when their emotions cause them to act before they can think about doing something else.

Children learn to manage aggression when supportive adults help them learn social problem-solving skills and connect consequences with aggression. Using aggression to stop aggression only teaches children that they must submit to adults who are bigger and more powerful. Replacing aggressive behavior with more sophisticated skills is a lifelong process.

The following are some examples of ways supportive family members can meet aggression with consequences.

- When your child grabs another child by the hair and pulls, separate the two and hold the other child until he or she calms down and gets under control. Help the hurt child say, "Stop pulling my hair!" Tell both children, "Pulling hair didn't solve the problem." Then offer an alternative, such as, "Tell him or her to stop. Use words." Then focus on the child who was aggressive, exploring other ways the problem could be solved.
- When your child hurts another child, tell your child that he or she will have to play alone for a while. When he or she wants to return to playing with his friend, remind your child that they can only play together if no one is hurt.

Early experiences with the consequences of aggression help children learn over time that aggressive behavior doesn't accomplish much. After children learn this lesson, they can begin the process of becoming assertive enough to prevent being victimized and authoritative enough to be a leader. Both of these important lessons are learned when parents and teachers help children to manage normal aggression and convert it into constructive assertion and social problem solving.

Dear Parents

TO

Television and Young Children

Parents hear many concerns about television and media exposure for young children. Viewing is definitely on the increase. On average, preschool children watch 35 hours of television and other media each week. Some children will watch over 4,000 hours of television before they start kindergarten and see over 100,000 acts of violence and over 20,000 commercial advertisements before they finish elementary school. Children's cartoons and action programs average over 20 acts of violence per hour compared with 5 acts per hour in prime time shows.

Television and other media have many negative effects on children. Research shows that the media culture has some dramatic consequences for children, including:

- Increasing children's verbal and physical aggressive behavior, teaching children that fighting is an acceptable way to solve conflicts,
- Desensitizing children to violence, teaching children that violence is a common, normal part of everyday life,
- Validating disrespectful and rude behavior as legitimate,
- Undermining children's view of the world as a safe place to be,
- Encouraging negative stereotyping of race, class, and gender,
- Delaying children's language development, and
- Teaching them that every problem has a simple and identifiable solution that is readily at hand.

Television can have some positive effects. Good children's television has been reported to teach children positive social behavior (Mr. Rogers' Neighborhood), support an increased in interest in reading (Reading Rainbow, Arthur), and expose children to new places, people, customs, and experiences (The Puzzle Factory).

Think about what your children are watching. It matters.

Family Television Viewing

Children model the behavior of their families. Experts caution parents to start by monitoring their own television viewing and media exposure. If the television or computer comes on as adults enter the house and gets turned off as adults leave, children's television exposure will be much higher than recommended.

Set some very basic rules about how often and for how long television and other media will be available to preschool children. Connect these rules to your child's age and stage. Use the following as you explore what might work for you and your family.

Make television or media exposure a family activity. Watch television or play with your child on the computer to establish that these are shared experiences rather than solitary ones.

Limit solitary viewing. If you are not available to watch with your child, limit solitary viewing to one show, videotape, or computer game. Say "no" to requests for repeated viewing of the same videotape or computer game over and over again.

Offer other options. Offer your child a variety of other experiences, such as reading books, going outside for a walk, playing games, drawing pictures, listening to music, and doing chores together.

Don't eat in front of the television. Mealtime is an important time for children. It is the time for sharing—sharing food and experiences.

Plan television watching or media usage. Review the television listings on Sunday and decide which, if any, television programs deserve your child's time and attention. If you don't put it on your weekly plan, don't watch it.

Television and media are a part of most families' lives. Diane Levin, author of *Remote Control Childhood? Combating the Hazards of Media Culture* says, "Media is a teacher that competes with all of us for the hearts and minds of our children." Start now, and you can make sure that media has a positive impact on your child.

Resource for Families

Add this helpful book to your library or post this title on your family bulletin board.

Levin, D. (1998). ***Remote control childhood? Combating the hazards of media culture.*** Washington, DC: National Association for the Education of Young Children (NAEYC).

Post these websites on your family bulletin board for parents to further explore the topics in this chapter:

- Coalition for Quality Children's Media (www.cqcm.org/kidsfirst): rates and review children's videos and provides information on choosing appropriate videos and CDs.
- Child Care Aware (www.childcareaware.org): connects parents to local resources and information within their communities.

INNOVATIONS IN ENVIRONMENTS

During the task of Expressing Feelings with Parents, Teachers, and Friends, teachers analyze the environment for evidence that it supports emerging self-regulation and the internalization of self-control. They also create, maintain, and refresh Movement/Outdoor Possibilities, stocking it with a wide variety of appropriate toys and materials. Also considered in this section is documenting children's learning and growth through projects.

Bring Indoor Materials Outside

When thinking of outdoor play, many adults think of traditional physical education activities. Most of these, of course, are not appropriate for preschool children. Instead, preschool children need opportunities for lots of physical exercise and exploration. Running, climbing, playing chase, throwing balls and catching them, riding tricycles, digging in the sand, working on construction projects, rearranging moveable equipment and materials, acting out dramas, singing songs, saying rhymes and fingerplays, experimenting with balance, playing with water and other sensory materials, and exploring the natural world are all appropriate outdoor experiences. In addition, some of the same activities that children need and enjoy inside are appropriate to bring outside. Try some of these:

- Books provide a special time for reading on a blanket outside.
- Dramatic play takes on a new dimension when activities take place under a shady structure or tree.
- Messy art projects that may be difficult to do in the classroom are often easier to clean up outside.
- Writing materials have a place outside, too. Adding paper to fences and attaching crayons or markers to the fence with string will encourage children to add literacy experiences to their play.
- Music sounds different outside, and can lead to spontaneous movement and dance activities or dramatic interpretations of activities on a new stage.

Activity Areas

Movement/Outdoor Possibilities

Outdoor time is an important part of the day for young children. Preschool children need opportunities to use all of the large muscles of the body. The fresh air is a nice change from the classroom. In addition, activities that are moved from the inside to the outside take on a new meaning.

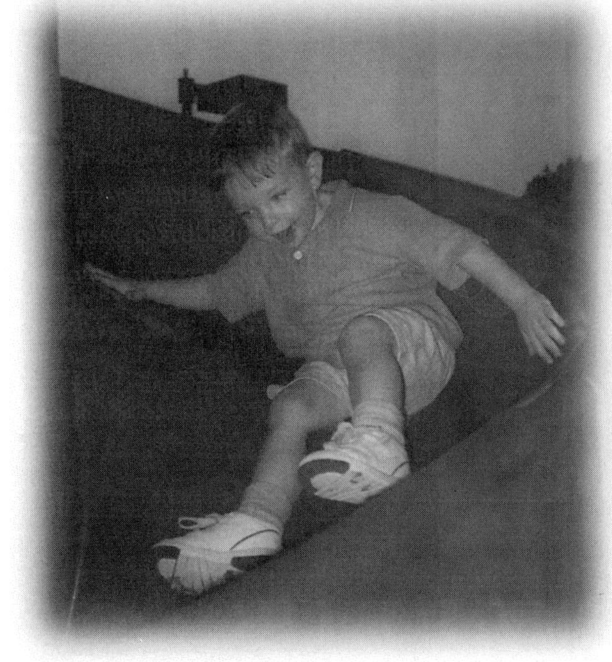

Motor skills get a good workout in appropriate outdoor environments. Children can use the large muscles of the body to run, climb, skip, hop, and explore outdoor spaces. Small muscles of the body are stimulated as children play in the sand, dig in the dirt, and explore natural things.

Outdoor play areas need to have many components—a place to run and experience active play, climbing equipment with appropriate fall zones and appropriate cushioning material, areas where children can dig in and manipulate sand, dirt, and other natural materials, and places to sit and rest.

To enhance and support movement and outdoor exploration, a well-planned Movement/Outdoor area will have the following supplies and equipment, perhaps not available at the same time, but accessible as needed to enhance children's physical development and outdoor movement experiences:

- A good collection of inflated balls of various sizes;
- A child-height basketball goal;
- Large manipulatives, such as waffle blocks, giant building cubes, interlocking blocks, and foam blocks;
- Balance boards and beams;
- A variety of tricycles, scooters, shared tricycles, and wagons, along with helmets to wear when riding them;
- Signs and traffic cones to use to direct traffic;
- Sand and water play tables or bins, a water source, and a collection of sensory materials to use in the bins and tables;
- Sand toys, including shovels, rakes, scrapers, sifters, funnels, buckets, scoops, and molds;
- Water play toys including pumps, scoops, buckets, tubing, measuring cups of different sizes, and funnels;
- Trucks, bulldozers, and wheelbarrows;
- A battery-operated CD or tape player;
- Bubbles and bubble makers;
- A variety of moveable parts including square boxes, planks, boards of various lengths, cable spools, and so on.
- A parachute for parachute play;
- A collection of dramatic play props, in prop boxes, to add to the outdoor space;
- A fence easel, two-sided easels or Plexiglas easels, preferably ones that allow two children to paint, and are placed side by side; and
- Woodworking materials and equipment, stored in a locked cabinet, along with a good supply of soft wood, safety glasses, nails, screws, bolts, and other fasteners.

Project/Documentation Possibilities

Projects are opportunities for children to engage in thorough investigation as a classroom activity. Projects are important because they provide children with opportunities for reflection about what they think, continuity of experience, and an opportunity to practice, perfect, and enjoy experiences again and again. Documentation is a record of the project that communicates what children have learned and provides children, parents, and teachers with the opportunity to revisit what children have learned.

Innovations: The Comprehensive Preschool Curriculum advocates using observation of children at play to discover emergent curriculum themes and play themes that are meaningful and interesting to children. It also recommends webbing to make sure teachers consider many possibilities rather than exploring curriculum in one direction. Projects usually emerge from the content or processes teachers are already considering and planning. They can be teacher initiated, responding to observations of children's interests, or they can come totally from children's play and interests.

Suggestions are given in each of the Possibilities Plans for projects. These are predominantly teacher initiated in focus. Don't hesitate to abandon the suggested projects when children present indications of interest in different or divergent projects. Use these as springboards to consider the types of projects that might fit into your curriculum plans.

References

Albrecht, K & M. Forrester. (2001). ***Brief evaluation and intervention program: Teacher's guide***. Houston, TX: Texas Children's Hospital.

Berk, L.E. (1999). ***Infants and children***. Boston, MA: Allyn and Bacon.

Brazelton, T.B., & S.I. Greenspan. (2000). ***The irreducible needs of children: What every child must have to grow, learn, and flourish.*** Cambridge, MA: Perseus Publishing.

Bronfenbrenner, U. (1979). ***The ecology of human development: Experiments by nature and design.*** Cambridge, MA: Harvard University Press.

Brunson, M.B. (2000). Recognizing and supporting the development of self-regulation in young children. ***Young Children,*** 55(2): 32-37.

Buzzelli, C. A. (1992). Research in review. Young children's moral understanding: Learning about right and wrong. ***Young Children,*** 47 (6): 47-53.

Feeney, S. & K. Kipnis. (1999). ***Code of ethical conduct and statement of commitment.*** Washington, DC: National Association for the Education of Young Children (NAEYC).

Greenspan, S.I. (1997). ***Growth of the mind and the endangered origins of intelligence.*** Cambridge, MA: Perseus Books.

Greenspan, S.I. (1999). ***The six experiences that create intelligence and emotional growth in babies and young children.*** Reading, MA: Perseus Books.

Howes, C. (2000). Social development, family, and attachment relationships of infant and toddlers. In D. Cryer & T. Harms (Eds.) ***Infants and toddlers in out-of-home care*** (87-113). Baltimore, MD: Brookes Publishing.

Levin, D. (1998). ***Remote control childhood? Combating the hazards of media culture.*** Washington, DC: National Association for the Education of Young Children (NAEYC).

Marion, M. (1999). ***Guidance of young children.*** Upper Saddle River, NJ: Merrill.

Mooney, C.G. (2000). ***Theories of childhood: An introduction to Dewey, Montessori, Erickson, Piaget, and Vygotsky.*** St. Paul, MN: Redleaf Press.

Shonkoff, J.P. & D.A. Phillips (Eds.). (2000). ***From neurons to neighborhoods: The science of early childhood development.*** Washington, DC: National Academy Press.

Siegel, D.J. (1999). Relationships and the developing child. ***Child Care Information Exchange,*** 130, 48-51.

Vaughan, B.E., C.B. Kopp, & J.B. Krakow. (1984). The emergence and consolidation of self-control from eighteen-thirty months of age: Normative trends and individual differences. ***Child Development,*** 55: 900-1004.

Resources for Teachers

Greenspan, S. (1989). ***Floor time.*** Video. Produced by Jefferson City, MO: Scholastic, Inc.

Helms, J.H., S. Beneke & K. Steinheimer. (1997). ***Windows on learning: Documenting children's work.*** New York: Teacher's College Press.

Helms, J.H., & L. Katz. (2001). ***Young investigators:The project approach in the early years.*** New York: Teachers College Press.

Helms, J. H. & S. Beneke. (2002). ***The power of projects: Meeting contemporary challenges in early childhood classrooms, strategies and solutions.*** New York: Teacher's College Press.

Kreidler, W.J. & S. Wittall. (1999). ***Early childhood adventures in peacemaking.*** Cambridge, MA: Educators for Social Responsibility.

Miller, K. (1995). ***Crisis manual for early childhood teachers: How to handle the really difficult problems.*** Beltsville, MD: Gryphon House.

Smith, C.A. (1993). ***The peaceful classroom.*** Beltsville, MD: Gryphon House.

Schiller, P. & T. Bryant. (1998). ***The values book.*** Beltsville, MD: Gryphon House.

Weikart, P.S. (1997). ***Movement plus rhymes, songs, and singing games.*** Yspilanti, MI: HighScope Press.

Possibilities Plan—

Fantasy Figures and More

Getting Ready to Plan

During the preschool years, children actively build knowledge about the world and how it works by aligning new information and experiences with things they have already figured out. Gaining an understanding of the difference between fantasy and reality goes through the same active, experimental knowledge construction process.

Children are intensely interested in action characters that come to life in movies, on television, and in the toys they find in stores. In this Possibilities Plan, fantasy figures are approached from the perspective of engaging children in meaningful dialogues about what they are thinking about related to fantasy figures. Rather than approving or disapproving of taking on an action figure's persona in play, the focus is on understanding what children are thinking and on how fantasy figure characteristics are connected to everyday behaviors.

The purpose of Getting Ready to Plan is to support the planning process with a general overview of the content of this Possibilities Plan. Now is the time to think about what interests children and what you want them to learn about each of these topics. Topics are explored in general below.

Differentiating between Real and Fantastic Characteristics and Behaviors of Fantasy Figures: Fantasy and reality are close together in the early preschool years. A three-year-old child may really think there are monsters under his bed while a five-year-old child usually understands that there aren't. Through play, children move from *being* the superhero to taking on the role of superhero.

Recognizing Characteristics and Behaviors of Fantasy Figures in Others: It is not surprising that children are drawn to fantasy figures. They have many of the characteristics and behaviors that society values, such as helping others and solving problems. Help children determine which behaviors and characteristics they value and then how to use these traits in their relationships with others.

Exploring Purpose: Why fantasy figures do the things they do is a fascinating topic to young children. They discuss and review minute details of exploits, experiences, and adventures, with varying degrees of accuracy. By exploring reasons behind behavior—the purpose of the action or deed, we help children recognize benefits of goal-directed behavior.

Resolving Conflicts: As children play roles, conflicts often occur. Children are learning social problem-solving skills and how to resolve conflict peacefully. The steps in conflict resolution include identifying the problem, finding possible solutions, choosing one to try, evaluating the solution to see if it works, and applying what was learned to new situations.

Now that you have an idea about the general content of the Possibilities Plan, you are ready to proceed with developing your own plan to implement with the children.

Toys and Materials*

Purchased

action figures of all types
animal and people figures
assorted beads
bells
blank tape
box cutter (teacher only)
brushes of various types
bubble solution and wands
capes
chart paper
cloth of different types
collage materials
colored pens and pencils
colored salt or sugar crystals
confetti
cookware
cotton balls
craft knife (teacher only)
duct tape
Elmer's glue
glitter
hats, coats, and boots for different professions
index cards
karaoke machine
latex balloons
liquid starch
magnets of various types
magnet wands
markers
masking and packing tape
masks
microphones
microscopes
notebook
packing tape
paints of various types
paper plates
paper of various textures and colors
plastic cups
playdough
powerful fan on stand
rhythm stick
scissors
sensory table
spaghetti pasta
stickers, containing 6-12 super hero characters, 2 packs
super hero figures
tempera paint
thermometer
toy foods
toy medical kits
unit blocks
Velcro
white coats

Gathered

appliance box
balls
bandanas
boxes of different sizes
briefcases
boots
chairs
clothes
coat hanger
cornstarch
cups
drying rack
duffle bags
earphones
eyeglasses
flashlights
fork
headbands
heavy objects
jewelry (old)
lightweight boxes
magazines
magnifying glasses
marbles
metal objects
newspaper
old costume jewelry
pictures of fire stations, police stations, and hospitals
pictures of hats
ping-pong balls
plastic spoon
purses
ribbons
rocks
rubber bands
sand
sheet or light blanket
shirts, different colors
shoeboxes
spools
stapler
string and yarn
sunglasses and eyeglasses
table
tape recorder or CD Player
tennis balls
thread
towels
tree bark
utensils
waistbands
walkie-talkie, large
wristbands
wrist watches

*Note: Please consider the ages and abilities of the children in your classroom. Use only safe, non-toxic materials.

Fantasy Figures and More

WEB

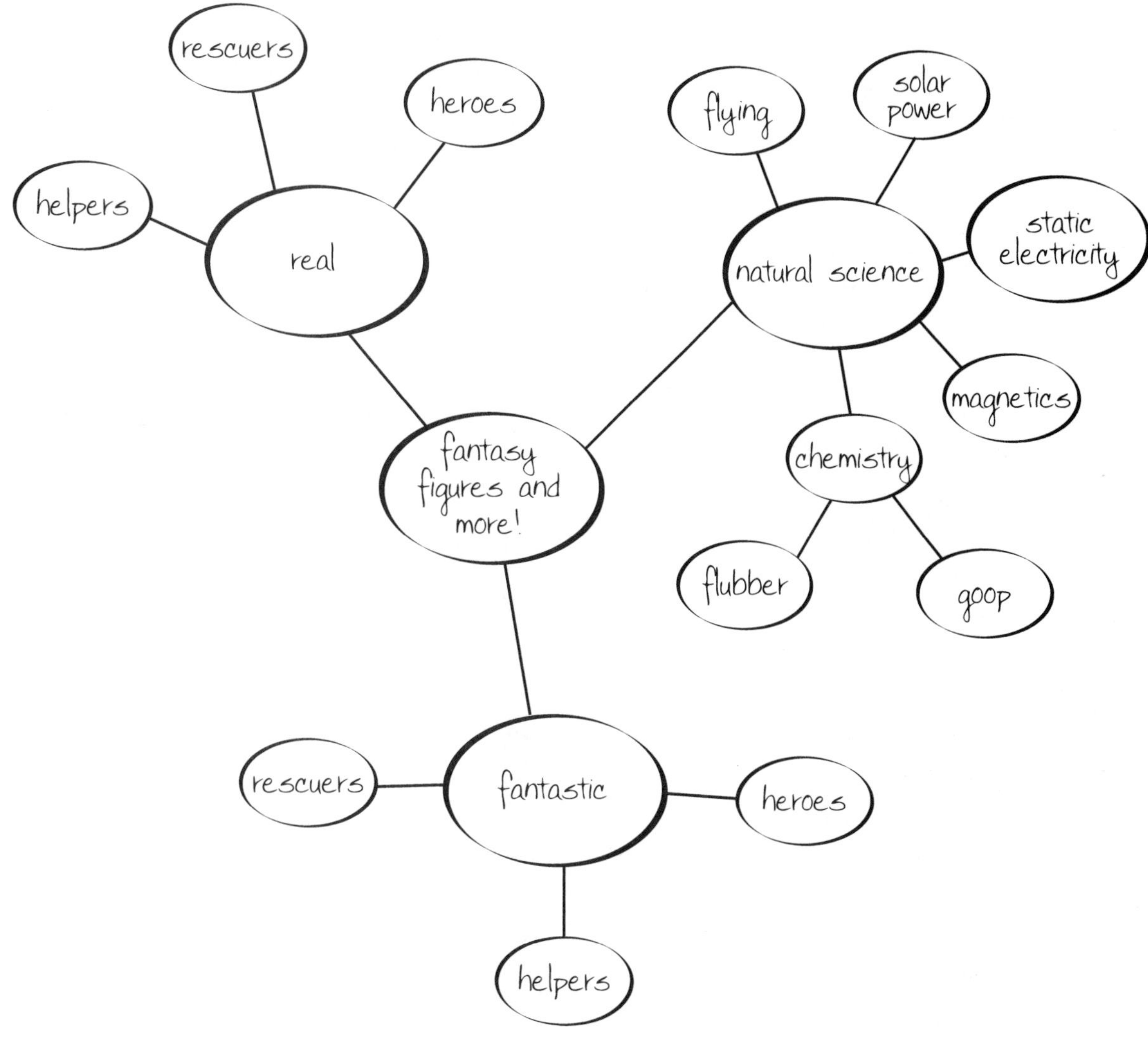

Fantasy Figures and More

PLANNING PAGES

Plan Possibilities

ACTIVITIES AND EXPERIENCES FOR FANTASY FIGURES AND MORE!

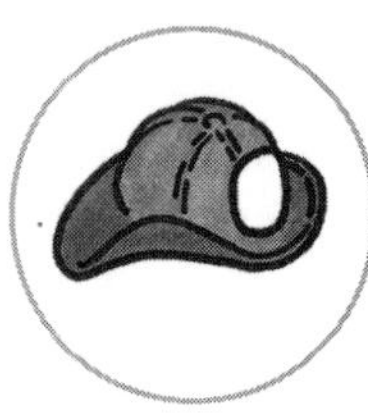

DRAMATIC POSSIBILITIES

Fantasy Figures in a Box

Materials
capes • wristbands • waistbands • headbands • towels • duct tape • Velcro • confetti • glitter • masks • paper plates • bandanas • cloth • boots • food

Teacher Talk
Talk about what fantasy figures do. "You are pretending to fight the bad guys." "What do the fantasy figures do before they fight the bad guys?"

Instructions
Add the props to the Dramatic Possibilities area. Consider adding prop boxes one at a time or adding several at one time, according to what is best for your group of children. Capes can be made from cloth or towels and Velcro. Wrist, waist, and headbands can be made from cloth or duct tape with Velcro and decorated with confetti and glitter. Masks can be made from paper plates, bandanas, or cloth.

Observation/Assessment
Takes on various roles in dramatic play

More than Fantasy Figures

Materials
blue shirts • white shirts • red felt • hats for different professions • boots • red or yellow raincoats • white coats • medical kits • duffle bags • briefcases • purses • books, such as *Firefighters A-Z* by Chris Demarest

Teacher Talk
"You are a firefighter." "What do you do to help people?"

Instructions
Real people who do many of the same things as fantasy figures are among us every day, including police officers, firefighters, doctors, and so on. Place props to support these roles in the Dramatic Possibilities area. Blue and white shirts can serve as great

uniform props. Cut the sleeves off if they are too long. For a doctor's white coat, cut out a red cross from felt and glue it on the pockets or on the sides of the sleeves.

Extension Possibilities: Help children think of everyday roles real people play in their lives. Explore who helps work things out when the washing machine breaks or traffic lights go out. Expand children's play options by adding these supporting props as well.

Observation/Assessment
Uses props to enhance dramatic play
Dresses and undresses in costumes

Dramatic Super Powers

Materials
unbreakable sunglasses and eyeglasses • magnifying glasses • microscopes • earphones • karaoke machine • microphones • books, such as *Seeing* by Helen Frost

Teacher Talk
"What powers can your glasses give you?"

Instructions
Provide materials that can help children see, hear, and talk in new and powerful ways. Include books in the area, such as *Seeing* by Helen Frost.

ART POSSIBILITIES

Super Duper Hats and More!

Materials
newspaper • masking tape • paints • paintbrushes • collage materials • glue • belts • wristwatches • pictures of hats from picture file (firefighter's hats, police officer's hats, etc.)

Teacher Talk
"What kind of hat would be helpful for a firefighter?" "What kinds of things would be helpful to add to your hat?"

Instructions
Ask families to provide newspapers for this activity. Place four different sheets of newspaper on the child's head. Hold down the newspaper to conform to the child's head shape. Wrap the masking tape around the newspaper a few times just above the child's eyebrows, tightly enough to hold the hat on. Take the newspaper off the child's head and roll the sides up. Encourage children to decorate the hat with things that would be helpful for the person who is wearing the hat.

Extension Possibilities: Expand this activity to include helpful things you might wear on your belt or wrist, or carry in your purse, briefcase, or backpack.

Observation/Assessment
Creates art using various media
Attaches items to a hat

Fantasy Figure Tracks

Materials
paints • spoons • cups • paper of different textures and colors • shoebox • tennis balls • ping pong balls • marbles (any size) • assorted beads • 1-inch blocks • Legos® • spools • other things that might roll and make tracks • drying rack

Teacher Talk
"Look at the tracks you made with the marbles." "What color will you choose next?"

Instructions
Pour different colors of paint into the cups. Place a spoon in each cup. After the child chooses which color or type of paper, place it securely in the bottom of the box. Each child can use the spoon to put a selected object into the paint, lift it out, and drop it in the shoebox. Find a variety of interesting objects for children to experiment with—especially ones that leave unusual shapes or textures of paint. Children can place more than one object and color into the box at a time for more fun. Pick up the shoebox and move the box from side to side. Repeat the process again for more tracks or with additional objects to vary the types of tracks. Help the child take the paper out of the box and place on a drying rack.

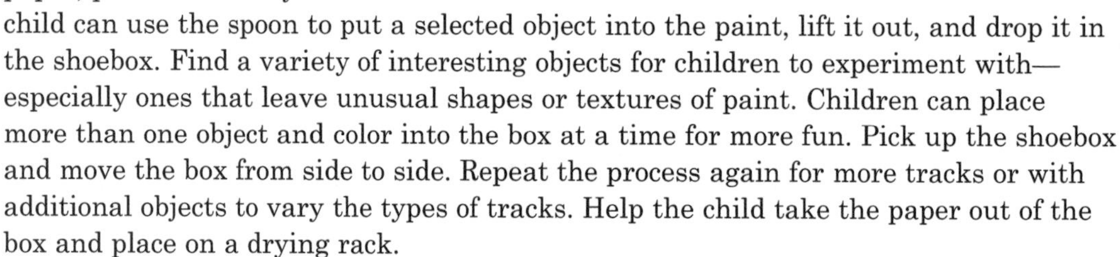

Observation/Assessment
Makes tracks with objects on paper
Chooses art materials from a selection

Masks and More!

Materials
scissors • paper plates • hole punches • yarn • rubber bands • tape • collage materials • glue • coloring materials

Teacher Talk
Ask children questions about how masks can be attached to the head. "Your mask is finished." "How are you going to put it on?"

Instructions
Use scissors to cut the plates in half using a zigzag or wavy pattern. Have a few of the plates pre-cut with two holes for the eyes, so children can discover ways to cut holes in

the other masks they make. Children decorate the masks with the materials provided. Once they are finished decorating, help them explore ways to put their masks on. Some ideas include using yarn, ribbon, string, rubber bands, or tape.

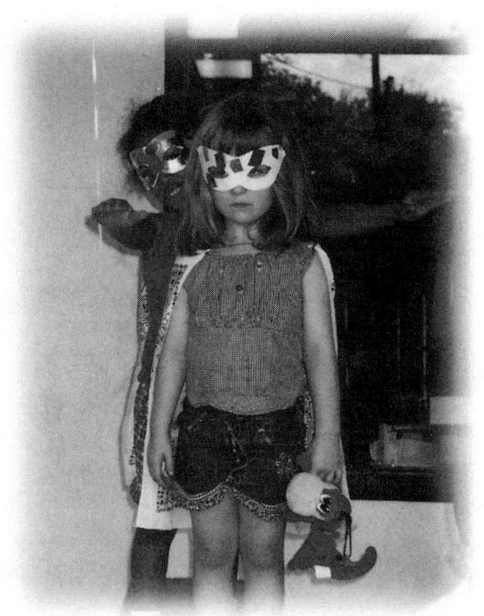

Observation/Assessment
Creates masks using various art media

Other Art Possibilities

- Use Band-Aids and other first aid materials to care for paper dolls that have "injuries."
- Use yarn, ribbons, or thread to weave a spider web on paper plates. Cut slits one-third of the way to the middle of the paper plate. Space slits one-half inch apart.

BLOCKS/CONSTRUCTION POSSIBILITIES

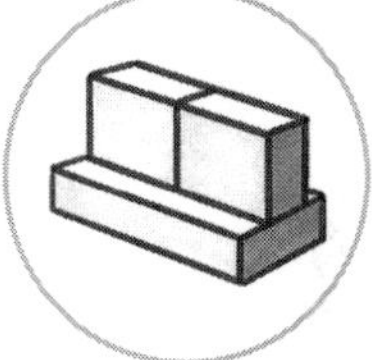

Home Base

Materials
blocks • action figures of all kinds including fantasy figures, community helpers, and family figures • transportation toys, such as fire engines, trucks, ambulances, helicopters, cars • pictures of fire stations, police stations, hospitals

Teacher Talk
"What do you think the home base of your favorite fantasy figure looks like?" "How is it different from (or similar to) a hospital? A police station?" Talk about the similarities and differences.

Instructions
Post the pictures of different types of home bases in the Block Possibilities area. Children can build a home base for their favorite fantasy or real figure.

Extension Possibilities: Observe children's play. Make anecdotal notes as they build. Synthesize your observations into a list of the similarities and differences between the children's fantasy and real figures' home bases.

Anecdotal Note Date:

Chip's home base	Meredith's home base	Paulo's home base
Has a telephone	Is behind a tall wall	Has only one way in
Has many rooms for figures to store gear	Has one room	Has bedrooms for sleeping
Has four barricades around it	Has a garage for vehicles	Is underground

Observation/Assessment
Builds with unit blocks

Masks and Capes

Materials
masks • capes

Teacher Talk
"Your muscles worked hard!" "You are able to move the entire building."

Instructions
Add fantasy figure costumes and props in the block area for children to dress in as they build in the area. Easy costumes can be made with large towels for capes and sunglasses for masks. Avoid using specific action figure costumes. Instead of commercial costumes, use props that encourage children to add details to them.

Observation/Assessment
Uses props and costumes to enhance block play

Other Blocks/Construction Possibilities

- Add fantasy figures to the block area.
- Use colored mats (blue, brown, yellow) to define areas for building.
- Provide cotton batting so children can build "in the clouds."

SCIENCE/DISCOVERY POSSIBILITIES

Solar Power

Materials
two containers of cold water or two blocks of ice the same size • thermometer • books, such as *You Smell and Taste and Feel and See and Hear* by Mary Murphy

Teacher Talk
"Do you think the sun has power?" "What do you think will happen to the water (or ice) if we leave one container (or block) directly in the sunshine and leave the other in the shade?"

Instructions
Feel the temperature of the water by touching it. Determine the exact temperature with the thermometer. Place one bucket of water directly in the sunshine and leave another in the shade. Check both of them later to determine the temperature of the water. Feel the difference.

Extension Possibilities: Make this activity more complex (and more scientific) by taking the temperature every 30 minutes and charting the results. Repeat the experiment with ice, measuring the temperature and how much it melts. Compare the results.

Observation/Assessment
Determines temperature by reading a thermometer
Makes and tests hypothesis
Conducts experiments

Magnet Power

Materials
magnet • notebook • markers

Teacher Talk
"Today I will give you a special power. The power is to determine if an object is made of iron metal or not." "Your job is to find as many objects as possible in the classroom that are attracted to the magnet."

Instructions
Give children a magnet and a notebook. Ask them to find metal objects, test them with the magnet, and draw a picture of the magnetic objects in the notebook. This makes a good partner activity. Children can work in pairs. The more magnets you can have in the classroom, the better. Horseshoe magnets are very easy for preschool children to handle.

Extension Possibilities: Try this activity on the playground or suggest that families help children do it at home. Provide instructions to children and families about what to do.

Observation/Assessment
Differentiates between magnetic and non-magnetic objects using a magnet

Static Electricity Power

Materials
colored salt or sugar crystals • paper plates • latex balloon • synthetic fabric square

Teacher Talk
"What is static electricity?" "Can you see it?"

Instructions
Place salt or sugar crystals on paper plates. Explore the power of static electricity by rubbing the balloon across a piece of synthetic fabric. After a few rubs, hold the balloon about two inches away from the crystals. They will jump up to attach to the balloon.

Other Science/Discovery Possibilities

- Use magnifying glasses, binoculars, and telescope for "super" vision.
- Use a tape recorder with microphone or headphone for "super" hearing.
- Create papier mâché blocks or paint Styrofoam blocks for large rocks, so children can show their superhuman strength.
- Use a karaoke machine for "super" singing.

SENSORY POSSIBILITIES

Gentle Touch

Materials
cotton balls • tree bark • rhythm stick • plastic cup • fork • spoon • playdough • rocks • sand • water • blindfold (optional)

Instructions
Help children understand the power of touch by exposing them to the way it feels to be touched gently by different things. Have one child lay his forearm on a table. Another child touches the first child's arm with the various objects. Encourage children to ask their partners to describe the "feeling" of the objects. Use the blindfold to heighten the sensitivity to the gentle touches. Participate in this activity by recording children's comments and responses.

Sand with Metal Objects and Magnet Wands

Materials
different magnetic and non-magnetic objects • sensory table or tub • sand • magnet wands

Teacher Talk
Talk about the magnetic wands and relate them to other magnets. "Wow, it looks like you have magnetic power. You sucked up all the iron objects in the sand. What else can you do with your magnetic wand?"

Instructions
Place different metal objects in a tub. Pour sand in the tub to cover the objects. Place magnet wands in the area. Provide two boxes labeled "yes" and "no," so children can sort objects by whether the magnet attracts them or not.

Extension Possibilities: Bury items in other ways (mud, sand, water, gel, goop, etc.) to determine if objects are still attracted by the magnet. Compare the outcomes from different experiments.

Observation/Assessment
Sorts objects by whether they are magnetic or not

Flubber and People/Animals

Materials
flubber (equal parts of liquid starch and Elmer's glue mixed together in a bowl or tub) • toy animals • people figures

Teacher Talk
"The animals are stuck in the flubber." "Can you help the people get the animals out?"

Instructions
Let children mix the flubber and then add the animal figures and people figures.

Helpful Hint: Use your hands to mix and knead the solutions together until the liquid is gone. Sometimes you might have to add a little bit of glue to absorb the excess amount of liquid starch. Add food coloring to the flubber to enhance children's interest. This is a wonderful science experiment about proportion because the mixture won't stay together unless the proportions of ingredients are correct.

Observation/Assessment
Mixes two materials to make a third material

LITERACY/WRITING POSSIBILITIES

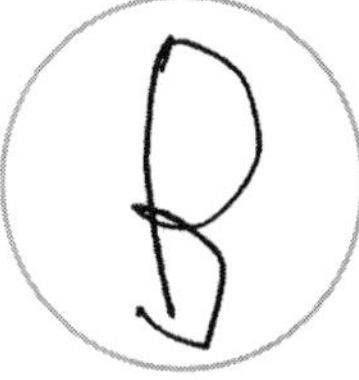

Super Ears

Materials
tape recorder • blank tape • photos • magazine pictures • books, such as *The Wind Blew* by Pat Hutchins

Teacher Talk
"Some fantasy figures can hear even very quiet sounds." "Who can identify this sound?" "Can you show me the picture of this sound?" "What does it say on the picture?"

Instructions
Use the tape recorder to record many different kinds of sounds, such as the sound of a car, airplane, truck, animals, household items, teachers, children, and adult voices. Play back the sounds and ask children to identify them. Collect photographs or magazine pictures of all the sounds you record. Label the pictures. The pictures can be a visual cue to help children identify the sound.

Extension Possibilities: Ask families to record sounds to get a greater variety.

Observation/Assessment
Identifies sounds
Matches sounds to the pictures of what makes them

Heroes among Us

Materials
newspaper articles about heroes • books, such as *Cat Up a Tree* by Ann Hassett

Teacher Talk
"What happened in this article?" "Let's write our own article."

Instructions
Collect examples of stories of heroic deeds from your local newspaper or periodical. Pick one article and read it to the children. Work with children to retell the story in their own words. Write the story on chart paper and read it periodically with the children. Add appropriate punctuation to the story, explaining what you are doing.

Observation/Assessment
Retells story

Other Literacy/Writing Possibilities

- Give children the opportunity to dictate stories about their favorite fantasy figure. Repeat this experience so that the stories have several chapters.
- Create a book to hold drawings of children as fantasy figures.
- Make cards with either the names of children's favorite fantasy figures or action words and/or illustrations on them. Use the cards to create sentences or as patterns for children's writing.

MATH/MANIPULATIVES POSSIBILITIES

Graph Favorite Fantasy and Real Figures

Materials
chart paper • markers

Teacher Talk
"If you don't like any of the fantasy figures on our list, you can vote for 'none.'"

Instructions
Throughout this Possibilities Plan, keep track of the fantasy and real figures that interest children. Then, ask children who their favorite fantasy figures are. If they don't have one (not everyone likes or is familiar with fantasy figures), record "None".

Create a graph to depict what you find out. Ask children to vote for their favorite fantasy figure. You could also create a graph for the real figures.

Helpful Hint: Draw symbols for the fantasy figures (their emblem or sign), so children can look at the symbols and connect them to the written words for the figure.

My Favorite Fantasy Figure

				None
Carlie	★			
Randolph			★	
Miller		★		
Lila	★			
Caroline			★	

Observation/Assessment
Reads a graph
Identifies preferences

Guess Who?

Materials
index cards • markers • paper plates

Teacher Talk
"You know a lot about Batman. You have all the cards that are about him."

Instructions
Choose three or more fantasy and real figures. On each index card, draw a characteristic that describes one of the fantasy or real figures you chose. The characteristics can be from the color or the design of the costumes or character's or person's abilities. Draw or paste a picture of each fantasy or real figure on each paper plate. The children place the cards on one of the plates to sort characteristics by the name of the figure.

Extension Possibilities: Increase the number of characters or people and characteristics to raise the difficulty level.

Observation/Assessment
Matches characteristics to character

Fantasy and Real Figure Lotto

Materials
two packs of stickers containing 6–12 fantasy or real figures • 24 index cards

Teacher Talk
"You made a match." "You remembered where that card was."

Instructions
Put stickers on index cards, so two of each type of figure are included. Place all the cards face down in rows. The person who is taking a turn gets to turn up two cards to see if they match. If the cards do not match, the person turns the cards back down again. Each child who is playing will need to try to remember what the figure was and where it was. If a child gets a match, he gets to have another turn. The game is over when all the cards are matched.

Helpful Hint: To help children see that the occupant of the winner's seat changes, play this game as a "best of" series. Keep track of winners over time to show that different children win.

Extension Possibilities: The same cards can be used for a "Go Fish" card game.

Observation/Assessment
Remembers an image after it is hidden
Matches identical cards

RHYMES/FINGERPLAYS/SONGS/MUSIC POSSIBILITIES

Wind Chime Doorbell

Materials
string • bells • metallic objects that make chiming noises when they strike each other, such as discarded keys, empty tin cans, and so on • coat hanger

Instructions
Attach string to the objects. Hang from the coat hanger. Use the wind chime as a doorbell for Home Base 1 (see page 515) or Home Base 2 (see page 525).

Five Little Firefighers

Instructions
Sing "One Little, Two Little, Three Little Firefighters" to the tune of "Bumping Up and Down in My Little Red Wagon." Hold up your fingers according to the numbers in the song.

Observation/Assessment
Sings familiar songs
Uses hand motions with songs

Other Rhymes/Fingerplays/Songs/Music Possibilities

- Sing "Little Miss Muffett" and "Itsy Bitsy Spider" and talk about real spiders as being different from Spiderman.
- Consider any of the following recorded selections:
  - "Itsy Bitsy Spider" from *Late Last Night* by Joe Scruggs
  - "Itsy Bitsy Spider" from *For Our Children* by Disney
  - "Earth Dance" from *Earth Quest* by Richard Searle
  - "Freeze Game" from *Kids in Motion* by Greg and Steve

GROUP TIME POSSIBILITIES

What Fantasy and Real Figures Do: Use selected comic strips to show what fantasy and real figures do at their regular jobs. Point out that fantasy figures know when to be superheroes and when to be regular people. Apply this idea to the classroom. When is it appropriate to pretend to be a fantasy figure? When is it inappropriate?

Peacemakers: Talk with children about solving problems without fighting. Suggest the following as possible strategies:

1) Ignore the person bothering you.
2) Move away from the person or situation.
3) Talk in a friendly way.
4) Talk firmly, but do not threaten.
5) Get an adult's help.

Stop, Drop, and Roll: Talk with children about fire safety. Real people do not have superpowers and can be injured by fire. Practice how to stop, drop, and roll in the event of clothing catching on fire.

Magnetic Objects Found: Invite the children who searched for magnetic objects with magnets to share their findings and field notes (drawings) with the group. If children repeated the activity at home, compare the differences between the objects found at school and those found at home.

Gentle Touch: Introduce this activity (see page 518) to children, demonstrating the activity directions. Revisit the outcomes and responses by children at another group-time session.

Other Group Time Possibilities

- Read any of the books from the Books List (page 530) in this Possibilities Plan.

MOVEMENT/OUTDOORS POSSIBILITIES

Super Crash

Materials

lightweight boxes • packing tape • balls • books, such as *Wind* by Susan Canizares and Betsey Chesson

Teacher Talk

"Some fantasy and real figures have special equipment that they use to help people."

Instructions

Close the flaps and tape the openings of the boxes closed. Children can stack them and crash them with a ball. Use activities like this one to redirect inappropriate fantasy figure play to acceptable alternatives.

Observation/Assessment

Hits a large box with a ball

Box Bodies

Materials

cardboard boxes • box cutter (teacher only) • tempera paint • paintbrushes • glitter • stickers • collage materials

Instructions

Collect several boxes that are about the size of the preschooler's body between the shoulders and the knees. Cut the top off of the box. Cut two circular holes in each side of the box (for arms) and one circular hole in the bottom of the box (for the head). Decorate the boxes with the additional materials. Use the boxes as costumes outdoors.

Other Movement/Outdoor Possibilities

- Play Follow the Leader using movements of fantasy and real figures.
- Blow bubbles and catch them using different parts of the body.
- Use crepe paper streamers or yarn to decorate tricycles.

PROJECTS/DOCUMENTATION POSSIBILITIES

Look! I'm a Fantasy and a Real Figure!

Materials
large paper • markers • construction paper • scissors • old jewelry

Teacher Talk
"What kinds of things would you wear as a fantasy figure?" "What are your special powers?"

Instructions
Trace each child's body on a large sheet of art paper. Let children design their own fantasy figure costumes. Children can use mirrors to see what their facial features are. Provide plenty of time over several days for children to decorate the figures completely. Interview children as the fantasy figures that they choose to be. Write their words or stories and display them with the figures.

Extension Possibilities: This project works well in two parts. Make two copies of the child's body. Decorate one as the child really is. Decorate the other as a fantasy figure. Interview children to discover how each image is viewed as different. Write their words and display them with both figures.

Observation/Assessment
Draws self-portrait
Uses various art media on large surfaces

Home Base 2

Materials
large appliance box • markers • paints • paintbrushes • craft knife (teacher only)

Teacher Talk
"Where does the princess live? I don't know either. What kind of a place do you think she would like?"

Instructions
Extend the Home Base activity listed in Blocks/Construction (see page 515) by providing large box, art materials, and other moveable parts to include in creating a home base on the playground. Add plenty of windows and doors for visual supervision. Use the notes you took about the home base created in Blocks/Construction for ideas about where to start.

Extension Possibilities: If children are interested in creating more than one home base, add additional boxes. Discard promptly when they become dilapidated or wet.

Solar Power

Materials
two containers of cold water or two blocks of ice the same size • thermometer

Teacher Talk
"Do you think the sun has power?" "What kind?" "What do you think will happen to the water (or ice) if we leave one container (or block) directly in the sunshine and leave the other in the shade?"

Instructions
Turn this activity (see page 516) into a project by repeating the experiment under a variety of different kinds of weather conditions across several seasons.

Observation/Assessment
Determines temperature by reading thermometer
Makes and tests hypothesis
Conducts experiments

FIELD TRIP POSSIBILITIES

Fire Station: Plan a trip to the fire station, so children can talk with real heroes.

Newspaper or Publisher: Plan a trip to show children how newspapers are published.

Bookstore or Library: Plan a trip to a bookstore or library, so children can explore different books about fantasy and real figures in print.

SNACK POSSIBILITIES

Spinach to Make You Strong: Make a fresh spinach salad using spinach leaves and Italian dressing. Talk about how healthy foods make us strong.

Fresh Carrots to Make You See Well: Provide vegetable peelers and fresh carrots, so children can peel carrots for snack. **Safety Note:** Supervise closely.

Rice Crispy Treats: Combine rice cereal and marshmallow creme or melted marshmallows to make gooey treats. The recipe is on the cereal box, or you can improvise and make your own recipe.

FAMILY PARTICIPATION POSSIBILITIES

Fantasy Figure Memories: Ask family members to tell their child about the fantasy figures that were popular when they were young. Ask families to bring in artifacts and examples if they still have them.

Stop, Drop, and Roll with Parents: Ask families to talk with their children about fire safety at home. They can practice Stop, Drop, and Roll together.

Dear Parents

TO

I Am Superman!: The Importance of Pretend Play

All of us remember the fun we had playing with friends during childhood. We want our children to have the same playful memories when they grow up. Yet, many parents wonder if the play time would be better spent in learning activities that are more structured—experiences that will help our children get ready to succeed in school.

The good news is that time spent in uninterrupted, child-directed play IS good preparation for school success. During the preschool years, children benefit from making their own toys and materials to enhance play and from playing for long periods of time alone and with friends with only facilitation, not direction or interruption, from adults. When children have these experiences, they are more successful in school—actually scoring higher on math and reading tests than children who were not able to spend as much time in pretend play. Play is how children integrate what they are learning academically and socially into their behavior. As such, it is a crucial early childhood experience.

Just as important, children learn how to make socially responsible choices through play. They learn to take turns, share resources, understand another child's point of view, solve problems that arise, and so on. All of these lessons challenge their thinking skills and lead them to act and respond in ways that keep the play going. So, let your child play. It IS the best way to prepare for the future.

Helping Children Differentiate between Fantasy and Reality

During the preschool years, children go through several stages of pretend play. At three, they "are" the princess or the firefighter—and love to dress and act the part. As children mature, they begin to "take" the role of the princess or firefighter, adding to the persona with props and costumes, clearly understanding that they stay themselves even when they have the costumes on. This progression from being the character to acting like the character shows children's process in separating real from pretend.

What can parents do to help children make this transition? First of all, don't rush it. Children construct their knowledge about what is real and what is pretend by having many successful experiences with real and pretend things. This awareness comes from testing their thoughts and ideas against the thoughts and ideas of others during play. For example, when children tell each other, "You can't be the princess. I'm the princess," they are testing the idea that there can't be more than one princess at a time.

Secondly, learn to ask good questions to challenge your child's critical thinking skills. Some examples are:

- How does Superman fly through the sky?
- Where does Spiderman get the strings of his web?
- How do you become a princess?

Questions that challenge thinking help children reconsider their ideas and lead to an understanding of whether their ideas are real or pretend.

Prop Boxes

Superheroes Prop Box
masks • tights • capes • walkie-talkie • whimsical sunglasses • flashlights for signals • wristbands • books about heroes

Firefighters Prop Box
helmet • hose • coat • small ladder • small fire truck • firefighter figures • road maps • boots • gloves • hats • bells or siren • books about firefighters

Books

Bugs, Bugs, Bugs by Mary Reid
Calling Dr. Amelia Bedelia by Herman Parish
Cat Up a Tree by Ann Hassett
Clifford Visits the Hospital (Clifford vista el hospital) by Norm Bridwell
Do Cowboys Ride Bikes? by Kathy Tucker
Doctor Maisy by Lucy Cousins
Dr. Desoto by William Steig
Even Firefighers Hug Their Moms by Christine Kole Maclean
Fireboat by Maira Kalman
Firefighters A to Z by Chris Demarest
Gilberto and the Wind by Marie Hall Ets
How Do You Lift a Lion? by Robert E. Wells
I Am a Rock by Jean Marzollo
The Itsy Bitsy Spider by Rosemary Wells
Jobs People Do by Christopher Maynard
Mama Zooms by Jane Cowen-Fletcher
Messages to Ground Zero: Children Respond to September 11, 2001 by Shelley Harwayne
A Million Visions of Peace by Jennifer Garrison
Mother! Mother! I Feel Sick! Call for the Doctor, Quick, Quick, Quick! by Remy Charlip and Burton Supree
Miss Spider's Tea Party by David Kirk
My Dad by Anthony Browne
Our Granny by Margaret Wild
Peace at Last by Jill Murphy
Peace Is a Circle of Love by Joan Walsh Anglund
Rip to the Rescue by Mat Mitter
Seeing by Helen Frost
Wind by Susan Canizares and Betsey Chessen
The Wind Blew by Pat Hutchins
You Smell and Taste and Feel and See and Hear by Mary Murphy

Observation/Assessment

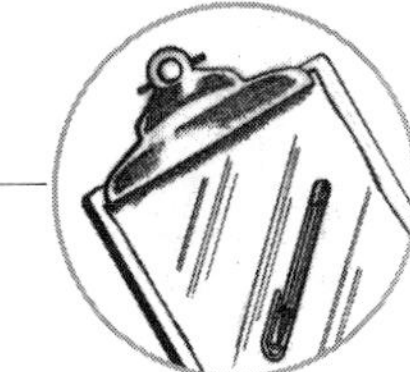

Takes on various roles in dramatic play, page 512
Uses props to enhance dramatic play, page 513
Dresses and undresses in costumes, page 513
Creates masks using various media, page 514
Attaches items to a hat, page 514
Makes tracks with objects on paper, page 514
Chooses art materials from a selection, page 514
Creates using various art media, page 515
Builds with unit blocks, page 515
Uses props and costumes to enhance block play, page 516
Determines temperature by reading a thermometer, pages 517 and 526
Makes and tests hypothesis, pages 517 and 526
Conducts experiments, pages 517 and 526
Differentiates between magnetic and non-magnetic objects using a magnet, page 517
Sorts objects by whether they are magnetic or not, page 518
Mixes two materials to make a third, page 519
Identifies sounds, page 519
Matches sounds to the pictures of what makes them, page 519
Retells story, page 520
Reads a graph, page 521
Identifies preferences, page 521
Matches characteristics to character, page 521
Remembers an image after it is hidden, page 522
Matches identical cards, page 522
Sings familiar songs, page 523
Uses hand motions with songs, page 523
Hits a large box with a ball, page 524
Draws self portrait, page 525
Uses various art media on large surfaces, page 525

Picture File/Vocabulary

boots
capes
costumes
chemistry
experiments
fantasy
firefighters
gloves
graph
hero
hypothesis
lotto
magnet
metal
patterns
portrait
reality
rescuers
roles
science
solar power
spiders
story-telling
sequence
strength
superheroes
target
temperature
thermometer
wind

Concepts Learned in Fantasy Figures and More

Content Knowledge

- ☐ Heroes have special characteristics or behaviors.
- ☐ A magnet attracts iron metals.
- ☐ A graph helps us compare.
- ☐ The sun has power.
- ☐ The sun can heat things up.
- ☐ Vegetables can make me strong.
- ☐ Many real people help others.

Process Knowledge

- ☐ I can create using various art media.
- ☐ I have different play partners.
- ☐ I can play various roles.
- ☐ I can dress and undress in costumes.
- ☐ I can use glue to attach things.
- ☐ I can weave simple patterns.
- ☐ I can cut using scissors.
- ☐ I can experience dramatic play in miniature.
- ☐ I can build with various blocks.
- ☐ I can differentiate between magnetic and non-magnetic objects.
- ☐ I can match cards.
- ☐ I can sing familiar songs.
- ☐ I can use hand motions to sing.
- ☐ I can throw objects.
- ☐ I can hit a target with a ball.
- ☐ I can move my body to catch bubbles.
- ☐ I can help others.
- ☐ I can apply first aid.
- ☐ I can make masks.
- ☐ I can differentiate between real and fantastic characteristics and behaviors.
- ☐ I can figure out why people do things.
- ☐ I can match sounds with pictures of what makes the sounds.
- ☐ I can play lotto games.

Pre-academic Skills

- ☐ I can retell stories.
- ☐ I can make and test hypotheses.
- ☐ I can sort objects by color or type.
- ☐ I can count using one-to-one correspondence.
- ☐ I can write using pens and pencils.
- ☐ I can read a graph.
- ☐ I can match characteristics to a character.
- ☐ I can remember a card face after it is hidden.
- ☐ I can arrange objects in a series.

Possibilities Plan—
Saying Goodbye

Getting Ready to Plan

Children often have to say goodbye. Sometimes they are saying goodbye to a friend who is moving away; at other times, they are saying goodbye to a well-liked teacher. At the end of the preschool years, most children will be saying goodbye to their preschool, their preschool friends, and familiar preschool teachers as they make the transition to elementary school.

Teachers have many opportunities to help children learn to say goodbye during the preschool years crop up from time to time. A child leaves because of a family move, a teacher takes leave to have a baby, or a child has a baby sister and stays home with Mom or Dad during her maternity leave. As these situations arise, teachers can support children's understanding of this life experience by supporting children in the process of saying goodbye.

As you explore this topic with children, you will be giving them tools to use as they make the important transition to elementary school as well as to handle the myriad, less dramatic separations that take place as a routine part of daily living.

Now is the time to think about what you want the children in your group to learn about each of these topics. Topics are explored in general below.

Transportation: Often when children say goodbye, the process of change involves transportation. Children enjoy active play, and the topic of transportation presents many opportunities for active play. Help children understand that transportation may vary according to where people live. Explore information related to trains, airplanes, buses, and cars.

Memories: Teachers have many ways to help children save their memories. Try photographs, address books, and drawings of favorite things. Help children realize that change is a part of life and that we can keep old friends even when we make new friends.

New Experiences: Children may be intimidated by new experiences and new places. Talk about how they have had many new experiences at school with you. Help children remember the many things they have learned and experienced.

Saying Goodbye: Children need to be able to express their feelings and concerns about saying goodbye in the activities and experiences in the classroom. Incorporate many celebrations of the things children cherish about their friends and experiences. Validate feelings of sadness and suggest many ways for children to stay in touch with each other.

Now that you have an idea about the general content of the Possibilities Plan, you are ready to proceed with developing your own plan.

Toys and Materials*

Purchased

blackboard
blocks
books about weather, transportation, and saying goodbye
camera (instant, 35mm, or digital)
colored pencils and pens
crayons
favorite costumes and props
film
full-length plastic mirror
glue
mirror markers (fine tip, broad tip, permanent, washable)
paint
paint tray
paintbrushes of various types
paper (craft, construction, cardboard, white)
people figures
pre-mixed concrete
road mat
scissors
scrapbooks
small fruit or shade tree
stapler
tempera paint
toy airplanes, trains, cars, and buses
toy buildings and trees, traffic signs, train tracks, vehicles
unit blocks
Vaseline™
wooden puzzles with travel themes

Gathered

address book
beach items
boxes, small and large
broom
buckets of different sizes
chairs
clothes and swimsuits
counting, sorting, or patterning cards
construction paper
containers
cotton balls
film canisters
garbage bag
gift boxes
keyboard
keys
hats
large and small boxes
magazines
manual typewriter
maps
phone book
photo albums or photos of children in the class
pictures of airplanes, trains, and buses
pictures of highways, roads, and overpasses
pillowcases, white or pastel
pitchers, small plastic
rotary telephone
pictures of travel
purses
sand
scrub brushes
sheet, white
shovel
small table
soap
stuffed animals
suitcases or travel bags
table, small
tickets (airplane, train, bus, metro)
tissues or toilet paper
transportation uniforms
travel clothes
travel kit
travel magazines
vehicles
white or pastel white sheet
zipper-closure plastic bags

*Note: Please consider the ages and abilities of the children in your classroom. Use only safe, non-toxic materials.

Saying Goodbye

WEB

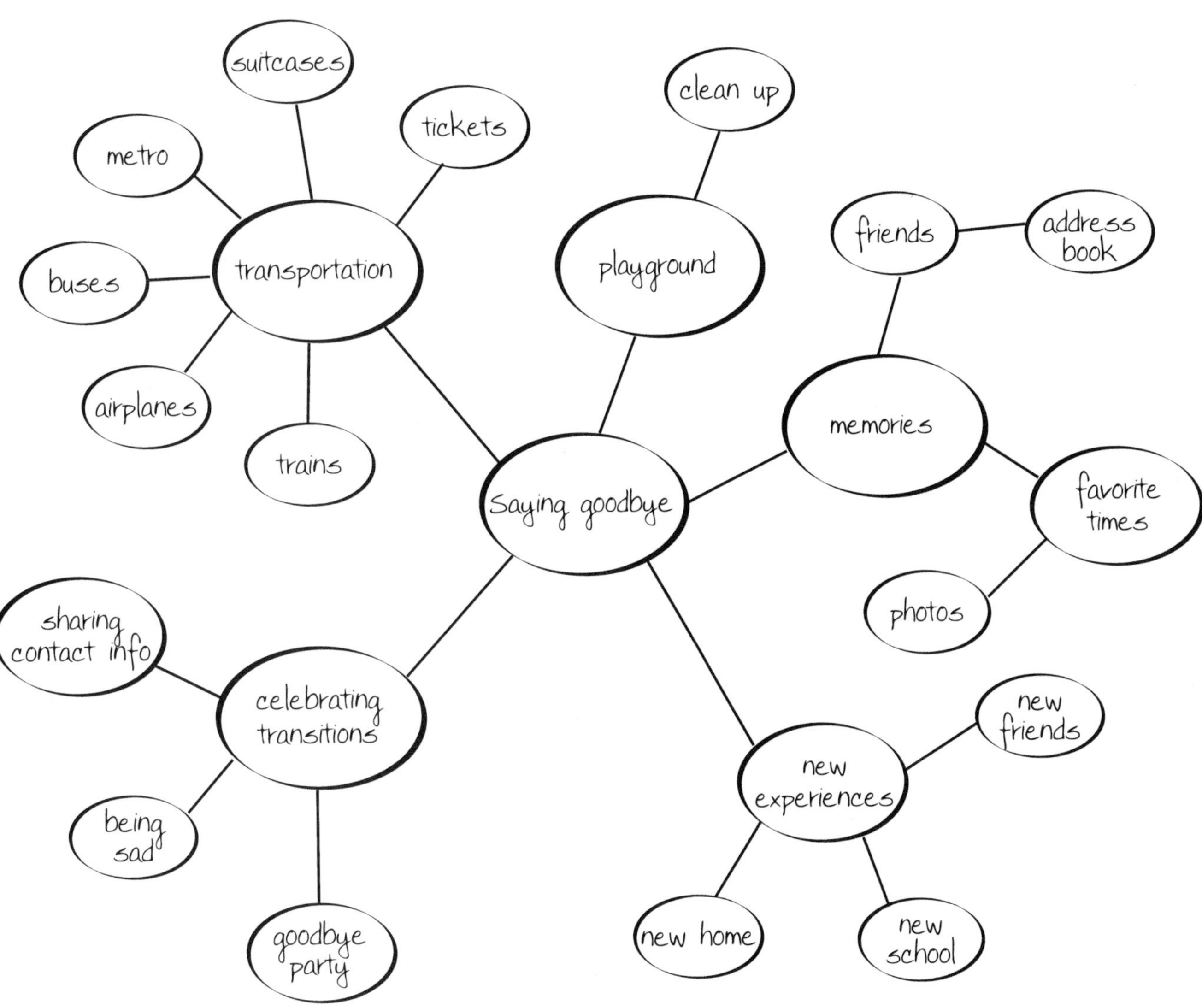

Saying Goodbye

PLANNING PAGES

Plan Possibilities

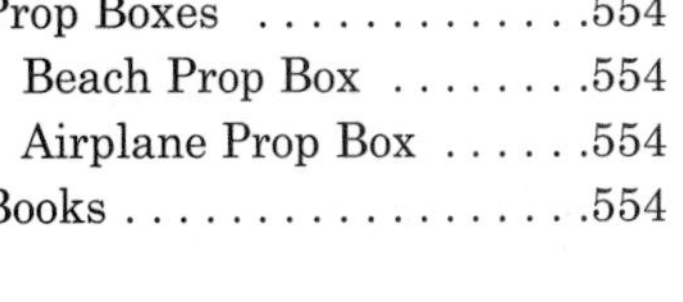

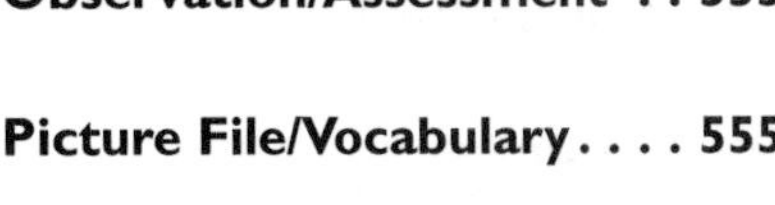

Dear Parents

ACTIVITIES AND EXPERIENCES FOR SAYING GOODBYE

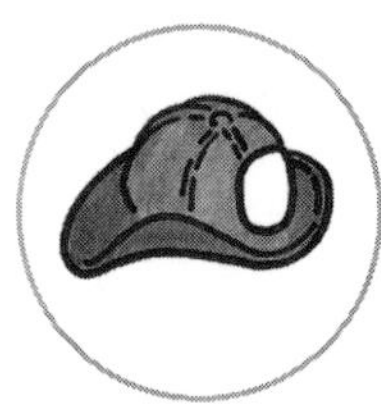

DRAMATIC POSSIBILITIES

See You at the Airport!

Materials
large boxes • table • old keyboard • airplane tickets • travel kit • variety of clothes people might wear on the airplane or as an airline or airport employee • suitcases • clothes • pictures of airplanes • hats • books, such as *Clifford Takes a Trip* by Norman Bridwell

Teacher Talk
"Have you ever been to the airport?" "Why did you go?" "What do people need to have to get on the plane?"

Instructions
Create airport props. Make a ticket counter with boxes and a table. Put the keyboard and papers on the table. Place the traveling kit, clothes, etc. in Dramatic Possibilities. Use the props to play different roles involved with air travel. Collect materials from someone who works for an airline or someone who travels frequently.

Extension Possibilities: Create a train station or bus terminal by collecting appropriate materials and props.

Observation/Assessment
Takes on various roles in dramatic play

Our Class Is Special

Materials
stuffed animals • chairs • small table • blackboard • books • classroom materials • clothes like ones the teacher wears • books, such as *David Goes to School* by David Shannon

Teacher Talk
"What do you like best about what we do in our class?" "Look, we have students (stuffed animals) who are ready to play and learn."

Instructions
Children can be the teacher in the Dramatic Possibilities area. Children or stuffed animals can be the students.

Things I Used to Do/Use/Wear

Materials
costumes • props • camera • film • construction paper • markers • pens • pencils • books, such as *I Am Not a Crybaby* by Norma Simon

Teacher Talk
"What costume do you plan to use for your memory photo?"

Instructions
Bring out all children's favorite costumes and props. Children choose their favorite things to do/use/wear for their memory photographs. When the pictures are developed, mount them on construction paper and children can write or dictate descriptions of the memory. Make double prints, so you will have one to display in the classroom and one to put in the child's portfolio.

Observation/Assessment
Writes or dictates to teachers about things that have happened in the classroom

ART POSSIBILITIES

Map and Travel Magazine Collage

Materials
travel magazines • old maps • scissors • glue • markers • large paper • books, such as *Round Trip* by Ann Jonas

Teacher Talk
"You have pictures of the beach in your collage. Do you like the beach?"

Instructions
Talk about what a collage is before beginning this activity. Show examples from the picture file. Provide materials for children to create collages of their own designs. Markers are for drawing on top of the collage and adding names and dates to the collages.

Observation/Assessment
Creates collages using various materials

Drawing a Happy Memory

Materials
photographs or photo albums of children in your classroom • variety of sizes of paintbrushes and paints • markers • colored pencils and pens • books, such as *Friends at School* by Rochelle Bunnett

Teacher Talk
"What photograph shows your favorite memory of school?" "Why is that your favorite?"

Instructions
Children talk about a favorite memory and then create a drawing related to the memory.

Helpful Hint: Add a collection of photos of children to the art table to give children ideas about what to draw. Compare the photographs to the drawing, discussing how they are similar and different.

Extension Possibilities: Take children's dictations about their drawings.

Observation/Assessment
Creates drawings

Other Art Possibilities

- Create a handprint banner.
- Make wheel art by rolling vehicles in paint and then rolling them on the paper.
- Make collages from magazine pictures by cutting out facial features (eyes, noses, ears, mouths, etc.) and pasting them to construction paper.

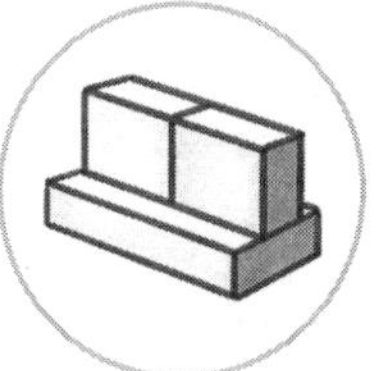

Block Airport

Materials
unit blocks • airplanes • buildings • paper runways • people figures • books such as *On the Go* by Ann Morris or *How I Spent My Summer Vacation* by Rochelle Burnett

Teacher Talk
"This is a large airport." "How many airplanes do we have?"

Instructions
Provide materials for building an airport. Provide an "under construction" sign, so children can continue building over time.

Observation/Assessment
Builds using unit blocks

Road Mat

Materials
vinyl or carpet road mat • shower curtain or butcher paper • variety of types of blocks • traffic signs • markers • vehicles

Teacher Talk
"What kind of traffic sign do we need at the intersection?"

Instructions
Provide a road mat for children to build on. You can create a road mat using a plastic shower curtain and permanent markers, a large sheet of butcher paper and markers, or a sheet and markers.

Observation/Assessment
Participates in dramatic play in miniature

Roads and Vehicles Galore!

Materials
vehicles of all types • lots of unit blocks perhaps borrowed from other classrooms • pictures of highways, roads, overpasses, and so on

Teacher Talk
"How many lanes do we need to build for all these vehicles?" Talk about lanes, ramps, bridges, etc. on the highway.

Instructions
Build a highway system throughout the classroom, using the characteristics you see in the pictures.

SCIENCE/DISCOVERY POSSIBILITIES

Nostalgia

Materials
old manual typewriter • old rotary phone • paper • phone book • address book • books, such as *The Quilt Story* by Tony Johnston

Teacher Talk
"This is the kind of typewriter people used to have long ago. Would you like to type a letter?" "The phone doesn't have buttons. Instead of pushing buttons, put your finger in a hole and turn the dial."

Instructions
Provide these bits of nostalgia for children to explore. Resale shops are a good source of historical items such as these. Ask parents and family members to participate in locating additional items.

Planting a Memory Tree

Materials
small fruit or shade tree • shovel

Teacher Talk
"Planting a tree is a wonderful way to make a memory." "Let's plant a tree in honor of our class."

Instructions
Purchase a tree at a local nursery. Find out the optimum circumstances under which the tree will grow. Plan a tree-planting ceremony and celebration. Give all children an opportunity to help dig the hole for the tree. Most trees come with a tag or some other kind of growing instructions. Place the tree tag or instruction in the Science/Discovery Possibility area, so children can review how the tree will grow.

Extension Possibilities: Extend this activity by researching tree types, taking a field trip to an area plant nursery, and tapping parents and family members who are interested in gardening or trees.

Observation/Assessment
Digs using a shovel

Other Science/Discovery Possibilities

- Provide stamps and magnifying glasses, so children can examine stamps for details.
- Make a plaque for the memory tree.
- Provide a travel atlas, globes, and books about other countries.
- Add a variety of weather maps.

Tissues and Water in the Sensory Table

Materials
tissues or toilet paper • water • sensory table • small plastic pitchers

Teacher Talk
"Sometimes people are sad when they have to say goodbye. They may cry and wipe their tears with tissues." "How do the wet tissues feel?"

Instructions
Children can tear apart tissues or toilet paper. Then they can pour water into the sensory table using small pitchers. Play with the mush. They can even make small shapes and let them dry. Add colored tissues for interest.

Observation/Assessment
Tears paper
Pours water from a small pitcher

Vehicles in the Sensory Table

Materials
sand • vehicles

Teacher Talk
"How many trucks did you find? How many cars?"

Instructions
Bury vehicles in the sensory table for children to find. Correlate the ones you hide to the transportation interests of the children and to what you are talking about related to transportation. Plan a clean-up activity using mild soap and water. Put vehicles outside to dry.

Observation/Assessment
Finds hidden items

What Is That?

Materials
cotton balls • film canisters

Teacher Talk
"What smell is that?" "What does it make you think of?"

Instructions
Put a cotton ball in each film canister. Place a drop of perfume or flavoring on each cotton ball. Place the top on the canister when children are not smelling it to lengthen the life of the activity.

Extension Possibilities: Send each child home with a film canister (labeled with the child's name), a cotton ball, and instructions for parents or family members to add a drop of cologne or a favorite flavoring to the film canister and return it to school. Offer children the opportunity to graph which fragrances they like and don't like.

Observation/Assessment
Identifies different scents

LITERACY/WRITING POSSIBILITIES

Goodbye Books

Materials
8 ½" x 11" sheets of paper • scissors • glue • stapler • markers • photos of the children taken throughout the school year • zipper-closure plastic bags • scrapbooks • colored pens and pencils

Teacher Talk
"When you came to our classroom, you had all of your teeth. Now you are missing your front teeth!"

Instructions
Display a collection of scrapbooks for children to understand the idea of collecting evidence of memories and putting them together in a book. Then, help children create goodbye books to chronicle their experiences at school. Put each child's photo collection in a zipper-closure bag. Work with children to create a scrapbook of their experiences at school using the photographs. Glue photos onto paper, encourage children to add drawings to the pages, and take dictation from children to add to the drawings and photos.

Extension Possibilities: Add to the book once a month to create it over time.

Friendship Books

Materials
8 ½" by 11" paper • markers • crayons • art supplies • stapler • books, such as *Friends* by Helme Heine

Teacher Talk
"What message did you want to write in Harrison's book?"

Instructions
Work with children individually to make a Friendship Book. Take children's dictation about their friends and what they like to do with them. Let children illustrate the pages. Collect all the pages about each child and bind into a book with a construction paper cover. Include children's books in the area, such as *Friends* by Helme Heine.

Other Literacy/Writing Possibilities

- Place old letters, business statements, letterhead paper, and postcards in the area for children to explore.
- Make a scrapbook using extra classroom photographs.
- Using permanent markers and one pillowcase for each child, create memory pillowcases that the children can take home. Each child writes his name or draws a picture on every child's pillowcase. (Ironed pillowcases work better. Place a piece of cardboard inside the pillowcase to make a good writing surface.)

MATH/MANIPULATIVES POSSIBILITIES

Train Tracks

Materials
trains • train tracks • model trees • model buildings

Teacher Talk
"You have built a really long train track." "Let's count the pieces of track you used."

Instructions
Create a bar graph of the types of track pieces and the props in your train set. Laminate it and store the chart with the set. As children play with the set, ask them how many pieces of track are in use. Help them use the bar graph to figure out the answer. As children clean up after playing with the train set, help them count the pieces to confirm that all of the pieces are accounted for.

Extension Possibilities: Make additional bar graphs for other manipulatives to support children in locating all of the pieces after playing with the toys. Expand this activity by adding bar graphs to puzzles, to block sets, and to marker, pencil, crayon, or chalk collections. This adds to children's numeracy experiences and helps them recognize when parts of the collection are missing or lost.

Observation/Assessment
Uses a bar graph to count objects
Builds using train tracks

Travel Puzzles

Materials

wooden puzzles with travel themes (transportation, different geography, etc.) • books, such as *Tattered Sail* by Verla Kay • glue • cardboard • travel pictures or maps • gift boxes or zipper-closure plastic bags

Teacher Talk

"You have put together all the pieces of the puzzle."

Instructions

Place puzzles in area for children to choose from and complete. Make additional puzzles by gluing travel pictures or maps to a piece of cardboard and cutting it into pieces. Number the pieces and store in gift boxes or zipper-closure plastic bags.

Extension Possibilities: As children get more proficient at putting together simple puzzles, increase the number of pieces and complexity.

Observation/Assessment

Completes 10-piece, then 20-piece, then 50-piece, then 100-piece puzzles

Counting/Sorting Vehicles

Materials

counting/sorting/patterning cards • small vehicles • construction paper • glue

Teacher Talk

"Follow the pattern on the card. That's right, red truck, blue truck, red truck, blue truck."

Instructions

Make cards by drawing or cutting out shapes of the vehicles you have collected. For counting, glue the vehicle shapes on a sheet of construction paper and write a number under each shape (1 through 10 or whatever number is appropriate for your class). For sorting, glue a shape on one side of the piece of construction paper. Draw a line down the center of the page. Then glue a different shape on the other side. Children sort vehicles and put them on the appropriate side of the sheet. To pattern the vehicles, glue a pattern of vehicle shapes on a piece of paper leaving blank spots after the pattern is established. For example, blue truck, red truck, white truck, blue truck, red truck, _________.

Extension Possibilities: Change cards periodically to reflect where children are in their skill development, increasing the complexity of the counting, sorting, or patterning over time.

Observation/Assessment
Counts using one-to-one correspondence
Sorts by one dimension, such as color, and two dimensions such as color and shape
Completes patterns
Continues patterns

RHYMES/FINGERPLAYS/SONGS/MUSIC POSSIBILITIES

The More We Get Together

Instructions
Teach children "The More We Get Together." Use the song for morning or afternoon group time as a gathering song.

Helpful Hint: Point to other children when the song says, "your friends," and point to yourself when the song says, "my friends."

Observation/Assessment
Uses hand motions for familiar songs

Row, Row, Row Your Boat

Teacher Talk
"This is a song we can sing in many different ways."

Instructions
Teach children the song, "Row, Row, Row Your Boat." Use the song at different times during the day. Vary the actions in subsequent verses to match children's experiences such as, "eat our snack," "go to sleep," "march outside," or "clean up the room."

Extension Possibilities: Sing variations of the song by substituting, "Drive, drive, drive your car," "Sail, sail, sail your boat," "Drive, drive, drive the bus," or "Board, board, board the plane."

Observation/Assessment
Sings variations on familiar songs

Other Rhymes/Fingerplays/Songs/Music Possibilities

- Consider any of the following recorded selections:
  - "Blanket for a Sail" from *For Our Children* by Disney
  - "Yellow Submarine" from *Rockin' Down the Road* by Greg and Steve
  - "Can a Jumbo Jet Sing the Alphabet?" from *Kimbo* by Hap Palmer
  - "We All Live Together" from *Kimbo* by Greg and Steve
- Sing "The Ants Go Marching" and use it as a transition during the day.

GROUP TIME POSSIBILITIES

PJ Party: Plan a PJ day when you and the children wear pajamas at school. Talk about having pleasant dreams and memories.

Messengers: Line children up in two lines. Whisper an instruction to the first child in each line, such as "fill the blue bucket with sand." Children whisper the instruction to the next child in line, and the last person in line follows the instruction. Children may be surprised at how different the actions of the last child in each line are than the initial instruction!

Nostalgia Introduction: Introduce this Science/Discovery activity by sharing some of the nostalgic items with children. Discuss how the items were used historically. Compare the items to the modern versions children might have today.

Goodbye Books: Introduce the idea of goodbye books by sharing your own scrapbook or scrapbooks collected from parents and family members. Talk about what is included in them. Share examples of goodbye books completed by children from previous classrooms as well.

Other Group Time Possibilities
- Read any of the books from the Books List (page 554).
- Talk about planting the memory tree.
- Introduce the name pillowcase activity (page 545), demonstrating how to keep the pillowcase straight and smooth for writing names.

Thank You, Playground

Materials
soap • scrub brush • old clothes or swimsuits • garbage bag • broom • large buckets • small buckets

Teacher Talk
"Have you enjoyed playing on the playground?" "What can we do to say thank you to our playground?"

Instructions
Bring cleaning materials outside, so children can wash climbing structures and outside toys. If the weather is cold, use small spray bottles with warm water in them.

Extension Possibilities: Invite families to help children say "thank you" to the playground.

Goodbye Outdoor Party

Materials
snacks • juice

Teacher Talk
"Will you show me what you can do on the playground?" Talk with children about their accomplishments.

Instructions
Give children a chance to reflect and be proud of their physical accomplishments on the playground. Let them demonstrate their skills. Children can serve their own snack on the playground. Plan a way to wash hands before snack.

Extension Possibilities: Repeat this idea in each activity area.

Observation/Assessment
Reflects on accomplishments
Climbs on playground equipment

Other Movement/Outdoor Possibilities

- Add transportation signs (taxi, bus, etc.) to riding toys.
- Add traffic signs to riding path.
- Use materials from Dramatic Possibilities to build a transportation hub outside.

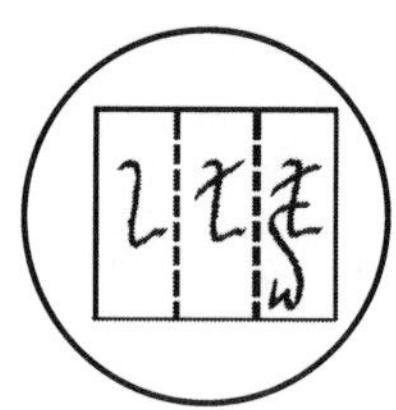

PROJECTS/DOCUMENTATION POSSIBILITIES

"Friends Love Me" Doll

Materials
two large sheets of craft paper for each child • stapler • markers • newspapers • full-length plastic mirror • crayons • markers • books, such as *Let's Be Friends Again* by Hans Wilhelm

Teacher Talk
"What do you love most about Sophia?"

Instructions
Trace around each child on a large sheet of craft paper. Place the paper on another large sheet of craft paper and cut out both at the same time. Each child decorates one of the body shapes as himself. Take children's dictation on the second body shape. Ask children to tell you what they like about each of their friends or what they like to do with their friends. Staple the two figures together leaving the head area open. Children crumple newspaper and stuff it in the figure. When the figure is stuffed, close the head area of the paper body shape with staples. Or, you may want to do the comments and the self-portrait on one large sheet of paper. Trace the child's body on the paper and let each child decorate the tracing to be himself. Around the edges of the figure write the sentences that the children dictate.

Helpful Hint: Hang a clothesline on the wall. Use clothespins to hang the shapes, so they will be out of the way when children are not working on them.

Group Map and Travel Magazine Collage

Materials
maps • travel magazines • scissors • glue • paste • tape • large paper

Instructions
Children can work on the giant collage over time. Initiate this activity by creating a list of collage materials that children would like to use and then collecting the materials.

A Moment in Time

Materials
camera • construction paper • fine-tip permanent markers • books, such as *The Night Before Kindergarten* by Natasha Wing

Teacher Talk
"You will be able to take three different photographs in the next two weeks. Let's plan carefully, so you will have pictures of things that you want to remember."

Instructions
Give each child an opportunity to take a set number of photographs of anything at school that he wants to remember after he says goodbye. When children decide on a particular photograph, ask them to dictate to you why they want to take that picture. Write children's words on one half of a sheet of construction paper. After the picture is taken and developed, glue the picture to the other half of the paper.

Helpful Hint: Make the choice of photographs to be taken an extended and thoughtful process.

Observation/Assessment
Takes photographs
Dictates to teacher

Goodbye Stepping Stones

Materials
pre-mixed concrete • water • containers (pizza boxes, aluminum pie tins, large cardboard ice cream tubs, etc.) • Vaseline • pencil

Instructions
Make goodbye stepping stones. Use pre-mixed concrete that only needs to have water added. Mix the concrete according to directions on the bag. Use a variety of containers as forms. Coat the containers with Vaseline before adding the concrete. For stepping stones, pour at least two inches of concrete into the containers. After the concrete begins to set, children can press their hands or feet into the concrete and write their names using a pencil. After 24 hours, carefully remove concrete from containers. Allow concrete stones to cure completely before moving them and using them as stepping stones. Children need to wear latex or vinyl gloves when working with the concrete mix and wash their hands thoroughly after completing their handprints. Recess the stones to ground level.

FIELD TRIP POSSIBILITIES

Transportation Trips: Plan a trip to the airport, train station, or bus terminal, so children can observe people saying hello and goodbye.

Post Office: Plan a trip to your neighborhood post office. Talk with someone about how to change an address.

Tourism Bureau: Plan a trip to a tourism bureau or welcome center, so children can see what newcomers to the area might learn. Collect brochures and maps to take back to school. Plan future field trips on brochures collected.

SNACK POSSIBILITIES

Teddy Bear Picnic: Invite children to bring teddy bears or stuffed animals to school. Children can eat snack outside on sheets or blankets with their teddy bears.

Porridge: Read children's favorite versions of "Little Red Riding Hood." Serve oatmeal (porridge) and talk about the story.

Travel Snack: Fresh fruit or breakfast bars make great travel food. Wash hands, give children their snack, and then travel to the playground to eat it.

FAMILY PARTICIPATION POSSIBILITIES

Goodbye Party: Hold a Goodbye Party, so families and children can say goodbye to each other at the end of the year or when a child leaves. Provide a signup sheet for party supplies: napkins, paper plates, snacks, juice.

Friends' Addresses: Ask each of the parents to bring an address book or small notebook to leave in a basket in the classroom. Label them clearly. Ask parents to write down their child's name, address, and phone number in each book. Children and parents can add their own names and address to each other's address books.

Thank You, Playground with Families: Invite parents to help children say "goodbye" and "thank you" to the playground.

Say "Yes" More Than "No"

Here is a suggestion guaranteed to decrease your child's questioning, tantrumming, and demanding behavior. The tip is to say "yes" more often than "no." This doesn't mean that you turn decision making over to your child. It simply means that you tell your child that he or she can "do" more things than he or she "can't do." For example, when your child asks for a cookie before supper, tell him or her, "Yes, you can have a cookie right after we eat dinner."

Often, we try too hard to make every interaction a teaching and learning experience. We want our children to understand that cookies spoil appetites. Explanations are appropriate. They tell our children that we have valid reasons for our limits and rules. But, they often lead to conflict when children see rules and limits as barriers to getting what they want. Your child needs to know that you are in touch with his or her desires. Tell your child often that he or she will get what he or she wants, and when.

The lesson learned is that your child can wait to get what he or she wants—a powerful lesson in delaying gratification that will serve your child well.

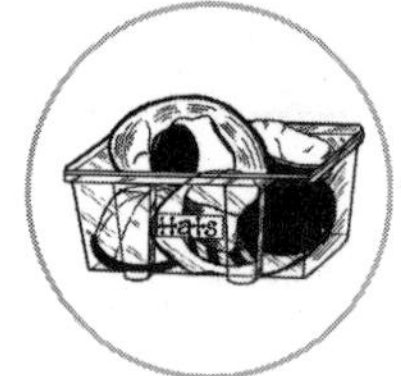

Curriculum Resources

Prop Boxes

Beach Prop Box
Beach umbrella • beach bag • sunscreen bottle • swimsuits • T-shirts • suitcases • travel bag • books • purses • keys

Airplane Prop Box
Airplane tickets • suitcases or travel bags • clothes • pictures of airplanes • large boxes • hats • table • travel kit • old keyboard • variety of clothes people might wear on the airplane or as an airline or airport employee

Books

Alicia Has a Bad Day by Lisa Jahn-Clouch
Billy and the New School by Laurence Anholt
The Bus for Us by Suzanne Bloom
Chicken Sunday by Patricia Polacco
Clifford Takes a Trip by Norman Bridwell
David Goes to School by David Shannon
The Doorbell Rang by Pat Hutchins
Eight Hands Round: A Patchwork Alphabet by Ann Whitford Paul
Friends at School by Rochelle Bunnett
Friends by Helme Heine
Goldilocks and the Three Bears by James Marshall (or children's favorite version)
Guess How Much I Love You by Sam McBratney
How Do I Feel? by Norma Simon
How I Spent My Summer Vacation by Mark Teague
I Am Not a Crybaby! by Norma Simon
I Read Signs by Tana Hoban
Let's Be Friends Again! by Hans Wilhelm
Little Bunny's Preschool Countdown by Maribeth Boelts
Making Friends by Fred Rogers
Miss Bindergarten Gets Ready for Kindergarten by Joseph Slate
Monster Goes to School by Virginia Mueller
The Night Before Kindergarten by Natasha Wing
On the Go by Ann Morris
The Quilt by Ann Jonas
The Quilt Story by Tony Johnston
Round Trip by Ann Jonas
Row, Row, Row Your Boat by Pippa Goodhart
Tattered Sails by Verla Kay
Tom Goes to Kindergarten by Margaret Wild
Will I Have a Friend? by Miriam Cohen

Observation/Assessment

Takes on various roles in dramatic play, page 538
Writes or dictates to teachers about things that have happened in the classroom, page 539
Creates collages using various materials, page 540
Creates drawings, page 540
Builds using unit blocks, page 541
Participates in dramatic play in miniature, page 541
Digs using a shovel, page 542
Tears paper, page 543
Pours water from a small pitcher, page 543
Finds hidden items, page 543
Identifies different scents, page 544
Uses a bar graph to count objects page 545
Builds using train tracks, page 545
Completes 10-piece, then 20-piece, then 50-piece, then 100-piece puzzles, page 546
Counts using one-to-one correspondence, page 547
Sorts by one dimension, such as color, and two dimensions such as color and shape, page 547
Completes patterns, page 547
Continues patterns, page 547
Uses hand motions for familiar songs, page 547
Sings variations on familiar songs, page 547
Reflects on accomplishments, page 549
Climbs on playground equipment, page 549
Takes photographs, page 551
Dictates to teacher, page 551

Picture File/Vocabulary

address
airplane
airport
bar graph
beach
bus station
camera
collage
concourse
engineer
film
friends
goodbye
hello
highway
lane
negative
phone book
photographs
pilots
relatives
road
rotary phone
runway
scents
self-portraits
shovel
station
terminal
train station
train tickets
travel
truck
typewriter
vacation
vehicle

Concepts Learned in Saying Goodbye

Content Knowledge

- ☐ Vehicles ride on wheels.
- ☐ Vehicles have different purposes.
- ☐ Vacations are trips for fun and relaxation.
- ☐ People go to the airport to fly on a plane.
- ☐ People go to the train station to ride a train.
- ☐ People go to the bus station to ride a bus.
- ☐ Weather maps show changes in weather.
- ☐ Maps are to scale.
- ☐ Maps show details of a particular area.
- ☐ Trains travel on tracks.
- ☐ Airplanes fly in the sky and land on runways.
- ☐ Buses, cars, and trucks ride on roads.

Process Knowledge

- ☐ I can create art using various media.
- ☐ I can draw my self-portrait.
- ☐ I can clean up my own messes.
- ☐ I can build with various blocks.
- ☐ I can dig with a shovel.
- ☐ I can tear paper.
- ☐ I can pour liquid from a small pitcher.
- ☐ I can sing familiar songs.
- ☐ I can make hand motions to familiar songs.
- ☐ I can march to music.
- ☐ I can clean using soap and water.
- ☐ I can climb on equipment on the playground.
- ☐ I can crumple newspaper.
- ☐ I can take photographs.
- ☐ I can dictate to my teacher.
- ☐ I can reflect on my accomplishments.

Pre-academic Skills

- ☐ I can read picture books and maps.
- ☐ I can write my name.
- ☐ I can write simple words.
- ☐ I can count using one-to-one correspondence.
- ☐ I can sort by one dimension and two dimensions.
- ☐ I can continue a pattern.
- ☐ I can put together puzzles.
- ☐ I can recognize simple words.

Appendix Contents

Tools to Support Observation and Assessment

Three tools are included in the Appendix to help you collect and use the assessment information embedded in Developmental Tasks and Possibilities Plans. Each is designed to simplify and systematize the assessment process into usable and easily understandable information for families, as well as for documenting children's developmental progress and skill acquisition.

Observation Classroom Summary

The Observation Classroom Summary provides a technique for easily tracking teacher observations. Write children's names on the vertical lines. When you make an observation, check off and date the observation item. You will be able to tell at a glance what observations have been completed for each child. Observations can also be gleaned from reviewing anecdotal notes that are written during Possibilities Plans. When an anecdotal note is the source of the observation data, simply write AN (anecdotal note) and the date the note was written. If you are creating your own Possibilities Plans to supplement the 12 Possibilities Plans included in ***Innovations***, identify observation items for the activities you plan and create your own Observation Classroom Summary using the blank form included in the Appendix on page 571.

Concepts Learned Classroom Summary

Each Possibilities Plan includes a list of concepts that children will learn during each Plan. There are three kinds of concepts: Content Knowledge, Process Knowledge, and Pre-Academic Skills. The summary allows teachers to tell at a glance which children have mastered each concept. Use the blank form to identify concepts learned when you develop your own Possibilities Plans.

Child Accomplishment Record

The Child Accomplishment Record is a tool to use when sharing information concerning children's accomplishments with families during conferences or at regular reporting intervals. The Child Accomplishment Record informs parents and family members about their child's accomplishments and experiences at school. It shares the teacher's observations and indicates what concepts have been mastered. It also provides an opportunity for both families and teachers to comment on the child's accomplishments and explore other topics of interest or concern. Use the Child Accomplishment Report to connect families to their child's classroom experiences.

Observation Classroom Summary

Chapter 2 Possibilities Plan

Saying Hello

Name																									
Takes on various roles in dramatic play																									
Dresses and undresses in costumes																									
Has particular play partners																									
Uses props to enhance dramatic play																									
Draws, sketches, or paints using a variety of art media																									
Draws self-portrait																									
Accomplishes level of detail in felt people																									
Observes similarities and differences																									
Uses tools appropriately																									
Builds using various materials																									
Builds using unit blocks																									
Examines/observes using magnifying glass																									
Counts sequentially with birthday candles																									
Uses one-to-one correspondence with birthday candles to years of age																									
Uses letter-like symbols or scribbles to represent print																									
Identifies initial letter of own name																									
Identifies initial letter sound of own name																									
Indicates preferences and interests																									
Recognizes family members																									
Sorts by one dimension (eye color) and two dimensions (eye color and hair color)																									
Uses graphing skills																									
Counts sequentially from 1-10, counts by 5's, 10's, etc.																									
Breaks words down into syllables																									
Listens to stories, rhymes, fingerplays, and songs																									
Identifies patterns in words and numbers																									
Adds details to self-portrait																									

Observation Classroom Summary

Chapter 2 Possibilities Plan

Castles

	Name																								
Takes on various roles in dramatic play																									
Uses props to enhance dramatic play																									
Dresses and undresses in costumes																									
Uses collage materials to decorate paper																									
Builds using a variety of materials																									
Spreads and pounds playdough																									
Uses wet sand to create shapes																									
Compares building with wet and dry sand																									
Uses correct pencil grip																									
Traces letters																									
Draws using paintbrushes and watercolors																									
Creates a simple pattern																									
Matches photos and pictures																									
Moves to the musical beat																									
Freely explores space while dancing																									
Throws beanbags at target																									

Chapter 3 Possibilities Plan

Making Messes and Cleaning Them Up

Observation Classroom Summary

	Name																								
Washes dishes																									
Dries dishes																									
Classifies laundry by type																									
Uses mathematical language, such as more, less, same, bigger, smaller, most, least, and so on																									
Recognizes that different coins have different values																									
Uses problem-solving skills																									
Throws a ball																									
Follows safety rules																									
Paints using different methods																									
Hits golf tees with hammer																									
Makes plans for using materials																									
Uses materials independently or with others																									
Works cooperatively to extend resources																									
Uses positional vocabulary, such as over, under, by, on top of, below, and between																									
Groups objects by size																									
Builds using various materials																									
Sorts items by whether they sink or float																									
Mixes, stirs, and measures materials																									
Draws shapes																									
Writes letter-like marks																									
Writes letters																									
Groups similar containers																									
Sorts items according to how they are used																									
Creates simple patterns																									
Uses small muscles of hand to squeeze paint from gloves																									

Observation Classroom Summary

Chapter 3 Possibilities Plan
Creepy Crawlies & Germs

	Name																								
Takes on various roles in dramatic play																									
Uses props to enhance dramatic play																									
Dresses and undresses in costumes																									
Observes insects using magnifying glass																									
Paints using various media																									
Constructs bug box																									
Builds using blocks and other materials																									
Observes using magnifying glasses																									
Matches shapes and colors																									
Creates simple patterns using shapes and colors																									
Dictates ideas																									
Dictate sentences																									
Uses one-to-one correspondence to 10 or 20																									
Adds numbers 1 to 5, then 1 to 10																									
Sorts insects by likes/doesn't like, flies/doesn't fly																									
Recites and acts out fingerplays																									
Makes field notes (drawings)																									
Uses field notes to explain ideas or observations																									
Records observations																									

Observation Classroom Summary

Chapter 4 Possibilities Plan

Maps

	Name																								
Takes responsibility for others' possessions																									
Shares resources for play																									
Paints using various materials																									
Builds using blocks and other materials																									
Experiences dramatic play in miniature																									
Uses the five senses for exploration																									
Makes simple diagrams and maps																									
Explores maps, globes																									
Shows curiosity about where places are on maps																									
Estimates distance																									
Counts using one-to-one correspondence																									
Repeats familiar stories																									
Labels directions by name—north, south, east, west																									
Balances on a beam																									
Knows home address																									
Understands the concept of directions																									
Knows name of city or location of residence																									

Observation Classroom Summary

Chapter 4 Possibilities Plan

Spin Me a Tall Tale

Name																									
Tells stories with a beginning, middle, and end																									
Expresses emotions using puppets																									
Participates in art activities																									
Makes sock puppets																									
Creates collages using various art media																									
Adds details to block constructions																									
Constructs with blocks																									
Uses geometric pegboard to create designs																									
Records sketches of designs																									
Differentiates among sounds by listening																									
Tells stories using puppets																									
Paints using various materials																									
Traces letters																									
Uses one-to-one correspondence																									
Uses basic graphing skills																									
Counts objects in book illustrations																									
Labels objects according to size																									
Acts out stories																									
Acts out stories using props																									
Follows directions																									

Observation Classroom Summary

Chapter 5 Possibilities Plan

What Will I Be ?

	Name																								
Uses props to enhance dramatic play																									
Takes on various roles in dramatic play																									
Draws using markers																									
Builds a variety of structures using blocks and block supports																									
Observes plant growth																									
Names plant parts including the stem, leaves, roots																									
Matches nuts and bolts																									
Creates landscape using various materials																									
Matches pictures with objects or tools																									
Plays simple games																									
Measures using a tape measure, ruler, or yardstick																									
Creates a matching pattern of materials																									
Listens to and repeats rhymes																									
Matches animal sounds to animal names																									
Sings songs																									
Uses tools for gardening																									
Digs holes in dirt using tools																									
Matches pairs of shoes																									
Draws self-portrait using crayons and markers																									

Observation Classroom Summary

Chapter 5 Possibilities Plan

Space

	Name																								
Uses props to enhance dramatic play																									
Takes on various roles in dramatic play																									
Finds items hidden from sight																									
Uses fine motor skills for art expression																									
Builds using blocks																									
Counts backwards from 5, from 10																									
Paints using paint and brushes																									
Writes own name																									
Sequences planets according to position																									
Matches names of planets to their images																									
Matches colors																									
Matches shapes																									
Counts to 5, then 10, using one-to-one correspondence																									
Moves body to the rhythm of a song																									
Paints using various media																									
Creates using papier-mâché																									
Participates in group projects																									
Makes circles on paper using patterns																									

Observation Classroom Summary

Chapter 6 Possibilities Plan

Where Does It Come From and Where Does It Go?

	Name																								
Uses props to enhance dramatic play																									
Manipulates small objects																									
Takes on various roles in dramatic play																									
Has particular play partners																									
Sorts recycled materials according to how they can be used in art																									
Paints using salad spinner																									
Builds sculptures using toothpicks, apples, and carrots																									
Builds using food boxes of various sizes and shapes																									
Builds using unit blocks and a variety of box blocks																									
Observes and discussed how water is purified																									
Makes recycled paper																									
Observes and discusses worm farm																									
Rolls playdough to form worms																									
Dictates ideas to teacher																									
Identifies food according to its place on the food pyramid																									
Associates written words with their pictures																									
Identifies logos																									
Sorts materials into recycling categories.																									
Plays using racket and ball																									
Categorizes food according to where it belongs on the food pyramid																									

Observation Classroom Summary

Chapter 6 Possibilities Plan
Building Up and Tearing Down

Name																									
Takes on various roles in dramatic play																									
Uses props to enhance dramatic play																									
Follows simple directions																									
Creates three-dimensional art																									
Rebuilds block constructions after knocking them down																									
Uses tools to take apart appliances																									
Forms shapes using playdough																									
Observes and discusses chemical reaction																									
Uses sandpaper to sand wood																									
Wears safety glasses when working with wood																									
Builds using Legos®																									
Explores house plans and blueprints																									
Draws house plans																									
Turns pages in a book																									
Builds using a variety of blocks																									
Measures using construction tools																									
Counts using one-to-one correspondence																									
Keeps time to the beat of music																									
Builds using big boxes																									
Cooperates with classmates to reach a goal																									
Paints and draws on large surfaces																									

Observation Classroom Summary

Chapter 7 Possibilities Plan

Fantasy Figures and More

	Name																								
Takes on various roles in dramatic play																									
Uses props to enhance dramatic play																									
Dresses and undresses in costumes																									
Creates art using various media																									
Attaches items to a hat																									
Makes tracks with objects on paper																									
Chooses art materials from a selection																									
Builds with unit blocks																									
Uses props and costumes to enhance block play																									
Determines temperature by reading a thermometer																									
Makes and tests hypothesis																									
Conducts experiments																									
Differentiates between magnetic and non-magnetic objects using a magnet																									
Sorts objects by whether they are magnetic or not																									
Mixes two materials to make a third																									
Identifies sounds																									
Matches sounds to the pictures of what makes them																									
Retells story																									
Reads a graph																									
Identifies preferences																									
Matches characteristics to character																									
Remembers an image after it is hidden																									
Matches identical cards																									
Sings familiar songs																									
Uses hand motions with songs																									
Hits a large box with a ball																									
Draws self portrait																									
Uses various art media on large surfaces																									
Determines temperature by reading thermometer																									
Makes and tests hypotheses																									
Conducts experiments																									

Observation Classroom Summary

Chapter 7 Possibilities Plan

Saying Goodbye

Name																									
Takes on various roles in dramatic play																									
Writes or dictates to teachers about things that have happened in the classroom																									
Creates collages using various materials																									
Creates drawings																									
Builds using unit blocks																									
Participates in dramatic play in miniature																									
Digs using a shovel																									
Tears paper																									
Pours water from a small pitcher																									
Finds hidden items																									
Identifies different scents																									
Uses a bar graph to count objects																									
Builds using train tracks																									
Completes 10-piece, then 20-piece, then 50-piece, then 100-piece puzzles																									
Counts using one-to-one correspondence																									
Sorts by one dimension, such as color, and two dimensions such as color and shape																									
Completes patterns																									
Continues patterns																									
Uses hand motions for familiar songs																									
Sings variations on familiar songs																									
Reflects on accomplishments																									
Climbs on playground equipment																									
Takes photographs																									
Dictates to teacher																									

Observation Classroom Summary

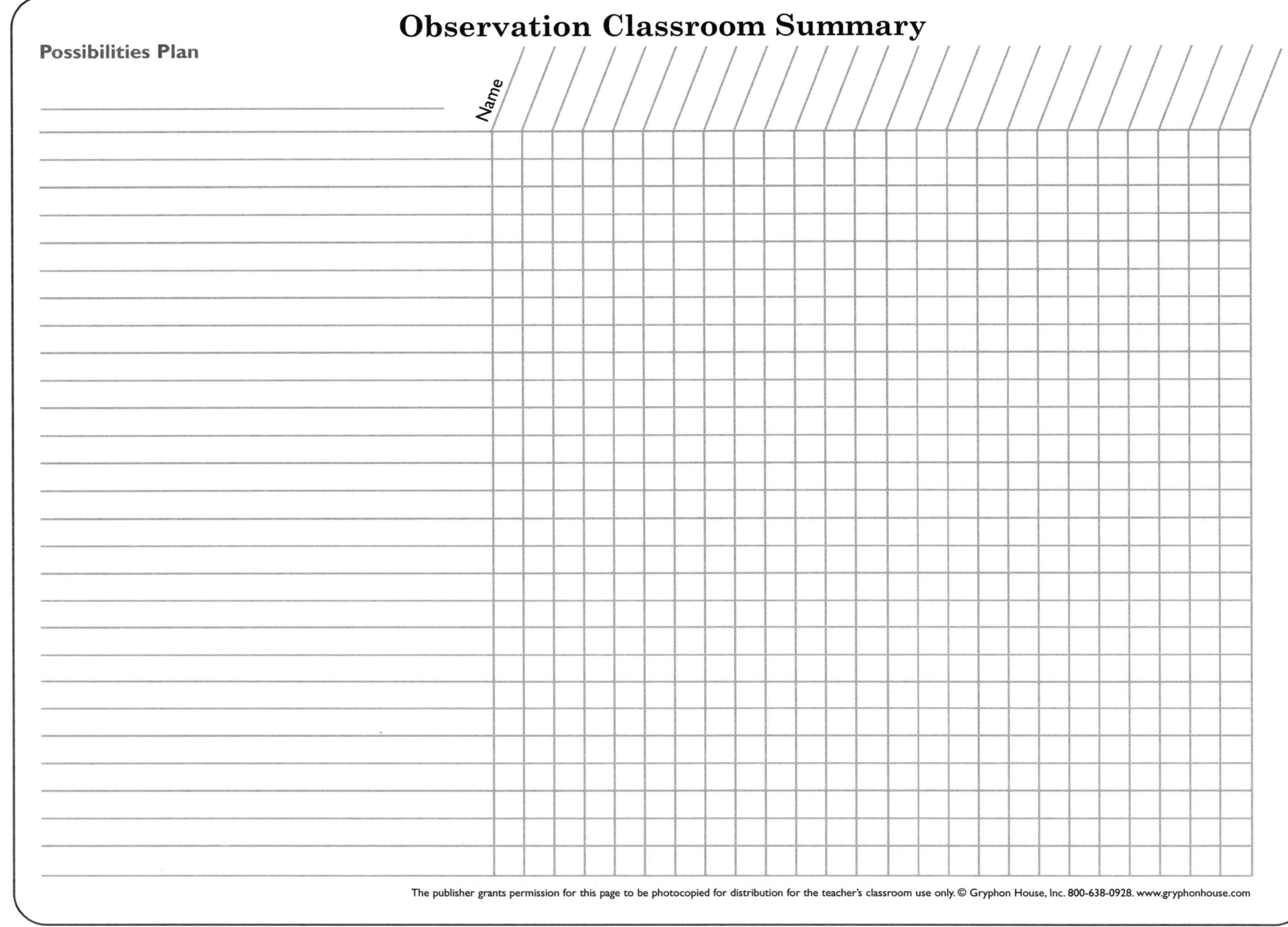

Concepts Learned Classroom Summary

Concepts Learned in

Saying Hello

	Name																								
Content Knowledge																									
All children are alike in some ways.																									
All children are different in some ways.																									
Fruits have different tastes.																									
I know the members of my family.																									
All families are not the same.																									
I can determine the color of my friend's eyes, hair, skin color, and so on.																									
Houses have different rooms.																									
I can identify my emotions.																									
I can count birthday candles.																									
I can say hello in many different ways.																									
Process Knowledge																									
I can cut with scissors.																									
I can play post office.																									
I can draw myself.																									
I can make puppets.																									
I can draw and paint to express my ideas.																									
I can trace.																									
I can make prints—handprints and footprints, and so on.																									
I can find out what is inside a telephone, intercom, answering machine, and so on.																									
I can build with blocks.																									
I can use a magnifying glass.																									

Concepts Learned Classroom Summary

Concepts Learned in

Saying Hello (continued)

	Name																								
Process Knowledge (continued)																									
I can taste different foods and tell others which ones I like.																									
I can paint with different parts of my body.																									
I can find things out from others by asking questions.																									
I can communicate my thoughts in drawings and with letter-like writing.																									
I know a lot about me.																									
I can follow a leader.																									
I can sing.																									
I can dance.																									
I can recognize my emotions.																									
I can wait just a minute for my turn.																									
Pre-academic Skills																									
I can count my fingers (one number to each finger).																									
I can count the beats (syllables) in my name.																									
I can identify the first letter of my name.																									
I understand that words have meaning.																									
I am interested in what words say.																									
I can make a graph.																									
I can listen to others.																									
I can ask questions.																									
I can answer questions.																									
I can observe likenesses and differences.																									

Concepts Learned Classroom Summary

Concepts Learned in

Castles

Name																									
Content Knowledge																									
Castles are a different kind of building than we have today.																									
Knights wore armor for fighting.																									
Castles from different countries look different.																									
Coats of arms are symbols or crests that identify particular families.																									
Castles have moats and drawbridges.																									
Castles were built during the medieval period.																									
People in castles worked in different ways.																									
Kings, queens, and nobles ruled the castles.																									
Knights rode horses.																									
Castles were used for protection.																									
Castles have walls and turrets.																									
Process Knowledge																									
I can cut using scissors.																									
I can play Bocce ball.																									
I can throw a beanbag.																									
I can build using different materials.																									
I can make sandcastles.																									
I can make stained glass windows.																									
I can create mazes.																									
I can dance.																									
I can hit a target with a beanbag.																									
I can roll balls.																									

Concepts Learned Classroom Summary

Concepts Learned in

Castles (continued)

Name

Process Knowledge (continued)

I can paint.

I can clean up.

I can put on and take off dress up clothes.

Pre-academic Skills

I can make hypotheses.

I can make a necklace out of beads and string.

I can weigh things with a balance scale.

I can sort by one dimension (color, weight, size, function, etc.).

I can sort by two dimensions (color and size, function and weight, etc.).

I can create a mathematical equation.

I can create patterns.

I can create a story with a beginning and an ending.

I can create a story with a beginning, middle, and an ending.

I can illustrate my words and thoughts.

I can tell how things are different.

I can match photographs and pictures.

I can estimate.

I can grip a pencil.

Concepts Learned Classroom Summary

Concepts Learned in
Making Messes and Cleaning Them Up

	Name																								
Content Knowledge																									
Some messes are easy to clean up and others are hard.																									
Coins have different values.																									
Recycling saves resources.																									
Cleaning up messes is the last step of making them.																									
Some things float in water, and others sink.																									
I need different tools to clean up different messes.																									
Handwashing has many steps.																									
Handwashing keeps me healthy.																									
Singing while you clean up makes it more fun.																									
Process Knowledge																									
I can make messes.																									
I can clean up my messes.																									
I can clean up my room.																									
I can wash things (clothes, dishes, my hands, tricycles).																									
I can sort (socks, mittens, laundry, coins).																									
I can paint with many different objects (balls, flyswatters, potato mashers, spatulas, mops, brooms).																									
I can hammer golf tees into Styrofoam.																									
I have creative ideas.																									
I can catch popcorn after it pops.																									

Concepts Learned Classroom Summary

Concepts Learned in

Making Messes and Cleaning Them Up (continued)

	Name																								
Process Knowledge (continued)																									
I can complete puzzles.																									
I can write letters.																									
I can draw shapes.																									
Pre-academic Skills																									
I can match soap bars to toilet paper rolls to see if we have the same number of each (one-to-one correspondence).																									
I can make simple patterns.																									
I can remember and repeat fingerplays and rhymes.																									
I can figure things out (how to drop eggs without breaking them, what floats and what sinks, how to make clean mud, how to mix flour and water together, how to make plastic wiggly worms stick to the sides of the sensory tubs).																									
I can trace figures, letters, and numbers with my fingers.																									
I can make plans.																									

Concepts Learned Classroom Summary

Concepts Learned in

Creepy Crawlies and Germs

Content Knowledge	Name																								
Beekeepers are called apiarists.																									
Bees live in an apiary or beehive.																									
Some bugs hide under logs, branches, rocks, etc..																									
Some insects fly, and some don't.																									
Bugs hatch from eggs.																									
Baby bugs can look different from adult bugs.																									
Caterpillars turn into moths and butterflies.																									
Some insects have patterns on them.																									
Insects use patterns and color to camouflage and protect themselves from predators																									
Spiders spin webs.																									
Webs catch insects so spiders can eat the body fluids.																									
Insects can climb because their feet are made for gripping.																									
Spiders crawl many different ways.																									
Worms live underground.																									
Worms make tunnels in the ground.																									
Germs grow.																									
Germs can make you sick.																									
Covering a sneeze keeps you from spreading germs to others.																									
Frequent handwashing keeps you from spreading your germs to others.																									

Concepts Learned Classroom Summary

Concepts Learned in Creepy Crawlies and Germs (continued)

	Name																								
Process Knowledge																									
I can create insects with playdough, collage materials, egg cartons, and pipe cleaners.																									
I can express ideas, thoughts, or feelings through creative dramatics.																									
I can move to music.																									
I can collect objects to observe likenesses and differences.																									
I can draw a two-dimensional image.																									
I can create a three-dimensional image.																									
Pre-academic Knowledge																									
I can count the beats of music.																									
I can research my ideas to learn more.																									
I can make predictions.																									
I can recognize shapes in the natural environment.																									
I can look at books to get information.																									
I can read pictorial context clues in books.																									
I am interested in print.																									

Concepts Learned Classroom Summary

Concepts Learned in

Maps

	Name																								
Content Knowledge																									
Maps are drawn to scale.																									
A scale represents distance.																									
Maps help us find things.																									
Maps give directions.																									
North, south, east, and west are directions.																									
Pirates sailed on the seas in ships.																									
Wind makes sailing ships move.																									
A compass shows direction.																									
Long ago, people navigated by using the stars.																									
Luggage carries clothes and personal belongings on a trip or on vacation.																									
People camp in tents.																									
People travel to different locations.																									
I can find my house on a map.																									
I can find my state and city on a map or globe.																									
I know what country my ancestors lived in.																									
Process Knowledge																									
I can balance on a "plank."																									
I can use a map.																									
I can search for hidden treasure.																									

Concepts Learned Classroom Summary

Concepts Learned in

Maps (continued)

	Name																								
Process Knowledge (continued)																									
I can play the role of pirate.																									
I can pack a suitcase.																									
I can make rubbings.																									
I can build a replica of my neighborhood.																									
I can build an airport.																									
I can build a train station.																									
I can build a working compass.																									
I can dig for treasure.																									
I can use a compass to find North.																									
Pre-academic Skills																									
I can read signs (stop, yield, no right turn, etc.).																									
I can count.																									
I can read a map.																									
I can categorize.																									
I can investigate and test my ideas.																									
I can predict.																									
I know my address.																									

Concepts Learned Classroom Summary

Concepts Learned in
Spin Me Tall Tale

Name

Content Knowledge

Stories have characters.

Quilts are made up of many squares.

There are many ways to tell a story.

Music can tell stories.

Hand signs can tell stories.

Pictures can tell stories.

Words can tell stories.

Invitations ask people to attend special events.

You can tell the same story many different ways.

Process Knowledge

I can perform.

I can make puppets.

I can produce a puppet show.

I can paint to music.

I can make books in several different forms.

I understand how sound moves through the air in waves.

I can follow a recipe.

I can act out stories.

Concepts Learned Classroom Summary

Concepts Learned in

Spin Me Tall Tale (continued)

Name

Pre-academic Skills

I can differentiate between sounds just by listening (auditory discrimination of sounds).

I can figure out pictures that tell a story (reading context clues to discern meaning).

I can identify how many characters there are in a story.

I can dictate a story with a beginning, middle, and ending.

I can predict what will happen next in a story.

I can sequence a story.

Concepts Learned Classroom Summary

Concepts Learned in
What Will I Be?

	Name																								
Content Knowledge																									
Adults have different jobs.																									
Firefighters, police officers, and medical workers are community helpers.																									
Farmers grow crops and animals.																									
Construction workers build.																									
Carpenters build using tools and wood.																									
Plumbers install pipes for water.																									
Teachers help children and adults learn.																									
Plants need light and water to live.																									
Process Knowledge																									
I can play different roles.																									
I can explore anything I want to be.																									
I can explore career options.																									
I can play with different partners.																									
I can dress/undress in different costumes.																									
I can build with blocks and boxes.																									
I can glue, paint, cut, and draw.																									
I can build a train station/airport.																									
I can match nuts and bolts.																									

Concepts Learned Classroom Summary

Concepts Learned in

What Will I Be? (continued)

	Name																								
Process Knowledge (continued)																									
I can use a tape measure.																									
I can use tools for gardening.																									
I can hammer nails.																									
I can draw my self-portrait.																									
Pre-academic Skills																									
I can count to 10.																									
I can observe and discuss my observations.																									
I can identify careers by uniforms and equipment used.																									
I can use printed words as a pattern for writing.																									
I can dictate.																									
I can copy numbers.																									

Concepts Learned Classroom Summary

Concepts Learned in

Space

	Name																								
Content Knowledge																									
A control center controls the space ship.																									
Different planets are different colors and sizes.																									
Planets rotate around the sun.																									
The moon rotates around the earth.																									
The sun is very hot.																									
Planets can be hot if they are close to the sun or cold if they are far away from the sun.																									
Gravity is different on different planets.																									
Astronauts travel in space.																									
Astronauts wear space suits in space.																									
Process Knowledge																									
I can find hidden objects.																									
I can paint with hot or cold paint.																									
I can build with blocks.																									
I can stack cups and glasses.																									
I can use a telescope/binoculars to see things.																									
I can punch holes in a pattern.																									
I can paint using colored ice.																									
I can shape playdough with cookie cutters.																									
I can build using Styrofoam balls and toothpicks.																									

Concepts Learned Classroom Summary

Concepts Learned in

Space (continued)

Name

Process Knowledge (continued)

I can sing and move to music.

I can carry a backpack.

I can create with papier-mâché.

Pre-academic Skills

I can identify planets.

I can sequence planets by position.

I can count backwards from 10.

I can use letters to represent words.

I can connect a sound to a letter.

I can write letters.

I can write my name.

I can recognize familiar words.

I can match colors and shapes.

I can count (forward or backward) using one-to-one correspondence to 5 (to 10).

Concepts Learned Classroom Summary

Concepts Learned in

Where Does It Come From and Where Does It Go?

	Name																								
Content Knowledge																									
I can make recycled paper.																									
Worms recycle fruits and vegetables into compost.																									
I can make mashed potatoes.																									
I know many different types of pizza toppings.																									
I can sort recycled materials into paper, plastics, and aluminum.																									
I know many songs and fingerplays about food.																									
I know about the food pyramid.																									
I can identify four different food groups on the food pyramid.																									
I can eat five fruits or vegetables a day.																									
Process Knowledge																									
I can play roles in Dramatic Possibilities.																									
I can create with recycled materials.																									
I can create sculptures.																									
I can construct things.																									
I can stock the shelves in the grocery store.																									
I can build with lots of different kinds of blocks.																									

Concepts Learned Classroom Summary

Concepts Learned in

Where Does It Come From and Where Does It Go? (continued)

Name

Process Knowledge (continued)

I can make my own snacks.

I can throw beanbags into milk jugs.

I can play paddle ball.

Pre-academic Skills

I can write alphabet letters.

I can sort kitchen utensils like forks, knives, spoons, etc..

I can recycle words and pictures from printed materials.

I can read the logos of my favorite snack foods.

I know the sounds that vowels can make.

I can count to 5, or 10, or 15, or 20.

Concepts Learned Classroom Summary

Concepts Learned in Building Up and Tearing Down

	Name																								
Content Knowledge																									
Blueprints and house plans are drawn to scale.																									
Blueprints are plans to help people build.																									
I can find my house on a map.																									
I can find my city on a county and state map.																									
People build using different tools and materials.																									
Demolition is when something is torn down.																									
Recycling is when something is used again.																									
Construction vehicles can be very big.																									
Safety is important at a construction site.																									
Process Knowledge																									
I can sort and recycle.																									
I can build using blocks and boxes.																									
I can create three-dimensional structures.																									
I can build a replica of a community.																									
I can cooperate with classmates to reach a goal.																									
I can keep time to music.																									
I can build using Legos®.																									
I wear safety glasses when I work.																									
I can use simple tools.																									
I can create using various art media.																									

Concepts Learned Classroom Summary

Concepts Learned in
Building Up and Tearing Down (continued)

Name

Pre-academic Skills

I know my colors.

I can count using one-to-one correspondence.

I can read a house plan.

I can predict what will happen.

I can plan before I begin an activity.

I can solve problems.

I can measure using rulers and measuring tape.

I can form letters.

Concepts Learned Classroom Summary

Concepts Learned in

Fantasy Figures and More

	Name
Content Knowledge	
Heroes have special characteristics or behaviors.	
A magnet attracts iron metals.	
A graph helps us compare.	
The sun has power.	
The sun can heat things up.	
Vegetables can make me strong.	
Many real people help others.	
Process Knowledge	
I can create using various art media.	
I have different play partners.	
I can play various roles.	
I can dress and undress in costumes.	
I can use glue to attach things.	
I can weave simple patterns.	
I can cut using scissors.	
I can experience dramatic play in miniature.	
I can build with various blocks.	
I can differentiate between magnetic and non-magnetic objects.	
I can match cards.	
I can sing familiar songs.	
I can use hand motions to sing.	

Concepts Learned Classroom Summary

Concepts Learned in Fantasy Figures and More (continued)

	Name
Process Knowledge (continued)	
I can throw objects.	
I can hit a target with a ball.	
I can move my body to catch bubbles.	
I can help others.	
I can apply first aid.	
I can make masks.	
I can differentiate between real and fantastic characteristics and behaviors.	
I can figure out why people do things.	
I can match sounds with pictures of what makes the sounds.	
I can play lotto games.	
Pre-academic Skills	
I can retell stories.	
I can make and test hypotheses.	
I can sort objects by color or type.	
I can count using one-to-one correspondence.	
I can write using pens and pencils.	
I can read a graph.	
I can match characteristics to a character.	
I can remember a card face after it is hidden.	
I can arrange objects in a series.	

Concepts Learned Classroom Summary

Concepts Learned in
Saying Goodbye

	Name
Content Knowledge	
Vehicles ride on wheels.	
Vehicles have different purposes.	
Vacations are trips for fun and relaxation.	
People go to the airport to fly on a plane.	
People go to the train station to ride a train.	
People go to the bus station to ride a bus.	
Weather maps show changes in weather.	
Maps are to scale.	
Maps show details of a particular area.	
Trains travel on tracks.	
Airplanes fly in the sky and land on runways.	
Buses, cars, and trucks ride on roads.	
Process Knowledge	
I can create art using various media.	
I can draw my self-portrait.	
I can clean up my own messes.	
I can build with various blocks.	
I can dig with a shovel.	
I can tear paper.	

Concepts Learned Classroom Summary

Concepts Learned in
Saying Goodbye (continued)

	Name																								
Process Knowledge (continued)																									
I can pour liquid from a small pitcher.																									
I can sing familiar songs.																									
I can make hand motions to familiar songs.																									
I can march to music.																									
I can clean using soap and water.																									
I can climb on equipment on the playground.																									
I can crumple newspaper.																									
I can take photographs.																									
I can dictate to my teacher.																									
I can reflect on my accomplishments.																									
Pre-academic Skills																									
I can read picture books and maps.																									
I can write my name.																									
I can write simple words.																									
I can count using one-to-one correspondence.																									
I can sort by one dimension and two dimensions.																									
I can continue a pattern.																									
I can put together puzzles.																									
I can recognize simple words.																									

Concepts Learned Classroom Summary

Concepts Learned in ______________________

Content Knowledge

Process Knowledge

Pre-academic Skills

Child Accomplishment Record

Concepts Learned for Saying Hello

Name

Date

Teacher

Teacher Comments

Parent Comments

Content Knowledge

- ☐ All children are alike in some ways.
- ☐ All children are different in some ways.
- ☐ Fruits have different tastes.
- ☐ I know the members of my family.
- ☐ All families are not the same.
- ☐ I can determine the color of my friend's eyes, hair, skin color, and so on.
- ☐ Houses have different rooms.
- ☐ I can identify my emotions.
- ☐ I can count birthday candles.
- ☐ I can say hello in many different ways.

Process Knowledge

- ☐ I can cut with scissors.
- ☐ I can play post office.
- ☐ I can draw myself.
- ☐ I can make puppets.
- ☐ I can draw and paint to express my ideas.
- ☐ I can trace.
- ☐ I can make prints—handprints and footprints, and so on.
- ☐ I can find out what is inside a telephone, intercom, or answering machine.
- ☐ I can build with blocks.
- ☐ I can use a magnifying glass.
- ☐ I can taste different foods and tell others which ones I like.
- ☐ I can paint with different parts of my body.
- ☐ I can find things out from others by asking questions.
- ☐ I can communicate my thoughts in drawings and with letter-like writing.
- ☐ I know a lot about me.
- ☐ I can follow a leader.
- ☐ I can sing.
- ☐ I can dance.
- ☐ I can recognize my emotions.
- ☐ I can wait just a minute for my turn.

Pre-academic Skills

- ☐ I can count my fingers (one number to each finger).
- ☐ I can count the beats (syllables) in my name.
- ☐ I can identify the first letter of my name.
- ☐ I understand that words have meaning.
- ☐ I am interested in what words say.
- ☐ I can make a graph.
- ☐ I can listen to others.
- ☐ I can ask questions.
- ☐ I can answer questions.
- ☐ I can observe likenesses and differences.

Innovations

Child Accomplishment Record

Concepts Learned for Castles

Name

Date

Teacher

Teacher Comments

Parent Comments

Content Knowledge

- ☐ Castles are a different kind of building than we have today.
- ☐ Knights wore armor for fighting.
- ☐ Castles from different countries look different.
- ☐ Coats of arms are symbols or crests that identify particular families.
- ☐ Castles have moats and drawbridges.
- ☐ Castles were built during the medieval period.
- ☐ People in castles worked in different ways.
- ☐ Kings, queens, and nobles ruled the castles.
- ☐ Knights rode horses.
- ☐ Castles were used for protection.
- ☐ Castles have walls and turrets.

Process Knowledge

- ☐ I can cut using scissors.
- ☐ I can play Bocce ball.
- ☐ I can throw a beanbag.
- ☐ I can build using different materials.
- ☐ I can make sandcastles.
- ☐ I can make stained glass windows.
- ☐ I can create mazes.
- ☐ I can dance.
- ☐ I can hit a target with a beanbag.
- ☐ I can roll balls.
- ☐ I can paint.
- ☐ I can clean up.
- ☐ I can put on and take off dress up clothes.

Pre-academic Skills

- ☐ I can make hypotheses.
- ☐ I can make a necklace out of beads and string.
- ☐ I can weigh things with a balance scale.
- ☐ I can sort by one dimension (color, weight, size, function, etc.).
- ☐ I can sort by two dimensions (color and size, function and weight, etc.).
- ☐ I can create a mathematical equation.
- ☐ I can create patterns.
- ☐ I can create a story with a beginning and an ending.
- ☐ I can create a story with a beginning, middle, and an ending.
- ☐ I can illustrate my words and thoughts.
- ☐ I can tell how things are different.
- ☐ I can match photographs and pictures.
- ☐ I can estimate.
- ☐ I can grip a pencil.

Child Accomplishment Record

Concepts Learned for

Making Messes and Cleaning Them Up

Name

Date

Teacher

Teacher Comments

Parent Comments

Content Knowledge

- ☐ Some messes are easy to clean up and others are hard.
- ☐ Coins have different values.
- ☐ Recycling saves resources.
- ☐ Cleaning up messes is the last step of making them.
- ☐ Some things float in water, and others sink.
- ☐ I need different tools to clean up different messes.
- ☐ Handwashing has many steps.
- ☐ Handwashing keeps me healthy.
- ☐ Singing while you clean up makes it more fun.

Process Knowledge

- ☐ I can make messes.
- ☐ I can clean up my messes.
- ☐ I can clean up my room.
- ☐ I can wash things (clothes, dishes, my hands, tricycles).
- ☐ I can sort (socks, mittens, laundry, coins).
- ☐ I can paint with many different objects (balls, flyswatters, potato mashers, spatulas, mops, brooms).
- ☐ I can hammer golf tees into Styrofoam.
- ☐ I have creative ideas.
- ☐ I can catch popcorn after it pops.
- ☐ I can complete puzzles.
- ☐ I can write letters.
- ☐ I can draw shapes.

Pre-academic Skills

- ☐ I can match soap bars to toilet paper rolls to see if we have the same number of each (one-to-one correspondence).
- ☐ I can make simple patterns.
- ☐ I can remember and repeat fingerplays and rhymes.
- ☐ I can figure things out (how to drop eggs without breaking them, what floats and what sinks, how to make clean mud, how to mix flour and water together, how to make plastic wiggly worms stick to the sides of the sensory tubs).
- ☐ I can trace figures, letters, and numbers with my fingers.
- ☐ I can make plans.

Innovations

Child Accomplishment Record

Concepts Learned for Creepy Crawlies and Germs

Name

Date

Teacher

Teacher Comments

Parent Comments

Content Knowledge

- ☐ Beekeepers are called apiarists.
- ☐ Bees live in an apiary or beehive.
- ☐ Some bugs hide under logs, branches, rocks, etc..
- ☐ Some insects fly, and some don't.
- ☐ Bugs hatch from eggs.
- ☐ Baby bugs can look different from adult bugs.
- ☐ Caterpillars turn into moths and butterflies.
- ☐ Some insects have patterns on them.
- ☐ Insects use patterns and color to camouflage and protect themselves from predators
- ☐ Spiders spin webs.
- ☐ Webs catch insects so spiders can eat the body fluids.
- ☐ Insects can climb because their feet are made for gripping.
- ☐ Spiders crawl many different ways.
- ☐ Worms live underground.
- ☐ Worms make tunnels in the ground.
- ☐ Germs grow.
- ☐ Germs can make you sick.
- ☐ Covering a sneeze keeps you from spreading germs to others.
- ☐ Frequent handwashing keeps you from spreading your germs to others.

Process Knowledge

- ☐ I can create insects with playdough, collage materials, egg cartons, and pipe cleaners.
- ☐ I can express ideas, thoughts, or feelings through creative dramatics.
- ☐ I can move to music.
- ☐ I can collect objects to observe likenesses and differences.
- ☐ I can draw a two-dimensional image.
- ☐ I can create a three-dimensional image.

Pre-academic Knowledge

- ☐ I can count the beats of music.
- ☐ I can research my ideas to learn more.
- ☐ I can make predictions.
- ☐ I can recognize shapes in the natural environment.
- ☐ I can look at books to get information.
- ☐ I can read pictorial context clues in books.
- ☐ I am interested in print.

Child Accomplishment Record

Concepts Learned for Maps

Name

Date

Teacher

Teacher Comments

Parent Comments

Content Knowledge

- ☐ Maps are drawn to scale.
- ☐ A scale represents distance.
- ☐ Maps help us find things.
- ☐ Maps give directions.
- ☐ North, south, east, and west are directions.
- ☐ Pirates sailed on the seas in ships.
- ☐ Wind makes sailing ships move.
- ☐ A compass shows direction.
- ☐ Long ago, people navigated by using the stars.
- ☐ Luggage carries clothes and personal belongings on a trip or on vacation.
- ☐ People camp in tents.
- ☐ People travel to different locations.
- ☐ I can find my house on a map.
- ☐ I can find my state and city on a map or globe.
- ☐ I know what country my ancestors lived in.

Process Knowledge

- ☐ I can balance on a "plank."
- ☐ I can use a map.
- ☐ I can search for hidden treasure.
- ☐ I can play the role of pirate.
- ☐ I can pack a suitcase.
- ☐ I can make rubbings.
- ☐ I can build a replica of my neighborhood.
- ☐ I can build an airport.
- ☐ I can build a train station.
- ☐ I can build a working compass.
- ☐ I can dig for treasure.
- ☐ I can use a compass to find North.

Pre-academic Skills

- ☐ I can read signs (stop, yield, no right turn, etc.).
- ☐ I can count.
- ☐ I can read a map.
- ☐ I can categorize.
- ☐ I can investigate and test my ideas.
- ☐ I can predict.
- ☐ I can identify letters in my name.
- ☐ I know my last name.
- ☐ I know my address.

Innovations

Child Accomplishment Record

Concepts Learned in Spin Me a Tall Tale

Name

Date

Teacher

Teacher Comments

Parent Comments

Content Knowledge

- ☐ Stories have characters.
- ☐ Quilts are made up of many squares.
- ☐ There are many ways to tell a story.
- ☐ Music can tell stories.
- ☐ Hand signs can tell stories.
- ☐ Pictures can tell stories.
- ☐ Words can tell stories.
- ☐ Invitations ask people to attend special events.
- ☐ You can tell the same story many different ways.

Process Knowledge

- ☐ I can perform.
- ☐ I can make puppets.
- ☐ I can produce a puppet show.
- ☐ I can paint to music.
- ☐ I can make books in several different forms.
- ☐ I understand how sound moves through the air in waves.
- ☐ I can follow a recipe.
- ☐ I can act out stories.

Pre-academic Skills

- ☐ I can differentiate between sounds just by listening (auditory discrimination of sounds).
- ☐ I can figure out pictures that tell a story (reading context clues to discern meaning).
- ☐ I can identify how many characters there are in a story.
- ☐ I can dictate a story with a beginning, middle, and ending.
- ☐ I can predict what will happen next in a story.
- ☐ I can sequence a story.

Child Accomplishment Record

Concepts Learned for What Will I Be?

Name

Date

Teacher

Teacher Comments

Parent Comments

Content Knowledge

- ☐ Adults have different jobs.
- ☐ Firefighters, police officers, and medical workers are community helpers.
- ☐ Farmers grow crops and animals.
- ☐ Construction workers build.
- ☐ Carpenters build using tools and wood.
- ☐ Plumbers install pipes for water.
- ☐ Teachers help children and adults learn.
- ☐ Plants need light and water to live.

Process Knowledge

- ☐ I can play different roles.
- ☐ I can explore anything I want to be.
- ☐ I can explore career options.
- ☐ I can play with different partners.
- ☐ I can dress/undress in different costumes.
- ☐ I can build with blocks and boxes.
- ☐ I can glue, paint, cut, and draw.
- ☐ I can build a train station/airport.
- ☐ I can match nuts and bolts.
- ☐ I can use a tape measure.
- ☐ I can use tools for gardening.
- ☐ I can hammer nails.
- ☐ I can draw my self-portrait.

Pre-academic Skills

- ☐ I can count to 10.
- ☐ I can observe and discuss my observations.
- ☐ I can identify careers by uniforms and equipment used.
- ☐ I can use printed words as a pattern for writing.
- ☐ I can dictate.
- ☐ I can copy numbers.

Child Accomplishment Record

Concepts Learned for Space

Name

Date

Teacher

Teacher Comments

Parent Comments

Content Knowledge

- ☐ A control center controls the space ship.
- ☐ Different planets are different colors and sizes.
- ☐ Planets rotate around the sun.
- ☐ The moon rotates around the earth.
- ☐ The sun is very hot.
- ☐ Planets can be hot if they are close to the sun or cold if they are far away from the sun.
- ☐ Gravity is different on different planets.
- ☐ Astronauts travel in space.
- ☐ Astronauts wear space suits in space.

Process Knowledge

- ☐ I can find hidden objects.
- ☐ I can paint with hot or cold paint.
- ☐ I can build with blocks.
- ☐ I can stack cups and glasses.
- ☐ I can use a telescope/binoculars to see things.
- ☐ I can punch holes in a pattern.
- ☐ I can paint using colored ice.
- ☐ I can shape playdough with cookie cutters.
- ☐ I can build using Styrofoam balls and toothpicks.
- ☐ I can sing and move to music.
- ☐ I can carry a backpack.
- ☐ I can create with papier-mâché.

Pre-academic Skills

- ☐ I can identify planets.
- ☐ I can sequence planets by position.
- ☐ I can count backwards from 10.
- ☐ I can use letters to represent words.
- ☐ I can connect a sound to a letter.
- ☐ I can write letters.
- ☐ I can write my name.
- ☐ I can recognize familiar words.
- ☐ I can match colors and shapes.
- ☐ I can count (forward or backward) using one-to-one correspondence to 5 (to 10)s.

Child Accomplishment Record

Concepts Learned for

Where Does It Come From and Where Does It Go?

Name

Date

Teacher

Teacher Comments

Parent Comments

Content Knowledge

- ☐ I can make recycled paper.
- ☐ Worms recycle fruits and vegetables into compost.
- ☐ I can make mashed potatoes.
- ☐ I know many different types of pizza toppings.
- ☐ I can sort recycled materials into paper, plastics, and aluminum.
- ☐ I know many songs and fingerplays about food.
- ☐ I know about the food pyramid.
- ☐ I can identify four different food groups on the food pyramid.
- ☐ I can eat five fruits or vegetables a day.

Process Knowledge

- ☐ I can play roles in Dramatic Possibilities.
- ☐ I can create with recycled materials.
- ☐ I can create sculptures.
- ☐ I can construct things.
- ☐ I can stock the shelves in the grocery store.
- ☐ I can build with lots of different kinds of blocks.
- ☐ I can make my own snacks.
- ☐ I can throw beanbags into milk jugs.
- ☐ I can play paddle ball.

Pre-academic Skills

- ☐ I can write alphabet letters.
- ☐ I can sort kitchen utensils like forks, knives, spoons, etc..
- ☐ I can recycle words and pictures from printed materials.
- ☐ I can read the logos of my favorite snack foods.
- ☐ I know the sounds that vowels can make.
- ☐ I can count to 5, or 10, or 15, or 20.

Innovations

Child Accomplishment Record

Concepts Learned for Building Up and Tearing Down

Name

Date

Teacher

Teacher Comments

Parent Comments

Content Knowledge

- ☐ Blueprints and house plans are drawn to scale.
- ☐ Blueprints are plans to help people build.
- ☐ I can find my house on a map.
- ☐ I can find my city on a county and state map.
- ☐ People build using different tools and materials.
- ☐ Demolition is when something is torn down.
- ☐ Recycling is when something is used again.
- ☐ Construction vehicles can be very big.
- ☐ Safety is important at a construction site.

Process Knowledge

- ☐ I can sort and recycle.
- ☐ I can build using blocks and boxes.
- ☐ I can create three-dimensional structures.
- ☐ I can build a replica of a community.
- ☐ I can cooperate with classmates to reach a goal.
- ☐ I can keep time to music.
- ☐ I can build using Legos®.
- ☐ I wear safety glasses when I work.
- ☐ I can use simple tools.
- ☐ I can create using various art media.

Pre-academic Skills

- ☐ I know my colors.
- ☐ I can count using one-to-one correspondence.
- ☐ I can read a house plan.
- ☐ I can predict what will happen.
- ☐ I can plan before I begin an activity.
- ☐ I can solve problems.
- ☐ I can measure using rulers and measuring tape.
- ☐ I can form letters.

Child Accomplishment Record

Concepts Learned for Fantasy Figures and More

Name

Date

Teacher

Teacher Comments

Parent Comments

Content Knowledge

- ☐ Heroes have special characteristics or behaviors.
- ☐ A magnet attracts iron metals.
- ☐ A graph helps us compare.
- ☐ The sun has power.
- ☐ The sun can heat things up.
- ☐ Vegetables can make me strong.
- ☐ Many real people help others.

Process Knowledge

- ☐ I can create using various art media.
- ☐ I have different play partners.
- ☐ I can play various roles.
- ☐ I can dress and undress in costumes.
- ☐ I can use glue to attach things.
- ☐ I can weave simple patterns.
- ☐ I can cut using scissors.
- ☐ I can experience dramatic play in miniature.
- ☐ I can build with various blocks.
- ☐ I can differentiate between magnetic and non-magnetic objects.
- ☐ I can match cards.
- ☐ I can sing familiar songs.
- ☐ I can use hand motions to sing.
- ☐ I can throw objects.
- ☐ I can hit a target with a ball.
- ☐ I can move my body to catch bubbles.
- ☐ I can help others.
- ☐ I can apply first aid.
- ☐ I can make masks.
- ☐ I can differentiate between real and fantastic characteristics and behaviors.
- ☐ I can figure out why people do things.
- ☐ I can match sounds with pictures of what makes the sounds.
- ☐ I can play lotto games.

Pre-academic Skills

- ☐ I can retell stories.
- ☐ I can make and test hypotheses.
- ☐ I can sort objects by color or type.
- ☐ I can count using one-to-one correspondence.
- ☐ I can write using pens and pencils.
- ☐ I can read a graph.
- ☐ I can match characteristics to a character.
- ☐ I can remember a card face after it is hidden.
- ☐ I can arrange objects in a series.

Innovations

Child Accomplishment Record

Concepts Learned for Saying Goodbye

Name

Date

Teacher

Teacher Comments

Parent Comments

Content Knowledge

- ☐ Vehicles ride on wheels.
- ☐ Vehicles have different purposes.
- ☐ Vacations are trips for fun and relaxation.
- ☐ People go to the airport to fly on a plane.
- ☐ People go to the train station to ride a train.
- ☐ People go to the bus station to ride a bus.
- ☐ Weather maps show changes in weather.
- ☐ Maps are to scale.
- ☐ Maps show details of a particular area.
- ☐ Trains travel on tracks.
- ☐ Airplanes fly in the sky and land on runways.
- ☐ Buses, cars, and trucks ride on roads.

Process Knowledge

- ☐ I can create art using various media.
- ☐ I can draw my self-portrait.
- ☐ I can clean up my own messes.
- ☐ I can build with various blocks.
- ☐ I can dig with a shovel.
- ☐ I can tear paper.
- ☐ I can pour liquid from a small pitcher.
- ☐ I can sing familiar songs.
- ☐ I can make hand motions to familiar songs.
- ☐ I can march to music.
- ☐ I can clean using soap and water.
- ☐ I can climb on equipment on the playground.
- ☐ I can crumple newspaper.
- ☐ I can take photographs.
- ☐ I can dictate to my teacher.
- ☐ I can reflect on my accomplishments.

Pre-academic Skills

- ☐ I can read picture books and maps.
- ☐ I can write my name.
- ☐ I can write simple words.
- ☐ I can count using one-to-one correspondence.
- ☐ I can sort by one dimension and two dimensions.
- ☐ I can continue a pattern.
- ☐ I can put together puzzles.
- ☐ I can recognize simple words.

Child Accomplishment Record

Concepts Learned for

____

____

Name

____

Date

____

Teacher

Teacher Comments

____

Parent Comments

Content Knowledge

- ☐ ______
- ☐ ______
- ☐ ______
- ☐ ______
- ☐ ______
- ☐ ______
- ☐ ______
- ☐ ______
- ☐ ______
- ☐ ______
- ☐ ______
- ☐ ______

Process Knowledge

- ☐ ______
- ☐ ______
- ☐ ______
- ☐ ______
- ☐ ______
- ☐ ______
- ☐ ______
- ☐ ______
- ☐ ______
- ☐ ______
- ☐ ______
- ☐ ______
- ☐ ______
- ☐ ______
- ☐ ______
- ☐ ______

Pre-academic Skills

- ☐ ______
- ☐ ______
- ☐ ______
- ☐ ______
- ☐ ______
- ☐ ______
- ☐ ______
- ☐ ______

Anecdotal Record (completed)

Child Tameka Harris **Date** September 18 **Time** 9:40am

What I observed

Several children were playing with dolls and stuffed animals in dramatic possibilities. Tameka approached Harrison and stood there watching him. Tameka then said, "I have a dog." Harrison stopped and said, "My dogs are Rex and Pogo." Tameka smiled and went to play in math possibilities.

Teacher Miss Alicia

Innovations

Anecdotal Record

Child **Date** **Time**

What I observed

Teacher

Communication Log

Simone Brown
Child's Name

Oct 18
Week oF

Day	Sign In	Bed Time	Wake up Time	Behavior Change?	Parent Comments	Snacks/Meals	NAP(S)	Activities/Teacher Comments	Sign Out
M	8:34 A	7:30 P	7:30 A	Normal		Snack A.M. (Y) N; P.M. (Y) N; Lunch 12:15	Y N	Simone completed the 11 piece puzzle we put out today. She was ready for this new challenge.	5:50 P
T	8:44 A	7:30 P	8:00 A	Normal	Simone has a cough and a runny nose	Snack A.M. (Y) N; P.M. Y (N); Lunch 12:35	Y N	Simone chose mostly quiet activities. She reported that she didn't feel well.	3:35 P
W	8:49 A	8:45 P	7:45 A	Normal	She has an entry on the med. chart	Snack A.M. (Y) N; P.M. Y (N); Lunch 12:15	Y N	Sensory activities kept Simone busy today. She liked taking apart the Lego® constructions covered with hair gel. Great for fine motor muscle strength and coordination.	6:25 P
Th	7:46 A	7:45 P	7:40 A	Normal Slight cough still	Jacket & breakfast are in room See med. chart	Snack A.M. (Y) N; P.M. (Y) N; Lunch 12:20	Y N	In group time Simone shared the map of her bedroom w/the other children. She told us about the special bed cover that her grandmother made.	6:18 P
F	9:02 A	8:45 P	7:15 A	Normal	ate some breakfast	Snack A.M. (Y) N; P.M. Y N; Lunch 12:15	Y N	Checked out the new prop box in Dramatic Possibilities. Simone loved the capes, crowns, and gloves. She wore them all morning.	5:08 P

Communication Log

Child's Name **Week of**

Day	Sign In	Bed Time	Wake up Time	Behavior Change?	Parent Comments	Snacks/Meals	NAP(S)	Activities/Teacher Comments	Sign Out
M						Snack A.M. Y N P.M. Y N Lunch	Y N		
T						Snack A.M. Y N P.M. Y N Lunch	Y N		
W						Snack A.M. Y N P.M. Y N Lunch	Y N		
Th						Snack A.M. Y N P.M. Y N Lunch	Y N		
F						Snack A.M. Y N P.M. Y N Lunch	Y N		

Possibilities Planning

Although ***Innovations: The Comprehensive Preschool Curriculum*** is emergent in nature, planning is critical. The purpose of a Possibilities Plan is to focus attention on all of the dimensions of planning curriculum and to support teachers' efforts to make both parents and others aware of the focus, events, activities, experiences, and interactions that are being considered and provided for children. The Possibilities Plan includes all the different components of curriculum addressed in ***Innovations: The Comprehensive Preschool Curriculum***.

Unlike traditional lesson plans that provide only activities, the Possibilities Plan provides a big picture of the possibilities that might emerge. It is designed to be a living document. Make additions, changes, or corrections to reflect children's experiences, reactions, preferences, emergent ideas, and changing development. You may find it helpful to write your original Possibilities Plan using one color of ink, and then use a different color to make modifications in the plan. You also can make notes on the Plan to show how the children responded to what actually happened in the classroom.

The following list provides an overview of the sections of the Possibilities Plan. Use the Possibilities Plan as it is (feel free to make additional copies), or modify it to reflect individual differences or preferences in format or space.

1. Web: A sample web is provided for each Possibilities Plan. Use it, modify it, or create your own web including ideas and activities that your children might enjoy, as well as to open up emergent possibilities. Then, use different ink colors to show how the web grows or changes as children show preferences for activities, experiences, materials, and so on.

2. Interactive Experiences: Each chapter in the curriculum includes a list of important interactive experiences for young children. These experiences emerge from warm, caring interactions and are rarely the result of planning or formal activities. Because this component of children's experiences is cumulative, interactions ARE curriculum and as such, belong on your curriculum plan.

3. Observation/Assessment Possibilities: A major focus of this curriculum is observation and assessment. Use indicators from assessment instruments to cue teachers' observation, as well as to create anecdotal records of children's emerging skills, abilities, reactions, responses, and activities. Keep observation tools close at hand to write down notes. Get into the habit of writing the date first, so it won't be omitted.

4. Possibilities: Choose from the many different possibilities provided, remembering the value of repetition for brain development. Space is included for the activities you select; list them on the form here.

5. Environment: A well-planned environment communicates volumes to children and supports children's play and work, teachers' activities and work, and family members' comfort. Here is where you include equipment and materials to make, add, take away, and change to keep the environment fresh and interesting.

6. Projects/Documentation: Some planned activities may have a project focus. List those activities here along with your notes or reminders about items to record or collect for documentation either in portfolios or displays.

7. Books: Include children's books that are favorites and support other literacy activities. You may also want to note books that relate specifically to the Plan's topic.

8. Rhymes/Fingerplays: Include the titles of rhymes that you will be using during the plan and place copies of the rhymes and fingerplays nearby.

9. Task Activities: List the developmental tasks that children are working on in this section, along with any of the specific skills or abilities taken from checklists within the chapters related to the task. Remember that children are working on developmental tasks as well as learning content, process, and pre-academic skills, and this section gives you an opportunity to highlight this interactional work.

10. Music/Songs: Include the titles of music and songs that you will use during the plan.

11. Prop Boxes: List prop boxes or itemize the contents here.

12. Picture File/Vocabulary: Write the new vocabulary words you will be using in this section and indicate the pictures you will add to the classroom from your picture file. Including these items in the plan will not only cue parents that you are supporting vocabulary development, but also that you are adding a wide variety of interest and images to the environment.

13. Snack: Use this space to write snacks that relate to the Plan.

14. Field Trip Plans: List field trip plans here.

15./16. Family Participation/Parent Postcards: Family and parent involvement needs planning as well. Be sensitive to different families' ability to participate in activities by selecting a range of participation activities. Also list the titles of the Parent Postcards that you plan to distribute to parents.

When you are finished considering all of these possibilities, you will have a rich and interesting plan. Then, it will be time to enjoy the educational experiences that you have prepared for the children in your classroom, knowing that everything you do IS curriculum.

Possibilities Plan

Teachers ______________________ Classroom ______________________

Possibilities Topic ______________________

1. Web

2. Interactive Experiences

3. Observation/Assessment Possibilities

4. Possibilities

Dramatic

Art

Blocks/Construction

Science/Discovery

Sensory

Literacy/Writing

Math/Manipulatives

Rhymes/Fingerplays/Songs/Music

Group Time

Movement/Outdoors

5. Environment

6. Projects/Documentation

3

7. Books

8. Rhymes/Fingerplays

9. Task Activities & Experiences

10. Music/Songs

11. Prop Boxes

12. Picture File/ Vocabulary

13.

Snack	AM	PM
M		
T		
W		
Th		
F		
S		

14. Field Trip Plans

15. Family Participation Activities

16. Parent Postcards

Other Assessment Instruments for Preschool

The Creative Curriculum Assessment Tool Kit
202-362-7543

This assessment tool is designed to be used in preschool, child care, and Head Start classrooms with three- to five-year-olds. The Tool Kit includes everything needed to assess one classroom of children and enough forms to record progress for a class of up to 25 children at three summary checkpoints each year.

Humanics Preschool Assessment Instrument
800-874-8844

This tool is designed for use in classrooms of children ages 3-6. Areas of child development in the assessment are: Social-Emotional, Motor Skills, Language, Cognitive, and the Hygiene/Self-Help. The handbook and observation checklist are a comprehensive guide to using the assessment form and utilizing the results in individualized education programs. The forms include educational objectives and the developmental significance of each activity.

High/Scope Child Observation Record (COR) for Ages 2 1/2–6 (COR)
800-40-PRESS

This is an observational assessment tool that can be used in a variety of early childhood settings. To use the COR, the trained teacher or observer assesses each child's behavior and activities in six categories of development: initiative, social relations, creative representation, music and movement, language and literacy, and logic and mathematics. Over several months, the teacher takes brief notes describing examples of children's behavior in these six categories. The notes are then used to rate the child's behavior on 30 five-level COR items within these categories.

Work Sampling System
Pearson Early Learning
800-552-2259

This is an ongoing classroom performance assessment system that is used in preschool through fifth grade. Its purpose is to document children's skills, knowledge, behavior, and accomplishments across a wide variety of curriculum areas on multiple occasions to enhance teaching and learning.

Index

D

Q

R

S

T

Book Index

C

D

E

F

G

H

I

J

K

L

M

N

O

P

Q

R

S

T

U

V

W

Y

Z